"COMPLETE . . . THOROUGH . . . PRESENTED WITH DEADLY ACCURACY . . . Unlike Marchetti who was so high in the CIA's administrative hierarchy that many of his notions of what goes on at operational levels are downright absurd, Agee was there. An authentic account."

—Miles Copeland,
former spy and high-ranking CIA official

"When Victor Marchetti's *The CIA and the Cult of Intelligence* was published, it contained intriguing blanks where material deemed too sensitive by the CIA had been. There are no blanks in Philip Agee's *Inside the Company: CIA Diary . . .* Among CIA agents (or contacts) Agee lists high-ranking political leaders of several Latin American countries, U.S. and Latin American labor leaders, ranking Communist Party members, and scores of other politicians, high military and police officials and journalists."

—*The Washington Post*

INSIDE THE COMPANY: CIA DIARY

Philip Agee

BANTAM BOOKS
TORONTO · NEW YORK · LONDON · SYDNEY

Dedicated to
Angela Camargo Seixas
and her comrades in Latin America
struggling for social justice,
national dignity and peace

This low-priced Bantam Book has been completely reset in a type face designed for easy reading, and was printed from new plates. It contains the complete text of the original hard-cover edition. NOT ONE WORD HAS BEEN OMITTED.

INSIDE THE COMPANY: CIA DIARY
A Bantam Book / published by arrangement with Stonehill Publishing Co.

PRINTING HISTORY
Stonehill edition / June 1975
2nd printing .... July 1975 3rd printing .... August 1975
4th printing .... September 1975
November 1975 alternate selection of Library of Political and International Affairs (a Macmillan Book Club)
August 1975 full selection of Saturday Review Book Club
First published in the United Kingdom by Penguin Books, Ltd. 1975.
Bantam edition / February 1976
2nd printing ...... January 1976 4th printing ...... January 1978
3rd printing .... February 1976 5th printing .... August 1979
6th printing .... May 1981

A small number of corrections, emendations and additions to the American edition have been made by the author.

Cover photograph by Dennis Rolfe shows a typewriter and bugged case planted on the author presumably by the CIA.

ISBN 0-553-20256-1

Bantam Books are published by Bantam Books, Inc. Its trademark, consisting of the words "Bantam Books" and the portrayal of a bantam, is Registered in U.S. Patent and Trademark Office and in other countries. Marca Registrada. Bantam Books, Inc., 666 Fifth Avenue, New York, New York 10103.

PRINTED IN THE UNITED STATES OF AMERICA

15 14 13 12 11 10 9 8

Contents

Introduction

This is a story of the twelve-year career of a CIA secret operations officer that ended in early 1969. It is an attempt to open another small window to the kinds of secret activities that the U.S. government undertakes through the CIA in Third World countries in the name of U.S. national security. It includes the actual people and organizations involved, placed within the political, economic and social context in which the activities occurred. An attempt is also made to include my personal interpretation of what I was doing and to show the effect of this work on my family life. My reasons for revealing these activities will be found in the text. No one, of course, can remember in detail all the events of a twelve-year period of his life. In order to write this book, I have spent most of the last four years in intensive research to reinforce my own recollections.

The officers of a CIA station abroad work as a team, often in quite different activities and with a considerable number of indigenous agents and collaborators. I have tried to describe the overall team effort, not just my own role, because all the station's efforts relate to the same goals.

The variety of operations that are undertaken simultaneously by a single officer and by the station team made an ordinary narrative presentation cumbersome. I have chosen a diary format (written, to be sure, in 1973 and 1974) in order to show the progressive development of different activities and to convey a sense of actuality. This method also has defects, requiring the reader to follow many different strands from one entry in the diary to another, but I believe it is the most effective method for showing what we did.

In order to ease the problem of remembering who all the characters are, I have included a special appendix, Appendix 1, which has descriptions of individuals and organizations involved or connected with the Agency or its operations (see note to Appendix 1). The reader is directed to this appendix by the use of a double dagger, ‡, in the text. It will be noted that many agents' names have been forgotten and that only cryptonyms (code names) can be given. Some of the original cryptonyms have also been forgotten, and in these cases I have composed new ones in order to refer to a real person by some name at least. Appendix 2 gives an alphabetical listing of all abbreviations used and an asterisk indicates those entries which appear in Appendix 1.

Several of the operational activities that I describe could not be placed at the exact date they really happened, for lack of research materials, but they are placed as close as possible to the date they occurred with no loss or distortion of meaning. Similarly, several events have been shifted a day or two so that they could be included in diary entries just before or just after they actually occurred. In these cases the changes make no difference.

When I joined the CIA I believed in the need for its existence. After twelve years with the agency I finally understood how much suffering it was causing, that millions of people all over the world had been killed or had had their lives destroyed by the CIA and the institutions it supports. I couldn't sit by and do nothing and so began work on this book.

Even after recent revelations about the CIA it is still difficult for people to understand what a huge and sinister organization the CIA is. It is the biggest and most powerful secret service that has ever existed. I don't know how big the KGB is inside the Soviet Union, but its international operation is small compared with the CIA's. The CIA has 16,500 employees and an annual budget of $750,000,000. That does not include its mercenary armies or its commercial subsidiaries. Add them all together, the agency employs or subsidizes hundreds of thousands of people and spends billions every year. Its *official* budget is secret; it's concealed in those of other Federal agencies. Nobody tells the Congress what the CIA spends. By law, the CIA is not accountable to Congress.

In the past 25 years, the CIA has been involved in plots to overthrow governments in Iran, the Sudan,

Syria, Guatemala, Ecuador, Guyana, Zaire and Ghana. In Greece, the CIA participated in bringing in the repressive regime of the colonels. In Chile, The Company spent millions to "destabilize" the Allende government and set up the military junta, which has since massacred tens of thousands of workers, students, liberals and leftists. In Indonesia in 1965, The Company was behind an even bloodier coup, the one that got rid of Sukarno and led to the slaughter of at least 500,000 and possibly 1,000,000 people. In the Dominican Republic the CIA arranged the assassination of the dictator Rafael Trujillo and later participated in the invasion that prevented the return to power of the liberal ex-president Juan Bosch. In Cuba, The Company paid for and directed the invasion that failed at the Bay of Pigs. Some time later the CIA was involved in attempts to assassinate Fidel Castro. It is difficult to believe, or comprehend, that the CIA could be involved in all these subversive activities all over the world.

The life of a CIA operations officer can be exciting, romantic. You belong to a special club: The Company. For most of my career with the CIA I felt that I was doing something worthwhile. There is not much time to think about the results of your actions and, if you try to do it well, the job of operations officer calls for dedication to the point of obsession. But it's a schizophrenic sort of situation. You have too many secrets, you can't relax with outsiders. Sometimes an operative uses several identities at once. If somebody asks you a simple question, "What did you do over the weekend?" your mind goes Click! Who does he think I am? What would the guy he *thinks* I am be doing over the weekend? You get so used to lying that after a while it's hard to remember what the truth is.

When I joined the CIA I signed the secrecy agreement. With this book, articles, exposure on radio and television, I may have violated that agreement. I believe it is worse to stay silent, that the agreement itself was immoral. My experience with the CIA has mostly been with its overseas operations. I trust investigations now going on in Washington into CIA activities will also expose CIA internal involvement which is, I suspect, much greater than anybody outside the CIA knows or the National Security Council realizes. I believe a lot of sinister things will come out and that Americans may be in for some very severe shocks.

In the *New York Review of Books* of 30 December 1971, Richard Helms, then CIA Director, was quoted from a rare address to the National Press Club. In justifying the CIA's secret operations, he said: "You've just got to trust us. We are honorable men." I ask that these words be remembered while reading this book, together with the fact that CIA operations are undertaken on instructions from the President himself and are approved in very detailed form on various levels within the CIA, and often at the Under-Secretary level or higher, outside the Agency. Finally, I ask that it be kept in mind that the kinds of operations I describe, which occurred for the most part in Latin America, were typical of those undertaken in countries of the Far East, Near East and Africa. I would also suggest that they are continuing today.

Revelations during the past year of the CIA's "destabilization" program against the Allende government in Chile, its illegal domestic operations and its complicity in political assassinations or assassination attempts have finally precipitated a long-overdue debate. I hope this book will contribute to it.

London
May 1975

Part 1

South Bend, Indiana — April 1956

Hundreds of companies come to the university to interview students for possible employment. I hadn't signed up for any interviews but I've just had my first, and probably only, job interview. To my surprise a man from the CIA came out from Washington to see me about going into a secret junior executive training program. Virginia Pilgrim must have recommended me. I'd forgotten she mentioned a program like this when she stayed with us in Tampa last year—said she would dearly love to see the son of her oldest friends come into the CIA. Somehow I have the impression she is one of the highest-ranking women in the CIA—worked on the Clark Task Force that investigated the CIA under the Hoover Commission.

I told Gus,‡ the recruiter, that I had already been accepted for law study. He was surprised. Virginia didn't know my plans. He said the JOT (Junior Officer Trainee) Program consists of six to nine months, in some cases even a year, of increasingly specialized training on the graduate school level. After the course you begin CIA work on analysis, research, special studies and reports writing, administration or secret operations. He said he couldn't say much about the course or the work because it is all classified.

Gus asked me about my military service situation and when I told him I would have to do it sooner or later he mentioned a possible combination. For JOT's who haven't done military service the CIA arranges for them to take a special course in the Army or the Air Force, which is really controlled by the CIA. It takes about a year to get an officer's commission and then you have to serve a year on a military assignment. Then it's back to Washington for the JOT training program and finally assignment to a job at CIA headquarters in Washington. According to his calculations it would take five or six years to be assigned overseas if I wanted to go into secret operations. Too long to wait before getting to the good part, I thought.

Gus knew a lot about me: student government, academic honors and the rest. I said that what I liked best was being Chairman of the Washington's Birthday Exercises in February when we gave the Patriotism Award to General Curtis Lemay. I told Gus that the Exercises are the most important expression of the "country" part of the Notre Dame motto ("For God, Country, and Notre Dame"). He said I should keep the CIA in mind if I changed my plans. I would consider the CIA if the military combination worked but Gus emphasized that they only want people prepared for a career in the CIA. That leaves me out.

I suppose the CIA works closely with General Lemay and his Strategic Air Command. This is the most important part of the speech he gave at the Exercises:

> Our patriotism must be intelligent patriotism. It has to go deeper than blind nationalism or shallow emotional patriotic fervor. We must continually study and understand the shifting tides of our world environment. Out of this understanding we must arrive at sound moral conclusions. And we must see to it that these conclusions are reflected in our public policies. . . . If we maintain our faith in God, our love of freedom, and superior global air power, I think we can look to the future with confidence.

Tampa, Florida — June 1956

It's a strange feeling being back in Florida for the summer with no plans to return to the cold north in the fall. The miserable weather and the long distance from home and all the other negative aspects of studying at Notre Dame seemed to fade away during Commencement Weekend.

No more bed check or lights out at midnight. No more compulsory mass attendance and evening curfew. No more Religious Bulletin to make you feel guilty if you didn't attend a novena, benediction or rosary service. And no more fear of expulsion for driving a car in South Bend. The end has come too, I hope, to the loneliness and frustration of living in an all-male institution isolated from female company.

What will it be like to live without the religion and discipline of the university? It may have been hard but they were teaching us how to live the virtuous life of a good Catholic. Even so, I still have this constant fear that after all I might die by accident with a mortal sin on my soul. Eternity in hell is a worry I can't seem to shake off. But the main thing is to keep on trying—not to give up. After having to take all those courses on religion the only person to blame, if I really don't make it, will be me. It is the discipline and religion that makes Notre-Dame men different, and after four years of training I ought to be able to do better.

Admiral Arleigh Burke, Chief of Naval Operations, discussed this in his speech at the graduation ceremony. He really impressed me:

> Notre-Dame symbolizes many virtues. It blends the virtues of religion and patriotism—service to God, service to country. Notre-Dame stands for faith—faith in self and faith in country. . . . Self discipline and determination and fighting spirit are an integral part of the curriculum . . . We are living in a great country where there is equality of opportunity, where justice is a reality. . . . We are a generous nation. . . . We will never wage a war of aggression. . . . We are a strong nation. . . . We have strong allies. . . . But greater than all this strength is the strength of our moral principles. . . . Our nation is the symbol of freedom, of justice and opportunity, regardless of flag or political beliefs. . . . Communism has been, and still is, a prison for the millions who are denied the opportunity to learn responsibility—who are compelled to let the few do the thinking for the many who will do the labor. . . . Should we relax our efforts, either spiritual or physical, we would find our ship without a rudder; we would find our strength not sufficient to cope with the strong adverse winds which at some time will confront us. It takes a man with strength and a stout heart to steer in a gale.

Admiral Burke writes a great speech—couldn't have been more accurate or more inspiring. At Notre Dame we learned how one's responsibilities extend beyond oneself to family, community and nation, and that respect for authority is the virtue of a respectable citizen.

I will be driving a truck this summer to earn money for law school in the fall.

Tampa, Florida — December 1956

Studying law at the University of Florida was a mistake. I didn't feel I belonged—I wasn't comfortable—in the fraternity whirl and the "hail fellow" routine. But I'm not an ascetic either. I suppose it was the lack of a sense of purpose or maybe I couldn't adjust to secular learning after four years of Jesuits and four at Notre Dame. At least I did realize it, and only stayed three months.

I checked with the draft board and they said I have about six months before I'll be called up. It's a sad prospect, two years wasted as a private, washing dishes and peeling potatoes. For a few months anyway I'll live with my parents in Florida and try to save some money. A draftee only makes about eighty dollars a month and that's hardly enough for booze and cigarettes.

The problem is what to do about the business. My father and grandfather are just starting a big expansion and they're counting on me to take my place with them. I know I'll make a lot of money but I can't get enthusiastic about it. Why the reluctance to go into a family business? When I switched to philosophy studies after a year of business administration at Notre Dame I thought I was doing it for the sake of a higher form of education. Like so many others I could learn to run a business once I got into it. Well now I'm in it and I feel the same as when I rejected business administration for philosophy. I wish I could speak to my father or grandfather about it but it would look as if I think

I'm too good for something they've dedicated their lives to.

No hasty decisions. I've got six months to work with them and then two years in the Army.

Tampa, Florida — February 1957

There has got to be a way to avoid two lost years in the Army. I've written to the CIA, reminding them of my meeting with Gus, and asking to be reconsidered. I've received application forms, returned them, advised Virginia Pilgrim by telephone, and now have to wait. Virginia said her friends in the personnel department would process my application as fast as possible because of the problem of the draft but it looks as if I may be too late. She said the security clearance takes about six months so the draft will probably win.

Gus said the JOT program is strictly for people who want to make the CIA a career and I've been wondering about this. No way to know until I learn more about what CIA work is like, but I really am interested in politics and international relations. And the more I live here the less enthusiastic I get for a lifetime in the family business.

We'll see what kind of alternative the CIA can provide. It will mean three years' military duty instead of two if they take me, but I'll be an officer—more pay, better work (especially at the CIA), and time to decide.

Washington, D.C. — April 1957

I've been called to Washington for an interview with the JOT office which is in Quarters Eye near the Potomac River. I waited in a reception room until a secretary came for me, filled out a visitor's pass form giving name, address and purpose of visit, and the receptionist added the hour and stamped in large letters MUST BE ACCOMPANIED. Then she gave me a plastic clip-on badge which I had to wear at all times. The secretary signed as responsible for me and I followed her to the JOT office.

The man who interviewed me is named Jim Ferguson.‡ We spent about a half-hour discussing Notre Dame, the family business and my interest in a career in foreign affairs. I remembered the conversation with Gus and emphasized that while I am interested in a CIA career I know so little about the Agency that my reasons are necessarily restricted to an interest in foreign affairs. He said that they had arranged a series of tests and interviews with officers in charge of the JOT program, including Dr. Eccles,‡ the Program Director. If the testing and interviews go well a complete security background investigation will be made which could take about six months. But in my case, with the problem of the draft, they could ask for priority action and hope for the best.

The secretary gave me a piece of plain white paper with the building names, offices and times I was to report for the testing—it would take three days in all. She explained that at each building I would have to report to the receptionist, who would call the office where I had the appointment for someone to come and sign me in. She also reminded me to wear the visitor's badge at all times in the buildings and to return it with the pink visitor's pass on leaving. I would use the shuttle, an exclusive Agency bus, to get around the different buildings.

During that first visit to the JOT office, I immediately sensed the fraternal identification among the CIA people. I suppose it was partly because they used a special "inside" language. No one spoke of "CIA," "Central Intelligence Agency," or even "The Agency." Every reference to the Agency used the word "company."

My first appointment was at the North Building with the Medical Staff and after that I alternated between those people and the office called "Assessment and Evaluation" in the Recreation and Services Building on Ohio Drive. Although it seemed that the Medical Staff were looking for physical and mental health, and that "A and E" were looking for the special qualities needed in an intelligence operative, there seemed to be little

distinction between them. It w
hours filling in answer sheets to vo
personality tests. I've read of the ela
cedures developed by the Office of S
during World War II and now I see it's
Stanford, Minnesota, Strong, Wechsler, Guil
Rorschach—some tests are administered a
just written. The worst was the interview w
psychiatrist at the Medical Staff—he really bugge

I finally finished about noon on the afternoon the third day, and I had a couple of hours before I had to report back to the JOT office so I decided to do some sightseeing. I grabbed a sandwich at a blind stand and then took the shuttle to the Executive Office Building. (Those blind stands—sandwich bars operated by blind people—are in practically every building. I guess it's a good thing for the blind people to have that work, and the company can let them in the buildings because they can't read secret papers. Everybody wins.)

Then out to the Washington Monument. Looking out from the top of the Monument at the buildings where our national life is guided, where our integrity in the face of grave external threat is defended, and where the plurality of conflicting domestic interests finds harmony, I admitted to myself that participation in government is my long-range goal. It won't matter if I live below my parents' material level or even without fixed roots in a community. Working in the Central Intelligence Agency, preferably overseas, with intimate knowledge of the functioning and decisions of friendly and hostile governments will provide a forever stimulating and exciting atmosphere as well as an intellectually challenging occupation. I'll be a warrior against communist subversive erosion of freedom and personal liberties around the world—a patriot dedicated to the preservation of my country and our way of life.

I left the Monument through the circle of American flags and walked back to Quarters Eye feeling more confident and self-possessed than at any time since arriving. After the usual sign-in, pink slip, badge and escort procedure, I was received again by Ferguson‡ who told me the first reports on the testing looked

Dr. Eccles, Ferguson
nilitary program they
warned me that the
to be discussed with
his request I signed a
at I learned was infor-
ty and promising that

program. When the
will be called back to
the Air Force. After
three months' basic training I will be assigned to the first available class at Officer Candidate School—all at Lackland Air Force Base in San Antonio, Texas. Following OCS I will be assigned to an Air Force base somewhere in the U.S., and, with luck, my duties will be in air intelligence. Ferguson explained that the company doesn't control assignments made by the Air Force after completion of OCS, but more and more of the company military trainees are getting intelligence assignments during the obligatory year of strictly military duties. After a year at the Air Force base I will be transferred to an Air Force unit in Washington that is actually a company cover unit, and my formal company training will begin.

The secretary appeared and said Dr. Eccles would see me. I still had to get past him and I had primed myself for this meeting. Virginia had told me that Dr. Eccles's approval was necessary for acceptance. He turned out to be a bushy-browed, bespectacled man of about sixty with an unavoidable authoritative glare. He asked me why I wanted to be an intelligence officer and when I replied that foreign affairs is one of my main interests he tried to make me uncomfortable. He said that foreign policy is for diplomats; intelligence officers only collect information and pass it to others for policymaking. He added that maybe I should try the State Department. I said maybe I should but that I don't know enough about the Agency yet to decide, adding that I'd like to come into the program to see. He then gave me a little lecture; they don't want men who will quit the CIA as soon as they finish military service. They want only men who will be career intelligence officers. After that he turned into a kind old grandfather and said we'd see how the security clearance turned out. He shook my hand and said they'd like to have me. Made it! I'm in—but it seems too easy.

Back in Ferguson's office where he continued to describe the program. At no time will I be connected openly with the company, and I am to tell no one that I am being considered by it for employment. Assuming the security investigation is favorable, they will arrange for me to be hired as a civilian by the Department of the Air Force, actually by an Air Force cover unit of the company, when I am called back to Washington. A few weeks later I will enlist in the Air Force and be sent to Lackland for basic training. While in the Air Force I will be treated just like any other enlistee and no one will know of my company connection. Keeping the secret will be part of my training—learning to live my cover. A violation of cover could lead to dismissal from the program. My assignments afterwards will also be determined in part by how well I have concealed my company affiliation. Back in Florida I must keep the plan secret, but notify Ferguson if I receive any orders from the draft board.

I'm beginning to feel a kind of satisfaction in having a secret and of being on the threshold of an exclusive club with a very select membership. I am going to be my own kind of snob. Inside the Agency I'll be a real and honest person. To everyone outside I'll have a secret lie about who and what I am. My secret life has begun.

Washington, D.C. — July 1957

Salvation! The security clearance ended before the call-up came, and I drove to Washington loaded with books, hi-fi, records and tennis gear. Georgetown is the "in" area where a CIA officer trainee feels most comfortable, so I've moved in with some former Notre Dame classmates who are doing graduate study at Georgetown University. We're living in a restored Federalist house on Cherry Hill Lane, a narrow brick street between M Street and the Chesapeake and Ohio Canal. I have that feeling of being just the right person in just the right place. These friends don't know I'm going into the CIA so this will be my first real test of living a cover.

At the JOT office Ferguson told me whom I am working for. My "employer" is the Department of the Air Force, Headquarters Command, Research and Analysis Group, Bolling Air Force Base, Washington. He gave me the names of my commander, an Air Force colonel, and of my immediate supervisor, a major, both of whom are fictitious. I have to memorize all this so I can reel it off to people I meet. My Bolling Air Force Base telephone number rings in the Agency Central Cover Division where they have some male telephone operators who roll dice each morning to see who will play the colonel and who will play the major.

I signed another secrecy agreement—the wording makes it permanent, eternal and universal about everything I learn in the company—and Ferguson sent me over to my first assignment at 1016 16th Street. I rushed over but discovered nobody was expecting me. Finally I was called up to the fourth floor and welcomed to the Personnel Pool. All we do is fold maps and have crossword puzzle competitions.

The Personnel Pool is a holding area for all prospective employees who lack the final *nihil obstat* for the security clearance—we're all waiting for the same happy event: the polygraph or lie detector. We're about thirty people. Some of them have been in the pool for over a month and they're the rumor-mongers. It seems that the polygraph, or "technical interview" as it's officially called, has been a real trauma for some. We have been warned that nobody talks about the "poly" and that makes the rumors all the more mysterious. It seems that the main part of the apparatus crosses the breasts, which makes some of the girls nervous, and the main questioning is on homosexual experience, which makes some of the boys nervous. There are stories of nervous breakdowns, ambulances and even suicide. There's no doubt, however, what's going to happen when you get advised of an appointment at Building 13.

Washington, D.C. — July 1957

After two weeks of folding maps my turn finally came. How stupid to think I could beat the machine! Yesterday I was "polyed" and now I'm back at the Personnel Pool but on a different floor and with people who've already taken the test. We're kept away from those who haven't taken it so they won't know much about it. The interrogators don't tell you right away about the results of the test—they make you wait. Nothing but gloom here.

The shuttle doesn't stop at Building 13 so I had to ask the driver to leave me as near as possible. When he acknowledged Building 13 in a loud voice (on purpose, I'm sure) the cold, knowing eyes of the other passengers focused right on me and I felt like a leper. They knew I was about to make a secret, intimate confession. Bad joke.

At 23rd Street and Constitution Avenue, the driver announced Building 13 and pointed me towards a complex of temporary buildings, barracks style, beyond a parking lot towards the Watergate. The buildings are surrounded by high chain-link fences topped by several strands of barbed-wire tilting towards the outside. At the windows have the same type of chain-link mesh and every third or fourth window has an air-conditioner. None of them are open and the buildings look impenetrable.

I made my way along the fence and the first building I noticed after getting to a gate was one with a discreet 13 near the entrance. After a short wait with the receptionist I was greeted by a man about thirty-five—clean-cut, clean-shaved and clear-eyed. He took me a short distance down a hallway, opened a door, and we passed into a small room with acoustical tile covering the walls and ceiling. There was a standard government leather easy chair that backed up to a desk-like construction with a built-in apparatus of dials, graph paper and odd, narrow, metal pens. In an effort to keep me from more than a swift glance at the machine, he conducted me immediately to a sitting position in the easy chair. From behind the desk he brought a straight chair and sat down in front of me.

The interrogator announced that I had reached the final phase of the security clearance procedure necessary for access to Top Secret material and, of course, for employment with the company. He assured me that all employees of the company, even Mr. Dulles, submit to the polygraph—not just once when they're hired, but periodically throughout their careers. Then he asked me to sign a prepared statement acknowledging that I was submitting to the test of my own volition and that I would hold no claim against any person or the company afterwards no matter what the outcome. I eagerly signed this quit claim—in advance—and also another secrecy agreement, pledging myself to speak to no one of the questions or other details of the interview.

We then reviewed the questions, all of which were to be answered simply "yes" or "no." Is my name Philip Burnett Franklin Agee? Was I born on 19 January 1935? Have I ever used any other name or identity? Have I filled out my job application form honestly? Have I ever been a member of any of the subversive organizations on the Attorney-General's list? Have I ever been a communist or belonged to any communist organization? Have I ever been in a foreign country? In a communist country? Have I known any officials of a foreign government? Of a communist government? Have I ever known an intelligence officer of a foreign country? Have I ever worked for a foreign government? For a foreign intelligence service? For a communist intelligence service? Have I been asked by anyone to obtain employment with the CIA? Have I told anyone outside the CIA of my attempt to obtain employment? Have I ever engaged in homosexual activities? Have I ever taken drugs? Have I taken tranquilizers today?

The pre-test interview lasted over an hour as the interrogator explored each question in depth, noting all names, dates, places, and finally rephrasing the question to include an "other than" or "except for" clause that would qualify the question and still allow for a "yes" or "no" answer. During this discussion the interrogator explained to me that the lie detector is used exclusively in the company by the Office of Security which is responsible for protecting the company against employment of security risks or against penetration by hostile intelligence services. He also assured me that everything I said during the interview is strictly confidential and will be restricted to my Office of Security File which is available only to security officers of the same office. I didn't have the courage to ask how many security officers that meant, but as I wondered I felt a creeping discomfort that behind one of those thousands of holes in the acoustical tiles there was a microphone secretly recording our conversation. I also began to wonder if I was having incipient symptoms of the paranoia that some people say is the personality trait *sine qua non* of the effective intelligence officer.

Now we were ready for the test. The polygraph consists of three apparatuses which are attached to the body of the person being interrogated and which connect by tubes or cords to the desk ensemble. Each apparatus measures physiological changes, marked on moving graph paper by three pens. There are, accordingly, a blood pressure cuff that can be attached either to the arm or leg, a corrugated rubber tube about two inches in diameter that is placed snugly around the chest and fastened in the back, and a hand-held device with electrodes that is secured against the palm by springs that stretch across the back of the hand. The cuff measures changes in pulse and blood pressure, the chest-tube measures changes in breathing rhythm, and the hand instrument measures changes in perspiration. I was hooked into the machine, told to look straight ahead at the wall, to be very still, and to answer only "yes" or "no" to each question. The interrogator was behind me at the desk ensemble facing the back of my head. He asked the questions to my back and I answered to the wall in front.

During the pre-test interview I had given my interrogator several half-truths, partly because I simply resisted his invasion of my life, and partly because I was curious about the effectiveness of the machine. Foolish child! As the cuff inflated I was conscious of increased pulse and my hands began to sweat profusely. Anticipating the questions that I should react on, I started to count the holes in the tiles in order to distract myself from the test. The interrogator passed very slowly from one question to another, pausing between each question. I answered "yes" or "no" and at the end he slipped in an unannounced question: had I answered all the questions truthfully? Dirty trick. I said "yes" and after a few seconds the cuff deflated.

I heard a shuffling of paper and he reviewed the chart as I remained still. He told me I could move a little but that if I was not particularly uncomfortable he would like me to remain seated and hooked up. Fine. He stayed behind the desk behind my chair behind my back and started asking me what I was thinking about when I answered the question on whether anyone had asked me to obtain employment with the CIA. Nothing in particular. He insisted but I couldn't come up with an answer other than that I was thinking that indeed no one had asked me. Discussion. Then he asked me what I was thinking when I answered the question about telling anyone outside the CIA of my attempt to obtain employment. Nothing in particular. Discussion. Then the question on homosexual experience. Then drugs. As we passed from question to question he insisted with increasing intensity that I try to remember what I was thinking when I answered the question, emphasizing that my cooperation is essential for a successful testing. Successful? I wondered if successful for him is the same as successful for me. Obviously not. I would stick to my half-truths. They weren't lies anyway, and besides I have heard that you can beat the machine if you stay consistent.

We started again. Up went the blood pressure cuff and out came the questions. In went the "yes's" and "no's" and up and down went the faintly scratching pens. I fiercely counted the holes in the tiles and was gaining in confidence. Down went the cuff followed by more post-test discussion. This time I was "having difficulty" on two more questions. I repeated and insisted that I was being truthful and that when answering each question I had been thinking only of the question and of its only possible truthful answer—which I gave.

The interrogator said we would go through the questions again and that I hadn't done too well on the first two runs, adding that there is no way for me to be hired without successfully passing the test. Was there anything I wanted to say or clarify? No. I was being truthful and maybe something was wrong with the machine. That hurt. His tone cooled, the cuff inflated and we did another test. At the end he said I was obviously having trouble. With an air of finality he unhooked me from the machine.

At that moment I got scared and feared I wouldn't be hired. As I was about to confess he said he would leave me alone to think things over for five or ten minutes. He closed a lid to the desk ensemble and left the room taking the charts with him. I stood up and looked at my watch which I had been asked to remove and place on the desk behind me. I had been at Building 13 for over two hours. The interrogator was gone for at least twenty minutes. During that time I decided to tell the full truth. Why risk losing the job out of silly pride or the illusion that I could beat the machine? But as the door opened and my interrogator rejoined me I suddenly became frightened of admitting deception. I decided not to change any answer. Besides, in the Personnel Pool I had heard that some people who have difficulty are called back for a second or third time for the polygraph. I would have another day if I really failed this time.

We passed through the questions two more times. After both tests the interrogator insisted that I was having trouble on the same questions and I insisted that I was answering truthfully no matter what difficulty I was having. At last he said that would be all. I asked if I had passed and he answered sceptically that he didn't know, that I would be advised after the Security Office had reviewed my case and the charts. He was very pessimistic, and as I was leaving I feared that they might not even call me back for another test. I was exhausted—went home, had a couple of drinks and slept for twelve hours.

When I called Virginia in the morning and told her I thought I'd failed the test, she said not to worry, that they always make people think they've failed. She thinks it's to avoid disappointment and fewer problems with those who really aren't going to be hired. Virginia's news is temporary relief, but the wait is agonizing. No more arrogant jokes about the polygraph in the Pool now—and nobody's reckless enough to discuss his interrogation with anyone else. Everybody's just sitting.

Washington, D.C. — July 1957

I couldn't stand it any longer. After three days' waiting, I called Ferguson to admit I was lying and to volunteer to take the test again. Before I could say anything he said he had some good news and to come over to his office. The tone of his voice gave infinite relief—I knew I had passed.

At the JOT office Ferguson told me he has started my processing for enlistment in the Air Force but it will take three or four weeks. Meanwhile he wants me to take a training course on international communism and, if there is time, a course on the bureaucratic organization of the company. These aren't the courses I'll be taking when I get back but they'll be useful, he thinks, even if they're pretty elementary. He also had the secretary arrange to get me a badge—I can come and go now without being signed in—and he made an appointment for me with Colonel Baird,‡ the Director of Training.

I missed the meeting with Baird and after being chastised at the JOT office I finally saw him in his office at T-3 (another of the Potomac Park temporaries). I hadn't realized how important Colonel Baird is—he set up the JOT program in 1950 under direct supervision of General Walter Bedell Smith who was then Agency Director. With Princeton, Oxford, and the headmastership of a boys' school behind him, Baird is considerably more formidable than his military rank. He oozes firm leadership, old hand super-confidence and a Dunhill special blend for special pipes. He's tall, greying, very tanned and very handsome—irresistible to the ladies,

I'm sure. He didn't say much—just to work hard at OCS.

Ferguson and everyone else, since the polygraph, have greeted me with "welcome aboard," as if these words are the official greeting for newcomers. Maybe there are a lot of ex-Navy men in the CIA—or maybe these people like to think they're on a ship because of the isolation imposed by cover and security.

Baltimore, Maryland — August 1957

The two weeks studying communism and two weeks reading organizational charts of the headquarters' bureaucracy leave me happy to leave Washington.

Yesterday morning Ferguson gave me my final briefing on joining the Air Force. Arrangements had been made, he said, at the main Air Force recruiting office in Washington for me to be taken into the Air Force on a normal five-year enlistment, which was the standard procedure for all Air Force enlistees. However, after basic training I will receive a special appointment by the Secretary of the Air Force to the first OCS class. I would have to be prepared to cover this appointment because we JOT's are the only exceptions to the Air Force regulation that five years' service is needed before an enlisted man can even apply for OCS. Ferguson said I can refer to a little known (so little known, in fact, that it doesn't exist) Air Force program for college graduates if I am pressed, but I can probably avoid giving explanations. He warned me, however, not to tell anyone that I am going to OCS until the assignment is actually announced to me at Lackland Air Force Base.

I signed another secrecy agreement and Ferguson said I'll have to take the polygraph again when I get back in two years' time. Then I took the bus to the recruiting office carrying only an overnight bag with some toilet articles and a change of underwear and socks.

I told the paunchy, weather-beaten recruiting sergeant my name as pleasantly as I could. He answered "yeah" and when I noticed it was a question I wondered whether to say "here I am" or "I want to enlist." I decided to say both, trying to sound unrehearsed, and I added that I thought I was expected. The recruiting sergeant understandably looked back as if he thought I thought the Air Force was about to be saved.

He gave me some forms to fill in and asked if I wanted to go in thirty, sixty or ninety days. I said cheerfully that I was ready to go right then, which made his eyes narrow and his mouth screw up into that "another case" expression. He motioned me over to a table across the room where I filled in the forms, wondering all the while whether the sergeant was really attached to the JOT office and was testing my ability to maintain the cover story. I returned the forms which he looked over and then he disappeared into a back office.

After a few minutes he returned with another recruiting sergeant and both expressed considerable scepticism. We spent the next half-hour discussing why a philosophy graduate wanted to enlist for five years in the Air Force in order to learn to be a radar mechanic. Finally I admitted that it was indeed kind of strange and I accepted their invitation to think it over for a few days. I carried my little bag of essentials out of the recruiting office wishing I could find somewhere to hide.

From a telephone booth I called Ferguson to advise that apparently the Air Force didn't want me—not that day anyway. He gulped and stammered for me to call him back in two hours. I wondered what clown had missed his cue while at the same time I dreaded facing the recruiting sergeant again. When I called back, Ferguson told me to go back to the recruiting office, that everything was all right now. When I pressed him for an explanation his voice turned cold and he warned me not to discuss classified matters over the telephone. Back in the recruiting office there was a new sergeant who simply gave me a ticket for the bus to Baltimore for the medical examination and swearing in.

At Fort Holabird they took me. Tonight I fly to San

Antonio to begin two years away from CIA headquarters —Ferguson said I must consider this time as part of the JOT training, a time for "maturing," I think he said.

San Antonio, Texas — Christmas 1957

Tony and I had Christmas dinner at the dining-hall, the low point of a miserable day. Next week, New Year's Eve to be exact, we report to OCS. We're going to live it up meanwhile except neither of us has any money.

There are only three of us going into this class; Tony, who's from Princeton; Bob, from Williams, and me. A couple of nights ago we met in a hotel downtown with the six JOT's who started OCS in the last class. They are going to be upper classmen now—the course is three months lower and three months upper class—which means they will be harassing us. That's normal and necessary for cover.

For the meeting we took security precautions as Ferguson instructed when he came to see us in October. No one can take any chances by a show of prior knowledge or special camaraderie between the triple Xer's. Those three X's which are in brackets after our names on all our documents, are the Air Force's way of keeping track of CIA trainees.

The guys from the upper class told us not to be surprised if they put the heat on us—they have to because of the resentment on the part of the others in the class who had to work years to get into OCS. It seems these non-coms aren't happy about our miniscule bunch (there are about 300 cadets altogether in OCS) being specially privileged by entering straight from basic training. I suppose we'll run into the same.

San Antonio, Texas — June 1958

In a few days I'll be a Second Lieutenant unless the OCS Commandant decides my insult was too much to take. A couple of weeks ago he called me in to tell me

I was going to be eligible for a regular commission instead of a reserve commission. Only the top six OCS graduates get regular commissions and for an aspiring career officer it's the end of the rainbow—you practically can't get discharged. The Commandant also said it looked as if I might graduate first in the class. I made a panic call to Ferguson and he told me to turn the regular commission down. I told the Commandant who said it might not help our cover situation (he's the only officer on the OCS staff who knows of our CIA sponsorship), if the top graduate refuses a regular commission. I got the hint and am holding back an academic paper which should drop me a notch or two. But the Commandant took my refusal of the regular commission like a slap in the face. Guess this hasn't come up before.

My orders after commissioning are for transfer to the Tactical Air Command. It's too good to believe: assignment as intelligence officer to a fighter squadron at a base just outside Los Angeles.

Victorville, California — June 1959

My orders finally came for transfer back to Washington —to the company bogus unit, I mean. It's been a marvelous year, driving up and down those motorways to Mexico, San Francisco, Yosemite, Monterey. I finally got busy training the pilots in targeting because we have the new F-104 and nuclear targets in China. I've also done some training in evasion and escape because some of the targets are one-way ditch missions. The only big mistake was volunteering for the Survival School at Reno, Nevada because they sent me to the January course and the week-long trek in the mountains was on snowshoes—pure misery.

I've been seeing Janet, my girlfriend from college, almost every weekend since last summer. I've told her about my work in the company and about my hopes to be assigned abroad. We've talked a lot about marriage but we're not sure what to do. She would like to stay in California, and I wonder if I should wait until after the JOT course is over a year from now. I'll be leaving for

Washington in a couple of weeks and we'll see how we endure the separation.

Washington, D.C. — September 1959

It didn't take a long time for us to decide. Less than a month after I left California we agreed we didn't want to wait any longer, so now we begin a life together. We were married at Notre Dame as a kind of compromise because Janet's family is Congregationalist and she felt a wedding in a Catholic Church in her home town might raise difficulties. We took a small apartment in the building complex where Vice-President Nixon and his wife first lived when they came to Washington after his election to the House. We have furniture to buy, but family and friends have been exceedingly generous and new gifts arrive every day. We can save some money by shopping at the military commissaries because I'm still on active duty.

My military cover unit is an Air Intelligence Service Squadron at Bolling Air Force Base in Washington. My cover telephone number has changed but the same two telephone operators are rolling the same dice to see who will be the colonel and who the major.

Ferguson said I probably won't be discharged until June or July of next year, which will coincide with the end of the JOT training program.

All the JOT's in the OCS class ahead of me, my class, and the one behind me are united in the JOT program. Even so, we make up only about fifteen of the sixty-odd in the class—which includes only six women. The JOT classes, which have just started, are held in the Recreation and Services Building, the same one where I was tested by the Assessment and Evaluation staff two years ago. The "A and E" routines are even longer now than before and I'm going through all of those monotonous tests again. The only thing we lack is a mammoth Potomac Park football stadium for Saturday afternoon frenzy—the rest is the old college routine once more.

The opening sessions in the training course were welcoming speeches by Allen Dulles, Colonel Baird, and others who have been showering us with affection and praise for following them into this life of deliberate self-abnegation, unknown sacrifice and silent courage as secret warriors in the battles of our time. Very romantic. Each one of us in the class represents the one in a hundred, or one in a thousand, of the total number of applicants for the JOT program who were finally accepted. The company leaders tell us we're entering the world's second oldest profession (maybe even the first, but that can't be proved) and if there are any uneasy consciences in the group they have been soothed by Biblical quotations showing that no less a figure than God himself instituted spying. So much for the moral question.

But our country had forgotten the lesson of Jericho. In 1929 Secretary of State H. L. Stimson closed the code-breaking operation known as the Black Chamber with the scolding that "gentlemen don't read other people's mail." Until Pearl Harbor foreign intelligence in the United States was all but forgotten. Then there were the heroics of the OSS during the war followed by the decision of President and Congress alike not to risk another surprise attack by leaving early warning to peace-time military neglect once again. So the civilian CIA was established in 1947 to provide a centralized agency for processing all foreign intelligence and for producing a national intelligence product blessed by enlightenment from all possible sources.

After two years away with the Air Force these first sessions have been stimulating and even exciting—almost like a raging thirst being finally quenched. The JOT office has arranged evening language courses for anyone interested, and Janet and I have a class in Spanish three nights a week. It's nice that the company includes the wives as much as possible. Otherwise they would really be at a distance, because everything we study and read, almost, is classified. We selected Spanish only because that was my language at school, but there is a monetary awards program for maintenance and improvement of foreign languages and it might be a way to earn a little extra. Things are working out just right.

Washington, D.C. — October 1959

We've just finished a month studying communism and Soviet foreign policy, and soon we'll began studying the government organization for national security, where the Agency fits in, and the bureaucratic organization of headquarters. Each of us has periodic sessions with one of the JOT counsellors to discuss possible future assignments and where to continue training after Christmas. Almost everyone seems to want to go into secret operations, which will mean six months' special training away from Washington at a place called "the farm." I told Ferguson I wanted to go to "the farm," but he was non-committal.

The lectures and readings in communism have been especially interesting. The Office of Training stays away from philosophy—dialectical materialism wasn't even mentioned—while concentrating on the Soviets. It's a practical approach, of sorts, because what the CIA is up against, one way or another, is Russian expansion directed by the Communist Party of the Soviet Union —CPSU. The Leninist concept of the party, particularly its élitist and secretive nature, and the CPSU's difficulties in reconciling pragmatism with ideology (Russian domination of the minority nationalities, NEP, collectivization and elimination of the kulaks, united front doctrine, the Molotov–Ribbentrop pact) are seen as related to one goal: obtaining, retaining and expanding power.

Subservience of foreign communist parties to the CPSU is another theme given considerable emphasis—it's hard to believe that the Soviets with a straight face preach that the first obligation of every communist, no matter what nationality, is to defend the Soviet Union. Institutions such as the Comintern and Cominform served that purpose in their time, but the KGB is the principal organ. Much importance, of course, is given to the Soviet security organizations, from the Cheka down.

The writings of defectors from communism were the most interesting: Louis Budenz, Howard Fast, *The God that Failed*, Kravchenko, Gouzenko, Petrov. But the most devastating for the Soviets, because of his criticism of Leninist party doctrine, is Milovan Djilas. The other day we split into small groups and interviewed Peter Deriabin‡—he's the highest-ranked KGB defector yet. It was done through closed-circuit television so that he could not see us (to protect our security) and he was disguised and spoke through an interpreter (to protect his security because he is living in the Washington area).

The central theory is that communist attempts to set up dictatorships around the world are really manifestations of Soviet expansion which in turn is determined by the need to maintain CPSU power at home. Our country is the real target, however, and the Soviets have said often enough that peace is impossible until the U.S. is defeated. Now we're going to study how the government, and the CIA in particular, are set up to counter the Soviet threat.

Washington, D.C. — November 1959

A theme that is continually repeated during these sessions is that the CIA does not make policy. The Agency's job is to provide the intelligence or information that is used by the President and other policymakers. It only executes policy, and collects information to be used in policy decisions by people outside the Agency. It doesn't make policy.

For several weeks we have been listening to lectures and reading documents on the government machinery for national security. The basic document is the National Security Act of 1947 which set up the National Security Council (NSC) as the highest body concerned with national security. Chaired by the President, the NSC is composed of the following statutory members: the Secretary of State, the Secretary of Defense, the Director of the Office of Civil and Defense Mobilization, and the Vice-President. Membership can be enlarged whenever the President desires by *ad hoc* appointments such as the Attorney-General or the Secretary of the Treasury. The Chairman of the Joint

Chiefs of Staff (JCS) and the Director of Central Intelligence (DCI) are NSC observers.[1]

The NSC has its own staff and offices in the Executive Office Building next to the White House and, in addition, has three important subordinate groups reporting to it: the NSC Planning Board, the Operations Coordination Board (OCB),[2] and the Intelligence Advisory Committee (IAC).[3] The NSC Planning Board works mostly on preparing materials for NSC meetings and on following up the implementation of NSC decisions. The OCB is of very special interest to the Agency because its function is to review and approve CIA action operations (as opposed to collection of information) such as propaganda, paramilitary operations and political warfare. The OCB is composed of the DCI, the Under-Secretary of State, the Deputy Secretary of Defense and *ad hoc* members at the Under-Secretary level.

The IAC is like a board of directors of the intelligence community, chaired by the DCI and having as members the Deputy Director of Central Intelligence, the intelligence chiefs of the Army, Navy, Air Force, Joint Chiefs of Staff, the Chief of Intelligence and Research (INR) of the Department of State and the Director of the National Security Agency. Intelligence chiefs of the FBI and the Atomic Energy Commission sit on the IAC when appropriate. The purpose of the IAC is to assign intelligence tasks among the different services according, at least in theory, to which service can best do the job. It is also designed to avoid both overlaps and gaps in the national intelligence effort, and it has several subordinate interdepartmental groups such as the Board of National Estimates, the National Intelligence Survey Committee and the Watch Committee, each of which is chaired by a CIA officer.

As part of the NSC mechanism the National Security Act of 1947 established the office of the DCI as the NSC's principal intelligence officer and the Central In-

---

1. See Chart I, p. 652.
2. Later known as the 54–12 Group, the Special Group, the 303 Group, the Forty Committee.
3. Later renamed the United States Intelligence Board.

telligence Agency as the organization that would effect the centralizing of the national intelligence effort. The CIA has five statutory functions:

1. To advise the NSC in matters concerning such intelligence activities of the government departments and agencies as relate to national security.
2. To make recommendations to the NSC for the coordination of such intelligence activities.
3. To correlate and evaluate intelligence relating to the national security, and provide for the appropriate dissemination of such intelligence within the government.
4. To perform, for the benefit of the existing intelligence agencies, such additional services of common concern as the NSC determines can be more efficiently accomplished centrally.
5. To perform such other functions and duties related to intelligence affecting the national security as the NSC may from time to time direct.

It is this fifth function which occupies most of the CIA's time and money. It's the dagger inside the cloak. Covert action, although it is not spelled out for us this way, is a form of intervention somewhere between correct, polite diplomacy and outright military invasion. Covert action is the real reason for the CIA's existence, and it was born out of political and economic necessity.

The DCI is described as a man with two hats. First, he is the principal intelligence advisor to the President and the NSC, and secondly, he is the Director of the Central Intelligence Agency. Formal commands are given by the NSC to the DCI through Top Secret Documents called National Security Council Intelligence Directives (NSCID's—pronounced non-skids). The NSCID's are put into effect by documents issued by the DCI to the concerned member of the intelligence community, including the CIA, these documents being called Director of Central Intelligence Directives (DCID's). Within the CIA the DCID's are particularized in the thick and continually changing volumes of regulations and other instructions. We have been studying, then, the very broadly worded NSCID's, the more particularized DCID's, and the specific CIA regulations. These are the documents that govern everything from foreign intelligence collection operations through political, psychological and paramilitary operations to communications and electronic intelligence efforts. Clearly, the documentation and the bureaucratic structure demonstrate that what the Agency does is ordered by the President and the NSC. The Agency neither makes decisions on policy nor acts on its own account. *It is an instrument of the President* . . . to use in any way he pleases.

We have also examined the question of Congressional monitoring of intelligence activities and of the Agency in particular. The problem resides in the National Security Act of 1947 and also in its amendment, the Central Intelligence Agency Act of 1949. These laws charged the DCI with protecting the "sources and methods" of the U.S. intelligence effort and also exempted the DCI and the Bureau of the Budget from reporting to Congress on the organization, function, personnel and expenditures of the CIA—whose budget is hidden in the budgets of other executive agencies. The DCI, in fact, can secretly spend whatever portion of the CIA budget he determines necessary, with no other accounting than his own signature. Such expenditures, free from review by Congress or the General Accounting Office or, in theory, by anyone outside the executive branch, are called "unvouchered funds." By passage of these laws Congress has sealed itself off from CIA activities, although four small sub-committees are informed periodically on important matters by the DCI. These are the Senate and House sub-committees of the Armed Services and Appropriations Committees, and the speeches of their principal spokesman, Senator Richard Russell, are required reading for the JOT's.

There have been several times when CIA autonomy was threatened. The Hoover Commission Task Force on Intelligence Activities headed by General Mark Clark recommended in 1955 that a Congressional Watchdog Committee be established to oversee the CIA much as the Joint Congressional Committee on Atomic Energy watches over the AEC. The Clark Committee, in fact, did not believe the sub-committees of the Armed Services and Appropriations Committees were able to exercise effectively the Congressional monitoring function. However, the problem was corrected, according to the Agency position, when President Eisenhower, early in 1956, established his own appointative committee to oversee the Agency. This is the President's Board of Consultants on Foreign Intelligence Activities,[1] whose chairman is James R. Killian, President of Massachusetts Institute of Technology. It can provide the kind of "private citizen" monitoring of the Agency that Congress didn't want. Moreover, our speakers have pointed out, the more Congress gets into the act the greater the danger of accidental revelation of secrets by indiscreet politicians. Established relationships with intelligence services of other countries, like Great Britain, might be complicated. The Congress was quite right at the beginning in giving up control—so much for them, their job is to appropriate the money.

Washington, D.C. — December 1959

Studying the Agency bureaucratic structure has been fascinating but at the same time exhausting—there's been no end to organizational charts and speeches by representatives from every one of the divisions, subdivisions, offices and sub-offices. Each of the speakers has a story of how his office broke an important case by having just the right piece of information or person for the job.

Woven into the training program since the first days in September are constant reminders of the need for tight security. Capabilities and intentions of the enemy must be discovered, whether in the Kremlin, in a Soviet nuclear weapons factory, at a missile development site, or in the meeting-hall of an obscure communist party in Africa. But of utmost importance, since knowledge of the enemy is necessarily limited, is the protection of our intelligence. We don't want the enemy to know what we know about him, for then he could

---

1. Renamed in 1961 the President's Foreign Intelligence Advisory Board.

take measures to annul our advantage. So we have to protect our intelligence by building a curtain of secrecy called "security." Receptionists, guards, badges, barred windows, combination safe-filing cabinets, polygraphs, background investigations, punishments for security violations, compartmentation and the "need-to-know" principle.

Compartmentation is the separation of activities whereby a person or group performing a particular task do not know what tasks other people are doing. The gap between people doing different jobs is bridged by the need to know. If a person working in intelligence has a definite need to know what others are doing on a specific job, he will be given access. If not, he is expected to subdue normal curiosity. The CIA is organized with built-in compartmentation designed to give maximum protection to the secret information collected for the policymakers.

The CIA bureaucracy is fairly complicated.[1] At the top of the pyramid are the executive offices composed of the Offices of the Director, the Deputy Director, the Inspector-General, the General Counsel, the Comptroller and the Cable Secretariat.

Below the executive offices are four deputy directorates, each responsible for distinct activities and each named after the title of the deputy director who heads it. They are the DDI, headed by the Deputy Director, Intelligence; the DDP, headed by the Deputy Director, Plans; the DDS, headed by the Deputy Director, Support; and the DDC, headed by the Deputy Director, Coördination. The DDC, we were told, is a small office dealing with management problems, and we have spent practically no time discussing it. The other three deputy directorates are the bone and muscle of the Agency. (See pp. 323–24 for organizational changes in the early 1960s.)

The DDI is the component that sets requirements, engages in some collection, evaluates and collates intelligence, and produces the finished product.[2] It consists

1. See Chart II.
2. See Chart III.

of several different offices, each of which provides a coordinating function for the entire intelligence community. They are the Office of Current Intelligence (OCI), the Office of National Estimates (ONE), the Office of Basic Intelligence (OBI), the Office of Scientific Intelligence (OSI), the Office of Research and Reports (ORR), the Office of Central Reference (OCR), the Office of Operations (OO), the Foreign Broadcast Information Service (FBIS), the National Photographic Interpretation Center (NPIC). We have been asked to write examples of the different types of specialized report prepared by these offices, and we have visited several of them. It is interesting to note that over 80 per cent of the information that goes into finished intelligence reports is from overt sources such as scientific and technical journals, political speeches and other public documents. The rest is obtained from secret agents or techniques, and the difference, of course, is in the quality and sensitivity of the covertly collected intelligence.

The clandestine collection part of the CIA is the DDP which is also known as the Clandestine Services (CS). It consists of a headquarters' organization with field stations and bases in almost all foreign countries. Although we reviewed the headquarters' organization of the DDP we were told that the details of how secret operations are run will be given only during the later instruction. Only the JOT's who express a desire to serve in the DDP and who agree in writing to take an assignment to any country will be given the advanced operational training at "the farm." Those who want to work in some area of the Agency other than the DDP will go on to specialized training in headquarters.

The bulk of the CS is divided into operating divisions and senior staffs.[1] The operating divisions are in charge of geographical areas and certain specialized services. The senior staffs are in charge of coordination and review of all operational activities within the functional category of each—which are reflections of basic CIA operational theory. There are three senior staffs: the Foreign Intelligence (FI) staff; the Psychological War-

1. See Chart IV.

fare and Paramilitary (PP) staff; and the Counter-Intelligence (CI) staff. The FI staff is concerned with intelligence *collection* operations, the PP staff with *action* operations and the CI staff with *protection* of FI and PP operations. The difference between collection and action operations is that collection should leave no sign, whereas action operations always have a visible effect. (See pp. 323–24 for organizational changes in 1960s.)

A collection operation might be the running of an agent in the Soviet Ministry of Defense who is reporting on military planning. An action operation might be an anti-communist intellectual journal, supported by CIA money, passed through a Russian *émigré* organization with headquarters in Paris. Collection operations respond to the needs of the DDI, for producing finished intelligence—which in turn depends on the needs of the NSC and other consumers such as the military services and the Department of State. Action operations consist of the control, guidance and support of individuals and organizations engaged in the battle against communism throughout the world. They include labor unions, youth and student organizations, public information media, professional societies such as journalists and lawyers, businessmen's organizations, politicians and political parties and governments. Action operations also include the training and support of irregular military forces such as guerrillas in Tibet or montagnards in Vietnam or saboteurs in Communist China. Protection operations consists generally of CIA efforts to protect the Agency against hostile penetration and to penetrate intelligence services of other countries in order to discover what operations those services are running against us.

The DDP area divisions are responsible for all activities of the CS within designated areas. These divisions are for Western Europe (WE) (which includes Canada), Eastern Europe (EE), Soviet Russia (SR), the Near East (NE), Africa (AF), the Far East (FE) and the Western Hemisphere (WH). Each area division is headed by a Division Chief and Deputy Chief whose offices include staffs responsible for review of FI, PP and CI operations within the geographical area.[1]

Within each division the geographical area is divided into branches which may include one or more countries as well as functional specialties peculiar to the division. The branches in turn are divided into country desks when more than one country is included in the branch. Thus the Polish branch of EE Division deals exclusively with matters on Poland while the Central American branch of WH Division has separate desks for six different countries.

A division and branch of the Clandestine Services in headquarters are responsible for supporting field stations and bases in the foreign countries within its area, as well as for keeping the senior staffs and the DDP advised on all matters related to those countries, informational as well as operational. A headquarters' division will provide personnel for the stations and bases, arrange training support by specialists and, most important, process the paper-work required for all field operations. Every operation, every agent and every report sent from the field to headquarters requires review and routing of documents. Area divisions are responsible for seeing that this enormous flow of paper is properly channeled to the appropriate offices of the CS for review, advice and approval or disapproval. *Intelligence* reports, as opposed to *operational* reports which deal with the mechanics of *how* information is obtained, also need processing for spelling, grammatical usage and routing to interested components of the CS, the DDI and the rest of the intelligence community. Processing of the operational and intelligence reports from the field is the job of desk officers in the area divisions.

The CS includes four divisions that serve the rest. The International Organizations Division (IO) supervises CIA relations with labor, youth, student, professional and news media organizations throughout the world. Activities in these fields are coordinated by IO with the PP staff and with the area divisions and branches concerned. Contact between the CIA and officials of

---

1. See pp. 323–24.

those organizations might be handled by an officer of IO or by a station officer where a particular operational activity takes place.

The Technical Services Division (TSD) provides support to operations in all area divisions through experts in listening devices, photography, lock-picking, invisible writing, clandestine opening and closing of correspondence, disguise, containers with hidden compartments, handwriting analysis, identification of persons through saliva analysis from objects such as cigarette butts, and many other technical services. Specialists are available for training agents as well as to perform tasks themselves. Several TSD support bases exist in foreign countries for regional support. The TSD also has a continuing research program for improving its capabilities and for developing protective measures against the devices of foreign services, especially the KGB.

Division D is the CS unit that supports the National Security Agency in cracking the codes of foreign governments. When it is necessary to mount operations in the field against the communications of other countries, NSA turns to its sister intelligence services, such as the military services, all of which have sizable monitoring operations going against communist countries' military communications. Or NSA could turn to Division D which coordinates CIA collection support for NSA. Thus Division D provides expert knowledge for the planning of operations to recruit code clerks or to install technical devices to enable the decrypting of coded messages. Division D seems to be the most hush-hush of the CS operating divisions, but, like IO Division, its activities are always coordinated with the geographical area divisions and with station chiefs abroad.

The Records Integration Division (RID) is to the Clandestine Services what OCR is to the DDI. It is somewhat different, however, because of the different needs of the DDP. Clearly the Agency has spared no expense with the best system for storage and retrieval that IBM can build. Numbering systems exist for topics and subtopics for every country for storing intelligence reports. They also exist for all agents and the different phases of each operation. Millions of names are indexed for easy electronic processing and retrieval and microfilm is automated so that copies of documents can be obtained simply by pushing buttons according to coding classifications—practically instant retrieval of one document from among millions. As the central repository for all CS intelligence and operational reports, RID serves the entire headquarters DDP organization and the field stations as well.

The DDS[1] is the support structure of the Agency, much of which serves the DDP. This is the deputy directorate that we belong to as JOT's. The most important offices of the DDS are Personnel, Security, Training, Finance, Communications and Logistics. Each of these offices has an important function, but most of us have been pushing hard for the special operations training and for assignment to the DDP.

A few days ago a list was read of those who have been accepted for "the farm." I was on the list—practically everyone was—and we had a special briefing on what lies ahead. "The farm" is officially known by the cryptonym ISOLATION (cryptonyms are always written in capitals), and is a covert training site run by the Office of Training under military cover. It is a few hours' drive from Washington, and we will spend most of the next six months there. On Friday evenings those who wish will be allowed to check out for the weekend. The briefing officer said that there is daily Agency air service (military cover) between Washington National Airport and ISOLATION, but the flights are used mostly by Agency personnel not assigned for long periods to the base. At the briefer's suggestion we have divided into groups of four or five for car pools so that as many wives as possible will be able to get around Washington during the week. Apparently we won't need transportation at ISOLATION anyway.

We have been given a Washington telephone number and told that it is a direct line to ISOLATION for families but only to be used for emergencies. The briefing officer finally told us the name and location of the base, the best route for driving and our instructions for

1. See Chart V.

reporting. He placed extreme emphasis on protecting the cover for the base and the sensitivity of its identification. He said that agents from all over the world are trained there and they are not supposed to know where they are. We probably won't even see them. The name of the base is so sensitive, in fact, that we were told not to tell any of the JOT classmates who weren't taking the operations training, nor any other Agency employees, nor even our wives. Nobody talks about ISOLATION, and in conversations and even formal briefing sessions it's just "the farm."

We report to "the farm" the first Monday after New Year's Day. I feel relaxed now—the customary over-eagerness has disappeared. I've been accepted into the work I want and only an utter catastrophe can wash me out. Six more months of training, study, learning a profession. Then an assignment to a DDP headquarters desk and in another year or two I'll be a secret overseas operative.

Camp Peary, Virginia — January 1960

The entrance to Camp Peary is an ordinary looking gatehouse manned by military police about fifteen minutes out of Williamsburg on the road towards Richmond. We showed our company badges to a guard and he instructed our car pool driver which turns to take to get to the JOT area. Our first session was in an amphitheater called the "pit" where we were welcomed by the ISOLATION Base Chief—formerly a Chief of Station in Mexico City. Then we were briefed by the Base Security Officer on the do's and don'ts of ISOLATION. At any one time there are a number of different training sessions being conducted here, some with foreigners who are not even supposed to know that they are in the U.S. These are called "black" trainees and are restricted to areas away from the JOT site and other "normal" activities. From time to time we will hear weapons firing and explosions as well as aircraft movement.

We are to stay in the general area of the JOT site except when coming or going from the base entrance, although we will have training sessions at sites all over the base where we will be taken by bus. Wherever we go on the base we are to take extreme caution with cigarette packages, beer cans or other objects that might reveal the location of the base to "black" trainees. We are to wear Army fatigues at all times on the base.

We are discouraged, although not forbidden, from leaving the base at night, but the Base Chief told us we will have night study and training sessions that will leave little time for visits to Williamsburg. Since all of us pertain to bogus Defense Department cover units in Washington, our cover story for ISOLATION is that we are Defense Department employees temporarily assigned to Camp Peary. The security officer gave us the name of an Army colonel and his Pentagon telephone extension in the unlikely event of verification of our status at Camp Peary becoming necessary. This Pentagon extension rings in the Camp Peary administration building where a CIA officer plays the part of the colonel.

The base is thickly wooded and surrounded by high, chain-link fences topped by barbed-wire with conveniently placed signs warning: "U.S. Government Reservation. No Trespassing." The northern boundary of the base is the York River and the base itself is divided internally into different tightly-controlled areas including administration, which is towards the entrance, the JOT training site, the staff housing area, the landing field, and distinct sites for training in border crossing, sabotage, weapons, air and maritime operations, ambush, evasion and escape, and clandestine meetings. Deer are plentiful as the base was once a wildlife refuge, and there are several ranges for hunting as well as a couple of stocked lakes.

After the fatigues were issued we checked into the old wooden-frame barracks that have double rooms rather than open bays. All the buildings, in fact, are World War II-style frame buildings except the new brick gymnasium. There are classroom buildings, the training office where instructors have their offices, mess hall, officers' club, movie theater, football fields and a softball diamond. For leisure time we have the club and sports facilities and even a language lab where we can work with tapes. ISOLATION won't be bad at all, and on Friday nights we can drive back to Washington for the weekends.

Each of us has been assigned an advisor from the teaching staff with whom we will meet from time to time to discuss our strengths and weaknesses. Mine is John Allen,‡ an "old NE hand" who served in Cairo. The training course will be divided along the usual lines of Foreign Intelligence (collection), Counter-Intelligence (protection) and Paramilitary and Psychological (action). We will also spend considerable time, they said, studying the tools of the clandestine operator, otherwise known as "tradecraft." Finally there will be many practical exercises in and around ISOLATION as part of the war-games technique used to create the training scenario.

As all clandestine operations take place within a political context, the first consideration is the set of objective factors that create the "operational environment or climate." These factors include the friendliness or hostility of the host government, the level of sophistication of the host internal security services and other intelligence services operating in the same area, the known and presumed aims of these services, the effectiveness and sophistication of the local communist and other revolutionary organizations, local language, dress and other customs, and the general political atmosphere of repression or liberalism. These are the objective conditions within which clandestine operations are undertaken, and they determine the manner in which these are executed. Running an agent-penetration of the Ministry of Defense in Baghdad obviously differs from running the same type of penetration in Paris or Prague or Bogotá. As the degree of clandestinity can vary according to the tools and techniques employed—operational security practices can be more extreme or less—the "operational environment" determines whether goals are realistic and how they are to be achieved. It includes a continuing evaluation of enemy capabilities.

Taking into account, then, the operational environment, each CIA station has a charter or general operational guide called the Related Missions Directive

(RMD). This is the document that establishes priorities and objectives and is, in effect, the DCI's instructions to the Chief of Station. In any country where there is an official Soviet presence, such as an embassy or trade mission, the first priority for the RMD is almost always the penetration of the Soviet mission through the recruitment of its personnel or by a technical device. Penetration operations against Chinese and other communist governments follow in priority as do intelligence collection efforts against indigenous revolutionary movements and local governments, whether friendly or hostile. CI and PP operations are also included in the RMD, and when a station requests headquarters' approval of new operations or continuation of existing operations, reference is made to the appropriate paragraphs of the RMD.

I suppose my problem will eventually disappear, but I find it all rather complicated because in the CIA cryptonyms and pseudonyms are used in place of true names. There are many standard ones and, when reading, one has constantly to refer from the text with cryptonyms to the cryptonym lists which give a number, and then look up the same number on a separate true name list. The cryptonym and true name lists are never kept in the same safe. Cryptonyms consist of two letters that determine a general category or place, followed by letters that form a word with the first two, or by another word.

Thus the United States government is ODYOKE. The Department of State is ODACID, the Department of Defense is ODEARL, the Navy is ODOATH, the FBI is ODENVY. All government agencies have a cryptonym beginning with OD. The CIA's cryptonym is KUBARK and all Agency components have cryptonyms beginning with KU. The Clandestine Services is KUDOVE, the FI staff (and FI operations generically) is KUTUBE, the CI staff (and CI operations) is KUDESK, the PP staff (and PP operations) is KUCAGE. Every foreign country and every agent and operation in that country has a cryptonym that begins with the same two letters—AE for the Soviet Union, BE for Poland, DI for Czechoslovakia, DM for Yugoslavia, SM for the United Kingdom, DN for South Korea, etc.

AELADLE, AEJAMMER and AEBROOM are cryptonyms for operations against the Soviets.

Cryptonyms are used to substitute for true names in order to protect the true identities of persons and places mentioned in correspondence. They are only used in documents of the Clandestine Services. The Records Integration Division assigns new cryptonyms whenever a new operation or agent is proposed, using the first two letters that correspond to the particular country. In certain cases agents and operations are given cryptonyms of which the first two letters refer to operations that occur in several countries—particularly the international organizations involving labor and students. In operational correspondence when no cryptonym has yet been assigned for a particular person, the word IDENTITY is substituted in the text and the truc name is sent in separate correspondence for reconciliation with the original document by the addressee.

All KUDOVE officers who engage in operations are assigned a pseudonym consisting of a first name, middle initial and last name which is used in the same fashion as cryptonyms—in order to preserve the officer's true identity should correspondence be lost or stolen. Pseudonyms are always written with the last name in capital letters, e.g. Rodney J. PRINGLE.

All this seems confusing at first—it's really like learning a new language. But it adds a certain spice to the work, like a special taste that helps develop institutional identity—more and more of the inside group syndrome.

Camp Peary, Virginia — February 1960

We still have plenty of snow on the ground and on Sunday nights when we return from Washington the deer are so thick along the base roads that we almost run into them. We've all gotten to know each other more since coming to ISOLATION. Almost any type of person you want can be found in the class. We have a physical training program three or four times a week at the gym—calesthenics, basketball, squash, volleyball, and weights. We also have training at the gym in defense, disarming, maiming, and even killing with bare hands—just how and where to strike, as in karate and judo. Our instructor in these skills (at first nobody believed his real name was Burt Courage) was formerly on Saipan in the South Pacific, which is another secret base of the Office of Training.

It's hard work. There is a physical-conditioning program, plenty of practice in the martial arts. How to disarm or cripple, if necessary kill an opponent. We have classes in propaganda, infiltration-exfiltration, youth and student operations, labor operations, targeting and penetration of enemy organizations. How to run liaison projects with friendly intelligence services so as to give as little and get as much information as possible. Anti-Soviet operations – that subject gets special attention. We have classes in framing Russian officials, trying to get them to defect. The major subject, though, is how to run agents—single agents, networks of agents.

In the classes we have been studying the different kinds of Foreign Intelligence—FI, or KUTUBE—operations conducted by the Clandestine Services. Although these operations are designed to discover the capabilities and intentions of foreign powers, particularly enemy or unfriendly governments, *vis-à-vis* the U.S., they are supposed to focus on secrets rather than on overt or public information. In addition to discovering ordinary state secrets, the CS is responsible for obtaining the most complete and accurate information possible on the global manifestations of Soviet imperialism, that is, on local communist parties and related political groups. The exceptions to the world-wide operating charter of the CS is the agreement among the U.S., the United Kingdom, Australia, Canada and New Zealand whereby each has formally promised to abstain from secret operations of any kind within the territory of the others except with prior approval of the host government. The governments of all other nations, their internal political groups and their scientific, military and economic secrets are fair game.

FI operations originate with the informational needs

of U.S. policymakers, specified in the voluminous requirements lists prepared by the various sections of the DDI that produce finished intelligence. These requirements are also reflected in the station RMD. The station, incidentally, is the CIA office in the capital city of a foreign country. Other major cities of the country may have CIA offices subordinate to the station and called bases. In most countries the stations and bases are in the political sections of the embassies or consulates, with some officers assigned for cover purposes to other sections such as economic or consular. In certain countries, however, such as Panama and Germany the CIA stations are on U.S. military installations with only the chief and a minimum of other officers having diplomatic status. Most of the others are under cover as civilian employees of the Department of Defense with assignment to the military bases.

The station's task is to determine the different ways desired information can be obtained and to propose to headquarters the method thought most appropriate. This task is called "targeting," and for every operation targeting receives its written expression in a Field Project Outline which is prepared at the station and includes all the operational details such as the purpose or desired outcome, specific target, the agents to be involved, any technical devices needed, support needed from headquarters or other stations, security and cover considerations with an assessment of the "flap potential" meaning the possible scandal if the operation is discovered, and costs. Most overseas CIA operations are described in Field Project Outlines, which are forwarded to headquarters for suggestions and approval or disapproval by all interested headquarters' sections of the CS.

Depending on the cost or sensitivity of an operation, the Project Outline is approved on a lower or higher level in headquarters, from Division Chief to Assistant DDP, to DDP, to DCI. Some operations require approval outside the CIA, but these are usually PP (action) projects that are submitted to the Operations Coordination Board of the National Security Council (the Under-Secretary level).

Projects for intelligence collection operations are generally approved for periods of one year and can be renewed. The request for Project Renewal is a document almost identical to the Field Project Outline and it includes details of the operation's progress over the past year such as productivity, costs, security problems, new agents and justification for continuation. Operations that have failed to meet expectations or that are compromised by a security flap or that have simply dried up are cancelled through a "Request for Project Termination" forwarded from the station to headquarters. This document includes the details on reasons for termination, disposal of agents and property, alternative sources, security and cover considerations and support requirements from other stations or from headquarters.

Correspondence among CIA stations, bases and headquarters is the lifeline of Agency operations. There are two basic types: operational reporting and intelligence reporting. In operational correspondence matters discussed include security problems, cover, finances, agent access to targets, levels of production (but not the facts themselves), proposals for new recruitments or termination, equipment requirements, agent motivation, and any other occurrences that affect the operation. On every operation an Operational Progress Report is required by headquarters every three months, but much more frequent correspondence is usually necessary.

Intelligence reporting from overseas operations comes in the form of a Field Information Report (FIR) which contains facts related usually to one subject but possibly from several sources. The FIR relates the facts as obtained from the sources although source or field comments may be added. FIR's are prepared in the stations on special mats for printing which are forwarded to headquarters for reproduction and distribution. FIR's contain a heading that includes the name of the country or countries concerned, the subject-matter of the report, a description of the source (prepared to protect his identity), an evaluation of the source's reliability and an evaluation of the accuracy of the contents of the report. The body of the report follows with the clarifying comments or opinions of source, station or headquarters at the end. In headquarters the FIR's are given CS numbers for retrieval purposes, and copies are sent, for instance, to DDI sections, the Departments of State and Defense, the FBI or the White House.

Both operational reports and intelligence reports may be sent to headquarters or other stations and bases either via the diplomatic pouch or by cable or wireless. Practically all stations and bases have radio transmitting and receiving equipment although commercial telegraph service is frequently used.

How do we get the information that goes into the intelligence reports of FI operations? Mostly through paid agents. On the highest level there is the politician, scientist, economist or military leader who is actually creating the events that the Agency would like to forecast. This kind of person, however, because of his position of leadership, is the least likely to tell the CIA or the U.S. government his own country's official secrets. There are some, however, who can be convinced that the interests of the U.S. and their own country are so close, even identical, that nothing is lost by providing the information wanted by the CIA. In other cases what the high level official says or plans may be placed on paper to which access may be obtained by a whole variety of secondary level officials, functionaries or colleagues. People of this level may betray their leader's confidence for a great variety of motives. Then there is the third level of prospective agents who simply have physical access to a target area but not to documents themselves. These people may be trained to place listening devices where sensitive conversations are held or to open secure document storage containers or to photograph documents. Finally there is a great variety of people who can assist in operations but who have no direct access to the sources themselves. These are the support agents who rent houses and apartments, buy vehicles, serve as couriers, and perform countless additional necessary tasks.

There are, then, in addition to operations involving high-level, primary sources, a category of extremely important secondary operations called "support operations." Often targeting to primary sources is effected through support operations. These operations involve the use of surveillance teams to follow people in the streets, observation posts to watch the comings and goings from buildings, multiple forms of photography, interception of correspondence from the mails, access to important statistics and identification files of police and other security services, airline, rail and ship passenger and freight lists, devices for listening, telephone tapping and telegraph records. These operations may very well yield sensitive, high quality intelligence but more often they are used to identify the people we really need to get at, who may be recruited as intelligence collection agents. Support operations are also indispensable for knowledge of target personalities in order to discover motives that might make them accept or decline a recruitment approach: strengths, weaknesses, problems, ambitions, failures, enmities, vulnerabilities.

Another type of FI operation that is very common throughout the free world results from the working relationships between the CIA and the intelligence and security services of foreign countries. Contacts with foreign services are known as liaison operations and their purpose is to exchange information, mount joint operations and penetrate foreign services. The general rule on exchange of information is to give nothing unless necessary. But since foreign services usually press for an exchange, and often in poor countries they collect very little useful information on their own, the second rule is to preserve a net gain, or favorable balance towards the CIA in the exchange. Regulations determine the types of information that can be exchanged and the record-keeping required.

The "third agency rule" is an important operating principle in liaison operations. Information passed from one agency to a second agency cannot be passed by the second agency to a third agency without prior approval of the first. The purpose of the rule, obviously, is to preserve the security of operations and the secrecy of information as well as the secrecy of the existence of the liaison relationship between the first two services. If, for example, the British equivalent of the CIA, MI-6, passed to the CIA station in London a certain piece of information, the CIA in turn could not pass that information to the Dutch Intelligence Service even though the information might be of great interest to the Dutch. In such a case the London station would either suggest that MI-6 pass the information directly to the Dutch (which may already have happened) or permission might be requested for the CIA itself to pass on the MI-6 information. In the event of a first agency agreeing that a second agency may pass information to a third, the first agency may not wish to be revealed to the third agency as the source, so that adequate concealment of the true source will be arranged. Sometimes it can get complicated.

The most important liaison operation of the CIA is with MI-6, whose cryptonym is SMOTH. It has been almost ten years since Burgess and Maclean disappeared, and SMOTH has apparently tightened its loose, "old boy," clubby security practices. The inner club also includes the services of Canada, Australia and New Zealand although the CIA receives relatively little from these. Liaison with the Dutch is considered excellent because they facilitate support operations against targets of mutual interest, as do the Italians who tap telephones and intercept correspondence for the CIA station in Rome. The West German services are considered to be thoroughly penetrated by the Soviets while liaison with the French has become difficult and sensitive since the return of de Gaulle.

In theory no operations should be undertaken by CIA stations with liaison services if the same operations can be mounted without the knowledge of the local service (excluding the U.K., Canada, Australia and New Zealand). Those operations undertaken without the knowledge or cooperation of a liaison service are called "unilateral," whereas bilateral operations are those mounted for the CIA with the knowledge and support of local services. As we examine various liaison relationships it becomes clear that the major FI results in Western Europe come from local services, particularly with support operations such as travel control, telephone tapping, physical surveillance, postal intercepts and cormunist party penetration operations. However, in underdeveloped, less sophisticated countries, local services usually lack the knowledge and technical capability to mount effective intelligence operations. Thus the station in many cases can choose whether to mount joint or bilateral operations, or to undertake the operations without the knowledge of the local service. The decision is often based on the local services' internal security but also on the CIA personnel available in a given country; when this is limited, it can balance the scales in favor of bilateral operations.

Finally, there is the matter of penetration of local services by the CIA. For many reasons, not the least of which is protection of the CIA itself, operational doctrine demands the continued effort to recruit controlled agents within liaison services. These agents, or prospective agents, are usually spotted by CIA officers assigned to work with the local service to exchange information, to train the local service and to work on the operations mounted by the local service to support the CIA. Thus a CIA station may have an information-exchange program going with a local service, a joint telephone-tapping operation with the local service and an officer or two of the local service on the payroll as a penetration of the same service. Penetration of liaison services, however, is more properly a counter-intelligence function.

FI operations, then, are those undertaken to obtain information on the capabilities and intentions of foreign governments, especially enemy and unfriendly governments. Ultimately the FI collection effort is aimed at recruiting or placing an agent in the Kremlin with access to the decision-making process of the Soviet Praesidium. From that dream situation, collection operations spread out and down to practically all other governments and their political, scientific and economic secrets, and from there to the most obscure communist or other revolutionary grouping of the extreme left.

As we study the different types of FI operations we engage in practical exercises, both here at ISOLATION and in cities near by such as Hampton, Norfolk, Newport News and Richmond. My main FI case has been a series of meetings with a leader of an opposition, nationalistic political party. I play the role of the station case officer under diplomatic cover while one of my instructors plays the foreign political leader. This is a developmental case and I have to work carefully to convince him that the best interests of his country and of the United States are so closely aligned that by helping me he will be helping his own country and political party. One more meeting and I'm going to offer him money.

Camp Peary, Virginia — March 1960

Counter-intelligence (CI or KUDESK) operations differ from foreign intelligence collection because by definition they are defensive in nature, designed to protect CIA operations from detection by the opposition. The opposition in this sense is every intelligence and security service in the world, from the KGB to the municipal police in Nairobi. Since many countries separate their foreign intelligence service from their internal security service, much as the FBI is separated from the CIA, CI operations are targeted against both the foreign and the internal services.

The CIA counter-intelligence function begins with the Office of Security of the DDS and its responsibility for physical and personnel security. By protecting buildings from entry by unauthorized persons and documents from perusal, the Office of Security serves to protect the overall CIA effort. Similarly, the lengthy and costly background investigations, together with the polygraph (cryptonym: LCFLUTTER) help to prevent the hiring of penetration agents. Continuing review of the security files of CIA personnel as well as periodic LCFLUTTER examinations are designed to reduce the risk of continued employment in the CIA of employees who might have been recruited by opposition services.

The use of cover and compartmentation also serves to protect secret operations by concealing the true employer of Agency members so as to prevent discovery. The same is true of organizations, buildings, apartments, vehicles, aircraft, ships and financing methods.

Cover protects operations by making them appear to be something legitimate that in reality they are not. Compartmentation reduces the chance that exposure of a single operation, for whatever reason, can lead to the exposure of additional operations. A CIA officer or agent could gain knowledge of what other officers or agents were doing only if it were necessary for him to do so for his own work.

Whether to use or not to use a particular prospective agent is determined, from the CI viewpoint, by the "operational approval" process. It is an integral part of every relationship between the CIA and foreign agents no matter what a given agent's tasks might be. The operational approval process begins with the initial spotting and assessment of a prospective agent and continues through field and headquarters' file checks and background investigation to the operational approval system established in the CI staff of the DDP.

No person may be used in an operational capacity by a field station without prior approval by the Operational Approval Branch of the Counter-Intelligence Staff of the DDP in headquarters (CI/OA). Requests for approval start from the field stations and are outlined in a document known as the Personal Record Questionnaire (PRQ) which is divided into two parts. The PRQ Part I contains some seven pages of basic biographical data including full name, date and place of birth, names of parents, names of family members, schools attended, employment history, marital history, military service, present and past citizenship, membership in political organizations, hobbies, any special qualifications, and use of drugs or other vices. In itself the PRQ Part I reveals no operational interest or plans. The PRQ Part II, which never carries the prospective agent's true name or other identifying data, is a document of similar length with all the details of operational plans for the agent. It is reconciled with the PRQ Part I by a numbering system and usually bears the cryptonym assigned to the prospective agent. In the PRQ Part II the proposed task for the agent is described, the means through which the information in PRQ Part I was obtained and verified is detailed, the cover used by the person who spotted and assessed the agent is given, and all the operational risks and advantages are discussed.

The officers in CI/OA run a series of name checks in headquarters and, after studying the case, give final approval or disapproval for the proposed use of the prospective agent. Assuming no serious problems exist, CI/OA issues a Provisional Operational Approval (POA) on the agent, effective for six months, at the end of which an Operational Approval (OA) is issued, based on additional investigation by the station and the CI staff.

Files are maintained on all agents and they always begin with the number 201—followed by a number of five to eight digits. The 201 file contains all the documents that pertain to a given agent and usually start with the PRQ and the request for POA. But the 201 file is divided into two parts which are stored separately for maximum security. One part contains true name documents while the other part contains cryptonym documents and operational information. Compromise of one part will not reveal both the true name and the operational use of the agent.

In addition to the continuing station assessment and evaluation of agents from a CI point of view (which is to protect the Agency from hostile penetration) and continuing file review in headquarters, almost all agents are polygraphed from time to time. We call this "fluttering," from the polygraph cryptonym LCFLUTTER. Agents are "fluttered" by the same polygraph officers of the Office of Security in headquarters who interview prospective Agency employees in Building 13. They travel, usually, in teams of two on periodic visits to several countries in the same geographical area, although special trips on the spur of the moment can be arranged for serious cases.

The polygraph is usually sent to field stations through the State Department diplomatic pouch, and is mounted snugly inside a suitcase, usually the two-suite size, caramel color made by the Samsonite company. These suitcases look innocuous and facilitate carrying the polygraph in and out of embassies and the places where agents are tested. Arrangements are made for agents to be "fluttered" in safe sites with interpreters as needed.

The questions usually concentrate on whom the agent has told about his relationship with the CIA and any contacts he may have had with other intelligence services. The purpose of using the "flutter" on agents is to root out double agents, although other matters inevitably arise such as honesty in reporting and in the use of money.

Communist Party (CP) Penetration Operations

Communist party penetration operations are all those efforts made to penetrate the communist and extreme leftist revolutionary movements around the world. Their purpose is to collect information on the capabilities, plans, officers, members, weaknesses, strengths and international connections of every revolutionary organization outside the communist bloc. They are considered primarily of a counter-intelligence nature because of the conspiratorial nature of communism and the similarity between communist parties and hostile intelligence services. The focal point of headquarters for specialized skill and advice on CP operations is the International Communism Division of the Counter-Intelligence Staff (CI/ICD). Although intelligence operations involving officials of communist-bloc countries may be included in the general definition of CP operations, because most government officials of interest in communist countries are also party members, these are more properly considered Soviet or satellite operations rather than CP operations.

A CIA station's approach to penetration of a communist party or of any revolutionary organization is determined by the operational environment and particularly on the measure of repression exerted against the revolutionary left. Another factor of major importance is the general economic and cultural level of a given country which will reflect markedly on the sophistication and vulnerability of the revolutionary groups. As a general rule, penetration of a communist party is more difficult in the degree that local security forces compel it to operate clandestinely. If a given party is completely forced underground, for example, there is no obvious way of penetrating it. Similarly, recruitment is easier to the degree that members of the party are forced to live in penury, and this generally corresponds to the overall level of a country's economic development. A communist in La Paz will be more likely to spy for money than a communist in Paris.

A proper interpretation of the operational climate is therefore an essential first step in any station's CP program. Next comes the matter of studying all the overt material available on the party. This can be very considerable in the case of a large and open party such as those of Italy, and France, or very limited in the case of a proscribed party that operates clandestinely, as in Paraguay. Such a study is based on the party press, speeches by its leaders, its propaganda notices, activities of front organizations and its degree of adherence to the party line that emanates from Moscow.

Penetration of communist parties and other local revolutionary organizations by agents are standard bread-and-butter operations of practically every CIA station. These agents are members of the revolutionary organizations on which they report through clandestine communications arrangements with the station. They are recruited in several ways. The first type is known as the "walk in." The walk-in is a member of the party who, from need of money, ideological disillusionment or other motive decides to offer his services to the U.S. government. He makes his initial contact either by walking into the U.S. Embassy or Consulate or by a more discreet path designed to protect him from discovery and party wrath.

It is the duty of every Chief of Station to make sure that the Embassy Security Officer (State Department) briefs the receptionists (usually local employees) and the Marine Guards about the possibility that nervous people who do not want to give their names may show up from time to time asking to speak to someone in the embassy about "politics" or the like. In such cases, a legitimate State Department officer, usually in the political section, will be notified and will hold a private, noncommittal interview letting the walk-in do most of the talking. In this way the station officers are protected.

The interviewing officer will advise an officer in the station and a decision will be made about the walk-in's *bona fides* and the advisability of direct contact by a station CP officer. A file check and background investigation is always made before risking an initial contact with the walk-in, since every precaution must be taken to avoid provocation.

If the walk-in looks favorable and contact is established a series of long sessions follow in which the walk-in details his political activities and his reasons for having contacted the U.S. government. His capabilities and willingness for future work as a spy against the party will be determined and sooner or later he will be "fluttered." The clearance process for POA will be initiated and if all goes well secret communications are established and a new CP penetration operation will be under way.

Another way of penetrating the CP is through the non-communist who is recruited to join the party and work his way up from the bottom. This is a long-haul approach and usually undertaken only as a last resort.

Perhaps the most difficult is the recruitment of members of a revolutionary organization who are in good standing. This type of operation depends on reports from other CP penetration operations because extensive knowledge of the prospective recruit is needed to determine vulnerabilities and possibilities for success. CIA stations are continually engaged in trying to recruit in this manner and files grow thicker until a decision is made to recruit or not to recruit.

The recruitment approach may be "hot" or "cold." In the first case a station agent, usually not a CP penetration agent, who knows or can get to know the target, will make the proposition, sometimes after long periods of nurturing the relationship and sometimes rather quickly. The cold approach may be made by a CIA officer or agent, perhaps wearing a disguise or called in from a neighboring country or from headquarters. He may accost the target in the street or at the target's home without prior personal acquaintance with him. This type of approach known as the "cold pitch" can backfire when knowledge of the target's vulnerabilities is defective, and a ready escape plan for the recruiting officer is advisable.

In both the hot and the cold approaches, prior arrangements are made for immediate debriefing at a safe site, or for secure communications afterwards should the target decline at first but reconsider later. The cold approach may also be undertaken, on a small or large scale, by sending letters or notices to possible recruits advising them of interest in their political work and suggesting that they share it with others. A serviceable but non-compromising address such as a post-box in the U.S. may be furnished as well as a separate identifying number for use by each prospective recruit. If the target answers by number he will be contacted by an officer under secure conditions.

Finally, there is the bugging of the homes or meeting-places of party officers. Such operations can be mounted successfully only if considerable information is available on people, places and the importance of meetings. These are not always available, given the secrecy required of conspiratorial revolutionary activity. But bugging yields excellent intelligence because it lacks the human factor that may color, exaggerate or otherwise distort the reports from agents.

A station's support operations may be used to assist in the CP program. Surveillance teams may discover secret meeting-places that may be bugged. Postal interception may provide interesting party correspondence, both from the national and the international mails. Observation posts may reveal participants in clandestine meetings or serve as listening posts for audio devices. Telephone tapping can reveal voluminous information on party functionaries and the routines of party leaders. Surreptitious entry may produce party records and membership lists.

Aside from the penetration program directed against revolutionary organizations, CIA stations also direct the offensive weapons of psychological and paramilitary operations against them. These include the placing of anti-communist propaganda in the public media, the frame-up of party officials for police arrest, the publishing of false propaganda attributed to the revolutionary group in such a way that it will be difficult to deny and damaging as well, the organizing of goon squads to beat up and intimidate party officials, using stink bombs and other harassment devices to break up meetings, and the calling on liaison services to take desired repressive action. But we shall study these types of operation later. Next we are concerned with the CI aspects of liaison operations.

Liaison Operations

From the standpoint of pure doctrine all liaison operations are considered compromised, since even the existence of a liaison relationship implies the giving of something by the CIA: at the very least the identity of a CIA officer. It is always hoped that the virtues of liaison operations with other intelligence services outweigh their defects, but the judgment is sometimes hard to make. The two most basic principles of liaison operations from the counter-intelligence point of view are: first, there is no such thing as a friendly intelligence service, and, second, all liaison services are penetrated by the Soviets or by local revolutionary groups. Thus any operations undertaken jointly by the CIA with a liaison service are by definition compromised from the start. It is for this reason that some CIA intelligence reports (FIR's) include the NOFORN or NO FOREIGN DISSEM indicators which restrict reports to U.S. officials only. The indicators are used so that foreign liaison services will not receive information from sensitive sources in the course of normal exchange programs.

Why get involved with other services? Basically, liaison operations are conducted because they are useful. They extend a station's limited manpower however shaky the extension may be. They give the CIA a foot in the door for penetration of the liaison service. And they may also result in a local service taking action, such as an arrest or raid, at station request.

In non-communist countries it is the policy of the Agency to assist local security services to improve their capabilities if, of course, these services want the help and their government is not openly hostile to the U.S.

By giving money, training and equipment to local services like the police, the CIA is able to receive information that might otherwise not be available because, for example, of the shortage of station officers. Travel control, for instance, involves obtaining airline and ship passenger lists from the companies or from local immigration services. Often it is easier to obtain them from a liaison service than from five or ten different companies. Telephone tapping is often possible only through a local service, especially when many lines are to be monitored. Mails can be opened much more easily by a local service than by the lengthy process of unilateral agent recruitment in post offices. Above all, if flaps (scandals) occur, the local service, not the CIA, will take the rap.

Usually a Chief of Station will handle the contact with the chief of a local service. Some stations may have whole sections of liaison officers at the working level both in operational planning and in information exchange. The general rule, of course, is to expose the absolute minimum of station officers to a local service and, if possible, only those officers engaged in liaison operations. Officers engaged in unilateral operations, that is, operations undertaken without the knowledge of the local government, should be protected against compromise with the local service.

Some local services are so pitifully backward that they need overt U.S. government assistance. Thus the International Cooperation Administration (ICA)[1] technical assistance missions in many countries include Public Safety Missions made up of U.S. technicians who work with police departments. They seek to improve the local service's capability in communications, investigations, administration and record keeping, public relations and crime prevention. The Public Safety Missions are valuable to the CIA because they provide cover for CIA officers who are sent to work full time with the intelligence services of the police and other civilian services. Station officers under other cover may work with

---

1. Predecessor of the Agency for International Development (AID).

military intelligence and, at times, officers under cover as businessmen, tourists or retired people may be assigned to work with local services.

CIA assistance to local services through Public Safety Missions or other forms of cover are not only designed to help improve the professional capability of the local service. Operational targeting of the local service is guided by CIA liaison officers so that the local service performs tasks that are lacking in the overall station operational program. In other words local services are to be used for the benefit of the CIA, and this includes keeping the local service away from station unilateral operations.

The personal relations between CIA liaison officers and their colleagues in local services are very important, because the CIA liaison officers are expected to spot and assess officers in the local service for recruitment as penetration agents. Liaison officers make money available to officers of the local service and it is expected that the local colleague will pocket some of the money even though it is supposed to be strictly for operations. The technique is to get the local police or intelligence officer used to a little extra cash so that not only will he be dependent on the station for equipment and professional guidance but also for personal financing.

Security officers such as police are often among the poorest paid public servants and they are rarely known to refuse a gift. Little by little an officer of a local service is called upon to perform tasks not known to anyone else in his service, particularly his superiors. Gradually he begins to report on his own service and on politics within his own government. Eventually his first loyalty is to the CIA. After all, that is where the money comes from. Penetration operations against local services are often of very considerable importance because of the place of security services in local political stability. Reporting from these agents is sometimes invaluable during situations of possible *coup d'état*.

Finally, CIA stations may undertake unilateral operations through officers of liaison services who have been recruited as penetration agents. That is the final goal. Recruited liaison officers may also report on efforts by their services to uncover unilateral station operations. This, too, is a happy situation.

Soviet/Satellite Operations

Operations against the Soviets and the satellite governments are designed to produce, in the long run, positive information as opposed to counter-intelligence. But both types of information, FI and CI, are so intertwined that they are practically inseparable in specific operations. The reason is that operations are extremely difficult to mount inside the target countries because of the effectiveness of the communist internal security services. Those that do originate within the Soviet Union or the satellites are usually surprise offers of services that have little to do with targeting, spotting, assessment and recruitment. Rather they are the result of inner processes hidden somewhere in the psyches of communist officials which surface at an unpredictable moment of strain. In effect, these people usually recruit themselves.

On the other hand, access to Soviet and East European officials outside the communist bloc is relatively easy and an elaborate operational method for attacking them has developed in the CIA over the years. The operations that result from this are generally more of a CI than an FI type, that is, they reflect more of the protective function than the collection of intelligence information, although they are in no way lacking in aggressive character.

The first rule is that all the bordering property around a Soviet embassy should be considered for purchase by station support agents. The most appropriate and the most promising of these properties will be purchased and kept available for use whenever needed. As Soviet embassies are often sizeable plots of land with large mansions and surrounded by high walls, there may be as many as seven or eight houses contiguous with the Soviet property. These houses may be used as visual observation posts and for the setting up of technical collection equipment. For example, when the Soviets are known or suspected to be using electronic encrypting machines, radiations emanating from them may be captured, enabling the message to be decrypted. Such an operation is undertaken in support of the National Security Agency. But observation posts are more routinely used for identifying, by associations, the KGB and GRU (military intelligence) residences within the Soviet mission as well as the general pecking order in the Soviet colony.

Wherever possible all the entrances to the Soviet compound as well as the gardens within are placed under visual observation. Such coverage may necessitate as many as three or four observation posts. Each OP is manned by agents, often elderly couples, who maintain a log of the comings and goings of every Soviet employee as well as those taking part in, and characteristics of, the frequent garden conversations. Photography is frequently used to get up-to-date photos of Soviet personnel as well as for less successful purposes as close-up movies shot of garden conversations and passed to Russian lip-readers. The logs from the observation posts are studied with the transcripts of telephone tapping, which is standard operational practice against all Soviet and satellite missions outside the bloc together with the transcriptions of bugging operations against their installations, if bugging has been possible. From these studies the functional duties within the Soviet colony are revealed and the daily routines of everyone become fundamental operating knowledge of the CIA Soviet and satellite operations officers.

Coverage of Soviet and satellite officers begins, however, long before they arrive in a foreign country. Almost always the first notice of a new arrival results from the visa request made by the Soviet Foreign Ministry to the embassy of the country concerned in Moscow. The visa may be granted by the embassy, which will advise its own Foreign Ministry, or the request will be transmitted to the Foreign Ministry for approval. These communications are often made in coded diplomatic messages. The CIA station in the capital city where the Soviet is to be posted receives the decrypted messages from the National Security Agency via headquarters where file checks immediately start on the

Soviet official in question. Thus if the Soviet Foreign Ministry requests from the Indian Embassy in Moscow, a diplomatic visa for Ivan Ivanovitch the CIA station in New Delhi may receive its first indication of the assignment through the monitoring of Indian government communications.

Before the Soviet arrives the station will have all the available information on him and his family together with photographs if possible. The information would have been collected and filed from coverage of the Soviet (or satellite) officer on previous tours of duty abroad, from defector debriefings, from communications intelligence and from other miscellaneous sources. When no traces exist a new file is opened and the target's history with the CIA begins.

The final purpose of the operations is to recruit Soviet and satellite officials as agents for spying and this can be done only by getting to know them. In this work the "access agent" is the station's most sensitive and effective means of obtaining data on target officials. Access agents are people who, for a great variety of reasons, can establish a personal relationship with a Soviet or satellite officer and through whom the CIA can observe the officer as closely as possible. The access agent can also guide conversations very carefully to selected topics so as to discover weakening beliefs, character defects, personal problems and basic likes and dislikes. Sometimes an access agent's role may change to that of double agent if the Soviet attempts to recruit him, but double-agent operations are discouraged except in special circumstances because there are too many problems in the continual need to be certain that the agent has not been doubled back against the CIA. An access agent may be anyone so long as the target official can be kept interested: a host country Foreign Ministry official, a third country diplomat, someone who shares the same hobby, a man with an attractive wife.

In most countries the foreign diplomats have a club with monthly luncheons, dinners and excursions. State Department and CIA officers under State cover are members of these clubs and can thereby develop personal relationships with Soviet officials. The Ambassador's permission is necessary for a station to guide a State Department officer in a personal relationship with a communist diplomat, who is almost always an intelligence officer, and at times CIA officers themselves develop personal relationships with communist officials. But such relationships are usually not as productive as the personal relations developed by access agents, with whom the target official may relax and let down his guard.

Soviet and satellite embassies usually employ a small number of local people as gardeners, cleaners and occasionally as chauffeurs. These people are always screened by the embassy for loyalty to communism, but sometimes they too can be recruited by the CIA. They have very little physical access to embassy offices so they usually cannot plant listening devices, but they can report interesting information on superior–inferior relationships, gossip and back-biting, wives and children and visitors to the embassies.

The bugging of Soviet and satellite official installations abroad is a very high priority but possible only in rare circumstances such as when a defector can plant a device after contact with the CIA but before disappearing. However, as the Soviets, satellites and Chinese expand their diplomatic and commercial relations around the world, they always need buildings. From the moment a preliminary mission by a communist country is planned, the CIA station brings everything to bear in order to discover the buildings selected and, during the period before occupancy, every effort is made to install listening devices. Soviet and satellite officials usually live in embassies, consulates or other official buildings with their families or alone, but a few live in apartment buildings. Their apartments are also bugged whenever there is reason to believe intelligence of value can be obtained.

Almost all CIA stations have surveillance teams equipped with cameras, vehicles and radio communications. Their primary targets are known Soviet and satellite intelligence officers and efforts are made to discover through the surveillance teams the operational habits, and, with luck, the clandestine contacts of the communist officer.

Soviet operations are closely controlled by the Soviet Russia (SR) Division of the DDP in headquarters. They are the specialists and much operational correspondence on Soviet operations bears the cryptonym REDWOOD, indicating SR Division action and control. In certain cases, however, the indicator may be REDCOAT which means action and control by the area division concerned. SR Division also coordinates a number of other operations that have world-wide significance.

The REDSOX program of illegal infiltration of agents into the Soviet Union and satellite countries had started during the early 1950s but failed miserably. It is still conducted, however, when the need is great and when a Russian *émigré* with suicidal tendencies can be found. The REDSKIN program of legal travellers, on the other hand, has been highly successful even though several agents have been lost. This program includes tourists, businessmen, scientists, journalists and practically anyone who can obtain legal entry into the Soviet Union or the satellites and who is willing to perform operational tasks.

Then there is the REDCAP program which is a machine-listing system of all Soviet nationals who travel abroad: scientists, technicians, military advisors and commercial officers as well as diplomats. Intelligence officers, of course, use all of these types of cover. The ZOMBIE listings are also machine runs, listing all non-Soviet/satellite nationals who travel to the bloc, and the ZODIAC machine program lists travel of citizens of satellite countries to the West. SR Division activities are particularly intense at international scientific and technical congresses, and prior notices are sent to stations around the world describing the meetings and requesting station nominees to attend the meetings and establish contact with Soviet or satellite colleagues.

Our instructors here, and the visiting lecturers from SR and EE Divisions, freely admit that the communist intelligence services have discovered numerous examples of all categories of operation against them. Thus they are aware of our methods. Nevertheless, the leaders of the Soviet Russia Division keep driving home the theme that the Soviets are the only nation on earth with the capability and the avowed intention of destroying the United States of America. This alone requires every possible effort to carry the attack to the enemy.

Practical exercises continue. We've been spending about one afternoon per week in nearby towns practicing surveillance and having "agent meetings" with instructors. My liaison case was to convince the officer of the sister service to accept money for personal expenses and to begin performing tasks for me without the knowledge of his superiors. The communist party penetration exercise was focused on building up the "agent's morale" and encouraging him to take a more active role in the party work he despises. The Soviet operation was a series of developmental meetings with a "third country" diplomat (in my case an Indian) leading to his recruitment as an access agent to a KGB officer. I also had a legal travel case in which I recruited a reluctant American scientist who was to attend a scientific conference. Then we had a series of briefing and debriefing sessions before and after his trip. His main task was to befriend a Soviet colleague who we know has access to sensitive military information. Hopefully they will meet at future conferences and eventually my agent will recruit the Soviet scientist.

Camp Peary, Virginia — April 1960

Psychological and paramilitary, known as PP or KUCAGE, operations differ from those of FI or CI because they are action rather than collection activities. Collection operations should be invisible so that the target will be unaware of them. Action operations, on the other hand, always produce a visible effect. This, however, should never be attributable to the CIA or to the U.S. government, but rather to some other person or organization. These operations, which received their Congressional charter in the National Security Act of 1947 under "additional services of common concern," are in some ways more sensitive than collection operations. They are usually approved by the PP staff of the DDP, but when very large amounts of money are required or especially sensitive methods are used approval may be required of the OCB (Under-Sècretary level), the NSC or the President himself.

PP operations are, of course, risky because they nearly always mean intervention in the affairs of another country with whom the U.S. enjoys normal diplomatic relations. If their true sponsorship were found out the diplomatic consequences could be serious. This is in contrast to collection operations, for if these are discovered foreign politicians are often prepared to turn a blind eye—they are a traditional part of every nation's intelligence activity.

Thus the cardinal rule in planning all PP operations is "plausible denial," only possible if care has been taken in the first place to ensure that someone other than the U.S. government can be made to take the blame.

PP programs are to be found in almost every CIA station and emphasis on the kinds of PP operations will depend very much on local conditions. Psychological warfare includes propaganda (also known simply as "media"), work in youth and student organizations, work in labor organizations (trade unions, etc.), work in professional and cultural groups and in political parties. Paramilitary operations include infiltration into denied areas, sabotage, economic warfare, personal harassment, air and maritime support, weaponry, training and support for small armies.

Media Operations

The CIA's role in the U.S. propaganda program is determined by the official division of propaganda into three general categories: white, grey and black. White propaganda is that which is openly acknowledged as coming from the U.S. government, e.g. from the U.S. Information Agency (USIA); grey propaganda is ostensibly attributed to people or organizations who do not acknowledge the U.S. government as the source of their material and who produce the material as if it were their own; black propaganda is unattributed material, or it is attributed to a non-existent source, or it is false material attributed to a real source. The CIA is the only U.S. government agency authorized to engage in black propaganda operations, but it shares the responsibility for grey propaganda with other agencies such as USIA. However, according to the "Grey Law" of the National Security Council contained in one of the NSCID's, other agencies must obtain prior CIA approval before engaging in grey propaganda.

The vehicles for grey and black propaganda may be unaware of their CIA or U.S. government sponsorship. This is partly so that it can be more effective and partly to keep down the number of people who know what is going on and thus to reduce the danger of exposing true sponsorship. Thus editorialists, politicians, businessmen and others may produce propaganda, even for money, without necessarily knowing who their masters in the case are. Some among them obviously will and so, in agency terminology, there is a distinction between "witting" and "unwitting" agents.

In propaganda operations, as in all other PP activities, standard agency security procedure forbids payment for services rendered to be made by a CIA officer working under official cover (one posing as an official of the Department of State, for instance). This is in order to maintain "plausible denial" and to minimize the danger of embarrassment to the local embassy if anything is discovered by the local government. However, payment is made by CIA officers under non-official cover, e.g. posing as businessmen, students or as retired people; such officers are said to be working under non-official cover.

Officers working under non-official cover may also handle most of the contacts with the recruited agents in order to keep the officer under official cover as protected as possible. Equally, meetings between the two kinds of officer will be as secret as may be. The object of all this is to protect the embassy and sometimes to make the propaganda agents believe that they are being paid by private businesses.

Headquarters' propaganda experts have visited us in

ISOLATION and have displayed the mass of paper they issue as material for the guidance of propaganda throughout the world. Some of it is concerned only with local issues, the rest often has world-wide application. The result of the talks was to persuade most of us that propaganda is not for us—there is simply too much paperwork. But despite that, the most interesting part of propaganda was obviously the business of orchestrating the treatment of events of importance among several countries. Thus problems of communist influence in one country can be made to appear of international concern in others under the rubric of "a threat to one is a threat to all." For example, the CIA station in Caracas can cable information on a secret communist plot in Venezuela to the Bogotá station which can "surface" through a local propaganda agent with attribution to an unidentified Venezuelan government official. The information can then be picked up from the Colombian press and relayed to CIA stations in Quito, Lima, La Paz, Santiago and, perhaps, Brazil. A few days later editorials begin to appear in the newspapers of these places and pressure mounts on the Venezuelan government to take repressive action against its communists.

There are obviously hosts of other uses to which propaganda, both black and grey, can be put, using books, magazines, radio, television, wall-painting, handbills, decals, religious sermons and political speeches as well as the daily press. In countries where handbills or wall-painting are important media, stations are expected to maintain clandestine printing and distribution facilities as well as teams of agents who paint slogans on walls. Radio Free Europe‡ (RFE) and Radio Liberty‡ are the best known grey-propaganda operations conducted by the CIA against the Soviet bloc.

Youth and Student Operations

At the close of World War II, the Communist Party of the Soviet Union began a major propaganda and agitation program through the formation of the International Union of Students (IUS) and the World Federation of Democratic Youth (WFDY), both of which brought together national affiliates within their respective fields in as many countries as possible. These organizations promoted CPSU objectives and policy under the guise of unified campaigns (anti-colonialism, anti-nuclear weapons, pro-peace groups, etc.), in which they enlisted the support of their local affiliates in capitalist countries as well as within the communist bloc. During the late 1940s the U.S. government, using the Agency for its purpose, began to brand these fronts as stooges of the CPSU with the object of discouraging non-communist participation. In addition to this the Agency engaged in operations in many places designed to stop local groups affiliating with the international bodies. By recruiting leaders of the local groups and by infiltrating agents, the Agency tried to gain control of as many of them as possible, so that even if such a group had already affiliated itself to either the IUS or the WFDY, it could be persuaded or compelled to withdraw.

The Agency also began to form alternative youth and student organizations at local and international level. The two international bodies constructed to rival those sponsored by the Soviet Union were the Coordinating Secretariat of National Unions of Students‡ (COSEC)[1] with headquarters in Leyden, and the World Assembly of Youth‡ (WAY) situated in Brussels. Headquarters' planning, guidance and operational functions in the CIA youth and student operations are centralized in the International Organizations Division of the DDP.

Both COSEC and WAY, like the IUS and WFDY, promote travel, cultural activities and welfare, but both also work as propaganda agencies for the CIA—particularly in underdeveloped countries. They also have consultative status as non-governmental institutions with United Nations agencies such as UNESCO and they participate in the U.N. special agencies' programs.

One very important function of the CIA youth and student operations is the spotting, assessing and recruiting of student and youth leaders as long-term agents,

1. Later known as the International Student Conference (ISC).

both in the FI and PP fields. The organizations sponsored or affected by the Agency are obvious recruiting grounds for these and, indeed, for other CIA operations. It is particularly the case in the underdeveloped world that both COSEC and WAY programs lead to the recruitment of young agents who can be relied on to continue CIA policies and remain under CIA control long after they have moved up their political or professional ladders.

Apart from working through COSEC and WAY the Agency is also able to mount specific operations through Catholic national and international student and youth bodies (Pax Romana and the International Catholic Youth Federation) and through the Christian democratic and non-communist socialist organizations as well. In some countries, particularly those in which there are groups with strong communist or radical leaderships, the Catholic or Christian Democratic student and youth organizations are the main forces guided by the Agency.

Agents controlled through youth and student operations by a station in any given country, including those in the U.S. National Students Association‡ (NSA) international program run by headquarters, can also be used to influence decisions at the international level, while agents at the international level can be used for promoting other agents or policies within a national affiliate. Control, then, is like an alternating current between the national and international levels.

Largely as a result of Agency operations, the WFDY headquarters was expelled from France in 1951, moving to Budapest. The IUS headquarters, on the other hand, was never allowed to move to the free world after its founding at Prague in 1946. Moreover, the WFDY and IUS have been clearly identified with the communist bloc, and their efforts to conduct conferences and seminars outside the bloc have been attacked and weakened by WAY and COSEC. The WFDY, for example, has been able to hold only one World Youth Festival outside the bloc, in Vienna in 1959, and then it was effectively disrupted by CIA-controlled youth and student organizations. The IUS has never held a congress in the free world. More important still, both WAY and COSEC have developed overwhelming leads in affiliate members outside the communist bloc.

Labor Operations

Agency labor operations came into being, like student and youth operations, as a reaction against the continuation of pre-World War II CPSU policy and expansion through the international united fronts. In 1945 with the support and participation of the British Trade Unions Congress (TUC), the American Congress of Industrial Organizations (CIO) and the Soviet Trade Unions Council, the World Federation of Trade Unions (WFTU) was formed in Paris. Differences within the WFTU between communist trade-union leaders, who were anxious to use the WFTU for anti-capitalist propaganda, and free-world leaders who insisted on keeping the WFTU focused on economic issues, finally came to a head in 1949 over whether the WFTU should support the Marshall Plan. When the communists, who included French, Italian and Latin American leaders as well as the Soviets, refused to allow the WFTU to endorse the Marshall Plan, the TUC and CIO withdrew, and later the same year the International Confederation of Free Trade Unions (ICFTU‡) was founded as a non-communist alternative to the WFTU, with participation by the TUC, CIO, American Federation of Labor (AFL) and other national centers. Agency operations were responsible in part for the expulsion of the WFTU headquarters from Paris in 1951 when it moved to the Soviet sector of Vienna. Later, in 1956, it was forced to move from Vienna to Prague.

The ICFTU established regional organizations for Europe, the Far East, Africa and the Western Hemisphere, which brought together the non-communist national trade-union centers. Support and guidance by the Agency was, and still is, exercised on the three levels: ICFTU, regional and national centers. At the highest level, labor operations congenial to the Agency are supported through George Meany,‡ President of the AFL, Jay Lovestone,‡ Foreign Affairs Chief of the AFL and

Irving Brown,‡ AFL representative in Europe—all of whom were described to us as effective spokesmen for positions in accordance with the Agency's needs. Direct Agency control is also exercised on the regional level. Serafino Romualdi,‡ AFL Latin American representative for example, directs the Inter-American Regional Labor Organization (ORIT)‡ located in Mexico City. On the national level, particularly in underdeveloped countries, CIA field stations engage in operations to support and guide national labor centers. In headquarters, support, guidance and control of all labor operations is centralized in the labor branch of the International Organizations Division.

General policy on labor operations is similar to youth and student operations. First, the WFTU and its regional and national affiliates are labelled as stooges of Moscow. Second, local station operations are designed to weaken and defeat communist or extreme-leftist dominated union structures and to establish and support a non-communist structure. Third, the ICFTU and its regional organizations are promoted, both from the top and from the bottom, by having Agency-influenced or controlled unions and national centers affiliate.

A fourth CIA approach to labor operations is through the International Trade Secretariats‡ (ITS), which represent the interests of workers in a particular industry as opposed to the national centers that unite workers of different industries. Because the ITS system is more specialized, and often more effective, it is at times more appropriate for Agency purposes than the ICFTU with its regional and national structure. Control and guidance is exercised through officers of a particular ITS who are called upon to assist labor operations directed against the workers of a particular industry. Very often the CIA agents in an ITS are the American labor leaders who represent the U.S. affiliate of the ITS, since the ITS would usually receive its principal support from the pertinent U.S. industrial union. Thus the American Federation of State, County and Municipal Employees‡ serves as a channel for CIA operations in the Public Service International,‡ which is the ITS for government employees headquartered in London. And the Retail

Clerks International Association,‡ which is the U.S. union of white-collar employees, gives access to the International Federation of Clerical and Technical Employees,‡ which is the white-collar ITS. Similarly, the Communications Workers of America‡ is used to control the Post, Telegraph and Telephone Workers International‡ (PTTI) which is the ITS for communications workers. In the case of the petroleum industry the Agency actually set up the ITS, the International Federation of Petroleum and Chemical Workers‡ (IFPCW) through the U.S. union of petroleum workers, the Oil Workers International Union.‡ Particularly in underdeveloped countries, station labor operations may be given cover as a local program of an ITS. Within the Catholic trade-union movement similar activity is possible, usually channelled through the International Federation of Christian Trade Unions‡ (IFCTU).[1] And for specialized training within the social-democratic movement, the Israeli Histadrut‡ is used.

Labor operations are the source of considerable friction between the DDP area divisions and the stations, on the one hand, and the International Organizations Division (IOD) on the other. The problem is mainly jurisdiction and coordination. The labor operations agents on the international and regional level (ICFTU, ORIT, ITS, for example) are directed by officers of IOD either in Washington or from a field station such as Paris, Brussels or Mexico City. If their activities in a particular country, Colombia, for example, are not closely coordinated with the Bogotá station, they may oppose or otherwise interfere with specific aims of the Bogotá station's labor operations or other programs. Whenever IOD labor assets visit a given country, the Chief of Station who is responsible for all CIA activities in his country, must be advised. Otherwise the IOD agent, lacking the guidance and control that would ensure that his activities harmonize with the entire station operational program, not just in the labor field, may jeopardize other station goals. Continuing efforts are made to ensure coordination between IOD activities in

1. Later renamed the World Confederation of Labor.

labor and the field stations concerned, but this is also hampered at times by the narrow view and headstrong attitudes of the agents themselves.

On the other hand, IOD agents can be enormously valuable in assisting a local station's labor program. Usually the agent has considerable prestige as a result of his position on the international or regional level, and his favor is often sought by indigenous labor leaders because of the travel and training grants and invitations to conferences that the agent dispenses. He accordingly has ready access to leaders in the local non-communist labor movement and he can establish contact between the station and those local labor leaders of interest. Such contact can be established through third parties, gradually, so that the IOD agent is protected when a new operational relationship is eventually established. Field stations may call on IOD support in order to obtain the adoption of a particular policy or program in a given country through the influence that an IOD agent can bring to bear on a local situation, again without the local labor leader, even if he is a station agent, knowing that the international or regional official is responding to CIA guidance.

Measuring the effectiveness of labor operations against their multi-million-dollar cost is difficult and controversial, and includes the denial-to-the-communists factor as well as the value of indoctrination in pro-Western ideals through seminars, conferences and educational programs. In any case, free-world affiliation with the WFTU has been considerably reduced, even though several leading national confederations in non-communist countries still belong.

Operations against the World Peace Council

Agency operations against the World Peace Council (founded in Paris in 1949) are undertaken to neutralize the Council's propaganda campaigns against the U.S. and its allies, particularly with regard to military pacts. Although no rival organization has been established, media operations are directed against WPC activities in order to expose its true sponsorship as a propaganda front of the CPSU. Some success can be claimed in the expulsion of WPC headquarters from Paris to Prague in 1951 although it moved to Vienna in 1954. Efforts are also made to prevent the WPC from holding congresses and other meetings outside the communist bloc through operations involving media, students, youth, labor and especially political-action agents for denial of permissions and other harassment.

Journalists

Founded in Copenhagen in 1946, the International Organization of Journalists (IOJ) brought together writers from both communist and non-communist countries. Although the original headquarters of the IOJ was in London, the Second Congress was held in Prague in 1947 where it was decided to move the IOJ headquarters. Following the leadership of the national journalists' organizations of the United States, Great Britain and Belgium, most non-communist membership had been withdrawn by 1950, and its activities were generally confined to Iron Curtain countries.

In addition to propaganda against the IOJ and operations to deny Western capitals for IOJ meetings, the Agency promoted the founding of an alternative international society of journalists for the free world. In 1952 the World Congress of Journalists reestablished the International Federation of Journalists‡ (IFJ) which had been founded originally in 1926, but had been disbanded in 1946 when the IOJ was formed.

Benefits to the Agency from the IFJ operation include the spotting and operational development of potential propaganda agents. Moreover, local station support to IFJ member organizations can be used to combat the local communist and pro-communist press and the efforts at penetration by the IOJ, especially in underdeveloped countries.

Lawyers

In 1946 the International Association of Democratic Lawyers (IADL) was founded in Paris with the participation of lawyers from some twenty-five countries.

Dominated from the beginning by pro-communist forces, especially the French participants, the IADL soon lost most of its non-communist members and in 1950 was expelled from France, moving its headquarters to Brussels where it has remained. The IADL's main function has been to serve as a propaganda mechanism for the CPSU post-war themes of peace and anti-colonialism.

In 1952, an international legal conference was held in West Berlin from which a permanent committee emerged to carry on the work of exposing communist injustice in East Germany. In 1955 this committee became the International Commission of Jurists (ICJ) with headquarters in The Hague, moving to Geneva in 1959. The ICJ is composed of twenty-five prominent lawyers from countries around the world, and its main work consists of investigating and reporting on abuses of the "rule of law," wherever they occur.

The Agency saw the ICJ as an organization which it hoped would produce prestigious propaganda of the kind wanted on such issues as violations of human rights in the communist bloc. Reports on other areas like South Africa would, so far as the CIA was concerned, merely lend respectability to this object.

Political-Action Operations

Communist expansion brought forth still another type of PP operation: political action. Operations designed to promote the adoption by a foreign government of a particular policy *vis-à-vis* communism are termed political-action operations. While the context of these operations is the assessment of the danger of communist or other leftist influence in a given country, the operations undertaken to suppress the danger are pegged to specific circumstances. These operations often involve promotion through funding and guidance of the careers of foreign politicians through whom desired government policy and action can be obtained. Conversely, these operations often include actions designed to neutralize the politicians who promote undesirable local government policy regarding communism.

Although political-action operations after World

War II began with electoral funding of anti-communist political parties in France and Italy in the late 1940s, they are now prevalent in the underdeveloped countries where economic and social conditions create a favorable climate for communist advance. The obvious human elements in political-action operations are political parties, politicians and military leaders, although agents in other PP operations including labor, student and youth, and media are often brought to bear on specific political-action targets.

In order to obtain political intelligence as well as to develop relationships with potential political-action agents, most stations have continuing programs for cultivating local politicians from opposition as well as from government parties. Making acquaintances in local politics is not usually difficult because CIA officers under diplomatic cover in embassies have natural access to their targets through cocktail parties, receptions, clubs and other mechanisms that bring them together with people of interest. Regular State Department Foreign Service Officers and Ambassadors as well may also facilitate the expansion of station political contacts through arranging introductions. When a local political contact is assessed favorably for station goals, security clearance and operational approval is obtained from headquarters, and the station officer in contact with the target begins to provide financial support for political campaigns or for the promotion of the target's political group or party. Hopefully, almost surely, the target will use some of the money for personal expenses thereby developing a dependency on the station as a source of income. Eventually, if all goes well, the local politician will report confidential information on his own party and on his government, if he has a government post, and he will respond to reasonable station direction regarding the communist question.

A station's liaison operations with local security services are also a valuable source of political-action assets. Because of frequent political instability in underdeveloped countries, the politicians in charge of the civilian and military security forces are in key positions for action as well as for information, and they are often drawn into an operational relationship with the station when they enter office merely by allowing ongoing liaison operations to continue. They are subjected to constant assessment by the station for use in political action and when deemed appropriate they may be called upon for specific tasks. Financial support is also available for furthering their political careers and for a continuing relationship once they leave the ministry.

As final arbiters of political conflicts in so many countries, military leaders are major targets for recruitment. They are contacted by station officers in a variety of ways, sometimes simply through straightforward introduction by U.S. military attachés or the personnel of U.S. Military Assistance Missions. Sometimes the liaison developed between the Agency and local intelligence services can be used for making these contacts. Again CIA officers can make contact with those military officers of other countries who come to the U.S. for training. As in the case of politicians, most Agency stations have a continual program for the development of local military leaders, both for the collection of intelligence and for possible use in political action.

The political actions actually undertaken by the Agency are almost as varied as politics itself. High on the list of priorities is the framing of Soviet officials in diplomatic or commercial missions in order to provoke their expulsion. Politicians working for the Agency are expected to take an active part in working for expulsion of "undesirables." Similarly, where the Soviet Union tries to extend its diplomatic or commercial activities, our politicians are expected to use their influence to oppose such moves. They are also expected to take a hard line against their own nationals engaged in left-wing or communist activities. In the last of these instances success means the proscription of the parties, the arrest or exile of their leaders, the closure of their offices, publications and bookstores, the prohibition of their demonstrations, etc. Such large-scale programs call for action both by anti-communist movements and by national government—where possible the Agency likes to use the same political-action agents for both purposes.

But it is not just a matter of financing and guiding local politicians. In situations regarded as dangerous to the U.S., the Agency will conduct national election operations through the medium of an entire political party. It will finance candidates who are both "witting" and "unwitting." Such multi-million-dollar operations may begin a year or more before an election is due and will include massive propaganda and public-relations campaigns, the building of numerous front organizations and funding mechanisms (often resident U.S. businessmen), regular polls of voters, the formation of "goon-squads" to intimidate the opposition, and the staging of provocations and the circulation of rumors designed to discredit undesirable candidates. Funds are also available for buying votes and vote counters as well.

If a situation can be more effectively retrieved for U.S. interests by unconstitutional methods or by *coup d'état,* that too may be attempted. Although the Agency usually plays the anti-communist card in order to foster a *coup,* gold bars and sacks of currency are often equally effective. In some cases a timely bombing by a station agent, followed by mass demonstrations and finally by intervention by military leaders in the name of the restoration of order and national unity, is a useful course. Agency political operations were largely responsible for *coups* after this pattern in Iran in 1953 and in the Sudan in 1958.

Paramilitary Operations

At times the political situation in a given country cannot be retrieved fast or effectively enough through other types of PP operations such as political action. In these cases the Agency engages in operations on a higher level of conflict which may include military operations—although these should not be seen as U.S.-sponsored. These unconventional warfare operations are called paramilitary operations. The Agency has the charter from the National Security Council for U.S. government unconventional warfare although the military services also sustain a paramilitary capability in case of general war. These operations seem to hold a special fascination, calling to mind oss heroism, resistance, guerrilla warfare, secret parachute jumps behind the lines. Camp Peary is a major Agency training base for paramilitary operations.

The need for getting agents into denied areas like certain parts of the Soviet Union, China and other communist countries, is satisfied in part by illegal infiltration by land, sea or air. The agents, usually natives of the denied area, are given proper clothing, documentation and cover stories and, if infiltrating by land, may be required to pass secretly through heavily guarded borders. Training in border crossing is given in a restricted area of Camp Peary where a mile or so of simulated communist borders is operated with fences, watchtowers, dogs, alarms and patrols. Maritime infiltration involves the use of a mother ship, usually a freighter operated by an Agency cover shipping company which approaches to within a few miles of the shore landing-site. An intermediate craft, often a souped-up outboard, leaves the mother ship and approaches to perhaps a mile off the shore where a rubber boat with a small silent outboard is inflated to carry the infiltration team to the beach. The rubber boat and auxiliary equipment is buried near the beach for use later in escape while the intermediate craft returns to the mother ship. Infiltration by air requires black overflights for which the Agency has unmarked long- and short-range aircraft including the versatile Helio Courier that can be used in infil–exfil operations with landings as well as parachute drops. Restricted areas of Camp Peary along the York River are used for maritime training and other parts of the base serve as landing-sites and drop zones.

Once safely infiltrated to a denied area, a lone agent or a team may be required to perform a variety of jobs. Frequently an infiltration team's mission is the caching of weapons, communications equipment or sabotage materials for later retrieval by a different team which will use them. Or, an infiltration team may perform sabotage through the placing of incendiary devices or explosives at a target-site timed to go off days, weeks or even months later. Sabotage weapons include oil and gasoline contaminates for stopping vehicles, contaminates for jamming printing-presses, limpets for sinking ships, explosive and incendiary compounds that can be moulded and painted to look like bread, lamps, dolls or stones. The sabotage instructors, or "burn and blow boys," have staged impressive demonstrations of their capabilities, some of which are ingeniously designed so as to leave little trace of a cause. Aside from sabotage, an infiltration team may be assigned targets to photograph or the loading or unloading of dead drops (concealed places for hiding film, documents or small containers). Escape may be by the same route as entry or by an entirely different method.

The Economic Warfare Section of the PP staff is a sub-section under Paramilitary Operations because its mission includes the sabotage of key economic activities in a target country and the denial of critical imports, e.g. petroleum. Contamination of an export agricultural product or associated material (such as sacks destined for the export of Cuban sugar), or fouling the bearings of tractors, trucks or buses destined for a target country may be undertaken if other efforts to impede undesired trade fail. As Economic Warfare is undertaken in order to aggravate economic conditions in a target country, these operations include in addition to sabotage, the use of propaganda, labor, youth, student and other mass organizations under CIA control to restrict trade by a friendly country of items needed in the target economy. U.S. companies can also be called upon to restrict supply of selected products voluntarily, but local station political-action assets are usually more effective for this purpose.

Also coordinated in the Paramilitary section of the PP staff is the effort to maintain Agency supplies of weapons used in support of irregular military forces. Although the Air and Maritime Support section of the staff supervises standing Agency operations to supply insurgents (Air America and Civil Air Transport in the Far East, for example) additional resources such as aircraft can be obtained from the Defense Department. These operations included the Guatemalan invasion in 1954 (aptly given the cryptonym LCSUCCESS); Tibetan resistance against the Chinese in 1958–9 and the rebellion against the Sukarno government in Indonesia in 1957–8; current training and support of irregular forces in South Vietnam and Laos; and increasing sabotage and paramilitary operations against the Castro government in Cuba. Leaflet drops as part of the propaganda aspect of paramilitary operations are also arranged through the Air and Maritime Support section.

Closely related to paramilitary operations are the disruptive activities known as militant action. Through organization and support of "goon squads" sometimes composed of off-duty policemen, for example, or the militant sections of friendly political parties, stations attempt to intimidate communists and other extreme leftists by breaking up their meetings and demonstrations. The Technical Services staff of the DDP makes a variety of weapons and devices for these purposes. Horrible smelling liquids in small glass vials can be hurled into meeting halls. A fine clear powder can be sprinkled in a meeting-place becoming invisible after settling but having the effect of tear-gas when stirred up by the later movement of people. An incendiary powder can be moulded around prepared tablets and when ignited the combination produces ample quantities of smoke that attacks the eyes and respiratory system much more strongly than ordinary tear-gas. A tasteless substance can be introduced to food that causes exaggerated body color. And a few small drops of a clear liquid stimulates the target to relaxed, uninhibited talk. Invisible itching powder can be placed on steering wheels or toilet seats, and a slight smear of invisible ointment causes a serious burn to skin on contact. Chemically processed tobacco can be added to cigarettes and cigars to produce respiratory ailments.

Our training in PP operations includes constant emphasis on the desirability of obtaining reportable intelligence information from agents engaged in what are essentially action (as opposed to collection) operations. A well-run action operation, in fact, can produce intelligence of extremely good quality whether the agents are student, labor or political leaders. Justification for continuing PP operations in Project Renewals includes references to the operation's value in strictly collection activities as well as effectiveness in achieving action goals. No action agent, therefore, can be allowed to neglect the intelligence by-product of his operation, although the action agent may have to be eased into the intelligence reporting function because of the collaborative nature of his early relationship with the Agency. Nevertheless with a little skill even leaders of some rank can be manipulated into collecting information by letting them know indirectly that financial support for them is based partly on satisfaction of intelligence reporting requirements.

The funding of psychological and paramilitary projects is a complex business. Project Outlines (see p. 41) are prepared either in the station or at headquarters, depending on which of these is proposing or running the operation. Included in this, apart from those elements already mentioned for FI projects, will be a statement on the need for coordination with other U.S. government agencies such as the State Department or the Department of Defense. Where appropriate further reports are attached giving greater detail on finances, personnel, training, supply and cover mechanisms.

Operational progress reports are required each trimester in the case of routine operations, but such reports may be more frequent in special cases. Intelligence received as a result of PP operations is processed in the same way as that which comes from FI operations.

Funding action operations, especially those involving labor, student, youth or other organizations is a perpetual problem. Under certain circumstances it can be done through foundations of one sort or another which have been created as fronts for the Agency, but before this, or any other, method can be employed there first has to be a decision about the level at which the funds should be passed. If money is to be put into an international organization like WAY, for example, then it might be possible to do this through an American organization affiliated to it. The money can then be disguised as a donation from that organization. In other circumstances it might be possible to supply the money through a "cutout," that is, through a person who can claim that the money is either a donation on his own account or from his business. If this system is used the money is sometimes paid by the "cutout" to a U.S. organization affiliated to the international group for whom the money is finally intended.

If it is paid direct then it is usual for the secretary-general or the finance committee chairman of the organization in question to be a "witting" agent. The decision about the method to be used is subject to several considerations. First the matter of security and cover is considered; second comes the question of which method would best ensure that the recipient or recipients will then do what they have been paid for. Thus funds become a very effective method of guiding an action agent. When cover foundations or companies are used for funding they may be chartered in the U.S. or in countries such as Lichtenstein, the Bahamas and Panama, where commercial secrecy is protected and governmental controls are minimal.

Camp Peary, Virginia — May 1960

The practical exercises are more pleasant now that spring has arrived. Except that we pick up hordes of ticks during the paramilitary training. We have had training in evasion and escape and border crossing—also night exercises in maritime infiltrations and air drops. At the ranges we have firing sessions with a variety of pistols, rifles and sub-machine-guns. In July, after the regular JOT training course ends, there will be a three-month specialized course in paramilitary operations. Ten or fifteen of the class have volunteered for the course and afterwards they'll be assigned to operations already underway against Vietnam, Laos and Cuba.

The instructor who was my nationalistic political leader in the FI exercise became a wild man in the political-action case. He went around without my knowledge trying to recruit colleagues to overthrow the government and telling them he was working for me in the U.S. Embassy. The word got back to the Ambassador (another instructor) and I had to convince him not to send me home. Then I paid the agent a generous termination bonus and picked up with one of his party subordinates.

Still, we have had a serious upheaval in the JOT class. None of us is quite sure whether this is a training exercise or real or partly both. The training staff has been ranting and raving, both in individual sessions with advisors and in the classroom and pit sessions, that we aren't taking the work seriously enough. They cancelled a couple of weekends off and we all had to stay here and practice report writing. Morale among the JOT's is down and resentment against the staff gets higher every day. Four of the outstanding trainees have quit—two of them in order to take appointments as Foreign Service Officers with the State Department.

The problem grew out of the way most of us handled the practical exercises with the political-action agent—practically all of us were crucified in the criticism sessions for not having developed proper control over the agent before moving into sensitive assignments. The instructors accused us of adopting whimsical attitudes—what they call derisively the "cowboy approach." Besides agent-control failure, the staff is down on us for not taking pains with tradecraft in the practical exercises. A couple of weeks ago several teams got arrested while photographing a huge chemical plant about twenty miles from here—they were caught by security patrols, turned over to the police, and then had to be bailed out through the base administration office. It was supposed to be a clandestine photography assignment in a denied area and those guys climbed over the fence and started snapping like they were at the beach in August.

The extra night sessions in tradecraft are supposed to emphasize the dangers in taking shortcuts on *how* clandestine operations are performed—as opposed to *what* is done (FI, CI and PP operations). Tradecraft is all the techniques and tools of the trade used to keep a secret operation secret. The tradecraft one selects depends on a correct analysis of the operational environment—the set of conditions that determine the degree of clandestinity needed, including the capabilities of local services, and the strength of the local target organizations against which our operations are directed. The more relaxed the operational environment, the more simple and uncomplicated the tradecraft and the more mileage obtained from each CIA officer.

Tradecraft is used to keep an operation secure and free from discovery because, among many reasons, people's lives are often at stake. The instructors keep driving home the importance of care to protect the agent, and they toss out example after example of fatal and near-fatal consequences of poor tradecraft. The techniques include how to select a meeting-site, counter-surveillance before and after clandestine meetings, the use of disguise, safety and danger signals before meetings, concealment devices, precautions in the use of telephones, ways to counter possible audio penetration of meeting-sites, the use of cutouts or go-betweens to avoid frequent direct contact between agents and CIA officers, and communication techniques.

Cover is closely related to operational security because it is the lie established to make a secret operation appear to have a legitimate purpose. A foundation may serve as a cover funding mechanism. A shipping company may serve as cover for maritime operations. An airline may serve as cover for air support to paramilitary operations. A legitimate business activity may serve as ostensible employment for a CIA officer in a foreign country. The State Department, Defense Department and the International Cooperational Administration may also serve as cover employment for CIA officers.

Communications with agents is perhaps the most crucial element of tradecraft and operational security. Personal meetings between CIA officers and their agents are often the most efficient type of communication but they are also the most dangerous and require elaborate security precautions and cover. Meetings can take place in hotels or apartments obtained for this purpose (safe houses), vehicles, subways, parks, isolated woods, tourist attractions. Normal communications may also be through cutouts and dead drops (hiding-places like the hollows of trees where messages can be placed). Brush contacts, such as the momentary contact for passage of a report, can be used in public lavatories or pedestrian tunnels where motion is uninterrupted and hostile surveillance difficult.

Communications with agents in denied areas (Iron Curtain countries) where counter-intelligence forces are most effective, is often through encoded radio transmissions to the agent, which can be heard on ordinary home radios—while the agents' reports are made in invisible writing and sent to a drop address in a non-communist country through the international mails. In such cases personal meetings would be restricted to emergencies or when the agent is able to travel to a non-communist country. Elaborate signal systems can be established to indicate safety, danger, discovery, loading or unloading a dead drop, request for meeting, postponement of meeting.

In every clandestine operation some form of training is usually involved, from simple reminders on security precautions to highly specialized instructions in the use of complicated technical equipment. In FI operations, continuous training is needed for refinement of the agent's reporting in such areas as separation of fact from rumor and opinion, specification of sources, correct dates, places and names, and spelling and format in written reports. The Office of Training has a staff of multilingual training officers in its Covert Training Branch who travel the world giving specialized operational training to agents on station request. The Technical Services Division personnel are also heavily engaged in agent training as is the Office of Communications which is in charge of training agents in the use of radio equipment and cryptographic materials.

Shortcuts in tradecraft on the practical exercises is not the main reason for the training staff's toughening up. The real reason is attitudes—they want us to get as serious about all this as they are, and they are focusing on agent-control factors in order to drive this home. Maybe we'll all have to become heavies in order to pass the course.

The importance of agent control is paramount because agent control means the ways an agent is made to do what the CIA wants him to do. Each agent is different and not everyone is always willing to do exactly what we want him to do—sometimes he has to be coaxed, sometimes cajoled, sometimes threatened.

"Agent" is a word that is used to signify the people who work at the end of the line. Usually they are foreigners and the instruments through which CIA operations are executed. The word "agent" is never used to describe the CIA career employee who functions in a station as an operations officer—more commonly known as a case officer. We are all being trained to be case officers, not agents.

There are different types of agents in CIA parlance. Many operations are structured under the leadership of a single agent to whom other agents respond either as a group working together or in separate, compartmented activities. The single agent who runs an operation under station direction is known as the *principal agent* and the others as *secondary* or *sub-agents*. The chief of a five-man surveillance team is a *principal agent* while the foot-men and drivers are *sub-agents*. An *action agent* is a person who actually provides secret information, e.g. a spy in a communist party, whereas a *support agent* performs tasks related to an operation but is not the source of intelligence, e.g. the person who rents an apartment for meetings between an action agent and the station case officer.

Case officers must constantly be searching for new agents to improve ongoing operations and to mount new, better operations. *Agent spotting,* therefore, is the activity whereby potential new agents are brought under consideration. *Agent development* is the manner in which a potential agent is cultivated and tested while *agent assessment* is the evaluation of whether and how the potential agent can be used effectively. If, after weighing all available data, a positive decision is reached for recruitment, the formal clearance procedure is completed through the Headquarters Operational Approval system. *Agent recruitment* can take many forms, often determined by the type of operation for which the agent is needed and by the history of agent development.

If your objective is to penetrate a leftist political

party, the first thing to do is to probe for a weak spot in the organization. You might bug the phone of a leading party member and find out he's playing around with the party's funds. In that case, perhaps he can be blackmailed. Or perhaps one of your agents plays on the same soccer team as a party member, or goes out with his sister. The agent might learn something about the party member that seems to make him a good prospect. Then you move in and make an offer.

On certain occasions recruitments are made in the name of the CIA, especially when involving U.S. citizens and high-level targets for PP operations. But often recruitment can be effected without explicit sponsorship with the target simply expected to assume that the CIA is the sponsor. Thousands of policemen all over the world, for instance, are shadowing people for the CIA without knowing it. They think they're working for their own police departments, when, in fact, their chief may be a CIA agent who's sending them out on CIA jobs and turning their information over to his CIA control. On other occasions *false flag recruitments* are more appropriate so that the target believes a service or organization other than the CIA is the sponsor, perhaps his own government, or even Peking or Havana. You don't let the recruit know he'll be working for the United States, because if he knew that, he might not consent to do it. Coercive recruitment of a communist party member in an underdeveloped country (under a threat made to appear to come from a local security service) may be more effective to start with than revealing CIA sponsorship. Later, when financial and other means of control have been established, the recruited agent may be brought gradually to the knowledge of true sponsorship.

In nearly all cases involving agents aware of their CIA sponsorship, a direct, personal relationship is established between the agent and the case officer. Since control of agents is so much more effective by persuasion than by threat, the development of personal *rapport* by the case officer with the agent receives constant emphasis from our instructors. On the other hand, agent-handling officers are expected always to maintain the upper hand and to avoid dangers that can give an agent a handle against him, or any of the different varieties of "falling in love with your agent."

However, as almost all operations depend upon money, delicate treatment of financial matters can be used as a constant control factor without insulting the agent by treating him as a mercenary. In rich countries a man might become an agent for ideological reasons, but in poor countries it's usually because he's short of cash. A man with a hungry family to support will do almost anything for money. The amounts paid to agents depends on local conditions. In a poor country $100 a month could get you an ordinary agent. In many countries $700 a month could get you a cabinet minister. Payment is made in cash—you can't pay spies by check. At the end of every month officers deliver pay envelopes to their agents around town; they meet in cars or safe houses. Agents should be made to count the cash in front of the officer so that any mistakes can be corrected immediately.

Firm guidance of agents, especially those involved in PP operations, where a wide variety of alternatives is usually presented, depends largely on the personalities of the agent and the case officer, and the twin requirements of control and *rapport* present continuing problems. Capability for detached manipulation of human beings is a cardinal virtue of the CIA case officer and nobody makes any bones about it.

Agent termination and disposal is the way an agent is unloaded when he's no longer needed or wanted. It can be touchy and complicated. Much depends on whether the termination is friendly or hostile and the reasons for it. Once the principle of terminating an operational relationship is established with an agent, the procedure usually becomes one of negotiating a financial settlement and quit-claim. The financial settlement may depend ostensibly on past services rendered by the agent, but under the surface both sides often negotiate on the basis of the damage a dissatisfied agent could cause if termination were not to his liking. Again the control exercised by case officers over the agent during the entire period of employment will reflect on termination negotiations. Efforts by terminated agents to get back on the payroll after having spent their termination bonus are not uncommon. When asked just how drastic agent termination and disposal might become in difficult circumstances, the instructor declined comment without disallowing "final solutions."

Camp Peary, Virginia — June 1960

This month the emphasis has been on technical operations and we have had to incorporate these skills in the practical exercises, including the training of our "agents." The heat from the training staff over tradecraft and agent control is still on, but we're getting used to it now. It looks as if they're trying to build up to a peak of tension for the final week of practical exercises—five or six days of intense operations in the same war-games scenario either in Baltimore or New York. But the past weeks have mostly been dedicated to long hours in laboratories learning basic skills in the four main technical functions: audio, photography, flaps and seals, and secret writing.

Audio operations include telephone tapping and all the different techniques of bugging. The most common and secure way to tap telephones is through connections made in the telephone exchange—sometimes by a unilateral agent but usually through a request to the local liaison service. But in certain circumstances telephone intercepts "off the line" (meaning connections made somewhere between the target telephone and the exchange) are more advisable. There are also small transmitters that can be placed inside a telephone and TSD has developed a pencil-sized transmitter that can be attached to telephone wires outdoors for reception in a listening post (LP) not far away.

Telephones and telephone lines can also be valuable for full audio penetration of the rooms where the telephones are located. This technique calls for the activation of the telephone mouthpiece so that it will pick up all conversations in the room, even when the telephone is cradled, and transmit these conversations down the telephones lines. This technique is called the "hot mike."

The simplest and most dependable audio operation is the "mike and wire" job, consisting of a concealed microphone with a wire leading to a listening-post where an amplifier and recorder are located. But this technique is also insecure because the wire can be followed and unpleasant surprises given to the LP keepers. So the mike and wire can be connected to a hidden low-powered radio transmitter for reception in an LP protected by being separated from the bugging equipment. Transmitters can be connected to house current or operated with batteries.

Switches on transmitters are often desirable especially in audio operations against the Soviets, Chinese and satellite governments because of their regular counter-audio sweeps in which wide-range receivers are used to detect radio transmissions. Visiting sweep teams pose as diplomatic couriers sometimes, and transmitters have to be shut down when they are in town. This necessitates constant reporting from station to station on the movements of diplomatic couriers and suspected sweep officers.

The carrier-current technique is similar to the regular transmitter installation except that the transmission is made through electric power lines instead of through the air. This technique is convenient for easy switching and has an unlimited power supply, but LP location is complicated because the transmissions will not jump electric power transformers.

Installation of audio devices often requires drilling through walls, floors or ceilings, for which TSD has demonstrated a large variety of drills, some with diamond bits, but drilling isn't recommended for the inexperienced. Even TSD technicians have been known to make the irreparable mistake of drilling large holes all the way through the wall or ceiling of a target room. Reducing the size of drilling equipment in order to reach the final pinhole takes fine calculation and infinite patience. Audio installations often require concealment afterwards, for which TSD has their Plaster Patching and Paint Matching Kit. This consists of super-quick-drying plaster, some fifty color chips with mixing formulas for color approximation, plus odorless super-quick-drying paint.

Listening-post equipment for telephone taps usually consists of a Revere tape-recorder and an actuator/dial recorder that starts the recorder when a telephone rings or when it is uncradled. Numbers called from the target telephone are also recorded on a paper tape. LP equipment for other audio operations may include FM radio receivers such as the military-supplied SRR-4 with a 50–200 megacycle range, headphones and a variety of tape-recorders. When switches are used the LP has a suitcase-package radio transmitter that transmits one frequency to turn a switch on, and another frequency to turn a switch off. But switches haven't been perfected yet and they cause problems by jamming in the *on* or the *off* positions.

The research and development programs of the TSD Audio Branch are dedicated to improving equipment like the switch systems and to development of sub-miniature microphones and transmitters for casting into innocuous objects like light-switches and electrical outlets—also to the development of new techniques. One new technique is the activation of cradled telephones (the "hot mike") by sending a current down the line to the telephone without the need to make a complicated installation in the telephone itself. Another fascinating technique under development is the use of infra-red beams that can be bounced off windows and that carry back to the receiving equipment the conversations being held in the room where the target window is located. This technique captures the conversations from the vibrations of voices against the window-panes.

Still another new technique involves the use of cavity microphones like the one discovered in the eagle's beak of the Great Seal given by the Soviets to the American Ambassador in Moscow and which he placed in his office. The cavity microphone is a simple plastic spoon-shaped object that can be activated by a radiowave of a certain frequency. The spoon reacts by transmitting another radio signal that carries the voice vibrations from the room to an appropriate receiver. That Soviet-made Great Seal was included in a display of audio equipment with the admission that the Soviets are far ahead in this particular field.

In photography we have learned to use a variety of cameras for general purpose and documents. 35-mm cameras like the Exacta, Leica and Pentax are the favorites of the instructors, although the tiny Minox is more secure for agents. We've been practicing also with clandestine photography using cameras that can be concealed in a briefcase or innocuous package—even underneath a shirt with the lens opening disguised as a tie clasp. Darkroom training-sessions have concentrated on selection of films, paper and developing chemicals. In the practical exercises each of us incorporated both document and outdoor photography with developing and printing in the dark-rooms.

The really boring technical skill is Flaps and Seals (F & S). This is the surreptitious opening and closing of letters and other containers such as diplomatic pouches. For a week we practiced with hot plate, tea kettle and the variously shaped ivory tools fashioned from piano keys and used for gently prying open envelope flaps. But the most effective technique for letters is the flat-bed steam table (about the size of a briefcase) that contains a heating element encased in foam rubber. Steam is created by placing a damp blotter on the top of the heated table, and most letters open in a matter of seconds after being placed on the blotter. Careful resealing with cotton swab and clear glue completes the process.

Secret writing (sw) is the communications system used for concealing or making invisible a secret message on an otherwise innocent letter or other cover document. sw systems are categorized as wet systems, carbons and microdot. The wet systems use chemicals, usually disguised as pills, which dissolve in water to form a clear "ink." The secret message is written on a sheet of paper, preferably high-quality bond, using the end of a wooden swab stick that has been tapered with a razor-blade and soaked in the "ink" to reach the proper tip flexibility. Before and after writing the message the paper must be rubbed with a soft cloth on both sides in all four directions to help conceal the writing within the texture of the paper. The paper with the secret message is then steamed and pressed in a thick book and after drying, if no trace of the message can be seen under ultra-violet and glancing light, a cover letter or innocuous message is written.

Carbon systems consist of ordinary bond paper that has been impregnated with chemicals. The carbon is placed on top of the message sheet and the secret message is written on a sheet placed on top of the carbon. Applying the proper pressure when writing the secret message with a pencil on the top sheet transfers the invisible chemical from the carbon to the message sheet on the bottom. The cover letter is then written on the opposite side of the message sheet from the secret message.

On receipt of an SW letter, an agent applies a corresponding chemical developer, rolling the developer with a cotton swab on to the page, and soon the secret message appears.

The microdot system involves a small camera kit with which a letter-sized page can be photographed on an area of film no larger than the dot of an "i." The microdot is glued over the dot of the "i" or a period of a cover letter. Although the equipment for microdots is incriminating, the microdots themselves are very secure and practically impossible to discover. On the other hand they require very tedious processing and can only be read with a microscope.

Secret messages can be written either in clear text or encoded for greater security. The SW branch of TSD has a continuous intelligence collection program on the postal censorship procedures in most foreign countries for protective procedures in SW operations. The operational environment in which the agent works determines the other details of SW correspondence: whether the SW cover letter will be posted nationally or internationally, to a post-box or a support agent serving as an accommodation address, with false or true return addresses or none at all, the content of the cover letters, signals to indicate safety or the absence of which could indicate that the writing is being done under control of a hostile service.

The SW branch also has a technique for "lifting" SW from suspect correspondence. The process involves placing a suspect letter in a letter press with steamed sheets on either side. By cranking down pressure enough of the chemicals will come off on the steamed sheets to allow for testing with other chemicals for development. The suspect correspondence can be returned to the mails with no traces of tampering.

The TSD instructors have also demonstrated some of their techniques in safe-cracking, surreptitious entry and lock-picking. But these are such highly specialized activities that TSD technicians almost always travel to countries when these talents are needed. As ordinary case officers we will need only the basic skills and enough knowledge of the really special techniques to know how to plan and when to ask for TSD technicians.

A few weeks ago I was discharged from the Air Force. Now I'm a civilian employee of the Department of the Air Force, as I was when I came to Washington three years ago. The cover unit is another bogus Pentagon office with the major, the colonel and all that routine. But I'm keeping my commission (I'm a First Lieutenant now) by joining an Agency Air Force reserve unit. This is a cover unit too.

Last week Ferguson came down from headquarters and he opened his session with me with a speech on the increasing demand in the Western Hemisphere Division for new case officers—apparently Castro and the Cuban Revolution are causing more and more problems all over Latin America. My reaction is disappointment, what with all my old fantasies of being a cloak-and-dagger operative in Vienna or Hong Kong. But Ferguson said I could ask for a transfer if after six months I still don't like it. It looks like ten or fifteen of us are destined for the Western Hemisphere Division so maybe it won't be so bad. Besides, all those hours in the language lab may at last be useful.

Part 2

Washington, D.C. — July 1960

The training program has ended at last. We spent the last week of June in Baltimore running in and out of department stores chasing our instructors on surveillance exercises. It was just like earlier exercises in the cities in Virginia except it went on day and night and included bugging hotel rooms, loading and unloading "dead drops," writing invisible messages, and several difficult agent meetings. Most of us spent the few free hours at night at the Oasis on East Baltimore Street—without par in really raunchy, fleshy, sweaty stripping.

My feelings were mixed about leaving Camp Peary. It was an isolated sort of life but the club was fun—the bar, ping-pong, chess. What I'll miss most is the athletic program and that nice gym.

After a short vacation I checked back with Ferguson‡ and he sent me over to the personnel officer in the Western Hemisphere (WH) Division. He didn't seem to have expected me and after waiting a couple of hours he sent me to the Venezuela desk, which, I discovered, consists of the desk officer, a secretary, and now me. We are part of Branch 3 of WH Division which covers the Bolivarian countries: Venezuela, Colombia, Ecuador, Peru and Bolivia—and we also handle matters related to the Dutch islands, Aruba and Curaçao, British Guiana and Surinam. Branch 1 has Mexico and Central America, Branch 2 has the Caribbean, Branch 4 has Brazil and Branch 5 has the *cono sur*: Uruguay, Paraguay, Argentina and Chile. Cuban affairs are centered in a special branch and the paramilitary operation (it looks like a repeat of the Guatemala operation but I can't get many details) has taken over a wing of Quarters Eye. All the rest of the division is in Barton Hall near Ohio Drive and the Potomac.

WH Division is the only area division of the DDP that isn't over in the buildings along the Reflecting Pool, and more and more I've been getting the impression that this division is looked down upon by the rest of the DDP. It seems that the physical separation of the division from the rest of the DDP has created the concept of WH as a fiefdom of Colonel J. C. King‡—he's been WH Division Chief now for some years. The other reason for disdain towards WH (I hear these stories from JOT's who have been assigned to other divisions) is that most of the division leadership—the branch chiefs and the station chiefs in the field—are a fraternity of ex-FBI officers who came into the CIA in 1947 when the CIA took over FBI intelligence work in Latin America.

It's embarrassing because they call us the "gumshoe division," even though the best communist party penetration operations are in Latin America—WH in fact was responsible for getting the secret Khrushchev speech to the 20th CPSU Congress, which the Agency made public long before the Soviets wanted it to be. And everybody knows about Guatemala. The problem is that the glory for super-spooky achievements is enjoyed mostly by EE officers—old hands from Berlin and Vienna. We'll see how they treat us after Castro gets thrown out!

I can't say I'm wild about the work I've been given. I inherited a desk full of dispatches and cables that nobody had done anything about and trying to make sense out of all this is frustrating—I have to keep bothering people to find out what all the office symbols mean on the routing sheets, who takes action on what, and which is more and which is less important. Most of my work is processing name checks and reports.

The name checks are even duller than processing reports. The first one I did was on some Jose Diaz and I didn't realize it was such a common name. When I got the references back from Records Integration Division (RID) there were over a thousand traces on people of that name. Trace requests for RID have to be narrowed down by date and place of birth and other identifying data. The bulk of the name checks are for the Standard Oil subsidiary in Venezuela—the company security officer is a former FBI man and he checks the names of prospective Venezuelan employees with the CIA before hiring—trying to keep out the bad guys.

This work routine has to improve—I can't spend a couple of years on reports and name checks.

Washington, D.C. — August 1960

I must be living right—and I'm almost too afraid to think about it—but I may just get a field assignment sooner than I could ever imagine. Yesterday morning my desk chief, C. Harlow Duffin,‡ asked me if I was interested in working overseas as he knows of an operations officer slot opening up next month in Quito, Ecuador, and if I'm interested he'll see what he can do. But he said nobody talks about field personnel assignments before they're approved so I've got to keep it secret until he says I can talk. Next month! But he said I wouldn't go right away. First, I'll have really to learn Spanish, then process into the Department of State—lots of details to take care of first.

Yesterday morning I picked up a book and some briefing material from the Ecuador desk, and I've been reading this instead of doing my work. I can't seem to lay it aside. Talk about banana republics and underdevelopment! Ecuador must be classic: torn apart as it is by internal contradictions and ruled by privileged oligarchies while bigger neighbors gobbled up enormous territories that Ecuador couldn't defend.

The overwhelming international reality for Ecuador is Peru and the 1942 Protocol of Rio de Janeiro whereby Peru made good its claim to over one third of what until then Ecuadoreans had considered national territory. In July and August 1941, after several months of negotiations had failed, Peruvian troops overwhelmed Ecuadorean defenses in the south—and in the eastern Amazonian region. The Rio Protocol was signed after new negotiations and Peru got the disputed territory, mostly Amazonian jungle. There is a Peruvian side to the story, of course, but Ecuador will never forgive having to sign the Rio Protocol under duress. The U.S. was already at war and we needed peace in

South America for our own war effort. Although the Peruvian victory in 1941 was only the latest in a series of disputes that go all the way back to pre-hispanic history, for Ecuador, easily defeated and claiming dismemberment by force, the Rio Protocol is a source of national humiliation less than one generation removed. The U.S. government is deeply involved because we promoted negotiation of the Rio Protocol and are still responsible for enforcing it—along with the other guarantor powers: Brazil, Chile and Argentina.

While Peru is the great international reality for Ecuador, the dominant national reality is the division of the country between sierra and coast. Although the Andes split the country down the middle, the eastern region is mostly tropical jungle divided by Amazonian tributaries. Some years ago exploration was made for petroleum but the cost of a pipeline over the Andes wasn't justified by the discoveries. The oriente, then, with its sparse population (including head-shrinking Indians) counts very little in the national life. The other two regions, the Andes highlands and the Pacific coast, are almost equally divided in area and population, and their interests are traditionally in conflict.

Liberal revolution came to Ecuador in 1895 and the main victim was the Church, as the dominant coastal forces behind the revolution took control of national policy out of the hands of the traditional sierra landowners. Church and State were separated, lay education was established, civil marriage and divorce were instituted, and large Church properties were confiscated.

Following the revolution in 1895 the Liberal Party dominated Ecuadorean politics as liberals joined conservatives in the land-owning aristocracy while conditions changed very little for the overwhelming mass of the population completely outside the power structure. Even so, Ecuadorean politics in the twentieth century is not just another history of violent conservative–liberal struggle for spoils of office—it is indeed that, but much more. Ecuador has one of the most amazing Latin American politicians of the century: Jose Maria Velasco Ibarra—elected President once again just two months ago. This is the fourth time he's been elected President and none of his terms have been consecutive. And of his three previous times in power, two ended before the constitutional term was over because of military *coups* against him.

Velasco is the stormy petrel of Ecuadorean politics, a spell-binding orator whose powers of rhetoric are irresistible to the masses. He is also an authoritarian who finds sharing power with the Congress very difficult. His politics are as unpredictable as his fiery temperament and he has taken conflicting positions on many political issues, thereby attracting support from all established political parties, at one time or another. He won the June elections by the largest margin ever attained by an Ecuadorean presidential candidate and he did it in his typically clever fashion. Running as an independent he allied himself with the impoverished masses in violent tirades against the ruling oligarchies who, he claimed, were behind the candidates of the Liberal and Conservative parties. He called for fundamental economic and social change, an end to rule by oligarchies and political bosses, and a fairer distribution of the national income. On this populist appeal Velasco got almost 400,000 votes, a smashing victory, and his denunciations of the Rio Protocol during the campaign made him the champion of Ecuadorean nationalism.

Velasco is due to take office in September but the station in Quito isn't taking any bets on how long he'll last. After three consecutive Ecuadorean presidents have served out their terms, perhaps the instability of the past is ending. Velasco's term is for four years, but taking into account the fact that he is Ecuador's 70th President in 130 years of independence one can't be too sure. I hope I'll be there to see.

Washington, D.C. — August 1960

I know I'm over-eager and impatient but I thought I'd go mad during the week they were deciding. Duffin finally called me in and said the Branch Chief, Edwin

Terrell,‡ had approved my nomination and that the reaction in Colonel King's office was also favorable. The officer who is in the position now is being transferred to Guayaquil as Base Chief in September and the station is calling for a replacement right away. The WH personnel officer is arranging for me to go into full-time Spanish training with a tutor so that I can get to Quito as soon as possible. Cover for the job is Assistant Attaché in the U.S. Embassy political section, which means I'll have diplomatic status and "integration" with the State Department as a Foreign Service Officer.

Then Duffin let me in on a secret. He said he is scheduled to go to Quito as Chief of Station (COS) next summer which is why he picked me. Meanwhile, he said, I'll be working with one of the best-liked COS's in WH Division: Jim Noland.‡ Even with the Spanish training and the time needed for State Department integration, Duffin says I'll be in Quito before Christmas.

Duffin then set up a meeting for me with Rudy Gomez,‡ the Deputy Division Chief who gives the final approval on all lesser personnel assignments. He's a gruff sort. Without looking up he said that if I didn't have a good reason for not going to Quito, then I'd have to go. I said I wanted to go, played it real straight and got his approval. Apparently I'm one of the first of our JOT class to get a field assignment—the only one I've heard of so far who will get out before me is Christopher Thoren‡ who's being assigned this month under State Department cover in the U.S. mission at the United Nations.

Washington, D.C. — August 1960

Getting to know Ecuador is at once stimulating and sobering. The new Congress, elected in June with Velasco, opened on 10 August although Velasco doesn't take office until 1 September. If the tactics of Velasquistas in the Congress are any indication, the new government may dedicate itself more to persecuting the Poncistas of the outgoing régime than to governing the country. The Velasquistas have a wide plurality in Congress but are just short of a majority. At the opening, which consisted of the annual messages of President Ponce and the President of the Supreme Court, Ponce was overwhelmed by the insults and jeers from the screaming Velaquista-packed galleries, unable to be heard during the entire three-and-a-half-hour speech. The President of the Supreme Court, however, followed Ponce and was heard with silence and respect. Congressional sessions since then have been dedicated to efforts by the Velasquistas to discredit the Ponce government, and Ponce's two most important ministers, Government (internal security) and Foreign Relations, have resigned rather than face humiliation in interpellations (political interrogations) by the Congress.

Attacks by Velasquistas against Ponce and his supporters reflect traditional rivalries but are especially acute now because the Velasquistas are beginning to take revenge for government repression against them during the electoral campaign and even earlier. The most notorious incident was at a Velasquita demonstration on 19 March when five Velasquistas were killed and many wounded. The demonstration was to celebrate Velasco's arrival in Quito to begin the political campaign after several years of self-imposed exile in Argentina. The Velasquista campaign that followed was as much a campaign against Ponce and traditional Ecuadorean oligarchies as it was in favor of political policies proposed by Velasco. While reform proposals for a fairer distribution of the national income and more efficient government administration were central to the Velasco campaign, many are sceptical of his personal stability as well as his ability to break the power of the one hundred or so families that have controlled the country for generations.

The people, nevertheless, liked what they heard from Velasco because this country's extreme injustices and poverty are so acute. Not only is Ecuador the next-to-the-poorest country of South America in terms of *per capita* annual income (220 dollars—about one third of Argentina's and less than one tenth of ours) but even this low average amount is extremely unevenly divided.

The top 1 per cent of the population receives an income comparable to U.S. standards while about two thirds of the population get only on average a monthly family income of about 10 dollars. This lower two thirds, consisting largely of Indians and people of mixed blood, are simply outside the money economy, completely marginalized and without social or economic integration or participation in the national life.

Except among those who would be adversely affected, there is wide agreement that the root of Ecuador's extremes of poverty and wealth is in land tenure. As in other countries the best lands belong to large landowners who employ relatively few rural workers and thereby contribute to the growing urban unemployed. The small plots usually cannot produce more than a subsistence income due to land quality and size. Even on the coast where the cash crops of bananas, coffee, caçao and rice are raised on small- and medium-sized properties, fluctuating prices, marketing difficulties, scarce credit and low technification combine for low productivity and a precarious existence for salaried workers.

Thus land reform and a stable market for export crops are fundamental for the economic development necessary before Ecuador can begin to invest adequately in facilities for education, health-care, housing and other possible benefits. Indicators are typical of poor countries: poor diet; high incidence of debilitating diseases caused by intestinal parasites from bad drinking water; 370,000 children unable to attend school this year because no schools exist for them; a housing deficit of 580,000 units in a country of 4.3 million.

Solutions to this misery are being sought both externally and internally. In the external sector the Ecuadoreans are making efforts to stabilize the falling prices that in recent years have forced them to produce ever greater quantities in order to sustain imports. Also of great importance is foreign aid obtained in part from the International Cooperation Administration (ICA) which has a technical assistance mission in Ecuador. Internally, the Ecuadorean government must embark on a program of reforms: agrarian reform to raise productivity and increase rural employment; fiscal reform to increase government revenues and redistribute income; administrative reform to improve the government administration and the myriad agencies that currently enjoy autonomy—and to reduce corruption. Already a movement is underway to abolish the *huasipungo*, a precarious form of tenure, although government land policy is mainly orientated towards colonization and opening of new lands with limited success. Lowering the population growth, now up to 3.1 per cent annually, is of obvious importance, but is hindered by tradition and Catholic Church policy. Somehow all of these programs will contribute to raising the rate of economic growth and to increasing the benefits available to the marginalized two thirds of the population. Promises for these reforms and increased benefits won Velasco his sensational victory, and he'll soon have the chance to deliver.

Washington, D.C. — September 1960

For several weeks I've been studying Spanish full-time with a tutor in Arlington, and on the tapes in the language lab. I'll probably be in this routine until November when I get integrated to the State Department and take the two-week orientation course at the Foreign Service Institute. Meanwhile I stop in each morning to see Duffin and read more background material at the Ecuadorean desk.

Velasco is now President. He has embarked on two early policies that affect operations of the Quito station and other matters of concern to us. First, he is trying to purge all the supporters of Ponce from government employment, and secondly, he is stirring up the border problem with Peru by declaring the Rio Protocol null and void.

Immediately after taking power Velasco relieved forty-eight military officers from their assigned duties and placed them at the disposition of the Ministry of Defense. Velasco also started a purge in the National Police, starting with the two senior colonels who were the station's main liaison agents. They were arrested and charged with participating in the 19 March riot.

More serious was the forced departure of our Station Operations Officer under Public Safety Cover with the United States Operations Mission (USOM) of the ICA program. Our Station Officer, Bob Weatherwax,‡ had been in the forefront directing the police during the 19 March riot, and he was clearly identified because of his very blond hair and red face—practically an albino coloring. As soon as Velasco was inaugurated Weatherwax and Jim Noland, the COS, were notified by Jorge Acosta Velasco,‡ the President's nephew and family favorite (he has no children), that Weatherwax should leave the country for a while to avoid being dragged into the prosecutions for the 19 March affair. Acosta, who is a close friend of both Weatherwax and Noland, made the suggestion only to be helpful, not as an official act. Nevertheless, Noland agreed and Weatherwax is now back in Washington killing time until he can return.

The government purge is being run mostly by Manuel Araujo Hidalgo who was elected to the Chamber of Deputies from Pichincha Province (the Quito region) and who is now Minister of Government. He was appointed after Velasco fired his first Minister of Government only a week after taking office. Araujo had to resign the Deputies seat but he is clearly the leader of the Velasquista mobs.

Araujo is an extreme leftist and ardent defender of the Cuban Revolution—exactly the wrong man for the most important internal security job. He is particularly hostile to the U.S., and the station is fearful that he may jeopardize the Public Safety Program because he is also in charge of the National Police. The real danger is that all our efforts to improve the government's security capabilities in preparation for the 11th Inter-American Conference—now just six months away—may go down the drain.

Araujo's purge is running not only into the military services and the police. The civilian government employees are also being purged of Ponce supporters—helped especially by the Congress's repeal of the Civil

Service Career Law passed during the Ponce administration. Velasco obviously wants to pack the government with his own people.

Velasco's declaration in his inaugural speech that the Rio Protocol is void has been followed by rising tension and fears that the dispute may jeopardize the Inter-American Conference. Ecuadoreans are without doubt behind Velasco on the matter, but Velasco is using the issue to denounce any opposition to his policies as anti-patriotic and prejudicial to a favorable solution of the boundary problem. So far the Conservative Party and the Social Christians, while defending the Ponce administration, have not declared open opposition to Velasco.

Washington, D.C. — October 1960

Headquarters files on the operations of the Quito station and its subordinate base in Guayaquil reflect the very careful analysis of the operational environment that is always the framework within which operations are undertaken. Although the analysis includes assessments of such factors as security and cover, the most important part deals with the enemy.

The Communist Party of Ecuador (PCE)

Although the PCE has been a legal party since World War II, it has never been able to obtain the 5000 signatures necessary for inscribing candidates in national elections. However, Pedro Saad, the PCE Secretary-General, held the seat as Functional Senator for Labor from the coast from 1947 until last June when he was defeated through a Guayaquil base political-action operation. (The Ecuadorean Senate has a number of "functional senators" from coast and sierra representing special interest groups, e.g. labor, commerce, education, agriculture, the military services.) Membership in the PCE is estimated by the station at around 1000 with perhaps another 1000 members in the Communist

Youth of Ecuador (JCE). Almost all of the members of the PCE National Executive Committee reside in Guayaquil. With respect to the emerging Sino-Soviet differences the PCE national leadership supports the Soviets although some PCE leaders in the sierra, particularly in Quito, are beginning to lean towards the more militant Chinese position.

In the elections this year the PCE joined with the left wing of the Socialist Party and the Concentration of Popular Forces (CFP) to back a leftist candidate for President, the Rector of Guayaquil University, who received only about 46,000 votes—just 6 per cent of the total. PCE strength, however, is not measured in voter appeal but in the strength of labor, student and youth organizations in which its influence is strong.

The Socialist Party of Ecuador (PSE)

Although much larger than the PCE, the Socialist Party has cooperated for many years with the Communists in the leadership of the labor movement. Recently the Socialists have split into a right wing which formed an alliance with the Liberal Party in the unsuccessful presidential campaign of Galo Plaza this year, and a left wing which voted with the PCE and the CFP.

Because of its support for the Cuban Revolution and of violent revolutionary principles, the left-wing Socialists are dangerous and inimical to U.S. interests. Their successes, however, are concentrated in the labor movement and intellectual circles. The President of the Ecuadorean Workers' Confederation is a left-wing Socialist as is the Functional Senator for Labor from the sierra.

The Ecuadorean Workers Confederation (CTE)

Founded by the Communists and the Socialists in 1944, the CTE is by far the most dominant labor confederation in Ecuador and a member of the World Federation of Trade Unions (WFTU). Although the Secretary-General of the PCE, Pedro Saad, headed the CTE at the beginning, a Socialist took over in the late 1940s and this party is still in nominal control. However, the Communists retained the number two position and are now considered to exercise dominant if not complete control in the CTE. CTE membership is estimated at 60,000—less than 10 per cent of the poorly organized labor force, but enough to cause serious trouble.

The Ecuadorean Federation of University Students (FEUE)

Consistent with the traditional leftist-activist student movement in Latin America, the FEUE—the principal Ecuadorean national student union—has been under frequent, if not continuous, control by PCE, JCE and left-wing Socialists. Its loud campaigns are directed against the U.S. presence in Ecuador and Latin America, mainly U.S. business, and strongly in support of the Cuban Revolution. When appropriate issues are presented the FEUE is capable of mobilizing the students, secondary students included, for strikes and street manifestations as well as propaganda campaigns. It is supported by leftist professors and administrators in the five state universities in Quito, Guayaquil, Portoviejo, Cuenca and Loja.

The Revolutionary Union of Ecuadorean Youth (URJE)

In 1959 the youth organizations of the Communists, the Socialists and the Concentration of Popular Forces formed URJE which has become the most important leftist-activist youth movement. It engages in street demonstrations, wall-painting, circulation of fly-sheets, intimidation—agitation of many kinds of revolutionary causes. Although URJE denies that it is a communist front, the station considers it under PCE control and the most immediate and dangerous threat for terrorism and armed insurgency. It is stronger in Guayaquil than in Quito, and its membership in both places totals about 1000. URJE gives unqualified support to the Cuban Revolution and several URJE leaders have traveled to Cuba, probably for revolutionary training.

Hostile Elements in the Ecuadorean Government

The Velasquista movement, as a heterogeneous populist movement, contains political colorings from extreme right to extreme left. The Minister of Government, Manuel Araujo Hidalgo, is our most important enemy in the government, but others, such as the Minister of Education and various appointees to lesser posts, are also dangerous. The station has a continuing program for monitoring leftist penetration in the government, and the results are regularly reported to headquarters and to the Ambassador and the State Department. Aside from the National Government, the mayors of the provincial capitals of Ambato and Esmeraldas are Revolutionary Socialists.

The Cuban Mission

The Cuban Embassy consists of the Ambassador and four officials. The station lacks concrete information on support by the Cuban Embassy to Ecuadorean revolutionary organizations, but their overt contacts with extreme leftists leave little doubt. Araujo is their angel in the government and of course they are supported by leftists throughout the country. While the station is making efforts to penetrate the Embassy—and the Guayaquil base is doing the same against the one-man Cuban Consulate—the main CIA drive is to promote a break in diplomatic relations through propaganda and political-action operations.

The Czech Mission

Ecuador broke diplomatic relations with Czechoslovakia in 1957 but during his last week in the presidency, Ponce received the Czech Minister to Brazil and relations were again established. The station expects that within a few weeks or a little longer the Czechs will try to establish a diplomatic mission in Quito which undoubtedly will include intelligence officers.

Operations of the Quito station and the Guayaquil base are directed against these targets and are laid down in the Related Missions Directive (RMD) for Ecuador, which is a general statement of priorities and objectives.

PRIORITY A
Collect and report intelligence on the strength and intentions of communist and other political organizations hostile to the U.S., including their international sources of support and guidance and their influence in the Ecuadorean government.

Objective 1: Effect agent and/or technical penetrations at the highest possible level of the Communist Party of Ecuador (PCE), the Socialist Party of Ecuador (PSE-revolutionary), the Communist Youth of Ecuador (JCE), the Revolutionary Union of Ecuadorean Youth (URJE) and related organizations.

Objective 2: Effect agent and/or technical penetration of the Cuban missions in Ecuador.

PRIORITY B
Collect and report intelligence on the stability of the Ecuadorean government and on the strength and intentions of dissident political groups.

Objective 1: Maintain agents and other sources at the highest levels of the government, the security services and the ruling political organization.

Objective 2: Maintain agents and other sources in opposition political parties, especially among military leaders favorable to opposition parties.

PRIORITY C
Through propaganda and psychological warfare operations: (1) disseminate information and opinion designed to counteract anti-U.S. or pro-communist propaganda; (2) neutralize communist or extreme-leftist influence in principal mass organizations or assist in establishing or maintaining alternative organizations under non-communist leadership.

Objective 1: Place appropriate propaganda in the most effective local media.

Objective 2: Support democratic leaders of political, labor, student and youth organizations, particularly in areas where communist influence is strongest (Ecuadorean Federation of University Students [FEUE]; Ecuadorean Workers' Confederation [CTE]), and where democratic leaders may be encouraged to combat communist subversion.

That is a sizeable order for such a small station and base—although the CIA budget for Ecuador is a little over 500,000 dollars for this fiscal year. The Quito station consists of the Chief, James B. Noland;‡ Deputy Chief (this job is vacant and will not be filled until early next year); one operations officer which is the job I'm being sent to; a reports officer, John Bacon,‡ who also handles several of the most important operations; a communications officer; an administrative assistant (she handles the money and property and doubles as Noland's secretary); and a secretary-typist. The entire station is under cover in the political section of the Embassy with the exception of Bob Weatherwax,‡ the operations officer under Public Safety cover in USOM.

The Guayaquil base forms the entire small political section of the Consulate, consisting of a base chief, Richard Wheeler,‡ (my predecessor in Quito); one operations officer; an administrative assistant who also handles communications; and a secretary-typist.

The general directives of the RMD are put into practice through a number of operations, making use of agents we have recruited, and which are summarized now in some detail, first so far as the main station at Quito is concerned, then for the Guayaquil base.

Quito Foreign Intelligence and Counter-Intelligence Operations (FI–CI)

ECSIGIL. This is our most important penetration operation against the Communist Party of Ecuador and consists of two agents who are members of the PCE and close associates of Rafael Echeverria Flores, principal PCE leader in the sierra. The agents are Mario Cardenas,‡ whose cryptonym is ECSIGIL–1, and Luis Vargas,‡ who is ECSIGIL–2. They have been reporting for about four years since their recruitment as "walk-ins" after their disillusionment with the PCE. Although the agents are close friends and originally came to the station together, they have since been discouraged from associating too closely, so that if one is ever blown, the other will not be contaminated. The separation is also designed to prevent their collaborating over what they report.

Cardenas is directed through a cutout, Mario Cabeza de Vaca,‡ a Quito milk producer who became a U.S. citizen through military service in World War II but returned to Ecuador afterwards. He is married to an American who runs the food and liquor commissary of the U.S. Embassy. Vargas is directed through another cutout, Miguel Burbano de Lara,‡ who is the Quito airport manager of Pan American–Grace Airways. The cutouts are not supposed to know each other's identity, although each knows that Vargas and Cardenas are reporting, and they meet separately with the station Reports Officer, John Bacon, who handles this operation.

Although neither of these agents holds important PCE elective positions, they are extremely close to Echeverria and the decision-making process in Quito. They receive information on practically all matters of importance, and the ECSIGIL project accounts for an average of about five or six disseminated intelligence reports in Washington each week.

ECFONE. This operation consists of an agent penetration of the PCE and his cutout who also reports on the policy and plans of the Velasco government. The recruitment of the PCE agent, Atahualpa Basantes Larrea,‡ ECFONE–3, is one of the more interesting recent station accomplishments. Early in 1960 when the leaders of Velasco's political movement began to organize for Velasco's return from Buenos Aires and the presidential campaign, Oswaldo Chiriboga,‡ ECFONE, was a Velasquista leader reporting to the station on Velasco's political campaign. Chiriboga advised one day that he had recently seen his old friend, Basantes, who had been active in Ecuadorean communism but had drifted away and was now in dire financial straits. Noland, the COS, directed Chiriboga to suggest to Basantes that he become more active in the PCE and at the same time become an adviser to Chiriboga on PCE reaction to the Velasco campaign. Care was taken from the beginning to establish a secure, discreet relationship between Chiriboga and Basantes, and Noland provided Chiriboga with modest sums for Basantes's "expenses" as adviser—the classic technique for establishing a developmental agent's dependence on a station salary. Basantes had no trouble expanding his activities in the PCE and soon he was reporting valuable information. Chiriboga, of course, moved carefully from innocuous matters to more sensitive information while easing Basantes into an agent's dependency. Although the original rationale for Basantes's reporting ended with the elections in June, Chiriboga has since been able to convince Basantes of the continuing need for his "advice."

ECOLIVE. An agent penetration of the Revolutionary Union of Ecuadorean Youth (URJE), ECOLIVE-1,‡ is a recent walk-in who is considered to have long-range potential for penetrating the PCE or other revolutionary organizations into which he may later be guided. For the moment he is reporting on the activities and plans of URJE for street demonstrations in support of Velasco's attempt to nullify the Rio Protocol.

ECCENTRIC. This agent is a physician, Dr. Felipe Ovalle,‡ with a history of collaboration with the U.S. government that goes back to FBI days during World War II. Although he is a Colombian he has lived in Ecuador for many years where he has a modest medical practice, most of which comes from his inclusion on the U.S. Embassy list of approved medical examiners for Ecuadorean applicants for visas. Ovalle's 201 agent file reveals that verification of his medical degree, supposedly obtained at a Colombian university, has proved impossible. Through the years he has developed a close relationship with President Velasco, whom he now serves as personal physician. Ovalle reports the results of his weekly meetings with Velasco to the station. Occasionally the information from this operation is interesting enough to disseminate in Washington, but usually the information is inferior to that of other agents.

ECAMOROUS. The main station activity in security preparations for the Inter-American Conference is the training and equipping of the intelligence department of the Ecuadorean National Police. The intelligence department is called the Department of Special Services of the National Police Headquarters, and its chief is Police Captain Jose Vargas,‡ ECAMOROUS–2, who has been given special training here and in headquarters. Weatherwax, our case officer under Public Safety cover, works almost exclusively with Vargas, who has been in trouble recently for being the leader of a secret society of pro-Velasco young police officers. Secret societies in the police, as in the military, are forbidden.

In spite of all our efforts, Vargas seems incapable of doing very much to help us, but he has managed to develop three or four marginal reporting agents on extreme leftist activities in his home town of Riobamba, a sierra provincial capital, and in Esmeraldas, a coastal provincial capital. Reports from these sources come directly to Vargas, and from him to the station, because there is little interest in this type of information further up the line in the Ecuadorean government. On the contrary, with Araujo as the minister in charge of the National Police, intelligence collection by a police officer is a risky activity.

Intelligence needs during the Inter-American Conference will have to be satisfied largely by the station directly through unilateral operations but before information of this kind is passed to Vargas it will have to be disguised to protect the source. Although strictly speaking ECAMOROUS is a liaison operation, the police intelligence unit is completely run by the station. Vargas is paid a salary by Noland with additional money for his sub-agents and expenses. Some technical equipment such as photo gear and non-sensitive audio equipment has been given to Vargas by the station, and we have trained his chief technician, Lieutenant Luis Sandoval.‡

Vargas is young and rather reckless but very friendly, well-disposed and intelligent. Although he is considered to be excellent as a long-term penetration of the National Police, he could be worked into other operations in the future. His first loyalty is undoubtedly to the station, and when asked he is glad to use his police position as cover for action requested by the station.

ECOLE. This is the station's main penetration operation against the Ecuadorean National Police other than the intelligence side, and it also produces information about the Ecuadorean Workers Confederation (CTE). The principal agent, Colonel Wilfredo Oswaldo Lugo,‡ ECOLE, has been working with the U.S. government since hunting Nazis with the FBI during World War II. Since 1947 he has been working with the Quito station, and in the police shuffle and purge during Velasco's first weeks in office, Lugo was appointed Chief of the Department of Personnel of the National Police Headquarters.

In contrast with the fairly open contact between Noland and Weatherwax and Captain Vargas, the intelligence chief, contact between Noland and Lugo is very discreet. The agent is considered to be a penetration of the security service and in times of crisis his reporting is invaluable, since he is in a position to give situation reports on government plans and reactions to events as reflected in orders to police and military units.

Over the years Colonel Lugo has developed several agents who report on communist and related activities. Two of these agents are currently active and are targeted against the CTE. Their reporting is far inferior to PCE penetration agents such as Cardenas, Luis Vargas and Basantes, but they are kept on the payroll as insurance in case anything ever happens to the better agents. Noland also pays a regular monthly salary to Colonel Lugo.

ECJACK. About two years ago the Army established the Ecuadorean Military Intelligence Service (SIME) under Lieutenant-Colonel Roger Paredes,‡ ECJACK, who then made contact with Noland. Paredes had been trained by the U.S. Army at Fort Leavenworth some years earlier. In 1959, however, discouraged by the lack of support from his government for SIME, Paredes suggested to Noland that he might be more effective if he retired from the Army and worked full time with the station. At this point SIME was only a paper organization, and even today is still useless.

Paredes's suggestion to Noland came just at the time the station investigations and surveillance team was discovered to be falsifying reports and expenses. The old ECSERUM team was fired and Paredes retired from the Army to form a new team. He now runs a five-man full-time team for surveillance and general investigations in Quito and, in addition, he has two reporting agents in the important southern sierra town of Loja. These two agents are on the fringes of communist activities there.

Station direction of this operation is entirely through Lieutenant-Colonel Paredes, who uses the SIME organization as cover and as ostensible sponsor for the other agents in the operation. Another sub-agent is the chief of the identity card section of the Ministry of Government. As all citizens are required to register and obtain an official government-issued identity card, this agent provides on request the full name, date and place of birth, names of parents, occupation, address and photograph of practically any Ecuadorean. His main value is to provide this data for the station LYNX List, which is a list of about 100 communists and other activists of the extreme left whom the station considers the most dangerous. The LYNX List is a requirement for all Western Hemisphere stations, to be maintained in case a local government in time of crisis should ask (or be asked by the U.S. government) for assistance in the emergency preventive detention of dangerous persons. The ECJACK team spends part of its time updating addresses and place of employment of current LYNX

List members and in getting the required information on new additions.

The team is also used for following officers of the Cuban Embassy or for following and identifying persons who visit the Embassy. Their surveillance work is recognized by the station as clumsy and indiscreet, but plans call for additional training, vehicles (they have no team transportation) and perhaps radio equipment. Paredes, of course, maintains close contact with military officers in SIME so that the station can monitor that service and confirm the reporting from the U.S. Army Major who is the Military Assistance Advisory Group (MAAG) intelligence advisor.

ECSTACY. In the central Quito post office, ECSTACY–1‡ is the chief of the incoming airmail pouch section. As pouches arrive from Cuba, the Soviet bloc and Communist China, he sets them aside for his brother, ECSTACY–2,‡ who passes them to the station. John Bacon, the station reports officer, processes the letters and returns them the same day for reinsertion in the mails. Payment is made on a piecework basis. Processing requires surreptitious opening, reading, photography of letters of interest, and closing. Each week Bacon reports by dispatch the gist of the letters of main interest, with copies to headquarters and other interested stations.

As most of the letters are from Ecuadoreans who are visiting the countries from which the letters are mailed, this postal intercept operation enables the station to monitor travelers to communist countries and their potential danger when they return. The letters also reveal leads to possible recruitment of Ecuadoreans who have been invited to visit communist countries, as well as those selected for scholarships to schools such as Moscow's People's Friendship University. Still other letters are from residents of the country where the letter originates, who are writing to Ecuadoreans who have visited that country. Attention is paid to possible political disaffection of the writers, for recruitment as agents in the country where the letter originates.

Since the letter intake amounts to about thirty to forty letters per day, the ECSTACY operation is time-consuming for the station officer in charge. Nevertheless it is a valuable support operation and of considerable interest to the Cuban, Soviet, Eastern Europe and Communist Chinese branches in the DDP in headquarters.

ECOTTER. Travel control is another standard support function enabling the station to monitor the movements of communists, politicians and other people of interest on the flights between Quito and other cities and on the international flights. ECOTTER–1,‡ an employee of the civil aviation office at the Quito airport, passes copies of all passenger lists to ECOTTER–2,‡ who brings them to the station in the Embassy. The passenger lists, which arrive in the station only one day after the flights, are circulated for perusal by each station officer and returned when the new batch is delivered.

ECOTTER–1 has arranged with airport immigration inspectors to note on the lists whenever a traveler's passport indicates travel to a communist country or to Cuba, and this information is reported to headquarters and indexed for station files. Any travel by people of importance, mainly local communists or communist diplomats, is reported to headquarters and appropriate stations and bases where the passenger list indicates they are traveling.

ECTOSOME. The principal station agent for intelligence against the Czechs is Otto Kladensky,‡ the Oldsmobile dealer in Quito. His reporting has diminished since the Czechs were expelled three years ago, but now that relations have been reestablished he will undoubtedly be in close contact with Czech officials when they open a Quito Embassy. For the time being he reports on the occasional visits of Czech trade officials, and he provides the link to a high-level penetration of the Velasquista movement, ECOXBOW–1.

ECOXBOW. Before this year's political campaign, Noland began cultivating a retired Army lieutenant-colonel, Reinaldo Varea Donoso,‡ ECOXBOW–1, whom he met through Kladensky. Recruitment of Varea, an important leader of Velasquistas in military circles, proceeded with the assistance of Kladensky. Funds were provided by Noland via Kladensky for Varea's successful campaign for the Senate, and in August he was elected Vice-President of the Senate. He reports on military support for Velasco and he maintains regular contact with the leadership in the Ministry of Defense and the principal military units.

Varea's station salary of 700 dollars per month is high by Ecuadorean standards but his access to crucial intelligence on government policy and stability is adequate justification. The project also provides funds for a room rented full-time in Kladensky's name in the new, luxurious Hotel Quito (built for the Inter-American Conference) where Kladensky and Varea take their playmates. Noland occasionally meets Varea in the hotel, but he is trying to keep the relation with Varea as discreet as possible by channeling contact through Kladensky.

AMBLOOD. Early this year the Miami Operations base, cryptonym JMWAVE, was established to support operations against the Castro régime in Cuba. The Havana station is preparing to continue operations from Miami when relations with Cuba are broken and the Embassy in Havana is closed. As part of the Cuban operation stay-behind procedures, the Quito station was asked to provide accommodation addresses for communicating with agents in Cuba by secret writing. Lieutenant-Colonel Paredes, the chief of the surveillance and investigative team, rented several post-boxes which have been assigned to Cuban agents who are part of a team located in Santiago, Cuba. The chief of the team is Luis Toroella,‡ AMBLOOD–1, a former Cuban government employee who has been trained in the U.S. and is now being sent back to Cuba to head the AMBLOOD team.

The messages to Cuba are written in secret writing (sw) in Miami and forwarded by pouch to the Quito station where a cover letter is written by Francine

Jacome,‡ ECDOXY, who is an American married to an Ecuadorean and who performs occasional support tasks for the station. The messages from Cuba to Quito are also written in a liquid SW system and are retrieved from the post-boxes by Paredes, passed to the station, and forwarded to the JMWAVE base in Miami.

Quito Psychological and Paramilitary Operations (PP)

ECURGE. The major station agent for placing propaganda is Gustavo Salgado,‡ an ex-communist considered by many to be the outstanding liberal political journalist in the country. His column appears several times per week in *El Comercio*, the main Quito daily, and in several provincial newspapers. Salgado also writes under pseudonyms for wider publication.

Proper treatment of Ecuadorean and international themes is worked out in the station by John Bacon, who is in charge of this operation too, and passed to the agent for final draft. Headquarters guidance on propaganda subjects is also passed over in considerable volume and, on request from other stations, Salgado can comment on events in other countries to be later replayed there.

Salgado is also extremely useful for publishing intelligence received from agent penetrations of the PCE and like-minded groups, and for exposing communist backing for disruptive activities. The agent is paid on a production basis.

ECELDER. Fly-sheets and handbills are a major propaganda medium in Ecuador and the ECELDER operation is a secret means for printing these kinds of throwaway notice. Five brothers, most of whom have other employment, divide the work of operating a small family printing business. The family name is Rivadeneira and the brothers are Marcelo,‡ Jorge,‡ Patricio,‡ Rodrigo,‡ and Ramiro.‡ The brothers are well known in local basketball circles and have been the mainstays of the principal Catholic preparatory-school team, La Salle, in its traditional rivalry with the principal lay preparatory school, Mejia. Noland, who is also active in basketball circles, handles the contact with whichever brother is running the printing plant at a particular moment.

The text of the fly-sheets is usually written in the station by John Bacon and passed to Gustavo Salgado for final draft. After printing they are given to a secret distribution team. The ECELDER printing plant is a legitimate operation with regular commercial orders. For the station handbills, fictitious print-shop symbols are often used because Ecuadorean law requires all printed material to carry the print-shop symbol. The shop also has symbols for the print shop used by the communists and related groups, for use when a station-written handbill is attributed to them.

ECJOB. A team of Catholic university students directed by ECJOB–1‡ is used to distribute the station handbills printed at the ECELDER shop. Because the handbills have false print-shop symbols and the team distributes without official permits, techniques for fast, efficient distribution are necessary. Usually several trucks are rented and as they move swiftly along the crowded Quito streets the handbills are hurled into the air. Several times team members have been arrested but ECJOB–1 has been able to buy their freedom without difficulty. None of the team except the leader himself knows about U.S. Embassy sponsorship of the operation.

The team is also used for wall-painting, another major propaganda medium in Ecuador. Usually the team works in the early hours of the morning, painting slogans on instruction by the station or painting out and mutilating the slogans painted by communist or pro-communist groups. Extreme caution is taken by the team in order to avoid street clashes with the opposition wall-painters who sometimes roam the streets searching for the anti-communists who spoil their work. John Bacon is also in charge of this operation.

ECACTOR. The most important station operation for anti-communist political action consists of funding and guidance to selected leaders of the Conservative

Party and the Social Christian Movement. The operation developed from the most important station penetration agent of the Ponce government, Renato Perez Drouet,‡ who was Secretary-General of the Administration under Ponce and has since returned to manage his Quito travel agency. Through Perez, the station now finances the anti-communist propaganda and political action of the Social Christian Movement, of which Perez is a leader.

Before the 1960 election campaign Perez proposed to Noland the support of a young engineer, Aurelio Davila Cajas,‡ ECACTOR–1, whom Noland began to cultivate. Davila intensified his activities in the Conservative Party and with station financing he was elected in June to the Chamber of Deputies, representing the distant and sparsely populated Amazonian province of Napo. Davila is now the fastest rising young leader in the Conservative Party and very closely associated with the Catholic Church hierarchy which the party represents in politics. He is an outspoken and militant anti-communist and is considered by Noland, moreover, to have an enlightened stance on social reform. The station is now helping him to build up his personal political organization, which is branching out into student politics at the Catholic university. Normal communications between Noland and Davila, and the passage of funds, is through Renato Perez. In emergencies, however, messages and money are passed via Barbara Svegle,‡ the station secretary-typist, who rents an apartment in Davila's apartment-building where the agent also lives.

Also through Renato Perez, Noland cultivated and eventually recruited Carlos Arizaga Toral,‡ ECATOR–2, who is the principal leader of the Conservative Party in Cuenca, Ecuador's third largest city. Through this agent Noland financed Conservative Party candidates in Cuenca including the agent's son, Carlos Arizaga Vega,‡ ECACTOR–3, who was elected to the provincial council of Azuay—the province of which Cuenca is capital. Communications with this branch of the ECACTOR operation are difficult, but usually Noland travels to Cuenca for meetings although the principal agent may go to Quito. Funds channeled through this project are now being spent on anti-communist propaganda, student politics at the University of Cuenca, and local militant street-action by Conservative Party youth groups.

Another agent has recently been added in order to fulfil the project's goals in Ecuador's fourth largest city, Ambato, another sierra provincial capital. The agent is Jorge Gortaire,‡ ECACTOR–4, a retired Army colonel who has recently returned from service on the Inter-American Defense Board in Washington. Gortaire is on the list of pro-Ponce military officers now being purged. In 1956 he was elected as functional Senator for the Armed Forces, but he served only part of his term before being assigned by Ponce to the Inter-American Defense Board. In Washington he was cultivated by a CIA headquarters officer assigned to spot and assess potential agent material in the delegations to the Defense Board, and reports on Gortaire were forwarded to the Quito station. Noland has initiated contact with Gortaire and the Ecuadorean desk is processing clearance for use of this agent in anti-communist political action and propaganda in Ambato. Special importance is attached to this new agent because the mayor of Ambato is a Revolutionary Socialist and is using the municipal government machinery to promote infiltration by the extreme left there. Gortaire has excellent potential because he would be a likely candidate for Minister of Defense if Ponce is re-elected in the next elections. Meanwhile he will also be reporting on any rumors and reports of discontent in the military commands.

ECOPTIC. The socialists, it will be remembered, have split into two rival groups: the Democratic Socialist Party of Ecuador (PSE) and the Revolutionary Socialist Party (PSR). Through his work in the University Sport League which sponsors one of the best Ecuadorean professional soccer teams, Noland met, cultivated and finally recruited Manuel Naranjo,‡ ECOPTIC–1, a principal leader of the PSE. With financial support from Noland, Naranjo, an outstanding economist, was elected to the Chamber of Deputies in June, representing Pichincha (Quito) Province. Financial assistance is continuing so that this agent, like the others, can build up a personal political organization and influence his party to take desired action on issues such as communism and Castro, while fighting the PSR.

ECBLOOM. Labor operations are perhaps the weakest part of the Quito station operational program, although considerable potential exists in political-action agents such as Aurelio Davila and Manuel Naranjo. However, because of Velasco's appeal to the working class and the poor, Noland has continued to support a long-time agent in the Velasquista movement, Jose Baquero de la Calle.‡ Baquero has presidential ambitions and is the leader of the rightist wing of the Velasquista movement, closely identified with the Catholic Church hierarchy. He is now Velasco's Minister of Labor and Social Welfare, and Noland hopes that non-communist labor organizations can be strengthened through his aid. His close identification with the Church, however, is restricting his potential for labor operations to the Church-controlled Catholic Labor Center‡ (CEDOC) which is a small, artisan-oriented organization. Noland pays Baquero a salary and expense money for his own political organization and for intelligence on the government and Velasquista politics.

ECORT. Student operations are run for the most part from the Guayaquil base. However, the Quito station finances and directs the most important Ecuadorean anti-communist student newspaper, *Voz Universitaria.*‡ The agent in this operation is Wilson Almeida,‡ ECORT –1, who is the editor of the newspaper. Almeida gives the publication a liberal orientation because the Catholic student movement is supported through Renato Perez, of the Social Christian Movement and Aurelio Davila of the Conservative Party. Propaganda against the Cuban Revolution and against communist penetration in the FEUE (university students federation) is the main function of the ECORT newspaper.

The following are the main operations of the Guayaquil base:

FI–CI *Operations*

ECHINOCARUS. There are already increasing signs of a policy split in the Communist Party of Ecuador (PCE) over the problem of revolutionary violence *v.* the peaceful road to socialism. The PCE leadership grouped around Pedro Saad, the Secretary-General, generally favor the long struggle of preparing the masses, while the sierra leaders grouped around Rafael Echeverria Flores, leader of the Pichincha Provincial Committee, tend towards early initiation of guerrilla action and terrorism. Thus the communists themselves are beginning to split along sierra-coast lines, and the Guayaquil base is charged with monitoring the Saad group.

The best of several base penetration agents is ECHINOCARUS 1‡ whose access is superior to cell-level, but far from the secrets of Saad's Executive Committee. The Guayaquil base is hoping to snare a really first-class penetration agent, or mount a productive technical penetration, on the basis of a new targeting study now underway.

ECLAT. The counterpart to the ECJACK surveillance and investigative team in Quito is the ECLAT operation to Guayaquil. This is a team of five agents who have access to government identification and police files. The team is directed by an ex-Army officer who also reports information picked up among his former colleagues in the coastal military garrisons. As in Quito, the investigative team in Guayaquil keeps the LYNX contingency list current for quick action against the most important activists of the extreme left.

ECAXLE. The main political intelligence collected by the base is through Al Reed,‡ an American who has spent a large part of his life in Guayaquil. He inherited a family business there, which has been doing rather badly, but he manages to keep close relations going with a variety of business, professional and political leaders.

Guayaquil PP *Operations*

ECCALICO. What the base lacks in intelligence collection is made up in labor and student operations. ECCALICO is the labor operation through which the base formed an organization to defeat Pedro Saad in the coast election of a Functional Senator for Labor earlier this year. The same organization forms the nucleus for a new coastal labor confederation that will soon be launched.

The principal agent in the operation is Emilio Estrada Icaza,‡ the general manager of one of the country's largest banks. The main sub-agents are Adalberto Miranda Giron,‡ a leader of the Guayas Provincial Federation of Employees (white-collar workers) and the base candidate who defeated Saad; Victor Contreras Zuniga,‡ anti-communist Guayaquil labor leader; and Enrique Amador Marquez,‡ also an anti-communist labor leader. Through Estrada the base financed Miranda's electoral campaign, which mainly consisted of the forming and registering of new, anti-communist unions in the coastal provinces, mostly in Guayas (Guayaquil). The election was based on a point system weighted according to the numbers of workers in the unions recognized by the electoral court. Although the new unions registered through the operation were really only company social clubs, for the most part, and were generally encouraged by management as a result of the prestigious but discreet support from Estrada, the protests from the CTE and other communist-influenced labor groups were disallowed by the electoral court. On the contrary, just before the election the electoral court disqualified some fifteen pro-Saad unions following protests from the ECCALICO agents. The balance swung in favor of Miranda, and he was elected. Blair Moffet,‡ the Guayaquil Base Chief, received a commendation from headquarters on this operation, which eliminated the PCE Secretary-General from a Senate seat he had held since the 1940s.

The base plan now is to follow through with the formation of a new coastal labor confederation using the same unions, agents and cover as in the election. The CIA labor programs and the ORIT labor representative will also be used, as they were in the electoral campaign, although they are not in direct contact with the base. The long-range strategy in labor operations, obviously, is to weaken the communist and revolutionary socialist-dominated CTE while establishing and strengthening the station and base-controlled democratic union structure.

ECLOSE. Student election operations for control of the Ecuadorean Federation of University Students (FEUE) are run by the Guayaquil base through Alberto Alarcon,‡ ECLOSE, who is a businessman active in the Liberal Party. At different times each year, the five Ecuadorean universities elect new FEUE officers. An annual convention is also held when the national seat of FEUE goes in rotation from one university to another. Alarcon manages teams of agents at these electoral conventions, who are armed with anti-communist propaganda and ample funds for purchasing votes and other activities designed to swing the elections away from the communist and pro-communist candidates. Through this operation national control of the FEUE has been kept out of communist hands for several years, although communist influence is still very strong nationally and at several of the local FEUE chapters. Nevertheless, efforts to have the FEUE pull out of the communist International Union of Students in Prague, and to affiliate with the CIA-controlled COSEC‡ in Leyden, have been unsuccessful.

Washington, D.C. — November 1960

Tension and crisis prevail in the most important breakthrough in operations against the Cubans in Quito. In October the Cuban Embassy chauffeur, a communist, offered his services to the Embassy through an intermediary and was immediately picked up by the station.

His motivation is entirely mercenary but his reporting so far has been accurate. His access is limited, of course, but he will be an extremely valuable source for information about the Cuban diplomats which we can use in trying to recruit some of them.

The problem is that the agent, ECALIBY–1,‡ missed a meeting several weeks ago and has also failed to appear for later alternative meetings. Blair Moffet, the former Guayaquil Base Chief who has gone temporarily to Quito until I arrive, is handling the case and has even checked at the agent's home. Nobody there knew anything of his recent movements. Moffet is afraid the chauffeur is in some kind of trouble because the ECJACK surveillance team has reported that he hasn't been showing up at the Embassy. For the time being Moffet will continue to work the alternative meeting-sites with extreme caution against a possible Cuban provocation.

The station's campaign to promote a break in diplomatic relations between Ecuador and Cuba is stalled because Manuel Araujo, the Minister of Government and an admirer of the Cuban revolution, is the principal leader of Velasco's program to denigrate the Ponce administration and to purge the government of Ponce's supporters. Araujo's campaign has been fairly effective, at least enough to keep our Conservative and Social Christian political-action agents, on whom we must rely for increasing pressure for the diplomatic break, on the defensive. Araujo has also been effective in his public campaign to equate support to the government with patriotism because of increasing tension over the Rio Protocol and the Peruvian boundary issue.

Last month, for example, Araujo accused the Conservative Youth Organization, through which Aurelio Davila carries out station political-action programs, of treason because it called on the Conservative Party to declare formal opposition to Velasco. Araujo was then called to the Chamber of Deputies by Conservatives to answer charges that he had violated the Constitution with his remarks about treason. The session lasted from 10 p.m. until 5 a.m. the next morning. Araujo, cheered on by the screaming Velasquista galleries which shouted down the Social Christians and Conservatives, turned the session into another denunciation of corruption in the Ponce administration. He even accused the forty-eight purged military officers of treason. Because of the deafening roar from the galleries' wild cheering for Araujo, the Conservative, Social Christian, Liberal and Socialist deputies who had planned to question him were forced to leave the session.

Araujo's new accusation of treason caused a big ripple in the military services, and the Minister of Defense and Velasco himself followed with denials that any of the officers were guilty of treason.

Since those events of early October the Velasquistas have continued to equate patriotism on the Peruvian question with support for the government. Thousands turned out on 18 October in Guayaquil for a street demonstration to support Velasco and Araujo, and a similar mass demonstration was held in Quito the following day. On 20 October, the FEUE sponsored what was described as the most massive demonstration in the history of Quito. Students, government workers and people from all walks of life joined in the march and rally at a Quito soccer stadium where Velasco and others denounced the Rio Protocol.

Early in November, Araujo was called again before the Congress to answer questions. He made the trip from his Ministry to the Legislative Palace riding a decrepit old horse that he claimed had been sold by Ponce's Minister of the Interior (a Social Christian and close station collaborator) to the National Police for 30,000 sucres—about 2,500 dollars. He said the former Minister had made his brother appear as the seller and that the useless nag ought to be embalmed and placed in a museum as a monument to the Ponce Administration.

During the ride from the Ministry to the Congress Araujo picked up a large crowd of followers—the spectacle of this physically deformed man less than five feet tall with a Van Dyke beard ridiculing the Poncista élite was just the sort of conduct that makes him so popular with the poor masses. The Velasquistas again packed the galleries to cheer Araujo wildly during his interpellation while shouting down any attempts by Conservatives or Social Christian legislators to criticize him. Later the same day a group of Velasquistas attacked a demonstration by a Conservative student group, and the police—controlled by Araujo as Minister of Government—first attacked the students and later persuaded the Velasquista mob to disperse.

The day after the "horse parade" Araujo nearly uncovered our ECJOB propaganda distribution team. Four of the team were distributing a fly-sheet against communism and Castro when by chance they were seen by Araujo himself. Araujo personally made the arrests, and our agents were charged with distributing fly-sheets without a print-shop symbol—the ECELDER print shop had erred in failing to use one of its fictitious symbols that take longer to trace. The distribution team leader couldn't buy their release this time so Noland had to get Aurelio Davila to use his Congressional leverage to get them out.

The station started a campaign to get Araujo thrown out, but it is progressing slowly. Through Davila a fly-sheet was circulated calling Araujo a communist because of his support for the Cuban revolution, but Velasquista agents like Baquero, the Minister of Labor, and Reinaldo Varea,‡ Vice-President of the Senate, haven't been able to shake President Velasco's confidence in Araujo. The campaign is difficult because it's bound together with the political battle of Velasco against the Conservatives and Social Christians—almost negating the effectiveness of our Velasquista agents against Araujo. Care is being taken, in the campaign through the rightist political agents like Davila, to focus on identifying Araujo with communism and to avoid criticizing Velasco himself.

Our forces came off second best just a few days ago, however, when the Social Christians sponsored a wreath-laying ceremony in commemoration of the death of a student killed during Velasco's previous administration when police invaded a school to throw out strikers. During the days before the ceremony, which was planned to include a silent march, Araujo's subsecretary denounced the ceremony as a provocation designed to cause a clash between Catholic students and the government. When the march arrived at the Independence Plaza in front of the Presidential Palace, groups of Velasquistas attacked with clubs and rocks. The marchers were forced out of the Plaza, and their floral offering left at the Independence Monument was destroyed. The Velasquista mob, now in control of the Plaza, cheered Velasco wildly when he returned to the Palace after a speech in another part of town. Numerous clashes followed during the afternoon and evening as the Velasquista mobs roamed the streets attacking the remnants of the Social Christian march which was also repressed by police cavalry. The government, however, clearly prefers to use its political supporters rather than the police to suppress opposition demonstrations, and the same tactics used in the Congress are now proving their worth in the streets.

As if all this weren't bad enough, Araujo just expelled one of our labor agents: John Snyder,‡ the Inter-American Representative of the Post, Telegraph and Telephone Workers International‡ (PTTI) who for two years has been organizing Ecuadorean communications workers. Araujo accused him of planning a strike to occur just before the Inter-American Conference, but the real reason was a CTE request for Snyder's expulsion because he was so effective. Jose Baquero de la Calle,‡ our Minister of Labor, could do nothing to help —he just doesn't carry the weight with Velasco that Araujo carries.

The campaign against Araujo has been hampered by the crisis atmosphere over the boundary problem with Peru. In September Velasco sent his Foreign Minister to the UN General Assembly where he repeated the denunciation of the Rio Protocol because it was signed while Peruvian troops still occupied parts of Ecuador. The Minister added that Ecuador would raise the issue at the Inter-American Conference. Peru countered by calling for a meeting of the Guarantor Powers and threatening not to attend the Conference. The Guarantor Powers, including the U.S. delegation, met in Rio de Janeiro in October but no public statement was issued. However, State Department documents at the Ecuador desk reveal that the Guarantors voted to disallow Ecuador's unilateral abrogation of the Protocol, but they followed with private appeals to both countries for a peaceful settlement. In early December, nevertheless, a public statement is going to be issued rejecting Velasco's position. The reaction in Ecuador will be strong—in Guayaquil in September our Consulate and the Peruvian Consulate were stoned because of the Rio Protocol.

The station has received isolated reports that Velasco might turn to the Soviets or Cubans for support when he sees that the boundary issue is going against him. Moreover, the Minister of Education is suspected of having opened negotiations for an arms purchase during his recent trip to Czechoslovakia, although the announced purpose of the trip was for the purchase of technical equipment for Ecuadorean schools.

In Ecuador the Congressional sessions are set by the Constitution from 10 August until 7 October, but extension for up to thirty days is possible. This year's Congress voted the extended session, but in the battling between rightists and Velasquistas there was no significant legislation on any reforms, particularly agrarian reform, which had been one of the central promises of the Velasquista campaign. On the other hand repeal of the Civil Service Career Law set administrative reform back a few years. Worse still, the Congress in secret session just before going into recess, voted a 50 per cent increase in its own salaries retroactive to the opening of the session in August. The new amount is equivalent to 25 dollars per day—by Ecuadorean standards rather generous considering that two thirds of the population have a family income of only 10 dollars per month.

During the final two weeks before I was appointed to the Foreign Service I had to take a special course in labor operations. Although the course was supposed to be for mid-career labor operations specialists, the WH Division training officer told me I was needed to fill a quota while he assured me that I wouldn't have to run labor operations just because the course is on my record.

Nominally the course was under the Office of Training, but the people who really run it are from IO/4 (Branch 4, labor, of the International Organizations Division). The course was dominated by bickering between the IO officers and the area division case officers over use of the labor agents controlled by IO Division under Cord Meyer.‡ Officers from WH Division were practically unanimous in condemning ORIT‡ which is the regional organization for the Western Hemisphere of the International Confederation of Free Trade Unions.‡ They said ORIT is hopeless, discredited and completely ineffective for attracting non-communist labor organizations in Latin America. Agency leaders (at the apparent urging of George Meany‡ and Serafino Romualdi‡) are convinced, however, that ORIT can be salvaged, and so WH Division must try to help.

Much emphasis was given to the advantages of using agents in the different International Trade Secretariats in which, in Latin America at least, the Agency has considerable control. Lloyd Haskins,‡ Executive Secretary of the International Federation of Petroleum and Chemical Workers,‡ gave us a lecture on how he can help in organizing Latin American workers in the critical petroleum industry. Also having interesting possibilities for Latin America is the International Federation of Plantation, Agricultural and Allied Workers‡ (IFPAAW) which was founded last year to carry on the rural organizing begun several years ago through the ICFTU Special Plantation Committee which had special success in Malaya. In Latin America its affiliate works to deny the peasant base of guerrilla movements through the organization and support of peasant unions within the larger area of agrarian reform and development of cooperatives. Overall, the course emphasized that Agency labor operations must seek to develop trade unions in underdeveloped countries that will focus on economic issues and stay away from politics and the ideology of class struggle. This is the Gompers tradition of American trade-unionism which, when promoted in poor countries, should raise labor costs and thereby diminish the effect that imports from low-cost labor areas have on employment in the U.S.

After the labor course I took the two-week orientation course at the State Department's Foreign Service Institute. Although the course was generally boring, and I only took it because of cover requirements, it got me thinking about the place Agency operations occupy within the larger context of U.S. foreign policy towards Latin America. There seem to be two main programs that the Latin American governments must promote: first, economic growth through industrialization; and second, economic, social and administrative reforms so that gross injustice can be eliminated.

For economic growth they need capital, technology and political stability. U.S. government programs are helping with these needs, particularly since Vice-President Nixon's trip two years ago: the Inter-American Development Bank was founded last year, Export–Import Bank financing is being increased, the technical assistance programs of ICA are being expanded, and now the Social Progress Trust Fund is to be established with 500 million dollars from the U.S. for health, housing, education and similar projects. From Kennedy's speeches on Latin America, some people conclude that these programs will be expanded still more when he becomes President.

CIA operations are crucial to the economic growth and political stability programs, because of the inevitable capital flight and low private investment whenever communism becomes a threat. The Cuban revolution has stirred up and encouraged the forces of instability all over the hemisphere and it's our job to put them down. CIA operations promote stability through assisting local governments to build up their security forces—particularly the police but also the military—and by putting down the extreme left. That, in a nutshell, is what we're doing: building up the security forces and suppressing, weakening, destroying, the extreme left. Through these programs we buy time for friendly governments to effect the reforms that will eliminate the injustices on which communism thrives.

The Cuban Revolution has swung to the far left, the State Department, and American businesses, are fearful that Cuba will try to export its revolution to other countries in the hemisphere, which might result in nationalization of holdings. The top priority of the United States in Latin America is to seal off Cuba from the continent. In Quito, our orders are to do everything possible to force Ecuador to break diplomatic and economic relations with Cuba, and also to weaken the Communist Party there, no matter what the cost.

For weeks Janet and I have been getting shots, for every known disease, I think, and she's been attending sessions on Foreign Service protocol and on what's expected of an embassy wife. Bob Weatherwax has been telling us a lot about housing and the life there. It sounds just too fantastic. He brought a Christmas shopping list from the Noland family and we're sending all their gifts down with our air freight. It won't be long now.

Today I made my last stop in the division on final check-out. It was in the Records Branch for assignment of pseudonym—the secret name that I'll use for the next thirty years on every piece of internal Agency correspondence: dispatches, cables, reports, everything I write. It will be the name by which I'll be known in promotions, fitness reports and other personnel actions. I signed the forms, acknowledging with my true name that in secret employment with the CIA I will use the assigned official pseudonym. Then I read the name—how can I miss with JEREMY S. HODAPP?

Quito, Ecuador — 6 December 1960

Finally here. Our plodding DC–7 took over ten hours to get to Quito, including stops in Panama and Cali, but Janet and I were in the first-class section thanks to government policy allowing the extra expense for long flights. Former Ecuadorean President Galo Plaza, the Liberal Party leader who lost to Velasco this year, was sitting behind us and it would have been interesting to talk to him, but I was afraid it might seem presumptuous.

The weather was clear and sunny as we approached Quito, and through the windows of the aircraft we could see snowcapped volcanos and green valleys that extended up the sides of mountains to what seemed like almost vertical cultivations. I wonder how they plough at such an angle. Everyone's heard of the Andes mountains but actually to see this breathtaking scenery is almost overwhelming.

At the Quito air terminal, an ultra-modern building just completed for the Inter-American Conference, we were welcomed by Blair Moffet who gave us the Embassy orientation folder, mostly pointers on Ecuadorean health hazards. Then he dropped us at a small hotel in a residential section less than a block from the Embassy itself. A little while later Noland came to greet us with a pleasant surprise; he had tickets for us to see the bullfight this afternoon with his wife and some of their friends.

Today is Quito's most important annual festival: the celebration of the city's liberation from Spanish rule. The festivities have been going on for some days with bullfights, parades and livestock shows. I'm not sure I liked the bullfight. It was exciting all right, and the music and *olés* were stirring, but if Paco Camino is really one of the world's best I wonder what second-raters are like. He practically butchered that bull trying to get him to fall.

Afterwards we went to a party with the Nolands at the home of the family that controls the movie theaters. Everyone there seemed to be related by blood or marriage, almost, and among the guests was Jorge Acosta,‡ Velasco's nephew and one of the station's best friends in the government. He runs the National Planning Board, not a terribly powerful job, but as President Velasco's family favorite he is not far from decision-making. Just recently Acosta advised that Weatherwax, our officer under Public Safety cover, can now return without danger.

Tension on the political scene has increased, if anything, in the past week. On 1 December the Quito Municipal Government, which is under Liberal Party control, began its new sessions. There was serious rioting between Liberal and Velasquista mobs, and when

Araujo's police intervened they threw their first tear-gas grenade at the Liberal Mayor.

Tomorrow the Guarantor Powers will release their decision denying Ecuador's claim that the Rio Protocol is void. Noland doesn't think the announcement will be taken calmly.

Quito — 8 December 1960

They say it takes a while to get used to this 9000-feet-plus altitude. The air is thin and I seem to be unusually sleepy, but neither of us has had any sign of the terrible headaches some people get. The nights are cool, and there is quite a difference between being in the shade and the sunshine, but because it is so dry here, people wear woollen clothing even on hot days. The nicest thing about Quito, so far, are the flowers. It seems just like springtime, in fact, and someone told me that here there are only two seasons, wet and dry, but flowers all year. As soon as we can we're going to visit the monument north of town where the equator passes. It's about a half-hour drive and you can take photographs with one foot in the northern hemisphere and one in the southern.

Noland says he wants me to take over the operations that Blair Moffet has been running so that he can return to Washington. But Blair said he can't return until he finds out what happened to the Cuban Embassy chauffeur.

The announcement on the Rio Protocol was a bitter blow in the face of all the recent civic demonstrations and new hopes fomented by Velasco since he took office. A really big demonstration is being organized for tomorrow at the Independence Plaza.

Quito — 9 December 1960

Emotions have overflowed. Today, my fourth day in Quito, I saw my first mob attacks against a U.S. Embassy. I was late leaving the hotel and the manager warned me that rioters had already been stoning the Embassy. When I arrived only a small group was still chanting in front, but I entered at the rear and saw that many windows were broken during the earlier raids.

Throughout the day the station telephones were ringing as agents called to report the movements of the URJE-led rioters who returned to attack the Embassy a number of times. Araujo kept the police away, so the mobs could operate almost at will. I watched from the station offices on the top floor. Their favorite chant, as they hurled their stones, was: "Cuba, Russia, Ecuador." The Ecuadorean–North American Cultural Institute which is run by USIS and the Peruvian Embassy were also attacked, as was our Consulate in Guayaquil.

While the Embassy was being attacked almost all the Quito buses suspended service and gathered north of town where they began a caravan into Independence Plaza picking up loads of people along the way. The Plaza was jammed with thousands when the speeches began, which included attacks on the Rio Protocol by Velasco and his Foreign Minister. Araujo, for his part, called for diplomatic relations with the Soviets if that were necessary for Ecuador to attain justice. The crowd chanted frequent denunciations of the Guarantor Powers and the OAS. Later the Foreign Minister announced that two Czech diplomats will be arriving shortly to open the Czech Legation here.

Quito — 14 December 1960

Attacks against the Embassy have continued but they now seem smaller and more sporadic. Police protection has been improved and there were even some Army units sent to the Embassy. Araujo was forced to send the police protection back by cooler heads in the government like Acosta. The riots spread to other cities, too, where bi-national cultural centers were attacked. More public demonstrations have been held, the largest of which was yesterday when a "March of Justice" brought thousands again to the Independence Plaza.

URJE continues to be the most important force behind the attacks although the marches and demonstrations are sponsored by a variety of organizations and are inspired mostly from civic motives.

Two important labor organizations have just been formed but for the time being only one is ours. In Guayaquil the ECCALICO agents who ran Miranda's‡ campaign to defeat the PCE General Secretary, Saad, as Functional Senator for Labor, held a convention on 9–11 December and formed the Regional Confederation of Ecuadorean Coastal Trade Unions‡ (CROCLE) as a permanent mechanism to fight the CTE on the coast, mainly in Guayas Province. Both of the principal-action agents, Victor Contreras‡ and Enrique Amador,‡ are on the Executive Committee, Contreras as President. The ORIT representative was very helpful, especially in providing unwitting cover for our agents. The plan now is to affiliate CROCLE with the ORIT ICFTU structure in place of the current Ecuadorean affiliate, the small and ineffective Guayas Workers Confederation (COG) which our Guayaquil base had been supporting.

In Quito the USOM labor division, whose main work consists of giving courses in free trade-unionism throughout the country, has taken the first step towards the formation of a national, non-communist trade-union confederation. Under their direction during the first week this month the Coordinating Committee of Free Trade Unionists of Ecuador was established. This committee will soon begin establishing provincial coordinating committees which will develop into provincial federations. Eventually a national confederation will be established. The station plan is to let USOM direct these early stages and later, after the new Deputy Chief of Station arrives, we will probably move in on the formation of the national confederation. For the moment, getting Miranda in the Senate and forming CROCLE are as much as we can manage.

Bill Doherty,‡ the Inter-American Representative of the PTTI,‡ and another of IO Division's international labor agents, arrived a few days ago to pick up the pieces from John Snyder's‡ expulsion. He's trying to arrange for continued PTTI support to the communications workers' union, FENETEL,‡ in organization, training and housing, but Araujo's hostility hasn't changed. Noland is reluctant to show our connections with Doherty to Baquero de la Calle, the Minister of Labor, by insisting on special treatment, but even if he tried, Baquero probably couldn't out-maneuver Araujo.

Guayaquil student operations have also had a big success. The FEUE National Congress was held in Portoviejo earlier this month, and the ECLOSE forces under Alberto Alarcon‡ finally attained a long-sought goal. The Congress adopted a new system for electing officers of the various FEUE chapters. From now on the elections will be direct, obligatory and universal as opposed to the old indirect system that gave the communist and other leftist minorities a distinct advantage. The national seat for the coming year will be Quito where FEUE leadership is in moderate hands.

I've met Ambassador Bernbaum—he arrived only a few weeks before I did and this is his first post as Ambassador. He is a career Foreign Service man and not very colorful. Noland said he knows nothing about our operations, not even the political-action operations, and doesn't want to. Today the Ambassador visited Velasco with a message from Kennedy, and he took advantage of the visit to announce that loans for certain public works and development projects have been approved in principle by U.S. lending institutions. The announcement is supposed to assuage anti-U.S. sentiment.

Press reports have alleged that several governments are seeking a postponement or change of site for the Inter-American Conference, partly because of the riots, and the Cuban press and radio are suggesting that Ecuador may follow Cuba in repudiating the Inter-American System.

Quito — 15 December 1960

Aurelio Davila,‡ one of the main political-action agents of the ECACTOR project, won an important and clever victory today. He was behind a mass demonstration of support to Velasco's policy on the Rio Protocol which backfired on Araujo. Students from all the Catholic schools and the Catholic university marched to Independence Plaza where they chanted slogans against communism. Velasco was on the platform and the Minister of Defense had begun to speak when a small group of counter-demonstrators began chanting "Cuba, Russia, Ecuador," which prompted a flurry of "down with communism" from the mass of students.

Araujo, who was also on the speaker's platform, descended to join the counter-demonstrators. Almost immediately a riot began and Velasco had to grab the microphone and ask for calm. The speeches continued, including one by Velasco, but the President was clearly annoyed at Araujo's having disrupted this huge demonstration of support.

At the instigation of Davila and other Conservative Party leaders the Cardinal issued a pastoral letter which was released today. The Cardinal, whose influence is at least equal to that of any politician including Velasco, warns that religion and the fatherland are in grave and imminent danger from communism, adding that Ecuador should not move towards Cuba and Russia in search of support on the boundary issue.

Tonight another demonstration of support for Velasco's Peruvian policy was held—but it was by a leftist organization called the Popular Revolutionary Liberal Party (PLPR) which is an offshoot of the youth wing of the Liberal Party but with many Velasquista supporters. The speakers included Araujo and Gonzalo Villalba, a Vice-President of the CTE and one of the leaders of the Communist Party in Quito. They called for diplomatic and commercial relations with the Soviets while condemning the U.S. and conservatives.

Quito — 16 December 1960

Araujo's out! Late this afternoon it was announced at the Presidential Palace that Araujo's resignation had been accepted, but we had been receiving reports all day that Velasco was getting rid of him. We have poured out a steady stream of propaganda against him for some weeks and his behavior at yesterday's demonstration clinched matters. The Foreign Minister, who is a good friend of the U.S., has also been working to get Araujo fired, and of course Araujo's own identification with the extreme left gave him little room to maneuver.

Since Araujo's resignation was announced, street clashes have been continuous between his supporters, mostly from the URJE, and anti-Araujo Velasquistas. Right now the downtown area is full of tear-gas but we learn from several agents that the rioters are finally dispersing.

Quito — 22 December 1960

Civic demonstrations on the Peruvian question have continued but they have lost their anti-U.S. flavor. In fact they have almost been replaced by a campaign by Catholic groups to show support for the Cardinal in response to an attack against his pastoral letter on communism, made by the Revolutionary Socialist Labor Senator. Aurelio Davila is leading the campaign, funded from the ECACTOR project, which includes letters and signatures published in the newspapers by Catholic organizations like CEDOC, the labor confederation, and the National Catholic Action Board, of which Davila is a Vice-President.

Today the campaign reached a peak with a demonstration by thousands who marched through the Quito streets in the rain chanting slogans against Cuba, communism and Russia. The Cardinal himself was the main speaker and he repeated his warning in the pastoral letter of the imminent danger of communism. He's almost ninety years old, but he's really effective.

I've taken over my first operations and met my first real-live agents—at last I'm a genuine clandestine operations officer.

The first operation I took over was ECJACK, the surveillance and general investigations team run by Lieutenant-Colonel Paredes. Blair took me out to meet him a couple of days ago, and through him I'm continuing to keep a watch near the Cuban Embassy for any signs of the missing chauffeur. With this operation I also took over the secret-writing correspondence with the agents in Cuba, and I've proposed to headquarters that we could save time if a trainer were sent to teach me to write and develop the letters. That way we could cable the messages and save the time required to pouch the sw letters. In a few days Noland will introduce me to Francine Jacome,‡ who writes the cover letters.

Blair also turned over the ECFONE operation to me. The principal agent, Oswaldo Chiriboga,‡ was appointed Ecuadorean Chargé d'Affaires to Holland and The Hague station is going to use him against Soviet and satellite diplomats. We had to get a new cutout to Basantes,‡ the Communist Party penetration agent, and Noland chose Velasco's physician, Dr. Ovalle,‡ in order to sustain the cover story used from the beginning on this operation. Dr. Ovalle will advise by telephone when he gets reports from Basantes, and I'll go to his office to get them. This operation took on even greater significance in October when Basantes was elected to the Pichincha Provincial Committee. With the schism growing between the PCE coastal and sierra leadership this is equivalent to having an agent on the local executive committee.

The station seems to have turned into a Santa Claus operation these last few days. At Noland's house all the wives with their servants have been wrapping bonbons, cartons of cigarettes, boxes of cigars, bottles of whiskey, cognac, champagne and wine—and dozens of golf-balls. These are operational Christmas gifts to agents and to "contacts"—(friends who might eventually be useful agents).

Most officers in CIA stations are expected to develop personal relationships with as wide a variety of local leaders as possible, whether in business, education, professions or politics. State Department cover in WH Division facilitates the cultivation of these "contacts" while station funds for entertainment, club dues, gifts and supplements to the regular housing allowances give us considerable advantages over our State Department colleagues.

Noland is clearly a great hit with the Ecuadoreans. He seems to know everyone in town who counts. He's a former college football star and coach with lots of personal charm and energy. His wife is the national women's golf champion and an ex-Captain in the WAC's. Together they are the most effective couple in the Embassy and are lionized by the local community. Mostly they've developed these "contacts" through Noland's political and sports work and the very active role both have at the Quito Tennis and Golf Club.

Quito — 30 December 1960

There seems now to be little doubt that the Inter-American Conference will be postponed. Peru insists it won't attend because of Ecuador's intention of raising the Protocol issue; Venezuela and the Dominican Republic are still in a crisis over Trujillo's attempt to assassinate Betancourt; and U.S.–Cuban relations are getting still worse. We all know the invasion is coming but certainly not until Kennedy takes over.

Peru's break in relations with Cuba today hasn't helped prospects for the Conference. The break is partly a show of appreciation to the U.S. for the October ruling by the Guarantors on the Protocol, but it's also the result of a Lima station operation in November. The operation was a commando raid by Cuban exiles against the Cuban Embassy in Lima which included the capture of documents. The Lima station inserted among the authentic documents several that had been forged by TSD including a supposed list of persons in Peru who received payments from the Cuban Embassy totalling about 15,000 dollars monthly.

Another of the forged documents referred to a non-existent campaign of the Cuban Embassy in Lima to promote the Ecuadorean position on the Rio Protocol. Because not many Peruvians believed the documents to be genuine, the Lima station had great difficulty in getting them publicized. However, a few days ago a

Conservative deputy in the Peruvian Congress presented them for the record and yesterday they finally surfaced in the Lima press. Although the Cubans have protested that the documents are apocryphal, a recent defector from the Cuban Embassy in Lima—present during the raid and now working for the Agency—has "confirmed" that the TSD documents are genuine. The Conservative Peruvian government then used the documents as the pretext for breaking relations with Cuba. We could do something similar here but Velasco probably wouldn't take action. He wants Cuban support against Peru on the Protocol issue, if he can get it.

The disappearance of the Cuban Embassy chauffeur is now solved. He tried to impress the Embassy gardener by telling him about working for us. The gardener told one of the Cubans and the chauffeur was fired. He panicked and has been hiding out in a provincial village, convinced that the Cubans will try to kill him.

He came into the Embassy yesterday and Blair met him. There's no saving the operation but Blair gave him a modest sum to get him back to the village and help him for a little while. Noland is really angry with Blair because he thinks Blair didn't take enough pains teaching the agent good security. Too bad—I was hoping I might get this operation too. Blair returns to Washington now.

Quito — 4 January 1961

The Inter-American Conference will definitely be postponed now that the U.S. has broken relations with Cuba. All cables and correspondence formerly sent to the Havana station are now to be sent to the JMWAVE station in Miami. I suppose the Conference won't be held until after the JMARC invasion by the exiles. Holding it after the Cuban revolution is wiped out will change the security situation here. For one thing we won't have the Cuban Embassy's support to URJE to worry about, and all these would-be protesters and agitators may not be so enthusiastic.

Two Czech diplomats have just arrived to open a

Legation. Headquarters had traces on only one of them who is a suspect intelligence officer. At headquarters' request we will watch closely, through agents like the Oldsmobile dealer, Kladensky, for indications on the permanent building they intend to buy or rent. Before their expulsion in 1957 we had their code-room bugged and headquarters wants to try again.

Weatherwax, our Public Safety officer, is back and through him we hope to improve intelligence collection in rural areas, which is now almost nil. Contraband operations complicate the problem. Some areas, particularly those from just north of Quito to the Colombian border, live from the contraband traffic, and rural security forces, if they're not in the pay of the contraband rings, are often engaged in small wars against them. The weakness of rural security forces is practically an invitation to guerrilla operations, so we hope to strengthen them through the Public Safety Mission and get some rural intelligence collection going at the same time.

Quito — 29 January 1961

Today is the anniversary of the signing of the Rio Protocol and we thought we might get some attacks on the Embassy. The only violence, however, was among the Ecuadoreans. In Guayaquil the Minister of Foreign Relations gave a speech on the boundary problem and in a procession afterwards to Guayaquil University he was jeered and booed as a traitor. Araujo and his friends in URJE are determined to get the minister fired because he was one of the forces behind Araujo's expulsion and he's also a good friend of the U.S. The campaign against him is based on his having been a member of the Ecuadorean commission that signed the Protocol in 1942.

I've taken over the ECSTACY letter intercept from John Bacon. He has been using old-fashioned techniques that took a lot of time so I asked for a TSD photographic technician to come and overhaul the station darkroom where I have to process the letters. The

TSD photographic and SW technicians have now both finished their work. The darkroom looks brand new. Everything's in order and the technician will send some new equipment in coming weeks. An SW technician has also come to train me to write and develop the messages to and from the agents in Cuba, and she left a supply of developer and ink pills. Now the Miami base will cable messages for me to send and I'll cable the incoming messages after development.

Quito — 1 February 1961

Velasco's low tolerance of opposition is about to touch off another crisis. Two days ago at the opening ceremony of the National Medical Association Convention he exchanged angry words with the Liberal Quito Mayor. Then yesterday, at the inauguration of a new fertilizer plant where both were present Velasquistas hissed and booed the Mayor and threw tomatoes at him, forcing him to leave the ceremony. Last night supporters of both Velasco and the Mayor held street demonstrations and the Minister of Government is making threats against people who disturb public order —not to be mistaken for the Velasquistas, of course.

Today the Minister of Government closed a Quito radio station under an administrative pretext (failure to renew its license on time) following an opinion program in which listeners were encouraged to call and participate in the program by expressing their support for the Mayor. The Minister himself called the radio station during the program and his threats against the station were broadcast as part of the program. Later he closed the station. More Velasquista street demonstrations tonight.

Quito — 8 February 1961

There has been a serious uprising at a large *hacienda* in Chimborazo Province south of here. Some 2000 Indians turned against the hacienda owner and the local authorities. Three policemen were injured, the Army was called out, two Indians were killed and over sixty arrested. The leaders of the Indians were organizers from the Campesino Commission of the CTE, and the Revolutionary Socialist Labor Senator (also a CTE leader) has started a campaign for the Indians' release.

The Indians' grievances were legitimate enough—they often are badly treated on these enormous estates. In this case the owner hadn't paid them since last year and wasn't keeping accounts of their daily work. The CTE is also demanding an investigation into alleged torture of the Indians who were arrested, and recognition of their demands: wages, housing and schools.

Several people have told me that this is the type of incident that chills the blood of the landowners here. If only one of these risings got out of hand and began to spread there would be no telling where it would end. Probably right in the Presidential Palace.

Quito — 15 February 1961

Our new Deputy Chief of Station, Gil Saudade,‡ arrived early this month. He's taking over the labor and student operations but Bacon will keep the ECURGE media operation. Saudade and I are working closely on preparing agents to send to the Latin American Conference for National Sovereignty, Economic Emancipation and Peace, scheduled for the first week of March in Mexico City.

Gil's agents are Juan Yepez del Pozo, Jr.,‡ ECLURE–2, and Antonio Ulloa Coppiano,‡ ECLURE–3. Until he arrived they were treated as developmental prospects by Noland who was helping finance their takeover of the Popular Revolutionary Liberal Party‡ (PLPR). This party is attracting a considerable following among young supporters of Velasco, and we hope to use it to channel these radicals away from support to Cuba and from anti-Americanism. Araujo's supporters are among those we most hope to attract, and Gil will be certain that the party keeps its leftist character and firm opposition to the traditional Ecuadorean political parties.

The agent really in control is Juan Yepez del Pozo, Sr.,‡ a writer who is also director of the Ecuadorean Institute of Sociology. He has larger political ambitions and is the party's chief advisor.

The Conference in Mexico City is sponsored by the leftist, former President of Mexico, Lazaro Cardenas, as a propaganda exercise in support of the Cuban revolution. Because communists and leftists from all over the hemisphere will be there, headquarters asked stations months ago to propose agents who could attend for intelligence gathering.

Besides Gil's agents, we're sending Atahualpa Basantes,‡ one of our best PCE penetration agents. Both headquarters and the Mexico City station were pleased that he can attend, and I've sent requirements to him in writing through Dr. Ovalle. If possible he will try to get invited for a visit to Cuba after the Conference is over.

Our propaganda operations have been promoting considerable comment adverse to Cuba. The general theme is the danger of penetration by international communism in the Western Hemisphere through Cuba, but recently specific stories have highlighted statements by Cuban exile leaders Manuel de Varona‡ and Jose Miro Cardona.‡ Alarmist accusations of Cuban subversive activities included one report coming from Cubans in Miami that Castro has sent arms to guerrillas in Colombia and arms to Ecuador to use against Peru—these stories originally surfaced in *El Tiempo* in Bogotá and were repeated in *El Comercio* in Quito. Still another story which came from Havana alleged that Castro's efforts to penetrate South America are concentrated mainly through Ecuador and Brazil. This story also accused Castro of contributing 200,000 dollars to the Mexico City Conference.

Araujo has helped our propaganda operations by appearing on television in Havana and promising the support of the Ecuadorean government and people to the Cuban revolution. The reaction here was strong, and both Velasco and the Foreign Minister issued statements rejecting Araujo's generosity.

Gustavo Salgado,‡ the well-known columnist, is placing most of this material for us, and he also arranged for a replay of follow-up propaganda about the exile assault on the Cuban Embassy in Lima last November. The commando leader has recently been interviewed by the *Agencia Orbe Latinoamericano*‡ news service which is a hemisphere-wide propaganda operation of the station in Santiago, Chile. He said that other documents captured during the raid (besides the list of Peruvians paid by the Cuban Embassy in Lima) revealed that Cuba was using certain Peruvians and Ecuadoreans in the hope of setting off an armed conflict between the two countries, which in turn would prepare the atmosphere for a communist rising in Peru. In his column today Salgado rehashed the background and the interview and called for the publication of the names of the Ecuadoreans working in this Cuban adventure. Araujo, of course, would be first on the list. The "other documents" are, of course, also Agency produced.

The purpose of the campaign is to prepare public opinion so that reaction to the Cuban invasion, when it comes, will be softened. Other stations in Latin America are doing the same, but here we can also tie the propaganda to Cuban interference in the boundary dispute.

Quito — 18 February 1961

Velasco is reacting strongly to the leftist campaign to force the Foreign Minister to resign, and some of our reports suggest this may be the beginning of the end for his fourth term.

Yesterday morning the Foreign Minister had accompanied a distinguished Colombian jurist (an expert in international law and proponent of the Ecuadorean thesis on the nullity of the Rio Protocol) to the Central University where he had been invited to speak. As they arrived several hundred students began jeering the Foreign Minister and throwing tomatoes at him. Several tomatoes hit him but he found shelter in the building and the Colombian made his speech. Velasco was furious because the scandal has upset his propaganda campaign for using the Colombian against Peru, even though it was the Foreign Minister who was attacked.

Today the government arrested five URJE members for taking part in the incident, which in turn has caused another spate of protests. The CTE condemned the arrests and also demanded freedom for the PCE Indian organizer Carlos Rodriguez, who is in jail in Riobamba over the recent Chimborazo Indian rising. The Revolutionary Socialists are protesting because three of those arrested are members of its youth group. The FEUE is protesting because the five arrested are university students. The protests include demands for the resignations of both the Foreign Minister and the Minister of Government, the latter for illegal arrest of the students and the closing of the radio station on 1 February.

Quito — 20 February 1961

This has been a day of great violence. Yesterday the Minister of Government ordered the release of the five students but they refused to leave the jail. They demanded a *habeas corpus* hearing because that would be held under the Quito Mayor and could be used to embarrass Velasco and force the resignation of the Minister. During the early hours of this morning the students were forced into police cars and driven separately to isolated sectors of town where they were forced out of the cars.

The law and philosophy faculties led by members of URJE began an indefinite strike this morning for the resignations of the Ministers of Government and Foreign Relations.

The strike committee is supported by the Quito FEUE leadership which has called a forty-eight-hour strike for the whole university, and the university council headed by the rector has issued its own protest against the government.

After the strike was announced this morning a Velasquista mob composed mostly of government employees in the state monopolies and customs service gathered at the downtown location of the philosophy faculty. After a verbal confrontation with the striking students the mob began stoning them to force them inside the faculty building. For much of the morning they continued to control the streets around the faculty and to menace the students with terrible violence.

The university administration and the students formed a special committee to visit the Minister of Government to plead for police protection for the striking students against the mob. The minister simply advised that the government would not move against the strikers, leaving open the question of police protection.

About five o'clock this afternoon the mob gathered again, this time in Independence Plaza where they chanted praise to Velasco and condemnation of the students. From there they marched to the Ministry of Government where the minister spoke to them from a balcony, saying he had acted legally in arresting the five students for throwing tomatoes at the Foreign Minister, but that no sooner were they released than they declared a strike.

I've had the surveillance team under Colonel Paredes scattered about the downtown area since the strike began this morning. Paredes has given us their reports on the movements of the mob and the danger that the students might be lynched. We've cabled reports to headquarters but Noland isn't making predictions yet on whether Velasco will last—he thinks there will have to be some bloodshed before the military gets restless.

Quito — 21 February 1961

Guayaquil was the center of today's action. A street demonstration by FEUE and URJE this morning was attacked by Velasquista mobs controlled by the Mayor (unlike Quito, in Guayaquil the Mayor is a powerful supporter of Velasco). The marchers were forced several times to seek refuge in the buildings of Guayaquil University when shots were fired from the mob. Police eventually broke up the clash with tear-gas, and university authorities have protested to the government and asked for protection for the students.

Another demonstration by the students in Guayaquil was held tonight and was again attacked by Velasquista mobs. Eventually the marchers returned to the university and who should be the main speaker but Araujo! He had just returned from Cuba today and was carried by the students on their shoulders from his hotel to the university. In his speech he lavished praise on the Cubans and described recent protest demonstrations in Havana against the killing of Patrice Lumumba.

Manuel Naranjo,‡ Noland's agent who is a Deputy of the moderate Socialist Party, got the party to publish a statement today criticizing the role of URJE in the student strike and in the tomato attack against the Foreign Minister. Wilson Almeida,‡ the editor of our main student propaganda organ *Voz Universitaria,* also published a statement against URJE participation and in support of the Foreign Minister. The Velasquista association of professionals published a statement supporting the Minister of Government.

The main propaganda item today, however, was from the Cuban Embassy which released a sensational statement alleging that during the coming Holy Week attacks will be made against religious processions by persons shouting "Viva Fidel, Cuba and Russia." Blame for the attacks would be placed on the Cuban Embassy. In the statement the Cubans also denied the allegation circulated recently that sixty Cubans had come to Ecuador to make trouble—adding that agents paid by the U.S. are entering the country from Peru. The statement also tried to clarify Araujo's television remarks in Havana as an expression of solidarity between Ecuadoreans and Cubans such as Velasco has repeatedly expressed. The statement went on to defend the Cuban photographic exhibit now on display in Quito as expressive of the works of the revolution, not communist propaganda as suggested in recent rightist criticism of the exhibit, adding that the exhibit is sponsored by the CTE, the National Cultural Institute and Central University as well as the Embassy. The statement ended by alleging that all these recent provocations are designed to disturb the good relations between Cuba and Ecuador and to impede Cuban participation in the Inter-American Conference. The real culprit, according to the statement, is the U.S. government with assistance from Peru because of Cuba's support to Ecuador on the Rio Protocol issue. The statement ended with words of praise for Velasco.

From what I gather this is an extraordinary statement for a diplomatic mission to make. It shows, among other things, that our propaganda is hurting the Cubans, and Noland hopes to get the political-action agents like Renato Perez and Aurelio Davila to charge the Cubans with meddling in Ecuadorean politics.

Quito — 22 February 1961

In response to the Cuban press release yesterday, our Ambassador issued a statement today that had everyone in the station smiling. The Ambassador said that the only agents in Ecuador who are paid and trained by the United States are the technicians invited by the Ecuadorean government to contribute to raising the living standards of the Ecuadorean people. He added that the U.S. has promoted a policy of order, stability and progress as demonstrated in our technical and economic assistance programs, and he suggested that the Cuban Embassy present their accusations and appropriate proof to the Ecuadorean government.

In Havana the Cuban Embassy statement has been prominently replayed for distribution over the whole continent, with emphasis that collaboration between the U.S. and Peru is part of a plan to isolate Cuba from the rest of Latin America and to impede Cuban participation in the Inter-American Conference. They couldn't be more accurate on the matter of isolation—that's the central theme of our propaganda guidance.

Today Guayaquil had the worst violence yet. The striking students in the university buildings were attacked by a much larger group of Velasquista students and government employees who forcibly ejected the strikers. Eight people were hospitalized before the morning was over. In the afternoon two bombs caused extensive damage at the Guayaquil Municipal Palace, although there were no victims, and another bomb was reported by the Mayor's office to have been hurled through a window into his office but without exploding. Expressions of support to the Mayor have begun to pour in, and tonight he announced that terrorists had tried to kill him. The Guayaquil base reported that several of their agents believe the bombs were planted by the Mayor himself.

Press reports confirmed by our National Police agents indicate opposition to the government has spread to Cuenca. Yesterday a group of students held a march to the provincial governor's office to plead for payment of certain money that is due to the school. They had nothing to do with the strikers here or in Guayaquil, but police didn't know this and the march was attacked by the cavalry with sabers and several students were wounded. Cuenca is a very conservative city and this was bound to cause a reaction against Velasco. Today the university students held a demonstration of support for the students in Quito and Guayaquil, and in protest against the police stupidity yesterday. They also joined in the call for the resignation of the two Ministers.

Quito — 23 February 1961

Important efforts by the ECACTOR project agents, especially Aurelio Davila, to focus attention on communism and Cuba are getting results. Today the Cardinal issued another pastoral letter—this one signed by all the archbishops, bishops and vicars in the hierarchy. Davila had been rallying the leadership of the Conservative Party to call on the Cardinal for this new letter for some weeks. The letter calls on all Catholics to take serious and effective action against the communist menace in Ecuador, while accusing the communists of trying to take advantage of the border problem for their own subversive purposes. The letter also laments the weakening of the Ecuadorean case on the border issue because of these communist tactics.

More important still was the call today by the Conservative Party for a break in diplomatic relations with Cuba. This is the first formal call for a break with Cuba by any of the political parties, and it is based partly on the Cuban Embassy statement of two days ago.

The new pastoral letter and the call for a break in relations are designed to use patriotism and the border issue rather like Velasco does, but more subtly, in order to discredit the extreme left and the Cubans. We hope a wave of mass opinion can be created, especially among Catholics, that will equate URJE, Araujo, the CTE and the PCE—and the Cuban Embassy of course—with divisive efforts to weaken Velasco's campaign against the Rio Protocol. Hopefully this will strengthen the Foreign Minister's position and suck Velasco himself into the current. But because of Velasco's attacks against the political right, the animosity is so great that he may resist and lash out again at our ECACTOR crowd. In that case we will simply continue the campaign through all our propaganda machinery to deny the enemy the banner of patriotism on the Protocol issue.

Through the same political-action agents we are promoting the formation of an anti-communist civic front that will concentrate on getting a break in relations with Cuba and on denouncing penetration of the Ecuadorean government by the extreme left. Right now the signature campaign is coming to a close and formation of the front will be announced in a few days.

John Bacon is starting a new program through Gustavo Salgado,‡ his main media agent, which will consist of a series of "alert" notices to be placed in the newspapers as paid advertisements against communism, the Cubans and others. They will be short notices, and if Bacon can write them fast enough they'll appear two or three times each week. The ostensible sponsor will be the non-existent Ecuadorean Anti-Communist Front, not to be confused with the political-action civic front which is going to be a real organization.

Quito — 28 February 1961

Yesterday was National Civics Day and suddenly it seemed that the whole country had forgotten its internal hatreds in the government-promoted demonstrations against Peru. The demonstrations were sharply anti-Peruvian because in recent days regular accusations have emanated from Lima that Ecuador has accepted support on the boundary problem from Castro and communism in general. The accusations are inspired by the Lima station in order to preclude Cuban support to Ecuador and Ecuadorean acceptance if support were ever offered.

Today things were back to normal. Our ECACTOR-financed anti-communist civic front was launched with a two-page newspaper notice containing about 3000 signatures and announcing the formation of the National Defense Front.‡ In the statement at the beginning, the signatories, mostly Conservatives and Social Christians, denounce communist penetration of the government, the CTE and the FEUE, together with the selection of Ecuador by the international communist movement as the second target after Cuba for conquest in America. The purpose of the Front is described as defense of the country against communist subversion, and the first objective is the break in relations with Cuba.

Although the political coloring of the rightist forces behind the Front is well known, Noland hopes that the Front will have more maneuverability than the political parties because it focuses on only one political issue: communism and Cuba. As such the Front should be a more effective tool for pressure on Velasco to break with Cuba and curb URJE, Araujo, the CTE and the rest. This will take some doing—in a speech in a provincial capital today Velasco said that communism in Ecuador is impossible. Today El Salvador became the seventh Latin American country to break with Cuba.

Quito — 5 March 1961

The student strikes have subsided and Velasco seems to have survived although opposition to him is growing steadily, particularly among the poor classes who voted for him, because of inflation and corruption in the government.

Our propaganda operations relating to communism and Cuba are intensifying opposition to Velasco among the rightists, if that's possible. With financing from the ECACTOR and ECURGE projects, we've been turning out a stream of handbills, editorials, declarations, advertisements and wall-painting, mostly through Salgado and the National Defense Front. Bacon's "alert" notices in *El Comercio* have also started.

Because of a new spate of rumors that the Inter-American Conference will be postponed, the government has issued several statements on its determination to maintain order at the Conference. Nevertheless, only on 1 March were the first arrests made in Guayaquil for the 22 February attack against the university strikers. A higher court forced the lower court to take action and those arrested were revealed to have been commanded by an assistant to the Guayaquil Mayor. The FEUE and URJE leaders arrested during the strike have also been released. This won't help the Conference.

The Mexico City Conference on National Sovereignty, Economic Emancipation and Peace opened today. Three of the five Ecuadorean delegates are our agents: if this were the case with all our stations the possibilities would be endless. No word yet on whether Basantes, my PCE penetration agent, will go on to Cuba.

Quito — 7 March 1961

The Soviet Ambassador to Mexico arrived in Quito today for a goodwill visit. He'll be here for about three days, discussing, among other things, Ecuador's desire to sell bananas to the Soviets. We have a program planned for disruption and propaganda against him. It began today with a statement by the National Defense Front calling for his expulsion. Another announcement arranged by Davila is from the Catholic University Youth Organization, denouncing the millions of dollars spent each year by the Kremlin to infiltrate Latin

America, adding that the budget against Ecuador for propaganda, agitators' salaries, secret go-betweens and instructors in sabotage, explosives and weapons is 250,721.05 dollars.

John Bacon's "alert" is directed against this visit. It runs:

> On the alert, Ecuadoreans, against communist agitators! The official Soviet newspaper is Pravda—which means Truth, one of the tremendous sarcasms of contemporary history.
>
> If we unmask the actors of this farce, we will find that it is not the plain truth, but distorted, calumnied truth. That's Russia and that's communism. And that is now Cuba and Fidelism. Disciples used by the great international fakes, and at the same time masters in deceit and subversion, try to introduce methods in Ecuador similar to those that their dictatorship employs. First, in order to avoid being responsible, the authorized agents wash their hands like Pilate even though the first terrorist bombs are heard elsewhere. Alert, Ecuadoreans, there is friendship that could dishonor us.

Still he has run into a problem in this campaign of "alert" notices attributed to the Ecuadorean Anti-Communist Front. He was surprised to read this morning that a real organization with that name has been founded. They published their first bulletin today with the theme: "For Religion and the Fatherland We Will Give Our Lives." The symbol of the group is a condor destroying with his powerful claws a hammer and sickle.

Quito — 10 March 1961

Six anti-communist organizations including the National Defense Front have been denied permits to hold street demonstrations against the Soviet Ambassador. Nevertheless, Davila sent some of his boys around to the Hotel Quito the other night and they made a small fuss. Police protection of the Soviet delegation is considerable and so far there's been no violence.

The Soviet Ambassador has seen the Ministers of

Foreign Affairs and Education as well as President Velasco, and it was announced that an Ecuadorean commercial mission will soon visit the Soviet Union. The government wants to sell bananas, Panama hats and balsa wood in exchange for agricultural and road-building equipment. The overwhelming police protection, which has included the cavalry, when the Ambassador visits colonial churches and other tourist sites, is helping our propaganda campaign.

Today's "alert" notice was also against the Soviets:

> Alert, Ecuadoreans! Communism enslaves. Communism imposes the hardest slavery known through the centuries, and once it is able to enslave a people it is very difficult for the victim to break the chains.
>
> Hungary tried in 1956. The valiant Hungarians in an unsuccessful and heroic struggle rose up demanding bread and freedom. But they were destroyed by Soviet tanks that massacred more than 32,000 workers and reduced the whole country to still worse slavery. In this terrible crime against humanity the puppet traitor Janos Kadar went over to the side of the muscovite hordes that assassinated his brothers and enslaved his fatherland. Alert! There are puppets of the same kind who want to sell out Ecuador.

Tonight the Defense Front held an indoor rally at a theater where Velasco was attacked for his permissive policies towards communism, particularly his continued favoritism towards Araujo. He was also attacked for inflation and the increased benefits for representation and housing given to members of his Cabinet. After the rally, participants were attacked in the street by a mob of Velasquistas and URJE members shouting *vivas* to Araujo. Our Embassy-sponsored bi-national cultural center was stoned and shots were fired at the home of a Social Christian leader.

If the opposition to Velasco over Cuba and communism is getting serious, it's even more serious over economic policy. In the past three days the Monetary Board (comparable to the U.S. Federal Reserve Board) has reversed the fiscal and economic policies begun when Velasco took office—largely because of the growing opposition of the sierra Chambers of Agriculture, Commerce and Industry.

The problem derives from the competing economies of the coast and sierra and from Velasco's having placed monetary policy in the hands of Guayaquil Velasquista leaders. Just after the election these people started a campaign against the old leadership of the Monetary Board and the Central Bank which under Ponce had followed policies of stability through tight money and balanced foreign trade. The coastal Velasquista leaders, however, claimed that such policies were strangling economic development and they proposed expansion of the money supply. When Velasco took power this group received the most important government financial positions, including the Ministries of Economy and Development, and eventually the chiefs of the Monetary Board and the Central Bank resigned and were replaced by people from the same Guayaquil financial circle.

Quito — 11 March 1961

The Peace Conference in Mexico City is over, and a cable arrived from the Mexico City station advising that Basantes has been able to get an invitation to visit Cuba. He will be there for two or three weeks at least, and when he returns to Mexico City he'll be debriefed by an officer from the Miami station. The Mexico City station was quite pleased with our agents' work at the Conference. The Conference adopted the predictable resolutions: support to the Cuban revolution; annulment of all treaties that tend to revive the Monroe Doctrine; opposition to the military, technical and economic missions of the U.S. in Latin America; nationalization of heavy industry and foreign companies: establishment of cultural and diplomatic relations with the Soviet bloc and Communist China; support to Panama in its efforts to gain possession of the Panama Canal.

Since most visitors of importance to Quito stay at the Hotel Quito I suggested to Noland that we could provide better coverage of their visits by taking advantage of the U.S. company that manages the hotel in order to bug the rooms. I suggested that we get a couple of the standard hotel lamps and send them to headquarters for installation of transmitters that we will be able to monitor from other rooms in the hotel. Through the American manager (whom we all know) we can get the lamps placed in the appropriate rooms before the guests arrive.

Noland liked the idea and is going to get two lamps through Otto Kladensky‡ who rents the room used in the operation with Reinaldo Varea,‡ Vice-President of the Senate. After we get them back we'll decide whether to use the manager or some other means for placing them. I'm going to suggest battery-operated equipment so that it will work if the lamp is unplugged.

Quito — 15 March 1961

President Kennedy's speech to the Latin American Ambassadors in Washington on the Alliance for Progress has caused much excitement here and almost unanimously favorable comment. We're using Castro's speech the day after Kennedy's against him: he said the Cuban revolution is supported by Ecuador, Uruguay and Brazil. Through the National Defense Front we're generating continuous propaganda against Velasco's policy on Cuba which may well be what caused the stoning of Ponce's house two nights ago. The attackers got away but they were probably Velasquistas.

Other propaganda is generated through coverage of the Cuban exiles. We are getting fairly good presentation of the bulletins of the main exile group, the Revolutionary Democratic Front,‡ and statements made by exiles when they arrive, usually in Guayaquil, but so far Noland hasn't wanted to get into direct contact with Cuban exiles in Ecuador.

Noland is financing the formation of the Anti-Communist Christian Front in Cuenca, Ecuador's third largest city. The principal agent is Carlos Arizaga Toral,‡ ECACTOR–2, a leader of the Conservative Party there whose son, Carlos Arizaga,‡ ECACTOR–3, is a Provincial Councillor and will be active in the Front. Formation of the Front has just been announced.

Bacon has solved his problem by changing the name of his non-existent organization to "Ecuadorean Anti-Communist *Action*" instead of "Front."

Quito — 19 March 1961

The lines are drawing tighter, which is just what we want. The leftists have conducted a signature campaign of their own to support Velasco over maintaining relations with Cuba. Two days ago they published a declaration accusing the Defense Front of aiding Peru by calling for a break in relations with Cuba. The announcement was followed by three pages of signatures including Araujo and other leftist political, educational and cultural figures.

Velasco himself, in a speech yesterday commemorating the deaths of his supporters which occurred a year ago, when he arrived in Quito to begin campaigning, insisted that Ecuador will never break with Cuba while he is President. He also emphasized that Ecuador is not communist, but he alluded to a subversive plot against him—a reference no doubt to recent rumors of rightist plotting in the military. Araujo was a speaker at the same rally. If this keeps up we will isolate Velasco on the Cuban issue so that his main support will be from the extreme left.

On our side Gil Saudade, the Deputy Chief of Station, has had Juan Yepez del Pozo, Jr., National Coordinator of the Popular Revolutionary Liberal Party, issue a manifesto on his return from the Mexico City Peace Conference. The manifesto, which is just being put out today, condemns the Conservative and Social Christians for their current campaign against communism and Cuba while also criticizing strongly the Liberal Party and the communists. In his appeal to the Velasquista masses of poor people, Yepez calls for an integral revolution favoring the poor, but insists that it be effected within the law. The manifesto also denounces *de facto* régimes and totalitarianisms from both left and right. If this party can really get moving we will bring under control much of Velasco's leftist support, gradually bending it against the Cuban solution. Gil is now going to have Yepez establish an organization in Guayaquil.

Quito — 27 March 1961

Velasco is showing signs of erratic behavior, partly at least as a result of our propaganda. On 23 March he had the former Army commander under Ponce arrested for subversion, but two days later he was released by the Quito Mayor at the *habeas corpus* hearing. The government looked so ridiculous that Velasco had to fire his Minister of Government, who today resigned "for reasons of health." In announcing the appointment of his new minister, Velasco criticized what he called the tendentious notices appearing almost daily in the press. With his habitual reference to his 400,000 votes he accused the propagandists of trying to provoke disorder. Velasco's physician, Dr. Ovalle,‡ is examining Velasco almost every week and he told me Velasco is feeling considerable strain over loss of popular support, which he attributes to the rightist campaign against Cuba and communism.

Atahualpa Basantes, my PCE penetration agent who went to Cuba after the Mexico City Peace Conference, is back. He returned via Mexico City where he was debriefed by an officer from the Miami station. In his first report, which I just got from Dr. Ovalle, Basantes strongly insinuates he knows he's working for the Agency, undoubtedly because of his meetings with officers in Mexico City. Noland wants to continue the Velasquista pretext for the time being, however, so I won't be meeting him personally yet. The agent can't stop praising the Cuban revolution—I'm not sure what to do about this.

Quito — 2 April 1961

Pleasant surprises for the station this week. Yesterday the University Sports League professional soccer team elected new officers and Noland was named as a Director. Manuel Naranjo,‡ the Socialist Party Deputy whom Noland met and recruited thanks to the Sports League, was elected President of the club. This is a matter of some prestige for Noland, an American Embassy official, to become an officer of Quito's top soccer club. Partly, it reflects his ability to move in the right circles and partly, no doubt, it is because he brought in uniforms and equipment for the team via the diplomatic pouch and contributed generously from his representation allowance. More important, the Socialist Party has been holding its annual convention, the first since the party split last year into the moderate wing and the extreme-left Revolutionary Socialist Party. Naranjo was elected Secretary-General today which means we will have still more influence in keeping the party moderately oriented. Naranjo and his colleagues call themselves Marxists but they reject the concepts of class struggle and dictatorship of the proletariat. It's important that we have some influence in a group that will attract people of social-democratic persuasion.

Propaganda remains intense. The Catholic University Youth Organization has just held a convention which we helped to finance through Davila. The convention received considerable publicity, including a visit by a convention delegation to the Cardinal, and a closing declaration against communism and Cuba was issued.

Quito — 4 April 1961

Velasco continues to struggle against the rightist campaign against communism and Cuba. He again lashed out against the National Defense Front,‡ accusing the rightist political parties of using the Front to turn people against his government for economic as well as political reasons. He was answered later by the Deputy Director of the Conservative Party, who is also on the Executive Committee of the Defense Front, with accusations that Velasco is letting himself be carried away emotionally in his attacks on the Front. He also belittled Velasco's accusations that the Front is being manipulated like an opposition political party.

Velasco's nervousness is evident in a new purge in the Army leadership, and in the resignation today of his Minister of Defense. The new minister is from a clique of Guayaquil Velasquistas, and his appointment will intensify charges that the President is being manipulated by the coastal Velasquista oligarchy.

Quito — 15 April 1961

The invasion against Cuba has started with the bombing of Cuban airfields by "defectors." A leftist rally was held against the bombing in Independence Plaza with Araujo as main speaker, but no attack has yet been made on the Embassy. Noland has arranged with Colonel Lugo‡ and also with Captain Vargas‡ to be sure we get good protection during the next few days. The invasion will give URJE and the others all the excuse they need for another round of window-breaking.

Quito — 18 April 1961

The invasion really got going today but reports are conflicting and headquarters hasn't said anything yet. There have been anti-U.S. riots all day in Quito and Guayaquil and the Army was called out to protect the Embassy, USOM and the bi-national cultural center. Araujo is leading the mobs here in Quito.

Davila tried to get a demonstration going in support of the invasion but they were outnumbered this time and had to be protected by police. Sentiment in general is running against the invasion even though many of those against it understand perfectly what would happen here if there was a communist revolution. They just hate U.S. intervention more than they hate communism.

The main Jesuit church in downtown Quito, a relic of colonial architecture, was stoned tonight during the URJE riot, and later tonight a bomb exploded in our Embassy garden. Things could be much worse however.

Quito — 19 April 1961

Things are indeed much worse. This morning we received a propaganda guidance cable—it was sent to all WH stations—with instructions on how to treat the Bay of Pigs invasion. The cable said we should describe the invasion as a mission to re-supply insurgents in the Escambray mountains, not to take and hold any territory. As such the mission has been a success. Noland says this means the whole thing has failed and that heads are going to roll in headquarters. I've never seen him so glum.

The Defense Front got together a sizable demonstration of support for the invasion, which included speeches against Castro and communism. There was also a march through downtown Quito with the burning of a Russian flag and chants against Fidel, URJE and the stoning of the Jesuit church.

I don't know what to think about the invasion. It's like losing a game you never even considered losing. I'm also worried about the AMBLOOD agents in Cuba. Press reports indicate that thousands have been arrested, many simply on suspicion of not supporting Castro. We have exchanged only five or six letters with secret writing, and they weren't very revealing. Toroella‡ has large sums of money, weapons and a yacht but apparently he communicates with Miami by radio as well as by the SW via Quito. I wonder if he is all right.

Quito — 24 April 1961

Mostly through the efforts of Davila the anti-communist reaction to the Bay of Pigs failure has driven the leftists off the streets. There was another pro-Castro demonstration three days ago but then the government banned all outdoor demonstrations for a week in order to let tempers cool. On the 21st the formation of the Ecuadorean Brigade for the struggle against Castro was announced with a call for inscriptions and the claim that among those already signed up are military officers, students, workers, nurses, priests and white-collar workers. The same day an indoor rally supporting the invasion was held at the Catholic University.

By coincidence the traditional Novena to the Sorrowful Mother going on right now is serving as a pretext to evade the ban on outdoor demonstrations. The sermons have focused on the imminent danger of communism, which is penetrating the country by passing itself off as Velasquismo. This can't please the President because this is one of the most heavily attended religious occasions, and is held at the Jesuit church that was attacked during the URJE demonstration against the invasion. Yesterday the novena service ended with a street procession that included thousands of people who turned it into a political rally against communism and URJE. Today a one-and-a-half-page notice was published in the newspaper condemning the attack against the Jesuit church. Araujo and URJE have denied the attack and the chances are high that the Conservative Party Youth or a Social Christian squad actually did it.

Through all the commotion Gil Saudade has been working on an international organization. Last month the Secretary-General and the Administrative Secretary of the International Commission of Jurists‡ (ICJ) arrived in Quito in order to lay the groundwork for an Ecuadorean affiliate of the ICJ. Saudade managed to arrange for them to meet Juan Yepez del Pozo, Sr., the sociologist and leader of the Bolivarian Society who is chief advisor to the Popular Revolutionary Liberal Party.‡ The visit by the ICJ officials was part of a tour of Latin America to form affiliates where they don't already exist and to generate publicity for the ICJ's work.

Today the Ecuadorean affiliate of the ICJ was formally established, and Velasco was named Honorary President. The Rector of Central University, a Liberal-leaning independent, is President of the provisional Executive Board, which also includes the President of the Ecuadorean Supreme Court. Other distinguished lawyers and legal associations are also taking part, including Carlos Vallejo Baez,‡ who with Yepez runs the learned magazine *Ensayos* to which Saudade gives financial assistance. Vallejo is also active in the PLPR, and Yepez was named Secretary-General of the ICJ affiliate.

Gil is also working with the Inter-American Federation of Working Newspapermen‡ (IFWN), which was founded in Lima last year with the American Newspaper Guild‡ as cover. This organization is more like a trade union, as opposed to the Inter-American Press Society which is mostly composed of publishers. The IFWN serves to promote freedom of the press and as a mechanism for anti-communist propaganda. Its annual conference has just taken place in Quito, with statements against Cuba and the rightist dictatorships in the hemisphere. They also called for economic, social and political reforms. U.S. journalists in attendance were used to spot and assess possible new media agents for different stations, while Saudade worked through the host organization, the Ecuadorean National Union of Journalists.‡

Quito — 30 April 1961

USOM has made its contribution towards countering the Bay of Pigs humiliation. They delivered a check for half a million dollars to our Minister of Labor and Social Welfare, Baquero de la Calle,‡ for colonization and integration of the campesino. Present at the well-publicized ceremony was Jorge Acosta,‡ who is head of the National Colonization Institute. Acosta has a strange relationship with the station. Most of us know him fairly well and he's closer than being just a "contact." Since we don't pay him he's not really a controlled agent, but he tells us as much as he can. The problem he has is that Velasco seems bent on losing all his support except the extreme left rather than break with Cuba. Not even Acosta can overcome that stubbornness.

The Inter-American Conference is definitely off. Velasco publicly accepted a proposal made jointly by the Presidents of Colombia, Venezuela and Panama that it be postponed indefinitely. We weren't surprised because now security would really be a problem. The rumors have never ended that one country or another was proposing postponement because of security hazards, and recent discoveries here of contraband arms shipments from the U.S. haven't helped to allay the fears.

The day before Velasco announced the postponement he called for national unity and the easing of partisan political passions. But the same day the Quito Chamber of Commerce denounced the failure of the government to publish the weekly statistical bulletin of the Central Bank. It hasn't come out for five consecutive weeks and the Chamber insists the government is making a deliberate effort to hide the worsening economic situation. The government is indeed considering a number of possible emergency economic decrees but has announced ahead of time that none of them involve new taxes.

Quito — 5 May 1961

Pressure on Velasco from the National Defense Front and from the Cardinal has been helped by Velasco himself. On 30 April the Cardinal was expelled from the prestigious National Defense Board which is composed of eminent citizens and is responsible for advising on how secret defense funds are to be spent. Since the announcement of Velasco's action many Catholic groups have made well-publicized visits of solidarity to the Cardinal, including one today from the Defense Front. The visits have usually included speeches on the inhumanities of communism and the imminent danger of a communist takeover in Ecuador. Velasco's action in expelling the Cardinal is clearly retaliation for the Cardinal's criticism of the government on the communist issue, and sympathy for the Cardinal especially among the poor and illiterate can only further erode Velasco's power base.

Quito — 7 May 1961

We have just had a remarkable breakthrough. One of our most valuable PCE penetration agents, Louis Vargas,‡ recently reported on what he thought was the beginning of serious guerrilla operations here. Vargas was not in the group currently being trained but his close and frequent association with the leaders of the group gave significant intelligence. Rafael Echeverria Flores, the number one PCE leader in the sierra, and Jorge Ribadeneira Altamirano, also a PCE leader in Quito and a principal leader of URJE, were the leaders, and the training was being conducted by a foreign specialist whose nationality was unknown to the agent.

Vargas the agent got the word in time to the station and Noland advised Captain José Vargas, the Chief of the Police Intelligence. This morning Lieutenant Sandoval‡ laid a trap and during the course of the morning twenty members of URJE were arrested on the mountain that rises above Quito. Ribadeneira and Echeverria are among those arrested. The foreigner conducting the training is a Bolivian and we're getting traces on him from the La Paz station for police intelligence. Too bad he isn't Cuban, but the propaganda dividend is going to be considerable anyway.

Quito — 9 May 1961

The guerrilla arrests are headlines this morning! Yesterday the Sub-Secretary of Government gave a press conference in which he distributed the police report written by the intelligence unit. At Noland's suggestion the police report described those arrested as only one small group among many other groups that have been receiving guerrilla training for some time at secret sites around the country. The press stories very effectively sensationalize the police report, which described the training as including explosives, guerrilla warfare, street fighting and terrorism.

The foreigner is Juan Alberto Enriquez Roncal, a thirty-two-year-old Bolivian who came to Ecuador last month and had been training URJE members in Guayaquil before coming to Quito. He has admitted everything to the police including giving training sessions in Ribadeneira's law office.

Velasco issued a statement today that he will severely repress any terrorists, but he has released all those arrested except Ribadeneira, Echeverria and Enriquez. In Guayaquil the leader of the previous trainees was arrested, but the release of the others is sure to provoke a negative public reaction, since last night a power plant in Guayaquil was bombed.

Quito — 13 May 1961

Basantes, another PCE penetration agent and a retired Army major, reported that the PCE leadership in Guayaquil (Pedro Saad and company) is furious with Ribadeneira and Echeverria. They think Enriquez may be a CIA *agent provocateur* and that Echeverria and Ribadeneira fell into the trap.

However, the guerrilla trainer admitted today that he is really an Argentine, aged thirty-six, named Claudio Adiego Francia. He told police intelligence that he had no money and was giving the guerrilla training so that he could continue traveling, Cuba is his destination but he said he has no invitation. He described his long background in Argentine revolutionary activities, and then changed his story, now claiming he wasn't really giving training but only recounting to the URJE and PCE people his experiences in Argentina.

This new twist is keeping the story in the newspapers and the case has been a help to our signature campaign for mercy for the Bay of Pigs prisoners. The campaign has been promoted by stations all over Latin America. In Quito the ECACTOR political-action agents have circulated the petition: today the telegram to Castro pleading mercy was published, followed by two pages of the more than 7000 signatures obtained.

Student operations of the Guayaquil base have had a series of successes in recent months culminating two days ago with the disaffiliation of the FEUE from the Prague-based International Union of Students.

This final victory began with the change in FEUE election procedures at Portoviejo last December, followed by election victories at the University of Cuenca in March and the Central University in Quito last month. In both instances the forces led by Alberto Alarcon defeated the candidates for FEUE offices put up by the Velasquistas and the extreme left. Our only defeat was at the University of Loja where the leftist candidate won. The picture is confused in Guayaquil because the FEUE has split between a Velasquita group that supports the Mayor and an extreme-leftist group led by members of URJE.

The vote today by the National FEUE Council in Quito will have to be ratified by the FEUE Congress later this year, but in the meantime relations between the FEUE and the Agency-controlled COSEC‡ in Leyden can be cemented.

Quito — 15 May 1961

Ambato is the site of the most recent action. Yesterday in Ambato a Cuban photographic exhibit was inaugurated under sponsorship of the Ambato chapter of the Cuban Friendship Society. The ceremony was held in the Municipal Palace approval for which had been granted by the Ambato Mayor, a Revolutionary Socialist. The Mayor in his speech went so far as to call the Quito Cardinal a traitor, and the Cuban Ambassador gave a fiery speech against the U.S.

Following the speeches an unexplained electrical failure prevented the showing of a film on Cuba and later a group of about twenty men invaded the Palace and destroyed most of the photographs and mountings. The police arrived after the damage was done and the group left quickly, firing their revolvers into the air as they went. No arrests were made.

Jorge Gortaire,‡ a retired Army colonel and leader of the Social Christian Movement in Ambato, was the organizer of the raid. Noland has been financing him from the ECACTOR project since last year to help build up a militant action organization and to promote a political campaign against the Mayor. Careful planning of the attack, especially through coordination with the police, was the reason it was so successful. Even so, the Mayor is getting more photographs down from Quito so that the exhibit can stay open.

Quito — 22 May 1961

In Guayaquil the police recently arrested, at base request, three Chinese communists who arrived some days ago. They had been given courtesy visas by the Ecuadorean Ambassador in Havana and supposedly were here representing the Chinese Youth Federation. The base tried to arrange for them to be held for a long period, so that recruitment possibilities could be studied, but the order for their expulsion had already been issued.

The police are carrying out the base request to sensationalize the case. The official report charges them with propaganda and subversion, claiming they had a powerful radio transmitter in their hotel room, with which they were in communication with Cuba and other communist countries in the evenings after ten o'clock. Preposterous charges, but there's so much fear and tension in the atmosphere right now that most people will believe it.

The same day the Chinese communists were deported, a sensational plot to assassinate Velasco surfaced. The attempted assassination was reported by a Guayaquil radio station (falsely, for which the radio station was ordered to be closed) but on checking sources the trail led straight to the Cuban Consul. The Consul refused to testify in the investigation and has been expelled by the Ecuadorean government. His departure has given us another propaganda peg for demonstrating Cuban intervention in Ecuador, even though he was simply a victim of provocation because he had reported the plot to security authorities in Guayaquil. It appears to us that the provocation was rigged by Velasco or his lieutenants in order to appease the Defense Front and other anti-communists.

Here in Quito the National Defense Front has been more strident than ever in its propaganda created through public meetings, press conferences and published statements. The Front is criticizing Velasco for his policy towards Cuba, demanding the firing of the Ecuadorean Ambassador to Cuba over the presentation of a portrait of Castro "in the name of the Ecuadorean people," demanding that Velasco suppress communism, and demanding the expulsion of the Cuban Ambassador for his anti-U.S. speech in Ambato. The Front continues to insist that Velasco define himself on communism even though he recently insisted in a speech that while he is President Ecuador will not become communist. The Conservative Party has also joined the campaign for expulsion of the Cuban Ambassador.

In Cuenca, Carlos Arizaga Vega,‡ a leader of the ECACTOR operation there, circulated a petition and sent it to Velasco demanding the firing of the Ambassador to Cuba over the portrait presentation. Velasco, for his part, has dismissed the military commander of the Cuenca zone who is a well-known anti-communist—provoking renewed criticism there.

In Ambato, the Mayor was severely denounced by Municipal Councillors for his remarks about the Cardinal and for having granted use of the Municipal Palace for the Cuban photographic exhibit. But at the closing of the exhibit yesterday the Mayor, Araujo, CTE and PCE speakers all repeated the anti-clerical themes. They began a march in the street afterwards, but were met by a Catholic counter-manifestation organized by Gortaire and armed with rocks, clubs and firearms. A pitched battle followed and, although shots were fired, no one seems to have been wounded. The much larger counter-demonstration easily overwhelmed the leftists and at one point Araujo was in danger of being lynched. If the police hadn't intervened something serious might have happened.

Somehow amidst all these crises labor operations continue to move, although not without some serious problems. CROCLE, our coastal organization, has served consistently for anti-Cuban and anti-communist propaganda, but our agents in it are not as effective in trade-union activities as we would like. They are constantly feuding among themselves and failing to get out and organize. However, they won't be terminated until Gil Saudade is able to move some of his agents from the PLPR‡ into the leadership of the national free labor confederation now in its embryonic stage. Miranda,‡ our Coastal Labor Senator, is also ineffective and he is feuding with the CROCLE agents. Finally, Jose Baquero, our Minister of Labor, is determined to promote the small and ineffective Catholic labor group, CEDOC, instead of our budding secular organizations. His effectiveness is also limited because as Minister he is responsible for the public-health service, the social-security system, protection of minors, the fire departments and cooperatives as well as labor matters.

On two recent occasions the International Organizations Division in headquarters has sent in agents to help us. In March William Sinclair,‡ the Inter-American Representative of the Public Service International‡ (PSI), and William H. McCabe,‡ also a PSI representative, came to assist in planning for a congress of municipal employees that a few weeks later launched a new National Federation of Municipal Employees. McCabe's‡ main operation is in British Guiana where the Georgetown Station is building up trade-union opposition to the government of Cheddi Jagan, a Marxist. Also, an exploratory visit was made by an international representative of the International Federation of Plantation, Agricultural and Allied Workers‡ (IFPAAW) for possible assistance in organizing Ecuadorean rural coastal workers.

Quito — 28 May 1961

The Cubans have made a timely maneuver. Yesterday Carlos Olivares, the Cuban Sub-Secretary of Foreign Relations and their most important trouble-shooter, arrived in Guayaquil. He is on a "goodwill" tour trying to bolster Cuban relations with South American countries, capitalizing, of course, on the Bay of Pigs invasion. Today he saw Velasco, but we haven't been able to get a report on their private meeting.

Olivares's visit coincides with new reports on the considerable publicity given in Cuba to recent speeches by the Ecuadorean Ambassador at Cuban universities. According to Cuban press releases the Ambassador has attacked the U.S., alleging that Ecuador, like Cuba, has been the victim of the "arbitrary, unjust and rapacious American imperialism." The reports have provoked new outrage against Velasco on his Cuban policy.

Today Velasco gave another speech and made no attempt to hide the damage our campaign is doing. He condemned persons unnamed for trying to divide the country between communists and anti-communists, and he repeated that while he is President, Ecuador will never become communist.

Our campaign through Salgado, Davila, Perez, Arizaga, Gortaire and other agents goes on. John Bacon is also continuing to publish the "alert" notices every two or three days, and other propaganda themes include concern over the Bay of Pigs prisoners and the recent guerrilla arrests in Quito.

In Ambato, Gortaire has managed to launch an Anti-Communist Front that includes Liberals as well as the Conservatives, the fascist ARNE and others. This is the first instance of significant Liberal Party participation in anti-communist fronts and clearly reflects the prestige and organizing ability of Gortaire.

Quito — 29 May 1961

If our propaganda and political-action campaign doesn't force Velasco to take the right action, the worsening economic situation will. Today the President of the Monetary Board, appointed by Velasco himself, resigned in protest against the damage to the economy that uncertainty over Cuba and communism is causing.

Since the return in early March to policies of monetary stability, inflation has failed to slow down while Velasco has created a considerable number of new indirect taxes that are very unpopular. While Velasco and his lieutenants continue their theme of "forty years of Velasquismo" most of the people have been struggling against their declining purchasing power. One indication of how bad the situation is getting is the decline in free-market value of the sucre: from about eighteen per dollar six months ago to over twenty-two right now.

The President of the Monetary Board, in resigning, attributed the worsening economic situation to lack of confidence based on Velasco's tolerance towards communism internally and his ambiguity towards Cuba. He insisted that Velasco must take action instead of making philosophical statements, and he pinpointed the following specific problems: the activities of the Ecuadorean Ambassador to Cuba; the agitation emanating from the Cuban Embassy in Quito and the Cuban Consulate in Guayaquil; the Cuban Ambassador's speech in Ambato; and the lack of clear definition by Velasco on communism.

Velasco is really embarrassed by this resignation which Noland says is bound to have some effect. The resignation statement couldn't have been better if we had written it ourselves. Exactly what we want.

Quito — 30 May 1961

Finally Velasco is taking action. Several of the Velasquista penetration agents have reported that Velasco asked Olivares to withdraw the Cuban Ambassador. There is not going to be a *persona non grata* note—simply a quiet exit. This is a significant start and it shows Velasco is facing reality: he just can't continue ignoring the pressure of the Social Christians, Conservatives,

Catholic Church and all the other anti-communists—and us. As soon as we learn of the Cuban Ambassador's travel plans we'll pass word for a hostile farewell committee.

On the negative side a judge today released Echeverria and Ribadeneira for lack of evidence. He's the best friend of the extreme left in the court system and was the last hope for those two. Earlier the *habeas corpus* proceeding had failed them and the CTE campaign for their release hasn't been very effective. The judge ordered documents from the police on the original sources of the police information, including names of their informants. As the station is the only source, this effectively killed the legal case.

Quito — 3 June 1961

Velasco made a very important speech tonight. At a political rally he tried to make the political definition that the Defense Front and the rightist political parties have been demanding. He announced a doctrine of liberalism which for him means cooperation rather than conflict between classes. He denounced communism, praised representative democracy, and described his own course as between the extremes of left and right. He also said that communism should be attacked not by police repression but through the elimination of misery, hunger, sickness and ignorance. He showed the effect of our campaign, charging the anti-communists with trying to take away the bases of his support by dividing the 400,000 Ecuadoreans who voted for him on the pretext of anti-communism.

This speech, coming on the heels of the Cuban Ambassador's expulsion, will tend to soften the campaign. Our goal is a complete break in relations with Cuba, not just an expulsion. Economics will probably help us. The sucre is now down to twenty-three per dollar from eighteen six months ago, and a controversy is raging over inflation, especially the prices of medicines which are among the highest in Latin America.

Quito — 7 June 1961

Velasco's "anti-communist" speech has been very well received and even the Conservative Party has issued a statement of guarded approval. What most people are watching, however, are his actions and we have some distance to cover before relaxing. The day after Velasco's speech, the Minister of Defense made it clear that Velasco now considers his position defined as anti-communist—a clear attempt to stop erosion of support from the station-backed anti-communist campaign.

The Liberal Party has rather suddenly taken a strong stance against the President, partly no doubt because of a recent attack by a Velasquista mob on their paper *El Comercio*. At the annual celebration of the Party's founding it was said that the past thirty years of Velasquismo have pulled down the country in a cataleptic state and, of course, that only the Liberal Party can save it. The Liberals' complaints are mostly founded on the worsening economic situation: the sucre has now fallen to twenty-five.

Some relief has become available, however, largely because of Velasco's anti-communist actions of the past two or three weeks. Today in Washington the International Monetary Fund announced a ten-million-dollar stand-by loan for a stabilization program in Ecuador. In the announcement the IMF also said that the Central Bank, which requested the loan, is going to adopt a policy of credit restriction and other measures to end the flight of capital, recognizing also that measures have already been taken to slow the fall in foreign-exchange reserves.

The IMF announcement was embarrassing to the government here, which didn't want publicity. The Minister of Economy even declined to comment on the announcement, saying that questions should be directed to the IMF in Washington.

Quito — 12 June 1961

This past week, since Velasco made his "anti-communist" speech, has been the first fairly calm period since

I arrived. In the hectic pace as we've passed from crisis to crisis I almost haven't noticed how far my Spanish has come along. Noland is especially pleased with my progress on the language and also with the way I have been developing friends among the Ecuadoreans, impossible, of course, without the language. Mostly I've been spending time meeting people at the golf-club while learning to play.

Janet has a mental block on the language and it's growing as a source of friction between us. Among other things this limits her friends to those who speak English and it also hinders her running servants and shopping. Politics, unfortunately, are not interesting to her either. But these are small complaints and common, I'm told, at overseas posts. And they certainly pale before the big news: in October our first child is due, something we didn't exactly plan but we were both happily surprised.

The work routine at the station is arduous—nights, weekends, whenever things are happening. After reading the newspapers each morning we begin writing and distributing papers: pouched dispatches on operations, intelligence reports, cables for urgent matters. Noland insists that each day we all read the cable chronological file so that we're up to date on all the incoming and outgoing traffic. The pouched material, both out and in, is circulated so that each officer will know exactly what the others are doing, their successes and their problems. Each of us also looks over the flight passenger lists each day, and Noland insists that we also read the State Department cables and pouched material handled by the Embassy staff. With all this reading, I'm pressed to get out for agent meetings, although I am only meeting directly about five. The worst is writing intelligence reports because the special usage and format must be followed.

The propaganda and political-action campaign against Araujo, Cuba and communism in general has clearly been the major station program since I arrived six months ago. The ECACTOR project has accounted for much of this activity. It costs about 50,000 dollars a year and in a place like Quito a thousand dollars a week buys a lot. The feelings I have are that we aren't running the country but we are certainly helping to shape events in the direction and form we want. The other main station activity, the PCE penetration program, has consistently provided good information. There's no question that Echeverria and his group here in the sierra are doing all they can to prepare for armed guerrilla operations. We have to keep the pressure on Velasco to break with Cuba and clamp down on the extreme left.

Quito — 15 June 1961

Velasco apparently thinks his "anti-communist" definition had ended the campaign. In a speech the other day he repeated his old theme that Ecuador will never become communist under him, but he insisted that he will not break relations with Cuba without a diplomatic cause.

On the other hand Jorge Ribadeneira, the URJE leader arrested on the guerrilla training exercise, has been sent to an isolated Amazon jungle outpost to do his military service. His absence will be a severe blow to the URJE leadership in Quito and also to the PCE.

Through Gustavo Salgado we are trying to relate the guerrilla arrests last month to exile reports on guerrilla training in Cuba. The JMWAVE station in Miami recently released an article on guerrilla training in Havana of groups of ten to fifteen who have been arriving from various Latin American countries. The article was passed to Salgado who added the URJE training episode of last month and arranged for publication on two consecutive days. Somehow we have to retain the sense of urgency in the propaganda campaign on communism and Cuba.

Today the Foreign Ministry announced that the Ecuadorean Ambassador to Cuba is retiring from the post "at the convenience of the Foreign Service." Velasco is certainly making an attempt to placate the rightists, but the fact is that he has no other choice now.

Quito — 16 June 1961

It was recently announced that Vice-President Arosemena will leave on 18 June for a trip to the Soviet Union, Czechoslovakia and Poland. We've known about this trip for some time. The invitation is from the Supreme Soviet and the group will include several legislators as well as Arosemena. Formally this is a "private" trip with no diplomatic or commercial purposes, but Arosemena is well known for his leftist ideas—he is also an alcoholic—and some mischief will come from the trip for sure.

Velasco is against the trip because Adlai Stevenson arrives the day Arosemena leaves, and Velasco is desperate for economic assistance. Stevenson is touring Latin America promoting the Alliance for Progress and trying to pick up the pieces from the Bay of Pigs fiasco, and Velasco is going to give him a list of requirements. He doesn't want Arosemena's trip to jeopardize his requests for aid to Stevenson, especially after expelling the Cuban Ambassador and firing his own anti-U.S. Ambassador to Cuba to prepare a favorable atmosphere. So Arosemena's trip has sparked a sharp public exchange between him and Velasco. The Foreign Minister announced today that the Cabinet unanimously resolved that Arosemena's trip at this time is "inconvenient" with emphasis that the trip is on Arosemena's own account with no official standing. Arosemena for his part defended the trip by denouncing unnamed Velasquista government leaders as money-crazed. Dr. Ovalle reports that Velasco is furious.

Quito — 20 June 1961

Arosemena left as planned and today Ambassador Stevenson also leaves. Velasco presented Ecuador's development needs in a seventeen-page memorandum that lists initial requirements totaling about 200 million dollars. Stevenson also met with moderate leaders of the Quito FEUE chapter and with leaders of the free trade-union movement. I had a short chat with him in the Embassy yesterday. In a few days an Ecuadorean delegation headed by the Minister of Development will leave for Washington to press for new loans. Arosemena's trip doesn't seem to have damaged Velasco's requests to Stevenson, but the split between the two won't be mended easily.

Today Velasco changed his Minister of Government again. He named a former Defense Minister under Ponce in what is an obvious move to make adequate security arrangements before the Congress reconvenes in August.

Quito — 29 June 1961

Noland has decided to move ahead on coverage of the Cubans here by putting a telephone tap on the Embassy. He asked me to take charge of this new operation, and a few days ago he introduced me to Rafael Bucheli,‡ the engineer in charge of all the Quito telephone exchanges. Bucheli is an old friend of Noland because his brother (cryptonym ECSAW) was our principal political-action agent in the Ponce government until he was killed in an automobile accident. Bucheli is going to make connections in the exchange where his office is located and which serves both his home and the Cuban Embassy. Noland also introduced me to Alfonso Rodriguez,‡ the engineer in charge of all the telephone lines system outside the exchanges. Noland met Rodriguez through his work on the University Sports League soccer team where Rodriguez is also active. He recruited Rodriguez who suggested that Bucheli might also help, not knowing yet that Bucheli had also agreed.

The two engineers, Noland and I began planning the operation but Noland is going to let me handle it alone. The first thing I must do is get headquarters approval for the operation and some equipment from the Panama station where the TSD has just set up a regional support base. The Panama station is located at Fort Amador in the Canal Zone where they have various support staffs who are able to save several days travel time to most of the WH stations. Then Rodriguez will run a special line to Bucheli's house where we'll set up the LP. I'll ask Francine Jacome, who was writing the cover letters for the AMBLOOD SW messages, to do the transcribing.

Quito — 7 July 1961

Good news from Velasco for a change. Today he appointed Jorge Acosta Velasco‡ as Minister of the Treasury. Until now Acosta has been Director of the Colonization Institute and the Vice-President of the National Planning Board, somewhat removed from his uncle, the President. He has been keeping Noland informed on Velasco's obstinacy over breaking with Cuba, but now he'll be able to work on the problem from within the Cabinet.

Ambassador Bernbaum is also trying to soften up Velasco on the Cuban problem. Thanks to his insistence a five million dollar development loan for housing has just been approved, and he also arranged an invitation for Velasco to visit Kennedy, which will be announced in a few days, probably to take place in October.

Davila and the Conservatives continue to squeeze. Today the Party forbade any of its members to accept jobs in the Velasco administration.

Quito — 11 July 1961

The Cardinal issued an anti-Cuban pastoral yesterday which may have overshot the mark. It's inflammatory, alarmist, almost hysterical in its warning against Cuba and communism. He urges all Ecuadorean Catholics to take action against communism but he doesn't say what action. The statement is so emotional it may be counterproductive, but Noland has faith that the Davila crowd, who at our instigation urged the Cardinal to produce it, know what they are about.

Today we distributed an unattributed fly-sheet through the ECJOB team. This severely attacked the Cardinal for these statements. The Catholic organizations are at once, as expected, beginning their protests.

Quito — 15 July 1961

The political situation has taken a new turn that promises to obscure the Cuban and communist issues. Opposition to the government has suddenly united behind Vice-President Arosemena, thanks largely to Velasco himself.

Three days ago Velasco appointed a new Minister of the Economy who is a paving contractor with large government contracts. He is also associated with the Guayaquil financial interests surrounding Velasco and his appointment immediately rekindled the criticisms that Velasco is dominated by the Guayaquil clique. Yesterday the government announced the unification of the exchange rate which will mean that importers of machinery, raw materials, medicines and other basic materials will have to pay about 20 per cent more in sucres for each dollar of foreign exchange purchased through the Central Bank for their imports. The unification measure is practically the same as an official devaluation of the sucre and will cause prices to rise immediately, because no compensatory measures such as tax adjustments or tariff exemptions were included. The economic sector most affected will be sierra agriculture but prices generally will rise throughout the country.

The unification decree has come just as a series of new indirect taxes has been announced on carbonated beverages, beer, official paper, unearned income, highway travel and other articles. These taxes will also cause prices to rise or buying power to drop and they violate Velasco's own recent statements that taxes are already too high.

In Washington the International Monetary Fund has issued a statement supporting the measure on unification, which is not surprising because everyone knows unification was a condition for the ten-million-dollar standby announced last month. In Ecuador, however, almost every significant political organization, and other groups such as the FEUE and the CTE have announced opposition to both unification and the new indirect taxes.

Announcement of the new economic decrees couldn't have been made at a worse time for Velasco, because the other event yesterday was Arosemena's return from his trip to Moscow. His supporters, including leaders of the extreme left, had been promoting a big reception for him for over a week. At the Quito airport several thousand turned out with Araujo as one of the leaders. Posters were prominent with slogans such as "Cuba si, Yankees no," "Down with Imperialism" and "We Want Relations with Russia."

Velasco is going to have to struggle hard to keep his balance. Just possibly he will break with Cuba in order to gain rightist support, but we aren't taking bets.

Quito — 23 July 1961

Arosemena has become undisputed leader of the opposition to Velasco. Although the Conservatives and Social Christians continue their opposition on the Cuban and communist issue, the new economic decrees have given the FEUE, CTE, URJE, the PCE and the Revolutionary Socialists the perfect pretext to line up behind Arosemena. Even the reactionary Radical Liberal Party and the moderate Socialist Party under our agent Manuel Naranjo have joined the extreme left in supporting Arosemena as the opposition leader.

Velasco is rattled by Arosemena's sudden popularity. During the reception for him at Guayaquil the local tank units were placed on alert to create fear and (unsuccessfully) to cut down attendance. While trying to defend the economic measures on the grounds that the government needs more income for public works, Velasco has bitterly attacked Arosemena for dividing the Velasquista Movement. As Arosemena and some of his supporters are still calling themselves Velasquistas even though they have turned against Velasco, the President has told them to leave the Movement and form another group with a different name.

Guayaquil student operations have just had a setback. Elections were held a week ago for FEUE officers at the University of Guayaquil—possibly the most important FEUE chapter because of the high level of militancy of the students there. Our forces, financed from the ECLOSE project and led by Alberto Alarcon, lost to the extreme left. A leader of URJE was elected FEUE President. The election came at a bad time just as the extreme left was making noisy support for Arosemena against Velasco on the economic issues.

Quito — 27 July 1961

Gil Saudade, our Deputy Chief of Station, decided to risk the future of his ECLURE party, the Popular Revolutionary Liberal Party (PLPR), on Velasco's longevity in the Presidency. His hope is still to attract the Velasquista left away from Araujo even if this means open and direct support for Velasco. When the party's first national convention opened in Quito a couple of days ago, Velasco was named Honorary President.

Preparations for the convention have been underway for several months and have included public statements on major issues. In late June, for example, the PLPR published a statement supporting Velasco on his Cuba policy (a conscious maneuver by Saudade) but strongly denouncing "the twenty families that have been exploiting Ecuador since before Independence and that seek to conserve their privileges by keeping the country under the landlords and bosses." The statement also affirmed that the real enemies of the Ecuadorean people are the Conservative Party, the Social Christian Movement, the Radical Liberal Party and the Socialist Party —all of whom represent the rich oligarchies who oppress the poor masses of the country.

Two weeks later the PLPR published another statement sharply criticizing the most recent pastoral letters of the Cardinal, whom our agents accused of being just one more oligarch using the communist scare for his own purposes. Right now Gil has on the payroll the party's National Director, Juan Yepez del Pozo, Jr.; the National Coordinator, Antonio Ulloa Coppiano;‡ the Legal Counsel, Carlos Vallejo Baez;‡ and the mastermind behind the operation, Juan Yepez del Pozo, Sr. who holds no office.

Saudade is very pleased with the PLPR convention which ended last night with Velasco as the principal speaker. The final session got ample publicity and was overflowing with people. Although the party had to support Velasco on his Cuban policy for tactical purposes, Saudade was careful to have Juan Yepez, Jr. in his opening speech describe the PLPR as opposed to the extremes of left or right, adding that the party could never approve of the despotism of Soviet Marxism.

Gil has also picked up two new agents from the convention, both of whom he plans to guide into the free labor movement to ensure station control beyond the CROCLE operation of the Guayaquil base. One of the new agents is Matias Ulloa Coppiano,‡ brother of Antonio Ulloa who is PLPR National Coordinator. Matias is a leader of a collective transportation cooperative. The other new agent is Ricardo Vazquez Diaz,‡ a leader of the Guayaquil PLPR delegation, who was one of the secretaries of the convention.

Quito — 31 July 1961

Velasco and the Cubans seem to be on the verge of establishing a mutual-aid society. Yesterday an interview with the new Ambassador was published wherein the Ambassador claims that Cuba was the first country to back Ecuador in its demand for revision of the Rio Protocol, comparing the forceful imposition of the Protocol to the imposition by the U.S. of the Platt Amendment and our retention of the Guantanamo naval base. Today the Foreign Ministry issued a statement emphasizing Ecuador's opposition to any form of collective or multilateral intervention in Cuba.

The Defense Front forces, however, haven't relaxed.

At a pro-Cuba rally three nights ago Araujo's speech was interrupted by an unexplained power failure. Police troops and cavalry outside the theater prevented another riot with counter-demonstrators. Similarly, when the new Cuban Ambassador presented his credentials at the Presidential Palace, an anti-Castro group sent by the Defense Front clashed with an URJE group that had come to the Palace to cheer the Ambassador. A riot followed and was finally broken up by the police with tear-gas.

The TSD support office in Panama sent tape-recorders, dial-recorders and actuators for setting up the telephone tap on the Cuban Embassy (cryptonym ECWHEAT). Last week the audio technician, Larry Martin,‡ was here to train Rafael Bucheli‡ to use the equipment, and Bucheli made the connections in the exchange aided by an assistant. Bucheli and the assistant are both active in the Quito model airplane club and I'm going to get a catalogue from headquarters so that they can select items that I can order through the pouch. Later we'll talk of salaries.

Quito — 4 August 1961

Velasco's tactics of bullying the opposition have cost him another Minister of Government. In a recent open polemic between the Minister and the National Director of the Radical Liberal Party the Minister launched such severe personal insults that he was challenged to a duel by the Liberal leader. Yesterday the Minister resigned so that he could accept the challenge, since dueling in Ecuador is illegal. The Liberal leader, who is from Guayaquil, flew up to Quito yesterday for final preparations, but he was met at the airport by several hundred rioting Velasquistas, most of whom were plain-clothes policemen and employees of the government monopolies and customs. The Liberal leader barely escaped lynching while several international flights were disrupted because of the tear-gas used by police and the general chaos. The duel was later called off, however, because the seconds somehow arranged for satisfactory excuses by the ex-Minister and honor was satisfied.

During the riot at the Quito airport a touring Soviet goodwill delegation flew in unexpectedly. We've had reports from other WH stations on their tour but the exact date they would proceed to Quito was undecided, probably to avoid a hostile reception. Our National Defense Front agents will publish statements and demonstrate against the visit. They are staying at the Hotel Quito but we still have not received the bugged lamps back from our technical support base in Panama.

Quito — 31 August 1961

Our propaganda and political-action campaign to keep the opposition to Velasco focused on Cuba and communism is being diverted because of the greater importance of last month's economic decrees on unification of the exchange rate and new taxes. Inflation has also become a major public issue. The government, however, is determined to retain the economic decrees in order to stimulate exports. Similarly, the new taxes are being justified as needed for the police, armed forces, education and public works. Nevertheless, the decrees have become the unifying issue for Velasco's opposition, and tomorrow the Chambers of Commerce of the entire country will call for repeal of the unification decree.

The Congress, which reconvened three weeks ago, is the center of opposition political debate, and already the Velasquista tactics of intimidation by hostile mobs in the galleries have been renewed. During one session, when the acting Minister of Government was called to answer questions about police repression in Guayaquil, nothing could be heard over the screaming of the galleries. Orange and banana peelings and showers of spittle fell on the opposition Deputy who was trying to question the Minister. Nevertheless, the Deputy spoke for several hours against repression in Guayaquil, but he was vilified continuously by the galleries, finally being forced to seek shelter. Meanwhile, fights broke out on the Chamber floor between Deputies, ashtrays were hurled by opponents, and the Chamber's security forces refused to eject the rioters in the galleries.

Arosemena, as President of the Congress, continues as the leader of the opposition to Velasco. Although loyal Velasquistas have been elected to offices in both houses, the exact party balance is unclear because of uncertainty over defections of Velasquistas to Arosemena—as in the case of Reinaldo Varea,‡ who was reelected Vice-President of the Senate and has declared for Arosemena. Two weeks ago a delegation from the CTE was invited by Arosemena to a joint session of Congress with Arosemena presiding. Members of the delegation asked the Congress to nullify the July decrees on unification and new taxes, adding that if the decrees are not canceled the CTE will call a general strike. This time Arosemena had the Velasquista mob ejected when they started shouting.

Quito — 2 September 1961

Saudade is certainly moving his Popular Revolutionary Liberal Party (PLPR) along—this time with help from the Bogotá station. Since arriving in Quito Saudade has been corresponding with the Bogotá station which supports a leftist wing of the Liberal Party called the Revolutionary Liberal Movement (MLR). Experience with the MLR in Colombia has been important for Saudade here because he hopes to achieve success with the PLPR comparable to the Bogotá station's success with the MLR.

Some weeks ago Saudade had Juan Yepez del Pozo, Jr. of the PLPR invite the leader of the MLR, Alfonso Lopez Michelson,‡ to visit Quito to exchange experiences and to promote PLPR organizational work. Saudade, of course, didn't reveal the CIA interest in the MLR but the Bogotá station assured acceptance of the invitation. I wonder whether Lopez is witting and contact with him is direct or whether the Bogotá station's access to him is through other MRL leaders.

Lopez arrived yesterday and will see Velasco and Arosemena and make a number of speeches. He will also visit Guayaquil. Saudade is picking up the tab, and good publicity is already coming out.

Quito — 4 September 1961

Arosemena is cementing his political support from the CTE. Today the Senate under his prodding gave 50,000 sucres to the CTE for its national convention, scheduled for later this month in Ambato. The CTE responded with thanks from the Revolutionary Socialist sierra Labor Senator and invited Arosemena to address the convention's closing session; he accepted.

The CTE's campaign against the decrees on unification and taxes continues, along with promotion of a general strike, the date of which still hasn't been set.

Our PCE penetration agents report joy in the party over Arosemena's cooperation with the CTE and the extreme left generally—but leftist leaders are worried about his alcoholism and will be careful not to get burned by getting too closely associated with him.

In a few days we are going to bug the Czech Legation. For months Noland has had Otto Kladensky eliciting information from the Czechs on possible permanent locations for the Legation, and they finally signed a contract on a large house now nearing completion. On checking the building records, Noland discovered that the engineer in charge of construction is a friend of his from the University Sports League. Noland also knows the owner of the house, but after discussions with the engineer he decided not to speak to the owner for fear he would oppose risking his contract.

Equipment has arrived from headquarters for five or six installations, and the audio technicians are already here studying the building plans to determine how the rooms will be used. Their first priority is the code-room, followed by the Minister's office, and then studies and bedrooms.

Since the house is in one of Quito's nicest new areas,

we have plenty of support bases available for use during the installation. The plan is for the two audio technicians to enter the house at night with the engineer who luckily speaks English. I will be in an observation post overlooking the house which is a back bedroom of the home of an Embassy USIS officer. Noland and Captain Vargas,‡ Chief of Police Intelligence, and several of Vargas's strong-arm boys, will be in a support base in the apartment of Noland's administrative assistant who lives only two blocks from the target house. We will have walkie-talkie communications between the target house, my OP and the support base. If anything goes wrong, we will call on Vargas and his boys to step in and take over "officially" while our audio technicians make a getaway. Vargas and his boys won't know why they're on standby unless they're needed.

Quito — 20 September 1961

The first try for the audio operation against the Czech Legation failed. It was the technicians' fault and they were lucky not to have been caught. Bunglers! Everything went perfectly until about five o'clock in the morning when, as I was fighting to keep awake, I noticed the two technicians hurrying out of the house with their suitcases of equipment and running down the street to the getaway car. The engineer went running after them and they all drove away. I advised Noland by walkie-talkie and we went to the Embassy to rejoin the technicians.

Incredible story. They worked all night making three installations in the walls and were about to plaster over the transmitters when they were surprised by four Indian guards who had been asleep in another room all night. The engineer is known to the Indians, who were told by the owner not to let anyone enter the house, and he told them our frightened technicians were simply some electricians he brought to work. At five o'clock in the morning? While the engineer occupied the Indians, the technicians ripped the installations out of the walls and packed up.

The Czechs are visiting the house every day and are bound to notice the big holes left where the installations were ripped out. Noland gave the engineer some money to buy silence from the Indians but the engineer will have difficulty making explanations to the Czechs. He'll just have to play dumb and hope the Indians keep quiet.

It may be too late to try again because the Czechs will soon be moving in, so I suppose headquarters will ask for telephone tapping instead. We have technical problems on this operation too—the tap on the Cuban Embassy still isn't working right. Headquarters wanted us to try a new type of equipment that actuates the tape-recorders from the sound on the telephone wires instead of from changes of voltage. The trouble is that the wires pick up a near-by radio station and all we're getting is reels and reels of music.

The only real casualty of this botched job will probably be my dog. Poor Lanita. I tested the dog tranquilizer on him last week just in case the Czechs suddenly put guard dogs at the house—several years ago the station spent about five nights using this special powder mixed with hamburger meat, but they couldn't get the Czechs' dogs to sleep so they could make an entry. Now, however, only a few minutes after I gave Lanita the prescribed dose he began to fade away. Hours passed and he just went into a coma. The vet came the next day and took him away, saying his central nervous system was paralyzed. He's still at the kennels and if he dies I will send a big bill to the TSD.

Quito — 24 September 1961

The CTE convention got underway in Ambato yesterday and it was almost like the Congress. Arosemena was one of the guests, and when the ceremonies began a group of Velasquistas who had infiltrated the theater began shouting *vivas* to Velasco and *abajos* to Arosemena and communism. The CTE people started shouting *vivas* to Cuba and Arosemena and a vast fist-fight ensued. Pistols were fired into the air, stink-bombs were set off, and only when the police arrived and filled the theater with tear-gas could the brawl be stopped. It continued in the street outside, however, while the inauguration ceremony began in the lingering stench of tear-gas combined with stink-bombs.

Velasco simply cannot learn to compromise; this episode can only be counter-productive.

Quito — 25 September 1961

Now I know what happened to the agents in Cuba on the other end of the secret-writing channel. *El Comercio* this morning carries a front-page article on the arrest of Luis Toroella‡ and the other AMBLOOD agents and a story about their plan to assassinate Castro. The article is a wire-service dispatch from Havana based on yesterday's Cuban government press release and the *El Comercio* article is naturally headlined with reference to the Quito–Havana secret-writing channel.

Apparently the agents told everything, but the story doesn't include the number of the Quito post-office box, which is under Colonel Paredes's true name. I sent a priority cable to the Miami station asking that they inform us if the box number was revealed, because Colonel Paredes will need to cover himself to protect the surveillance team. The agents undoubtedly were arrested several months ago, perhaps at the time of the Bay of Pigs invasion, but Miami should have told us so we could cancel the box and perhaps destroy the records of the name of the holder.

I hadn't known they were planning to assassinate Castro but the press report reveals a detailed plan using bazookas in an ambush near the Havana sports complex. The radio channel must have been used for this operation. No indication on how they were caught—I hope it wasn't from my bad sw technique. No indication either of when they'll get the *paredón*[1]—maybe already.

---

1. Wall against which people are executed by the firing-squad.

Quito — 3 October 1961

The CTE set tomorrow as the day for the twenty-four-hour general strike against the July economic decrees. They claim 500 unions will participate and have been joined by the FEUE and by the Socialist Party of Manuel Naranjo. Velasco described the strike as a proclamation of revolution against his government, adding that if the new taxes are repealed there will be no money for "teachers, police and military."

For the past few days the government has been promoting a propaganda campaign against the strike. Large numbers of "unions" which are really Velasquista political organizations have been publishing statements of boycott. But the only real unions boycotting the strike are the Catholic CEDOC and our own free trade-union movement including CROCLE, both of which are for annulment of the taxes but against strengthening the CTE.

Tonight Baquero de la Calle, our Minister of Labor, made a nationwide radio broadcast in which he called the strike a subversive political action having nothing to do with labor matters, to counter CTE insistence that the strike is purely for economic motives having nothing to do with politics. Both are wrong because the strike is both political and economic, but we're against it because of its extreme-left promotion.

No one doubts there will be violence when the strikers set up road-blocks to stop transportation. We've set up special communications with our police agents to get timely news on their reports from around the country. Tension is high.

Quito — 4 October 1961

Velasco is truly incomprehensible. This morning most of the commercial activities in Quito and Guayaquil were normal and it was evident that the strike would be only partially successful. However, by noon the police cavalry and Army tanks had made such a show of force that everything closed, and as the afternoon went on the strike became total in both cities. If the government hadn't created such a climate of fear the strike would probably have been a failure. But there was considerable violence in the provinces, especially at Tulcan, on the Colombian border. Several have been killed and wounded there.

Quito — 6 October 1961

The strike continues in Tulcan. Yesterday a Congressional Commission that included Manuel Naranjo went there along with the Minister of Government and other high police and security officials. The meeting of the Congressional Commission, the Minister's group, and the Tulcan strike commission turned into a political rally against Velasco and the government. The crowd, in fact, became so menacing that the Minister had to seek refuge in a government building under military protection.

Today a popular strike committee in the coastal province of Esmeraldas decided to follow the lead in Tulcan by extending the strike indefinitely.

Velasco continues the hard line. Four of the principal CTE leaders are being held since the day before the strike, and an arrest list of nineteen others has been published.

Quito — 11 October 1961

Velasco ended the strikes in Tulcan and Esmeraldas by promising public works, and tomorrow he goes to Tulcan to listen to complaints. A few days ago in Guayaquil he again defended unification and the new taxes, but he had the Mayor accuse Arosemena of subverting public order from the Presidency of the Congress. The Congress is now in its thirty-day extraordinary period, but there is little sign that anything of significance will result—probably more riots and clashes with Velasco. No one expects the lull of the past two days to continue.

Today the national golf tournament ended: I was awful but Noland and his wife played well. I'm skipping the celebrations at the club tonight because Janet is due to deliver any day. Her obstetrician is the Quito golf champion and will be leading the party tonight. I hope his early prediction of delivery on Columbus's Day will be slightly off because he won't be in condition tomorrow.

Quito — 12 October 1961

He was right! I had to get Alberto out of the golf-club at five o'clock this morning. Miraculously everything was perfect—a boy.

Quito — 16 October 1961

The political security office of the Ministry of Government has invented a "plot" as a pretext for arresting opposition leaders. It's so unlikely that it will probably make Velasco look worse than ever. For the past three days political-security agents have been arresting opposition leaders, including a leftist deputy who tried to question the Minister of Defense last August, and some of the rightist leaders of the National Defense Front. Luckily none of our agents is among the sixteen arrested although the security agents are looking for communists and conservatives alike.

The "plot" was announced today by the Director-General of Security who runs the political security arm of the Ministry of Government—an office we've purposely stayed far away from. Leaders of the "plot," which was to break out tomorrow night, are from the extreme right and the extreme left. A sizeable quantity of arms was put on display, said to be of Iron Curtain origin and found in the homes of communists during raids. No thinking person could believe such a transparent fabrication, but Velasco obviously hopes it will rekindle the support he needs from the poor and uneducated if he decides to close the Congress by force.

In answer to the arrests and "plot" the Liberals, Conservatives, Social Christians, democratic Socialists and the fascist ARNE all joined today in a coordinating bureau to fight assumption of dictatorial powers by Velasco.

Jorge Acosta,‡ the Minister of the Treasury, returned from Washington today. He tried to make the trip sound successful by telling reporters of several loans that are "pending" and "ready to be signed," but he wasn't able to bring immediate relief. Velasco must certainly be disappointed.

Almost unnoticed in this atmosphere of crisis was the resignation today of Jose Baquero de la Calle, our Minister of Labor. Velasco wanted to get him out, so he let him fire the Guayaquil Fire Chief for irregular use of funds, then canceled Baquero's action, leaving the agent no choice but to resign. He has been an ineffective minister and not a particularly effective agent either, so Saudade isn't too sorry to see him fired. Now he'll try to ease him off the payroll.

Quito — 17 October 1961

A shoot-out in the Congress last night has the whole country in an uproar, and rumors are beginning to circulate that there may be a military move against Velasco.

At a joint Congressional session last night the loyalist Velasquista mob packed the galleries and began hurling orange and banana peelings as well as the worst insults they could articulate. Loyalist Velasquista legislators joined the rioters in the galleries, and when Arosemena, who was presiding, ordered the galleries to be cleared the police refused to act. Stones began to fly from the galleries and opposition legislators sought shelter under their desks while others formed a protective shield around Arosemena.

By one o'clock this morning, after nearly four hours

of rioting, shots also began to be fired from the galleries, some directed right at Arosemena's desk. He finally pulled out his own revolver, emptied it into the air, and left the chamber, claiming that over forty policemen were in the galleries in civilian dress with their service revolvers.

Today Velasco denied that he is seeking to install a dictatorship, while the loyalist Velasquista legislators are justifying last night's riots as necessary for the preservation of Ecuadorean democracy. Arosemena said today he will charge Velasco before the Supreme Court with trying to assassinate him. In Guayaquil today police with tear-gas, firing weapons into the air, broke up a FEUE manifestation against the government. This can't go on forever.

Quito — 24 October 1961

Yesterday the Minister of Government resigned rather than face political interrogation by Congress over repression since the general strike three weeks ago. Velasco named Jorge Acosta as Acting Minister of Government, which is a break for the station, but Noland thinks the situation may be too desperate to hope for productive work with Acosta.

Today Velasco finally made his expected move for Conservative Party support. Noland has been insisting with Davila that he do all he can to sustain the Conservatives in making a break with Cuba their condition for supporting Velasco. Thus Velasco's offer today of the Ministry of Labor was rejected by the Conservatives, and Velasco's position continues to weaken. Acosta told Noland that Velasco is as stubborn as ever on breaking with Cuba, but he is going to do all he can to convince his uncle that the only hope of survival for the government is to break with Cuba and gain Conservative backing.

I haven't seen anything in writing on whether the Agency or State Department want to see Velasco survive or fall—only that our policy is to force a break with Cuba. The obvious danger is that Velasco will fall because of his obstinacy and that a pliable Arosemena, strongly influenced by the CTE, FEUE and other undesirables, will end up in power. This makes Acosta's influence on Velasco for the break absolutely crucial.

Quito — 27 October 1961

We weren't able to re-enter the Czech Legation before they moved in, so the audio operation is definitely lost.

A couple of nights ago someone fired shots through the huge front windows of the Legation, but a bomb placed in the garden at the same time failed to explode. The windows are very expensive and have to be imported from the U.S., so that will keep the Czechs off balance for a while—what's left of the windows is all boarded up. We didn't instruct any agents to make this terrorist attack, but Noland thinks it was Captain Vargas, our Chief of Police Intelligence. Vargas's office is in charge of investigating the attack.

I've just taken over a new operation—the Tulcan portion of the ECACTOR political-action project. Noland had been meeting irregularly with a leader of the Conservative Youth organization there, Enrique Molina,‡ but guidance and funding were difficult because the agent could come to Quito only infrequently and Noland lacks the time to go there: two long days to drive to the Colombian border and back.

The drive between Quito and Tulcan is so spectacular that it's beyond adequate expression. There are green fertile valleys, snow-capped volcanoes, arid canyons eroded by snaking rivers, lakes smooth as glass, panoramic views from heights almost as from an airplane. All the way the cobble-stoned Pan-American highway winds around and up and down the mountains, passing through colorful Indian villages where every few kilometers the hats, ponchos, even the hairstyles change to distinguish one community from another.

I took money to Molina and told him to use it for the anti-communist front in Carchi province but he'll probably use it mainly for propaganda against Velasco.

I also set up a communications channel for him to report intelligence on political unrest and we will try to alternate meetings; one month he'll come to Quito and the next I'll go there.

Quito — 1 November 1961

New violence broke out yesterday in Cuenca when a FEUE manifestation against the government was severely repressed by police. The students had been joined by a large number of people and when the demonstrators attacked government buildings the Army was called in. Seven persons were wounded in the shooting.

Velasco announced that in spite of the violence he will make an official visit to Cuenca for its provincial independence celebrations the day after tomorrow. There is much speculation that more violence will occur because the people in the Cuenca area are so angry at Velasco's failure to alleviate the effects of declining prices of the area's products—especially Panama hats. Hunger migrations from the province, a rare occurrence even in Ecuador, have been going on for some time, and representatives of the Quito government are increasingly unpopular in this strongly Conservative and Catholic region.

Reports from our police agents indicate that the rioting in Cuenca is continuing today.

Quito — 3 November 1961

Military rule was imposed yesterday in the province of Azuay (of which Cuenca is the capital) as at least ten more people were wounded during a popular uprising. Velasco fired the provincial governor and other leading government officials and sent Jorge Acosta, Acting Minister of Government, to Cuenca for a first-hand inspection. Acosta's trip only caused further protest, which was followed by more arrests. Municipal authorities in Cuenca canceled the independence celebrations scheduled for today and asked Velasco not to come.

But Velasco is in Cuenca right now, and many reports are coming from the radio and the police that serious new rioting and shooting is going on.

Quito — 4 November 1961

In Cuenca yesterday at least two were killed and eight more wounded. On arrival Velasco headed a procession on foot from the airport into town—a grave provocation against the local hostility reflected in funeral wreaths and black banners decorating the houses in sign of mourning. Along the way Velasco and his committee were jeered, taunted and finally attacked with stones and clubs. Shooting followed as the riot was suppressed, but Velasco insisted on presiding at the military parade. Afterwards, however, he was forced to give his speech in an indoor hall where he blamed the violence on opposition political leaders.

From Cuenca Velasco is motoring to several small towns for speeches and then to Guayaquil. In the Congress today the debate over events in Cuenca went on for eight hours. The CTE, FEUE and Revolutionary Socialists have condemned Velasco, along with the Conservative Party and the Social Christian Movement. A strange alliance for our political-action agents but momentum against Velasco dominates the scene.

Jorge Acosta, Acting Minister of Government, got Velasco's approval to expel another Cuban—this time it's the Chargé d'Affaires because the Ambassador is in Havana right now. After meeting today with the Cuban Chargé, the Minister of Foreign Affairs announced that the Chargé will be leaving. He gave vague reasons, suggesting an association between certain Ecuadorean political figures and the Cuban government, but he emphasized that the Chargé's departure does not mean any change of policy towards Cuba. The Chargé on the other hand said he is leaving for Cuba voluntarily. It's clear that the Foreign Minister was reluctant to follow Acosta's order to expel the Cuban—and it's equally doubtful that this desperate move by Velasco to obtain support from the Conservative Party and other rightists will work. Acosta told Noland that Velasco still refuses to break completely with the Cubans, but he is also going to move against the *Prensa Latina* representative.

Velasco finally got some good news on economic aid. Two large loans have just been signed in Washington: one a 4.7 million dollar loan for development of African palm oil and sheep ranching and the other a 5 million dollar loan for middle-class housing. Good publicity but no early effects expected.

Quito — 5 November 1961

Today Jorge Acosta announced that the Cuban Chargé is being expelled as *persona non grata.* His clarification has been broadcast continually over the government radio network. The Cuban Embassy, however, insisted (in order to save face) that the Chargé was never told that he is being expelled, while at the Foreign Ministry confirmation was made of expulsion rather than voluntary return to Cuba.

Quito — 6 November 1961

If he goes, Velasco will not have gone quietly. More violence today, both in Quito and in Guayaquil, where eleven have been killed and at least fourteen wounded —all students and workers. We've been sending one report after another to headquarters and the Guayaquil base is doing the same.

Congress went into session at noon and Arosemena accused Velasco of having violated the Constitution. A FEUE delegation visited the Congress to express support, and about three o'clock this afternoon the Congressional Palace was sealed off by Army troops and telephone communications were cut.

This morning the entire Cabinet resigned, and Velasco, who only arrived from Guayaquil at noon, spent most of the afternoon visiting military units. He also made a radio broadcast in which he accused Arosemena of proclaiming himself a dictator, adding that he was firing Arosemena as Vice-President.

I'll be spending the night here in the Embassy listening to the police and military radios and taking calls from agents in the street. The latest is that Arosemena and other legislators were allowed to leave the Congressional Palace just after midnight, and as they walked towards Arosemena's house a few blocks away they were arrested by Velasco's Director-General of Security. Arosemena and the others have been taken to jail, but several agents believe that it's a deliberately dangerous scheme on the part of Arosemena to force Velasco to unconstitutional action—which could provoke the military to move against him.

In spite of the Cabinet resignations, Acosta continues to function as Minister of Government. This morning he expelled the *Prensa Latina* correspondent, a Cuban who had been expelled last year under Ponce but had slipped back into the country while Araujo was Minister of Government. We're sending situation reports to headquarters practically every hour.

Quito — 7 November 1961

It's all over for Velasco but the succession isn't decided. About five o'clock this morning the engineers battalion in Quito rebelled on the grounds that Velasco had violated the Constitution in arresting Arosemena, but was attacked by loyalist Army units. A ceasefire occurred about 8 a.m. for removal of dead and wounded and later in the morning the Military High Command decided that both Velasco and Arosemena had violated the Constitution. They later named the President of the Supreme Court to take over as President of an interim government. Velasco has accepted this decision and the Supreme Court President has taken over the offices in the Presidential Palace.

Velasco visited several of the loyalist military units after leaving the Presidential Palace this afternoon and according to military intelligence reports he is at the home of friends but asking for asylum in a Latin American embassy. Acosta received asylum earlier today in the Venezuelan Embassy.

Arosemena is making a fight of his own to succeed to the Presidency. He and the other legislators were released from prison tonight and went immediately to the Legislative Palace where Arosemena convoked a joint session and was himself named President. The constitutional limit on Congress's extended session ends at midnight tonight, but the Congress is remaining in the Palace with Arosemena.

Tonight I sleep in the Embassy again—just in case the Military Command decides to move in favor of either of our two Presidents. Let's hope they stick with the President of the Supreme Court, a rightist who would be favorably disposed to a break with Cuba and suppression of the extreme left in general.

Quito — 8 November 1961

It's Arosemena! This morning the Legislative Palace was surrounded by Army paratroopers and tanks but just after noon Air Force fighters flew low over the Palace firing their guns into the air to intimidate the Army units. When it became clear that the Air Force was backing Arosemena and the Congress, the Supreme Court President resigned—he has lasted as President only eighteen hours—and the Army units were withdrawn from the Palace. The Military High Command recognized Arosemena later this afternoon.

During the hours before the outcome was known today, URJE and FEUE demonstrations in favor of Arosemena broke out in different parts of Quito and later expressions of support to Arosemena have poured in from all over the country, especially from the CTE organizations, FEUE and URJE.

While the Legislative Palace was still surrounded this morning Arosemena named a centrist Cabinet consisting of two Liberals, two Democratic Socialists, one Social Christian, one Conservative and three independents. One of the Socialists is Manuel Naranjo who was named Minister of the Treasury. This afternoon

Arosemena has been meeting with supporters, including Araujo whom Arosemena described as "that great fighter." But when Araujo got up on a chair and tried to give a speech to the crowd milling about, he only got out "Noble people of Quito," when he was shouted down with much ridicule. Arosemena's first act, even though he won't be inaugurated until tomorrow, was to convoke a special session of Congress for election of a new Vice-President and other business. Reinaldo Varea Donoso was presiding officer at the first session today.

Velasco hasn't given up—quite. From the Mexican Embassy he issued a statement that he hasn't resigned and he again reminded everyone of the 400,000 votes he got last year. Four times elected and three times deposed: a winner on the stump but a loser in office. If he had only broken with Cuba he could have won Conservative and other right support and weathered the left campaign over economic issues.

Quito — 9 November 1961

This morning before the inaugural ceremony the FEUE organized "Operation Clean-up" which was a symbolic scrubbing down and sweeping up at the Presidential Palace to cleanse the place before Arosemena took over.

Arosemena and his new Cabinet then led a march of thousands from the Legislative Palace to the Presidential Palace at Independence Plaza. In his speech Arosemena described Velasco's régime as one that started with 400,000 in favor and ended with 4,000,000 against. In promising action instead of flowery speeches, he pledged that his government will be one of peace and harmony and that he will be President of all Ecuadoreans, not just the privileged few. But from our point of view the most important of his remarks was his pledge to continue diplomatic relations with Cuba.

In other ominous indications from the inaugural speeches the President of the CTE attacked "yankee imperialism" while praising the Cuban revolution and calling for the formation of a Popular Revolutionary Front.

(Formation of the Front has already been reported by our PCE penetration agents and will include the CTE, Revolutionary Socialists, PCE, URJE, Ecuadorean Federation of Indians, and a new student front called the Revolutionary University Student Movement.) The FEUE President also spoke, recounting the participation of the students in Velasco's overthrow. Although he's a moderate and was elected with support from the Guayaquil base student operation, opposition to Velasco has been growing too strongly in recent months for economic and other motives to permit Alberto Alarcon and his agents to keep the moderate FEUE leadership from supporting Arosemena.

Diplomatic relations with the Ecuadorean government are continuing as if Velasco had died or resigned —which means there is no question of formal recognition of the new government. Everything's been legal and constitutional.

Quito — 11 November 1961

The general political atmosphere is one of relief, optimism, satisfaction—almost euphoria. After fourteen months of intimidation by Velasco, supporters of the traditional parties are happy to see Arosemena in power, at least for the moment.

Davila was elected President of the Chamber of Deputies for the Extraordinary Congressional Session. Reinaldo Varea was elected Vice-President of the Senate—offering, in his acceptance speech, to die before violating the legal norms "of this new and unmerited honor." Congress then recessed for two days and on Monday they will reconvene to elect a new Vice-President. There's going to be plenty of tension over the weekend as deals are made to see who becomes number two to Arosemena. The importance of this election is very great because no one knows how long Arosemena can last with his frequent drinking bouts. Noland thinks Varea, one of the leading candidates, has a good chance. The Rector of Central University, a Liberal-leaning independent, is the main contender and is backed by the FEUE and extreme left.

Velasco was put on a Panagra flight to Panama this afternoon. Most of the country is peaceful again and the vandalism and looting of stores has disappeared. From the general strike on 4 October until now, at least thirty-two have died in five cities and many more were wounded, forty-five in Quito alone. It wasn't exactly a bloodless *coup*.

Quito — 13 November 1961

Noland has pulled off a *coup* of his own. Over the weekend Varea called for a meeting at the Hotel Quito safe house. He wanted to know if Noland knew where he might get support for election as Vice-President, particularly whether Noland thought the Conservatives might support him. Noland said he thought so, but naturally had to be tactful in order not to reveal any relation with Davila or other rightist agents.

Later Noland met with Davila who asked for advice on whom the Conservatives should support for Vice-President. Noland was able to promote Varea discreetly, reasoning that if the Central University Rector were elected, the Vice-Rector, a Revolutionary Socialist, would take over the University. Davila pledged to throw the Conservative vote to Varea. Later Davila and Varea met for agreement, and Noland is convinced that neither knew of the other's meeting with him.

This morning a notice in *El Comercio* placed through Gustavo Salgado compromised the Rector pretty badly. It was an announcement of support attributed to the Ecuadorean Communist Party and URJE. Denial will come but too late because Congress reconvened at noon to elect the Vice-President.

The galleries were packed by the CTE and FEUE militants screaming for the Rector's election. Davila was the presiding officer and on the first ballot Varea got sixty-four votes—the most of the four candidates but twelve short of the two-thirds needed. When the results of this vote were announced the galleries began to riot.

Varea was elected on the next ballot and the FEUE and CTE people really broke loose, showering Davila with stones, spit and wads of paper. No police around as usual.

Varea, in his inaugural speech after Davila proclaimed him Vice-President, seemed a little too humble: "You will see that I lack the capacity to be Vice-President of the Republic. I am full of defects, but against this is my life, which I have filled with modesty and sacrifice. You and I with the help of God can solve little by little the great problems that affect the Ecuadorean people." Noland said he's going to raise Varea from seven hundred to one thousand dollars a month, and if he gets to be President we'll pay him even more.

Senator Humphrey arrived yesterday and we're reporting on possible demonstrations against him. He'll visit Arosemena and address the Congress, but yesterday he was right on target in remarks to newsmen: the U.S. is ready to finance the development of poor countries but their governments have to effect agrarian, tax and administrative reforms. Otherwise the U.S. will just be financing eventual bolshevization.

Quito — 17 November 1961

Arosemena's government is not yet two weeks old but there are clear signs that he will have significant leftist participation in his régime. Appointments at the Minister and Sub-Secretary level like Manuel Naranjo, the new Minister of the Treasury, are certainly acceptable. But jobs on the middle level are increasingly falling into hands of Marxists and other leftists who are unfriendly to the U.S. even though they may not be formally affiliated with the PCE or the Revolutionary Socialists. The objectionable appointments are mostly in education and the welfare and social-security systems, although the new governments of Guayaquil and Guayas Province are also taking on an unfortunate coloring.

Both in the station and at the Guayaquil base we have been preparing memoranda on the new faces in Arosemena's government for the Ambassador, the Consul-

General and the State Department in Washington. The memoranda are based on our file information and also on queries to our PCE penetration agents on Party reaction to the appointments. First indications are that influence from the extreme left will be much greater under Arosemena than under Velasco.

Reaction from the State Department and from headquarters is moderately alarmist and headquarters has sent special requirements on continued close monitoring of Arosemena appointments. The worry is that this is only the beginning and that Ecuador will continue sliding to the left much as Brazil is moving that way already. On the Cuban question the Foreign Ministry announced today that the Cuban Chargé expelled by Velasco can now remain—in the confusion during Velasco's last days he had stayed on in Quito.

To counter these developments we are going to start a new round of propaganda and political-action operations through the ECACTOR agents such as Davila, Perez, the National Defense Front and propaganda agents such as Gustavo Salgado. Reinaldo Varea, the Vice-President, will also be extremely important because he is well-known as an anti-communist. He's a retired lieutenant-colonel in the Army and he studied at Fort Riley and Fort Leavenworth in the U.S. He was also Ecuadorean military attaché in Washington and advisor to the Ecuadorean representative on the Inter-American Defense Board, Sub-Secretary of Defense and later Minister of Defense.

As an opening and somewhat indirect thrust, the Guayaquil base had the CROCLE labor organization publish a half-page statement in the newspapers yesterday on the danger of communism and the subservience of the CTE to the WFTU in Prague. It called for repression of communism, warned against opening diplomatic relations with the Soviet Union, and forecast the establishment of the Ecuadorean Confederation of Free Trade Union Organizations as a democratic alternative to the CTE.

Arosemena has started a shake-up in the internal security forces. Today an investigation was started to verify the lists of agents on the role of the National

Security Directorate, the political security office responsible for Arosemena's arrest on the night of 6–7 November. It is expected that many of the agents listed simply do not exist and that their salaries were pocketed by top officers of the NSD.

The top echelons of the National Police are also being shaken up. Captain Jose Vargas, Chief of the Police Intelligence organization, will undoubtedly be purged because he is well known as the leader of a secret pro-Velasco organization within the police. We're hoping, however, that Lieutenant Luis Sandoval,‡ the chief technician under Vargas and fairly apolitical, will not be moved.

Quito — 20 November 1961

The station program for penetrating the PCE is suddenly in better shape than ever. The Pichincha PCE members have just elected a new Provincial Committee and not only was Basantes re-elected but Cardenas and Luis Vargas‡ were elected too. This gives us three agents on the eight-member committee which is comparable to a national Central Committee because of the growing split between the coastal leadership under PCE Secretary-General Pedro Saad and the sierra leadership under Rafael Echeverria, chairman of the Pichincha Provincial Committee.

I've taken over another operation from Noland—this time it's Colonel Oswaldo Lugo,‡ our highest-level penetration of the National Police. The other night Noland introduced me to Lugo who advised that he has been appointed Chief of the National Police in the Southern Region with headquarters in Cuenca. He won't be leaving for a few weeks, and meanwhile he will introduce me to his stepson, Edgar Camacho,‡ a university student who will serve as cutout for reports from Lugo's sub-agents in the CTE. Lugo expects to come to Quito at least once a month when we'll meet, but he'll send urgent reports through Camacho. A very friendly, intelligent and sharp officer.

Operations at the Guayaquil base got a jolt yesterday

when their most important labor and political intelligence agent died suddenly. He was Emilio Estrada Icaza,‡ director of one of Ecuador's largest banks, president of a fertilizer company, former Mayor of Guayaquil and well-known collector of pre-Hispanic artifacts. It was through Estrada that the base organized the successful campaign to oust Saad from the Senate and then formed the CROCLE labor organization.

Quito — 19 December 1961

There has been a flurry of activity prior to the Christmas lull, with little of particularly happy significance to us. Three days ago Arosemena was the principal speaker at the Congress of the CTE-controlled Ecuadorean Indian Federation. He shared the platform with the CTE President, a Revolutionary Socialist; Carlos Rodriguez, the PCE organizer in charge of the Indian Federation; and Miguel Lechon, an Indian and PCE member who was elected President of the Federation. In his speech to the thousands of Indians trucked into Quito for the ceremony, Arosemena promised quick action to abolish the *huasipungo*.

The Indian Congress was followed yesterday by the Congress of coastal campesinos which is the CTE's organization for rural workers on the coast. Arosemena was also the principal speaker at this Congress which, like the Indian Congress, was highly successful for the extreme left.

Student operations of the Guayaquil base under Alberto Alarcon have suffered another defeat. The National FEUE Congress recently ended in Guayaquil and the extreme left dominated. Guayaquil University, with the FEUE chapter run by URJE militants, will be the national seat for the coming year. Delegations from the universities of Cuenca and Portoviejo, which are controlled by Alarcon, walked out of the Congress when resolutions, supporting the Cuban revolution and condemning the Alliance for Progress, were passed. Protests against the take-over by the extreme left were also made through Davila and the Catholic University Youth

Organization and through Wilson Almeida, editor of *Voz Universitaria.*

We also had a setback in student operations when a Revolutionary Socialist was elected President of the Quito FEUE chapter. After the voting the new officers issued a statement supporting Arosemena on the need for agrarian reform and on "non-intervention" with regard to Cuba.

Now both the Quito and the Guayaquil FEUE chapters, as well as Loja, are in extremist hands. Meanwhile URJE continues to dominate the streets. A few days ago a group of Cuban exiles (several hundred have arrived to reside in Guayaquil) was attacked by URJE militants as they reported to a government office to register.

Operations with the National Police are in transition. Jose Vargas‡ was not only relieved of command of the Police Intelligence unit—he is under arrest along with other members of his secret Velasquista police organization. Luckily Luis Sandoval was left untouched and will continue in the unit. I've been seeing him much more frequently since Vargas was removed and until we can evaluate the new Police Intelligence Chief, Major Pacifico de los Reyes,‡ Sandoval will be our main Police Intelligence contact—in effect he's a paid penetration agent. De los Reyes came to the station under a pretext related to some equipment we gave Vargas, but the visit was obviously to begin contact. Noland and I will alternate contact with him without telling him that I am meeting regularly with Sandoval.

Colonel Lugo has taken command in the Cuenca Zone. Regular communications with him will be through Edgar Camacho, his stepson, except on the trips he makes to Quito every month or so. He wants me to hold his salary and the salaries of his sub-agents for passing directly to him, so I imagine he'll come every month.

Progress continues on the formation of a national free labor confederation. On 16–17 December the existing free labor organizations led by CROCLE‡ held a convention for naming the organizing committee for the Constituent Congress of the national confederation—to be called the Ecuadorean Confederation of Free Trade

Union Organizations‡ (CEOSL). Enrique Amador, one of the Guayaquil base labor agents, was President of the convention and Adalberto Miranda Giron,‡ the base agent elected last year as Labor Senator from the coast, was a principal speaker. The Constituent Congress was set for late April of next year.

Nevertheless, serious problems are growing behind the facade of progress among the free trade-union groups. Mainly it's a question of job security and bureaucratic vanity among the leaders of the different organizations. Competition among them to get the best jobs in CEOSL, when it's established, is creating jealousies and friction. In early November, IO Division's most important Western Hemisphere labor agent, Serafino Romualdi‡ (AFL–CIO representative for Latin America), came to Guayaquil and tried to establish a little harmony. The convention just over was a result of his trip, but the various leaders are still fighting.

Now that Velasco is out, Gil Saudade's Popular Revolutionary Liberal Party is bound to decline if not disappear completely. He is going to move some of his agents from that party as fast as possible into the CEOSL organization, so that with salaried agents in place the organization will have some discipline and order. Otherwise it will be forever weak and no match for the CTE.

Our National Defense Front has issued another call for a break in relations with Cuba, but at the recent Conservative Party Convention it was decided to give general support to Arosemena while still insisting on a break with Cuba. (The photographs published on the Conservatives' meetings are embarrassing—they keep a crucifix, about half life-size, on the front of the speakers' table, and it looks like a Jesuit retreat.) Davila was elected Sub-Director-General of the Party. All the other political parties of importance have also held conventions, and all are continuing general support to Arosemena.

The State Department, too, is going to gamble on Arosemena and, perhaps, on the anti-communist tradition in the military. A few days ago a new loan was announced: 8 million dollars for budget support from the U.S. government—forty years at no interest. It had originally been negotiated by Jorge Acosta as Minister of the Treasury under Velasco.

Congress recessed until next August with practically no legislation to show for its 112-day session that cost over ten million sucres. Incredibly, Congress took no action to repeal the decree on unification of the exchange rate that had unified the opposition to Velasco. Arosemena and the CTE also seem to have forgotten their big issue.

Quito — 23 December 1961

The pace is slowing for the end-of-the-year celebrations and we've been taking advantage to make the rounds with whisky, cigarettes, golf-balls and other gifts. Noland is taking the new Administrative Assistant, Raymond Ladd,‡ around to meet the Quito travel-agent and tourism crowd so that he can take over and expand the station travel-control operations. The new principal agent will be Patricio Ponce,‡ an old friend of Noland and prominent bullfight figure, whom Ladd is going to set up in a cover office as soon as possible. In January I'll also turn the ECSTACY letter intercept over to Ladd.

We were fortunate to get Ladd for the administrative job, which is usually filled by a woman, because he can handle some operations too. During his previous assignment in San José, Costa Rica, he learned some operational techniques, and although he was refused the operations training (for lack of formal education) Noland wants to use him on non-sensitive matters. He works in perfectly because he's a champion golfer, poker addict and general hustler.

When I stop to think about the excitement and continual state of crisis over the past year, I realize that we've tried to attain only two goals and have failed at both. We haven't been able to bring about a break in diplomatic relations with Cuba, and we haven't been able to get the government to take action against the growing strength of local communist and related movements. With Velasco, we made no direct effort to overthrow his government. But by financing the Conservatives and Social Christians in the quasi-religious campaign against Cuba and communism, we helped them destroy Velasco's power base among the poor who had voted so overwhelmingly for him. By the time Velasco introduced the new taxes and unification of the exchange rate, our campaign, led by the rightists and assisted by inflation, had already turned popular opinion against him. It was an easy matter then for the CTE, URJE, FEUE and others with extreme-left inclinations to usurp the anti-Velasco banner using Arosemena as their anti-oligarchical symbol and as legitimate successor.

Our principal tasks in the coming months will be to renew the campaign against relations with Cuba through the National Defense Front and other operations while monitoring carefully the penetration by the extreme left of Arosemena's government—and their preparations for armed action. Although both the second and third in succession to Arosemena are on our payroll, it would be difficult to argue that the present security situation is an improvement on the Velasco régime.

The fundamental reasons why there is any security problem at all remain the same: concentration of wealth and power in the hands of the very few with marginalization of the masses of the people. Such extreme injustice can only encourage people to resort to extreme solutions, but there is still no sign of the reforms that everyone talks about. I wonder about reforms. Certainly the attitudes of my friends—whether blue-blood conservatives, new-rich liberals or concerned independents—are not encouraging. Their contemptuous term for the poor who supported Velasco—the *chusma*—shows how much distance has still to be traveled.

My son is only ten weeks old but already he's beginning to show some personality and awareness. Proud father, yes I am—he was baptized three weeks ago in the old church in Cotocollao in a beautiful white dress given by the families in the station.

I'm not sure what to do about Janet. We continue to grow apart for lack of common interests. She knows practically nothing of my work, and her lack of interest in politics and the language has turned her to bridge with other American wives who tend to complain over trivia. I must help her, but the strain of daily events leaves so little energy—except for golf where I'm spending most of my free time. It's an unfair escape, I know, but it's also a relaxation.

Quito — 2 January 1962

The Cuban Sub-Secretary of Foreign Relations, Carlos Olivares, is back in Ecuador—this time drumming up support in advance of the OAS Foreign Ministers Conference scheduled for later this month in Punta del Este, Uruguay. At the Conference, the U.S. government hopes to get some collective action going against Cuba—at least a resolution that all countries still having diplomatic and commercial relations with Cuba move to break them. Yesterday Olivares met with Arosemena at a beach resort and Arosemena reaffirmed his policy of non-intervention towards Cuba. Today he said, Ecuador will be against any sanctions against Cuba at the Punta del Este Conference.

One reason why we're trying to isolate Cuba is that headquarters believe the Cubans are training thousands of Latin Americans in guerrilla warfare, sabotage and terrorism. Every station is required to report on travel to Cuba, or to Moscow or Prague, which are longer but also widely used routes to Cuba. Right now there are at least sixty-two Ecuadoreans in Havana invited for the celebrations of the third anniversary of the revolution. Some no doubt will be funneled off to the training camps. Miguel Lechon, President of the Ecuadorean Federation of Indians, is in the group.

Quito — 16 January 1962

Our new campaign is off to a bang—literally. The national convention of URJE was to have opened in Cuenca two days ago but during the night before bombs exploded in the doorways of two Cuenca churches. There were no injuries from the bombs—the anti-communist militants under Carlos Arizaga Vega were careful—but large "spontaneous" demonstrations against the bombings occurred on the day the convention was to start. Public authorities then banned the URJE convention in order to avoid bloodshed.

The Conservative Party under Davila's direction has called on Arosemena for a definite political statement on Cuba and communism (the prelude to new Conservative pressure). He answered that Ecuadoreans should concentrate on national problems that are "above" the problem of Cuba. Davila is organizing a demonstration for the day after tomorrow in Quito in solidarity with the Cuenca one.

Yesterday the Popular Revolutionary Movement (formed by the PCE, URJE and other extreme leftist organizations when Arosemena took over) sent a delegation to visit the Minister of Government. They told him that the bombings in Cuenca were not their work and that they reject terrorism as a political instrument. Last night in Guayaquil Pedro Saad's home was bombed—again no one injured.

The main theme of our propaganda in recent days has been the shooting last month in Havana when a group of Cubans tried to obtain asylum in the Ecuadorean Embassy by crash-driving an automobile on to the grounds. Cuban security forces opened fire to impede them and several bodies were carried away.

Gil Saudade keeps grinding away with his international organizations. This time it's the Ecuadorean affiliate of the World Assembly of Youth‡ (WAY)—called the National Youth Council.‡ It groups together students, workers, sports organizations, rural and religious youth groups, Boy and Girl Scouts and the Junior Red Cross. Gil runs this operation through Juan Moeller‡ who is President of the Ecuadorean Junior Red Cross and who just put in another leader of the Junior Red Cross as Secretary-General of the Youth Council. The main business in coming months will be to arrange for Ecuadorean participation in the WAY Congress scheduled for August and to pass headquarters' guidance to the Ecuadorean leader on which issues to support and which to oppose.

Quito — 19 January 1962

The campaign is back in full swing in Quito. Yesterday's rally against Cuba and communism was enormous—and considerably helped by the government. After days of promotional work by the ECACTOR-financed organizers, yesterday morning the Minister of Government, a Liberal, prohibited public political demonstrations throughout the country until further notice including the rally planned for yesterday afternoon. His decision was based on the recent wave of bombings and the tension caused by our renewed campaign.

The organizers sent the word around that the rally would take place in spite of the prohibition as a show of solidarity with the recent demonstrations in Cuenca and Guayaquil. The crowd gathered at a theater on the edge of the downtown area, soon grew into thousands, and began to move towards the Independence Plaza. Police tried to stop it with tear-gas and cavalry but lost the pitched battle that followed in spite of wounding twelve people. The demonstrators also attacked an URJE counter-demonstration which quickly disappeared.

Once in the Independence Plaza the crowd frequently shouted against the government and Arosemena. Speakers attacked communism and Castro and called for a break in relations with Cuba while urging Ecuadorean support for a program of sanctions against Cuba at the coming Punta del Este Conference.

Yesterday, when the Minister of Government announced the prohibition of demonstrations he denounced the right's "battle plan" founded on the government's lack of definition on communism and Cuba. Today the Minister called for a pause in the fighting between Ecuadoreans over "external problems," while the Cardinal issued another anti-communist pastoral letter accusing the communists of the bombings in the Cuenca churches.

The campaign is getting under way in Tulcan as well. Yesterday an anti-communist demonstration was held in spite of the prohibition and afterwards the demonstrators clashed with leftists in a counter-demonstration.

The Ambassador is also active making propaganda that nicely complements ours. Yesterday with considerable publicity he presented a check to Manuel Naranjo‡ representing the second instalment of the 8 million dollar budget support loan announced just after Arosemena took over. Photographs of the Ambassador handing over the check were prominent in the newspapers this morning.

Quito — 21 January 1962

In Guayaquil the base financed a demonstration yesterday. Thousands turned out after a bomb exploded in the morning at the entrance to one of the main churches —again with no injuries. These bombings are mostly being done by a Social Christian squad in order to whip up emotions. One would think the people would realize this, but Renato Perez, Noland's principal Social Christian agent, says they can keep it up as long as is needed. Participating organizations in the Guayaquil demonstration were the Defense Front, our CROCLE labor organization, the Liberals, Conservatives, Social Christians and the fascist ARNE.

An anti-communist demonstration was also held yesterday in Riobamba thanks to the efforts of a new agent of Noland's named Davalos.‡ Through Renato Perez and Aurelio Davila, Noland is also getting money out for demonstrations in Loja and other provincial cities in days to come.

The Punta del Este Conference opens today but in spite of all the pressure we're bringing on the government through the right it appears that Ecuador will not support any joint move against Cuba.

Quito — 31 January 1962

The Punta del Este Conference finally ended yesterday. All our efforts to get sanctions against Cuba failed, thanks to opposition from countries like Ecuador. Even on the resolution to expel Cuba from the OAS only fourteen countries voted in favor with Ecuador among the abstentions.

Today the Social Christian Movement formally ended its participation in the Arosemena government, and the Conservative Party is issuing a statement against the government's position at Punta del Este. The Foreign Minister, a prominent Social Christian, will either have to resign or quit the party.

Last night, the Czech Legation was bombed again and the huge new windows just installed because of the October attack were completely shattered. I drove by the Legation on my way to work this morning and the carpenters were already at work boarding up again. The bombers escaped through the heavy fog last night—must have been the Social Christian squad.

Quito — 28 February 1962

Most of the important political parties have held conventions this month to begin preparations for the local, provincial and Congressional elections scheduled in June. Where possible we have instructed agents to push for resolutions on the Cuban and local communist issues.

Manuel Naranjo was only partially successful at the Socialist Party convention where his party decided to join again with the Liberals in the National Democratic Front as a joint electoral vehicle. The statement on re-establishing the Front called for struggle against the totalitarian movements now operating in Ecuador—but also affirmed the party's belief in Marxist philosophy as "adapted to the Ecuadorean political and economic reality." In a foreign policy statement issued two days after the convention closed, the principle of non-intervention in Cuba was sustained along with opposition to expulsion of Cuba from the OAS and to the economic blockade.

The Conservative Party has issued another statement insisting that Arosemena dismiss communists and pro-communists from the administration while alleging that a communist plot is underway for uprisings to occur soon throughout the country. The Conservatives in Azuay Province (Cuenca) have elected Carlos Arizaga Vega,‡ one of our principal ECACTOR agents there, as a party director.

Araujo is also active trying to build an organization that will attract leftist Velasquista voters. His new People's Action Movement held an assembly today in preparation for the elections.

Our own campaign continues to consist of stimulating charges of communist leanings of appointees in the government. Debate has also continued over Ecuadorean failure to back resolutions against Cuba at Punta del Este, and Arosemena is being forced on the defensive. Through political action and propaganda operations we are trying to repeat what we did with Velasco: cut away political support on the Cuban and communist issues so that only the extreme left is left on his side. For his part Arosemena has been protesting frequently in public that communists will never become an influence in his government.

The Argentine break with Cuba a few weeks ago, which was the climax of increasing military pressure on President Frondizi, has already generated a spate of new rumors that the Ecuadorean military will bring similar pressure on Arosemena. The rumors are mostly rightist-inspired as suggestive propaganda targeted at the military, but they may well have an effect—especially since less than three weeks after the break Argentina got 150 million dollars in new Alliance for Progress money. Now only Ecuador and five other Latin American countries still have relations with Cuba.

Quito — 1 March 1962

In another effort to create military ill-feeling towards the left, the Social Christians infiltrated a FEUE march today in order to shout insults against the military that appeared to come from the marchers. The march was through the downtown area to the Independence Plaza where Arosemena spoke and the leaders of the march presented a petition for increased government support to the universities. The situation is indeed grave—professors at Central University, for example, haven't been paid since last December.

The Social Christian plan worked perfectly. The march was headed by the President of the FEUE, the Rector and Vice-Rector of the University and the Ministers of Education and Government. At the Independence Plaza just before the speeches began, shouts were clearly heard of "Death to the Army" and "More universities and less Army." An almost electric current is passing through the officer corps of the military services and new rumors, not ours this time, are beginning on possible military reactions.

Quito — 3 March 1962

Reactions to the Social Christian infiltration of the FEUE march have been most satisfactory. Yesterday the Minister of Defense and the chiefs of all the services issued a statement in which they admitted breaking a long silence on the many activities going on that are designed to sow chaos in the armed forces and separate them from the Ecuadorean people and the government. These activities, according to the statement, are directed by international communism through campaigns in periodicals, magazines, radio, rumor, strikes, work stoppages, rural risings, militia training and, most recently, the FEUE demonstration of 1 March. Instead of a demonstration for greater economic resources, according to the statement, the march was perverted to make propaganda against the armed forces. The statement ended with an expression of the determination of the Minister and the service chiefs to take whatever measures are necessary to defend military institutions.

The military statement yesterday coincided nicely with a rally we financed through Aurelio Davila with participation of the Conservatives, Social Christians, ARNE, and Catholic youth, labor and women's organizations. The purpose of the rally was another demand for a break in relations with Cuba, and Davila was the principal speaker. He blamed the insults of 1 March against the military on communists and Castroites who seek to form their own militias. He accused Arosemena, moreover, of giving protection to the communist menace and, as President of the Chamber of Deputies, he sent a message of support to the Minister of Defense and the chiefs of the services.

Quito — 16 March 1962

Fate's heavy hand has just fallen on our Vice-President, Reinaldo Varea. Yesterday the government announced that a million dollars' worth of military equipment purchased by a secret mission sent to the U.S. last year by Velasco has turned out to be useless junk. The announcement came just a couple of days after one of Velasco's ex-ministers made a public call for Velasquistas to begin organizing for the June elections. Obviously the announcement was made to begin a campaign to discredit the Velasquista movement prior to the elections.

Varea is implicated because as Vice-President of the Senate he was chief of the purchasing mission. There is no accusation that any money was stolen, but to be swindled out of a million dollars by a U.S. surplus parts company is sheer incompetence on someone's part. Photographs of the tanks and armored personnel carriers are being published—some without motors, others with no wheels, others simply rusted and falling apart.

Varea had told Noland that the case might come to the surface but he had hoped to keep it under cover. There's no telling how badly this will affect Varea's position as Arosemena's successor, but Noland is in a really black humor.

The PCE has just held one of its infrequent national congresses. Basantes and Cardenas attended as members of the Pichincha delegation. Divisions within the party over whether to resort to armed action soon or to continue working with the masses indefinitely are continuing to grow. Rafael Echeverria, the Quito PCE leader, is emerging as the most important leader of those favoring early armed action, although Pedro Saad was re-elected Secretary-General and remains in firm control. Unfortunately neither of our agents was elected to the new Central Committee.

Quito — 25 March 1962

For some days the anti-communist (Social Christian and Conservative) forces in Cuenca have been preparing for another mass demonstration against relations with Cuba and communist penetration of the government. Noland financed it through Carlos Arizaga who will use it to show solidarity with the important military command there. The affair was very successful. In spite of police denial of permission thousands turned out with posters and banners bearing the appropriate anti-communist, anti-Castro and anti-URJE themes. Demands were also made for the resignation of Arosemena and his leftist appointees, and expressions of solidarity with the military services against their extremist attackers were also prevalent. A petition with 2000 signatures was presented to the provincial governor, Arosemena's chief representative.

Colonel Lugo, National Police commander in Cuenca, advised that although he was unable to grant permission for the street march because of orders from Quito, he was able to avoid taking repressive measures. The march in fact had no police control and there was no disorder.

Quito — 28 March 1962

The Cuenca military garrison under Colonel Aurelio Naranjo has suddenly sent a message to Arosemena giving him seventy-two hours to break relations with Cuba and fire the leftist Minister of Labor. The whole country is shaken by the revolt although the outcome is uncertain because so far no other military units have joined.

Arosemena spoke this afternoon with Vice-President Varea and with the press. He's taking a hard line promising severe punishment for those responsible for the rebellion. The traditional parties are ostensibly supporting Arosemena and the Constitution, but the Conservatives have issued a statement insisting on a break with Cuba and Czechoslovakia and a purge of communists in the government. The FEUE, CTE, URJE and other extreme leftists are of course backing Arosemena.

The key is the reaction of the Minister of Defense and the armed services commanders here in Quito. We're checking various agents who have access but haven't been able to get straight answers because apparently the military leaders are taking an ambiguous position.

This Cuenca revolt is clearly a result of the renewed agitation we have been promoting since January through the Conservatives and Social Christians. There was no way to tell exactly when action of this sort would occur but several sensational events of the past two days have probably had an influence. Yesterday news reached Quito of an uprising at the huge Tenguel Hacienda on the coast which is owned by a subsidiary of United Fruit and where communist agitation has been going on for some time. Eight hundred workers are striking over the company's contracting of land to tenant farmers, and the strike has touched off rumors of other risings in rural areas. At a Social Christian rally yesterday where Renato Perez was one of the speakers the Tenguel rising was attributed to the communist leadership of the workers. Also yesterday, in Cuenca, the provincial committee of the Conservative Party called on the National Committee to declare formal opposition to the Arosemena régime. Key figures in this move are Carlos Arizaga Vega in Cuenca and Aurelio Davila Cajas‡ on the National Committee.

The other sensation is the overthrow of President Frondizi by the Argentine military. Although the Peronist victory in this month's elections is the immediate reason for the military move there, we will interpret the *coup* in our propaganda as related strongly to Frondizi's reluctance to break with Cuba and his general policy of accommodation with the extreme left.

Quito — 29 March 1962

The crisis continues. Today the Cuenca garrison issued a public statement on the need to break relations with Cuba and Czechoslovakia and to purge the government of communists. The Minister of Defense, the Chief of Staff and the commander of the Army are all indirectly supporting the Cuenca commander by not sending troops to put down the rebellion. In response to today's statement by the Cuenca garrison, the Army commander publicly ordered the Cuenca commander to refrain from political statements, but he also sent an open statement to the Minister of Defense that the armed forces are in agreement on the need to break with Cuba.

Demonstrations have occurred today in most of the major cities: in Quito one in favor and one against Arosemena; in Guayaquil in favor of Arosemena; and in Cuenca against—marchers there carried posters reading "Christ the King, Si, Communism, No."

Arosemena is trying to strike back but in the absence of cooperation from the military he's almost powerless. He had the entire Cabinet resign today, accepting the resignations of the Ministers of Government (for allowing the security situation to degenerate), Labor (as a gesture to the rightists who have focused on him as an extreme leftist), and Economy (for being one of the Conservative Party leaders of the campaign against communism and relations with Cuba).

Quito — 30 March 1962

The stand-off between Arosemena and the Cuenca garrison has continued for a third day although Arosemena is grasping for an alternative to save face. He announced today that within ten or fifteen days a plebiscite will be held on relations with Cuba. The idea of a plebiscite has already been proposed by several groups including the Pichincha Chamber of Industries whose members are suffering the effects of all the tension and instability of recent months.

Arosemena may not have ten or fifteen days left for the plebiscite. This afternoon in Quito a massive demonstration calling for a break with Cuba was sponsored by the anti-communist forces including a four-hour march through the streets. At the Ministry of Defense the Chief of Staff, a well-known anti-communist, told the demonstrators that he and other military leaders share their views on Cuba. The demonstration also had pronounced anti-Arosemena overtones. Similar demonstrations have occurred today in Cuenca and Riobamba. In the press we are stimulating statements of solidarity with the movement to break with Cuba including one from the Popular Revolutionary Liberal Party‡ which Gil Saudade had to wring out of Juan Yepez, Jr.

In spite of all the crisis other activities continue. Today Noland was honored at a ceremony presided by Manuel Naranjo for his year as a Director of the University Sports League. He got a medal and a diploma of appreciation—plenty of good publicity.

Quito — 31 March 1962

A solution is emerging. The Conservatives today formally ended their participation in Arosemena's government, and conversations betwen Arosemena and the National Democratic Front—composed of the Liberals, Democratic Socialists and independents—have begun. One of the Front's conditions for continuing to support Arosemena is a break with Cuba and Czechoslovakia. Meanwhile the Electoral Court quashed the plebiscite idea for constitutional reasons.

Conservative withdrawal from the government was highlighted by the publication today of an open letter from the Conservative ex-Minister of the Economy who resigned two days ago. In the letter the Cuenca rightist charged communists whom Arosemena has allowed to penetrate the government with thwarting the country's economic development.

The solution, interestingly, has resulted because Varea, the Vice-President, is unacceptable to the military high command because of his implication in the junk swindle. Otherwise Arosemena would probably have been deposed in favor of Varea for his resistance on the Cuban break. The Liberals and others in the Democratic Front expect to improve their electoral prospects from a position of dominance in the government. And the Conservatives and Social Christians will be able to campaign on the claim that they were responsible for the break with Cuba (if it takes place). Everyone is going to be satisfied except Arosemena and the extreme left—although Arosemena will at least survive for now.

The Social Christian bomb squad finally slipped up last night. Just after midnight they bombed the home of the Cardinal (who was sleeping downtown at the Basilica) and a couple of hours later they bombed the Anti-Communist Front. By a stroke of bad luck the two bombers were caught and have admitted to police that they are members of the Anti-Communist Front itself. So far they haven't been traced to the Social Christian Movement which planned the bombings. These produced lots of noise but little damage, to provide a new pretext for demonstrations of solidarity with the Cardinal.

Quito — 1 April 1962

The crisis is over and the Cubans are packing. Today the announcement was made that the National Democratic Front will enter the government with five Cabinet posts and that relations with Cuba will be broken. The new Minister of Government, Alfredo Albornoz,‡ is an anti-communist independent known personally by Noland. (His son is a friend of Noland's and of mine—he's President of the YMCA board on which I replaced Noland in January. The new minister is an important banker and owner of the Quito distributorship for Chevrolets and Buicks. Noland intends to begin a liaison arrangement with him as soon as possible.)

Today new anti-communist demonstrations and marches were held in Quito and down south in Loja celebrating the break with Cuba. The Conservatives and Social Christians are promoting still another massive demonstration in three days to show support for the Cardinal—in spite of the admission by the bombers (which in the newspapers was relegated to a small, obscure notice).

Quito — 2 April 1962

Success at last. Today the new Cabinet, in its first meeting with Arosemena, voted unanimously to break relations with Cuba, Czechoslovakia and Poland (which just recently sent a diplomatic official to Quito to open a Legation). After the meeting Arosemena lamented that the plebiscite was impossible while Liberal Party leaders claimed credit for the break.

Tomorrow the Foreign Ministry will give formal advice to each mission. Besides the Pole there are three Czechs and seven Cubans. The main problem for the Foreign Ministry is to find a country with an embassy in Havana that will take the asylees in the Ecuadorean Embassy—almost two hundred of them. The extreme left has been trying to promote demonstrations against the decision but they've only been able to get out small crowds.

This afternoon we had a champagne victory celebration in the station, and headquarters has sent congratulations.

Quito — 4 April 1962

The Social Christian and Conservative street demonstration today was said to be the largest in the history of Quito. Tens of thousands swarmed through the downtown streets to the Independence Plaza where the

Cardinal, who was the last speaker, said that, following the teachings of Christ, he would forgive the terrorists who had tried to kill him. Aurelio Davila was one of the organizers of the demonstration, and he arranged for a Cuban flag to be presented to the Cardinal by a delegation of the exiles. (The main exile organization, the Revolutionary Student Directorate, is run by the Miami station and in some countries the local representatives are run directly by station officers. In our case, however, Noland prefers to keep them at a distance through Davila.)

Noland is already meeting with the new Minister of Government, Alfredo Albornoz,‡ to pass information on communist plans that we get from our penetration agents. Today we got a sensational report from one of Jose Vargas's sub-agents to the effect that Jorge Ribadeneira, one of the principal leaders of URJE, has called his followers into immediate armed action in a rural area towards the coast. Communications with the sub-agent are very bad right now but Noland is trying to get more details. When Noland met with the Minister he learned that the Minister also has information on the guerrilla operation—it's concentrated near Santo Domingo de los Colorados, a small town a couple of hours' drive towards the coast from Quito. Tonight the Ministry of Defense is sending a battalion of paratroopers to the area to engage the guerrillas. As a precaution the Minister has banned all public demonstrations until further notice, but he and the Minister of Defense hope to keep the guerrilla operation secret until the size of the group is known. That may be impossible, however, because other agents including Lt. Col. Paredes,‡ the surveillance team chief, are beginning to report on the paratroopers' mobilization.

The thought of facing an effective guerrilla operation is one of our most persistent nightmares because of the ease with which communications and transport between coast and sierra could be cut. The difficult geography, moreover, is ideal for guerrilla operations in many areas, and if the imagination of the rural Indians and peasants could be captured—admittedly not an easy task because of religion and other traditional influences

—the guerrillas would have a very large source of manpower for support and for new recruits. This is why we have been continually trying to induce government action against the various groups of the extreme left in order to preclude this very situation.

Quito — 5 April 1962

Communications are impossible with Jose Vargas's agent in the guerrilla band and little news of substance is coming into the Ministry of Defense from the operations zone. I sent Lieutenant-Colonel Paredes down to Santo Domingo to see what he could pick up, but he hasn't been able to get close to the operations. Our best information from the Ministry of Defense is coming from Major Ed Breslin,‡ the U.S. Army Mission Intelligence Advisor. He has been in Quito only a short time but has already worked his way in with the Ecuadorean military intelligence people much more effectively than his predecessor. Both Noland and I have been working more closely with him on targeting for recruitments in the military intelligence services, and our relationship with him is excellent—he trained the tank crews that landed at the Bay of Pigs last year. Breslin reports the guerrillas are offering no resistance and that several arrests have been made.

At the Guayaquil airport last night two events related to Cuba will give us good material for propaganda. First, an Ecuadorean returning from a three-month guerrilla training course in Cuba was arrested. He is Guillermo Layedra, a leader of the CTE in Riobamba, whose return was reported to the base by the Mexico City station which gets very detailed coverage of all travelers to and from Cuba via Mexico through the Mexican immigration service. Data on Layedra's travel was passed to Lieutenant-Colonel Pedro Velez Moran,‡ one of the liaison agents of the base. Of propaganda interest are the books, pamphlets, phonograph records of revolutionary songs and, especially, a photograph of him in the Cuban militia uniform. Through Velez the base expects to get copies of his interrogation and will pass questions at headquarters' request.

The other case, also the work of Lieutenant-Colonel Velez, occurred during a refueling stop of a Cuban airliner bound from Chile to Havana. It was carrying some seventy passengers most of whom were Peruvian students going to study on "scholarships" in Cuba—most likely they were really guerrilla trainees. The base asked Velez to get a copy of the passenger list, an unusual demand for a service stop, which the base will forward to the Lima station. During the stop, however, the pilot was seen to give an envelope to the Third Secretary of the Cuban Embassy in Quito (the Cubans haven't left yet) and a customs inspector demanded to see the envelope. The Cuban diplomat took out a .45 pistol and, after waving it menacingly at the customs inspector, he was arrested by the airport military detachment. Only about 10 a.m. this morning was he allowed to go free, but he was allowed to keep the envelope.

Quito — 6 April 1962

The press carried its first stories of the Santo Domingo guerrilla operation this morning—sensational accounts of 300 or more men under the command of Araujo. The Ministry of Defense, however, announced later that thirty guerrillas have been arrested along with a considerable quantity of arms, ammunition and military equipment. First reports from interrogations indicate that the guerrilla group numbers less than 100 and that Araujo isn't participating, but military operations continue.

Although the early interrogation reports also indicate that the guerrilla operation was precipitated by the Cuenca revolt and very poorly planned, we will try to make it appear serious and dangerous in our propaganda treatment. Most of those arrested are young URJE members—followers of Jorge Ribadeneira who may well be expelled from the PCE if, as is likely, the

Executive Committee under Saad had nothing to do with the operation. Reports from PCE agent penetrations coincide in the view that Ribadeneira was acting outside party control.

Quito — 10 April 1962

The Santo Domingo guerrilla affair is wiped up. Forty-six have been captured with only a brief exchange of fire. Only one casualty occurred—a guerrilla wounded in the foot. All have been brought to Quito and we're getting copies of the interrogations through Major Breslin. In an effort to help Pacifico de los Reyes‡ make a good impression in his new job as chief of the intelligence department of the National Police, I have been giving him information on many of those arrested, which he is passing as his own to the military interrogation team.

Propaganda treatment is only partly successful. The Minister of Defense has announced that the weapons seized are not of the type used by the Ecuadorean Army and must have been sent from outside the country—although the truth is that the weapons are practically all conventional shotguns, hunting rifles and M–1's stolen from the Army. Interrogation reports released to the press allege (falsely) that the operation was very carefully planned and approved at the PCE Congress held last month.

Press comment, however, is tending to romanticize the operation. Participation of four or five girls, for example, is being ascribed to sentimental reasons. Those arrested, moreover, once they have been turned over to police and are allowed to see lawyers, are saying that they only went to Santo Domingo for training in the hope of defending the Arosemena government from overthrow by the Cuenca garrison. The FEUE has set up a commission of lawyers for the guerrillas' defense, and unfortunately the early public alarm is turning to amusement and even ridicule.

Of continuing importance will be two factors. First, the ease with which the guerrillas were rolled up has given the Ecuadorean military new confidence and may encourage future demands for government suppression of the extreme left. Second, the operation is bound to exacerbate the growing split on the extreme left, both inside and outside the PCE, between those favoring early armed action and those favoring continued long-term work with the masses. In both cases this pitiful adventure has been fortunate for us.

Quito — 23 April 1962

Back in the cool thin sierra air after a brief holiday. The Pole, Czechs and Cubans have all left so we have no hostile diplomatic missions to worry about any more. The telephone tap on the Cubans was only of marginal value because they were careful, but I'm going to begin soon to monitor Araujo's telephone and perhaps one other if I can arrange for transcription. The technical problems with the sound-actuated equipment were never solved so we reverted to the old voltage-operated machines.

Although we tried to keep the Santo Domingo guerrilla operation in proper focus it hasn't been easy. The Rio station helped by preparing an article on the communist background of one of the girls in the operation, a Brazilian named Abigail Pereyra. The story was surfaced through the Rio correspondent of the hemisphere-wide feature service controlled by the Santiago, Chile, station—*Agencia Orbe Latinoamericano*.‡ The story revealed that her father is a Federal Deputy and the personal physician of Luis Carlos Prestes, long-time leader of the Communist Party of Brazil, while her mother is the Portuguese teacher at the Soviet Commercial Mission in Rio de Janeiro. Both parents are leaders of the Chinese–Brazilian Cultural Society, and her mother went to Cuba early this year to visit Abigail —who was taking a guerrilla training course, according to the article. This may help keep her in jail for a while, but public opinion is favorable to early release.

Gil Saudade has established another of his front organizations for propaganda. The newest was formed a few days ago and is called the Committee for the Liberty of Peoples.‡ Through this group Gil will publish documents of the European Assembly of Captive Nations‡ and other Agency-controlled organizations dedicated to campaigns for human rights and civil liberties in communist countries. The agent through whom he established the Committee is Isabel Robalino Bollo‡ whom he met through Velasco's former Minister of Labor, Jose Baquero de la Calle. Robalino is a leader of the Catholic Labor Center (CEDOC), and is Gil's principal agent for operations through this organization. She was named Secretary of the Committee which includes many prominent liberal intellectuals and politicians.

Quito — 27 April 1962

The government has lifted the prohibition on public political demonstrations in effect since the turmoil over the break with Cuba, and the campaign for the June elections is picking up steam. Quite a number of our agents will be candidates but so far our main electoral operation is in Ambato where Jorge Gortaire, a retired Army colonel and Social Christian leader, is working to defeat the Revolutionary Socialist Mayor running for re-election.

Gortaire is also a leader of the Rotary Club and is President of the Ambato Anti-Communist Front which we finance through him. Because of his exceptional capability the Front is running a single list of candidates backed by the Conservatives, Liberals, Social Christians, independents and, of course, the fascist ARNE. Noland thinks Gortaire is one of the best agents he has —after Renato Perez and Aurelio Davila.

Gil Saudade is about to see a giant step forward in his and the Guayaquil base labor operations. Tomorrow the constituent convention of the free trade-union confederation to be called CEOSL‡ begins, and Gil is fairly certain that between the base agents in CROCLE and his Popular Revolutionary Liberal Party agents, we will come out in control. In recent months the PLPR agents have become increasingly active and Gil is counting on them to offset the divisive regionalism of the CROCLE agents.

Quito — 1 May 1962

The CEOSL—Ecuadorean Confederation of Free Trade Union Organizations—is formally established with several agents in control: Victor Contreras Zuniga‡ is President, Matias Ulloa Coppiano‡ is Secretary for External Relations, and Ricardo Vazquez Diaz‡ is Secretary of Education. Publicity build-up has been considerable, including messages of solidarity from ORIT in Mexico City and ICFTU and International Trade Secretariats in Brussels. Leaders of other Agency-controlled labor confederations such as the Uruguayan Labor Confederation‡ (CSU) were invited.

The main business of the first sessions was to seek affiliation with the ICFTU and ORIT which has just opened an important training-school in Mexico. Soon CEOSL will begin sending trainees to the ORIT school, which is run by the Mexico City station through Morris Paladino,‡ the ORIT Assistant Secretary-General and the man through whom IO Division controls ORIT. (The new Secretary-General of ORIT, Arturo Jauregui,‡ hasn't been directly recruited yet although he was here in March to promote the school.)

Gil Saudade will now have to coordinate closely with the Guayaquil base so that his agents, Ulloa and Vazquez, will work in harmony with the base's agent, Contreras. None is supposed to know of the others' contact with us.

Unfortunately the controversy between the Guayaquil base agents from CROCLE and the ECCALICO election operation of two years ago came to a head. Adalberto Miranda Giron, the Labor Senator from the Coast, was terminated by the base several months ago because certain of his inappropriate dealings with companies became known. At the CEOSL constituent convention he was denounced as a traitor to the working class, the beginning of a campaign to get him completely out of the trade-union movement.

Quito — 3 May 1962

The "junk swindle" has become Ecuador's scandal of the century and is being used increasingly by the left to ridicule the military. Today the Chief of Staff and the Commander of the Army issued a joint statement defending themselves from attacks by CTE leaders in May Day speeches and other recent attempts to connect them with the junk swindle. Final liquidation of the armed forces, they warned, is the purpose of the leftist campaign. Resentment is also growing in the military over recent leaflets and wall-painting labeling them "junk dealers."

A new crisis has developed in rural areas violently demonstrating the backwardness of this country. For the past two months the government has been trying to conduct an agriculture and livestock census to aid in economic planning. Numerous Indian uprisings have occurred because of rumors that the census is a communist scheme to take away the Indians' animals. On several occasions there were dead and wounded, as in Azuay Province, for example, where a teacher and his brother, who were taking the census, were chopped into pieces with machetes and only the arrival of police impeded the burning of what remained of their bodies.

Because priests serving rural areas are often responsible for the rumors, the government had to ask the Church hierarchy to instruct all priests and other religious to assist in the census wherever possible. In Azuay, nevertheless, the census has been suspended.

One has to wonder about the strength of religious feeling here. On Good Friday two weeks ago tens of thousands of Indians and other utterly poor people walked in procession behind images from noon till 6 p.m.—despite heavy rain. The same occurred in Guayaquil and other cities.

Quito — 12 May 1962

Some of our agents are running solid electoral campaigns but others have pulled out for lack of support. Both Jose Baquero de la Calle, ex-Minister of Labor under Velasco and running as an independent Velasquista, and Juan Yepez del Pozo, Sr., General-Secretary of the Ecuadorean affiliate of the International Commission of Jurists,‡ and running for the Popular Revolutionary Liberal Party,‡ declared for Mayor of Quito. When Baquero's candidacy was repudiated by the Conservative Party, he resigned, and when Yepez failed to attract significant Velasquista backing, he resigned. Oswaldo Chiriboga,‡ long-time penetration of the Velasquista movement, also declared for Mayor but is pulling out. For all of these candidates station support was only nominal because their possibilities for success were obviously rather limited.

On the other hand the candidacies of Renato Perez for the Municipal Council, Aurelio Davila for the Chamber of Deputies and Carlos Arizaga Vega for Deputies are going very well. Alfredo Perez Guerrero, President of the ICJ‡ affiliate and reform-minded Rector of Central University, is heading the Deputies list of the National Democratic Front (Liberals, Socialists and independents) and will win without our help. Other candidates of the Social Christian Movement and the Conservative Party are being financed indirectly through funds passed to Perez and Davila.

Quito — 13 May 1962

Because Arosemena continues to resist firing extreme leftists in his government—penetration in fact continues to grow—Noland recommended, and headquarters approved, expansion of the political operations financed through the ECACTOR project. Not only will continued and increased pressure be exerted through the regular agents in Quito, Cuenca, Riobamba, Ambato and Tulcan, but we have made two new recruitments of important Social Christian leaders in Quito. I am in charge of both these new cases.

The first new operation is with Carlos Roggiero,‡ a retired Army captain and one of the principal Social Christian representatives on the National Defense Front. Roggiero is chief of the Social Christian militant-action squads, including the secret bomb-squad, and I have started training him in the use of various incendiary, crowd dispersement and harassment devices that I requested from TSD in headquarters. Through him we will form perhaps ten squads, of five to ten men each, for disrupting meetings and small demonstrations and for general street control and intimidation of the Communist Youth, URJE and similar groups.

The other new operation is with Jose Maria Egas,‡ a young lawyer and also a leading Social Christian representative on the National Defense Front. Egas is a fast-rising political figure and a really spellbinding orator. Through him I will form five squads composed of four to five men each for investigative work connected with our Subversive Control Watch List—formerly known as the LYNX list. The surveillance team under Lt. Col. Paredes simply hasn't the time to do the whole job and is needed on other assignments. With the group under Egas's control we will have constant checking on residences and places of work so that if the situation continues to deteriorate and a moment of truth arrives, we will have up-to-date information for immediate arrests. If Egas's work warrants it, we may train him in headquarters and even extend the operation to physical surveillance.

In another effort to improve intelligence collection on the extreme left I have arranged to add another telephone tap through Rafael Bucheli‡ and Alfonso Rodriguez.‡ The new tap will be on the home telephone of Antonio Flores Benitez, a retired Army captain and somewhat mysterious associate of Quito PCE leader Rafael Echeverria Flores. We have several indications from PCE penetration agents Cardenas and Vargas that Flores is a key figure in what seems to be an organization being formed by Echeverria outside the PCE structure properly speaking. The chances are that Echeverria is developing a group that may be the nucleus for future guerrilla action and urban terrorism, but he hasn't yet taken any of our agents into it. I will tap Flores for a while to see if anything of interest develops—Edgar Camacho will do the transcribing as Francine Jacome has only time for transcribing the Araujo line. The LP remains in Bucheli's home under the thin cover of an electronics workshop.

Raymond Ladd,‡ our hustling administrative officer, has been very active in the basketball federation, teaching a course in officiating and helping to coach the local girls teams. Through this work he met Modesto Ponce,‡ the Postmaster-General of Ecuador, who soon insisted that Ladd review in the Embassy all the mail we are already getting through the regular intercept. In order to avoid suspicion that we are already getting mail from Cuba and the Soviet Bloc, Ladd accepted Ponce's offer, and now we get the same correspondence twice. We may attempt certain new coverage through Ponce so Ladd has begun giving him money for the mail under the normal guise of payment for expenses.

Quito — 21 May 1962

Arosemena struck back for his humiliation at the hands of the military when he was forced to break with Cuba. Last week he fired the Minister of Defense, sent the Army Commander to Paris as military attaché and sent the Air Force Commander to Buenos Aires as military attaché. Immediate protests came from the Social Christians, Conservatives and others over the removal of these staunchly anti-communist officers with new charges of communist penetration of the government.

Then Alfredo Albornoz,‡ the Minister of Government appointed only seven weeks ago, resigned. Next, all the other National Democratic Front Ministers resigned. The issue is Arosemena's refusal to honor his promise of last month, when the Front came into the government, to dismiss two key leftist appointees: the Secretary-General of the Administration and the Governor of Guayas Province.

Noland is sorry to lose Albornoz because they were developing a worthwhile relationship both from the point of view of intelligence collection through Albornoz and from action by Albornoz on undesirables within the government. Arosemena is searching for new support, but the Front is holding out for the resignations.

But yesterday new ministers were named after Arosemena made another promise in secret to fire the Governor of Guayas Province. Today the resignation was announced. Although this is a step in the right direction, the Secretary-General of the Administration remains (he is like a chief of staff with Cabinet rank) along with many others of the same coloring. Among the new ministers is Juan Sevilla,‡ a golfing companion of mine who was named Minister of Labor and Social Welfare. Gil Saudade will decide whether Sevilla could be of use in his labor operations.

Quito — 4 May 1962

Traditional violence flared up in several cities during the final days before the elections which were held yesterday. The right was split, as were the center and the Velasquistas—with a profusion of candidates all over the country excepting the extreme left which didn't participate.

The Conservative Party won the most seats in the Chamber of Deputies (although not quite a majority), and victories in most of the municipal and provincial contests. Aurelio Davila, who managed the Conservative campaign in Quito, was elected Deputy for Pichincha. Renato Perez was elected Quito Municipal Councillor from the Social Christian list. And Carlos Arizaga Vega was elected Conservative Party Deputy for Azuay Province.

The Velasquistas have had a disaster, winning only six deputies and two mayors' races—one of which was in Ambato. Jorge Gortaire's candidate there, backed by the Anti-Communist Front,‡ was second but Gortaire is being given overall credit for the defeat of the Revolutionary Socialist incumbent.

The elections are a clear indication of the effectiveness of the Conservatives' campaign against communist penetration in the government and are a severe defeat both for Arosemena and for the National Democratic Front. When Congress opens there can be little doubt that the Conservatives will exert new and stronger pressure for elimination of extreme-leftists in the government.

Reinaldo Varea has been taking a severe beating in the continuing controversy over the junk swindle. The case is coloring the whole political scene and unfortunately for us Varea isn't very effective in what is a very difficult defense. In a few days he'll go to Washington for treatment of stomach ulcers at Walter Reed Hospital—Davila will be acting Vice-President.

Quito — 15 June 1962

The International Monetary Fund has just announced another stabilization credit to Ecuador of five million dollars over the next twelve months for balance of payments relief. The announcement was optimistic and complimentary, noting that Ecuador since mid-1961 has stopped the decline in its foreign exchange reserves and obtained equilibrium in its balance of payments. The new standby, of course, is conditional on retention of last year's exchange-rate unification, that contributed to Velasco's overthrow.

Two programs are getting under way this month as part of a new U.S. country-team effort in staving off communist-inspired insurgency. One is the Civic Action program of the Ecuadorean military services and the U.S. military assistance mission—in fact under way for a couple of years but now being expanded and institutionalized. The purpose of Civic Action is to demonstrate through community development by uniformed military units that the military is on the side of the people so that tendencies of poor people to accept communist propaganda and recruitment can be reversed. It's a program to link the people, especially in rural areas, to the government through the military who contribute visibly and concretely to the people's welfare.

The Civic Action program just announced as the first of its kind in Latin America calls for contributions in money and equipment by the U.S. military-assistance mission worth 1.5 million dollars plus another 500,000 dollars from the AID mission. Projects will include road-construction, irrigation-canals, drinking-water systems and public-health facilities, first in Azuay Province to be followed by Guayaquil slums and by the Cayambe–Olmedo region north of Quito. Widespread publicity will be undertaken to propagandize these projects in other areas in order to generate interest and project proposals in these other regions.

In the station, we will work with Major Breslin,‡ the intelligence advisor of the U.S. military mission. He will use the mission personnel who visit and work at the projects as a type of scout—keeping their eyes open and reporting indications of hostility, level of communist agit-prop activities and general program effectiveness.

The other new program is more closely related to regular station operations and is Washington's answer to the limitations of current labor programs undertaken through AID as well as through ORIT and CIA stations. The problem is related to the controversy over the ineffectiveness of ORIT but is larger—it is essentially how to accelerate expansion of labor-organizing activities in Latin America in order to deny workers to labor unions dominated by the extreme left and to reverse communist and Castroite penetration. This new program is the result of several years' study and planning and is to be channeled through the American Institute for Free Labor Development‡ (AIFLD), founded last year in Washington for training in trade-unionism.

The reason a new institution was founded was that AID labor programs are limited because of their direct dependence on the U.S. government. They serve poorly for the dirty struggles that characterize labor organizing and jurisdictional battles. ORIT programs are also limited because its affiliates are weak or non-existent in some countries, although expansion is also under way through the establishment of a new ORIT school in Mexico. Control is difficult and past performance is poor. The CIA station programs are limited by personnel problems, but more so by the limits on the amount of money that can be channeled covertly through the stations and through international organizations like ORIT and the ICFTU.

Business leaders are front men on the Board of Directors so that large sums of AID money can be channeled to AIFLD and so that the institute will appear to have the collaboration of U.S. businesses operating in Latin America. Nevertheless, legally, AIFLD is a non-profit, private corporation and financing will also be obtained from foundations, businesses and the AFL–CIO.

The AIFLD is headed by Serafino Romualdi, IO Division's long-time agent who moved in as Executive Director and resigned as the AFL–CIO's Inter-American Representative. Among the Directors are people of the stature of George Meany,‡ J. Peter Grace‡ and Joseph Beirne,‡ President of the Communications Workers of America‡ (CWA) which is the largest Western Hemisphere affiliate of the Post, Telegraph and Telephone Workers International‡ (PTTI). AIFLD, in fact, is modeled on the CWA training school of Front Royal, Virginia where Latin American leaders of PTTI affiliates are being trained. Day to day control of AIFLD by IO Division, however, will be through Romualdi and William Doherty,‡ former Inter-American Representative of the PTTI and now AIFLD Social Projects Director. Prominent Latin American liberals such as Jose Figueres,‡ former President of Costa Rica and also a long-time Agency collaborator, will serve on the Board from time to time.

The main purpose of AIFLD will be to organize anti-communist labor unions in Latin America. However, the ostensible purpose, since union organizing is rather sensitive for AID to finance, even indirectly, will be "adult education" and social projects such as workers' housing, credit unions and cooperatives. First priority is to establish in all Latin American countries training institutes which will take over and expand the courses already being given in many countries by AID. Although these training institutes will nominally and administratively be controlled by AIFLD in Washington, it is planned that as many as possible will be headed by salaried CIA agents with operational control exercised by the stations. In most cases, it is hoped, these AIFLD agents will be U.S. citizens with some background in trade-unionism although, as in the case of ORIT, foreign nationals may have to be used. The training programs of the local institutes in Latin America will prepare union organizers who, after the courses are over, will spend the next nine months doing nothing but organizing new unions with their salaries and all expenses paid by the local institute. Publicity relating to AIFLD will concentrate on the social projects and "adult education" aspects, keeping the organizing program discreetly in the background.

This month, in addition to training in Latin American countries, AIFLD is beginning a program of advanced training courses to be given in Washington. Spotting and assessment of potential agents for labor operations will be a continuing function of the Agency-controlled staff members both in the training courses in Latin America and in the Washington courses. Agents already working in labor operations can be enrolled in the courses to promote their technical capabilities and their prestige.

In Ecuador, the AIFLD representative from the U.S. who is now setting up the training institute—the first course begins in three weeks—is not an agent but was sent anyway in order to avoid delays. However, Gil Saudade arranged for Ricardo Vazquez Diaz,‡ the Education Secretary of CEOSL, to be the Ecuadorean in charge of the local AIFLD training programs. Carlos Vallejo Baez,‡ who is connected with the Popular Revolutionary Liberal Party,‡ will also be on the teaching staff. Eventually Saudade will either recruit this first AIFLD representative or headquarters will arrange for a cleared agent to be sent.

These two new programs, military Civic Action and the AIFLD, are without doubt being expanded faster here than in most other Latin American countries. Recently I read the report by a special inter-departmental team of experts from Washington called the Strategic Analysis Targeting Team (SATT), which in months past secretly visited all the Latin American countries. Their purpose was to review all U.S. government programs in each country and to determine the gravity of the threat of urban terrorism and guerrilla warfare. We prepared a secret annex for the SATT Report, and among their recommendations were expansion of the Subversive Control Watch List program and updating of contingency planning in order to continue our operations from a third country—in case we lose our Embassy offices. Ecuador, in fact, shared with Bolivia and Guatemala the SATT Report's category as the most likely places for early armed insurgency. Emphasis on immediate expansion of Civic Action and labor programs is probably a result of the SATT Report.

Quito — 21 July 1962

A breakthrough in Guayaquil student operations. The anti-communist forces led by Alberto Alarcon have just won the FEUE‡ elections. They replace extreme-leftist officers who are members of URJE. Less than two weeks ago, Alarcon was here in Quito for a golf tournament sponsored by Ambassador Bernbaum, and he and Noland made final preparations for the FEUE elections.

Gil Saudade has launched another new operation—an organization of business and professional people to promote economic and social reform. Civic organizations of this sort have been established by other stations and have been effective for propaganda and as funding mechanisms for elections and other political-action operations. Our group is called the Center for Economic and Social Reform Studies‡ (CERES) and is headed by two agents, Mario Cabeza de Vaca‡ and Jaime Ponce Yepez.‡ Cabeza de Vaca formerly was the cutout to PCE penetration agent Mario Cardenas but they had a personality clash of sorts so John Bacon shifted Cardenas to Miguel Burbano de Lara‡ who was already handling another PCE penetration agent, Luis Vargas.‡ Bacon then turned Cabeza de Vaca over to Saudade to front in the CERES organization. Jaime Ponce is the Quito Shell Oil dealer and already a friend of mine and Noland's. Noland recruited him to work in CERES and then turned him over to Saudade. The Bogotá station is helping by sending a delegation from its reform group called Center of Studies and Social Action‡ (CEAS). They are here now.

Quito — 2 August 1962

Arosemena's back from a state visit to Washington. During his main business meeting with Kennedy he was feeling no pain and proved he could name all the U.S. Presidents in order from Washington on. He also claimed he couldn't remember the Ecuadorean Presidents, there have been so many, for the last half-century. Kennedy apparently was amused, but the State Department reports on the trip are somber.

Thanks to Arosemena the last of the Santo Domingo guerrillas have been released. In recent months they've trickled out slowly with little publicity, and unless Davila and others can create an issue during the Congressional session opening in a week, the cases will just sink away into the bureaucratic swampland. Several of the guerrillas have already gone to Cuba for additional training.

The telephone tap on Antonio Flores Benitez is producing better information right now than any of our PCE penetration agents. Flores has ten or fifteen persons who call and say very little, only code-phrases for arranging meetings, obviously using code-names. Using the ECJACK surveillance team under Lt. Col. Paredes I've been trying to identify Flores's contacts but the work is very slow, especially because Flores simply cannot be followed—partly it's the size and low proficiency of the team, but mainly Flores is watching constantly and taking diversionary measures.

Even so, I have identified Rafael Echeverria, principal PCE leader in Quito, as one of the clandestine contacts, along with a non-commissioned officer in the Ministry of Defense Communications Section, the chief of the archives section of the Presidency and the deputy chief of Arosemena's personal bodyguard. Analysis of the transcripts has been most helpful because even though Flores is careful when he speaks by telephone, his wife is very garrulous when he's out of the house. Several important identifications have been made from her carelessness.

My impression at this point is that Flores, who is not a PCE member, is in charge of the intelligence collection branch of an organization Echeverria is continuing to form outside the established PCE structure. If he is doing as well in the guerrilla and terrorism branch we will have to act soon to suppress the organization before armed operations begin.

In order to speed up transcriptions we have brought in another transcriber. He is Rodrigo Rivadeneira,‡ one of the brothers who run the clandestine printing press. Rodrigo is one of Ecuador's best basketball players and was on a scholarship in the U.S. obtained for him by Noland. He returned to Ecuador in June and because of family financial problems he will probably have to give up the scholarship. Francine Jacome will be unable to work for a few months so Rodrigo will take over the Araujo line which, while interesting, is not producing as much as the Flores line.

Two police agents have been transferred to new assignments. Pacifico de los Reyes,‡ Chief of Police Intelligence, left yesterday for the FBI course at Quantico, Virginia. We got the scholarship for him through the AID Public Safety office and he will be gone until the end of the year. Before he left he asked me if I would like to keep up contact with the Police Intelligence unit while he is away. He selected Luis Sandoval,‡ chief technician of the Police Intelligence unit, with whom I have been meeting since last year but without de los Reyes's knowledge. He introduced Sandoval to me three days ago and somehow we both kept a straight face. Before leaving, de los Reyes was promoted from captain to major. With the Office of Training in headquarters I am arranging special intelligence training for him to follow the FBI course.

Colonel Oswaldo Lugo, our oldest and most important penetration agent of the National Police, has been reassigned from the Cuenca district to the job as Chief of the Fourth District with headquarters in Guayaquil. This new job puts him in command of all the National Police units on the coast and will be an important addition to the Guayaquil base operations. In a few days I will make a quick trip to Guayaquil to introduce Lugo to the Base Chief.

Guerrilla training in Cuba is on headquarters' highest priority list for Latin America and instructions have been sent to all stations asking that efforts be made to place agents in the groups sent for training. We haven't been able to get an agent sent for training yet, but I've been meeting lately with the new Director of Immigration, Pablo Maldonado,‡ who has expressed interest in helping impede travel to Cuba by administrative procedures where prior knowledge of the travel is available. Maldonado, whom I met through mutual friends, is also willing to arrange close searches of Ecuadoreans who return from Cuba. I have begun passing on information which comes from the Mexican and Spanish liaison services using the immigration documents of travelers to and from Cuba through the two main travel points: Mexico City and Madrid.

Quito — 10 August 1962

Congress opened a new session today and acknowledged that agrarian reform is one of the first items on its order of business. In the Senate the National Democratic Front is in control while in the Chamber of Deputies the Conservative Party has a slight edge when backed by the leftist Concentration of Popular Forces' two or three deputies.

The Conservatives are out to get Varea's‡ resignation and Noland has no way either to stop it or to salvage Varea. Once Varea is thrown out over the junk swindle the Conservatives will try to get Arosemena thrown out or force his resignation for physical incapacity. Unfortunately Varea has to go first because ousting Arosemena with Varea as Vice-President will be almost impossible.

Varea continues as President of the Senate and Carlos Arizaga Vega,‡ our ECACTOR political-action agent from Cuenca, was elected Vice-President of the Chamber of Deputies. He has quickly replaced Davila as leader of the rightist bloc—Davila is concentrating on organizational work and wasn't a candidate in the Chamber of Deputies.

Quito — 29 August 1962

After four days of political crisis, including the resignations of all Cabinet ministers, Arosemena finally had to dismiss his leftist Secretary-General. Without doubt this is a significant victory for the Conservatives and Social Christians, although certain Liberals and Socialists are also aligned in the campaign since last year against the key administration leftist.

The only other Cabinet resignation accepted was that of Manuel Naranjo,‡ Minister of the Treasury and Noland's agent leading the democratic Socialist Party. His resignation comes as a result of increasing opposition from businessmen to his austerity policies although he is widely and favorably recognized for his personal honesty and the beginnings of tax-reform.

The situation worsens for another of Noland's agents. Two nights ago the Chamber of Deputies voted to impeach Varea for his participation in the junk swindle—still the supreme issue in current Ecuadorean politics. He's not being charged with stealing any of the money, just with negligence and ineptitude. The Minister of Defense at the time of the swindle is being prosecuted by the Chamber along with the Vice-President. Carlos Arizaga Vega is leading the attack.

Araujo has arrived back in Guayaquil after a trip to China that started late last month. At the airport five rolls of training film on street-fighting techniques were confiscated as well as propaganda. In China he was received by the Vice-Premier—we're going to try and discover if he got other assistance too.

Quito — 3 September 1962

Labor operations proceed with their usual mixed accomplishments. The CROCLE leadership within the CEOSL has insisted in attacking Adalberto Miranda, the Labor Senator from the coast, because of his dealings with the Guayaquil Telephone Company. Now they are accusing him of being involved with efforts by the United Fruit subsidiary to fire certain employees who are members of the subsidiary's trade union which recently affiliated with CROCLE and CEOSL. The same Guayaquil CROCLE leaders tried to get Miranda disqualified from the Senate but that move failed too. This campaign against Miranda is justified in some ways, according to the base, but undesirable right now because of its divisive nature. Soon the base plans to terminate the CROCLE agents who also insist on retaining the regional identity of CROCLE in opposition to our efforts to replace it with coastal provincial federations. When that happens, Gil Saudade will move his Quito agents into full control of CEOSL; he is now preparing for that development.

Meanwhile the AIFLD program is continuing to progress with close coordination with CEOSL through Ricardo Vazquez Diaz. Next month Vazquez will conduct a seminar for labor leaders from which four will be selected for the three-month AIFLD course starting in October in Washington.

Two weeks ago a PTTI delegation was here to discuss organization and a low-cost housing program with their Ecuadorean affiliate, FENETEL,‡ which is one of the most important unions in CEOSL. The PTTI is training FENETEL leaders at their school in Front Royal, Virginia, and the visit was also used to create publicity for the AIFLD seminar program. Included in the delegation was the new PTTI Inter-American Representative and a Cuban who is leader of the Cuban telephone workers' union in exile. This PTTI organization is without doubt the most effective of the International Trade Secretariats currently working in Ecuador under direction of IO Division.

One has to wonder how the Ecuadorean working class can even stay alive to organize. Two weeks ago the President of the National Planning Board, in a general economic report to the Chamber of Deputies, revealed that the worker in 1961 received an average monthly income of only 162 sucres—about seven dollars.

Quito — 10 September 1962

Noland has turned over another branch of the ECACTOR political-action project to me. From now on I'll be handling the Ambato operation with Jorge Gortaire.

Two weeks ago I went with Noland down to Ambato to meet Gortaire and to plan a bugging operation that we think may reveal information on Chinese support to Araujo, if any. Previously, the manager of the Villa Hilda Hotel in Ambato, a Czech *émigré*, reported to Gortaire that Araujo had made reservations for one of the cottages. This will be Araujo's first trip to visit his Ambato followers since returning from Communist China and Gortaire suggested that we bug the cottage —which he will monitor when Araujo goes there at the end of the month.

Last weekend I returned with the equipment and spent a couple of days with Gortaire. He had taken the cottage which Araujo will use and we installed a microphone, transmitter and power supply behind the woodwork of the closet door. It works perfectly and Gortaire can monitor at ease from his house, which is only two blocks from the Villa Hilda. The only problem was that Gortaire forgot to lock the door and, when I was standing on a table in the closet making the installation, a couple of maids burst in on us. They were clearly puzzled by my strange activity, but Gortaire believes they simply could not imagine what I was really doing.

He will stop by to see the manager from time to time to find out if the maids mentioned seeing me on the table.

Quito — 3 October 1962

Arosemena has survived another attempt at impeachment for incapacity, largely because the Conservatives fell apart on the issue, and because Varea is so discredited.

Through my work with Pablo Maldonado,‡ Director of Immigration, on attempting to stop or delay Ecuadoreans from traveling to Cuba and to carefully review their baggage on return, I have met the Sub-Secretary of Government, Manuel Cordova Galarza,‡ who is Maldonado's immediate superior.

Cordova expressed willingness to cooperate in trying to cut off travel to Cuba, and he said Jaime del Hierro,‡ the Minister of Government, is also anxious to see effective controls established. He added that any time I wish, I can call on him or on the Minister to propose new ideas.

Noland isn't anxious to get involved with Cordova or del Hierro because, according to him, Arosemena won't allow them to take really effective action. He said they are probably just trying to appear to be cooperative since serving as Minister and Sub-Secretary of public security in this government is beyond redemption. In his view they're like the other Liberals serving Arosemena: disgraceful opportunists. For the time being I'll continue with Maldonado and avoid contacts with Cordova and del Hierro.

Today Cordova went to Cuenca to investigate a macabre incident that occurred in an Indian village about twenty kilometers outside Cuenca. A medical team of the Andean Mission, an organization supported by U.N. agencies and dedicated to teaching social progress and self-help to rural Indians in several countries, was making the rounds of villages when they encountered strange hostility just outside a community they had already visited several times. They stopped the jeep and the doctor and social-worker proceeded on foot leaving the nurse and chauffeur in the vehicle. In the village the doctor and the social-worker found the Indians assembled in the church for a religious service, but when they entered the church they were greeted with extreme hostility by the Indians who began to jostle them about. When they did not return for some time the nurse also left the jeep and entered the village, but at the church she too was menaced as she joined the others. By now the Indians were whipped into a rage by several of their leaders who thought the Andean Mission people were communists. As matters grew worse the Mission team fled to the sacristy for safety but were followed by the Indians who surrounded them and would not let them leave. The elderly priest, who had been in the parish thirty-eight years, appeared and the team begged him to confirm to the Indians that they were not communists, but were simply there to help them. The priest refused to intervene even as the team knelt before him begging protection, and he simply blessed them and disappeared. The team was then severely beaten—the nurse left for unconscious while the doctor and the social-worker were dragged to the street.

The nurse escaped, returned to the jeep and obtained a police patrol from Cuenca. When they returned to the village the doctor and social-worker had been killed with stones, clubs and machetes while a local schoolteacher who tried to intervene had also been attacked. The Indians, in fact, were about to burn him, thinking he was dead, when the nurse and police arrived.

Preliminary investigation revealed that the priest had earlier instructed the Indians to resist the agriculture and livestock census because it was a communist plot, and that the priest also spread the story that the Andean Mission team were communists. My friends tell me that the priest will probably be sent to a religious retirement house as punishment.

Arosemena rewarded Manuel Naranjo‡ by naming him Ecuadorean permanent delegate to the U.N. General Assembly. He has gone to New York and Noland has arranged for contact to be established with him by officers from the Agency's New York office. We expect that the CIA will try to use him for special operations at the U.N.

Quito — 7 October 1962

Brazilian elections are being held today as the climax of one of WH Division's largest-ever political-action operations. For most of the year the Rio de Janeiro station and its many bases in consulates throughout the country have been engaged in a multimillion dollar campaign to finance the election of anti-communist candidates in the federal, state and municipal offices being contested. Hopefully these candidates will become a counter-force to the leftward trend of the Goulart government—increasingly penetrated by the communists and the extreme left in general.

Noland's transfer back to Washington, expected by him for many months, is now official. After five years here he is being replaced in December by Warren L. Dean,‡ currently Deputy Chief of Station in Mexico City. No one here knows anything about the new chief except that he's a former FBI man who wants Noland to arrange for immediate release of his dogs, that are coming on the same flight from Mexico City.

Quito — 15 October 1962

The Santo Domingo guerrilla adventure has reached a conclusion as far as the PCE is concerned. At a Central Committee Plenum just ended Jorge Ribadeneira was expelled from the party for his "divisionist" work in URJE and for leading PCE and JCE members into the guerrilla operation. The expulsion was in agreement with a resolution of the Pichincha Provincial Committee following their investigation in August. Ribadeneira was an alternate member of the Central Committee and a full member of the Pichincha Provincial Committee under Rafael Echeverria. Our PCE agents report that the struggle will now turn to URJE where the Ribadeneira forces are struggling with the forces controlled by the PCE and Pedro Saad. One can only wonder what the Central Committee would think of Echeverria's parallel activities outside the PCE as reports continue to reveal preparations by his group for armed action and terrorism. This comes through the ECWHEAT telephone tap on Antonio Flores.

I continue working with my two Quito Social Christian leaders, Carlos Roggiero and Jose Maria Egas, in their respective fields of militant action and subversive watch-control. Egas has been under rather intense cultivation by the chief of the Embassy political section (ostensibly my boss) who doesn't know he is my agent. Egas has just left on a State Department leader grant to observe the U.S. electoral campaign. He'll spend most of his time in California but after the elections he'll return to Washington where headquarters will give him a month of intense training in clandestine operations, mainly surveillance and investigations.

Velasco is again beginning to haunt the political scene and the specter of his return for the 1964 elections looms not far over the horizon. Through the *Agencia Orbe Latinoamericano*‡ news service we arranged to have Velasco interviewed recently in Buenos Aires, and he affirmed his plans to return in January 1964 for the campaign. Publication of the interview here has caused just the ripple we want so that the ECACTOR agents will begin plotting to keep him from returning or from being a candidate.

Noland has a new Velasquista agent who began calling on him at the Embassy some weeks ago to offer tidbits on organizational work of Velasquista leaders in Quito. The new agent is Medadro Toro‡ and he has Noland extremely nervous because of his reputation as a gunman. He was one of the four people arrested for firing at Arosemena during the shoot-out in the Congress in October last year, and he was jailed from then until February when the Supreme Court threw out the case. He was back in jail in April for insulting Arosemena and in May he was a Velasquista candidate for Deputy in the June elections. He lost and is obviously looking for some way to keep body and soul together.

So far his information has helped resolve persistent rumors of Velasco's imminent return and Noland, although personally fearing this man, thinks he has long-range potential. What bothers Noland are Toro's beady eyes looking through him, but he'll either have to begin discreet meetings outside the Embassy very soon or forget the whole thing. Politically Toro is dynamite.

Gil Saudade is trying to salvage his Popular Revolutionary Liberal Party‡ (PLPR), although several of the agents are now firmly entrenched in the CEOSL labor organization. After the fall of Velasco the struggle resumed in the PLPR between our agents and a group of extreme-leftists who were close to Araujo, coming to a head last week with the expulsion of Araujo's friends. Now Gil will try to get his agents active again in the organization, again to attract the Velasquista left away from Araujo, so that the PLPR will have some influence if Velasco returns for the 1964 election campaign.

Quito — 6 November 1962

At long last Reinaldo Varea's impeachment proceedings, which have dominated the political scene since August, have ended. Today he was acquitted by the Senate although Velasco's Minister of Defense at the time of the junk swindle lost his right to hold public office for two years. Varea may have survived as Vice-President but his political usefulness is practically wiped out. The only hope is for him to work very hard to rebuild his reputation so that when Arosemena's next drunken scandal occurs Varea might not be such an obstruction to ousting Arosemena for physical incapacity. Even so, there is little or no indication that Varea could ever overcome the Conservative and Social Christian opposition to him—he is, after all, a Velasquista.

Quito — 8 November 1962

Congress's final session last night kept tradition intact. In addition to a fistfight involving Davila, the national

Budget was adopted. Discussion of the Budget only began yesterday and was, of course, shallow and precipitate. There is a general agreement that it will be very difficult to finance in spite of new tax measures.

The 1962 Congressional session, as in 1961 and 1960, ended with no agrarian, tax or administrative reform. The session was controlled by the Conservatives and Social Christians who sought to use the Congress as a political forum, with the junk scandal as the issue, to attack both the Arosemena administration and the Velasquista movement. Significant legislation was never seriously considered.

Quito — 20 December 1962

Another crisis—the worst yet—broke today. President Allesandri of Chile stopped in Guayaquil this afternoon for an official visit to Arosemena after a trip to see Kennedy. At the airport Arosemena was so drunk he had to be held up by aides on both sides and later at the banquet he had to call on a guest to make the welcome toast.

News of this disgrace has spread around the country like a flash and already Carlos Arizaga Vega is moving to gather signatures for convoking a special session of Congress to throw Arosemena out. This time Arosemena may well have to resign.

The new Chief of Station arrived with his wife and dogs and next week the Nolands leave. Today Jim was given a medal by the Quito Municipal Council in recognition of his work with youth and sports groups in Quito. Renato Perez, Acting Council President, presided at the ceremony. Tomorrow at the golf-club the Nolands will be honored at a huge party, and the following day Janet and I have invited about a hundred friends to a farewell lawn party for the Nolands at our house.

Quito — 28 December 1962

The Nolands left and the new Chief of Station, Warren Dean,‡ hasn't wasted any time letting us know how he works. The other day, even while Noland was still here, Ray Ladd and I went off to spend the afternoon with a crowd of friends, mostly from the tourism business, at a bar and lounge of questionable respectability called the Mirador (it overlooks the whole city). The next day Dean gave us a verbal dressing down in a staff meeting and left no doubts he wanted to know where everyone is at all times. Afterwards Noland gave me another of his friendly advice sessions, warning me that my wilder habits may not sit well with Dean and that I'd better be a little more discreet. Frankly I think this new chief is pulling the old military shakedown technique—a mild intimidation to establish authority. Surely, with the extra hours worked at night and on weekends, an afternoon taken off now and then is justified.

This new chief is a big man, about six feet four inches and somewhat overweight. He's obviously having difficulty with the altitude even though he has come from Mexico City—each afternoon after lunch he sits behind his desk fighting to keep his eyes open. So far the main changes he has indicated are increased action against the extreme left in collection of information through technical operations and new agent recruitments. He also wants me to increase my work with Major Pacifico de los Reyes, the former Chief of Police Intelligence who has just returned from training at the FBI Academy in Virginia and at headquarters, where he was given several weeks training in clandestine intelligence operations. He's just been appointed Chief of Criminal Investigations for Pichincha but will continue to oversee the intelligence department.

Jose Maria Egas, the young Social Christian leader, is also back from his State Department trip and from our special training program. Dean also wants me to intensify the use of this agent because headquarters is getting frantic that serious insurgency may be imminent. Programs like the Subversive Control Watch List are getting increased emphasis and Egas's teams are crucial for this effort. From now on I'll pay him the equivalent of 200 dollars a month, which is very high by Ecuadorean standards but consistent with Dean's instructions.

Quito — 12 January 1963

In Guayaquil last week a national convention of URJE voted to expel Jorge Ribadeneira and nine other URJE leaders, most of whom were involved in the Santo Domingo guerrilla operation. The expulsions reflect PCE control of the convention and the specific charge against those expelled was misuse of 40,000 dollars that Ribadeneira and his group were given by the Cubans for guerrilla operations around Quevedo rather than Santo Domingo.

The best report on the convention was from a new agent of the Guayaquil base who is one of the URJE leaders expelled. Although the agent, Enrique Medina,‡ will no longer be reporting on URJE the base will try to ensure that he participates in the organization that these former URJE leaders will now form.

From now on the URJE ceases to be the main danger for insurgency from our point of view. The most important leaders have been thrown out and now that the PCE is back in control the emphasis will be on organization and work with the masses rather than armed action, not to eliminate, of course, selective agitation through bombings and street action. Our main concern now will be to monitor any new organization set up by Ribadeneira and the others who were expelled, together with improving our penetrations of the Araujo and the Echeverria groups in Quito. In a few days the base will bring out an appropriate story in the Guayaquil press on the URJE convention and we'll give it replay here in Quito. This will be a blow to URJE and to those expelled, since normally they try to keep these internal disputes quiet. Ribadeneira couldn't have been more effective for our purposes if he had been our agent.

My year as a director of the YMCA is ending, but now I am going to organize a YMCA basketball team. Dean has approved the use of station funds for players' salaries so we will be able to attract some of the best in Quito. We'll also buy uniforms and bring in shoes from the U.S. by diplomatic pouch. The station administrative assistant, Ray Ladd, will coach the team. The advantage to the station is to continue widening our range of contacts and potential agents through the YMCA, which was only established here a couple of years ago.

Quito — 16 January 1963

Reorganization of CEOSL is moving ahead although termination of the old CROCLE agents by the Guayaquil base required a visit in November by Serafino Romualdi, Executive Director of AIFLD and the long-time AFL–CIO representative for Latin America. The struggle between the old CROCLE‡ and COG‡ agents, who favored retention of their unions' autonomy within CEOSL, and our new agents, who insisted (at our instruction) that CROCLE and COG disappear in favor of a new Guayas provincial federation, finally led to the expulsion a few days ago of the CROCLE and COG leaders from CEOSL. Those expelled included Victor Contreras‡ who only last April became CEOSL's first President. Matias Ulloa Coppiano is now Acting Secretary-General of CEOSL and Ricardo Vazquez Diaz is Acting Secretary of Organization. Both are agents of Gil Saudade who originally recruited them through his Popular Revolutionary Liberal Party.

Ricardo Vazquez Diaz has been very effective in expanding the AIFLD education program along with Carlos Vallejo Baez.‡ In recent months, courses have been held in Guayaquil and Cuenca as well as Quito. Other courses are being planned for provincial towns in order to strengthen the CEOSL organizations there.

Quito — 18 January 1963

Student election operations through Alberto Alarcon have again been successful in Quito. In December the elections for officers of the Quito FEUE chapter were so close that both sides claimed fraud and the voting was annulled. Today another vote was held and Alarcon's candidate, a moderate, won. The national FEUE seat is now in Cuenca where anti-communist forces are also in control.

The Guayaquil base has made several PCE documents public, by having Colonel Lugo, Commander of the National Police in the coastal provinces, add them to a three-ton haul of propaganda he captured last October. In a few days these documents will come to light in the report emerging from a Senate commission's investigation of the propaganda. Included is the PCE Central Committee resolution expelling Ribadeneira. Dean is determined to create as much fear propaganda as possible as part of a new campaign for government action against the extreme left.

Quito — 30 January 1963

Our new station officer under Public Safety cover has arrived and Dean put me in charge of handling his contact with the station. His name is John Burke‡ and he's the most eager beaver I've ever met. Seems to think he'll be crawling in the attic of the Presidential Palace next week to bug Arosemena's bedroom. His problem is that he broke his leg training, and while it mended for the past year and a half he took every training course offered by the Technical Services Division, for lack of anything else to do. In recent months he has sent to the station masses of audio, photo and other technical equipment including about 200 pounds of car keys—one for every Ford, General Motors and Chrysler model built since 1925. Dean finally blew up over this equipment and fired off a cable telling headquarters not to send one more piece of technical gear unless he specifically asks for it. Poor Burke. He's not off to a very good start, and Dean has told me to make him stick exclusively to the AID police work until further notice. His first AID project, it seems, will be to take a canoe trip down in the Amazon jungles to survey rural law enforcement capabilities there—not exactly clandestine operations but it could get interesting if he runs into any Auca head-shrinkers.

In fact Burke will have plenty to keep him busy in the straight police work. Under the Public Safety program this year AID is giving about one million dollars' worth of weapons and equipment to the police: 2000 rifles with a million rounds of ammunition, 500 .38 caliber revolvers with half a million rounds, about 6000 tear-gas grenades, 150 anti-riot shot-guns with 15,000 shells, almost 2000 gas-masks, 44 mobile radio units and 19 base radio stations, plus laboratory and investigations equipment. In addition to training the national police here in Ecuador, the Public Safety office is also sending about seventy of them to the Inter-American Police Academy‡ at Fort Davis in the Panama Canal Zone. This Academy was founded by our Panama station last year and is intended to be a major counter-insurgency facility similar in many ways to the training programs for Latin American military officers under the military aid programs.

Quito — 15 February 1963

Dean is getting more determined each day to avoid a surprise insurgency situation. He wants to increase coverage of two groups in particular and he wants me to do most of the work. The two groups, not surprisingly, are those led by Araujo and Echeverria.

We've had a breakthrough in coverage of the Araujo group through the recent recruitment of one of his close collaborators, a Velasquista political hack named Jaime Jaramillo Romero.‡ Jaramillo was arrested last month with Araujo and two of the expelled PLPR leaders while recruiting in the provinces. Soon after, he was a "walk in" to the Embassy political section, and after being informed by the State Department officer who spoke with him we decided to make a discreet contact with him using the non-official cover operations officer of the Guayaquil base. I arranged for this officer, Julian Zambianco,‡ to come to Quito and with automobiles rented through a support agent, José Molestina,‡ Zambianco called on Jaramillo at his home. A meeting followed in Zambianco's car, which I recorded in another car from which I was providing a security watch for Zambianco. Earlier I had rigged the Zambianco car with a radio transmitter to monitor their conversation. Jaramillo's information looks good—including information about an imminent trip by Araujo to Cuba for more money. As Dean is a great believer in the polygraph I have requested that an interrogator come as soon as possible to test Jaramillo. If he's clean I'll turn him over to a new cutout so that we won't have to call Zambianco to Quito for each contact. Telephone coverage continues on Araujo but it hasn't produced good information.

On the other hand telephone coverage of Antonio Flores Benitez—one of Echeverria's principal lieutenants—is still providing excellent information. Flores is obviously getting very good intelligence from his agents in the Ministry of Defense, the Presidential Palace and the police. Our problem is inadequate coverage of Echeverria's plans and of his organization for terrorism and guerrilla warfare, although we are getting some information from Mario Cardenas, one of our PCE penetration agents who is close to Echeverria. On Dean's instruction I am studying three new operations for increasing coverage of Echeverria.

First, we will try to install an audio penetration of the Libreria Nueva Cultura, the PCE bookstore in Quito run by José Maria Roura, the number two PCE leader in Quito and Echeverria's closest associate. The two of them often meet at the bookstore, which is a rendezvous for PCE leaders in general and consists of a street-front room on the ground floor of an old colonial house in downtown Quito. On checking records for the owner of the house I discovered that it belongs to a golfing companion of mine, Ernesto Davalos.‡ Davalos has agreed to give me access and security cover during the audio-installation which we will make from the room above the bookstore on a Sunday when it is closed. For a listening post (LP) I hope to obtain an office in a modern, multi-storey building across the street from the bookstore, where we could also photograph visitors and monitor the telephone.

Second, we will try to bug Echeverria's apartment. He lives in a fairly new building in downtown Quito but access for the installation will be difficult. On the floor beneath his apartment is the Club de Lojanos (the regional club of people from Loja), from which we might be able to drill upwards to install the microphone and transmitter. This installation would be very slow and difficult, especially if we have to do it while Echeverria or his wife are at home, but Cardenas believes Echeverria has important meetings at home and probably discusses all his activities with his wife, who is a Czech. I am also checking on whether I can get an apartment across the street from Echeverria's that would serve as listening and observation post for this operation.

The third new operation is another technical installation, this time against Antonio Flores Benitez. He has recently moved into a modern multi-storey apartment-building where we might be able to monitor both his telephone and an audio-installation from the same LP. Although there seems to be little chance for access to his apartment or to those around it for the installation, an apartment above and just to the side of his is coming free in a few weeks. I may take that apartment in order to begin monitoring the telephone from there (rather than from the LP in Rafael Bucheli's house) and see later whether the audio technicians can drill to the side and down or whether we will have to make the bugging by surreptitious entry. Already we know that Flores meets many of his contacts in his apartment, and he discusses most of his activities with his wife—who gossips about them by telephone when he's not at home.

On the government side Dean also wants me to intensify my work with Pablo Maldonado,‡ the Director of Immigration, and to work into a liaison relationship with Manuel Cordova, the Sub-Secretary of Government and with Jaime del Hierro,‡ the Minister of Government. Although I have avoided until now regular contact with Cordova and del Hierro (on Noland's instruction last year) picking up with them now should not be difficult. The reason, Dean said, is to discover and to monitor their willingness to take action on information we give to them. Once we determine willingness on the high level, we'll be able to determine more accurately what information will bring action when passed through police agents such as Pacifico de los Reyes and Oswaldo Lugo.

With all this technical coverage I'll need some new agents for transcribing, photographic work and courier duties—but if they work we'll not be surprised by either Araujo or Echeverria. The team for processing the telephone taps will be Edgar Camacho and Francine Jacome with Francine as courier. Rodrigo Rivadeneira can switch to transcribing the new audio penetration and Francine will serve as courier for receipt of his material as well. I'll have Francine come by my house each morning at eight to leave transcripts and pick up any instructions for the others.

One other effort coming up that could be important: I've given money to Jorge Gortaire so that he can buy a used Land Rover to make a trip to military garrisons in the southern sierra and on the coast. The purpose of this trip is for Gortaire to sound out military leaders on all the rumors going around about a move against Arosemena while at the same time weighing the predisposition of the military leaders to such an action, even if the rumors aren't true.

Quito — 1 March 1963

This morning's newspapers give prominent coverage to Mr. McCone's testimony to the Senate yesterday in Washington on training for guerrilla warfare in Cuba. The Director mentioned Ecuador as one of the countries from which the largest number of trainees has been recruited, and he explained how the Cuban Embassy in Mexico City tries to conceal travel to Cuba by issuing the visa on a slip of paper with no stamp in the passport. His report follows another headquarters' report, issued last month by the State Department, that between 1000 and 1500 Latin American youths were given guerrilla training in Cuba during 1962.

In commenting on the press reports this morning Dean told me that one of his operations in Mexico City was the airport travel-control team. There the passports of travelers to Cuba are stamped by the Mexican immigration inspectors with "arrived from Cuba" or "Departed for Cuba" to make sure the travel is reflected in the passports. The station there also photographs all the travelers' passports and with large press-type cameras photographs are taken as they embark or deplane. Results of the Mexico City travel-control operation are combined with other data on travel, mostly from the other important routes to Cuba via Madrid or Prague, for machine processing. In order to intensify operations with Pablo Maldonado, Dean wants me to pass him copies of the monthly machine runs on Ecuadoreans traveling to Cuba. In addition, Mexico City is cabling the names and onward travel data to stations throughout the hemisphere so that the travelers can be detained or thoroughly searched when they arrive home. I'll also pass this type of information to Maldonado and use it as an entrée to Cordova and del Hierro.

I tried to get Dean to reveal why he wants me to work with the Minister and Sub-Secretary, because usually a Chief of Station handles the high-level liaison contacts. He says he wants me to get the experience now because it will help me later. He's bitter about Winston Scott,‡ the Chief of Station in Mexico City. Scott has very close relations with both the President, Adolfo Lopez Mateos,‡ and the Minister of Government, Gustavo Diaz Ordaz.‡ When Scott left the country from time to time or went on home leave he made arrangements for communications to be kept open with the President and the Minister but would never let Dean make personal contact even though he was Acting cos when Scott was away.

Guayaquil — 31 March 1963

The best part of being a CIA officer is that you never get bored for long. On Friday, two days ago, I flew down from Quito to recruit someone I've known for about a year and whom the Base Chief, Ralph Seehafer,‡ wants to use as a cutout to one of his PCE penetration agents. The recruitment went fine and tomorrow I'll introduce the new agent, Alfredo Villacres,‡ to Seehafer.

I came down on a Friday so that I could spend the weekend out of the altitude, but mostly because Alfredo and I usually spend Saturday nights making the rounds of Guayaquil's sleazy dives. Last night was typical and we left the last stop about eight o'clock this morning with Alfredo roaring down the unpaved, potholed streets of a suburban shanty town, firing his .45 into the air while his dilapidated, windowless old jeep station wagon practically shook apart.

This afternoon he called me at the hotel to advise that we had barely escaped involvement in a new Arosemena scandal. It seems that a few minutes after we left the "Cuatro y Media" last night (it had been an early stop and we left about 1 a.m.) Arosemena and his party arrived. The story is all over town now of how Arosemena and his friends began to taunt the waiters—all are homosexuals there—finally ordering one of them to put a lampshade on his head. Arosemena took out the pistol he always carries and instead of shooting off the lampshade he shot the waiter in the head. No one is certain whether the waiter died or is in the hospital, but the blame is going to be taken by Arosemena's private secretary, Galo Ledesma (known to all as "Veneno" (poison) Ledesma). Ledesma apparently left today for Panama where he's going to wait to see what happens here. Alfredo said that if we had been there when Arosemena and his group arrived we would have had to stay since it's a small, one-room place and Arosemena always invites everyone to join his group. I can see the Ambassador's face if that had happened and my name was included in the story: good-bye Ecuador.

Guayaquil — 2 April 1963

I was to have returned to Quito on the first flight this morning but a very interesting situation suddenly developed yesterday. After introducing Villacres to the Base Chief over lunch, Seehafer and I returned to the Consulate and had a visit from the chief of the USIS office. He told us that a young man had come into the Consulate this morning asking to speak to someone about "information" and was eventually directed to him. The person said he was a Peruvian and that he had information on the revolutionary movement in Peru and on Cuban involvement. The USIS chief said the Peruvian was so nervous and distracted that he is probably a mental case, but Seehafer asked me to see him if I had nothing better to do. We arranged for the USIS chief to give him my hotel-room number (the Peruvian was to return to the Consulate in the afternoon), where he would call in the evening.

The Peruvian came around to the hotel and we talked for two or three hours. I took copious notes because I know none of the names on the Peruvian scene and sent off a cable this morning to Lima and headquarters. The Peruvian is DUHAM–1‡ and is a middle-level militant of the Movement of the Revolutionary Left (MIR). He has just finished a three months' training course in Cuba along with several hundred other MIR members. They are all reinfiltrating to Peru right now, overland from Colombia and Ecuador.

The important aspect of this future agent, if he's telling the truth, is that he was selected out of the MIR group to receive special training in communications. He showed me a notebook full of accommodation addresses throughout Latin American to which secret correspondence will be sent. Moreover, he also showed me a dictionary that serves as the key to a code system that he will use in secret writing and radio communications with Havana.

This afternoon we got cables back from both headquarters and Lima confirming DUHAM–1's status in the MIR and warning us not to let this one slip away. The MIR is the most important potential guerrilla organization in Peru with hundreds of people trained in Cuba and with advanced plans for armed insurgency.

Lima sent a list of questions for DUHAM–1 which I'll go over with him tonight. He really is a case of nerves and won't like working with a tape-recorder but I'm going to insist we record everything so that we don't have to depend on my notes. This way I can get more out of him too. It's not going to be easy getting him to stay with us—what he wants is financial assistance to get his wife and child out of Peru and to resettle in some other country. He says he became disillusioned during the training in Cuba, but my guess is that he's lost his nerve now that he's almost on the battlefield.

Quito — 5 April 1963

This MIR case has people jumping all around headquarters it seems. Not just the Peruvian and Ecuadorean desks—the Cuban branch and even the Soviet Russia Division are also getting into the act. As a cut-out and handling officer I brought in Julian Zambianco,‡ and yesterday Wade Thomas‡ arrived from headquarters to take close charge of the case—he's a specialist in CP penetration operations. Meanwhile I had sessions each day with DUHAM–1 on the tape-recorder, summarizing the results in cables to Lima and headquarters. The guy is definitely coming clean—everything seems to check out—and yesterday I finally got him to agree to spending at least a short period back in Peru with his former friends. From the sound of the cables from Lima, DUHAM–1 is going to be their first important MIR penetration. My participation ended today when I came back to Quito.

Quito — 12 April 1963

A report is just in from Mario Cardenas, one of our best PCE penetration agents and a close but not intimate associate of Echeverria. Cardenas reported that Jose Maria Roura, Echeverria's principal lieutenant in Quito, has left for Communist China where he expects to get payments started that will enable the Echeverria group finally to begin armed action. Echeverria has told Cardenas to stand by for travel to Colombia at a moment's notice; so that he can receive money and documents that Roura, who is very well-known, should not bring into the country himself.

We discussed in the station whether to advise Jaime del Hierro, the Minister of Government, or Manuel Cordova, the Sub-Secretary, but for better security we decided to post a special watch on Roura's return through Juan Sevilla,‡ the Minister of the Treasury. Sevilla, who has been a golfing companion of mine for over a year, jumped at the chance, just as I thought he would, and he assigned his personal secretary, Carlos Rendon Chiribaga,‡ to watch for Roura's return at the Quito airport. Now we can only hope that Roura comes straight back to Quito with no stop in Colombia so that we're not forced to protect Cardenas. If by chance we learn that Roura will arrive in Guayaquil, Sevilla can send his secretary there to await Roura. Meanwhile I'm moving along with the audio operation against Roura's bookstore and in a couple of days Larry Martin,‡ the audio technician from the Panama station support unit, will arrive to make the installation.

Besides Roura's trip we are also monitoring for Araujo's return. He is in Cuba right now and perhaps he too will bring back money, although the chances are slim that either he or Roura will be so careless as to bring back money on their persons. So that we can get timely information after his return I've had Zambianco come up from Guayaquil again to turn over Jaime Jaramillo‡ to a new cutout, Jorge Andino,‡ who is a hotel owner and Ecuador's best polo player. Andino is another acquaintance from about the time

I arrived and he too was quite willing to help. He'll receive the reports at the hotel but pass them to me at another business he owns a couple of blocks away. One of the mysteries we're trying to solve right now is whether there is any close relationship between Araujo's group and Echeverria's group, because Echeverria has given several indications that he is in contact with the Cubans.

Medardo Toro,‡ the Velasquista gunman whom Noland picked up in a developmental status last year, is now reporting on a regular basis. Dean told me to get him into the groove so I brought Zambianco into the case in an arrangement similar to the one we used with Jaime Jaramillo two months ago. Until I get a good cutout for Toro we'll have to keep it going with Zambianco, but this way it's very secure. Mainly we want to keep abreast of Velasco's plans to return for next year's elections. Too bad Toro is so far from Araujo's group.

Quito — 14 April 1963

Each day, it seems, a new wave of rumors spreads around the country signaling the imminent outbreak of guerrilla warfare and terrorism. Partly the rumors reflect our continuing propaganda campaign to focus attention on communism in order to provoke a serious crackdown by the government. But partly the tension is based on real cases such as captures of propaganda by Colonel Lugo's police in Guayaquil and the recent near-death of a terrorist when a bomb exploded during a training session. Our worry is that the Ecuadorean police and military wouldn't be able to cope with a determined guerrilla movement.

A recent incident underlines our doubts. Two nights ago a Navy logistics ship was returning from the Galapagos Islands with a group of university students who had been in the islands on an excursion. A coastal Navy patrol was lurking in the darkness just off-shore in wait for an expected incursion by a contraband vessel. The coastal patrol mistook the logistics ship for the contraband vessel and a two-hour gun battle between the two Navy ships followed. The coastal patrol finally called by radio to Guayaquil for help and the Navy communications center called off the battle. What was worse was that their firing was so bad that no serious hits were made during the two-hour battle and only one sailor was wounded. After arriving in Guayaquil the students spread the story, which was published in Guayaquil today, but the Navy isn't talking.

When Dean heard this story this morning he told me to get moving faster on the new technical operations—he said headquarters will get all over us if we get surprised by Araujo, Echeverria or others, what with the guerrilla movements already under way in Peru, Venezuela and Guatemala, and Brazil steadily going down the drain under Goulart. Here the only encouraging sign of late has been increasing willingness by the Minister of Government and Sub-Secretary to increase general travel-control efforts and to allow police action such as Colonel Lugo's recent operations. However, del Hierro and Cordova are clearly being restrained by Arosemena from really effective action.

Quito — 19 April 1963

Another important trip to wonder about—this time it's Antonio Flores Benitez, one of Echeverria's lieutenants, who left today for Cuba. What we can't figure out is why Echeverria would send Flores to Cuba when Araujo is there and Roura is in China. Roura's trip to China, according to Cardenas, was made without the authorization of the PCE Executive Committee in Guayaquil and if Pedro Saad finds out there will be serious trouble for Roura, a member of the PCE Central Committee, and possibly for Echeverria. No doubt now that Echeverria is moving ahead fast with his organization outside the party.

Flores was very careful not to mention his trip by telephone, but his wife let it slip out a couple of days ago. We're monitoring the telephone now from the apartment above and to the side of Flores's. Rodrigo

Rivadeneira‡ moved into the apartment with his brother Ramiro‡ and his mother, and between him and Ramiro the transcriptions are kept right up to date. The connection was easy because the building is completely wired for telephones and Rafael Bucheli‡ and an assistant simply made the connections in the main terminal box in the basement of the building. While Flores is away we'll try to get going on the audio operation although the audio technician isn't enthusiastic about drilling through reinforced concrete at such a difficult angle.

I also decided to use Rodrigo Rivadeneira in the listening and observation post for the technical operation against the PCE bookstore. On Sunday Larry Martin and I made the installation from the room above with Ernesto Davalos‡ giving us security and cover. Davalos was very nervous because his caretaker is a communist and spends most of the time in the bookstore. Although I assured him that we would be very quiet, Martin decided to make the installation behind the baseboards and underneath several of the floorboards. The noise when we ripped them up was so screeching, what with their centuries-old spikes, that Davalos almost had a coronary. The same thing happened when we hammered the boards back into place but luckily the caretaker showed no signs of suspicion—at least according to Davalos. The audio quality is good (Echeverria is running the bookstore while Roura is in China) although street noise at times drowns the conversations.

Rivadeneira rented the office across the street as an LP and he sits in a false closet I had built by Fred Parker,‡ a U.S. citizen support agent who has a furniture factory in Quito. Parker built the closet so that it could be carried in by pieces, and Rivadeneira sits in it looking through a masked side, listening, recording, snapping pictures of visitors to the bookstore, and keeping a log.

I had good luck also in getting just the right apartment across the street from and slightly above Echeverria's apartment. This observation and listening post (OP-LP) has just been rented through Luis Sandoval, the chief technician of police intelligence, who accepted my offer to work with us full-time for the foreseeable future. Sandoval is resigning from the police and will open a cover commercial photography studio in the OP-LP. I've given him enough equipment to start—more is coming later—and he will do the developing and printing of the photographs taken by Rivadeneira at the bookstore. As soon as we have a chance, we'll get Larry Martin back and try for the audio installation against Echeverria's apartment—probably by drilling up from the Loja Club that occupies the entire floor underneath Echeverria's place.

Quito — 24 April 1963

A sensational case that may be our first real breakthrough has just developed, but it looks as though interference from Arosemena may hamper follow-up. A few days ago, the Guayaquil base received information from one of its penetration agents that a Cuban woman was training URJE members there. The base passed the information to Colonel Lugo who managed to arrest her. Her name is July da Cordova Reyes, at least that's what her documentation says, and we may well have here the first case of the Cubans sending out training missions to work in Latin American countries where they don't have diplomatic missions—certainly it's the first case of its kind in Ecuador.

Colonel Lugo, however, reported that after her arrest he was ordered not to conduct an extensive interrogation. I took up the matter with Jaime del Hierro, the Minister of Government, in order to emphasize the great importance of this case for discovering the extent of Cuban involvement, especially whether there are other Cubans here besides the woman and all the details about when she arrived, whom she trained, where and whom she has trained before, her intelligence service in Cuba, communications, and much more. We are prepared, I told the Minister, to bring down an expert from Washington who could assist in the interrogation but who would not be recognizable as an American. All I got from the Minister was evasion, and we've concluded that Arosemena gave the order not to exploit the case. Two days ago the Governor of Guayas ordered her expulsion from the country: we're trying to salvage the case but right now we're not hopeful.

The extreme left has been forced into the dubious position of supporting the very government that broke with Cuba. Arosemena certainly isn't fooling the extreme left, or anyone else for that matter, on how hard he must fight for political support. Two days ago he canceled a provision of last November's Budget Law prohibiting any government salaries higher than the President's. The purpose of the law was to limit the very high salaries and benefits being received by the heads of certain autonomous government agencies and by other officials who hold more than one government job. Some, for example, were making the equivalent of 1000 dollars per month—twice as much as Arosemena. Obviously he canceled the law in order to glue on a little more firmly his Liberal Party supporters and others who had been hurt by the salary limitation bill. Disgusting for a desperately poor banana republic where over half the population receives less than 100 dollars per year.

Quito — 1 May 1963

Some success on the da Cordova case. On 27 April she was deported to Mexico but was refused entry and returned to Guayaquil. Colonel Lugo can't proceed with interrogation until he gets the go-ahead from the ministry, so I'll bring up the case again with del Hierro or Manuel Cordova. Warren Dean is happy—he told me very confidentially that Gustavo Díaz Ordáz, the Mexican Minister of Government, is really in the Chief of Station's pocket and that's where I ought to try and get del Hierro. The way to do it, according to Dean, is to provide money for a high government official's mistress-keeping: the *casa chica* rent, food, clothing, entertainment. In Mexico, he said, the Chief of Station got an automobile for the Minister of Government's girlfriend. The Mexican President, with whom the COS also works closely, found out about the car and demanded one for his girlfriend too. That must be an interesting station.

Gil Saudade has made some progress in labor operations. Last month a provincial trade-union federation for Guayas (FETLIG)‡ was established as the CEOSL affiliate there, replacing CROCLE. This was a long-sought after development and perhaps will now end the dissension that has wracked CEOSL for so long. The AIFLD courses, largely the work of our agents, Ricardo Vazquez Diaz and Carlos Vallejo Baez, continue to expand. Vazquez was recently confirmed as permanent CEOSL Organization Secretary and Matias Ulloa Coppiano was confirmed as permanent Secretary-General. They had been acting in these jobs since the expulsions in January of the old CROCLE agents.

Today only the CTE and the Catholic CEDOC were in the streets to celebrate Labor Day. Instead of a parade, which would have turned out very few people, the CEOSL group were invited by our Ambassador to a reception at his residence which was highlighted with entertainment by Matias Ulloa.‡

Quito — 11 May 1963

Today a sensational new case has solved at least some of the recent bombings and kept the city in a commotion all day. It started just after midnight this morning when four terrorists (two from URJE) hailed a taxi, overpowered and drugged the driver, tied him up and placed him in the trunk. The terrorists then drove around town passing various embassies where they intended to throw the bombs they were carrying—along with a quantity of weapons and ammunition. Because of recently increased police protection at the embassies, however, they decided against the bombings. Just after dawn the driver regained consciousness and after slipping out of his ropes managed to open the trunk of the taxi. The terrorists saw him escaping but he got away and went for the police.

Major Pacifico de los Reyes took charge of the case. The terrorists panicked and drove to the edge of town where they tried to escape on foot up the volcano that rises on one side of Quito. The manhunt during the day caused widespread alarm and exaggerated fears in Quito but eventually the terrorists were captured. They have already confessed to various recent bombings and armed robberies, through which they were raising funds to finance guerrilla operations. Most sensational of all, however, is that their leader is Jorge Ribadeneira of Santo Domingo guerrilla fame and another member is Claudio Adiego Francia, the Argentine who was arrested in 1961 for training URJE members.

We didn't know about this new Rivadeneira group, and I've told de los Reyes to try to determine if there is any connection between them and the Echeverria group.

Quito — 17 May 1963

Major de los Reyes has arrested Francia but Ribadeneira is still in hiding. He has also arrested Echeverria and Carlos Rodriguez, Echeverria's chief lieutenant for Indian affairs, but they protested their innocence and he had to let them go. Propaganda play on the case is sensational, with photographs of the weapons and ammunition spread all across the newspapers. Dean wants to press ahead with propaganda exploitation of every possible case: Layedra, da Cordova, this one—also the current trips of Araujo, Roura and Flores. Somehow Arosemena has got to be forced into taking repressive action.

It's too soon to be sure but perhaps a change of policy is already under way. Today Pablo Maldonado's Immigration Service denied passports to ten young Ecuadoreans who have scholarships to "study" in Cuba. I've given Maldonado this type of information before but this is the first time he has taken strong action and it may work. The students asked for passports saying they were only going to Mexico (where they would arrange visas and onward travel). The protests have already started and we shall see how long del Hierro, Maldonado's superior, takes to weaken.

Quito — 19 May 1963

Roura's hooked! Juan Sevilla,‡ Minister of the Treasury, called me this morning to advise that Roura arrived at the airport and was discovered to be carrying 25,000 dollars in cash. Carlos Rendon, Sevilla's personal secretary, was at the airport and made the body search, and right now Roura is being held incommunicado by the police with the money impounded. I suggested to Sevilla that he add to the sensation of the case by starting a story that Roura was also carrying false documents, compromising papers and other similar material. This is going to be a big one.

Jorge Gortaire‡ was back here in Quito a couple of days ago. He has finished his trip to the military garrisons in the south and on the coast—making several long delays through breakdowns. He's going to write up a complete report back in Ambato, but he said there is very considerable disgust with Arosemena in the military commands. If it weren't for Reinaldo Varea, in fact, there would be nothing to keep the military leaders, once they got organized, from forcing Arosemena's resignation. For now they see nothing to do because they still favor constitutional succession. Varea is still the fly in the ointment, because the junk swindle led to so much ridicule of the military. All the officers with whom Gortaire spoke seriously are concerned about communist infiltration in the government and preparations for armed action, but something more serious will have to happen before they begin to move against Arosemena. So we must keep up the pressure, exploiting every case to the maximum through propaganda media and political-action agents. On Varea, Dean is considering whether or not to ask him to resign, with encouragement in the form of a generous termination bonus, but he hasn't decided.

Quito — 21 May 1963

The Roura case is headlines—supersensational! Everyone in the country is talking about it. Jaime del Hierro has taken charge and is keeping up the suggestions about "compromising documents." He told the press that Roura's documents are more important than the money and relate to recent reports from the U.S. that Che Guevara is leading guerrilla-warfare planning for several South American countries including Ecuador. The documents are also said to include a "secret plan" for guerrilla warfare and terrorism in Ecuador.

Last night del Hierro asked me if I could get someone in Washington to determine whether the bills are counterfeit because the Central Bank experts here believe they're real. I suppose he and his friends want to keep the money, so I cabled headquarters to see what can be done.

Del Hierro's action puzzles me somewhat because of his sudden enthusiasm. Perhaps Sevilla is pushing him hard because he was responsible for the arrest, yet del Hierro still refuses to give the go-ahead on interrogation of the Cuban, July da Cordova Reyes.

Quito — 23 May 1963

Del Hierro is getting worried because the press and others keep urging him for the compromising Roura documents. There aren't any, of course, and now Roura's lawyers are beginning to move. Nevertheless both del Hierro and Sevilla are keeping the publicity going by calling the Roura case an example of the importation of foreign ideology to enslave the country. Del Hierro is also citing the case of the ten students who were refused passports as another example of falsification of documents for travel to Cuba for guerrilla-warfare training. Yesterday Sevilla's secretary, who made the airport arrest, said in a press statement that the Roura documents include instructions on how to organize a Marxist revolution, how to intensify hatred between classes, and how to organize campesinos and salaried agricultural workers.

Yesterday del Hierro ordered the arrest in Guayaquil of the local correspondent of the New China News Agency, whose press carnet was in Roura's pocket when he arrived. The correspondent only returned from Europe a few days ago, and his trip must have been related to Roura's.

Roura's defense began yesterday with publication of a statement that shows he is worried about repercussions from Saad and the PCE leadership in Guayaquil. He defended having the money, saying that he had been invited to London by Gouzi Shudian (International Bookstore of Peking) and that his trip was sudden and without authorization of the PCE. Because of recent confiscations by the government of material purchased for sale in his bookstore, Roura said, he had obtained 25,000 dollars for a printing shop to reproduce the materials provided by Gouzi Shudian. From London he went to Peking, he said, and he denounced the confiscation of his notes on visits to communes and other sites.

No doubt Roura will end up in terrible trouble with the PCE—possibly even expulsion like Ribadeneira. More important, his arrest will drive the wedge deeper between the Saad and the Echeverria groups. What a ridiculous cover story.

Quito — 24 May 1963

Roura has had a bad day all around. He made his formal declaration to the court alleging that he discussed the new printing facility in Peking with one Chan Kung Wen. The money, however, was given to him, so he said, in Berne on his return by someone named Po I Fo. We're checking these unlikely names with headquarters—Roura's imagination knows no bounds.

Roura's lawyer also had a session before the Council of State (the highest body for appeal against government violation of personal liberties) which refused Roura's plea for liberty and took under advisement Roura's charges against Sevilla and del Hierro for violating the Constitution. Now he'll have to stand trial on the basis of the "documents" and the money. We'll have plenty of time to fabricate appropriate documents for del Hierro to use against Roura but first we're working on something else.

John Bacon, the Station Reports Officer, and I suggested to Dean that we prepare an incriminating document to be used against Antonio Flores Benitez—to be planted on Flores when he arrives at the airport. There's a chance, of course, that he'll come overland from Colombia or that he'll arrive in Guayaquil, but Dean likes the plan and asked us to go ahead. The document will appear to be Flores's and Echeverria's own report to the Cubans on the status of their organization and on their plans for armed action. We are describing what we know about the organization, filling in with imagination where necessary, on the basis of the information from the ECWHEAT telephone tap and reports from Cardenas and Vargas, our two best penetrations of the Echeverria group. We are emphasizing (for propaganda afterwards) Flores's penetration agents in the Ministry of Defense, Army communications, the presidential bodyguard and the presidential archives. We are also planning to mention relations with Araujo's group and Gonzalo Sono Mogro, who seems to be training a separate organization in explosives and weapons.

Quito — 26 May 1963

It has been a busy weekend. Bacon and I finished the "Flores Report" yesterday and he took it out to Mike

Burbano‡ to put in final form, correct Spanish and proper commie jargon. He knows this usage best because he's the cutout for Cardenas and Vargas. No question but that we've got a really sensational and damaging document.

Bacon included in the report a general analysis of the Ecuadorean political scene with appropriate contempt for the Saad PCE leadership for its "reformist" tendencies. He infers that the Echeverria group has already received funds from Cuba and that this report is the justification for new funds. The date for commencing an all-out terrorism campaign will be late July (since we already have a report that the CTE plans to announce a general strike for that date). Bombing targets and guerrilla attacks will be set for the homes of police and military officers as well as key installations such as the water-works and the telephone and electric companies.

Burbano passed it back and I typed it this morning —it filled five sheets of flimsy blue copy paper. Then Dean came to the office and we agreed that Juan Sevilla, the Minister of the Treasury, would be better for getting it planted than Jaime del Hierro, the Minister of Government. I went to see Sevilla; he agreed immediately and said he'll use Carlos Rendon, the same secretary and customs inspector who nailed Roura. When I got back to the Embassy Dean was acting like a little boy. He had gone over to the "Favorita" to buy a tube of toothpaste and had spent three hours squeezing out the paste and cleaning the tube. Then he crumpled the papers, ground them a little with his shoe, folded them to fit into the tube and pronounced the report genuine beyond doubt. I took the tube, now with the report neatly stuffed inside, back over to Sevilla and tomorrow he will give it to Rendon who will plant it if possible. Rendon won't move from the airport until Flores arrives, and if he comes via Colombia or Guayaquil, we'll figure out some other way to get the document out. One way or another this one should really provoke a reaction.

Quito — 29 May 1963

Yesterday still another sensation broke when Araujo arrived back from his trip to Cuba. Too bad we didn't have a document prepared for him but he did just what we wanted. Sevilla's customs people, whom I had advised through Sevilla of Araujo's imminent return, tried a body search but Araujo provoked such a scandal that he was taken to the central immigration offices for the search. He only had forty-one dollars, however, and was later released—but his screams at the airport that revolution will occur very soon in Ecuador were prominently carried in this morning's newspapers.

Other propaganda is coming out nicely. The Council of State meeting on the Roura case was in the headlines, featuring Sevilla's very effective condemnation of communism and Cuba in defense of his action against Roura. The case of Guillermo Layedra, who blew his hand off training URJE members to make bombs, is in the courts, and Jorge Ribadeneira's latest caper is still causing sensation. Still, we haven't been able to get an interrogation of the Cuban woman.

Quito — 31 May 1963

First try at the Echeverria bugging was a near disaster. The audio technicians, Larry Martin‡ and an assistant, came back from Panama during the week and I worked out an elaborate plan for security and cover. Gil Saudade brought up from Loja one of his agents who works in Catholic student activities there, Cristobal Mogrovejo,‡ who is the only agent we have who could easily rent the Loja Club which occupies the floor underneath Echeverria's apartment. I brought up Julian Zambianco from Guayaquil to be team leader and to direct Mogrovejo as the shield for cover. Luis Sandoval and I were in the OP-LP across the street, observing and communicating with Zambianco via walkie-talkie.

I also arranged for two getaway vehicles through Pepe Molestina.‡

Mogrovejo earlier this week arranged to rent the entire club for this afternoon, a Friday, and to have an option to rent it for the rest of the weekend if his "business conversations" with the foreigners required additional meetings. From observation we knew which room Echeverria uses as a study and we selected the proper spot beneath from which to drill up.

The team entered the club about ten o'clock this morning and Martin and his assistant began quietly drilling, slowly and by hand in order not to arouse Echeverria or his wife who were coming and going. About four o'clock this afternoon the club manager burst in with about a dozen flower-hatted ladies to whom, he said, he wanted to show the club. Mogrovejo protested that he had been promised absolute privacy but because of the insistence of the club manager and the ladies, Zambianco had to intervene to keep them from proceeding to the room where the drilling was going on. The incident produced enough suspicion in the club manager and enough panic in Mogrovejo to warrant calling the operation off for now. I radioed to Zambianco to have the technicians fill in their holes with plaster and to paint over. This only took a few moments and shortly the team had evacuated the building.

For the time being we'll let this one cool off while I try to discover another way to get access to the Loja Club. Mogrovejo was a bad choice. We won't forget it because Echeverria, according to Cardenas, has given several indications that he has some kind of communications with Cuba—possibly, one would suppose, with a secret writing and radio link. A photo technician from Panama was recently here and he said that TSD has large lenses that could be used to "see through" the curtains Echeverria sometimes draws in front of the table where he works so that readable photographs of documents on the table might be obtainable. This would be one way to read his communications.

Quito — 2 June 1963

Flores is hooked and we've got another big case! Juan Sevilla and I were playing golf together this morning when a caddy came running out to call him to the telephone. We rushed into the clubhouse and sure enough it was Carlos Rendon, his personal secretary, calling to say that Flores had arrived and that the plant had worked perfectly. Sevilla rushed straight to the airport and I went home to wait. Late in the afternoon he telephoned and when I went to his house he explained that Rendon had seen Flores arrive and had put the toothpaste tube up his sleeve. He let it fall out carefully while he was reviewing Flores's luggage, "found it" and began to examine it, finally opening it and "discovering" the concealed report.

Arriving with Flores was another well-known communist, Hugo Noboa, who was discovered to be carrying 1,400 dollars in cash in a secret pocket. This money, propaganda material, and phonograph records of revolutionary songs were confiscated along with the Flores report, and both Flores and Noboa were taken under arrest to the political security offices for questioning.

Now to get the publicity going.

Quito — 3 June 1963

We're going to have to fight for this one. Only a small notice appeared in the press today on the Flores and Noboa arrests, and the only reference to the "Flores Report" was an allegation that microfilm had been found in his suitcase. Flores, according to this notice, is protesting that if any microfilm was found it was planted either in San Juan, Puerto Rico, where he was in transit, or here in Quito.

I checked with Juan Sevilla and he told me that he thinks Arosemena is going to try to quash the whole case including the false document. This is why, according to Sevilla, Flores is still in custody of the political security office instead of the police investigations department under Major Pacifico de los Reyes. He added that the key figure is Jaime del Hierro, the Minister of Government and added that if I know del Hierro, I should confirm the importance of Flores and the document. (Neither Sevilla nor del Hierro knows that I am in a working relationship with the other.)

For most of the afternoon I've tried to get either del Hierro or Manuel Cordova, the Sub-Secretary of Government, by telephone. It's not like them to avoid me like this, and Dean is about to blow up because the report hasn't been surfaced.

Quito — 4 June 1963

There's no doubt now that Arosemena has tried to cover up the case and protect Flores, but we're prying it loose almost by the hour. Sevilla threatened to resign if the case were suppressed and the rumors of a new Cabinet crisis were so strong yesterday and today that the Secretary-General of the Administration made a public denial of the crisis.

Del Hierro finally called me back today, and when we met at Cordova's house he gave me the "Flores Report" asking that I check it for authenticity because it is so grave. I couldn't simply give it a moment's look and pronounce it genuine so I took it back to the station. When I told Dean of this he went into a fury, stamped up and down and said I'd better get that report surfaced or else. He's really disgusted with del Hierro, whom he thinks is trying to delay making it public in order to protect the Liberal Party from embarrassment; the document, after all, is pretty damaging to the government, even though it is primarily aimed at exposing the Echeverria group.

A positive sign is that Flores has been passed from the political security office to the police, which places him directly under del Hierro. In his declaration Flores only said that he had been in Europe on a forty-five-day trip as a journalist (he writes for the leftist weekly *La Mañana*) with no mention of travel to Cuba.

Quito — 5 June 1963

Dean's fit of temper shows no signs of diminishing. This morning he demanded Jaime del Hierro's private telephone number at the ministry, which I gave him. He called del Hierro and told him angrily that of course the document is authentic and that every Ecuadorean should read it. Dean was careful to record this call on his dictaphone just in case del Hierro complains to the Ambassador.

Then I proposed to Dean that I give a copy of the document to Jorge Rivadeneira Araujo, the brother of Rodrigo Rivadeneira—the transcriber of the Flores telephone tap. Jorge has long participated in the clandestine printing operation, along with his brothers, and is a writer for *El Comercio,* Quito's leading daily. We don't usually place propaganda through Jorge, but Dean agreed since it is the fastest way to put pressure on del Hierro to release the original document. Later I took a copy to Rodrigo which he is passing to Jorge who will show it to his editors at the newspaper. This may destroy my relationship with del Hierro and Cordova but Dean doesn't care—he doesn't think Arosemena and the Liberals can last much longer anyway.

Quito — 6 June 1963

Our ploy against del Hierro worked liked a charm. This morning about ten o'clock Cordova called me from the Embassy receptionist's desk and when I went down he took me out back to del Hierro who was waiting in his car. He said he urgently needed back the Flores document because the press had somehow got a copy and he would have to release the original later today. I rushed up for the document, returned it to del Hierro and told Dean who whooped for joy. Then I called Rodrigo Rivadeneira to alert his brother Jorge that the Ministry of Government would release the document later today. It may not be printed in today's evening newspapers but already the whole town is buzzing about it.

Today the Council of State formally rejected Roura's case against del Hierro and Sevilla, which wasn't unexpected. Roura will be on ice for a long time and now Flores's chances of getting off are nil. Tomorrow, Sevilla's formal statement to the Council of State will be published in the newspapers—a full page which we're paying for and which includes PCE data like membership figures and recruitment priorities that I passed to Sevilla for documentation.

Both Mario Cardenas and Luis Vargas report that Echeverria has been crushed psychologically by this blow. He fears that with the Roura arrest and now Flores he'll surely be reprimanded by the Saad leadership, possibly even expelled from the PCE. He has now gone into hiding and the agents are trying to find out where.

Quito — 7 June 1963

Finally it's in print and the sensation is immense. Everything's included: description of Saad and the PCE Guayaquil leadership as "old bureaucrats full of bourgeois vices, faithful to the Moscow line and acting as a brake on revolution." Also: "We (the Echeverria group) are faithful to the experiences of the Cuban revolution and the necessity to prepare for armed insurrection." Araujo is described as having a good number of trained and armed teams and the Ribadeneira group is cited as possibly useful for "our" purposes. All the different critical government offices where Flores has his contacts are mentioned—including the Presidential Palace—and the date for commencing operations (urban terrorism and rural guerrillas) is given as late July to coincide with "our" urging of the CTE to call a general strike for that time.

As if this document weren't enough in itself, by sheer coincidence the CTE yesterday announced a general strike for late July. Our agents had reported that this announcement would come some time and we had included it in the Flores document. This announcement was carried in the press today, alongside the Flores document, as proof that the latter is genuine. Moreover, Sevilla's statement to the Council of State also came out this morning.

Quito — 15 June 1963

Several pieces of good news. First, I've just received my second promotion since coming to Quito, to GS–11 which is about equivalent to captain in the military service. The other is that I'm being transferred to Montevideo, Uruguay, at the end of the year—this I learned informally in a letter from Noland the other day. I had asked to be transferred to Guayaquil as Base Chief if the job became vacant, but the Montevideo assignment is good news because we'll be near the seashore again. These mountains are getting oppressive lately, and besides, Noland says Montevideo is a great place to live with good operations going.

Meetings between Zambianco and Medardo Toro,‡ the Velasquista gunman, have been fruitful but Dean is getting nervous about collecting timely intelligence on Velasco's plans to return for next year's elections. Through Zambianco I have worked out a plan to send Toro to Buenos Aires under cover of medical treatment for a back injury that has needed special attention for some years. Toro will take the treatment in Montevideo but will contact Velasco in Buenos Aires and stay as close to him as possible. Our hope is that Velasco will take Toro into his confidence as a kind of secretary and general handyman—this shouldn't be difficult as Toro was at Velasco's side with two sub-machine-guns draped over his shoulders up to the moment Velasco left the Presidential Palace. I've notified the Buenos Aires station, set up a contact plan for an officer of that station, and requested that Toro be placed on the list for the polygraph the next time the interrogators come around. Hopefully Toro will have his affairs arranged so that he can leave by the end of the month.

Over the weekend I'm going to Guayaquil and to the beach for a day—then to Manta and Portoviejo, the two principal towns of Manabi province just north of Guayas. In Portoviejo I'll introduce Julian Zambianco to Jorge Gortaire's brother, Federico Gortaire,‡ an Army lieutenant-colonel and commander of the Army units in the province. Because of the extreme poverty in Manabi province, even by Ecuadorean standards, communist activities there have prospered in recent years. Zambianco has been working several operations in the province including support of a well-known anti-communist priest, and he'll be able to handle contact with Gortaire on his frequent trips there. Contact arrangements were made by Jorge Gortaire when he was in the province last month, so getting this new operation going will be easy. The purpose is to be able to pass information on communist activities in Manabi to Lieutenant-Colonel Gortaire who, according to his brother, will not hesitate to take strong and prompt action unfettered by the political restraints often imposed on Colonel Lugo in Guayaquil.

Warren Dean is leaving shortly for six or eight weeks' home leave. Too bad about Gil Saudade. Normally when a Chief of Station leaves the Deputy simply takes over as Acting cos. But with all the tension and instability right now Dean asked for a temporary replacement from headquarters. It'll be Dave McLean,‡ a Special Assistant to Colonel King,‡ the Division Chief who, surprisingly, managed to survive the head-rolling exercise after the Cuban invasion. While at headquarters Dean is going to push for one or two more slots for case officers under Embassy cover.

Quito — 22 June 1963

The struggle is growing within the government among the factions favoring different lines of action in the face of the growing tension and fear of imminent insurgency. Juan Sevilla, the Minister of the Treasury, is the leader of the hard-liners while Jaime del Hierro,

Minister of Government, is somewhere in between, trying to maneuver so that the Liberals can stay in the government and retain their emoluments. Arosemena leads the doves, who refuse to see the danger, and the leftists, who would like to see the power of the traditional parties broken. Thus the cooperation we're getting from del Hierro in the security field is mixed.

Today, for example, the government finally announced a program that I've been pushing since last year to restrict travel to Cuba. From now on travel to Cuba by Ecuadoreans is formally banned and all passports will be stamped "Not Valid for Travel to Cuba." This program is the work of Pablo Maldonado who told me only recently that such a drastic measure would still be very difficult to get approved. On the other hand del Hierro still evades all my requests for access to the Cuban woman who was training in Guayaquil—now she's been sent to Tulcan which is practically isolated and a place from which she could "escape" and disappear across the border in Colombia.

In Guayaquil two days ago, an anti-communist television commentator narrowly escaped when a bomb demolished his car. Yesterday Colonel Lugo's police raided a bomb factory and storage facility at the isolated house of Antonio Chang, a militant of an URJE faction, following a lead provided by a base agent. Chang's wife, two sons, a Spanish bomb technician and a helper were all arrested and have made sensational declarations, including the fact that they were trained by a Cuban. (The Cuban hasn't lived in Cuba since the 1940s but this item was hidden in small print in the propaganda coverage.)

Meanwhile we're trying to keep media coverage going on all the cases, old as well as new, and stations in countries nearby are helping. As each case breaks we advise Caracas, Bogotá, Lima, Rio de Janeiro, Santiago and others, mailing immediately the clips of what's been published. These stations generate editorial comment on the communist danger in Ecuador and send clips back to us which we use to generate still more comment based on the Ecuadorean image abroad.

Dean has made one last effort before going on home

leave to salvage a little mileage from Reinaldo Varea, our discredited Vice-President. He told Varea to get going on speeches related to all the recent cases revealing communist plans for action and the bombings. Yesterday Varea began with a speech at the national convention of the Chamber of Industries, denouncing communism as a cancer seeking to destroy the national life. Hopes for his succeeding Arosemena are ever so slim but three days ago the Supreme Court began hearing charges against three persons in the junk swindle and Varea, happily, wasn't one of them.

Quito — 25 June 1963

Yet another sensation broke today: this one without our help. The case began this morning when one of the revolutionary paratrooper group led by Lenin Torres, still under arrest since they were discovered last year trying to help the guerrillas they had arrested to escape, themselves escaped and joined with three others in order to hijack one of the Area Airlines DC–4's that fly between here and Guayaquil. The plan was to fly over Quito distributing fly-sheets from the aircraft telling people to mass at the Presidential Palace and demand the release of Torres and the other paratroopers still being held. Also while the aircraft was circling URJE members would have carried out a series of intimidation bombings and would have demanded the release of Flores, Noboa and Roura as well as the paratroopers. They would have landed, taken aboard the released prisoners and flown to Cuba.

The paratrooper who escaped had been outside the prison under guard on an urgent family matter, but the guard, who was overpowered, tied and gagged, and left behind, got loose and reported the planned hijacking which he had overheard. Pacifico de los Reyes,‡ Chief of Criminal Investigations in Quito, placed some of his men in maintenance uniforms at the airport and when the four hijackers arrived they were immediately taken into custody. Seized with them were arms, bombs, tear-gas canisters, walkie-talkies, and TNT—as well as the fly-sheets. After their arrest they implicated Araujo and Ribadeneira in the plan, although this may well be a little provocation by de los Reyes. The whole episode, in fact, may have been staged or at least well-penetrated.

The story is headlines in the afternoon papers and has sent another shock-wave across the country as it's the first political hijacking here.

Quito — 27 June 1963

Today is a bigger day for propaganda than most but it illustrates how our campaign to arouse concern over the communist problem has been going. The front page of *El Comercio* carries four articles related to it. The headlines report a press conference yesterday by Reinaldo Varea‡ in which he condemned communism for threatening the country with organized subversion, including acts of terrorism and massacre. He also pointed to Cuba, supported by Russia and China, as the focal point for communist terror in America, adding that when the Congress convenes in August a special law against terrorism should be passed, possibly to include the outlawing of communism. A second article reports a press conference by Jaime del Hierro, in which he promised to exterminate every center of communist terrorism in the country. A third article describes follow-up raids of Colonel Lugo's police in Guayaquil and the discovery of another bomb factory from which 150 bombs were seized—it also reports a strategy meeting held two days ago between Colonel Lugo, Manuel Cordova, the Commanding General of the National Police and the Governor of Guayas province. A fourth article describes the latest revelations in the frustrated airliner hijacking. Not to be forgotten, of course, is the junk swindle, and a fifth front-page article relates the latest development in this case. Aside from the front page, the lead editorial expresses alarm over the recent terrorist cases and still another editorial wishes success to some Cuban exiles who recently landed a raiding party in Cuba.

Quito — 28 June 1963

Police in Guayaquil under Colonel Lugo seized some 300 more bombs in raids yesterday, and arrests of terrorists there now number nineteen.

Also yesterday, Juan Sevilla,‡ Minister of the Treasury, was honored at a banquet given by the Chambers of Industry and Commerce and the Textile Association. In condemning communism Sevilla said: "The country is suffering a grave moral crisis. It is discouraging to walk through government offices and see how moral values have deteriorated. It is indispensable that we re-establish moral values." He was given a parchment in appreciation of his "clear democratic position in defense of free enterprise and of our country's Western ideology."

Media exploitation of the airliner hijacking continues as does the Roura case. Today it was announced that the money taken from Roura will be examined by experts to see if it is counterfeit. This is a delaying formality because I've already told Jaime del Hierro that the Treasury Department in Washington has refused to certify that the U.S. currency is counterfeit.

Quito — 5 July 1963

The chain of recent cases, particularly the Roura and Flores cases, has produced one of the results we wanted. At a special meeting of the PCE Central Committee the whole Pichincha Provincial Committee under Echeverria was dismissed, with Roura expelled from the party and Echeverria suspended. Already Jaime Galarza, one of Echeverria's lieutenants, has published an article suggesting that Pedro Saad, PCE Secretary-General, was behind the revelations in the Flores document and Roura's arrest, because such information could only come from highly placed party members.

The momentum of the last three months' campaign is having other effects. Most of our political-action agents, particularly the rightists in the ECACTOR project, are reporting improving disposition to a military rather than a Congressional move against Arosemena, what with the alarm and gravity of the current situation. At the Ambassador's reception yesterday, moreover, the politicians talked considerably of their surprise that communist preparations have progressed so far. Moreover, everyone seemed to be apprehensive over the spectre of Velasco's return and the probability that he'll win again next year. Some members of Congress are anxious to begin proceedings against Arosemena, but many realize the odds favor Arosemena and his patronage over a weak and divided Congress.

Quito — 8 July 1963

Rafael Echeverria is still hiding and has seen our agents only rarely. In order to get closer monitoring of his activities, and possibly to discover his hiding-place, I've arranged to turn over the Land Rover bought for Jorge Gortaire's trip to Luis Vargas, a PCE penetration agent. I gave the car to Jose Molestina,‡ a support agent and used-car dealer, to place on sale, and at the same time John Bacon sent Vargas around to make an offer. Molestina doesn't know Vargas, much less as a communist, and when he told me of the offer I told him to take it. Now Vargas will probably be asked by Echeverria (who has no private transportation) to drive him around for his meetings.

Media exploitation continues on the recent cases as well as on efforts to salvage Varea. The Guayaquil base placed an editorial in *El Universo*, the main daily there, praising Varea for his recent anti-communist speeches. We replayed the editorial here in *El Comercio*. We also used the CEOSL to condemn communist plans for terrorism.

Operations at the Georgetown station (British Guiana) have just brought a big victory against the Marxist Prime Minister, Cheddi Jagan. Jagan has led that colony down a leftist-nationalist path since coming to power in the 1950s on the strength of Indian (Asian) predominance over blacks there. The Georgetown station operations for several years have concentrated on building up the local anti-Jagan trade-union movement, mainly through the Public Service International‡ (PSI) which is the International Trade Secretariat for public employees. Cover is through the American Federation of State, County and Municipal Employees,‡ the U.S. affiliate of the PSI.

Last year through the PSI the Georgetown station financed an anti-Jagan campaign over the Budget that included riots and a general strike and precipitated British intervention to restore order. This past April, with station financing and direction, another crippling strike began, this one led by the Guiana civil servants union which is the local PSI affiliate, and it has taken until just now to force Jagan again to capitulate. Visitors here who have also been to the Georgetown station say eventually the Agency hopes to move the leader of the black community into power even though blacks are outnumbered by Jagan and the Indians.

Quito — 11 July 1963

Arosemena's out and a four-man military junta is in.

It began last night at a banquet Arosemena gave for the President of the Grace Lines—W. R. Grace and Co. has large investments in Ecuador—to which high-ranking Ecuadorean military men were invited because the Grace Lines President is a retired U.S. Navy admiral. During the toasts Arosemena made favorable commentary about U.S. business operating in Latin America but he insulted our Ambassador by derisive reference to U.S. diplomatic representatives. In his drunkenness Arosemena also demonstrated incredible vulgarity and finally left the banquet and his guests.

This morning the chiefs of the military services decided at a meeting at the Ministry of Defense to replace Arosemena with a junta and about noon the Presidential Palace was surrounded by tanks and troops. I went down to the Hotel Majestic just in front of the Palace where Jorge Andino,‡ a support agent and owner of the hotel, arranged a room where I could watch the action. I also monitored the military intelligence radio and reported by telephone and walkie-talkie back to the station where frequent progress reports on the *coup* were being fired off to headquarters and to Panama (for the military commands there who receive all Agency intelligence reporting in Latin America).

Several hours of tension passed as Arosemena, known to be armed, refused to receive a delegation from the new junta. He remained in the presidential living quarters while the junta members arrived and went to work in the presidential offices. Eventually Arosemena was disarmed by an aide and taken to the airport where he was placed on a military aircraft for Panama—the same place that Velasco was sent to less than two years ago.

As the *coup* was taking place a leftist protest demonstration was repressed by the military with three killed and seventeen wounded but these figures will probably be much higher if an accurate count is ever made. Also during the *coup* Reinaldo Varea tried in vain to convene the Congress in order to secure his succession to the Presidency, but it's no use—he's finished.

The junta is composed of the officers who commanded the Army, Air Force and Navy plus a colonel who was Secretary of the National Defense Council. The Navy captain is the junta chief but Colonel Marcos Gandara‡ of the Defense Council is said unanimously to be the brains and main influence. No question that these men are anti-communist and will finally take the kind of action we want to disrupt the extreme left before they get their serious armed operations underway.

Quito — 13 July 1963

No problem for the junta in consolidating power. Loyal messages were received from military units throughout the country, civil liberties have been suspended, and communist and other extreme leftists are being rounded up and put in jail, more than a hundred in Guayaquil alone. Communism is outlawed (the junta's first act), censorship has been imposed, there is a curfew from 9 p.m. to 6 a.m., and next year's elections are canceled.

It will take some days for formal U.S. recognition of the junta but we've already started passing data from the Subversive Control Watch List to Major de los Reyes here in Quito and to Colonel Lugo in Guayaquil which they are using with military colleagues in the arrests campaign. For the time being we'll keep working with these police agents, and after U.S. recognition of the junta and Dean's return, decisions will be made on new contacts in the government. The most likely liaison contacts are the Minister of Defense, Colonel Aurelio Naranjo, who was chief of the Cuenca garrison and leader of the movement that forced Arosemena to break with Cuba; the Minister of Government, Colonel Luis Mora Bowen;‡ and the junta leader, Colonel Marcos Gandara.

Besides outlawing communism the junta is looking favorably at the reforms that the civilians were never able to establish. In their first statement the junta said its purpose is to re-establish moral values because the country had reached the brink of dissolution and anarchy. Their rule will be limited to the time necessary to halt the wave of terrorism and subversion and to resolve the country's most urgent problems. They have also declared that their government will not be oligarchic and will have policies designed to stimulate economic and social development in order to raise the standard of living—not just through development, however, but also through the redistribution of income. Among its highest priorities are agrarian, tax and public administrative reforms.

In a press conference Colonel Gandara said that reforms will be imposed by decree and that after repressing the extreme left the junta will call for a constituent assembly, a new Constitution and elections. However, he added, the junta might stay in power for two years to accomplish these plans—which immediately caused a cry of outrage from politicians in all quarters. Today, rather sheepishly, the junta issued a statement saying that they will "not be in power for a long time."

In justifying their takeover the junta said that Arosemena had spotted the national honor with his frequent drunkenness and his sympathy for communism. Arosemena, for his part, is saying in Panama, as Velasco did, that he still hasn't resigned. Varea is also in Panama now, but he had a happy departure. At the Quito airport where he was taken under arrest yesterday he was given an envelope from the junta containing a month's pay.

Quito — 31 July 1963

The first three weeks of junta rule have been rather mild as military dictatorships go, in fact after all the crisis and tension in recent months one can even note a feeling of euphoria. Today the junta was recognized by the U.S. but all along we've kept busy getting information to Major de los Reyes and Colonel Lugo. Goes to show how important station operations can be at a time when conventional diplomatic contacts are suspended. Even so, the most important communist leaders from our viewpoint, Echeverria, for example, have eluded all efforts to catch them. Very possibly some have even left the country.

At least for the time being the junta has considerable political support from Conservatives, Social Christians and others—not formally as parties but as individuals. How long this will last is unknown because the junta is obviously determined to end the power struggle between Velasco and Ponce and the instability such *caudillismo* brings. Moreover, by stressing that they intend to wipe out special privilege and the rule of oligarchies while pledging projects in community development, housing, public-health and education, the junta is attracting considerable popular support.

From our standpoint the junta definitely seems to be a favorable, if transitory, solution to the instability and danger of insurgency that were blocking development. By imposing the reforms this country needs and by taking firm action to repress the extreme left, the junta will restore confidence, reverse the flight of capital and stimulate economic development.

Quito — 15 August 1963

Dean is back from home leave and is moving fast to get established with the junta. Already he is regularly meeting Colonel Gandara, the most powerful junta member, Colonel Aurelio Naranjo, the Minister of Defense and Colonel Luis Mora Bowen, the Minister of Government. With Gandara he is using as bait the weekly Latin American and world intelligence summaries (cryptonym PBBAND) that are received from headquarters each Friday, translated over the weekend and passed to Gandara on Monday. Already Gandara has given approval in principal to a joint telephone-tapping operation in which we will provide the equipment and the transcribers and he will arrange the connections in the telephone exchanges and provide cover for the LP. Tentatively they have agreed to set up the LP at the Military Academy. What Dean wants is a telephone-tapping operation to rival the one in Mexico City where, he said, the station can monitor thirty lines simultaneously. After this operation gets going we'll save Rafael Bucheli for monitoring sensitive political lines without the knowledge of the junta.

Gil Saudade has been transferred to Curitiba, Brazil (a one-man base in the Consulate) and his replacement, Loren Walsh,‡ doesn't speak Spanish. Walsh, who transferred to WH from the Far East Division after a tour in Karachi, had to cut short his Spanish course in order to take the interdepartmental course in counter-insurgency that is required now for every officer going out as Chief or Deputy Chief of Station. What this means to me is that I've got to take over most of Saudade's operations: Wilson Almeida‡ and *Voz Universitaria*; the CEOSL labor operation with Matias Ulloa Coppiano, Ricardo Vazquez Diaz and Carlos Vallejo Baez; and the media operation built around Antonio Ulloa Coppiano, the Quito correspondent of *Agencia Orbe Latinoamericano*. Most of these agents are also leaders of the Popular Revolutionary Liberal Party and Antonio Ulloa runs the PLPR radio-station that we bought through him and Juan Yepez del Pozo, Jr. as a media outlet. This development is more than a little aggravating because the new deputy won't be able to take over any of these operations as none of the agents speaks good English. Dean said relief will come soon because he got three new Embassy slots; two will be filled in coming months and one early next year. All I can do with these new agents is hold their hands until somebody with time can really work with them.

Right now there are about 125 political prisoners in Quito, including not only communists but Velasquistas and members of the Concentration of Popular Forces. The junta policy is to allow them to go into exile, although some will be able to stay in Ecuador depending on their political antecedents—judgment of which, in most cases, is based on information we're passing to Colonel Luis Mora Bowen, the Minister of Government. Processing these prisoners, and others in Guayaquil and elsewhere is going to take a long time because of interrogations and follow-up. Although Dean is working closely with the Minister of Government in processing the prisoners, he hopes to use these cases to start a new unit in the Ministry of Defense that will be solely dedicated to anti-communist intelligence collection—basically this is what we had previously set up in the police. In fact the Ministry of Defense will be better because politics sooner or later will come back into the Ministry of Government and the police, while the military unit should be able to remain aloof from normal politics, concentrating on the extreme left.

First on the junta's program of reforms are the universities and the national cultural foundation called the Casa de la Cultura, both of which have long traditions as centers of leftist and communist agitation and recruitment. Several station and base operations are focused on giving encouragement to the junta for university reform including agents controlled through Alberto Alarcon in Guayaquil and the student publication *Voz Universitaria* published by Wilson Almeida.

According to Gandara the first university reform decree will be issued in a few days with the important provision that student participation in university administration will be greatly reduced.

Quito — 30 August 1963

Labor operations always seem to be in turmoil but now and then they produce a redeeming flash of brilliance. Ricardo Vazquez Diaz, one of the labor agents I took over from Gil Saudade, told me the other day that his mistress is the official shorthand transcriber of all the important meetings of the Cabinet and the junta and that she has been giving him copies so that he can be well-informed for his CEOSL work. He gave me samples and after Dean saw them he told me to start paying her a salary through Vazquez. From now on we'll be getting copies of the record of these meetings even before the participants. In the Embassy we'll make them available just to the Ambassador and the Minister Counsellor, and in Washington short summaries will be given limited distribution with the entire Spanish text available on special request. The Ambassador, according to Dean, is most interested in seeing how the junta and Cabinet members react to their meetings with him and in using these reports to plan his meetings with them. Eventually we'll try to recruit Vazquez's mistress, ECSIGH–1,‡ directly, but for the moment I'll have to work this very carefully in order not to jeopardize the CEOSL operation. Vazquez claims he's told no one of the reports, which I believe, because, if he told anyone, it would be one of the other CEOSL agents who probably would have mentioned it to me. These reports are jewels of political intelligence—just the sort of intelligence that covert action operations should produce.

(There has been a change, incidentally, in terminology: the operations that used to be called PP operations—labor, youth and students, media, paramilitary, political action—are now called covert action, or CA, operations. In headquarters this change in terminology was made at the same time the old PP staff was merged with International Organizations Division to form what is now called the Covert Action Staff.)

In labor operations themselves we've had serious problems with the new government, partly as a result of the junta's arbitrariness—the right to strike, for example, is suspended. In this respect the junta tends to treat the CEOSL trade-union movement much in the same fashion as it treats the CTE. This general trend is aggravated by the Minister of Economy, Enrique Amador Marquez,‡ who is one of the former labor agents of the Guayaquil base terminated last year for regionalism. Amador is doing all he can to promote decisions favorable to his old CROCLE and COG friends and detrimental to CEOSL.

Right now the most serious case involves the junta's attempts to reorganize the railways which are one of the many inefficient government autonomous agencies that together spend about 65 per cent of public revenues. The lieutenant-colonel appointed to run the railways is favoring the CEDOC (Catholic) railway union which is backed by COG and CROCLE against the other railway union which is part of CEOSL and is an affiliate of the International Transport Workers Federation‡ (ITF) in London.

I arranged for Jack Otero,‡ the Assistant Inter-American Representative of the ITF and one of our contract labor agents, to come to Quito from Rio de Janeiro to help defend the CEOSL railway union. He is here now but instead of following my instructions to approach the matter with restraint he started threatening an ITF boycott of Ecuadorean products. The specter of boatloads of rotten Ecuadorean bananas sitting in ports around the world provoked counter-threats from the junta and we've had to cut Otero's visit short. The ITF railway union may have to suffer for a while but we're going to get action now from Washington, probably from someone like Andrew McClellan‡ who replaced Serafino Romualdi as the AFL-CIO Inter-American Representative when Romualdi set up the AIFLD. What the junta needs is a little education on the difference between the free trade-union movement and the CTE, but this may not be easy with Amador working behind the scenes for CEOSL's rivals.

The Minister of Government is very cooperative in following our advice over the matter of the political prisoners. We have a special interrogation team here now from the U.S. Army Special Forces unit in the Canal Zone: they're from the counter-guerrilla school there and are helping process the interrogation reports and prepare follow-up leads. The results aren't especially startling but they are providing excellent file information. As a result the prisoners are being released in a very slow trickle and most are choosing exile in Chile. Araujo is one of the big fish that was able to hide, but a few days ago he and six others got asylum in the Bolivian Embassy. Chances are he'll be there a long time before the junta gives him a safe conduct.

University reform continues. Already the universities in Loja and Guayaquil have been taken over and Central University here in Quito is due next. What this means is the firing of communists and other extreme leftists in the university administrations and faculties. The same process is under way in the primary and secondary schools and is in charge of the military governors of each province.

Reforms in the government administration are also widening. Already the Ministry of Foreign Affairs and the Ministry of Economy are being reorganized. So far the junta's not doing so badly—tomorrow Teodoro Moscoso, the Coordinator of the Alliance for Progress, arrives to negotiate new aid agreements.

Quito — 8 September 1963

These labor operations are so messy they're forcing me to put practically all my other operations on ice for lack of time. No wonder Saudade had so few agents: they talk on and on so that one agent-meeting can fill up most of an afternoon or morning.

Our call for help from McClellan backfired. He sent a telegram to the junta threatening AFL–CIO efforts to stop Alliance for Progress funds and appeals to the

OAS and U.N. if the junta doesn't stop its repression of trade unions. Three days ago the Secretary-General of the Administration denounced McClellan's telegram and showed newsmen documents from CROCLE and COG backing the junta and the colonel in charge of the railways. Now the junta is going to suspend the railway workers' right to organize completely. Somehow we have to reverse this trend and we asked for a visit from some other high-level labor figure from Washington, hopefully William Doherty,‡ the former PTTI Latin American Representative and now with the AIFLD. Doherty is considered to be one of our more effective labor agents and Dean thinks he might be able to change the junta's attitude towards our organizations.

Not long ago the CA staff sent two operations officers to the Panama station to assist in labor operations throughout the hemisphere much as the Technical Services Division officers in Panama cover the area. They came for a short visit to Quito, more for orientation than anything else, but they're going to get ORIT to send someone to see the junta about these problems. Recently, according to Bill Brown‡ who is one of the labor officers, the Secretary-General of ORIT, Arturo Jauregui,‡ was fully recruited so that now he can be guided more effectively. Before, our control of ORIT in Mexico City was exercised through Morris Paladino,‡ the Assistant Secretary-General and the principal AFL-CIO representative on the staff. Possibly we will get Jauregui himself to intervene.

We've also had two polygraph operators here for the past week testing agents. I decided finally to meet Atahualpa Basantes,‡ one of our PCE penetration agents who has been reporting since 1960 but who had never been met directly by a station officer, using the polygraph as the excuse.

The interview with Basantes was interesting because it showed how useful the LCFLUTTER is for things other than determining honesty in reporting and use of funds. In the case of Basantes, which is not unusual according to the operator, the polygraph brought out a flood of remarks about his motivation and his feeling towards us and his comrades in the party. He's certainly a confused man, drawn to us by money yet still convinced that capitalism is destructive to his country. Why does he work for us? Partly the money, but he rationalizes that the PCE leadership is rotten. From now on I'll try to see him at least once a month. His reporting has fallen off during the last six months, mostly because Dr. Ovalle‡ is such a poor agent handler, so I'm now looking for a new cutout. Instead of a raise in pay, which could be insecure, I've agreed to pay the premium on a new life-insurance policy for Basantes—it's expensive because he's in his late forties and his health is poor, but it'll be one more control factor.

The polygraph operator who worked with me on the Basantes case is Les Fannin.‡ Fannin was arrested in Singapore in 1960 while he was testing a local liaison collaborator whom the station was trying to recruit as a penetration agent of the Singapore police. The Agency offered the Singapore Prime Minister some three million dollars as a ransom for Fannin and Secretary of State Rusk even wrote a letter of apology in the hope of getting Fannin out. Nevertheless, he spent months in the Singapore jail before being released. He told me the Agency analysis of the case suggested that the British MI–6, which controlled the Singapore service at the time because Singapore was still a British colony, had been aware of the attempted recruitment from the beginning. In a strong reaction to this violation of the long-standing agreement that the CIA refrains from recruitments in British areas except when prior permission is granted, MI–6, according to Fannin, arranged for the Singapore security official to play along, and then at the moment of the polygraph they had Fannin arrested.

One of Saudade's agents whom he sent to Cuba has just been arrested on his return to Guayaquil and nobody seems to know what to do about him. The agent is Cristobal Mogrovejo,‡ the same Loja agent whom we used to front for the near-disaster audio installation in the Loja Club beneath Rafael Echeverria's apartment. Dean is taking a hard line on Mogrovejo because the agent was told not to return to Ecuador when he was met by officers from the Miami (ex-Havana) station after leaving Cuba. We had sent that instruction precisely to protect Mogrovejo, but since he refused to comply, Dean isn't anxious to spring him loose. He was arrested because he had Cuban propaganda material in his baggage (incredibly stupid) on his arrival. Already the arrest is causing wide comment in Loja where Mogrovejo is President of the University of Loja law-student association and well known as a staunch Catholic.

For the time being the audio operations against Echeverria's apartment and Flores's apartment are suspended. Sooner or later Flores will go into exile and Echeverria is still hiding. The audio-photo operation at the PCE bookstore is also suspended since the junta closed the bookstore right after the *coup*. Now we'll have to take out the audio equipment with more pounding and squealing of spikes.

Quito — 20 September 1963

This has been a month of constant movement of people: agents, visitors and new station personnel. The first of the new station operations officers has arrived—he's Morton (Pete) Palmer‡ and his cover is in the Embassy economic section. Unquestionably he'll be an excellent addition to the station and I'm already beginning to unload some of the covert action operations on him.

Dean appointed me to look after another visitor: Ted Shannon,‡ the former Chief of Station in Panama and now Chief of the section of the CI staff in headquarters responsible for CIA officers under AID Public Safety cover. Shannon was the founder of the Inter-American Police Academy‡ in Panama (which, incidentally, will be moving next year to Washington with a new name: the International Police Academy‡) and he was rather upset that we haven't been fully using our Public Safety cover officer, John Burke.‡ Dean explained to Shannon his fears about Burke's getting into trouble through his over-eagerness, but after Shannon left Dean told me to start thinking about what operations we can give to Burke. Dean is worried about criticism in headquarters that he's not using his people, but in fact there's lots of work Burke can do. The first thing will be to integrate him with the Special Forces interrogation team working on the political prisoners.

Reinaldo Varea‡ returned to Ecuador yesterday but his troubles are far from over. Immediately after the *coup* the junta canceled the impeachment case against Varea but announced that he would have to stand trial if he ever returned. His return means that his trial begins again, and he has also agreed to refrain from political activity. From Panama he had gone to Houston where a headquarters' officer gave him termination pay, but if Dean needs to see him he can establish contact through Otto Kladensky.‡

Manuel Naranjo was replaced as Ecuador's U.N. Ambassador and has also returned. Headquarters was highly impressed with his work for us at the U.N., and Dean feels the same—in fact he's going to nominate Naranjo, who is now back at work in the Socialist Party, for Career Agent status which would mean considerable income, fringe benefits, job tenure and retirement pay.

Juan Sevilla,‡ Arosemena's Minister of the Treasury, is the only one of our political-action assets in the old government to get a new job with the junta. Probably because of his firm action during the months before the junta took over, he's been named by the junta as Ecuador's new Ambassador to West Germany. We're forwarding the file to the Bonn station and making contact arrangements in case they want to use him in Germany. A few weeks ago I gave Sevilla money for Carlos Rendón,‡ his private secretary, who caught Roura and made the plant on Flores. Apparently Rendon has been threatened and is going to leave the country for a few months.

Lieutenant-Colonel Federico Gortaire was reassigned from Army commander in Manabi province to Military Governor of Chimborazo Province. For the time being we'll communicate with him through Jorge Gortaire in order to save time, but Dean wants to have one of the new officers begin going directly to Riobamba to see Colonel Gortaire as soon as possible.

Dean still refuses to intercede with the Minister of Government, Colonel Luis Mora Bowen, on behalf of Cristobal Mogrovejo. Mogrovejo told the police that he went to Cuba on our behalf, and his mother even came to see the Ambassador but Dean is playing real dumb. I think he ought to help the poor guy out of that stinking, miserable jail.

The country's honeymoon with the junta is fading fairly fast. The traditional political parties are getting worried that the junta may stay in power longer than they've admitted, and their massive promotions of military officers haven't been very popular. Especially since among the first to be promoted were the junta members themselves: now they are one colonel, one admiral and two generals.

Quito — 15 October 1963

Labor operations are still unsettled because of the junta's arbitrary actions. Since last month, a new national traffic law has been in preparation but the junta refuses to consult the national drivers' federation (taxi, truck and bus drivers), which will be the organization most affected by the law. Everyone understands the need to stop the general traffic chaos and the carnage that so frequently occurs on the roads, especially when overcrowded buses roll off the mountainside because of their poor mechanical condition: traditionally, the driver, if he's alive and can move, flies from the scene as fast as he can go. But the drivers' federation is our top priority to woo away from the CTE and eventually into the CEOSL. So we called Jack Otero‡ back from Rio de Janeiro to see if he could intercede with the junta on the traffic law question, even though the drivers' federation isn't affiliated with the ITF. Something may come from the effort, perhaps not with the junta but with the drivers' federation.

Even the AIFLD operation is beset with problems. The country program chief here isn't an agent and so we can't guide him (except through Washington) so that his program harmonizes nicely with ours. Doherty finally came to help straighten out the AIFLD program for us, but this isn't the end of it. He's going to arrange to have Emilio Garza,‡ the AIFLD man in Bogotá who is a recruited and controlled agent, come here for as long as is needed to make sure the AIFLD program is run the way Dean wants it run. Mostly it's a question of personnel assignments through which we want to favor our agents. Sooner or later all the AIFLD programs will be run closely by the stations—until now the expansion has been so fast that in many cases non-agents have been sent as AIFLD chiefs and can only be controlled through cumbersome arrangements of the kind we've had here.

Political prisoners are being released to go into exile as their cases are reviewed. There are still well over one hundred of them—Flores and Roura are both going to Chile in exile. Araujo finally got a safe conduct and left for Bolivia a week ago. Echeverria is still in hiding, rejecting the bait we set with the Vargas‡ Land Rover. Cardenas, Vargas, Basantes‡ and our other penetration agents have somehow managed to avoid arrest.

For a few days last week our Popular Revolutionary Liberal Party agents were also taken as political prisoners. They held a meeting in violation of the government's prohibition of all political meetings without prior permission, and among those arrested were Juan Yepez del Pozo, Jr., Carlos Vallejo Baez‡ and Antonio Ulloa Coppiano.‡ They were only held for a couple of days and later Vallejo and Ulloa admitted to me that they staged the whole thing for publicity. Pete Palmer‡ is going to take over these agents so that next time they will discuss this sort of caper with us first—otherwise they can't expect us to bail them out if the junta is slow in letting them go.

Another new station officer arived: Jim Wall,‡ an old friend who went through the training program with me at Camp Peary. Wall has just finished two years under non-official cover in Santiago, Chile, as a university student. He's going to take over some of my operations too—probably the ECACTOR political-action agents. His cover will be in the Embassy economic section, along with Palmer.

The polygraph operators are now in Buenos Aires and Dean wants to be sure that Medardo Toro‡ is "fluttered." Our impression is that the Buenos Aires station isn't taking this case very seriously—undoubtedly they have plenty of Argentine problems to worry about. In order to see why production from the operation is not better, Dean asked me to go to Buenos Aires to interpret for the polygraph examination of Toro. I'll also go to Montevideo because Toro is taking the treatment for his back there and has made contact on behalf of Velasco with an officer of the Cuban Embassy in Montevideo.

Moscoso's visit brought good news for the Ecuadoreans—ten million dollars in new loans from the Inter-American Development Bank have been announced this month.

Quito — 7 November 1963

It was a strange trip, disappointing on the Toro case but very encouraging for my coming assignment in Montevideo. In Buenos Aires the station considers the Toro case something less than marginal, just as we had suspected. About all we can hope for is to have an officer from the station meet Toro occasionally to receive his reports and pay his salary. In Montevideo it's worse—the Chief of Station there, Ned Holman,‡ doesn't want anything to do with Velasco. Holman was Noland's predecessor as Chief of Station in Quito so he's had plenty of chance to get soured by Velasco. Even so, the case is interesting because Velasco is opening a channel to the Cubans through Toro who has already met Ricardo Gutierrez two or three times. Gutierrez is carried by the Montevideo station as the Chief of the Cuban intelligence operation which the station believes is targeted in large part towards Argentina and the guerrilla operations now going on there. It will be interesting to see whether Velasco gets money from the Cubans—it wouldn't be too unlikely, if he were to become a candidate again for President, because he refused to break with Cuba and has often spoken highly of Castro.

In Buenos Aires, besides interpreting on the Toro case I interpreted on two other cases: one was a labor leader who is one of the station's best penetrations of the Peronist movement and the other was an Argentine Naval intelligence officer and his wife who are working together as a penetration of the Naval intelligence service.

Quito — 10 November 1963

On 31 October, the national drivers' federation was required by the government to undergo "fiscal analysis," which means they're going to bring under control the one organization that can stop the country completely. It'll be a long time before this union can be brought into the ITF. In fact it's not really a union because many of its members are owners of taxis, trucks and buses and even gasoline stations. Its orientation, then, is middle class rather than working class but for our long-range planning it's the most important of the organized trade groups to be brought under greater influence and control.

Bill Doherty‡ arranged for Emilio Garza,‡ the Bogotá AIFLD agent, to come to help us smooth out the problems between our CEOSL agents and the AIFLD operation. The agent was an excellent choice and I've already recommended that he be transferred to Ecuador when his assignment in Bogotá ends. He's the most effective of the career labor agents that I've worked with.

For the past six week there have been regular terrorist bombings, mostly against government buildings. They started in Quito—five occurred in one week in mid-October—but now they've spread to Guayaquil. None of our agents seems to know what group is behind the bombings and Dean's getting jittery. It's embarrassing because the bombings make the junta look inept in spite of all the arrests and forced exiles.

The day after tomorrow I'm going to try to recruit Jose Maria Roura who's been rotting away in the Garcia Moreno prison since May. He's being allowed to leave the country and will fly to Guayaquil, then to Lima, La Paz, and eventually to Chile.

Colonel Lugo has been in Quito for the past few weeks and he told me that the police interrogators report that Roura is very depressed, even disillusioned, about his political past. He is also extremely concerned about his family which is completely destitute and living on the charity of friends. This information coincides with what we've learned from the interrogation reports received through other sources and from information on Roura's family obtained through the PCE penetration agents. Lugo suggested to me that Roura may be ripe for a recruitment approach but he doesn't think it should be made in the prison.

After discussing the possibilities, Dean asked me to take the same Guayaquil–Lima flight as Roura and to try my luck on the plane. We've arranged for ECBLISS-1‡ the Braniff manager in Guayaquil, who is an American and a base support agent, to have me seated next to Roura. Headquarters' approval just came in and the Lima station is going to get the police to allow Roura to stay over for a few days if he wants because he only has about two hours between arrival from Guayaquil and departure for La Paz. For our purposes any possible follow-up after the flight should be in Lima rather than La Paz. When I talk to him I'll invite him to stay in Lima at my expense. After all these months in one of the world's gloomiest prisons he might just accept. In any case it's worth the risk of a scene on the plane—Roura is known to be extremely volatile—because we need a penetration of the exile community in Santiago and Roura would be an excellent source when he eventually returns here.

Quito — 13 November 1963

It didn't go perfectly, but it wasn't a disaster either. I took the noon flight to Guayaquil and to my surprise

Roura was on the same flight under police guard. Colonel Lugo had told me that Roura was going on the morning flight and the last thing I wanted was to be seen in Quito by Roura or in any connection with him at all. Arrangements by the base with the Braniff manager were perfect—he was waiting for me at the airport at three o'clock this morning and gave me the seat right next to Roura who would be released from his police guard when he boarded the aircraft.

When I walked on the plane I was shocked to see that there were only about ten passengers in the whole cabin. The stewardess conducted me to the seat next to Roura, who was already there, and my planned introduction and cover story began to crumble. I had wanted to begin the conversation as some anonymous traveler striking up a conversation with another anonymous traveler. And I wanted the seat next to Roura in case the flight were crowded—so that someone else wouldn't be sitting in that seat. But now it was too obvious.

A seemingly endless silence followed after I sat down next to Roura. I tried desperately to think of some new excuse to ease into a conversation—somebody had to say something because I was clearly there for a purpose. Suddenly the stewardess returned and suggested that I might like to move to where I could sleep since row after row was vacant. Time for recovery and a new plan. I went forward to a different seat, maybe ten rows ahead and began to get depressed.

We rolled down the runway and into the air. As the minutes began to go by, five, ten, twenty, I felt more and more glued to my seat. I was going into a freeze and beginning to think up excuses, like bad security, to offer later for not having talked to Roura. But somehow I had to break the ice and I finally stood up and began walking back to Roura's seat, in mild shock as when walking into a cold sea.

I introduced myself, using an alias and Roura agreed nonchalantly as I asked if I could speak with him. I sat down and went into my new introductory routine, relaxing a bit as I went on. I was an American journalist who had spent the past few weeks in Ecuador studying the problems of illiteracy, disease and poverty for a series of articles. At the airport before the flight, I learned to my happy surprise that he was going to be on the same flight and I wondered if he would mind discussing Ecuadorean problems with me from the point of view of a communist revolutionary. I added that I knew of his arrest earlier in the year and I expressed wonderment that such arbitrary and unfair proceedings could occur.

Over coffee we passed the flight discussing Ecuador. Roura spoke openly and relaxedly and we seemed to be developing a little empathy. About twenty minutes before we were to land in Lima I shifted the conversation to Roura's personal situation. He told me that he was taking a connecting flight to La Paz and after a few days would proceed to Santiago. He was bewildered over what to do about his family and was expecting hard times in exile.

Now I had to make my proposal, ever so gently, but clear enough for Roura to understand. I said I would be seeing friends in Lima who are in the same profession, more or less, as I am. They too would probably like to speak with him and I was certain that they would offer him a fee for an interview since they represent a large enterprise. He was interested, but said he had permission from the Peruvians only to remain in the airport until the connecting flight. I said my friends could probably arrange permission for him to remain a few days and that he should ask the immigration authorities if he could spend at least the day in Lima and proceed to La Paz on a later flight perhaps tonight or tomorrow. Who knows, I said, whether some kind of permanent financial support might be arranged for him in Santiago and for his family in Quito. Perhaps, even, he could arrange for the family to go to Santiago to live with him. I sensed he was taking the bait and was beginning to understand.

When the "fasten seat belt" light came on I took out a piece of paper with my alias typed on it and the number of a post-office box in Washington. I said I would be staying in Lima at the Crillon Hotel and if he was able to stay for a few days he could call me at the hotel and we could continue talking. If not, he could always reach me through the post-office box. He didn't say he would ask the airport authorities for permission to stay, but he didn't say no either. I thought he was deciding to stay. As a final touch, something I hoped would convince him I was knowledgeable, in fact I now hoped he realized I was CIA, I bade farewell pointedly calling him "Pepito," which is the name his PCE comrades call him. I returned to my other seat for the landing.

At the terminal building I walked down the steps and headed for the entrance where I was met by the Lima station officer who is in charge of liaison with immigration authorities. He had arranged for permission to be granted if asked by Roura, and indeed offered if Roura didn't ask—without, of course, creating suspicion that we were trying to recruit Roura. From just inside the terminal building we watched the Braniff aircraft because Roura had delayed inside. Eventually he appeared, descended the steps, but suddenly turned and rushed back up the steps and into the aircraft. At that moment about ten uniformed police who had been striding swiftly, practically rushing, towards the aircraft arrived at the steps. The leader boarded the aircraft and a long delay followed. The Lima station officer went to see his airport police and immigration contacts to find out what happened, and I went to the station offices in the Embassy to await news from the airport. If Roura stayed, I would check into the Crillon and wait for his call. If he proceeded to La Paz I would take the noon Avianca flight back to Quito.

When I reached the Embassy they gave me the bad news. Roura had been frightened by the police when they rushed towards him and thought something terrible might happen. In the aircraft he refused to descend to the terminal until the flight continued. Then he was extremely nervous in the terminal and interested only in being sure he didn't miss the flight to La Paz which he took as planned.

The Lima Chief of Station, Bob Davis,‡ apologized for the over-enthusiasm of their liaison service—the police approaching the aircraft were only trying to give him a warm welcome in preparation for immigration's offer of permission to stay for a few days. The Lima station botched the operation—I am convinced that Roura would have stayed—and now we can only wait for a telegram or letter to the post-box. On the other hand Dean is thinking of a follow-up visit to Roura once he gets to Santiago.

At the Lima station I asked how the penetration operation of the MIR is progressing—the one I had started in Guayaquil with the recruitment of Enrique Amaya Quintana. The Deputy Chief of Station, Clark Simmons,‡ is one of my former instructors at Camp Peary and is in charge of the case. He told me that Amaya's information is pure gold. He has pinpointed about ten base-camps and caching sites plus identification of much of the urban infrastructure with full details of each phase of their training and planning. The Lima station has a notebook with maps, names and addresses, photographs and everything else of importance on the MIR which the station considers to be the most important insurgency threat in Peru. The notebook is in Spanish and is constantly updated so that just at the right moment it can be turned over to the Peruvian military.

At the Lima station I sent a cable on the Roura recruitment to headquarters with information copies to Quito and La Paz. Dean had already seen the cable when I got back this afternoon and he's elated even though we can't be sure yet that Roura has accepted. Tomorrow I'll get Bolivian and Chilean visas for quick departure when Roura sends a telegram to the Washington post-box.

Quito — 17 November 1963

It didn't take long to resolve the Roura recruitment. This morning we had a cable from the La Paz station with the special RYBAT sensitivity indicator, reporting that Roura was in a secret meeting with two of the leading Bolivian communists. At the meeting he told them of my attempt to recruit him and he said if he ever sees me again he'll kill me. One of the two

Bolivians is an agent of the La Paz station, it would seem, although possibly the source is an audio operation. I won't need the visas now, but Dean still thinks Roura may change his mind in six months or a year or two. At least he knows we're interested and he has the post-box number.

I only have about three more weeks before leaving and as I turn over operations to the three new officers I am also terminating a number of the marginal cases—with provision, of course, for picking them up again if needed.

Among those I've terminated is Dr. Philip Ovalle, Velasco's personal physician and the cutout to Atahualpa Basantes, the PCE penetration agent. Ovalle is getting senile and is probably the main reason why Basantes's reporting has been in such a slide. Before termination I was able to get the Ambassador to have Ovalle placed back on the list of approved physicians for visas (the consular section had thrown him off because he sent some people with syphilis to the U.S.), or otherwise he might have been difficult. The chances of Velasco's coming back are now so slight that there's no reason to waste time seeing Ovalle for information on the Velasquistas. I recruited a new cutout for Basantes who I think can get the agent's reporting jacked up. He's Gonzalo Fernandez,‡ a former Ecuadorean Air Force colonel who was military attaché in London until he was forced to retire for political reasons. As Basantes is also a former military officer the chances are that they will work well together.

I also terminated the letter intercepts which I had taken back when the administrative assistant left a couple of months ago. The agents were pretty rattled at first but after I explained that we just don't have time for opening, reading, photography, closing, plus the two meetings for pick-up and return—they seemed to accept it. They liked the termination bonus and we made arrangements for meetings every two or three months to pay for propaganda they've burned. Not too bad at a couple of hundred dollars a ton. These postal intercepts are a waste of time, in my opinion, and only the headquarters desks that are ready to take anything, like the Cuban branch, will waste effort poring over letters and testing for sw.

Tampa — 10 December 1963

On the flight home I compared the existing situation in Ecuador with what I met when I first arrived there. Noland practically wouldn't recognize the place with all the growth. In the Quito station we now have eight officers, including Gabe Lowe‡ who will arrive in the spring to fill the last new slot, as opposed to five when I arrived, plus two additional secretaries, several new working wives and an additional communications officer. In Guayaquil we still have only two officers inside the Consulate but have added onc officer outside. Now Dean plans to add even more officers under non-official cover, particularly in Guayaquil. The station budget has also risen dramatically—from about 500,000 dollars in 1960, to almost 800,000 dollars now.

Operations are better now, too. The counter-insurgency program has improved, helped along by all the arrests, the exiling and the general repression undertaken by the junta. We have some new operations under way—particularly the new telephone tapping and military intelligence unit that Dean is setting up. Many of these activities are carried out in cooperation with the junta which, in turn, we have managed to penetrate through police and military officers and the junta's chief stenographer whom we have on our payroll. It looks as if operations in the student field are going to improve, and in our labor operations, both CEOSL and the AIFLD are well established in spite of all the problems they have had to face. The best of our PCE penetration agents have survived and we have added several more, including those of the Guayaquil base.

So far as the general political situation is concerned the position is even more favorable. When I arrived in Ecuador, Araujo was Minister of Government and for two and a half years the traditional parties made a mess of things, thus encouraging the people to look for extremist solutions. All politicians, Velasco and his followers, the Conservatives, the Social Christians, the Liberals and the Socialists, had struggled for narrow sectarian interests, sometimes under the leadership of our agents and close liaison contacts. But they failed to establish through the democratic process the reforms to which they all paid at least lip-service. Now, at last, these reforms can be imposed by decree and it seems certain that the order imposed by the junta will speed economic growth. Land reform is still the greatest need. In a report published earlier this year, the U.N. Food and Agricultural Organization noted that some 800,000 Ecuadorean families (over three million people) live in precarious poverty while 1000 rich families (900 landowners and 100 in business and commerce) enjoy inordinate wealth.

Part 3

Washington, D.C. — 8 February 1964

One can't help being impressed on a first visit to the new headquarters building out in Virginia. It's a twenty- or thirty-minute drive up the Potomac river from Washington—very beautiful parkway along the cliffs with the headquarters exit marked "Bureau of Public Roads" as if to fool someone. The building itself is enormous, about seven storeys with a somewhat "H" shape, surrounded by high fence and woods—extremely complicated to orient oneself on the inside. I read that it was built for ten thousand employees and from the numbers of cars in the vast parking lots it seems that number may already have been passed.

I spent two days with the Ecuadorean desk officer filling in the items that never get into formal reporting and catching up somewhat on the changes in the headquarters' bureaucracy. The most important change is the recent establishment of a new Deputy Directorate, the DDS & T (for Science and Technology), which was formed by merging the old Office of Scientific Intelligence and Office of Research and Reports, both of the DDI, with several other offices. This new unit has taken over all the processing of information and setting of requirements on progress around the world in the different key fields of science and technology with special emphasis, not surprisingly, on Soviet weapons-related developments. It is also responsible for developing new technical collection systems. The Deputy Directorate for Coordination has been eliminated.

The other major change is in the DDP[1] where the old International Organizations Division and the Psychological and Paramilitary Staff merged and adopted the new name: Covert Action Staff. Headquarters' coor-

1. See Chart VI.

dination and guidance for all CA operations (formerly known as PP operations) now centers in this staff. The people in the new CA staff, perhaps because many are veterans of the traditional friction between IO Division and the geographical area divisions over activities of IOD agents in the field, have developed a new terminology that provokes no little humor in headquarters' halls. Instead of calling their agents *agents* anymore, they now insist in their memoranda and other documents on calling them "covert associates." Problems relating to agent control—the old IOD wound that would never heal—seem now to have diminished simply by not calling CA operatives agents anymore.

Another change in the DDP that will take effect shortly is the merging of the Soviet Russia Division with the Eastern Europe Division—except that Greece will pass to the Near East Division. Now all the communist countries in Europe will be in the same area division which will be called Soviet Bloc Division. The communications indicator for action by SB Division is also changing: from REDWOOD to REDTOP.

Also, there is a completely new DDP division called the Domestic Operations Division (DOD) which is responsible for CIA intelligence collection within the U.S. (on foreign targets, of course). DOD engages mostly in recruiting Americans for operations, e.g. recruitment of scientists and scholars for work at international conferences. DOD has a "station" in downtown Washington, D.C. and offices in several other cities.

In WH Division the big news is that Colonel J. C. King‡ is finally on his way out as Division Chief. His power has gradually been chipped away since the Bay of Pigs invasion by separating Cuban affairs from regular Division decision-making and by surrounding King with various advisers such as Dave McLean,‡ who was Acting Chief of Station in Quito when the junta took over, and Bill Hood,‡ who has had the newly created job of Chief of Operations for the past year. King is being replaced as Division Chief by one of the senior officers who were brought into the Division after the Bay of Pigs from the Far East Division. He is Desmond FitzGerald,‡ Deputy Chief of WH Division for Cuban

Affairs—also a newly created job after the Cuban invasion. The regular Deputy Division Chief, Ray Herbert,‡ continues to handle personnel assignments and matters not related directly to operations against Cuba.

Washington, D.C. — 10 February 1964

I spent a night out at Jim Noland's house. They live in McLean not far from headquarters—everyone seems to have moved out that way. After return to headquarters Noland was assigned as Chief of the Brazil Branch in WH Division—a key job, with Brazil's continuing slide to the left under Goulart. Noland made several trips to Brazil last year and from what he says Brazil is the most serious problem for us in Latin America—more serious in fact than Cuba since the missile crisis.

Operations in Brazil haven't been helped by a Brazilian parliamentary investigation into the massive 1962 electoral operation, that began last May and is still continuing in the courts. The investigation revealed that one of the Rio station's main political-action operations, the Brazilian Institute for Democratic Action (IBAD) and a related organization called Popular Democratic Action (ADET),‡ spent during the 1962 electoral campaign at least the equivalent of some twelve million dollars financing anti-communist candidates, and possibly as much as twenty million. Funds of foreign origin were provided in eight of the eleven state gubernatorial races, for fifteen candidates for federal senators, 250 candidates for federal deputies and about 600 candidates for state legislatures. Results of the elections were mixed, with station-supported candidates elected governors in São Paulo and Rio Grande, both key states, but a leftist supporter of Goulart was elected governor in the critical north-east state of of Pernambuco. In the Chamber of Deputies the balance among the three main parties stayed about the same which in some ways was seen as a victory.

The parliamentary investigating commission was controlled somewhat—five of its nine members were themselves recipients of IBAD and ADEP funds—but only the refusal of the First National City Bank,‡ the Bank of Boston‡ and the Royal Bank of Canada‡ to reveal the foreign source of funds deposited for IBAD and ADEP kept the lid from blowing off. At the end of August last year President Goulart decreed the closing of both ADEP and IBAD, and the parliamentary report issued in November concluded that IBAD and ADEP had illegally tried to influence the 1962 elections.

Washington, D.C. — 12 February 1964

For the past few days I've been shuttling between the Uruguayan desk and the Cuban branch getting briefed on operational priorities against the Cubans, as my primary responsibility in Montevideo will be Cuban operations. Only five Latin American countries still have diplomatic relations with Cuba, and in Montevideo operations against the Cubans are the highest priority on the Station Related Missions Directive—the only station in the hemisphere where operations against a Soviet Embassy are in second place on the priorities list. The reason is that communist strength in Uruguay is growing considerably, particularly in the trade-union field, and is undoubtedly assisted by the Cuban Embassy there. Moreover, there have been strong indications that current guerrilla and terrorist activities in the north of Argentina are being supported from the Cuban Embassy in Montevideo.

Right now there are two main objectives for Cuban operations in Montevideo. First, in order to promote a break in relations, we are using all appropriate operations to support the Venezuelan case against Cuba for intervention and aggression based on the arms cache discovery on the Venezuelan coast last November. The arms have since been traced to a Belgian manufacturer who claimed to have sold them to Cuba. The purpose of the Venezuelan case is eventually to get a motion through the OAS calling on all Latin American countries with diplomatic relations with Cuba to break them. The hope is that such a motion, coming from Venezuela and not the U.S., would have sufficient momentum to get adopted by the OAS, particularly if enough propaganda of non-U.S.-origin can be generated over the coming months. For the sake of discretion I haven't asked, but the whole campaign built around the arms cache has looked to me like a Caracas station operation from the beginning. I suspect the arms were planted by the station, perhaps as a joint operation with the local service, and then "discovered."

While our overall objective in Uruguay is to effect a break in diplomatic relations with Cuba, we must meanwhile penetrate their Cuban mission in Montevideo either technically or by recruiting an agent, in order to obtain better intelligence about their activities. We already have a number of valuable operations going against the Cuban Embassy, but so far we haven't been able to penetrate it technically or to recruit any of its officers.

Not that the station hasn't tried. Last year several cold recruitment approaches were made and there was the unsolicited defection of Rolando Santana.‡ Unfortunately, in the case of Santana, he had been in Montevideo only a short while and had not had access to sensitive information because he wasn't an intelligence officer. The case served nevertheless for propaganda operations.

On another occasion we very nearly recruited the officer believed to be the Chief of Cuban Intelligence in Montevideo. This officer, Earle Perez Freeman,‡ had spurned a cold street approach for recruitment last December in Montevideo just before he was due to return to Cuba after some three years in Uruguay. In Mexico, where he was awaiting a flight to Havana, he suddenly appeared in the U.S. Embassy and in discussions with station officers agreed to take asylum in the U.S. The officer in charge was Bob Shaw,‡ one of my former instructors at ISOLATION, and headquarters' halls are still reverberating over his carelessness. After making all the arrangements to evacuate Perez in a military aircraft from the Mexico City airport, Shaw took Perez in a car to the airport. On the way to the airport Perez panicked, jumped out of Shaw's car and disappeared in a crowd. No one yet can understand how Shaw failed to follow the first rule in cases like these: to place Perez in the back seat with other officers by the doors on either side. Had he changed his mind before leaving Mexico City conversations in a controlled situation could perhaps have convinced him to come. At least a sudden panic and loss of contact would have been avoided. Perez returned to Havana and there has been no sign that his short contact with the Mexico City station became known to the Cubans, but opinion is unanimous in headquarters that the Mexico City station did a remarkably inept job on the case—not even an initial debriefing on Cuban operations in Montevideo.

On agent recruitment priorities in Montevideo the Cuban branch is most interested in the code clerk whom the station has identified as Roberto Hernandez. According to Division D officers in charge of Cuban communications matters, the Soviets are supplying the Cubans with cryptographic materials that are used for their diplomatic and intelligence traffic—impossible to break and read. If I could get the code clerk recruited, they said, arrangements could be made to have a headquarters technician copy the materials ("one-time" pads) for safe return to the code-room. Traffic afterwards, and perhaps traffic before—now stored by the National Security Agency for eventual breakthrough—could be read.

Miami — 14 March 1964

We divided our home leave between Janet's parents' home in Michigan and mine here in Florida. Two weeks ago another son was born, right on the day calculated by the doctor many months ago. Such joy—again everything went perfectly. When the new baby is able to travel in a few weeks, Janet and the children will fly to Montevideo, but I'm going now because the officer I'm replacing is in a rush to leave.

On my way down to Montevideo I've stopped off here and spent most of today discussing ways the JMWAVE (Miami) station can help our program against the Cubans in Montevideo. Charlie McKay,‡ the

JMWAVE officer who met me at the airport, suggested we spend the day discussing matters at the beach instead of at the station offices at Homestead Air Force Base so we relaxed in the sun until he finally brought me back to the airport. He was just the right person for these discussions because he was assigned to the Montevideo station in the early 1960s and is familiar with the operations there.

Miami CIA operations are vast but mainly, it seems, concerned with refugee debriefings, storage and retrieval of information, and paramilitary infiltration–exfiltration operations into Cuba. They have both case officers and Cuban exile agents who can assist hemisphere stations on temporary assignments for recruitments, transcribing of audio operations and many other tasks. Just recently the Montevideo station proposed that JMWAVE attempt to locate a woman who could be dangled before the Cuban code clerk, who is exceptionally active in amorous adventures. According to McKay they have just come up with the candidate—a stunning Cuban beauty who has done this sort of work before. Next week he will forward biographical data and an operational history on her, together with the photograph he showed me, to the Montevideo station.

The main Miami operation related to Uruguay, however, is the AMHALF project involving three Uruguayan diplomats assigned in Havana. They are the Chargé d'Affaires, Zuleik Ayala Cabeda,‡ and two diplomats: German Roosen,‡ the Second Secretary, and Hamlet Goncalves,‡ the First Secretary. No one of them is supposed to know that the others are working for the CIA but the Miami station suspects they have been talking to each other. Their tasks in Havana include arranging for asylum for certain Cubans, loading and unloading dead drops used by other agents, currency purchase and visual observation of certain port and military movements. Communications to the agents from Miami are through the One-Way-Voice-Link (radio) but every week or two at least one of them goes to Nassau or Miami on other tasks unrelated to the CIA, such as bringing out hard currency and jewels left behind by Cuban exiles. Such contraband serves as cover for their

CIA work but adds to the sensitivity of this operation—already extreme because of the implications of using diplomats against the country to which they're accredited. The Department of State would have no easy time making excuses to the Uruguayan government if this operation were to blow.

Montevideo — 15 March 1964

This is a marvelous city—no wonder it's considered one of the plums of WH Division. Gerry O'Grady,‡ the Deputy Chief of Station, met me at the airport and took me to the Hotel Lancaster in the Plaza de la Libertad where I stayed when I came last year. We then went over to his apartment, a large seventh-floor spread above the Rambla overlooking Pocitos beach, where we passed the afternoon exchanging experiences. O'Grady came in January but his family won't be down until after the children finish school in June. He's another of the transfers from the Far East Division—previous assignments in Taipei and Bangkok. Very friendly guy.

Montevideo — 18 March 1964

Moving from the next-to-the smallest country in South America to the smallest is nevertheless taking several giant steps forward in national development, for contrast, not similarity, is most evident. Indeed Uruguay is the exception to most of the generalities about Latin America, with its surface appearance of an integrated society organized around a modern, benevolent welfare state. Here there is no marginalized Indian mass bogged down in terrible poverty, no natural geographic contradictions between coastal plantations and sierra farming, no continuum of crises and political instabilities, no illiterate masses, no militarism, no inordinate birth-rate. In Uruguay I immediately perceive many of the benefits that I hope will derive from the junta's reform program in Ecuador.

Everything seems to be in favor of prosperity in

Uruguay. The *per capita* income is one of the highest in Latin America at about 700 dollars. Ninety per cent of the population is literate with over ten daily newspapers published in Montevideo alone. The country is heavily urban (85 per cent) with over half the 2.6 million population residing in Montevideo. Health care and diet are satisfactory while social-security and retirement programs are advanced by any standards. Population density is only about one third of the Latin American average and population growth is the lowest —only 1.3 per cent. Most important, Uruguay's remarkable geography allows for 88 per cent land utilization, most of which is dedicated to livestock grazing. Here we have a model of political stability, almost no military intervention in politics in this century, and well-earned distinction as the "Switzerland of America."

Uruguay's happy situation dates from the election in 1903 of José Batlle y Ordoñez, certainly one of the greatest and most effective of Western liberal reformers, who put an end to the violent urban–rural struggle that plagued Uruguay, as in much of Latin America, during the nineteenth century. To Batlle, Uruguayans owe social legislation that was as advanced as any of its time; eight-hour day; mandatory days of rest with pay each week; workers' accident compensation; minimum wage; retirement and social security benefits; free, secular, state-supported education. In order to set the pace in workers' benefits and to check concentration of economic power in the hands of private foreign and national interests, Batlle established government monopolies in utilities, finance and certain commercial and industrial activities. And in the political order Batlle established the principle of co-participation wherein the minority Blanco Party (also known as the National Party) could share power with Batlle's own Colorado Party through a collegiate executive that would include members of both parties. Through this mechanism patronage would be shared, fringe parties excluded and bloody struggles for political control ended. It is to Batlle, then, that Uruguayans attribute their political stability, their social integration, and an incomes redistribution policy effected through subsidies, the social welfare system, and the government commercial, financial and utility monopolies.

However, since about 1954 the standard of living in Uruguay has been falling, the GDP has failed to grow, productivity and *per capita* income have fallen, and industrial growth has fallen below the very low population growth rate. Investment is only about 11 per cent of GDP, an indication, perhaps, of Uruguayans' resistance to lowering their accustomed levels of consumption. Nevertheless, declining standards of living of the middle and lower classes have produced constant agitation and turmoil reflected in the frequent, widespread and crippling strikes that have come to dominate national life.

What has happened in this most utopic of modern democracies? The economic problem since the mid-1950s has been how to offset the decline of world prices for Uruguay's principal exports: beef, hides and wool. Because export earnings have fallen—they're below the levels of thirty years ago—Uruguay's imports have been squeezed severely with rising prices of manufactured and intermediate goods used in the substitution industries established during the Depression and the 1945–55 prosperity. Result: inflation, balance-of-payments deficits, economic stagnation, rising unemployment (now 12 per cent), currency devaluation.

In part Uruguay's problems are inevitable because recent prosperity was based on the unusual seller's market during World War II and the Korean War. However, the problems have been aggravated by certain government policies, particularly the creation of new jobs in the government and its enterprises in order to alleviate unemployment and to generate political support. Because of the "three–two system" for distribution of government jobs (three to majority party appointees and two to minority appointees) established during the 1930s, one could fairly say that both parties are at fault for the current top-heavy administration. Indeed government employees grew from 58,000 in 1938 to 170,000 in 1955 to about 200,000 now. Because of attractive retirement and fringe benefits the belief prevails that everyone has a right to a government job—

although salaries trail so far behind inflation that most government employees need more than one job to survive. But the overall result has been deficit financing for a public administration often criticized for ineptitude, slow action, interminable paper-work, high absenteeism, poor management, low technical preparation and general corruption.

Uruguay's system of paying for its state-employment welfare system is to retain a portion of export earnings through the use of multiple currency-exchange rates. Thus the exporter is paid in pesos by the central bank at a rate inferior to the free market value of his products with the retention being used by the bank for government operations. This system of retentions is at once a means for income redistribution and the equivalent of an export tax damaging to the competitiveness of the country's products in international markets. Retentions also serve as a disincentive to the primary producing sector, the cattle and sheep ranchers, who resist taxation to support the Montevideo government bureaucracy and the welfare system. The result in recent years has frequently been for ranchers to withhold wool and cattle from the market or to sell their products contraband—usually across the unguarded border to southern Brazil.

The contradiction between rural and urban interests, aggravated by decline in export earnings, resulted in Uruguay's falling productivity and declining standard of living. In 1958, after almost 100 years in opposition, the Blanco Party won the national elections in coalition with a rural pressure group known as the Federal League for Ruralist Action or Ruralistas. This coalition instituted programs to favor exports of ranching products but with little success at first. In 1959 major international credit was needed for balance-of-payments relief, and at the insistence of the International Monetary Fund fiscal reforms were adopted in the hope of stabilizing inflation, balancing trade and stimulating exports. The peso was devalued, retentions on exports lightened, import controls established and consumer and other subsidies curtailed. The recovery program failed, however, partly because industrial import prices continued to rise while inflation and other ills have also continued. The peso, which was devalued from 1.5 to 6.5 per dollar in 1959, has continued to fall and is now down to about 18 per dollar. The cost-of-living increase, a not extreme 15 per cent in 1962, went up by 33.5 per cent in 1963. In spite of continued economic decline, however, the Blancos were able to retain control of the executive in the 1962 elections, largely because of new government jobs created before the elections.

Perhaps more fundamental than the disincentives to ranchers and other contradictions in the income redistribution policies is the dilution of Uruguayan political power. The collegiate executive, conceived as a power-sharing arrangement between the two major parties and as a safeguard against usurpation of excessive authority, consists of nine members, six from the majority party and three from the minority party. In practice, however, the National Council of Government has many of the appearances of a third legislative chamber because of the factionalism in the major parties promoted by the electoral system. The current NCG, for example, consists of three members from one Blanco faction, two from another and one from a third faction. The Colorado minority members are similarly divided: two from one faction and one from another. Thus five separate factions are represented on the executive, each with its own program and political organization. Ability of the executive to lead and to make decisions is considerably limited and conditioned by fluctuating alignments of the factions, often across party lines, on different issues.

The Legislature is similarly atomized and moreover self-serving. A special law allows each senator and deputy to import free of duty a new foreign automobile each year which at inflated Uruguayan prices means an automatic double or triple increase in value. Legislation in 1961 similarly favored politicians, providing for privileged retirement benefits for political officeholders, special government loans for legislators and exceptionally generous arrangements for financing legislators' homes.

What are some of the solutions to this country's problems when already they have so much going in their favor? Some degree of austerity is necessary, but reforms are also needed in the government enterprises, the ranches, and, most of all, in the executive.

The twenty-eight government enterprises, commonly known as the autonomous agencies and decentralized services, are noted for inefficiency, corruption and waste. For such a small country the scope of their operations is vast: railways, airlines, trucking, bus lines, petroleum refining and distribution, cement production, alcohol production and importation, meat packing, insurance, mortgage and commercial banking, maritime shipping, administration of the port of Montevideo, electricity, telephones and telegraphs, water and sewerage services. Improved management and elimination of waste and corruption in the Central Administration—the various ministries as opposed to the autonomous agencies and decentralized services—is without doubt equally important.

In the ranching sector two major problems must be solved: concentration of land and income, and low capital and technology. On land concentration, some 5 per cent of the units hold about 60 per cent of the land while about 75 per cent of the units hold less than 10 per cent of the land—the latifundia–minifundia problem escaped Batlle's attention. Over 40 per cent of the land, moreover, is exploited through some form of precarious tenure with the corresponding disincentive to capitalize. Clearly the large landholdings must be redistributed in order to intensify land use both for production and employment.

As for the executive, commentary has started on constitutional reform such as a return to the one-man presidency or perhaps retention of the collegiate system but with all members elected from the same party.

No one seems to know just how Uruguay will solve these problems but all agree that the country is in an economic, political and moral crisis.

Montevideo — 21 March 1964

The Montevideo station is about medium-sized as WH stations go. Besides the Chief of Station, Ned Holman,‡ and O'Grady, we have four operations officers (one each for Soviet operations, communist party and related groups, covert-action operations and Cuban operations), a station administrative assistant, two communications officers and three secretaries—all under cover in the Embassy political section. On the outside under non-official cover we have two U.S. citizen contract agents who serve as case officers for certain FI and CA operations.

Uruguay's advanced state of development, as compared with Ecuador, is clearly reflected in the station's analysis of the operational environment which is much more sophisticated and hostile than in poor and backward surroundings. Although there are similarities in the stations' targets the differences are mostly the greater capability of the enemy here.

The Communist Party of Uruguay (PCU)

In contrast to the divided, weak and faction-ridden Communist Party of Ecuador, the PCU is a well organized and disciplined party with influence far beyond its vote-getting ability. Thanks in part to the electoral system (the *ley de lemas*) the PCU has only minimal participation in the national legislature: three seats of a total of 130. The party's strength is growing, however, largely because of the deteriorating economic situation. Whereas in the 1958 elections the PCU received 27,000 votes (2.6 per cent), in 1962 they received 41,000 (3.5 per cent). Station estimates of PCU are also rising: from an estimated 3000 members in 1962 to about 6000 at the present—still less than the PCU claim of membership in excess of 10,000.

The PCU's political activities are largely channeled through its political front: the Leftist Liberation Front, better known as FIDEL (for Frente Izquierda de Liberacion). Besides the PCU, FIDEL includes the Uruguayan Revolutionary Movement (MRO) and several small leftist splinter groups. Ariel Collazo, the principal leader of the MRO, holds a seat in the Chamber of Deputies which, with the three PCU seats, brings FIDEL congressional representation to four.

Uruguay's exceptionally permissive political atmosphere allows free reign for the PCU's activities in labor and student organizations as well as in the political front. The party's newspaper, *El Popular,* is published daily and sold throughout Montevideo—a fairly effective propaganda vehicle for the PCU's campaigns against "North American imperialism" and the corruption of the traditional Uruguayan bourgeois parties. While many communist parties are increasingly rocked with splits along the Soviet–Chinese model, the PCU is only minimally troubled and maintains unwavering support for the Soviets. Support for the Cuban revolution and opposition to any break in relations with Cuba are principal PCU policies.

The Uruguayan Workers Confederation (CTU)

Throughout its forty-odd years of existence the PCU has been active in the Uruguayan labor movement, peaking in 1947 when the party controlled the General Union of Workers which represented about 60 per cent of organized labor. Following the death of Stalin, however, ideological division led to a decline in PCU trade-union influence while the rival Uruguayan Labor Confederation‡ (CSU), backed by the Montevideo station, became the predominant organization. The CSU affiliated with ORIT‡ and the ICFTU,‡ but began to decline when the Uruguayan Socialist Party withdrew support and the PCU renewed its organizational efforts. In the early 1960s under PCU leadership the CTU was formed, and it has now become by far the largest and most important Uruguayan trade-union organization. Besides PCU leadership in the CTU, left-wing socialists are also influential.

Major policies of the CTU are support for the Cuban revolution and opposition to government economic policies, particularly the reform measures adopted at the insistence of the International Monetary Fund (devaluation, austerity) that hurt the lower-middle and low income groups. While only a small percentage of the workers are communists (most workingmen vote for the traditional parties), the PCU and other extreme-left influence in the CTU allows for mobilization of up to several hundred thousand workers, perhaps half the entire labor force, what with the prevalence of legitimate grievances. Action may range from sitdown or slowdown strikes of an hour or two, to all-out prolonged strikes paralyzing important sectors of the economy. As should be expected, the CTU is an affiliate of the Prague-based World Federation of Trade Unions.

The Federation of University Students of Uruguay (FEUU)

The situation in the national student union is similar to the labor movement: communists are a small minority of the student population but control the federation. There are two institutions of higher learning in Uruguay, the University of the Republic with an enrollment of about 14,000 and the National Technical School (Universidad de Trabajo) with about 18,000, both in Montevideo. FEUU activities, however, are concentrated at the University of the Republic but extend into the secondary system. A PCU member is Secretary-General of FEUU, and, when a cause is presented, large numbers of students can be mobilized for militant street action and student strikes. Campaigns of the FEUU include support for the Cuban revolution and CTU demands, and attacks against "North American imperialism."

The Socialist Party of Uruguay (PSU)

Although the pro-Castro PSU is waning as a political force in Uruguay—in the 1962 elections they were shut out of national office for the first time in many years—it retains some influence among intellectuals, writers and trade unionists. A considerable part of the Socialists' problem is internal dissension over peaceful versus violent political action. A portion of PSU militants under Raul Sendic, the leader of the sugar workers from Bella Union in northern Uruguay, have broken away and formed a small, activist revolutionary organization. They continue to be weak, however, and Sendic is a fugitive believed to be hiding in Argentina.

The Uruguayan Revolutionary Movement (MRO)

Although the MRO participates in FIDEL with the PCU, it retains its independence and a much more militant political posture than the PCU. Because it is dedicated to armed insurrection it is considered dangerous, but it is thought to have no more than a few hundred members which considerably limits its influence.

Trotskyists and Anarchists

The Revolutionary Workers Party (POR) under Luis Naguil is the Trotskyist group aligned with the Posadas faction of the Fourth International. They number less than one hundred and their influence is marginal. A similarly small number of anarchists led by the Gatti brothers, Mauricio and Gerardo, operate in Montevideo, but they too merit only occasional station coverage.

Argentine Exiles

Uruguay, with its benevolent and permissive political climate, is a traditional refuge for political exiles from other countries, especially Argentina and Paraguay. Since the overthrow of Peron in 1955 Montevideo has been a safe haven for Peronists whose activities in Argentina suffer from periods of severe repression. The Buenos Aires station is considered rather weak in penetration operations against the Peronists, particularly those on the extreme left. The Montevideo station, therefore, has undertaken several successful operations against Peronist targets in Uruguay through which Cuban support to Peronists has been discovered. One operation, an audio penetration of the apartment of Julio Gallego Soto, an exiled Peronist journalist, revealed a clandestine relationship between Gallego and the former chief of Cuban intelligence in Montevideo, Earle Perez Freeman—the would-be defector in Mexico

City. Our station, in fact, has made the most important analysis of the complicated arrangement of groups within Peronism—those of CIA interest are termed "Left-Wing Peronists and Argentine Terrorists"—but current signs are that the Argentine government is to allow Peronists to return, and much Argentine revolutionary activity will soon begin moving back to Buenos Aires.

Paraguayan Exiles

To an even greater extent than the Argentine extremists, the Communist Party of Paraguay (PCP) is forced to operate almost entirely outside its own country. Based mainly in Buenos Aires, Montevideo and São Paulo, the PCP is largely ineffectual with only about 500 of its three to four thousand members living in Paraguay. Harassment and prison for PCP activists under the Stroessner government is most effective. Nevertheless, the PCP has formed a political front, the United Front for National Liberation (FULNA), which includes some non-communist participation—mainly from the left wing of the Paraguayan Liberal Party and from the Febrerista movement, neither of which is allowed to operate in Paraguay. FULNA headquarters is in Montevideo.

The Soviet Mission

The Soviet Mission in Montevideo consists of the Legation, the Commercial Office and the Tass representative. About twenty officers are assigned to the Legation of whom only eight are on the diplomatic list of the Uruguayan Foreign Ministry with the rest listed as administrative and support officials. Of the twenty officers in the Embassy, twelve are known or suspected to be intelligence officers: six known and two suspect KGB (state security), and two known and two suspect GRU (military intelligence). The Commercial Office, located in a separate building that is also used for Soviet Mission housing, consists of five officers of whom two are known and one is suspect KGB. The Tass representative is known KGB. Thus of twenty-six Soviets in Montevideo sixteen are known or suspected intelligence officers, about the average for Soviet missions in Latin America.

Targets for Soviet intelligence operations in Uruguay, other than the U.S. Embassy and the CIA station, are fairly obvious although station operations have failed to turn up hard evidence except in rare circumstances. Thought to be high on the Soviet priority list are support to the PCU and CTU, penetration of the Uruguayan government and the leftist factions of traditional political parties through their "agents of influence" programs, propaganda publishing and distribution throughout Latin America through the firm Ediciones Pueblos Unidos among others, cultural penetration through various organizations including the Soviet–Uruguayan Friendship Society, travel support through the Montevideo office of Scandinavian Airlines System, and support for "illegal" intelligence officers sent out under false nationalities and identities.

The Cuban Mission

Like the Soviets, the Cubans have an Embassy and separate Commercial Office, but Prensa Latina, the Cuban wire service, is operated by Uruguayans and Argentines. The Embassy is headed by a Chargé d'Affaires with four diplomats, all either known or suspected intelligence officers. The Commercial Office is operated by a Commercial Counsellor and his wife, both of whom are thought to be intelligence officers. Contrary to Agency operations against the Soviets, however, there is no known framework for classifying Cuban intelligence operations, and practically nothing is known about the organizational structure of Cuban intelligence.

Nevertheless, the Montevideo station has collected valuable information on Cuban involvement with Argentine revolutionaries, and strong indications exist that the Cubans are providing support from their Montevideo Embassy to current guerrilla operations in northern Argentina. Other Cuban activities relate to the PCU, CTU, FEUU, artists, intellectuals, writers and leftist leaders of the traditional parties.

Other Communist Diplomatic Missions

Czechoslovakia, Poland, Bulgaria, Hungary, Romania and Yugoslavia also have diplomatic missions in Montevideo. The Czechs are considered the most important from a counter-intelligence viewpoint, but station personnel limitations preclude meaningful operations against any of these other communist missions.

There is also an East German trade mission. Because of the higher priorities, we don't cover their activities closely and the Chief of Station is trying through the Minister of the Interior to have them expelled.

As I read the files and briefing materials on Uruguay it becomes clear that the operational climate here, with the Soviet, Cuban and Czech intelligence services, and a sophisticated local political opposition in the PCU and related organizations, is rather less relaxed than in Ecuador. Care will have to be taken in operational security, especially in agent meetings and communications. Nevertheless, as Uruguayans are generally well disposed to the U.S., and because the station has a close relationship with the police and other security forces, the operational climate is generally favorable.

Montevideo — 22 March 1964

Until about a year ago the Montevideo station had the typical anti-communist political operations found at other hemisphere stations, the most important of which were effected through Benito Nardone,‡ leader of the Federal League for Ruralist Action, and President of Uruguay in 1960–61. Other operations were designed to take control of the streets away from communists and other leftists, and our squads, often with the participation of off-duty policemen, would break up their meetings and generally terrorize them. Torture of communists and other extreme leftists was used in interrogations by our liaison agents in the police. An outstanding success among these operations was the expulsion, in January 1961, just before Nardone's term as NCG President ended, of the Cuban Ambassador, Mario

Garcia Inchaustegui, together with a Soviet Embassy First Secretary, for supposedly meddling in Uruguayan affairs. The station's goal, of course, had been a break in diplomatic relations but resistance was too strong among other members of the NCG.

These operations had been expanded, much as the ECACTOR operations in Ecuador, under Tom Flores‡ who arrived in 1960 as Chief of Station. However, when Ambassador Wymberly Coerr arrived in 1962, he insisted that Flores put an end to political intervention with Nardone and to the militant action operations which had caused several deaths and given the communists convenient victims for their propaganda campaigns against the "fascist" Blanco government. Flores resisted, and in 1963 Ambassador Coerr arranged to have him transferred and the objectionable operations ended. Holman was sent to replace Flores, but he has maintained a discreet communication with Nardone, only for intelligence collection and without political-action implications. At this moment Nardone is in the terminal stages of cancer and for all practical purposes operations with him have ended.

The rest of the station operational program, however, covers all areas. First the Related Missions Directive:

PRIORITY A

Collect and report intelligence on the strength and intentions of communist and other political organizations hostile to the U.S., including their international sources of support and guidance.

Objective 1: Establish operations designed to effect agent and/or technical penetrations of the Cuban, Soviet and other communist missions in Uruguay.

Objective 2: Effect agent and/or technical penetrations at the highest possible level of the Communist Party of Uruguay, the Communist Youth of Uruguay, the Leftist Liberation Front (FIDEL), the Uruguayan Workers' Confederation, the Socialist Party of Uruguay (revolutionary branch), the Federation of University Students of Uruguay, the Uruguayan Revolutionary Movement (MRO) and related organizations.

Objective 3: Effect agent and/or technical penetrations of the Argentine terrorist and leftist Peronist organizations operating in Uruguay, the Communist Party of Paraguay, the Paraguayan United Front for National Liberation (FULNA) and other similar third-country organizations operating in Uruguay.

PRIORITY B
Maintain liaison relations with the Uruguayan security services, principally the Military Intelligence Service and the Montevideo Police Department.

Objective 1: Through liaison services maintain intelligence collection capabilities to supplement station unilateral operations and to collect information on Uruguayan government policies as related to U.S. government policies and to the communist movement in Uruguay.

Objective 2: Maintain an intelligence exchange program with liaison services in order to provide information on communist and related political movements in Uruguay to the Uruguayan government, including when possible information from unilateral sources.

Objective 3: Engage in joint operations with Uruguayan security services in order to supplement station unilateral operations and to improve the intelligence collection capabilities of the services.

Objective 4: Through training, guidance and financial support attempt to improve the overall capabilities of the Uruguayan security services for collection of intelligence on the communist movement in Uruguay.

PRIORITY C
Through covert-action operations: (1) disseminate information and opinion designed to counteract anti-U.S. or pro-communist propaganda; (2) neutralize communist or extreme-leftist influence in principal mass organizations or assist in establishing and maintaining

alternative organizations under non-communist leadership.

Objective 1: Place appropriate propaganda through the most effective local media, including press, radio and television.

Objective 2: Support democratic leaders of labor, student and youth organizations, particularly in areas where communist influence is strongest (the Federation of University Students of Uruguay, the Uruguayan Workers' Confederation) and where democratic leaders may be encouraged to combat communist subversion.

Foreign Intelligence and Counter-Intelligence Operations (FI–CI)

AVCAVE. Of the four agent penetrations of the Communist Party of Uruguay, AVCAVE–1‡ is the most important, classified as "middle-level" while the others are "low-level." The station's very limited success in running agents into the PCU in comparison with other countries, Ecuador, for example, is due in large part to the higher standard of living and welfare system: Uruguayan communists simply are not as destitute and harassed as their colleagues in poorer countries and thus are less susceptible to recruitment on mercenary terms. Of equal if not greater importance are the higher level of political sophistication in Uruguay, superior party leadership, minimal internal party dissension and the growth the party has experienced in recent years—there may even be a flicker of revolutionary hope given the mess the traditional parties are making of the country.

Not that the station hasn't tried to get a "high-level" agent. Periodic letter recruitment campaigns and approaches by "cold pitch" in the streets have been undertaken regularly but without success. AVCAVE–1's access derives from his membership in one of Montevideo's district committees and his close relation with an incipient pro-Chinese faction. His position enables the station to anticipate some PCU policies but he is far from the power locus of the Secretariat. Of some interest, however, is AVCAVE–1's guard duty at PCU headquarters.

AVPEARL. For many months Paul Burns,‡ the case officer in charge of operations against the PCU, has been studying ways to bug the conference room at PCU headquarters where meetings of the Secretariat and other sensitive conversations are held. Through AVOIDANCE–9,‡ one of the low-level penetration agents who is occasionally posted to guard duty at PCU headquarters, the station has obtained clay impressions of the keys to the conference room from which duplicate keys have been made. However, the twenty-four-hour guard service at PCU headquarters renders an audio installation in the conference room almost impossible by surreptitious entry.

AVOIDANCE–9 has also photographed the electrical installations in the conference room, which the guards check on their rounds of the building, and the station pouched to Washington identical electrical sockets of the bulbous, protruding type used in Uruguay. The Technical Services Division in headquarters is casting bugs (microphone, carrier-current transmitter and switches all subminiaturized) into identical porcelain wall sockets of their own manufacture. The Minox photographs of the conference-room sockets were also needed so that the slightest details of painted edges and drops can be duplicated on the bugs being cast at headquarters. Installation will consist simply in removing the current sockets and replacing them with those cast by TSD. If successfully installed the stereo audio signal will be transmitted down the electric power line as far as the first of the large transformers usually located on utility poles.

A study of the power lines has also been made in order to determine which apartments and houses are between the target building and the first transformer. One of these locations will have to be acquired as Listening Post because radio frequency (RF) signals cannot pass through the transformer. Several agents already tested in support operations are being considered for manning the LP. AVOIDANCE–9, however, has been kept as unaware as possible of the true nature of this operation because he is extremely mercenary, and there is some concern that he might use his knowledge of the installation, if he made it, to blackmail the station later. Thus AVCAVE–1,‡ whose loyalty is of a higher type, was instructed to volunteer for guard duty and he too is now spending one or two nights per month in a position to make the AVPEARL installation. At this moment the station is awaiting the devices from headquarters for testing before installation.

AVBASK. The station's only penetration of the Uruguayan Revolutionary Movement (MRO) is Anibal Mercader,‡ a young bank employee developed and recruited by Michael Berger,‡ the officer whom I am replacing. The agent's information is generally low-to-middle-level because he is some distance from the MRO leadership. He is well motivated, however, and there is some hope that he could rise within this relatively small organization. Nevertheless, as the MRO is terrorist-oriented there may be a problem over how far the agent should go, even if willing, in carrying out really damaging activities for his organization. The agent, moreover, is torn between emigrating to the U.S. (where his banking talents could provide a decent income) and remaining in Uruguay where he faces only turmoil and strain.

AVBUTTE. This is the support and administrative project for all matters to do with a U.S. citizen who is working under contract as an operations officer. His name is Ralph Hatry‡ and he is involved in FI operations. His cover is that of Montevideo representative for Thomas H. Miner and Associates,‡ a Chicago-based public relations and marketing firm. Hatry, who is about sixty years old, has a long history of work with U.S. intelligence, including an assignment in the Far East under cover of an American oil company. The immediate background to his assignment to Montevideo was a difficult contract negotiating period, in which Gerry O'Grady, the Deputy Chief of Station, was involved, and which revealed Hatry to be a very difficult person but with important sponsor. The Assistant DDP, Thomas Karamessines,‡ gave instructions to find Hatry a job somewhere and his file was circulated, eventually landing on the Uruguayan desk.

Hatry came to Montevideo last year and has been causing problems continuously, for the most part related to his personal finances and his efforts to increase fringe benefits. Holman, the Chief of Station, is trying to keep as much distance as possible between Hatry and himself—the opposite of Hatry's efforts. Because Berger is the junior officer in the station he was assigned to incorporate Hatry into his operations and to handle his needs in the station, and as is often the case with officers under non-official cover, the time involved in solving his problems inside the station practically wipes out the advantage of having him in the field. Nevertheless, Hatry is handling four operations: a letter intercept, an exiled Paraguayan leader, several penetration agents of the Paraguayan Communist Party and FULNA, and an observation post at the Cuban Embassy.

AVBALM. The contact in this operation is Epifanio Mendez Fleitas, the exiled leader of the Paraguayan Colorado Party. Although the Colorado Party provides the political base for the Stroessner dictatorship, Mendez Fleitas' past efforts to promote reform and to unite Colorados against Stroessner have earned him a position of leadership in the exile community. He is chiefly dedicated to writing and to keeping together his Popular Colorado Movement (MOPOCO) which he formed several years ago. We keep this operation going in Montevideo in order to assist the Asunción station and headquarters in following plotting by Paraguayan exiles against General Stroessner.

AVCASK. This operation is also targeted against Paraguayan exiles, specifically the Communist Party of Paraguay (PCP) and FULNA. The principal agent, AVCASK-1,‡ is active in a leftist group within the Paraguayan Liberal Party, and he reports on leftist trends within the party while serving as cutout and agent-handler for two lesser agents, AVCASK–2‡ and AVCASK–3.‡ AVCASK–2 is also a Liberal Party member but he works in FULNA and reports to AVCASK–1 on FULNA and PCP work in FULNA. AVCASK–3 is a PCP member who is currently moving into a paramilitary wing that is preparing for armed action against the Stroessner government. Only AVCASK–1, of these three agents, knows that CIA is the sponsor of the operation and he uses his own Liberal Party work as cover for the instructions and salaries he pays the other two. Yearly cost of this project is about five thousand dollars. Hatry meets with AVCASK–1 and reports back to Michael Berger.

AVIDITY. The station letter intercept provides correspondence from the Soviet bloc, Cuba, Communist China and certain other countries according to local addressee. The principal agent is AVANDANA,‡ an elderly man of many years' service going back to Europe during World War II. He receives the letters, which come from AVIDITY–9‡ and AVIDITY–16,‡ both of whom are employees of Montevideo's central post office. AVANDANA meets one of the sub-agents each day, receiving and returning the correspondence. Payment is made on the basis of the numbers of letters accepted.

The letters are processed by AVANDANA at his home, where he has photo equipment and a flat-bed steam table. He writes summaries of the letters of interest which he passes with microfilm to Hatry who passes them to Berger. This operation costs about 10,000 dollars per year.

AVBLINKER. When the station decided to set up an observation post in front of the Cuban Embassy it was decided to man the OP with AVENGEFUL–7,‡ who is the wife of AVANDANA, his assistant in the AVIDITY letter intercept, and an occasional transcriber for the AVENGEFUL telephone-tapping operation. The OP is in a large house across the street from the Embassy in the elegant Carrasco section of Montevideo. The station pays the rent for AVBLINKER–1 and 2, an American couple who live in the OP house (the husband is employed by an Uruguayan subsidiary of an American company) and

AVENGEFUL–7 spends each day in an upstairs front-room taking photographs of persons entering and leaving, and maintaining a log with times of entry and exit and other comment that she reconciles with the photographs which are processed by AVANDANA. AVENGEFUL–7's work with U.S. intelligence also goes back to World War II days when she worked behind enemy lines in Europe.

In addition to the logs and photographs, AVENGEFUL–7 also serves as a radio base for the AVENIN surveillance team which works most of the time on Cuban targets. From the OP she signals by radio when the subject to be followed leaves the Embassy—with different signals if by foot, by car, or by one street or another. The team waits in vehicles four or five blocks away and picks up the subject. The logs and photographs are passed to Hatry who also passes back instructions on surveillance targets.

AVENIN. The station has two surveillance teams, the oldest and most effective being the AVENIN team directed by Roberto Musso.‡ The team consists of seven surveillance agents, one agent in the state-owned electric company, and one agent in the telegraph company who provides copies of encoded telegrams sent and received by the Soviet bloc missions through commercial wire facilities. Most of the surveillance agents, like Musso, are employees of the Montevideo municipal government, and communications and instructions are passed by Paul Burns, the case officer in charge, at a safe office site a block from the municipal palace.

The team is well trained and considered to be one of the best unilateral surveillance teams in WH Division. Vehicles include two sedans and a Volkswagen van equipped with a periscope photography rig with a 360-degree viewing capability for taking pictures and observations through the roof vent. Concealed radio equipment is also used for communication between the vehicles, between the vehicles and the OP at the Cuban Embassy, and between the vehicles and the people on foot. These carry small battery-operated transmitter-receivers under their clothing and can communicate with each other as well as with the vehicles. They are also trained and equipped for clandestine street photography using 35-mm automatic Robot cameras wrapped to form innocuous packages.

The AVENIN team was formed in the mid-1950s with the original nucleus of agents coming from part-time police investigators. Until last year, when a new, separate team was formed, the AVENIN team was almost constantly assigned to follow Soviet intelligence officers or related targets. Their most sensational discovery was a series of clandestine meetings between an official of the Uruguayan Foreign Ministry and a Soviet KGB officer in which all the clandestine paraphernalia of signals and dead drops had been used. Photographs and other evidence passed by the station to Uruguayan authorities led to expulsion of the Soviet officer and considerable propaganda benefit. Last year, however, the AVENIN team was taken off Soviet targets and assigned to the Cubans, partly because of increasing importance of the Cubans and partly because the team was considered to be fairly well blown to the Soviets.

The AVENIN agent in the electric company is valuable because he has access to lists of persons who are registered for electric service at any address in Montevideo. Not only are the lists helpful in identifying the apartments or offices where surveillance subjects are followed, but the lists are also used to check building security of potential safe sites. The same agent also provides on request the architect's plans for any building served by the electric company and these plans are used for planning audio installations or surreptitious entries for other purposes. The same agent, moreover, can be called upon to make routine electrical inspection visits, ostensibly for the electric company, which gives him access to practically any office, apartment or house in Montevideo for inside casings.

AVENGEFUL. The station telephone-tapping operation is effected through the AVALANCHE liaison service (the Montevideo Police Department) with a history dating back to World War II when the FBI was in charge of counter-intelligence in South America. This is currently the most important joint operation underway between the station and an Uruguayan service. Connections are made in telephone company exchanges by company engineers at the request of the police department. A thirty-pair cable runs from the main downtown exchange to police headquarters where, on the top floor, the listening post is located.

The chief technician, Jacobo de Anda,‡ and the assistant technician and courier, Juan Torres,‡ man the LP, which has tables with actuators and tape-recorders for each of the thirty pairs. Torres arranges for lines to be connected by the telephone company engineers and he delivers the tapes each day to another courier, AVOIDANCE,‡ who takes them around to the transcribers who work either at home or in safe site offices. This courier also picks up the transcriptions and old tapes from the transcribers and passes them to Torres who sends them to the station each day with yet another courier who works for the Intelligence Department of the police. The police department thus arranges for connections and operates the LP.

The courier AVOIDANCE is a station agent known only to Torres among the police department personnel involved. Each of the transcribers is unknown to the police department but copies of all the transcriptions, except in special cases, are provided by the station to the police intelligence department. Each operations officer in the station who receives telephone coverage of targets of interest to him is responsible for handling the transcribers of his lines: thus the Soviet operations officer, Russell Phipps,‡ is in charge of the two elderly Russian *émigrés* who transcribe (in English) the Soviet lines; the CP officer, Paul Burns,‡ is in charge of the transcriber of the PCU line; and the Cuban operations officer is in charge of the transcribers of the Cuban lines. Most of the transcribers are kept apart from one another as well as from the police department.

The station, which provides technical equipment and financing for the operation, deals directly with the Chief of the Guardia Metropolitana, who is the police department official in overall charge of the telephone-tapping operation. He is usually an Army colonel or lieutenant-colonel detailed to run the Guardia Metropolitana, the paramilitary shock force of the police. Currently he is Colonel Roberto Ramirez.‡ Usually he assigns lines to be tapped as part of his operations against contraband operations which also provides cover for the station lines which are political in nature. Torres and de Anda work under the supervision of the Chief of the Guardia Metropolitana although approval in principle for the operation comes from the Minister of the Interior (internal security) and the Chief of the Montevideo Police Department. The station encourages the use of telephone tapping against contraband activities not only because it's good cover but also because police contraband operations are lucrative to them and such operations tend to offset fears of political scandal depending upon who happens to be Minister of the Interior at any particular time.

Only seven lines are being monitored right now. They include three lines on Soviet targets (one on the Embassy, one on the Consulate and another that alternates between a second Embassy telephone and the Soviet Commercial Office), two on Cuban targets (one on the Embassy and one on the Commercial Office), one on a revolutionary Argentine with close associations with the Cubans, and one line assigned to the headquarters of the Communist Party of Uruguay.

Security is a serious problem with the AVENGEFUL operation because so many people know of it: former ministers and their subordinates, former police chiefs and their subordinates, current officers in the Guardia Metropolitana and the Criminal Investigations and Intelligence Departments. Copies of the transcriptions prepared for the police intelligence department are considered very insecure because of the poor physical security of the department despite continuous station efforts to encourage tightening. Regular denunciations of telephone tapping by the police appear in the PCU newspaper, *El Popular,* but without the detail that might require shutting down the operation.

Telephone tapping in Montevideo, then, is very shaky with many possibilities for serious scandal.

AVBARON. The station's only agent penetration of the Cuban mission is a local employee who began working for the station as a low-level penetration of the PCU. He is Warner,‡ the Cuban Embassy chauffeur, whose mother works at the Embassy as a cook. About two months ago the Cubans fired their chauffeur and the station instructed this agent to try, through his mother, to get hired by the Cubans as their new chauffeur. Paul Burns, the station officer in charge, arranged for a crash course in driving lessons and suddenly this agent became a very important addition to the operational program against the Cubans. Through his mother's pleading he was hired, and in spite of an accident the first day he was out with the Embassy car, he has gained steadily in their confidence. Although he does not have access to documents or sensitive information on Cuban support to revolutionaries, he is reporting valuable personality data on Cuban officials as well as intelligence on security and other procedures designed to protect the Embassy and the Commercial Department. Meetings are held directly between the station officer and the agent, usually in a safe apartment site or an automobile.

ECFLUTE. The only potential double-agent case against the Cuban intelligence service here is Medardo Toro,‡ the Ecuadorean sent to Buenos Aires by the Quito station to report on exiled former President Velasco. Although Toro claims to have established a channel from Velasco to the Cuban government through Ricardo Gutierrez Torrens, a Cuban diplomat believed to be their chief of intelligence in Montevideo, and the Quito station and headquarters as well are extremely interested in monitoring the channel for signs of possible Cuban support to Velasco, Ned Holman, the Montevideo Chief of Station, continues to avoid handling the case in Montevideo. His reasoning is that we already have more than enough work to do and he is afraid to open the door to still more coverage of exiles. For the time being Toro's meetings with Gutierrez will be monitored through reports sent by pouch from Buenos Aires.

AVBUSY/ZRKNICK. The most important counterintelligence case against the Cubans in Montevideo consists of the monitoring of the mail of a known Cuban intelligence support agent. The case started in 1962 when encoded radio messages began from Havana to a Cuban agent believed to be located either in Lima or La Paz. The National Security Agency is able to decrypt the messages which contain interesting information but fail to reveal the identity of the agent who receives them. In one of the messages Havana control gave the name and address of an accommodation address in Montevideo to which the agent should write if necessary, including a special signal on the envelope to indicate operational correspondence. The addressee in Montevideo is Jorge Castillo, a bank employee active in the FIDEL political front, and the signal is the underlining of Edificio Panamericano where Castillo lives. Operational correspondence is expected to be written in secret writing.

In order to monitor this communications channel, should it be activated, the station has recruited the letter carrier who serves Castillo. Because the letter carrier, AVBUSY-1,‡ cannot be told of the special signal on the envelope (since it came from a sensitive decrypting process) the station officer has to review all the mail sent to Castillo—a very time-consuming process. So far no operational correspondence has been intercepted, but headquarters correspondence indicates that successful identification has been made of Cuban agents in similar ZRKNICK cases. (ZRKNICK is the cryptonym used for the entire communications monitoring operation against Cuban agents in Latin America.)

AVBLIMP. The Soviet Embassy here is a large mansion surrounded by a garden and high walls. In order to monitor the comings and goings of Soviet personnel, especially the intelligence officers, the station operates an observation post in a high-rise apartment building about a block away and in front of the Embassy. The OP operators are a married couple who live in the OP as their apartment and divide the work: keeping a log of entries and exits of Soviet personnel, photographing visitors and the Soviets themselves from time to time, photographing the license plates of cars used by visitors, signaling the AVBANDY surveillance team by radio in the same manner as the OP signals the AVENIN team at the Cuban Embassy. The AVBLIMP OP also serves for special observation of the superior–inferior relationships among Soviet personnel, which requires long training sessions with the Soviet operations officer. Such relationships are vital for identifying the hierarchy within the KGB and GRU offices. The apartment is owned by a station support agent who ostensibly rents it to the OP couple as their living-quarters.

AVBANDY. The new (1963) surveillance team formed to operate against the Soviets and Soviet-related targets consists of a team chief who is an Army major and five other agents. The team has two sedans and communications equipment similar to that used by the AVENIN team, with coordination when appropriate with the AVBLIMP observation post. The team chief, AVBANDY–1, originally came to the attention of the station through the liaison operations with the Uruguayan military intelligence service, and after a period of development he was recruited to lead the new team without the knowledge of his Army chiefs. The team is currently undergoing intensive training by Eziquiel Ramirez,‡ a training officer from headquarters who specializes in training surveillance teams. His period with the AVBANDY team will total about eight weeks by the time he is finished next month.

AVERT. For some years the station has owned, through AVERT–1, a support agent, the house that is joined by a common wall to the Soviet Consulate. The Consulate and the AVERT house are the opposite sides of the same three-storey building that is divided down the middle. The building is situated next to the Soviet Embassy property and backs up to the Embassy backyard garden. In the Consulate, in addition to offices, two Soviet families are housed, including the Consul who is a known KGB officer. The AVERT house has been vacant for several years and has been used operationally only for occasional visits by technicians with their sophisticated equipment for capturing radiations from Soviet communications equipment in the Embassy. When successful such electronic operations can enable encoded communications to be read but we haven't been successful so far in Montevideo.

Recently there has been considerable indecision about what to do with the AVERT property: whether to use it as an additional OP, since it allows for observation of the garden where Soviet officers are known to have discussions; whether to use it to bug the Consulate offices and living-quarters; whether to sell it; or whether to retain it for some unknown future use. For the time being it is being retained for possible future use although the station strongly suspects that the Soviets are aware that it is under our control. They have, in fact, probably bugged our side as a routine matter of protection.

SOVIET ACCESS AGENTS

The weakest aspect of Soviet operations in Montevideo is the access agent program—Uruguayans or others who can develop personal relationships with Soviet officials in order to report personality information, and, if appropriate, to recruit or induce defection. Although three or four station agents are in contact with Soviet officers their relationships are weak and their reporting scanty.

AVDANDY. Part of the station program against the Cubans, Soviets and other communist diplomatic missions in Montevideo is keeping up-to-date photographs and biographical data on all their personnel. Although the observation posts against the Cubans and Soviets provide good photographs, their use is limited because of the necessity to protect the OP's. The Uruguayan Foreign Ministry, on the other hand, obtains identification photographs on all foreign personnel assigned to diplomatic missions in order to issue the identity card that each is supposed to carry. AVDANDY–1,‡ is a medium-level official of the Foreign Ministry who gives copies of all these photographs to the Chief of Station as well as tidbits of information. Although efforts have been made to obtain passports of communist diplomatic personnel for a period long enough to photograph them, this agent has been reluctant to take the added risk of lending the passports when they are sent with the application. Nevertheless his willingness to turn over the Foreign Ministry Protocol Office files for copying in the station is a valuable, if routine, support function.

ZRBEACH. One of the activities of the CIA in support of the National Security Agency's code-cracking task is to maintain teams of radio monitors in certain U.S. embassies. Often but not only where Soviet diplomatic missions exist, CIA stations include a contingent of monitors who scan frequencies with sophisticated equipment and record radio communications which are passed to NSA for processing. The program is called ZRBEACH. Such a team has been operating for some years in the Montevideo station. The monitors also place mobile stations as close as possible to target-encrypting machines for capturing radiations—as in the use of the AVERT house next to the Soviet Embassy here. ZRBEACH teams work under the direction of Division D of the DDP although locally they are supervised by the Chief of Station.

When Ned Holman arrived in Montevideo he recommended that the ZRBEACH team be withdrawn for lack of production. Gradually their activities were curtailed and in recent weeks they have been packing equipment. Several have already departed for other stations and soon Fred Morehouse,‡ the ZRBEACH team chief, will leave for his new assignment in Caracas.

AVBALSA. Liaison with the Uruguayan military intelligence service is in charge of Gerry O'Grady, the Deputy Chief of Station, who meets regularly with Lieutenant-Colonel Zipitria,‡ the deputy chief of the service. Holman also occasionally meets Zipitria and when necessary Colonel Carvajal,‡ the military intelligence service chief. For some years the Montevideo station has tried to build up the capabilities of his liaison service through training, equipment donation and funding but with very little success. Even now, their main collection activity is clipping from the local leftist press. The main problem with this service is the Uruguayan military tradition of keeping aloof from politics, as is shown by Carvajal's reluctance to engage the service in operations against the PCU and other extreme-left political groups. On the other hand the Deputy Chief, Zipitria, is a rabid anti-communist whose ideas border on fascist-style repression and who is constantly held in check by Carvajal. For the time being the station is using the Deputy Chief as a source of intelligence on government policy towards the extreme left and on rumblings within the military against the civilian government. Hopefully Zipitria will some day be chief of the service.

AVALANCHE. The main public security force in Uruguay is the Montevideo Police Department—cryptonym AVALANCHE—with which liaison relations date to just before World War II when the FBI was monitoring the considerable pro-Nazi tendencies in Uruguay and Argentina. In the late 1940s, when the CIA station was opened, a number of joint operations were taken over from the FBI including the telephone-tapping project. Although police departments exist in the interior departments of Uruguay, the technical superiority and other capabilities of the Montevideo police almost always produce decisions by Ministers of the Interior that important cases be handled by AVALANCHE even when outside Montevideo.

As in Ecuador, the Minister of the Interior is in charge of the police, and station liaison with civilian security forces begins with the Minister, currently a Blanco politician named Felipe Gil‡ whom Holman meets regularly. Holman also meets regularly, or whenever necessary, Colonel Ventura Rodriguez,‡ Chief of the Montevideo Police; Carlos Martin,‡ Deputy Chief; Inspector Guillermo Copello,‡ Chief of Investigations; Inspector Juan José Braga,‡ Deputy Chief of Investigations; Commissioner Alejandro Otero,‡ Chief of the Intelligence and Liaison Department; Colonel Roberto Ramirez,‡ Chief of the Guardia Metropolitana (the anti-riot shock force); Lieutenant-Colonel Mario

Barbe,‡ Chief of the Guardia Republicana (the para-military police cavalry); and others. Of these the most important are the Minister, Chief of Police, Chief of Intelligence and Liaison and Chief of the Guardia Metropolitana, who supervises the telephone-tapping operation.

As in Argentina, the political sensitivity of an AID Public Safety Mission for improving police capabilities has precluded such a Mission in Uruguay and restricted police assistance to what overall demands on station manpower allow. But whereas in Argentina a non-official cover operations officer has for some years been ostensibly contracted by the Argentine Federal Police‡ to run telephone-tapping and other joint operations, in Uruguay these tasks have been handled by station officers under official cover in the Embassy. Until January all the tasks relating to AVALANCHE were handled by the Deputy Chief of Station, but Holman took over these duties when Wiley Gilstrap,‡ the Deputy, was transferred to become Chief of Station in San Salvador and replaced by O'Grady, whose Spanish is very limited. The station long-range plans continue to be the establishment of an AID Public Safety Mission that would include a CIA officer in order to release station officers in the Embassy for other tasks. However, such a development will have to wait until a strong Minister of the Interior who will fight for the Public Safety Mission appears on the scene. On the other hand Uruguayan police officers are being sent by the station for training at the Police Academy, which has changed its name to the International Police Academy and is moving from Panama to Washington.

Of the activities undertaken by the police on behalf of the station, the most important is the AVENGEFUL telephone-tapping operation. Other activities are designed to supplement the station unilateral collection program and to keep the police from discovering these operations. Apart from telephone tapping these other activities are effected through the Department of Intelligence and Liaison.

Travel Control. Each day the station receives from the police the passenger lists of all arrivals and departures at the Montevideo airport and the port where nightly passenger boats shuttle to Buenos Aires. These are accompanied by a special daily list of important people compiled by I & E personnel, including those traveling on diplomatic passports, important political figures, communists and leftists and leaders of the Peronist movement. On request we can also obtain the lists of travelers who enter or leave at Colonia, another important transit point between Montevideo and Buenos Aires. Daily guest lists from the hotels and lodgings in Montevideo are also available. The main weakness in travel control is at the Carrasco airport, which is the main airport for Montevideo but is in the Department of Canelones just outside the Department of Montevideo, and there is considerable rivalry between the Montevideo and the Canelones police. More important, however, is the lucrative contraband movement at the airport which jealous customs officials protect by hampering any improvement of police control. Thus station efforts to set up a watch list and a document photography operation at the airport have been unsuccessful.

Name Checks. As a service to the Embassy visa office, information is requested constantly from the police department, usually on Uruguayans who apply for U.S. visas. Data from the intelligence and criminal investigations files is then passed by the station to the visa office for use in determining whether visas should be granted or denied.

Biographical Data and Photographs. Uruguay has a national voter registration that is effectively an identification card system. From the AVALANCHE service we obtain full name, date and place of birth, parents' names, address, place of work, etc., and identification photos of practically any Uruguayan or permanent resident alien. This material is valuable for surveillance operations of the AVENIN and AVBANDY teams, for the Subversive Control Watch List and for a variety of other purposes.

License Plate Data. A further help to station analysis of visitors to the Soviet and Cuban embassies are the names and addresses of owners of cars whose license plate numbers are photographed or copied at the observation posts. The police make this information available without knowing the real reason. The same data is also used to supplement reporting by the two surveillance teams.

Reporting. The Intelligence and Liaison Department of the Montevideo Police Department is the government's (and the station's) principal source of information on strikes and street demonstrations. This type of information has been increasing in importance during the past few years as the PCU-dominated labor unions have stepped up their campaigns of strikes and demonstrations in protest against government economic policies. When strikes and demonstrations occur, information is telephoned to the station from I & E as the events progress. It includes numbers of people involved, degree of violence, locations, government orders for repression, and estimates of effectiveness, all of which is processed for inclusion in station reporting to headquarters, the Southern and Atlantic military commands, etc. At the end of each month I & E also prepares a round-up report on strikes and civil disturbances of which the station receives a copy.

While contact between the various officers in the police department and the station is no secret to the Chief of Police—they are described as "official" liaison—the station also maintains a discreet contact with a former I & E chief who was promoted out of the job and now is the fourth- or fifth-ranking officer in Investigations. This officer, Inspector Antonio Piriz Castagnet,‡ is paid a salary as the station penetration of the police department, and he is highly cooperative in performing tasks unknown to his superiors. The station thus calls on this agent for more sensitive tasks where station interest is not to be known by the police chief or others. Piriz also provides valuable information on government plans with respect to strikes and civil disorder, personnel movements within the police and possible shifts in policy.

The overall cost of the AVALANCHE project, apart from AVENGEFUL telephone tapping, is about 25,000 dollars per year.

SMOTH. The British Intelligence Service (MI-6), known in the CIA by the cryptonym SMOTH, has long been active in the River Plate area in keeping with British economic and political interests here. The station receives regularly copies of SMOTH reports via headquarters but they are of very marginal quality. Because of budget cutbacks the British are soon closing their one-man office in Montevideo but before returning to England the SMOTH officer will introduce Holman to the Buenos Aires Station Commander who will be in charge of MI-6 interests in Montevideo. Basically a courtesy arrangement between colleagues of like mind, the SMOTH liaison is of little importance to the Montevideo operational program.

ODENVY. The FBI (cryptonym ODENVY) has an office in the Embassy in Rio de Janeiro (Legal Attaché cover) whose chief is in charge of looking after FBI interests in Uruguay and Argentina. Occasionally the FBI chief comes to Montevideo for visits to the police department and he usually makes a courtesy call on the Montevideo Chief of Station. Soon, however, the FBI will be opening an office in the Embassy in Buenos Aires which will take over FBI interests in Uruguay.

Covert Action (CA) *Operations*

AVCHIP. Apart from Ralph Hatry the other non-official cover contract officer is a young ex-Marine who is ostensibly the Montevideo representative for several U.S. export firms. The cover of this officer, Brooks Read,‡ has held up well during the three or four years that he has been in Montevideo, mainly because he has socialized mostly with the British crowd he met as a leader of the English-speaking theater group in Montevideo. Although he originally worked in the station FI program, during the past year he was transferred to the CA side as cutout and intermediate case officer for media and student operations. Although time-consuming, handling Read's affairs inside the station is a joy for O'Grady, the inside officer in charge, by comparison with the plethora of problems constantly caused by Hatry.

AVBUZZ. Because of the large number of morning and afternoon newspapers in Montevideo, press media operations are centralized in AVBUZZ–1,‡ who is responsible for placing propaganda in various dailies. As each newspaper of the non-communist press is either owned by or responds to one of the main political factions of the principal political parties, articles can be placed more easily in some newspapers than in others depending upon content and slant. AVBUZZ–1 has access to all the liberal press but he uses most frequently the two dailies of the Union Blanca Democratica faction of the Blanco Party (*El Pais* and *El Plata*), the morning newspaper of the Colorado Party List 14 (*El Dia*), and the morning newspaper of the Union Colorada y Batllista (*La Mañana*) to a lesser extent. AVBUZZ–1 pays editors on newspapers on a space-used basis and the articles are usually published as unsigned editorials of the newspapers themselves. O'Grady is in charge of this operation which he works through Brooks Read who deals directly with AVBUZZ–1. All told the station can count on two or three articles per day. Clips are mailed to headquarters and to other stations for replay.

AVBUZZ–1 also writes occasional fly-sheets at station direction, usually on anti-communist themes, and he operates a small distribution team to get them on the streets after they are secretly printed in a friendly print shop. Television and radio are also used by AVBUZZ–1, although much less than newspapers because they carry less political comment.

AVBLOOM. Student operations have had very limited success in recent years in spite of generous promotion of non-communist leaders for FEUU offices. Recently the station recommended, and headquarters agreed, that student operations be refocused to concentrate on the secondary level rather than at the University—on the theory that anti-communist indoctrination at a lower level may bring better results later when the students go on to the University. Brooks Read works with several teams of anti-communist student leaders whom he finances for work in organization and propaganda. O'Grady is also the station officer in charge of student operations.

AVCHARM. Labor operations for some years have been designed to strengthen the Uruguayan Labor Confederation‡ (CSU), which is affiliated with the ORIT–ICFTU‡ structure, but we have been unsuccessful in reversing its decline in recent years. A crucial decision on whether to continue support to the CSU must soon be made. If the CSU is to be salvaged the station will have to replace the present ineffectual leaders, not a pleasant prospect because of their predictable resistance, and begin again practically from the beginning. The fact is that the CSU is largely discredited, and organized labor is overwhelmingly aligned either inside, or in cooperation with, the CTU and the extreme left. Apart from the CSU, station labor operations are targeted at selected unions that can be assisted and influenced, perhaps eventually controlled, through the International Trade Secretariats that operate in Latin America, such as the International Transport Workers Federation.‡

The most important new activity in labor operations is the establishment last November of the Montevideo office of the American Institute for Free Labor Development.‡ This office is called the Uruguayan Institute of Trade Union Education‡ and its director, Jack Goodwyn,‡ is a U.S. citizen contract agent and the Montevideo AIFLD representative. Alexander Zeffer,‡ the station officer in charge of labor operations, meets Goodwyn under discreet conditions for planning, reporting and other matters. In addition to training locally at the AIFLD institute, Uruguayans are also sent to the ORIT school in Mexico and to the AIFLD school in Washington.

AVALON. This agent, A. Fernandez Chavez,‡ has for many years been used for placing propaganda material and as a source of intelligence on political matters. At times when AVBUZZ–1 cannot place things the station wants in the papers, Fernandez may be successful because of his very wide range of friends in political and press circles. He is the Montevideo correspondent of ANSA, the Italian wire service, and of the Santiago station-controlled feature news service *Agencia Orbe Latinoamericano*.‡ Although he occasionally meets Holman, his usual station contact is Paul Burns, the CP officer.

AVID. Although the political-action operations formerly effected through Benito Nardone have largely ended, Holman continues to see Nardone, Nardone's wife Olga Clerici de Nardone,‡ who is very active in the Ruralist movement, and Juan Jose Gari,‡ Nardone's chief political lieutenant. Gari has the major political plum assigned to the Ruralists in the current Blanco government—he's President of the State Mortgage Bank. Should a policy change occur and the station return to political and militant action, one place we would start is with Mrs. Nardone and Gari—even if Nardone himself fails to survive his struggle with cancer.

AVIATOR. Holman recently turned over to O'Grady the responsibility for keeping up the developmental contact with Juan Carlos Quagliotti,‡ a very wealthy right-wing lawyer and rancher. This man is the leader of a group of similarly well-to-do Uruguayans concerned with the decline in governmental effectiveness and in the gains made by the extreme left in recent years. He is active in trying to persuade military leaders to intervene in political affairs, and would clearly favor a strong military government, or military-dominated government, over the current weak and divided executive. Although the station does not finance or encourage him, an attempt is made to monitor his activities for collecting intelligence on tendencies in military circles to seek unconventional solutions to Uruguayan difficulties. Should the need arise for station operations designed to promote military intervention, Quagliotti would be an obvious person through whom to operate.

SUPPORT AGENTS

As in other stations we have a fairly large number of support agents who own and rent vehicles or property for use in station operations. These agents, mainly social acquaintances of station officers, are usually given whisky or other expensive and hard-to-get items that can be brought in with diplomatic free-entry, rather than salaries. Tito Banks,‡ a wool dealer of British extraction, is one of the more effective of these agents.

As in Ecuador, the station in Montevideo is getting no small milage from a relatively small number of officers. The station budget is a little over one million dollars per year. Major improvement is needed in the access agent program against the Soviets, direct recruitment against the Cubans, higher-level penetrations of the PCU, improvement in the capabilities of police intelligence, and greater effectiveness in labor and student operations.

Next week I begin to take over all the operations targeted against the Cubans, not all of which are being handled at present by the officer I am replacing, Michael Berger. This officer has had difficulty in learning Spanish and on the whole has been able to work only with English-speaking agents. He's being married to an Uruguayan girl next weekend and afterwards will depart for a honeymoon, home leave and reassignment to the Dominican Republic.

The operations I'm taking over are the following: the AVCASK operations against the Paraguayans; the AVIDITY letter intercept; Ralph Hatry and his problems (unfortunately); the telephone-tap transcriber AVENGEFUL–9; AVANDANA; the chauffeur at the Cuban Embassy; the observation post at the Cuban Embassy; the AVENIN surveillance team; the AVBASK penetration of the MRO; the Foreign Ministry protocol official who provides photographs and other data on communist diplomats; and the postman who delivers letters to the ZRKNICK Cuban intelligence support agent. I'm also temporarily (I hope) taking over Holman's contacts with Inspector Antonio Piriz,‡ our main penetration of the Montevideo Police Department, and with Commissioner Alejandro Otero,‡ the Chief of the Intelligence and Liaison Department.

Montevideo — 26 March 1964

The ruling Blanco Party is in a deepening crisis right now that illustrates both the complexity and the fragmentation of Uruguayan politics—and the effect these conditions have on our operations.

In January the Chief of Police of Canelones, the interior department that borders on Montevideo, was involved in a bizarre bank robbery in which the two robbers were gunned down by police just as they were leaving the bank. Press reporting revealed that there was a third member of the gang who had been working for the Canelones Police Chief and had previously advised which bank was to be robbed, the day and time of the robbery and the hideouts to be used by the robbers afterwards. The Police Chief provided weapons for the robbers that had been altered so that they would not fire. In the fusillade of bullets fired by the police ambush, a policeman and a passer-by were wounded, but the Police Chief defended such exaggerated firepower, on the grounds that the robbers had first fired several shots at the police. The most ironic note for the murdered robbers was that the Montevideo press had carried several articles during the week before the robbery that unusual police movements in Canelones at that time were due to a tip-off on a probable robbery. Had the robbers read the newspapers they would have known they were betrayed.

An uproar followed this irregular police procedure, producing an investigation in the Ministry of the Interior and a movement to fire the Police Chief and prosecute him for not having prevented the robbery. Lines are now drawn in the Blanco Party between those supporting the Police Chief, who comes from one Blanco faction, and those supporting Felipe Gil,‡ the Minister of the Interior, who comes from another Blanco faction and who is leading the movement against the Police Chief. Supporters of the Chief, in fact, are charging that the Chief had kept the Minister fully informed on the case and that the Minister is to blame for any unethical procedures.

Benito Nardone‡ died yesterday but almost until the

end he was making radio broadcasts in support of the Canelones Police Chief. According to reports from Juan Jose Gari‡ there is no quick solution in sight, and so the Blancos continue to weaken—a process that reaches right up to the Blanco NCG majority. The Colorados aren't sitting idly by. The day after I arrived they got a Colorado elected President of the Chamber of Deputies by taking advantage of Blanco splits. Meanwhile Holman's chief project with the Minister, establishment of an AID Public Safety Mission in the police, continues in abeyance pending a decision by Gil.

Montevideo — 1 April 1964

It's all over for Goulart in Brazil much faster and easier than most expected. He gave the military and the opposition political leaders the final pretext they needed: a speech to the Army Sergeants' Association implying that he backed the non-commissioned officers against the officer corps. Coming right after acts of insubordination by low-ranking sailors and marines, the speech couldn't have been better timed for our purposes. The Rio station advised that Goulart is probably coming to Uruguay which means Holman's fears about new exile problems were real. U.S. recognition of the new military government is practically immediate, not very discreet but indicative, I suppose, of the euphoria in Washington now that two and a half years of operations to prevent Brazil's slide to the left under Goulart have suddenly bloomed.

Our campaign against him took much the same line as the ones against communist infiltration in the Velasco and Arosemena governments two and three years ago in Ecuador. According to Holman the Rio station and its larger bases were financing the mass urban demonstrations against the Goulart government, proving the old themes of God, country, family and liberty to be effective as ever. Goulart's fall is without doubt largely due to the careful planning and consistent propaganda campaigns dating at least back to the 1962 election operation. Holman's worry is a new flood of exiles to add to the Paraguayans and Argentines we already have to cover.

Montevideo — 3 April 1964

My first Cuban recruitment looks successful. A trade mission arrived from Brazil and will be here until sometime next week. An agent of the Rio station had reported that Raul Alonzo Olive, a member of the mission and perhaps the most important because he's a high-level official in the sugar industry, seemed to be disaffected with the revolution. In order to protect the Rio agent against provocation and because of the confusion in Brazil this past week, the Rio station suggested that a recruitment approach be made here or in Madrid which is their last stop before return to Havana.

The AVENIN surveillance team followed him after arrival and at the first chance when he was alone they delivered a note from me asking for a meeting. The note was worded so that he would know it came from the CIA. After reading it he followed the instructions to walk along a certain street where I picked him up and took him to a safe place to talk. Headquarters had sent a list of questions for him, mostly dealing with this year's sugar harvest, efforts to mechanize cane cutting, and anyone else he might know was dissatisfied. We spoke for about two hours because he had to rejoin his delegation, but we'll meet again several times before he leaves for Madrid. Contact instructions just arrived from the Madrid station.

He said sugar production from this year's harvest should be about five million tons and he rambled on at length about the problems with the cane-cutting machines, mostly caused when used on sloping or inclined surfaces. What was surprising was that he knows so many government leaders well even though he wasn't particularly active in the struggle against Batista.

I recorded the meeting, which he didn't particularly like, and reported by cable the essentials of what he said. He thinks he will be in Madrid for most of next week, or perhaps longer, so communications training can be done there. Strange he agreed so readily to return to Cuba and for his salary to be kept safe for him by the CIA, but he seemed honest enough. In Madrid he'll get the polygraph, which should help to resolve his *bona fides.*

Montevideo — 5 April 1964

Goulart arrived here yesterday and was greeted with a surprising amount of enthusiasm. The military takeover, in fact, has been rather badly received here in Uruguay because Goulart was popularly elected and a strong Brazilian military government may mean difficulties for Uruguay over exiles. Already officials of Goulart's government are beginning to arrive, and the Rio station is sending one cable after another asking that we speed up reporting arrivals. Our only source for this information is Commissioner Otero,‡ whose Intelligence and Liaison Department is in charge of processing the exiles. It's clear that the Rio station is going all out to support the military government, and the key to snuffing out any counter-*coup* or insurgency is in either capturing or forcing into exile Leonel Brizola, Goulart's far-left brother-in-law who is the Federal Deputy for Guanabara (Rio de Janeiro) and is now in hiding.

Headquarters has begun to generate hemisphere-wide propaganda in support of the new Brazilian government and to discredit Goulart. For example, Arturo Jauregui,‡ Secretary-General of ORIT, has sent a telegram pledging ORIT‡ support for the new Brazilian government. This may provoke a negative reaction in places like Venezuela because the CIA's policy before was to have ORIT oppose military takeovers of freely elected governments —not very realistic in view of the way events are moving.

Through AVBUZZ we're currently promoting opinion favorable to the Venezuelan case against Cuba in the OAS based on the arms cache discovered last year. One of our placements was a half-page paid advertisement in the Colorado daily *La Mañana* that came out yesterday. It was ostensibly written and signed by Hada Rosete,‡ the representative here of the Cuban Revolutionary Council‡ and one of the propaganda agents of the AVBUZZ project. In fact it was written by O'Grady and Brooks Read and based on information from headquarters and from station files. The statement relates the arms cache to overall Soviet and Cuban penetration of the hemisphere, including allegations attributed to Rolando Santana,‡ last year's Cuban defector here. Current insurgent movements in Venezuela, Honduras, Peru, Colombia, Argentina, Panama and Bolivia are described as being directed from Soviet and Cuban embassies in Mexico City, Buenos Aires and Montevideo, not to exclude the Chinese communists who were also mentioned.

Montevideo — 18 April 1964

Holman returned from a Chiefs of Station conference with the grudging acknowledgment that we'll have to devote more attention to the Brazilian exiles. The decision was made, apparently, by President Johnson himself, that an all-out effort must be made not only to prevent a counter-*coup* and insurgency in the short run in Brazil, but also to build up their security forces as fast and as effectively as possible for the long run. Never again can Brazil be permitted to slide off to the left where the communists and others become a threat to take things over or at least become a strong influence on them.

Here in Montevideo this policy means that we will have to assist the Rio station by increasing collection of information about the exiles. This will have to be through police intelligence for the time being and will be my responsibility since Holman, as I suspected, wants me to continue to work with Otero, Piriz, de Anda, Torres and others while he maintains the high-level contacts with the Minister of the Interior, Felipe Gil, and the Chief of Police, Colonel Ventura Rodriguez.‡ As a start I have gotten Otero to place his officers at the residences of Goulart and three or four of the most important exiles, according to the Rio station's criteria, and these officers will keep logs of visitors while posing as personal security officers for the exiles. We'll forward highlights of the reports to Rio by cable along with information on new arrivals with full copies following by pouch.

The political currents here are running against the new military government in Brazil and making favorable editorial comment very difficult to generate. The Brazilian government, nevertheless, has begun to pressure the Uruguayans in different ways so that Goulart and his supporters in exile here will be forbidden to engage in political activities.

Promoting sentiment in favor of a break in relations with Cuba is almost as difficult here as promoting favorable comment towards Brazil. Not that Uruguayans are fond of communism or well-disposed towards the Cuban revolution. The corner stone of Uruguayan foreign policy is strict non-intervention because of the country's vulnerability to pressures from its two giant neighbors. Since sanctions or collective action against Cuba can easily be interpreted as intervention in Cuba's internal affairs, the station program to promote a break in relations runs counter to Uruguayan traditional policies.

Even so, we are keeping up media coverage of Cuban themes in the hope that Venezuelan attempts to convoke an OAS Foreign Ministers conference over the arms cache will result not only in the conference but in a resolution for all OAS countries to break with Cuba. A few days ago the former Venezuelan Foreign Minister under Betancourt, Marcos Falcon Briseno, was here trying to drum up support for the conference but he couldn't convince the Uruguayans to join actively in the campaign.

Montevideo — 24 April 1964

We've just had a visit from the new WH Division Chief, Desmond FitzGerald,‡ who is making the rounds of field stations. Holman gave a buffet for all the station personnel and wives, and in the office each of us had a short session with FitzGerald to describe our operations. He was pleased with the Cuban recruitment but suspects he may have been a provocation because of his high estimate of the sugar harvest. Instead of five million tons, according to FitzGerald, production this year will probably be less than four million. He also encouraged me to concentrate on making an acceptable recruitment approach to the Cuban code clerk here. When we told him that one of our station offices has a common wall with an uncontrolled apartment in the building next door, he ordered that a large sign be immediately placed on the wall reading: "This Room is Bugged!" Rank has its privileges in the CIA too.

FitzGerald was very insistent that the Montevideo station devote attention to supporting the new Brazilian military government through intelligence collection and propaganda operations. Holman has given O'Grady the overall responsibility for Brazilian problems, and the Rio station is going to help by sending down one of its liaison contacts as military attaché in the Brazilian Embassy. He is Colonel Camara Sena,‡ and he is due to arrive any day. O'Grady will be meeting with him and will assist him in developing operations to penetrate the exile community.

In spite of Goulart's popularity here, the NCG voted yesterday to recognize the Brazilian government which should serve to ease tensions. Also, Goulart has been declared a political asylee rather than a refugee which is a looser status that would have allowed him more freedom for political activities.

Montevideo — 2 May 1964

Headquarters has approved my plan for recruitment of Roberto Hernandez, the Cuban code clerk, and we shall see if luck prevails. I'm using Ezequiel Ramirez,‡ the training officer from headquarters who's just finished training the AVBANDY surveillance team, to make the initial contact. He can pass for a Spaniard or Latin American and will be less dangerous for Hernandez (if he accepts) until we can establish a clandestine meeting arrangement. Today Ramirez begins working with the AVENIN surveillance team to follow Hernandez from the Embassy to wherever in town the first approach can be made.

It's very hard to tell what the chances are, although reporting from Warner,‡ the Cuban Embassy chauffeur, has been excellent in providing insight into Hernandez's personality. He not only is having problems with his wife, who has just had a baby, but he seems to be more than casually involved with Mirta, his Uruguayan girlfriend. Because of Mirta I rejected the girl offered by the Miami station and will concentrate on interesting Hernandez in eventual resettlement, possibly in Buenos Aires. In addition to his duties as code clerk he is the Embassy technical officer with proficiency in photography. Perhaps resettlement could include setting him up with a commercial photography shop. For the moment, however, we will offer him, per headquarters instructions, thirty thousand dollars for a straight debriefing on what he knows of Cuban intelligence operations; fifty thousand dollars for the debriefing and provision and replacement of the code pads; and three thousand dollars for each month he will work for us while continuing to work in the Embassy. I have a safe apartment all ready to use if Hernandez agrees and will take over from Ramirez as quickly as possible.

The other day I cornered Holman and proposed that I could do more with the police work and Cuban operations if I weren't bogged down with the Paraguayans, the letter intercept and Ralph Hatry. It was a dirty move because I suggested that Alex Zeffer,‡ the labor officer, could probably take over these operations. Holman agreed and then told Zeffer who hasn't spoken to me since. He knows all about Hatry's problems and of the drudgery involved in the letter intercept.

I'll continue to go occasionally at night to AVANDANA's‡ house in order to discuss problems of the Cuban Embassy observation post with his wife. I wouldn't want to miss that experience—the house is a low bungalow set far back off the street in a sparsely populated section on the edge of town and surrounded by thick woods, almost jungle. The house is protected by a high chain-link fence and perhaps a half-dozen fiercely barking dogs. Such isolation in this *addams-esque* setting is convenient in that AVANDANA is almost completely deaf and operational discussions are necessarily but insecurely loud when not screaming. Each time I have visited the home I have gone with Hatry, and the picture of these two aging men yelling furtively over their spy work is an interesting study in contradiction.

Another operation that I took over has resolved itself. Anibal Mercader,‡ the MRO penetration, decided to seek employment in the U.S. He was hired by a Miami bank and is leaving shortly—I arranged to keep his MRO membership off the station memorandum on his visa application.

I don't envy Alex Zeffer for his labor operations. He is going to have to start again, practically from scratch, because the decision was finally made to withdraw support from the Uruguayan Labor Confederation‡ (CSU). Last month the CSU held a congress and the leadership was unable to overcome the personality conflicts that have resulted in continuing withdrawals of member unions and refusals of others to pay dues. The real problem is leadership and when Andrew McClellan,‡ the AFL–CIO Inter-American Representative, and Bill Doherty,‡ the AIFLD social projects chief arrived last week they advised CSU leaders that subsidies channeled through the ICFTU, ORIT and the ITS are to be discontinued.

The situation is rather awkward because the CSU has just formed a workers' housing cooperative and expected to receive AIFLD funds for construction. These funds will also be withheld from the CSU and may be channeled through another non-communist union organization. Next week Serafino Romualdi,‡ AIFLD Executive Director, will be here for more conversations on how to promote the AIFLD program while letting the CSU die. One thing is certain: it will take several years before a new crop of labor leaders can be trained through the AIFLD program and from them recruitments made of new agents who can set up another national confederation to affiliate with ORIT and the ICFTU.

Montevideo — 5 May 1964

None of us can quite believe what is happening. Just as planned, Ramirez and the surveillance team followed Hernandez downtown, and at the right moment he walked up to Hernandez in the street and told him the U.S. government is interested in helping him. Hernandez agreed to talk but only had about fifteen minutes before he had to get back to the Embassy. He was a pale bundle of nerves but he agreed in principle to the debriefing and to providing the pads. Another meeting is set for tomorrow afternoon.

I sent a cable advising headquarters of the meeting and suggesting that they send down the Division D technician right away so that he can work on the pads on a moment's notice. If this recruitment works, as it seems to be working, we'll have the first important penetration of Cuban operations in this region.

More anti-Cuban propaganda. Representatives of the Revolutionary Student Directorate in Exile‡ (DRE), an organization financed and controlled by the Miami station, arrived today. They're on a tour of South America hammering away at the Cuban economic disaster. We don't have a permanent representative of the DRE in Montevideo so arrangements were made by Hada Rosete‡ and AVBUZZ–1. Also through AVBUZZ–1 we're generating propaganda on the trial in Cuba of Marcos Rodriguez, a leader of the Revolutionary Student Directorate in the struggle against Batista. Rodriguez is accused of having betrayed 26 of July members to the Batista police, and our false line is that he was really a communist and was instructed to betray the 26 of July people by the Cuban Communist Party. Purpose: exacerbate differences between the old-line communists and the 26 of July people. We're also playing up the Anibal Escalante purge. Both cases are causing serious divisions in Cuba where, according to AVBUZZ-1, "the repression is comparable to that under Hitler, Mussolini and Stalin as the revolution devours its own."

The internal crisis in the Blanco Party over the Canelones police case continues to grow. What is at stake, besides the reputations of the principals, is the division of spoils among the Blanco factions—a very delicate balance negotiated with difficulty and easily upset by internal struggle. Rumors abound of an impending Cabinet crisis.

Montevideo — 10 May 1964

All is not well on the Hernandez recruitment. He made the second meeting with Ramirez, but refused to talk about Cuban operations until he actually saw the money. He doesn't trust us an inch. Zeke set up a third meeting and I went with fifteen thousand dollars—practically all the cash we have right now in the station. Holman was nervous about me taking out all that money, but if we're going to get Hernandez to talk we have to at least show him the money and maybe even give him a little. O'Grady also came along for extra security, but Hernandez didn't show.

My plan was to give Hernandez up to one thousand dollars if he would begin talking and then try to convince him to let me keep everything for him in an Agency account until we finally arrange for him to "disappear." Otherwise he might be discovered with large sums of money he can't explain. For four nights now I've been waiting for him and if he doesn't show up tonight I'll get Zeke back into action with the surveillance team.

Yesterday the Division D technician arrived. He says he only needs the code pads for a few hours in order to open, photograph and reseal them. That's going to be a neat trick: the pads have adhesive sealers on all four edges so it's only possible to see the top page. But if we get them copied we'll be able to read all their traffic for as long as the pads last.

For me the most important thing is the debriefing on

their intelligence operations. Hernandez told Zeke that he knows absolutely everything they're doing here and I believe him. Tonight he's got to show.

Leonel Brizola, leader of the far-left in the Goulart government and Goulart's brother-in-law, arrived here in exile and the Brazilian government has asked that both he and Goulart be interned. If interned they will have to live in an interior city without freedom of movement around the country which would make control much easier. As the most dangerous political leader in the old government, Brizola's leaving Brazil is a favorable development. He had been in hiding since the fall of Goulart. The Rio station wants close coverage of him.

Montevideo — 15 May 1964

Something is definitely going wrong on the Hernandez recruitment. From the observation post at the Cuban Embassy I know Hernandez practically hasn't left the Embassy since the second meeting with Zeke Ramirez. For four days the surveillance team and Zeke have been waiting for the signal from the OP in order to intercept Hernandez again for another try. According to the telephone tap on the Embassy Hernandez isn't taking many calls either, and the chauffeur reported today that Hernandez hasn't spoken to him lately. I can't give him special instructions because I don't want him to suspect we have a recruitment going on. Nothing to do but just be patient and keep on trying.

Another nuisance assignment. The Santiago station has a really big operation going to keep Salvador Allende from being elected President. He was almost elected at the last elections in 1958, and this time nobody's taking any chances. The trouble is that the Office of Finance in headquarters couldn't get enough Chilean escudos from the New York banks so they had to set up regional purchasing offices in Lima and Rio. But even these offices can't satisfy the requirements so we have been asked to help.

The purchasing agent for currency in this area is the

First National City Bank,‡ but the Buenos Aires station usually handles currency matters because they have a "Class A" finance office empowered to purchase currency. As a "Class B" station we are restricted to emergencies for exchanging dollars for local currency. Nevertheless, headquarters sent down a check drawn on an account in the New York City Bank office which I took over to Jack Hennessy,‡ who is the senior U.S. citizen officer at the Montevideo Citibank. He is cleared by headquarters for currency purchases and had already been informed by Citibank in New York to expect the check. I gave him the check and he sent his buyers over to Santiago for discreet purchase. In a couple of days they were back—according to Hennessy they usually bring the money back in suitcases paying bribes to customs officials not to inspect—and Paul Burns and I went down to see Hennessy for the pick-up. When we got back to the station we had to spend the rest of the day counting it—over one hundred thousand dollars' worth. Now we'll send it to the Santiago station in the diplomatic pouch. They must be spending millions if they have to resort to this system and New York, Lima and Rio de Janeiro together can't meet the demand.

Montevideo — 20 May 1964

The Hernandez recruitment has failed—for the time being anyway. Today he finally left the Embassy and with the surveillance team Zeke Ramirez caught him downtown. Hernandez refused to speak to Ramirez or even to acknowledge him. The key to the operation now is whether Hernandez told anyone in the Embassy of his first conversations with Ramirez and all the signs are negative. Today, in fact, Hernandez turned pale when Zeke approached him. If he had reported the recruitment he wouldn't be so panicky because his position in the Embassy would be firm. Undoubtedly his fright derives from failure to report the first conversations with Zeke—meaning that his initial acceptance was genuine. Ramirez will return to Washington tomorrow and we'll let Hernandez get back into his old habits before approaching him again. According to his first conversations with Ramirez, Hernandez's political and cultural orientation is towards Argentina or Brazil rather than the U.S. Perhaps we will enlist help from the Buenos Aires or Rio stations with a security service penetration agent who could make the next approach in the name of the Brazilian or Argentine government.

Montevideo — 23 May 1964

Hernandez has panicked but we'll probably get him after all. This morning I had an emergency call from the Cuban Embassy chauffeur and when we met he reported that when he arrived this morning at the Embassy everything was in an uproar. Hernandez left the Embassy—he lives there with his family—sometime during last night leaving behind his wedding-ring and a note for his wife. The Cubans believed he has defected and that he's with us, either in hiding here or on his way to the U.S. From the worry and gloom at the Embassy the chances are that he took the code pads with him.

I told the chauffeur to stick around the Embassy all day, if possible—he doesn't usually work on Saturday afternoons—and to offer to work tomorrow. Then I got the Cuban Embassy observation post going—we usually close down on weekends—and with Holman, O'Grady and Burns we tried to decide what to do. What we can't figure out is where Hernandez is and why he hasn't come to the Embassy. We arranged for the front door to be left open so that Hernandez can walk right in instead of waiting after ringing the bell, and tonight (in case he's waiting for darkness) we'll have a station officer sitting in the light just inside the front door. Somehow we have to give Hernandez the confidence to walk on in. Sooner or later he's got to appear.

Montevideo — 24 May 1964

Hernandez is out of his mind. The chauffeur called for another emergency meeting and reported that Hernandez arrived back at the Embassy sometime after daybreak. He's being kept upstairs under custody. Several times yesterday and today the Chargé went over to the Soviet Embassy, probably because the Soviets are having to handle the Cubans' encoded communications with Havana about Hernandez. What possibly could have possessed Hernandez to change his mind again?

Montevideo — 26 May 1964

According to the chauffeur, Hernandez is going to be taken back to Cuba under special custody—Ricardo Gutierrez and Eduardo Hernandez, both intelligence officers, will be the escorts. They leave Friday on a Swissair flight to Geneva where they transfer to a flight to Prague.

The chauffeur also learned from Hernandez that when he disappeared from the Embassy last Saturday he went to see his friend Ruben Pazos and they drove together to the Brazilian border. Hernandez had the code pads with him and planned to defect to the Brazilian Consul in Rivera, but the Consul was out of town for the weekend. After waiting a while Hernandez changed his mind again and decided to take his chances with revolutionary justice—he told AVBARON–1, the chauffeur, that he'll probably have to do about five years on a correctional farm. I wonder.

We've decided to make the case public for propaganda purposes and also to try to spring Hernandez loose on the trip home. The decision to publish came after the Minister of the Interior, Felipe Gil, refused to get the Foreign Ministry or the NCG involved—Holman told him that Hernandez had been caught trying to defect to us and asked for official efforts to save him. The most the Minister would agree to was a police interview at the airport, in which Hernandez will be separated, by force, if necessary, from his escorts. Through AVBUZZ–1, meanwhile, we'll expose the case as a sensational kidnapping within the Cuban Embassy of a defector trying to flee from communist tyranny.

Montevideo — 28 May 1964

The story of Hernandez's kidnapping is splashed all over the newspapers and is provoking just the reaction we wanted. AVBUZZ–1 sent several reporters to the Embassy seeking an interview with Hernandez and they were turned away, adding to speculation that perhaps only Hernandez's corpse will eventually appear.

I've alerted each of the stations where Hernandez's flight will stop on the way to Geneva. So far the stations in Rio de Janeiro, Madrid and Berne are going to take action. Rio and Madrid will arrange for police liaison services to speak with Hernandez and the Geneva base will arrange for uniformed Swiss police to be in evidence while Hernandez is in transit, although forcing an interview is too sensitive for the Swiss.

We hope Hernandez won't get that far. Through the Chief of Police, Colonel Ventura Rodriguez, we have the interview arranged at the airport tomorrow before the flight leaves. Inspector Antonio Piriz‡ and Commissioner Alejandro Otero‡ will both be there, and Hernandez will be separated for a private interview in which our police agents will try to convince him to stay rather than face punishment on return. I'll also be at the airport to speak with him if he shows signs of agreeing to political asylum in Uruguay.

Montevideo — 29 May 1964

More propaganda but Hernandez couldn't be convinced. At the airport, Gutierrez, one of the escorts, tried to resist having Hernandez separated for the police interview. During the scuffle he pulled out a pistol and was forcibly disarmed. Hernandez, however, insisted that he was returning of his own will and eventually he and his wife and child boarded the flight with the two escorts. So far no news from stations along the way.

This morning before his departure the Cubans recovered somewhat from the adverse propaganda by inviting the press to the Embassy for an interview with Hernandez. Hernandez said he was returning to Cuba because he feared reprisals against his wife and son from certain persons (unidentified) who were trying to get him to betray his country. For the past twenty days, he admitted, certain persons whose nationality he couldn't place were accosting him in the street. They had first offered him five thousand dollars and later as high as fifty thousand. Even with this interview, however, press coverage makes it clear that Hernandez is being returned as a security risk, especially in view of the escorts.

The recruitment may have failed but we have certainly damaged the Cubans' operational capabilities here. The only officers they have left now are the Commercial Counsellor and his wife, and the Chargé who we don't believe is engaged in intelligence work. Suddenly they're cut from five to two officers and must use Soviet Embassy communications facilities until they can get a new code clerk. The propaganda, moreover, may have improved the climate here for a break in relations if the Venezuelan case in the OAS prospers. If we didn't get the pads and debriefing, at least we got good media play and disruption.

Perhaps indirectly related to the Hernandez case—we won't know for some time—are two very favorable recent developments relating to Cuban intelligence defections. In Canada, a Cuban intelligence officer, Vladimir Rodriguez,‡ defected a few weeks ago and is beginning to give the first details of the General Intelligence Directorate (DGI) which is housed within the Ministry of the Interior. Headquarters is keeping us up to date on the highlights of debriefings, which must be similar to the first KGB defector because nothing was known until now—not even the existence of the DGI.

More closely related to Cuban operations in Uruguay is another attempt to defect by Earle Perez Freeman,‡ their former intelligence chief in Montevideo, who had defected and then changed his mind in Mexico this past January. Perez has just obtained asylum in the Uruguayan Embassy in Havana where three of the four diplomats (the AMHALF agents) are working for the Miami station. One of these, the Chargé d'Affaires, is being replaced, but through the other two, German Roosen‡ and Hamlet Goncalves,‡ the Miami station will try for a debriefing on Cuban operations in Montevideo. Over the weekend I'll compile a list of questions based on what we already know and forward it to Miami for use with the AMHALF agents.

Montevideo — 6 June 1964

The struggle within the Blanco Party has reached a new crisis just as labor unrest also approaches a peak. Beginning on 21 May the Cabinet ministers began to resign, one by one, with the Minister of Defense resigning on 30 May and Felipe Gil, the Minister of the Interior, today. From initial concern over the Canelones police case, the Blancos have turned to fighting over assignment of government jobs, and rumors are getting stronger by the day that Blanco military officers are organizing a *coup* against the Blanco political leadership. So far the rumors are unfounded but we're sending regular negative reports to headquarters based mostly on reports from Gari and Colonel Ventura Rodriguez who are closely connected with the military officers said to be involved in the planning. Holman is hoping to get a new Minister of the Interior who will be strong enough to push through the Public Safety Mission for the police.

As the government grinds to a halt the unions of the autonomous agencies and decentralized services are getting more militant. Two days ago they struck for twenty-four hours for a 45 per cent increase in the budget for the government enterprises, and a twenty-four-hour general strike is already being organized by these unions and the CTU in protest against inflation.

Hernandez returned to Cuba although police agents of the Rio station had another scuffle with Gutierrez when they separated him for an interview alone with Hernandez. Cuban sugar production for this year's harvest was announced (much lower than my Cuban sugar official, Alonzo,‡ told me) so FitzGerald was probably right. Now I'll have to terminate the safe apartment I used with him. No indication from Madrid yet on results of the polygraph. Miami station reported that getting information from Perez in Havana may be more complicated than expected because they want to keep Goncalves and Roosen from working together on the case. For the time being they'll use only Roosen, and he only comes out to Miami or Nassau about once a month.

Montevideo — 17 June 1964

The Blancos finally solved their crisis. New ministers were announced and other jobs were realigned among the different disputing factions. The new Minister of the Interior is Adolfo Tejera‡ whom the Montevideo Police Chief, Rodriguez, describes favorably. Through the Chief, Holman will make an early contact with the new Minister using the AVENGEFUL telephone-tapping operation as the excuse and following with the AID Public Safety program later.

Today practically all economic activity is stopped thanks to a twenty-four-hour general strike, organized by the CTU and the unions of the government autonomous agencies and decentralized services, on account of inflation and other economic ills that adversely affect the workers. Last night, as the strike was about to start, Colonel Rodriguez,‡ Montevideo Police Chief and the government's top security official, issued a statement denouncing the wave of rumors of a military takeover as completely unfounded.

How different from Ecuador where a general strike is enough to bring down the government. Here traffic circulates freely and almost everyone, it seems, goes to the beach even if it's too cold to swim. Holman, in commenting on the Sunday-like atmosphere, said that Uruguayans are nothing more than water-watchers—content to sip their *mate* quietly and watch the waves roll in.

The Brazilian government is keeping up the pressure for action against political activities by Goulart, Brizola and other exiles. Although they have begun to allow some of the asylees in the Uruguayan Embassy to come out, which has temporarily relieved tension, they have also sent a Deputy here for a press conference to try to stimulate action for control of the exiles. But the Deputy's remarks were counter-productive because in addition to accusing supporters of Goulart and Brizola of conspiring against the military government through student, labor and governmental organizations in Brazil, he also said that Uruguay is infiltrated by communists and as such is a danger for the rest of the continent. The Uruguayan Foreign Minister answered later by acknowledging that the Communist Party is legal in Uruguay, but he added that the country is hardly dominated by them.

Brazilian pressures may create negative reactions in the short run but sooner or later the Uruguayans will have to take a similar hard line on communism because the country's just to small to resist Brazil's pressure. As an answer, I suppose, to Holman's resistance on covering the exiles, the Rio station has decided to send two more of its agents to the Brazilian Embassy here —in addition to the military attaché, Colonel Camara Sena.‡ One is a high-level penetration of the Brazilian Foreign Ministry, Manuel Pio Correa,‡ who is coming as Ambassador, and the other is Lyle Fontoura,‡ a protégé of Pio, who will be a new First Secretary. Until last month Pio was Brazil's Ambassador to Mexico where, according to the background forwarded by the Rio station, he was very effective in operational tasks for the Mexico City station. However, because Mexico hadn't recognized the new military government, Pio was recalled, and the Rio station arranged to have him reassigned to Montevideo which at the moment is the Brazilian government's diplomatic hot spot. When they arrive Holman will handle the contact with Pio while O'Grady works with Fontoura. One way or another the Rio station is determined to generate operations against the exiles, and Pio apparently is the persistent type who will keep up pressure on the Uruguayan government.

Montevideo — 28 June 1964

The Miami station is having trouble getting information out of Earle Perez Freeman, the Cuban intelligence officer who is in asylum in the Uruguayan Embassy in Havana. After several attempts at elicitation by German Roosen, one of the Uruguayan diplomats working for the Miami station, Perez accused him of working for the CIA and demanded that the CIA arrange to get him out of Cuba. He told Roosen that he will not reveal anything of Cuban operations in Uruguay until he is safely out of Cuba.

One of Roosen's problems is that he is unable to pressure Perez very effectively without instructions from the Foreign Ministry here. He denied, of course, Perez's accusation of his connections with us, but is reluctant to proceed without some instructions from his government. Holman agreed that I propose to Inspector Piriz that he go to Miami to provide official guidance to Roosen—but without Roosen knowing that Piriz is in contact with us. When I spoke to Piriz he liked the idea but cautioned that Colonel Rodriguez, the Chief of Police, should authorize his trip and coordinate with the Foreign Ministry.

Holman proposed to Rodriguez that he send one of his best officers to Miami to work with Uruguayan diplomats who are in contact with Perez in the Embassy, but without revealing either our contacts with Piriz or Roosen. As expected Rodriguez accepted the idea, obtained Foreign Ministry endorsement, and nominated Piriz. In a few days now, Piriz will go to Miami to give official guidance both to Roosen and to Goncalves, the other Uruguayan diplomat in Havana working for the Miami station (Ayala Cabeda had previously been transferred from Havana and was no longer used by the Agency). The Miami officer in charge will be meeting Roosen, Goncalves and Piriz separately, all of which seems cumbersome and inefficient, but we must protect the contact we have with each from being known by the others. In any case Roosen and Goncalves will have official encouragement for pressure against the Cuban intelligence officer. We've got to get information from him before any break in relations removes the diplomat-agents from Havana.

The campaign for isolating Cuba is another step closer to success. The OAS announced that sufficient votes have been obtained for a Conference of Foreign Ministers to consider the arms cache case and the Venezuelan motion that all OAS members still having relations with Cuba break them. Still no sign, however, that Uruguay will support the motion or break even if the motion is passed.

Propaganda against Cuba continues through the AVBUZZ media project. Among the many current placements are those of the canned propaganda operation, Editors Press Service,‡ which is based in New York and turns out quantitics of articles against the Castro government and communism in general, much of which is written by Cuban exiles like Guillermo Martinez Marquez.‡

Montevideo — 15 July 1964

The *coup* rumors have subsided since the general strike last month but several strikes have continued. Headquarters sent down a strange dispatch that Holman believes is a prelude to getting back into political-action operations. According to him the dispatch, although signed as usual by the Division Chief, was actually written by Ray Herbert‡ who is Deputy Division Chief and an old colleague of Holman's from their days in the FBI. In rather ambiguous terms this dispatch instructs us to expand our contacts in the political field to obtain intelligence about political stability, government policy concerning activities of the extreme left, and possible solutions to current problems such as constitutional reform. Holman believes that Herbert deliberately did not mention political-action operations (as opposed to political-intelligence collection) but that the message to prepare for renewal of these operations was clearly implied.

For preliminary organization Holman has given me the responsibility for reporting progress and for developing new political contacts. He will increase somewhat his meetings with Mrs. Nardone and with Gari and soon will introduce me to yet another Ruralista leader, Wilson Elso,‡ who is a Federal Deputy. We will not make contact with the other principal Ruralista leader, Senator Juan Maria Bordaberry, because he is already in regular contact with Ambassador Coerr, and Holman wants no problems with him. The importance of the Ruralistas is that they have already announced support for constitutional reform in order to return Uruguay to a strong one-man presidency. The other parties are openly opposed to such reform.

In addition to the Ruralistas, Holman asked me to arrange with one of the legitimate political section officers to begin meeting some of the more liberal leaders of the Colorado Party, mainly of the List 15 and the List 99. These two factions will be in the thick of the elections coming up in 1966, and they also constitute an attractive potential for access agents in the Soviet operations program.

For purposes of political reporting Holman will also have his new contact with Adolfo Tejera,‡ the Minister of the Interior, with Colonel Ventura Rodriguez, the Chief of Police, and with Colonel Carvajal, Chief of Military Intelligence. For the time being he will refrain from reinitiating contact with Colonel Mario Aguerrondo‡ who was Rodriguez's precedessor as Chief of Police and a close station liaison collaborator, because Aguerrondo is usually at the center of rumors of a move by Blanco military officers against the government. Also O'Grady will meet more regularly with Juan Carlos Quagliotti,‡ the wealthy rancher and lawyer who is active in promoting interventionist sympathies among military leaders.

In discussing expansion of political contacts Holman said we have to be very careful to avoid giving the Ambassador any reason to suspect that we're getting back into political-action operations. When the time comes, he said, the decision will be made in Washington and the Ambassador will be informed through department channels.

This is bad news. All the work with political leaders in Quito only emphasized how venal and ineffectual they were and in Uruguay the politicians seem to be even more so. I couldn't be less enthusiastic. I don't want to cultivate senators and deputies—not even for the Director.

Montevideo — 20 July 1964

Another purchase of Chilean currency at the Montevideo branch of the First National City Bank for shipping by pouch to the Santiago station. This time the Finance Officer who is in charge of the purchasing operations in Lima and Rio came to Montevideo to assist in the pick-up from Hennessy‡ and to count the escudos afterwards. This one was also worth over 100,000 dollars and, according to the Finance Officer, is only a drop in the bucket. He says we are spending money in the Chilean election practically like we did in Brazil two years ago.

We've had serious trouble in the AVENGEFUL/AVALANCHE telephone-tapping operation. AVOIDANCE,‡ the courier who takes the tapes around to the transcribers, reported to Paul Burns, his case officer, that a briefcase full of tapes was taken from the trunk of his car while he was on his rounds making pick-ups and deliveries. AVOIDANCE has no idea whether the tapes were taken by a common thief or by the enemy. Although he claims he has been very careful to watch for surveillance (negative), the chances are that the tapes will be listened to, even if only stolen by a thief, in order to determine saleability.

After a discussion with Holman and Burns, I advised Commisioner Otero and Colonel Ramirez, Chief of the Metropolitan Guard, that we had lost some tapes and believe all the lines except the Cuban Embassy should be disconnected. Ramirez agreed that the Cuban line should be retained because of our coming OAS meeting and the possibility of a break in relations with Cuba. He is also going to keep several of the contraband lines in operation for cover, although there is no way of denying the targets of the lost tapes.

For the time being AVIODANCE will be eliminated from the operation although he will go through the motions of a daily routine very similar to normal while continuing to watch for surveillance. The tapes of the Cuban line will be sent over to the station with the daily police intelligence couriers and we will give them to Tomas Zafiriadis‡ who is an Uruguayan employee of the Embassy Commercial Section. He will serve as courier between the station and his wife (AVENGEFUL-3)‡ who transcribes the Cuban Embassy line. His wife's sister (AVENGEFUL-5),‡ the transcriber of the PCU Headquarters line, will also help on the Cuban Embassy line since her line is being disconnected. Using an Embassy employee like this is against the rules but Holman is willing to risk the Ambassador's wrath to keep the Cuban Embassy line going.

Montevideo — 25 July 1964

News is in that the OAS passed the motion that all members should break diplomatic and commercial relations with Cuba and that except for humanitarian purposes there should be no air or maritime traffic. It took four years to get this motion passed—not only CIA operations but all our Latin American foreign policy has been pointing to this goal. The countries that still have relations, Chile, Mexico and Uruguay, voted against the motion, while Bolivia abstained. Whether Uruguay or any other of these countries honor the motion or not is another matter but headquarters' propaganda guidance is certain to call for an all-out campaign to force compliance with the motion.

Perhaps with the vote to break relations the AMHALF agents in the Uruguayan Embassy in Havana, Roosen and Goncalves, will be able to get information out of Perez Freeman. Even with the assistance of Inspector Piriz in Miami, the Uruguayan diplomats still were unable to exert enough pressure to force Perez to begin talking about Cuban operations in Montevideo. We need the information to support the campaign for a break by Uruguay with Cuba through Perez's revelations of Cuban intervention here. We could alternatively write our own document based on a little fact and a lot of imagination and attribute it to Perez, whose presence in the Embassy is public knowledge. Such a document could backfire, however, if Perez had actually been sent by the Cubans to seek asylum—this suspicion grows as he continues to refuse to talk—because after the document was surfaced Perez could escape from the Embassy and issue a public denial through the Cuban authorities. For the time being Inspector Piriz will return and we will hold up the false document project until we see how our media campaign progresses without it.

Station labor operations limp along with Jack Goodwyn‡ and the AIFLD‡ in the lead. This week we had a visit from Joaquin (Jack) Otero,‡ the representative of the International Transport Workers' Federation‡ (ITF) who worked with me in Quito last year. Otero is now the chief ITF representative for all of Latin America and the Caribbean, and he came to assist in a boycott against meat exports by non-union packing plants. The hope is that his assistance will help strengthen the democratic unions involved.

Agency-sponsored trade-union education programs through ORIT are being expanded. Through the ICFTU International Solidarity Fund, headquarters is pumping in almost 200,000 dollars to establish an ORIT training school in Cuernavaca. Until now the ORIT courses have been limited by the space made available in Mexico City by the Mexican Workers' Confederation‡ which is the most important ORIT affiliate after the AFL–CIO. Opening of the Cuernavaca school is still a year or two away but already the ORIT courses have become an effective combination with the AIFLD program in Washington.

As if we don't have enough problems with Argentines, Paraguayans and Brazilians now we have Bolivians to worry about. A week or so ago the new Bolivian Ambassador, José Antonio Arce,‡ arrived and the La Paz station asked that we keep up their relationship with him. He has been in and out of various government jobs since the Bolivian revolution, most recently as Minister of the Interior when he worked closely with the La Paz station. Holman will be seeing him from time to time, probably no more than is absolutely necessary, so that when he returns to La Paz this important supporter of President Paz Estenssoro can be picked up again for Bolivian operations.

Arce's main job here will be to watch the supporters of former Bolivian President Hernan Siles Suazo, and Siles himself if he settles in exile in Montevideo as is expected. Siles aspires to succeed current President Victor Paz Estenssoro in keeping with their custom, since the revolution of 1952, of alternating in the presidency. Paz, however, against the tradition, was reelected in May and must now contend with Siles's plots against him. The La Paz station is anxious to prevent Siles from returning to the presidency in Bolivia because of his recent leftward trends, and his friendly relationship with the Soviets when he was Bolivian Ambassador in Montevideo during 1960–62. As an initial move to support the La Paz station I have asked Commissioner Otero, Chief of Police Intelligence, to make discreet inquiries about Siles's plans among his political friends and to watch for signs that he will be settling here.

Montevideo — 11 August 1964

Uruguayan compliance with the OAS resolution on Cuba looks very doubtful. The Foreign Minister on his return from Washington announced that the NCG will now have to decide whether the OAS resolution should be passed to the U.N. Security Council for approval before it can be considered binding. This is only a delaying maneuver to avoid a difficult decision but the most damaging developments are that Mexico has announced that it will ignore the resolution and Bolivia is undecided. Unless Uruguay can be made to seem isolated in its refusal to break, the chances are not good. Moreover, although we have intensified our propaganda output on the Cuban issue through AVBUZZ–1 considerably, it's no match for the campaign being waged by the extreme left against breaking relations, which has been carefully combined with the campaign against the government on economic issues.

Today the National Workers' Convention (CNT), formed only a week ago as a loosely knit coordinating organization of the CTU and the government workers, is leading another general strike. Again most of the country's economic activity has stopped: transport, bars, restaurants, port, construction, wool, textiles, service stations, schools and many others. The strike was called to show support for continued relations with Cuba, admittedly a political purpose, but not unprecedented in Uruguay.

Apart from the strike today, the formation of the CNT is a very significant step forward by the communist-influenced trade-union movement, because, for the first time, government workers in the Central Administration (the ministries and executive) and the autonomous agencies and decentralized services are working in the same organization as the private-sector unions of the CTU. With continuing inflation and currency devaluation (the peso is down to almost 23 per dollar now) the CNT will have plenty of legitimate issues for agitation in coming months. Besides the Cuban issue the CNT campaign is currently targeted on pay raises, fringe benefits and subsidies to be included in the budget now being drawn up for next year.

Montevideo — 21 August 1964

Through the AVBUZZ media operation we're getting editorials almost daily calling for Uruguayan compliance with the OAS resolution to break with Cuba. President Alessandri in Chile has done this already, instead of waiting until after the elections. Today Bolivia announced it is breaking in accordance with the resolution, leaving only Uruguay and Mexico still with ties to Cuba.

The NCG will surely buckle under such isolation, but

getting decisions here is cumbersome. On important matters, the majority NCG members decide their position only after prior decisions within each of the Blanco factions represented on the NCG. Likewise the Colorado factions must decide. Eventually the NCG meets to formalize the positions taken by each faction earlier and a decision may emerge. In the case of Cuban relations the Foreign Minister has yet to present his report on the OAS Conference and related matters even with a month already passed since the Conference.

For additional propaganda, we have arranged for Juana Castro,‡ Fidel's sister, to make a statement favoring the break during a stopover next week at the Montevideo airport. She defected in Mexico this June and is currently on a propaganda tour of South America organized by the Miami station and headquarters. We'll get wide coverage for her statement, and a few days later still another Miami station agent will arrive: Isabel Siero Perez,‡ important in the International Federation of Women Lawyers,‡ another of the CA staff's international organizations. She'll describe the Havana horror show and emphasize the Soviets' use of Cuba as a base for penetration throughout the hemisphere.

Montevideo — 31 August 1964

The Montevideo association of foreign diplomats recently held their monthly dinner and Janet and I went along with several others from the Embassy. By chance we began a conversation with two of the Soviet diplomats and later joined them for dinner. I wrote a memorandum for headquarters on the conversation—one of the Soviets, Sergey Borisov, is a known KGB officer—and Holman later asked me to keep up the contact and see if Borisov is interested. Russell Phipps,‡ our Soviet operations officer, isn't the outgoing type and Holman is clearly not pleased with Phipps's failure to recruit any decent new access agents.

I'll go to the diplomatic association meeting next month but I'm not keen on getting deeply into Soviet operations. Just keeping the telephone transcripts analyzed and the files up to date is deadly dreary and requires far too much desk work. We shall see if Borisov is interested in continuing the contact—he's the Consul and lives in the Soviet side of the AVERT house.

I decided to try another Cuban recruitment with the possibility that the specter of a break in relations might help us. The target was Aldo Rodriguez Camps, the Cuban Chargé d'Affaires in Montevideo, whose father-in-law is an exile living in Miami. Last year the Miami station sent the father-in-law, AMPIG-1,‡ down to Montevideo to discover the political views on Castro and communism of the Chargé and his wife. He felt from his conversation that neither seemed to be particularly ardent communists although they were clearly loyal to the Cuban revolution. At that time it was decided not to try for the recruitment or defection of either Aldo or Ester but to wait for a future date.

At my request the Miami station proposed to the father-in-law that he come back to Montevideo as soon as possible for a more direct approach to his daughter, who appeared to be the more susceptible of the two. If Ester had agreed to defect we would have made arrangements to evacuate her to Miami, but only after she had had a few days to work on Aldo. The key to Aldo, the Chargé, is their two young children, to whom he is very attached and when confronted with their flight to Miami he just might have decided to come along.

Unfortunately, this recruitment failed. The father-in-law came as planned and made the initial meeting with his daughter but she cut him off at the beginning and refused any discussion of defection. After two days he went back to Miami, sad and broken, with no idea if he'll ever see his daughter and grandchildren again.

Montevideo — 4 September 1964

The main Blanco and Colorado newspapers are carrying a torrent of AVBUZZ-sponsored articles and statements calling for the government to heed the OAS resolution. However, maneuvering among the different

Blanco and Colorado NCG members and their factions is causing the outlook on the break with Cuba to change almost daily. In the past three days there have been a meeting of the NCG Foreign Relations Commission that was scheduled but didn't convene for lack of quorum, new scheduling of debate by the full NCG for 10 September, and finally last night an NCG decision to consider the OAS resolution at a special meeting on 8 September. So far only two of the NCG members have indicated how they'll vote—one for and one against—and there is a good chance we'll lose. Nevertheless, relations with Brazil are again at crisis point, and the thesis that Uruguay must go along with the majority in order to assure protection against pressures from Argentina or Brazil is gaining ground.

If they don't break relations this week, I'll write the "Perez Freeman Report" right away and we'll make it public either through Inspector Piriz or the AMHALF agents, Roosen or Goncalves. The Foreign Minister, who is against the break, is the first guy I'll burn as a Cuban agent—he probably is anyway.

Returns from the elections in Chile today show Eduardo Frei an easy winner over Allende. Chalk up another victory for election operations. Allende won't be a threat again for another six years.

Montevideo — 8 September 1964

A great victory. Forty-four days after the OAS resolution on Cuba the NCG has voted to comply. How the vote would go wasn't known for sure until the last minute when the NCG President changed his position and carried a Counsellor from his faction with him. Final vote: six in favor of breaking (five Blancos and one Colorado) and three against (one Blanco and two Colorados).

While the Councillors were debating several thousand pro-Cuban demonstrators gathered in Independence Plaza in front of Government House where the NCG was meeting. When the vote was announced a riot was on, and the crowd surged down the main street,

18 de Julio, breaking store fronts and clashing with the anti-riot Metropolitan Guard and the mounted Republican Guard. At least ten police were injured and twenty-six demonstrators arrested before the water cannons and tear-gas dispersed the mob. Somehow many of the demonstrators got back to the University buildings further down 18 de Julio, and right now the battle is continuing there with stones and firecrackers being hurled from the roof of the main University building.

I'm spending the night in the station just in case anything drastic happens that has to be reported to headquarters. Tomorrow we'll see if any of the Cubans can be picked off before they leave for home.

Montevideo — 10 September 1964

Rioting continues, mostly centered at the University of the Republic buildings on 18 de Julio. Although some demonstrators abandoned the University during the early morning hours yesterday at the urging of Colonel Rodriguez,‡ Chief of Police, and Adolfo Tejera,‡ Minister of the Interior, new riots began yesterday morning at about ten o'clock and have continued since. The demonstrators' tactics include, besides the throwing of stones from the University buildings, lightning street riots at different places to throw the police off guard. Shop windows and cars parked at our Embassy have also been stoned.

During the early hours of this morning, several U.S. businesses were attacked. A powerful bomb exploded outside the First National City Bank shattering the huge plate-glass windows and causing the hanging ceiling in the lobby to fall. Another bomb exploded at the Western Telegraph Company while an incendiary device started a fire at the Moore–McCormick Lines offices. General Electric's offices were also damaged.

The Cubans advised the Foreign Ministry that they'll be leaving on Saturday for Madrid. Last night with Roberto Musso,‡ the chief of the AVENIN surveillance team, I tried to talk to the new code clerk by telephone. Musso, using the name of someone we already know is in contact with the code clerk, got him on the telephone and passed it to me. I said I was a friend of Roberto Hernandez, his predecessor, and would like to make a similar offer of assistance. He told me to kiss his ass and hung up, but I'll try again if I have time after I've done the same with the other three—two of whom are new arrivals since the Hernandez episode.

The Cubans may have made a serious mistake yesterday, in their haste to tie up loose ends before leaving. They sent the chauffeur, my agent, to send a telegram to Tucuman, Argentina with the message, "Return for your cousin's wedding." This can only be a code phrase and the urgency attached to sending the telegram led the chauffeur to conclude that someone is being called for a meeting before Saturday. I've passed the addressee and address by cable to the Buenos Aires station for follow-up and will watch carefully the air and riverboat passenger lists for this and other names of possible Cuban agents. We know nothing about the person this was addressed to, but he is probably involved in the guerrilla activity in the Tucuman area.

Montevideo — 11 September 1964

Demonstrators continue to occupy the University and bombings have occurred at the OAS offices, the Coca-Cola plant, newspapers that promoted the break (*El Dia, El Pais* and *El Plata*), the homes of four councillors who voted for the break, and several of the neighborhood clubs of the factions that favored the break. At the University, which is still sealed off by police, minors were allowed to leave and the Red Cross entered with doctors to distribute blankets and examine the students, who were suffering from cold and hunger. Any who decide to leave, however, will have to be registered, identified and face possible arrest. Colonel Rodriguez's plan is to trap all the non-students among the 400 or so people occupying the University.

Not to be outdone by the students and political demonstrators, the municipal-transit system workers struck for three hours this afternoon and the workers of the autonomous agencies and decentralized services staged a huge demonstration at the Legislative Palace. Again the issue was budget benefits.

I've spoken to all but one of the Cubans and none has been willing to meet me. One of them last night invited me to the Embassy for coffee but I thought it prudent to decline in spite of the freezing wind howling through the telephone booth. When they leave tomorrow I'll be at the airport just in case—as will Otero,‡ Piriz‡ and other police officers who can take charge if a last-minute defection occurs.

Montevideo — 12 September 1964

This morning the demonstrators at the University surrendered and were allowed to leave after fingerprints, identification photographs and biographical data were taken. Forty-three non-students were arrested among the 400 who came out.

At the airport this afternoon several thousand demonstrators came together to bid the Cubans farewell. When the police began to force the demonstrators back to a highway some distance from the main terminal building another riot broke out followed by a pitched battle. The police won easily, using the cavalry effectively in the open areas around the terminal building, but many were injured on both sides.

All the Cubans left as scheduled. Only one remains behind: the Commercial Counsellor, who is being allowed to stay on for a couple of weeks to close a Cuban purchase of jerked beef.

Of all the Latin American and Caribbean countries only Mexico still has relations with Cuba. If Mexico refuses to break, as seems likely, the Mexican channel could be used for various operational ploys against Cuba—it's even possible that the Mexican government was encouraged by the station there not to break with Cuba. Here we've done our job, but poor O'Grady will be working until the end of the year to send headquarters all the clips on Cuba we've managed to place in the media.

Efforts by the Miami station to get information out of Earle Perez Freeman through the Uruguayan diplomats, Roosen and Goncalves, have ended, as these agents are returning to Montevideo. Although Switzerland is taking charge of Uruguayan affairs in Havana the Uruguayan Chargé is staying to close the Embassy and to transfer the eight remaining asylees, including Perez Freeman, to another Embassy. According to the Miami station Goncalves is too insecure and frivolous to consider incorporating into other operations so I've asked them to forward a contact plan for Roosen only. Just possibly he could develop a relationship with a Soviet officer here, but this will depend on a careful analysis of the possibility that he was known by the Cubans to be working with us.

No sooner do we get the Cubans out than the Chinese communists try to move in. Only yesterday the Foreign Minister told a reporter that the Chicoms have asked permission to set up a trade mission in Montevideo and that as far as he is concerned it would be all right. Holman gave O'Grady the responsibility for following this one up but as in the case of the Brazilians the details are mine because we'll use the police intelligence office to get more information.

Manuel Pio Correa,‡ the new Brazilian Ambassador, arrives tomorrow. He is pointedly visiting Brazilian military units along the Uruguay–Brazil border on his way here. Holman will establish contact with him next week.

Montevideo — 16 September 1964

In spite of the intensity of station operations against the Cubans and other matters like the Brazilians, and local communist gains in the trade-union field we have a serious morale problem that's getting worse as weeks go by. In most stations, I suppose, the day to day demands of work keep personal dissentions to a minimum because one doesn't have the time or energy to feud. But here the problem is with Holman and everyone in the station is affected.

The problem is that Holman expects all the station officers to give outstanding performances in their particular areas of responsibility but he's not willing to exert very much effort himself. Besides that he is a great player of favorites, and for better or worse he's chosen me as his favorite. He invites me to lunch several days each week and practically insists that I play golf on Saturday afternoons with his crowd out at the Cerro Club even though I've made it clear I'm not enthusiastic. When we're alone he speaks derisively of the other station officers, especially O'Grady, Phipps and Zeffer. O'Grady, in fact, has turned into a bundle of nerves under Holman's criticism, which he's sure is the cause of his increasingly frequent attacks of hives. Usually Holman's criticisms are about shortcomings in language or failure to make new recruitments but sometimes he even criticizes the wives.

His attitude would be understandable, perhaps, if his own work habits were more inspiring, but he avoids work as much as possible and requests from other stations like Rio or La Paz or Buenos Aires seem like personal insults to him. Just the other day when we were playing golf, Holman told me that in fact he was rather relieved when the recruitment of Hernandez, the Cuban code clerk, failed. He said he came to Montevideo for a relaxing last four years before retiring and only hoped to keep operations to a minimum and the Ambassador happy. If Hernandez had been recruited, headquarters would have bothered us constantly with advice and probably would have sent down "experts" to tell us how to run the operation.

Holman is not only determined to keep operations to a minimum. At night or on weekends when priority cables are received or have to be sent Holman refuses to go to the station to take action. He either sends O'Grady in to bring the cable out to his house in Carrasco—against all the rules of security—or he has the communications officer bring it out to him. If another officer has to take action he simply calls that officer to his house.

I'm not sure what to do since I'm the only officer Holman thinks is doing a good job—nothing to be proud of, it could even be the kiss of death. Warren Dean told me before leaving Quito that Holman isn't considered one of the more outstanding Chiefs of Station in the Division, but he's apparently protected by Ray Herbert, the Deputy Division Chief, who is Holman's best friend.

Montevideo — 25 September 1964

Today the Congress approved the new budgets for the state-owned banks with provisions for a 30 per cent salary increase retroactive to January of this year plus improved fringe benefits. Political motivation prevailed at the last moment even though the NCG had previously rejected such generous increases, which is not to say they aren't justified when inflation is taken into account. The main problem is that this increase of 30 per cent will set the standard for demands by all the other government employees which in turn will accelerate inflation with new budget deficits.

The new National Workers' Convention, heavily influenced by the PCU, is also intensifying its efforts to unify the government and private-sector workers through a series of rallies and marches in coming weeks, culminating in a mass meeting in early December to be called the Congress of the People with representation from the trade unions and other popular mass organizations. At the Congress of People they will formulate their own solutions to the problems afflicting this country—not a bad idea what with the mess they're in.

Relations between Uruguay and Brazil are back at boiling-point. Police in Porto Alegre, the capital of the Brazilian state bordering Uruguay, have just discovered a new plot by Goulart and his supporters to foment a communist-oriented takeover. A written plan, supposedly found on a university student, included the formation of terrorist commando units. Earlier, another plot was discovered in Porto Alegre involving Army officers loyal to Goulart. Here in Montevideo, the 300 Brazilian exiles have formed an association to help those unable to get along financially. However, at the first meeting considerable discussion was devoted to ways in which the military government could be overthrown, and Brizola's wife, who is Goulart's sister, was elected to the association's governing board.

In tracking down the possibility that the Chinese communists will establish a trade mission here, we discovered that permission has in fact been granted, not to the Chinese but to the North Koreans. They have just arrived and are taking a house on the same street as the Soviet Legation. Holman asked Tejera,‡ the Minister of the Interior, what could be done to keep them from staying permanently, but Tejera made no promises. Already headquarters is asking for a program to get them thrown out.

Two recent developments of note have occurred in our otherwise stagnated student operations. A new publication aimed at university and secondary students is now coming out: it's called *Combate*‡ and is published by Alberto Roca.‡ Also, at the Alfredo Vazquez Acevedo Institute, which is the secondary school associated with the University and as such the most important on that level, the student union supported by the station has just defeated the FEUU-oriented candidates for the fifth straight time. Sooner or later our work with this group, the Association of Preparatory Students,‡ is bound to be reflected in the FEUU.

Montevideo — 29 September 1964

Montevideo was alive with new rumors this morning that senior Blanco military officers are planning a *coup* against the government. Cause of the rumors is a dinner given last night by Juan José Gari, the long-time station agent in the Ruralist League and currently President of the State Mortgage Bank, in honor of Mario Aguerrondo,‡ former Montevideo Police Chief, who was recently promoted from Colonel to General. Among the guests at the dinner were other Ruralista leaders and practically all of the top military commanders from the Minister of Defense down. Holman checked out the rumors with Gari and with Adolfo

Tejera, the Minister of the Interior, while I checked with Colonel Roberto Ramirez, Chief of the Metropolitan Guard, who was also there. The dinner was simply an expression of homage to Aguerrondo but the rumors, entirely unfounded, reveal just how nervous people are that a military takeover may occur, what with the increasing strength of the PCU-dominated unions and the government's incapacity to slow inflation. New strikes are being planned.

Holman thinks he has at last got agreement from the Minister of the Interior, Adolfo Tejera, for setting up a Public Safety mission for work with the police under AID. For some time Colonel Rodriguez, the Chief of Police, has wanted the program but the delicate question of foreigners working openly with the police has caused Tejera to delay his decision. No wonder Tejera has now finally decided. He has just testified before the Budget Commission of the Chamber of Deputies that his ministry is too poor to buy paper, the police lack uniforms, arms, transport and communication, and the fire departments lack hoses, chemicals, trucks and other equipment.

It's not just a question of money and equipment for the police; they are also very poorly trained. Not only are bank robberies frequent, for example, but successful escapes often involve not only stolen cars but motor scooters, bicycles, trucks, buses—even horses. In one recent robbery the getaway car wouldn't start so the robbers simply walked down the street to the beach and disappeared into the crowd. In August four thieves were caught robbing a house on the coast near Punta del Este but escaped to the nearby hills, and after a two-day gun battle they slipped through a cordon of several hundred police. Their escape car, however, got stuck in the sand and they walked down the beach, robbed another house, were again discovered, but this time escaped in a rowing-boat. For six days the police chased them in cars, helicopters and on foot but they finally escaped completely—carrying their loot on their backs as they rode their bicycles down the main highway into Montevideo.

The competence of the AVALANCHE service is similarly limited in its attempts to suppress terrorist activities. Undoubtedly some of the bombings at the time relations with Cuba were broken were the work of the terrorist group led by Raul Sendic. Last March Sendic returned from several months in hiding in Argentina after an arms theft from a shooting club in Colonia. He arrived in a light aircraft at a small airport near Montevideo, but when discovered he simply rushed past the police guard and escaped in a waiting truck. The following month 4000 sticks of dynamite were stolen from a quarry and a few days later enough caps and fuses to explode it disappeared from another site. All the police could report was that these thefts may have been the work of the Sendic band.

Building up the police is like labor operations—we're still at the beginning with a long road ahead requiring training, equipment, money and lots of patience.

Montevideo — 7 October 1964

This is the final day of the forty-eight-hour strike in the autonomous agencies and decentralized services. Only the electric company and the state banks have been operating although the banks have been stopping work for one hour each shift in solidarity with the others. Yesterday the striking government workers, CNT unions and FEUU held a demonstration at the Legislative Palace to demand salary increases equivalent to the 30 per cent won two weeks ago by the government bank workers.

Two days ago all the privately owned gasoline stations were closed indefinitely in an owner's strike against the government for a higher profit margin from the state-owned petroleum monopoly, ANCAP, which also has a large number of gasoline stations. As the ANCAP workers are participating in the forty-eight-hour government workers' strike, no stations were open yesterday or today. More strikes and demonstrations coming up: teachers, the ministries, postal workers and some unions in the private sector.

Montevideo — 17 October 1964

Commissioner Otero and others have had a stroke of luck against the Sendic group of terrorists. Two leaders of the group, Jorge Manera, an engineer in the electric company, and Julio Marenales, a professor in the School of Fine Arts, were arrested in an unsuccessful bank robbery. They confessed that their purpose was to aid the sugar-cane workers of Bella Union and that the focal point for their activities is the School of Fine Arts. Police seized arms and are searching for two other members of the group. Otero's leads from these arrests are very important because this is the only active armed group. If he can get good information from the interrogations we may be able to target some recruitment operations against them. So far they've been completely underground.

We've decided to hook up the AVENGEFUL lines again on the Soviets and the PCU. I'll also put a line on *Prensa Latina* and another on the Czech Embassy which has taken over the Cubans' affairs. If the transcribers can manage I'll also put a tap on the telephone of Sara Youchak, a young activist in the FIDEL political front who has all the marks of being a Cuban intelligence agent.

Still no sign of who was behind the theft of the tapes from AVOIDANCE's car. He'll now take over the courier duties again so that we can stop using the Embassy employee. Colonel Ramirez, Chief of the Metropolitan Guard, is really happy about AVENGEFUL. A few days ago his men, acting on data from telephone taps, intercepted a truck containing 600 transistor radios that had been off-loaded from a light aircraft running contraband from Argentina. The 300,000 pesos that the haul is worth will be divided among Ramirez and his men.

Meanwhile the government announced that they simply had no money to start paying September salaries —even the police and the Army, always the first to be paid—have received nothing for September. Nevertheless, the NCG has just approved the 30 per cent increase for employees of the state-owned telephone, electricity and petroleum monopolies.

Montevideo — 25 October 1964

Perez Freeman has been killed trying to escape from the Uruguayan Embassy in Havana! The story was carried in wire-service reports this morning and said that he had been trying to hold the Uruguayan Chargé, who is still trying to arrange for another Embassy to take over the asylees, as hostage. The Miami station is attempting to check the story but no confirmation so far. If only the Mexico City station had handled his defection correctly in January we would have all his information and he'd be basking in the Miami sun.

Montevideo — 31 October 1964

On the Perez Freeman case the Foreign Ministry received what is being called the longest cable in its history—some 1300 groups in code from the Embassy in Havana. The communications office of the Foreign Ministry, however, was unable to decode it for "technical" reasons—meaning, probably, that too much effort was involved—so the Foreign Minister called the Embassy by telephone to get the story the Chargé had put in the cable.

Perez Freeman, according to the Chargé, was the leader of a group of four asylees who took the Chargé hostage and escaped from the Embassy in the Chargé's car. Cuban security forces gave chase and when the escaping group arrived at a roadblock Perez Freeman jumped out of the car and was shot running away. The others were taken to the fortress where executions are normally held. I've asked the Miami station to try to verify the Chargé's version.

Hernan Siles Suazo, the former Bolivian President, was caught plotting and was deported by President Paz Estenssoro. He's arrived back in Montevideo and we're supposed to report any signs that he may be returning to Bolivia. Paz Estenssoro is in serious trouble right now, and the La Paz station wants to head off any complications from Siles. Holman continues to meet with Jose Arce, the Bolivian Ambassador, to pass tidbits from police intelligence. Yesterday Arce gave a press conference to assure everyone that the rebellion now underway against Paz Estenssoro is communist-inspired and doomed to failure. He emphasized that Paz has the full support of the Bolivian people and that current problems have been blown all out of proportion—adding that the minority groups opposing Paz are so few in number that they could all be driven off together in a single bus. So far ex-President Siles hasn't moved from Montevideo but Otero has posted a special "security" guard for Siles in order to watch him more closely.

Montevideo — 6 November 1964

In Bolivia President Paz has been overthrown by the military and allowed to go to Lima in exile. Ambassador Arce has resigned and has announced that he plans to continue living in Montevideo for a while. Meanwhile ex-President Siles has started to pack and will be leaving for Bolivia within a few days. Holman's not very happy, though, because rumors are strong that Paz Estenssoro is coming to live in Montevideo—meaning exile-watching will continue, only with new targets.

Late tonight the Budget was finally passed by the Chamber of Deputies, ten minutes before the final constitutional deadline and after forty hours of continuous debate. Passage was made possible by a last-minute political pact between the Blancos, who lack a majority in the Chamber, and the Ruralistas, Christian Democrats and a splinter faction of the Colorados. Opinion is unanimous, even among Blancos, that the Budget is unworkable because of its enormous deficit and that not even the devaluation of the peso included in the Budget exercise—the third devaluation since the Blancos took over in 1959—will allow for printing enough new money to cover the deficit.

I've seen my Soviet friends at several recent diplomatic receptions and have become acquainted with a couple of Romanians and Czechs as well. Headquarters has reacted favorably and asked that I develop the relationship further with the Soviet Consul, Borisov. Tomorrow night I go to the Soviet Embassy as the Ambassador's representative for their celebration of the October Revolution. Phipps tells me to expect plenty of vodka, caviar and singing.

Montevideo — 28 November 1964

Relations between Uruguay and Brazil are heating up again although Goulart's importance is diminishing fast because he has heart trouble and recently underwent an operation. Brizola is the center of controversy now because of recent declarations against the Brazilian government that were published both here and in Brazil. Manuel Pio Correa,‡ the Brazilian Ambassador, has filed another official protest against Brizola's conduct. Perhaps more important are the recent arrivals of two former high officials in Goulart's government, Max de Costa Santos, formerly a Deputy, and Almino Alfonso, former Minister of Labor. Both are far-left and Pio has protested against their arrival here, claiming they entered Uruguay illegally and cannot obtain asylum because they had already been granted asylum in other countries following the military *coup*. The Minister of the Interior, Adolfo Tejera,‡ is studying the case and Holman is urging him to throw them out.

In Brazil, the federal government has been forced to take over the state of Goias, throwing out the state government because of what is being described as communist subversion there. Yesterday the Brazilian Foreign Minister blamed the intervention in Goias (the military government's worst crisis yet) on the activities of exiles in Montevideo. Today President Castelo Branco told the Brazilian Congress that he had ordered the takeover in Goias in order to forestall a plot led by Brizola from Montevideo. New protests from Pio Correa are certain.

Outright military intervention in Uruguay by Brazil is getting closer. We've had several alarming reports lately through the communications intelligence channel based on monitoring of the military traffic in southern

Brazil. According to these reports the Brazilian Army is ready at any time to implement a plan to invade Uruguay and take over Montevideo in a matter of hours.

Montevideo — 2 December 1964

I have been trying in recent weeks to follow up some of the mass of leads on probable agents and operations of the Cubans. Most of these leads have come from telephone tapping, surveillance, letter intercepts and monitoring of communications channels. Several of these cases have interesting aspects.

I continue to receive the mail addressed to the Cuban intelligence support agent, Jorge Castillo, through the postman AVBUSY–1. In May the Cubans changed the cryptographic system of their network in Latin America (the ZRKNICK agents), probably as a result of the near-recruitment of Hernandez here and of the defection of the Cuban intelligence officer, AMMUG–1,‡ in Canada. Since then the National Security Agency has been unable to decrypt the messages which continue, nevertheless, to be sent to agents operating in several parts of Latin America. Although I haven't intercepted any mail that would appear to be sent by the Cuban agent believed to be working in Lima or La Paz, I have received some very suspicious letters mailed from a provincial Uruguayan town.

Telephone tapping and surveillance of Sara Youchak, a frequent overt contact of one of the Cuban intelligence officers before the break in relations, revealed that she travels frequently to Buenos Aires, where she sees her cousin, whom the Buenos Aires station has connected with guerrilla activities in northern Argentina and with communist student organizing. Moreover, Sara has a first cousin (whom she has never seen) who is a State Department Foreign Service officer. Soon I'll ask headquarters to check with State Department security people to see if we might use the cousin to place an agent next to Sara.

Through monitoring of airline reservation communications the National Security Agency has discovered that the manager of the Montevideo office of the Scandinavian Airlines System, Danilo Trelles, is in charge of assigning pre-paid tickets for passengers from many Latin American countries on the SAS flights that start several times each week in Santiago, Chile, and arrive after a number of stops in Prague. The prepaid tickets are usually requested by the Prague office of Cubana Airlines and are intended for Latin Americans traveling to Cuba. Because the pre-paid tickets are sent as "no-name," Trelles can assign them and assure that the identity of the traveler is protected. What we are trying to discover is how Trelles is advised of the identities of the travelers. The answer may be through the Czech or Soviet embassies which Trelles's assistant, Flora Papo, often visits. Papo in fact takes care of the details of this travel-support operation and the AVENIN surveillance team has turned up interesting vulnerability data on her.

AVENGEFUL telephone tapping on the Montevideo office of *Prensa Latina,* the Cuban wire service, seems to reveal what I suspected—that PL is serving as a support mechanism for Cuban intelligence operations now that the Embassy is gone. The monthly subsidy for the office is about five thousand dollars, which is wired to the Montevideo branch of the Bank of London and Montreal from the Bank of Canada. The tap also revealed that the total of all the salaries, rent, services of *Press Wireless* and other expenses amount to only about half the subsidy. Headquarters is currently processing clearance for an Assistant Manager of the Bank of London and Montreal whom I already know rather well and whom I'll recruit for access to checks on the PL account. It would be interesting to discover the recipients of the unaccounted half of the subsidy, but right now I can still only suspect that it is used for intelligence operations.

We have a new case officer for operations against the Communist Party of Uruguay and related organizations. He's Bob Riefe‡ who was the chief instructor in communism for the headquarters' portion of the JOT course five years ago. Riefe has a Ph.D. and has spent his entire career in training, but he was able to wangle an assignment in the DDP as part of the Office of Training's "cross-fertilization" program. A couple of years ago he was to have been assigned to a WH station but a heart-attack delayed him. Hopefully I can convince Riefe to take back the former Cuban Embassy chauffeur, AVBARON–1, whom I've been unsuccessfully trying to push back into PCU work since the Cubans left.

Riefe's predecessor, Paul Burns, is returning to headquarters rather discouraged after four years here without getting a really high-level penetration of the PCU. In recent months he has spent most of his time struggling with the AVPEARL audio penetration of the PCU conference room. The bugged porcelain electrical sockets arrived from headquarters some months ago but when AVCAVE–1, the PCU penetration agent assigned to make the installation, got his next guard duty he found that the paint flecks were not quite exact. Back in the station the paint was corrected by Frank Sherno,‡ a TSD technician who is setting up a regional support shop in the Buenos Aires station to service Uruguay and Chile as well as Argentina. (This new shop will give us much faster service than the Panama station regional support base for technical operations.)

At last a listening post has also been found—it's a tiny apartment in a building behind the PCU headquarters but located where the carrier-current transmitters in the sockets can be picked up. Then AVCAVE–1 got guard duty again, Sherno came over from Buenos Aires again, and during the course of guard duty the agent was able to replace the original sockets with our bugged ones for testing. Sherno in the LP had transmitters to test the switches (one frequency to turn them on and another frequency to turn them off) and a receiver to test the RF and audio quality. Then AVCAVE–1 removed our sockets and replaced the original ones since there was no way to get a message from Sherno back to him if they hadn't worked properly.

The testing operation was very risky, both for AVCAVE–1 and for Sherno in the LP. Guard duty at PCU headquarters is always in pairs and for AVCAVE–1 to slip loose from his colleague and install the bugged sockets was difficult even though it only involved the use of a screwdriver. Getting Sherno in and out of the LP with the transmitters and receivers was also dangerous because almost all the people around the PCU headquarters are party members and suspicious of strangers. Somehow both AVCAVE–1 and Sherno came out undiscovered, and now Riefe will proceed with finding a permanent LP-keeper and with the final installation by AVCAVE–1. According to Sherno the signal is excellent.

Montevideo — 4 December 1964

Pio Correa,‡ the Brazilian Ambassador, is making a loud noise over the two former Goulart government leaders, Max da Costa Santos and Almino Alfonso. Adolfo Tejera, the Minister of the Interior, recommended to the NCG ten days ago that they be expelled because they had indeed entered Uruguay illegally. A week later the Foreign Minister announced that they can remain in Uruguay because their documentation is, after all, in order—according to a Ministry of the Interior investigation. Furious, Pio Correa has filed another protest note asking for their expulsion and Brizola's internment—complaining also that Brizola has several light aircraft at his disposal for courier flights to and from Brazil.

The NCG has passed this latest protest back to the Ministers of the Interior and Foreign Relations with an instruction to the latter that the Brazilian government be asked for an explanation of the recent repeated violations of the border by Brazilian military vehicles. Three aircraft belonging to Brizola were also grounded. Commissioner Otero's‡ Intelligence and Liaison Department of the Montevideo Police, however, have arrested one of Colonel Camara Sena's‡ spies—a Navy sergeant who came posing as a student but was caught surveilling one of the exiles. He was charged with spying but set free when the Brazilian Embassy intervened.

According to Holman, Pio Correa is going to keep protesting until Brizola either leaves Uruguay or is interned and until a favorable resolution of the Alfonso and Santos cases. Otherwise we can expect Brazilian military intervention.

Montevideo — 18 December 1964

A new victory for the station at Georgetown, British Guiana, in its efforts to throw out the leftist-nationalist Prime Minister and professed Marxist, Cheddi Jagan. In elections a few days ago Jagan's Indian-based party lost parliamentary control to a coalition of the black-based party and a splinter group. The new Prime Minister, Forbes Burnham, is considered to be a moderate and his ascension to power finally removes the fear that Jagan would turn British Guiana into another Cuba. The victory is largely due to CIA operations over the past five years to strengthen the anti-Jagan trade unions, principally through the Public Service International‡ which provided the cover for financing public employees strikes. Jagan is protesting fraud—earlier this year he expelled Gene Meakins,‡ one of our main labor agents in the operation, but it was no use.

Montevideo — 25 December 1964

Christmas in Uruguay is like the 4th of July at home. It's hot and everybody goes to the beach—and it's almost completely secular with the official designation "Family Day." (Holy Week is similarly changed to "Tourism Week" and most of the country goes on vacation.) How different from Ecuador where the Church is so powerful.

I stopped over at O'Grady's house this morning for a little Christmas cheer but ended up commiserating with him over the latest Holman outburst. A few days ago O'Grady and his wife gave a little cocktail party and buffet as a welcome for the new CP operations officer, Bob Riefe. Holman didn't hold his drinks very well that night and soon began to lash out at O'Grady and then at Riefe and Riefe's wife. It was all pretty unpleasant and now O'Grady's hives are back out in full bloom, in spite of the fact that we all know now that Holman is coming out the real loser.

Apparently certain powers in headquarters are not entirely pleased with the station's performance, particularly in the area of Soviet operations, and Holman is to be transferred in about six months to Guatemala. His replacement as Chief of Station will be a man named John Horton,‡ who came to WH Division from the Far East Division along with so many others after the Bay of Pigs invasion. Holman has only just got official notification but he heard the change was coming, some time ago from his protector Ray Herbert, the Deputy Division Chief. Although Herbert was able to salvage the situation somewhat by arranging Holman's reassignment to Guatemala, Holman's bitterness keeps growing. Russ Phipps, the Soviet operation officer, is now almost up to O'Grady's level on Holman's list of persons to blame, but Riefe was attacked because he's obviously part of the new crew being assembled by Horton. Clearly Holman resents being edged aside by newcomers from FE Division because his days in Latin America go back to World War II.

What O'Grady and Phipps, and Alexander Zeffer too, are worried about is that Holman's search for scapegoats will seriously damage their careers and chances for future promotions and assignments. A couple of months ago I chanced across the combination to Holman's safe-cabinet and out of curiosity began to read some of the "Secret-Informal Eyes Only" letters that he exchanges more or less weekly with Des FitzGerald,‡ the Division Chief. I was so shocked at the knives he was putting into everyone but me that I gave the combination to O'Grady. Now he's reading the letters—which only makes his hives worse—and I think he's passed the combination on to Zeffer and Phipps. The dangerous part is that Holman is not so damning in the official fitness reports on the other officers, but that he cuts them so badly in these letters that they aren't supposed to see. Reading these letters, in fact, is highly dangerous, but all these officers are competent and certainly harder workers than Holman. I wonder if we can hold together for these next six months without rebellion.

Montevideo — 15 January 1965

Some decisions on Brazilian affairs indicate the Blancos are persisting in efforts to elude Brazilian pressures. The NCG voted not to give political asylum to Almino Alfonso and Max da Costa Santos on the grounds that they had come to Uruguay after having received asylum in other countries. However, they were given ninety-day tourist visas which isn't going to please Pio Correa. No decision on Brizola was needed because he promised the Minister of the Interior that he'll be leaving Uruguay no later than 23 January. On the other hand Brizola will be allowed to return to Uruguay in which case he can request political asylum again.

Two important new exiles are now here. One, a former Brazilian Air Force officer and one of its most highly decorated men, escaped from a military prison in Porto Alegre and made it across the border. The other is a former deputy who was in exile in Bolivia until ex-President Paz was overthrown, but came here recently for fear the new rightist régime in Bolivia would expel him to Brazil. Both are important supporters of Brizola.

In a personal complaint to the NCG President, Pio Correa tried to get action started on the fourteen recent requests he has made regarding the exiles. This prompted several notes from the Uruguayan Foreign Ministry but resistance continues. The Brazilian press, meanwhile, probably at the government's instigation, has started a campaign to raise the tension by speculating that relations are about to be broken and that commercial pressures are being exerted on Uruguay. For their part the Uruguayan and Brazilian Foreign Ministers have denied that relations are about to be broken, while in the NCG a Colorado Councillor called for the Foreign Minister's resignation for his inept handling of Brazilian problems.

These Brazilian affairs are a nuisance for me because I have constantly to be checking rumors and requesting special reports from the police on the exiles for Holman or O'Grady to use with Pio Correa, Fontoura and Camara Sena. Who could believe a handful of exiles here could be a threat to the Brazilian military government? Even so, headquarters keeps insisting that we help the Rio station in their operations to support the military.

If the military in Brazil weren't so strongly anti-communist our support for them would be embarrassing. In recent weeks the Brazilians have had an internal crisis going over the question of whether the Navy or the Air Force is to operate the aircraft of their only aircraft-carrier—a decrepit cow discarded by the British. Two ministers of the Air Force have recently resigned over decisions by the President to have the Navy fly the airplanes, but he changed his mind again and yesterday the Minister of the Navy resigned. Now, it seems, the Brazilian carrier strike force will have Air Force pilots.

To make matters with Brazil worse, a few days ago the commercial offices of the Brazilian Embassy were bombed, although little damage was done because the bomb was poorly placed. However, written on a wall nearby was the name "Tupamaros" which appeared at several other recent bombings. Commissioner Otero, Chief of Police Intelligence, is trying to find out who these people are. He thinks they may be the Sendic group. Raul Sendic, the revolutionary socialist leader, who had been arrested on a contraband charge in an Argentine town near the border, was recently released, and may have returned to Montevideo.

Inability to curb these bombings illustrates the difference between good penetrations of the CP and related groups and bad ones. In Ecuador a group like this would have been wiped up by now. Nevertheless, Riefe doesn't take the bombings very seriously and seems intent on concentrating on the strictly-reformist PCU.

Montevideo — 4 February 1965

At Headquarter's instruction I'm continuing to develop the relationship with Sergey Borisov, the Soviet Consul and KGB officer.

Last Sunday Janet and I went with Borisov and his wife Nina to the beach. First they came out to our house in Carrasco and then Borisov drove us out to a beach near Solymar. His driving is very odd and made me nervous—practically like a beginner. Not so his chess, of course, where he beat me easily. Phipps tells me that Borisov knows I'm a CIA officer without any doubt, so I wonder sometimes why I bother meeting him. Headquarters says that's just the reason to keep the relationship going—on the chance that Borisov could be disaffected and trying to "build a bridge."

Holman has asked me to take over complete responsibility for the satellite missions, which include Czechs, Romanians, Bulgarians, Poles and Yugoslavs. For East European countries we have no elaborate operational procedure such as we do for the Soviets. Headquarters apparently has such high-level penetrations in those countries that the painstaking work of spotting and placing access agents next to them simply isn't justified. Successes in the case of the satellites have come from CIA officers in direct contact with them. As a start, however, I'm going to bring the files up to date on the personnel of each mission and next week I'll try to get the Foreign Ministry protocol files through AVDANDY–1 for that purpose. Then I'll start a photographic album and get reports from headquarters on the new arrivals. Right now I'm not even sure who they all are, because Phipps has been concentrating on the Soviets and ignoring the Eastern Europeans.

Last week I made my first visit to the AVENGFUL telephone-tapping LP at the Montevideo Police Headquarters. I took along a visiting TSD technician who wanted to see how the equipment is being maintained—in the operational files I couldn't find the last time it was visited by a station officer, probably some years ago. The room is located right over the office of the Deputy Police Chief on the same floor as Commissioner Otero's Intelligence and Liaison Department. However, there is a locked steel door between I and E and the LP—in fact the normal way to enter the LP section of the floor is by an elevator from the underground garage for which a special key is necessary. Off the same hallway as the LP are several rooms that I was told are used by the Chief and Deputy Chief as rest quarters.

De Anda‡ and Torres,‡ the technicians and LP operators, do an excellent job in keeping up the equipment but they have an uncomfortable situation with the heat. Those tube-operated Revere recorders give off so much heat that the room is stifling in the summer. I promised to get them an air-conditioner that they'll install either in a small high window to the inside hallway, or else they'll have to make another opening. The LP has no windows to the street and only the one small window to the hallway—good security but no ventilation.

Montevideo — 7 February 1965

Investigation of *Prensa Latina* (the Cuban wire service) has got more interesting. Because of procedural agreements I had to postpone recruitment of my friend at the Bank of London and Montreal until the intelligence chief of his country's service spoke to him and to his superior, the bank manager—whom I also know from the Cerro Golf Club. This cumbersome process completed, I started reviewing the *Prensa Latina* account. As checks are not returned to the account holder in Uruguay, it was easy to discover that practically all the money is paid out in cash. Legitimate expenses still total only about half of the monthly subsidy, so the rest of the money is clearly going into "other activities." The next step is to check the financial reports filed with government offices to see if we have a case for shutting down *Prensa Latina* for falsifying financial reports or similar irregular procedures inconsistent with the subsidy.

Montevideo — 11 February 1965

At last the NCG voted to intern Brizola—an accomplishment that has taken every ounce of Pio Correa's‡ considerable energy and persistence. Typically, however, the NCG decided to let Brizola pick the town where he wants to live—any except Montevideo and no closer than 300 kilometers to the Brazilian border. Now we can begin to relax about these messy Brazilian operations.

Pio Correa has done an excellent job bringing the Uruguayans into line over the exiles, which made possible the Foreign Minister's pleasant visit. Brizola, incidentally, has chosen the beach resort of Atlantida as the town where he'll be interned. Otero will continue the logs by "security guards" from police intelligence—it's only 35 kilometers from Montevideo where Brizola could still be fairly active—and right at the limit on proximity to Brazil: 301 kilometers.

Final approval for the AID Public Safety Mission was obtained by Holman from Tejera, the Minister of the Interior, and last month the first Chief of Public Safety arrived. For the time being we will refrain from putting one of our officers under Public Safety cover, and I'll continue to handle the police intelligence operation. After the Mission gets established through straight police assistance (vehicles, arms, communications equipment, training) we'll bring down an officer to work full-time with Otero's intelligence department. About the best I can do part-time is to keep AVENGEFUL going and increase Otero's subsidy for intelligence expenses.

These Montevideo police are getting the Public Safety assistance none too soon. In another bank robbery just three days ago the policeman on guard got excited and fatally shot one of the customers—

mistaking the customer for one of the robbers. Seeing this, the robbers, a man and a woman, rushed out of the bank leaving the money behind. They walked for several blocks and hailed a taxi which took them to the other side of the city. Since they had no money to pay the fare, the robber gave his pistol to the taxi driver in payment. The driver, however, heard of the robbery on the radio and turned the pistol over to the police. On checking the weapon the police discovered that it was the service revolver of one of their own policemen. He was arrested at home and admitted forcing his wife to go along with him on the robbery. The last time that particular bank had been robbed was in 1963 by two women (or men?) dressed as nuns who were never caught.

New strikes: Montevideo buses and trolleys for payment of subsidies and salaries; port workers for last year's Christmas bonus; city employees for retroactive fringe benefits. Inflation during 1964 was almost 45 per cent and last month reached the 3 per cent per month rate. The Blancos are trying to put through another devaluation, while the peso is unsteady and has now slipped to 30.

Montevideo — 25 February 1965

I got an important hit on the postal intercept operation against Jorge Castillo, the Cuban intelligence support agent used as an accommodation address for Agent 101 in Lima or La Paz. The letter-carrier, AVBUSY–1, offered me a large brown manila envelope the other day but it was addressed not to Castillo but to Raul Trajtenberg who lives in the same huge apartment building as Castillo. I took the envelope because it was sent from Havana and the words *Edificio Panamericano* in the address were underlined just as they were to have been underlined in correspondence to Castillo.

I arranged with AVBUSY–1 to keep the envelope for several days in case headquarters wanted to send down a secret-writing technician to test the contents. Inside were Cuban press releases and clippings from Havana newspapers. Headquarters answered my cable by sending a technician immediately from Panama (the Buenos Aires regional support technician is a specialist in audio and photo rather than SW techniques) and he was going to try to "lift" secret writing from the contents. However, we couldn't find a letter press fast enough so I had to return the envelope to AVBUSY–1 without the test.

On checking station files on Trajtenberg I found a letter that he had written from Havana two years ago that was intercepted through the AVIDITY operation. Strangely, the handwriting on the manila envelope was exactly the same as that of the Trajtenberg letter written from Havana—meaning, probably, that Trajtenberg addressed the envelope to himself and, along with other self-addressed envelopes, gave it to a Cuban intelligence officer for later use. Trajtenberg's mail will also be given to me regularly by AVBUSY–1 although Trajtenberg is leaving soon to study at the University of Paris. So far other Trajtenberg intercepts reveal that his father (he lives with his parents) is manipulating large sums of money in a numbered Swiss bank account. The Berne station advised that the Swiss security service will provide data from numbered accounts but insist on all the details and reasons—which headquarters doesn't want to give right now because of the sensitivity of other cases in this same Cuban network.

Montevideo — 18 March 1965

Washington Beltran, the new NCG President, has had plenty of labor unrest in spite of the recent carnival distractions: railway workers striking for the 1964 retroactive pay increases, the interprovincial buses stopped again for back salaries and subsidies, the Montevideo bus and trolley employees also striking for salaries and subsidies, and public-health clinics and hospitals struck by employees demanding their January salaries. Today there is no public transportation in

Montevideo except taxis, and the Sub-Secretary of the Treasury just announced that government receipts amount to only half the daily cost of the central administration.

We've been trying to find a little relief from the gloomy atmosphere of dissension in the station. Holman's letters to FitzGerald are getting even worse if that's possible and each time O'Grady reads the file his hives start up again. Bob Riefe, the CP officer, has a way of reading the news of each day's mismanagement by the Uruguayan government with loud rhetorical questioning broken by equally loud and contemptuous guffaws and cackles. His approval of the strikes and other agitation by his target group are shared by all of us, though perhaps for different reasons, as we watch political partisanship prevail over the reforms (land, fiscal) and austerity needed to stop the country's slide. Russ Phipps, who sits on the other side of me from Riefe, pores over his surveillance reports, telephone transcripts and observation post logs, muttering from time to time that's it not the PCU but the Soviets who deserve the honor of putting this country straight.

Riefe and Phipps always catch me in the middle because I'm supposed to be building up the police intelligence department and developing political contacts. When things get bad I usually call over beyond Riefe to Alex Zeffer but his morale is so low he can rarely summon more than an agonizing oath. Then I have to call on O'Grady for support because he works with military intelligence, such as it is, and is the most terrorized of all by Holman. The five of us then discuss solutions. Usually Holman is selected to save Uruguay—one plan is to send Phipps over to the KGB Chief to request that they defect Holman, with our help if they want it, but if they turn him down, as is likely, well, there's always AVALANCHE.

Officers from the Inspector-General's staff were just here on a routine inspection. This was the time to get the word back to headquarters about Holman's incompetence, but I don't think anyone opened his mouth.

Montevideo — 31 March 1965

The AVPEARL audio penetration of the PCU headquarters conference room is another step closer. AVCAVE–1, again on guard duty, permanently installed the two electrical sockets and final tests by Frank Sherno in the LP were successful. Now the problem is to find a good LP-keeper who can monitor the installation and record the meetings. Ideally this person could also transcribe, but chances are that transcribing will have to be done at first by AVENGEFUL–5,‡ transcriber of the PCU telephone tap, who already knows the names and voices.

Montevideo — 6 April 1965

The general strike today is very effective: Otero's office estimates that 90 per cent of organized labor is participating. No government offices are open, there are no taxis or buses, no restaurants, no newspapers. The theme is protest against government economic policies and marches have been loud and impressive although no violence is reported. Speakers have called for radical solutions to the country's problems—solutions that will attack the privileged classes, where the problems begin.

The strike is also being used to promote coming CNT programs, including the preparatory meeting for the Congress of the People that was postponed from last December and the annual protest march of the sugar-cane workers from Artigas in the far north to Montevideo. Recent statistics support the protests: the OAS reported this month that inflation in Uruguay during 1962–4 was 59.7 per cent—higher than Chile (36.6), Argentina (24.4) and even Brazil (58.4).

The government is getting uneasy about the CNT's successes of late. Adolfo Tejera, the Minister of the Interior, made a radio speech last night on the rights and duties of citizens in the context of today's general strike.

Holman keeps insisting that I develop more political contacts but I'm keeping the activity to a minimum. Even if we reached a level of effectiveness in political action similar to what we had in Ecuador, we would simply have better weapons to use against the PCU, CNT and others of the extreme left. What's needed here is intensification of land use, both for increasing export production and creating more jobs, but this can never happen without land reform. If we were to have a political-action program to promote land reform, as well as action against the extreme left, some justification might be found in the balance. But these Uruguayan politicians are interested in other things than land reform.

Montevideo — 14 April 1965

The government has taken a first step towards suppressing agitation organized by the extreme left. Last week the NCG designated an emergency commission with special executive powers to deal with the drought, now some months old, which is seriously endangering livestock. The commission includes the Ministers of Defense and Interior and similar commissions have been established in each department under the local police chief with representatives of the Ministry of Defense, a regional agronomist and a veterinarian. The same day the NCG also decreed special powers for the Minister of the Interior to limit public gatherings to twenty-four hours. This second decree, which the Minister later admitted is to be used against the march of the sugar-cane workers, was enacted in a manner designed to confuse it with the special drought measures and with the hope that it might pass without much comment.

The CNT immediately denounced the measure as directed against the sugar-workers' march, which prompted the Minister's admission, and the Colorado minority NCG Councillors unsuccessfully tried to rescind it. Because these decrees allow for restriction of civil liberties they were presented to the Legislature for approval. The Blancos, however, knowing that the Colorados and others would rescind the decree aimed at the marchers, have prevented a quorum from being constituted each day by simply staying away.

In passing the decrees the NCG clarified that they were not adopting emergency security measures as defined in the Constitution (equivalent to a state of siege) and Tejera has given assurances that his special powers will be used with reason. However, in a public statement two days ago he accused the marchers of taking along women and children as hostages, of not having proper health and educational facilities for children, and of allowing promiscuity dangerous to collective morals. Clearly we have a confrontation building up, aided by press reports coming from the Ministry of the Interior that the march will be broken up before it reaches Montevideo. Right now the marchers are in San José, only a few days away, where police are registering them by taking biographical data, fingerprints and photographs for Otero's intelligence files. If Tejera gives orders for the march to be broken up not too many people will notice because this is tourism week and most of the country is on vacation. From our viewpoint he ought to do just that because the sugar-cane workers are led by Raul Sendic, now a fugitive and believed to be the organizer of most of the terrorist bombings in the past year.

Montevideo — 25 April 1965

The march of the sugar-cane workers arrived in Montevideo yesterday—almost unnoticed and with no danger of intervention by the government. Something much bigger has suddenly attracted everyone's attention: one of Uruguay's major banks has failed and been taken over by the Bank of the Republic. The sensation is causing mild panic and fear that other banks may go under, which might not be a bad thing. In this small country there are about fifty private banks even though the government banks do about 65 per cent of commercial business. The peso has slipped to 39.

Montevideo — 27 April 1965

Inspector Piriz was assigned to handle investigations into fraud and other crimes related to the bank failure. So far eleven of the officers and directors have been jailed. Today, however, two more private banks were taken over by the Bank of the Republic, and for fear of a run on banks in general a holiday was decreed for all private banks. The holiday doesn't make much difference, though, because all the private banks have been closed since the first failure six days ago, when the unions struck to demand job security for employees of the bank that failed. Almost unnoticed today was the NCG's lifting of the emergency drought decree of 8 April although the special decree on limiting public gatherings was retained.

Montevideo — 28 April 1965

I don't quite understand this invasion of the Dominican Republic. Bosch was elected in 1962 thanks to the peasant vote organized by Sacha Volman.‡ Volman earlier set up the Institute of Political Education‡ in Costa Rica (cryptonym ZREAGER) where we sent young liberal political hopefuls for training. Bosch is from the same cut as Muñoz Marin, Betancourt and Haya de la Torre. He stands for the reforms that will allow for redistribution of income and integration. Rightist opposition to his land reform and nationalistic economic policies brought on his overthrow by the military in 1963 after only seven months in power. This was another chance for him to turn the balance towards marginalized peasants and to channel income from industry, mostly sugar, into education and social projects.

Now, just as the Constitutionalists have the upper hand to restore Bosch to power, we send in the Marines to keep him out. Nobody's going to believe Johnson's story of another Cuba-style revolution in the making. There has to be more to the problem than this—for some reason people in Washington just don't want Bosch back in. Uruguayans don't understand either. People here think Bosch stands for the kind of liberal reform that brought social integration to Uruguay. Already the street demonstrations against the U.S. have started. Very depressing. AVBUZZ-1 is going to look silly trying to place propaganda—headquarters says we must justify the invasion because of a danger to American and other foreigners' lives and a takeover of the Constitutionalist movement by communists.

Montevideo — 4 May 1965

Headquarters has sent about fifty operations officers to the Dominican Republic to set up outposts in rural areas for reporting on popular support for the Caamano forces. The officers were sent with communications assistants and equipment for radioing reports straight back to the U.S. All WH stations were notified to put certain officers on stand-by for immediate travel, but Holman is not going to let me go—probably because he would have to work a little harder. I would like to go and see for myself. Surely the Constitutionalist movement hadn't fallen into the hands of the communists. And this Johnson Doctrine! "Revolutions that seek to create a communist government cease to be an internal matter and require hemisphere action." Bullshit. They just don't want Bosch back in and the "they" is probably U.S. sugar interests.

We've had more protest demonstrations against the invasion, some violent. Targets of the attacks: U.S. Embassy, OAS, U.S. businesses. Today four demonstrators were wounded by gunfire when police broke up a street march following a meeting at the University. The private banks are still closed—fifteen days now—and there's no telling when government employees' salaries for April will begin being paid. Today both the Minister of Defense and the Minister of the Interior publicly denied the rumors of an impending *coup.*

Montevideo — 7 May 1965

Ambassador Harriman came to explain the Dominican invasion and to propose Uruguayan participation in the multilateral peacekeeping force. He spoke to President Beltran yesterday and afterwards held a press conference in which he blamed those fifty-eight trained communists for having taken over the Bosch movement, thereby creating the need for intervention. He admitted, though, that Caamano, the leader of the Bosch movement, isn't one of the fifty-eight. Then he said the U.S. government is not going to permit the establishment of another communist government in the hemisphere.

I can easily imagine the station in Santo Domingo in a panic compiling that list of fifty-eight trained communists from their Subversive Control Watch List. There were probably more than fifty-eight, but Caamano and the Bosch people were in control, not trained communists. The movement was put down not because it was communist but because it was nationalist. The Uruguayans weren't convinced by Harriman—after he left, the NCG voted not to participate in the peacekeeping force approved yesterday by the OAS. "Fifty-eight trained communists" is our new station password and the answer is "Ten thousand marines."

Montevideo — 12 May 1965

Protest demonstrations and attacks against U.S. businesses over the Dominican invasion continue. The CNT, FEUU and other communist-influenced organizations are most active in the demonstrations, but opposition to the invasion is a popular issue going all the way up to the NCG. All America Cables and IBM are among the businesses bombed.

The CNT is also leading protests against economic policies, and new revelations of corruption in the banking sector are coming up almost daily. Although the Congress passed a special law assuring jobs for the employees of banks that have failed, tension continues, with three more banks taken over by the Bank of the Republic yesterday. The bank workers' union voted to return to work but today the government announced that the banks won't open until 17 May. The reason is that they can't open until a shipment of 500 million new pesos arrives from London.

Coup rumors continue and yesterday Tejera told the NCG that he believes the 8 April decree limiting public gatherings is unconstitutional. He complained that the only law relating to public meetings dates from 1897, but he promised the NCG a new constitutional decree on the subject for next week. Port workers struck yesterday and judicial branch employees began partial work stoppages for payment of April salaries.

Montevideo — 20 May 1965

Financial corruption in Uruguay seems to have no end. Yesterday the NCG fired the entire board of directors of the Bank of the Republic. Nineteen officers and directors of banks taken over have been imprisoned and investigations are continuing. After being closed for twenty-six days the private banks have reopened but the falling peso—it's down to 41—suggests more scandal to come.

On the labor front, strike action for payment of April salaries has been started by government employees in the judiciary, public schools, port, petroleum monopoly, fishing enterprise, postal system, communications and University. Other strikes are being planned or threatened.

Coup rumors are so strong that the Ministry of Defense yesterday issued a denial. The latest rumors relate to speculation in the Brazilian press that Brazilian and Argentine military leaders are watching the increasing strikes and banking scandals in Uruguay closely, and that perhaps Uruguay is becoming a bad risk because of its opposition to intervention in the Dominican Republic and its tolerance of exile activities. Meanwhile the NCG is considering Pio Correa's latest protest on the exiles' meetings, finances and infiltration from Uruguay back to Brazil.

The PCU has in recent months been planning to host an international pro-Cuba conference to be called The Continental Congress of Solidarity with Cuba—now scheduled for 18–20 June. Headquarters is anxious to prevent the conference so Holman proposed to Tejera that it be prohibited because it might reflect badly on Uruguay in the U.S. (where emergency loans are going to be sought for financial relief), and in Latin America. Tejera immediately saw the connection with Brazilian problems, and promised to take up the matter with the NCG.

Montevideo — 29 May 1965

Suddenly we've had a flurry of security moves sparked by controversy over the activities of one of O'Grady's people, Juan Carlos Quagliotti,‡ and others of his group. Last night extraordinary police control was established in Montevideo and the interior departments, with special patrols, check points and security guards at radio stations, the telephone company, waterworks, railroad stations, bridges and crossroads. This morning Tejera said publicly that these measures were taken to help the electric company promote voluntary rationing of power, because of low generating capacity as a result of the drought last summer. The Minister of Defense also denied any special reasons for the police measures, but rumors are stronger than ever of a military move against the government.

According to Commissioner Otero of police intelligence, what really happened is that Quagliotti was arrested after Otero's investigation revealed that he had arranged for the printing and distribution of a distorted version of an article written in 1919 by President Beltran's father, on justification of military intervention in politics. The judge who heard the case refused to take jurisdiction, however, and Quagliotti was released pending action by military courts. Quagliotti's release caused a wave of ill-feeling in the police, while resentment also broke out in certain military circles against the police for having made the investigation and arrest.

So far the Quagliotti case hasn't been connected with the special security measures and for the time being O'Grady is going to avoid meeting him. Similarly when Otero asked me several days ago what I knew about Quagliotti I said nothing. Headquarters is very concerned that a breach is opening up between police and military leaders, but we've reported that the storm will probably pass. According to the Chief of Police, Colonel Ventura Rodriguez, the crisis is being resolved.

At an NCG meeting yesterday before imposition of the special security measures, Tejera asked for permission to ban the Continental Congress of Solidarity with Cuba. Using a report we had prepared on the Congress as his own, the Minister said the purpose of the Congress was to raise the question of relations with Cuba once more and to promote foreign ideologies that are incompatible with Uruguayan institutions. He said he wishes to avoid the pernicious proselytism by trained communist elements who promote infiltration by dangerous extremists, adding that Uruguay already has enough problems without this Congress. The NCG postponed a decision but chances are good that they'll prohibit the Congress in order to avoid jeopardizing their already difficult prospects for refinancing the Bank of the Republic, which is bankrupt, owing some 18 million dollars to New York banks. The President of the Bank has resigned, and the bank has been taken over by the NCG. The peso is now down to 52, and the scandals are moving into wool-exporting companies.

Montevideo — 2 June 1965

Last night the NCG discussed the Quagliotti case with speeches from Tejera and the Minister of Defense. Tejera admitted that the special security measures of last week—which are still in force—were a result of Quagliotti's agitation in military circles and of dissension over whether he will be prosecuted or not. Today

Quagliotti appeared before a military court which refused to take jurisdiction because he hadn't actually entered any military installation. It seems the crisis has passed for the time being thanks to Quagliotti's friends among the senior military officers, but resentment continues in the police over the failure to prosecute in both civil and military courts.

Tejera's request to the NCG to ban the pro-Cuban Congress went through. They voted to prohibit it on the principle of non-intervention. Headquarters will be pleased.

Montevideo — 4 June 1965

Only a few more weeks until Holman is transferred. What none of us can imagine is why he is going to Guatemala, where one of the most serious insurgency threats exists. Surely if he is bad enough to be transferred from Montevideo after only two years, he's bad enough not to be sent as Chief of Station where armed action is under way.

About the only success he can claim is getting the Public Safety program going. After the first AID officers arrived, Holman gave a couple of dinners to introduce them to the Minister of the Interior and senior police officers. As the station officer in charge of police liaison I had to go to Holman's house for these dinners, and soon he'll be giving more parties to introduce the new Chief of Station and say farewell. Strange man this Holman. Surely he can sense his isolation at the station but he never mentions it. He just keeps on denigrating the other officers.

Holman has asked me to take over another operation. This one is an effort, not yet off the ground, to make a technical installation against the Embassy of the United Arab Republic on the street behind our Embassy and on the floor above the AID offices. Phipps had been handling this operation without enthusiasm, but headquarters is getting anxious because if successful it will enable an important UAR cryptographic circuit to be read. As part of planning they asked for a floor plan of the Embassy, which I got through the AVENIN electric company agent, and soon a Division D officer will be coming to survey the place. As my office is in the back of our Embassy I can almost look out into the windows of the UAR Embassy.

I still can't believe the reasons for the Dominican invasion that we're trying to promote through AVBUZZ–1. Holman says it all goes back to the Agency's assassination of Trujillo. He was Chief of the Caribbean branch in headquarters at the time and was deeply involved in planning the assassination, which was done by Cuban exiles from Miami using weapons we sent through the diplomatic pouch. The weapons were passed to the assassins through a U.S. citizen who was an agent of the Santo Domingo station and owner of a supermarket. He had to be evacuated though, after the assassination, because the investigation brought him under suspicion.

Why is it that the invasion seems so unjustifiable to me? It can't be that I'm against intervention as such, because everything I do is in one way or another intervention in the affairs of other countries. Partly, I suppose, it's the immense scale of this invasion that shocks. On the other hand, full-scale military invasion is the logical final step when all the other tools of counter-insurgency fail. The Santo Domingo station just didn't or couldn't keep the lid on. But what's really disturbing is that we've intervened on the wrong side. I just don't believe "fifty-eight trained communists" can take over a movement of thousands that includes experienced political leaders. That's a pretext. The real reason must be opposition to Bosch by U.S. business with investments in the Dominican Republic. Surely these investments could have produced even while the land reform and other programs moved ahead.

Montevideo — 17 June 1965

We almost just lost one of our principal police liaison officers, Carlos Martin,‡ the Deputy Chief of the Montevideo Police. Martin is an Army colonel, as is the Chief, but he is also a chartered accountant and has been supervising the police investigations that have uncovered so much corruption since April. He resigned two days ago because a judge denied his request to interrogate one of the convicted officers of the first bank to fail about lists of payments to high government officials by that bank. The lists are purposely cryptic notes that Martin wants clarified to aid the investigation. Martin's resignation in protest against political suppression of the investigations provoked such a row that the NCG agreed to take up the matter of the lists, and today Martin withdrew his resignation. So far there have been thirty-one convictions.

Montevideo — 24 June 1965

The NCG now has the lists of political bribes paid by the first bank that failed in April. Names include an important Blanco Senator, the Vice-President of the State Mortgage Bank, a Blanco leader who has just been nominated as Uruguay's new Ambassador to the U.N., two high officers of the Ministry of the Treasury, the person in charge of investigating one of the banks that failed, and a person known only by the initials J.J.G. This last person can only be Juan Jose Gari, our Ruralista political contact from the Nardone days and now the President of the State Mortgage Bank.

Meanwhile the Bank of the Republic debt has been determined at 358 million dollars, with 38 million dollars currently due. Gold from the Bank of the Republic, perhaps as much as half the Bank's holdings, will have to be sent to the U.S. as collateral for refinancing. Such an emotional and humiliating requirement is sure to cost the Blancos heavily.

In an important policy decision on the labor front, the Blancos decided to apply sanctions against the central administration employees for a strike on 17 June. Justification for the sanctions is that strikes by government employees are illegal, although until now the government had been reluctant to invoke illegality because of inflation and the obvious political consequences. The decision was answered by another strike of central administration employees—this one began yesterday and will end tonight. The issues again are employees' benefits, agreed upon last year but still unpaid, payment of salaries on time, and now the sanctions. The strike is complete, with even the Montevideo airport and the government communications system closed. Other strikes continue in the judiciary, University and the huge Clinics Hospital. The peso is down to 69 and one of the Colorado Councillors has called for the resignation of the Minister of the Treasury.

Montevideo — 7 July 1965

The Movement of the Revolutionary Left (MIR) in Peru has finally gone into action and seems to have had several initial successes against Peruvian police. Three days ago the Peruvian government declared a state of siege and the military services have been called in to supplement police operations. Hundreds of leftists are being arrested all over the country but the guerrilla operation seems to be located mostly in the eastern slopes of the Andes towards the Brazilian border. Undoubtedly the Lima station's notebook of intelligence from DUHAM–1,‡ the MIR walk-in in Guayaquil two years ago, is now in the hands of Peruvian military liaison officers.

The Continental Congress for Solidarity with Cuba was shifted to Santiago, Chile, after we got the Uruguayans to ban it. Now the Santiago station has gotten the Chilean government to ban it and they'll have to try still another country. More likely it will be quietly forgotten.

Montevideo — 16 July 1965

Holman is gone. No one from the station went to see him off at the airport except John Horton, the new Chief of Station. Already the atmosphere in the station has changed beyond recognition. O'Grady's hives are much better although he got the bad news that he is going to be transferred so that a new Deputy Chief with better Spanish can come. Horton speaks almost no Spanish and has already told me he wants me to work closely with him on the high-level liaison contacts like the Minister and the Chief of Police. I suppose this means interpreting for him until he can get along, but anything is better than Holman. Horton is such a contrast: very approachable, good sense of humor, very anglophile from his years as Chief of Station in Hong Kong. He's even running a car pool with his chauffeur and office vehicle, picking us all up in the morning so that wives can get around easier.

Montevideo — 23 July 1965

Financing for the new government employees' benefits was passed by the Senate last night after days of increasing strike activity in the postal system, University administration, central administration, judicial system and public-health system. Even the Ministry of the Treasury tax collectors were on strike. The financing measure calls for putting out 1.7 billion new pesos, much less than the request of the Blanco NCG Councillors, which prompted senators of the NCG President's faction to vote against the bill. This faction had wanted five billion in new currency—almost double what is now in circulation. Payments are progressing for June salaries and many of the government employees on strike are now going back to work. The FEUU, however, is organizing lightning street demonstrations as a protest against government refusal to deliver some 100 million pesos overdue to the University. The next battle begins in a few days when the Chamber of Deputies starts work on the budget review, in which the government employees' unions will attempt to include salary increases for next year. Inflation during January–June this year was 26.3 per cent, which is one of the reasons why the government backed down on its threat to impose sanctions.

Horton is anxious to build up the capabilities of the police intelligence department—making it a kind of Special Branch for political work along the lines of British police practice. He wants me to spend more time training Otero, Chief of Intelligence and Liaison, and to give him more money for furniture, filing cabinets and office supplies. As soon as possible Horton wants Otero put in for the International Police Academy and for additional training by headquarters at the conclusion of the Academy course. Before leaving Washington Horton obtained AID approval for a CIA officer to be placed under Public Safety cover, and after we get approval from the Chief of Police and get the officer down here we will have him working full-time with Intelligence and Liaison.

Physical surveillance and travel control are the kinds of operations that we plan to emphasize from the beginning. Expansion of AVENGEFUL will come later, perhaps, along with recruitment operations against targets of the extreme left, but these changes will follow Otero's training in Washington. In travel control we will start by trying to set up the often-delayed passport photography and watch-list operation at the Montevideo airport.

The AID Public Safety program is moving along well. Vehicles, communications, riot-control equipment and training are the main points of emphasis. Until our Public Safety cover officer arrives, however, we plan to keep the police intelligence work strictly in our office. It's going to be a long and difficult job and I won't have time to do it adequately because of other work. Somehow we have to make them start thinking seriously on basic things like security and decent filing systems.

Headquarters is sending down a disguise technician in order to train the station operations officers in its use. The technician is Joan Humphries,‡ the wife of the audio technician at the Mexico City station. Equipment will include wigs, hair coloring, special shoes and clothing, special glasses, moustaches, warts, moles and sets of false documentation.

Montevideo — 15 August 1965

We have a new Soviet operations officer to replace Russ Phipps who has been transferred back to headquarters. The new officer is Dick Conolly,‡ a West Point graduate with previous duty in Cairo and Tokyo. Because Conolly can't handle Spanish yet, Horton asked me to help him on an operation that Phipps got going during his final weeks here. The operation is another chauffeur recruitment—this time it's AVAILABLE–1,‡ the chauffeur of the Soviet Commercial Office. Although the agent has Soviet citizenship, he is considered a local employee by the Soviet mission, because he was raised in Uruguay and is the son of Russian *émigrés*.

Phipps used one of the AVBANDY surveillance-team members for the recruitment. This agent, AVBANDY–4,‡ is the father of the team chief, an Army major. He had some visiting cards printed, identifying himself as Dr. Nikolich, a Buenos Aires import–export consultant. He approached the chauffeur as if interested in assistance in his efforts to promote imports to Argentina and Uruguay from the Soviet Union. In return for inside information on the Soviet Commercial Office in Montevideo Dr. Nikolich would pay the chauffeur a commission on all deals. Phipps's interest, however, was to use the chauffeur as an access agent to the Soviets working in the Commercial Office—two are known intelligence officers and one is suspect.

As the recruitment was made just as Phipps was leaving, AVBANDY–4 turned the chauffeur over to me as a Canadian business colleague working in Montevideo, claiming, as Dr. Nikolich, that he would return occasionally from Buenos Aires and if possible would see him. Phipps also got a new safe apartment site, a miserable basement room in a building on Avenida Rivera a couple of blocks from the Montevideo zoo. The room has only a small skylight and is extremely cold. Nevertheless, the chauffeur and I are meeting one night each week. His information on the five commercial officers and their families plus the secretary, all of whom live in the seven-storey building housing the Commercial Office, is not earth-shaking but it's better than anything we've had until now from the other access agents.

The Tupamaros terrorist group continues to be active, recently bombing the Bayer Company offices and leaving behind a protest note against U.S. intervention in Vietnam. Riefe still doesn't think they're important enough to justify a targeting and recruitment program, so I have begun to encourage Otero, Chief of Police Intelligence, to concentrate on them. There's no doubt now that this is the group led since 1962 by Raul Sendic, the far-left leader of sugar-cane workers who broke away from the Socialist Party.

Montevideo — 20 August 1965

The CNT-sponsored Congress of the People, postponed several times since originally scheduled last year, has at last begun and shows signs of considerable success. The PCU is playing the dominant role, of course, but quite a lot of non-communist participation has been attracted. Practically all the significant organizations in fields of labor, students, government workers and pensioners are participating along with consumer cooperatives, neighborhood groups, provincial organizations and the leftist press. Meetings continue in the University and at other sites where participants are drafting solutions to the country's problems along leftist-nationalist lines. Given the obvious failure of the traditional parties and Congress, this Congress of the People is attracting much attention and will undoubtedly provide the PCU and similar groups with new recruits as well as a propaganda platform.

It is too successful to ignore so we have generated editorial comment through AVBUZZ-1 exposing the Congress as an example of classic communist united front tactics. In fact the Congress isn't the same as a united front political mechanism, but our fear is that it might turn into one and be used as such in next year's elections. Through AVBUZZ-1 we also printed a black handbill signed by the Congress and calling on the Uruguayan people to launch an insurrectional strike with immediate occupation of their places of work. Thousands of the leaflets were distributed today, provoking angry denials from the Congress organizers. More editorial comment and articles against the Congress will follow in this campaign to dissuade non-communists from participating.

One of the campaigns of the Congress of the People is for resistance to the stabilization programs imposed by the International Monetary Fund, because these measures hurt the low- and middle-income groups harder than the rich. Right now a high-level group of Uruguayan political leaders is in New York trying to get new loans in order to refinance the bankrupt Bank of the Republic (Uruguay's central bank). The New York bankers, however, are insisting on new financial reforms that will meet IMF approval as a condition to granting the new loans—which may be as high as 150–200 million dollars.

At the NCG meeting last night, as the whole country awaited news from the refinancing mission in New York, it was revealed that two days ago an urgent confidential message from the mission arrived in Montevideo in the Uruguayan diplomatic pouch. No one can explain why, but the pouch, which for most countries is the government's most closely guarded system of communications, wasn't retrieved at the airport. It got sent back to New York on the next flight, and the NCG must wait until it's found and sent again before they can make their decisions.

The Blancos continue to fight among themselves over how to finance government employees. Yesterday the Acting Minister of the Treasury advised the NCG that salaries for this month simply cannot be paid without new resources, and he insisted on greater currency emission. Right now the deficit for this year is set at 6.3 billion pesos, and coins of five and ten centavos are disappearing because they're worth more as melted metal than as money.

Montevideo — 27 August 1965

One of Holman's last requests to the Minister of the Interior, Adolfo Tejera, was to find a way to expel the North Korean trade mission that has been here for almost a year. I have followed up with queries to the police on the Koreans but without adequate reply. As an enticement to cooperate I've taken the unusual step of obtaining support from the Miami station, and perhaps others, in order to follow the movements of an aircraft that loaded up in Miami with transistor radios and television sets for smuggling into Uruguay. Information on this contraband ring was obtained by the police through the AVENGEFUL telephone-tapping operation, but Colonel Ramirez, Chief of the Metropolitan Guard, asked me if the aircraft's movements in Miami could be watched. Ramirez and his colleagues were anxious to snare this shipment because under the law they get the value of all contraband they seize. The Miami station advised when it left, as did Panama, Lima and Santiago where technical stops were made. A few nights ago the aircraft made a secret landing on an interior airfield, unloaded and took off again. The Metropolitan Guard, however, intercepted the two truckloads of television sets and transistor radios—initial value is set at 10 million pesos. Still no action on the Koreans but we will remind the police chief on our next visit; he doesn't often get such valuable help as we have just given him.

Uruguayan Air Force Base No. 1 has just been the scene of the delivery of the first of eight new aircraft as part of our military aid program. Ambassador Hoyt made the presentation to the Uruguayan delegation composed of the Minister of Defense, Commanding General of the Air Force, Chief of Staff and other dignitaries. In his speech the Ambassador recalled that that day was the fourth anniversary of the signing of the Charter of Punta del Este beginning the Alliance for Progress. He cited President Johnson's declaration that the Alliance for Progress constitutes a change not only in the history of the free world but also in the long history of liberty. After the Dominican invasion one has to wonder. The photographs in the press yesterday show the Ambassador, the Minister and the others—they practically block from view the little four-seat Cessna that was the object of the ceremony.

Montevideo — 10 September 1965

Strike activity is in full swing again after more than a month of relative calm. The financing mission is back from New York. They got only 55 million dollars, enough to pay the 38 million dollars already overdue, but gold will have to be shipped as collateral. New credit will be needed soon, however, in order to prevent the Bank of the Republic from defaulting again, and conditions imposed by the IMF will surely include cutbacks on internal spending such as salaries to government employees and subsidies. There is much pessimism, with general agreement that even harder times lie ahead. The peso is down to 68.

Internal struggle among the Blancos has paralyzed the naming of the new board of directors of the Bank of the Republic. So much so that yesterday the Minister and Sub-Secretary of the Treasury resigned—only to withdraw their irrevocable resignations today. At issue is which Blanco factions will get seats on the board of directors. Rationing of electricity continues although the drought earlier this year has now turned to serious flooding and hundreds of families have had to be evacuated along the Uruguay river. We're also in the midst of a rabies epidemic—a disease believed to have been eradicated from Uruguay several years ago. In the past year some 4000 people have been bitten by dogs in Montevideo even though 10,000 stray dogs were picked up. Malaise everywhere.

New rumblings from Brazil and Argentina on possible intervention in Uruguay have provoked sharp reaction. During Brazilian Army Week the Minister of War made a public statement widely publicized here which praised the historic mission of the Brazilian Army: "defense of democratic institutions, not only within our frontiers but also in whatever part of America we believe menaced by international communism." A few days later the Argentine Army Commander, General Juan Carlos Ongania, said on returning from a trip to Brazil that the Argentine and Brazilian armies have jointly agreed to combat communism in South America, particularly of that of Cuban origin. Although he did not mention Uruguay by name his statement comes at a time of continuing public comment in Argentina and Brazil over economic and social problems in Uruguay. Ongania later denied the press version of his speech, but here the original version sticks. Protests by Uruguayan military officers have caused cancelation of an invitation to the Brazilian military commander of the border zone, while the Uruguayan Navy has withdrawn from joint exercises with U.S. and Argentine units. A conference to have been given in Montevideo by an Argentine military leader was also boycotted by Uruguayan officers. The Foreign Ministry, moreover, has issued a statement in the name of the NCG rejecting any tutelary role in Uruguay by foreign-armed forces.

I can't seem to avoid getting sucked further into Soviet operations. Besides Borisov (whom I continue to see occasionally) and Semenov (a First Secretary whose intelligence affiliation, if any, is unknown) and the Commercial Office chauffeur, we have a new lead involving the new KGB chief, Khalturin. Through AVENGEFUL we learned that Khalturin was searching for an apartment—any Soviet who lives outside the community compounds is surely an intelligence officer because all the rest must live under controlled circumstances. The apartment Khalturin wanted is owned by Carlos Salguero,‡ the head of Latin American sales for the Philip Morris Co. and a naturalized American of Colombian origin. Salguero lives in a large mansion in Carrasco where he moved with his family just before I took over his previous house. Salguero's apartment, which is an investment property, is located in a modern building overlooking the beach in Pocitos. Conolly asked me to speak to Salguero about the possibility of obtaining access to his apartment before Khalturin moved in.

Khalturin took the apartment, and at a "recruitment luncheon" at the golf-club, Salguero agreed to give us access prior to Khalturin's moving in. I turned Salguero over to Conolly, the Soviet operations officer, who will organize the audio installation with Frank Sherno, the technician stationed in Buenos Aires.

One reason for this audio operation is that Khalturin seems to be having a love-affair with Nina Borisova, the wife of my friend the Consul—also a KGB officer. Borisova works in the Embassy, possibly with classified documents, and might have interesting discussions with Khalturin if he takes her to the apartment. So far Khalturin's wife hasn't arrived although he has said on the telephone that he expects her soon. There is also a chance that Khalturin might use the apartment for entertainment of prospective agents or even for agent meetings.

Montevideo — 23 September 1965

Strikes intensifying: municipal workers, state banks, autonomous agencies and decentralized services. Yesterday the Blanco NCG Councillors and Directors of state enterprises decided to use police to eject employees of the state banks which have been paralyzed by work to rule for the past ten days. Any employees who fail to respond to calls to work will be dismissed—harsh measures by Uruguayan standards. Today work to rule continues but the Bank of the Republic and the State Mortgage Bank closed in lock-outs, while workers in the private banks are stopping for thirty minutes in the morning and thirty in the afternoon in solidarity with the state bank employees.

Blanco NCG Councillors and Directors of state enterprises meeting today decided to grant only 25 per cent increases for workers in all the autonomous agencies and decentralized services and without negotiations. Unions, however, persist in demanding 48 per cent increases for 1966, citing the government's own statistics for January–August inflation: 33.8 per cent. Blanco leaders are determined to hold the line, however, because of the critical need for IMF backing. This will require suppressing the bank workers, who also opened the floodgates for overall government salary increases at this time last year.

There are no signs of relenting on the union side. The peso is now down to 74. The Minister and Sub-Secretary of the Treasury resigned again, this time accepted by the NCG.

The 20 September resolution by the House of Representatives in Washington is causing an outrage here and in other parts of Latin America. The resolution attributes to the U.S. or any other American state the right to unilateral military intervention in other American states if necessary to keep communism out of the Western Hemisphere. Here the resolution is viewed as an encouragement to the interventionist-minded in Brazil and Argentina. If this resolution is meant to be a show of support for the Dominican invasion, as it seems to be, I can only wonder how so many U.S. political leaders could have been convinced that fifty-eight trained communists took over the Bosch movement.

Montevideo — 27 September 1965

We've had a visit from John Hart, the new Deputy Chief of WH Division for Cuban Affairs. He's a former Chief of Station in Bangkok and in Rabat and is an old friend of Horton's. As the officer in charge of operations against the Cubans I spent a lot of time with him briefing him on our operations and listening to his plea for more work against the Cubans.

Hart said that the Agency has practically no agent sources reporting from inside Cuba (although technical coverage through electronic collection and aerial surveillance is adequate) and he is pushing recruitment of agents by mail. The system is to monitor mail from Cuba very closely in order to watch for signs of discontent. If records at headquarters and the JMWAVE station in Miami do not rule out the disaffected writer as a prospective agent, the station concerned or another

WH station can write back a letter on an innocuous subject to the Cuban, with instructions to save the letter. If the Cuban replies to the given accommodation address, a second letter will be written instructing him how to develop secret writing contained on the first letter. The developed message will be a recruitment proposal and, if answered, secret-writing carbon sheets can be sent to the Cuban and regular correspondence established. Here in Montevideo we would use the AVIDITY intercept operation to monitor mail for possible agents.

Although I nodded politely and tried to show enthusiasm for this search for needles in a haystack, I thought to myself that this man must be mad to think we have time for such games. I can scarcely make a quick scan of letters from Cuba, much less begin a recruitment campaign with all that implies.

Hart's other pet project is to find Che Guevara. Guevara disappeared about six months ago and although there were signs of him in Africa nobody knows where he is right now. Hart thinks he may be in a hospital in the Soviet Union with a mental breakdown caused by spoilage of asthma medicine kept unrefrigerated. He asked us to watch passenger lists closely and promised to send a photograph now being prepared of how Guevara would look without his beard—an artist's conception because no photos of a beardless Guevara have been found. Hart also asked that we continue the campaign already underway to generate unfavorable press speculation over Guevara's disappearance, in the hope that he'll reappear to end it. Other stations are doing the same.

Hart's visit came at an opportune time for me because he liked the work I'm doing against the Cubans and in six months I'm going to be looking for a job in headquarters, if indeed I don't resign from the Agency. Right now I'm not sure exactly what I'll do but I told Horton that I plan to return to headquarters in March when my two years here are finished.

There are two problems, I suppose, and each seems to reinforce the other. At home the situation is worse than ever: no common interests except the children, no conversation, increasing resentment at being trapped in loneliness. I told Janet that I'm leaving when we get back to Washington—she seems not to believe me—and in fact would have insisted that she return some time ago but for being separated from the children which is a prospect I can't accept. This is a hellish situation and no good for anyone.

The other problem is even worse. The Dominican invasion started me thinking about what we are really doing here in Latin America. On the one hand the spread of the Cuban revolution has been stopped and the counter-insurgency programs are successful in most places. Communist subversion at least is being controlled. But the other side, the positive side of reforming the injustices that make communism attractive, just isn't making progress. Here the problem is a small number of landholders who produce for export and whose interests clash with those of most of the rest of the country. Until Uruguay has a land reform there can be no fair distribution of either the benefits or the burdens of the country's production. There will be no encouragement to the landholders to produce and export legally. Even if export prices were to rise dramatically the benefits would mostly go to the same handful of people who have the land—the same handful who are suffering the least during these hard times. For certain the landholders will resist, here as in other countries, but somehow the Alliance for Progress will have to stimulate land reform if other reforms are to be successful.

The more I think about the Dominican invasion the more I wonder whether the politicians in Washington really want to see reforms in Latin America. Maybe participation by the communists wouldn't be such a bad thing because that way they could be controlled better. But to think that fifty-eight trained communists participating in a popular movement for liberal reform can take control is to show so little confidence in reform itself. The worst of this is that the more we work to build up the security forces like the police and military, particularly the intelligence services, the less urgency, it seems, attaches to the reforms. What's the benefit in eliminating subversion if the injustices continue? I don't think the Alliance for Progress is working, and I think I may not have chosen the right career after all.

I'll need to keep working when I separate from Janet after we return to Washington because she'll need money for the children and she probably won't want to work. The object would be to find another job without a period of seriously reduced income or none at all. I told Hart I'd like to work in Cuban affairs when I get back. Maybe Riefe's kind of cynicism is the best way to stay with the Agency and assuage one's conscience.

Montevideo — 1 October 1965

The bugging of Khalturin's apartment was successful—transmitters inside the bed and inside a sofa. The batteries will last for six months or more because the transmitters have radio-operated switches. Now Conolly must find a listening post close enough for operating the switches and for recording. Then an LP operator and a transcriber. These audio operations are messy.

Montevideo — 3 October 1965

Strikes by the government employees, particularly the bank workers, continue and there are strong rumors circulating that the government is going to declare a state of siege in order to break the strikes. So far the only government action has been lock-outs at the banks and threats to impose economic sanctions against any employees engaging in new strikes. However, the unions of the autonomous agencies and decentralized services, which just completed a two-day walk-out, have announced a three-day walk-out for 13–15 October.

Colonel Ventura Rodriguez,‡ Chief of the Montevideo Police and the country's top security official, had gone to Miami for the U.S. police chiefs' convention, but he was recalled suddenly. Although the reasons for his recall were not related to the current strikes, his return created new rumors. Nevertheless, he told us that the decision on a state of siege hasn't yet been made. Headquarters is getting nervous and has asked for continuous reporting on the situation.

In Peru the state of siege was finally lifted. The MIR guerrilla movement is defeated and only mopping up remains. A recent visitor who went through Lima told me that the station there opened an outpost in the mountain village where the Peruvian military command had been set up. During the crucial months of July–September the outpost served for intelligence collection on successes and failures of the military campaign and for passing intelligence to the Peruvian military obtained from Lima station sources. During the roll-up of the MIR urban organization, the main penetration agent, DUHAM–1,‡ was arrested and during police interrogation he revealed his work for us. Eventually the station got him released and now he's been resettled in Mexico with, I'm sure, a generous retirement bonus.

Suppression of the MIR will be regarded as a classic case of counter-insurgency effectiveness when good intelligence is collected during the crucial period of organization and training prior to commencement of guerrilla operations. Given their large numbers and training in Cuba, suppression would have been difficult and lengthy without a penetration agent like DUHAM–1.

Montevideo — 7 October 1965

This afternoon the NCG voted to enact a state of siege (six Blancos in favor, three Colorados opposed) which in Uruguayan law is called "prompt security measures." Adolfo Tejera, the Minister of the Interior, made the proposal which he justified on the need to end labor unrest. The decree prohibits all strikes and all meetings for the promotion of strikes and related propaganda. Enforcement of the state of siege was given to the Ministers of the Interior and Defense.

This had in fact been decided secretly yesterday, because the whole country is on strike, in the government banks, judiciary and other key areas—the main issues being salaries, inflation, sanctions, fringe benefits. The police and Army have been paid their September salaries in preparation for action. Colonel Ventura Rodriguez, who had gone to the U.S. police chiefs' convention in Miami, has been recalled, and Commissioner Otero and Inspector Piriz have been to tell me that the police have been some days at the ready. Headquarters wants daily reports on strikes and violence while the siege is on.

Nobody was surprised—yesterday's "secret" decision by the Blancos was in this morning's newspapers—but the CNT went ahead with its plans for a street rally and march this afternoon from the Legislative Palace to Independence Plaza. At the moment of the NCG voting the demonstrators were massed in the Plaza in front of the NCG offices, but as soon as the vote was taken police moved in to break up the demonstration. So far tonight thirty-four workers have been arrested, all from the electric company, except two who are leaders of the bank employees' union.

Montevideo — 8 October 1965

Arrests have risen to over one hundred but practically all the important union leaders are in hiding. This afternoon sit-down strikes in the government banks continued but ejections and arrests followed. Lightning street demonstrations against the state of siege have been occurring in different parts of the city.

As required by the Constitution the decree imposing the state of siege was sent to the Legislature for approval. The Blancos, however, knowing that the Colorados and splinter groups will try to repeal it, are staying away in order to prevent a quorum.

The CNT has called a general strike for 13 October and the autonomous agencies and decentralized services will begin that day a three-day walk-out. The government is in trouble.

Montevideo — 15 October 1965

The police are no match for the well-organized unions. The general strike was a big success with over 200,000 government workers and most of the private organized workers out. Newspapers, public transport, wool, textiles, public health, schools, practically every activity stopped. Today is the last of the three-day strike in the autonomous agencies and decentralized services. Lightning street demonstrations have been frequent with much pro-strike wall-painting and handbill distribution.

Police have made several hundred more arrests but the important leaders are still free. The PCU radio outlet, Radio Nacional, was closed for seventy-two hours for broadcasting strike news while an entire issue of *Epoca,* a leftist daily newspaper, was confiscated yesterday. In protest, however, the press association and press unions struck again and no newspapers appeared today. Tejera‡ has publicly blamed the communist leadership of the government employees' unions for the state of unrest, and Blanco leaders are hardening. The directors of the four government banks announced the firing of eighteen employees for strike leadership, while the autonomous agencies and decentralized services have announced sanctions of wage discounts equaling two days for the first day of the current strike, three days for yesterday and five days for today. Dismissals will follow if strikes continue. Final arrangements are being made for the arbitrary 25 per cent salary increases although the unions are still insisting on 48 per cent and inflation for this year is now up to 50 per cent.

The PCU, according to our agents, plans to continue the street demonstrations and other agitation in order to force the government to back down on the firings and sanctions. Two of our agents, AVCAVE-1 and AVOIDANCE-9, are on the highly secret PCU "self-defense" squads engaged in the lightning demonstrations and propaganda distribution. Their reporting has been excellent but they've been unable to get to know the hiding-places of certain of the union leaders which, if we knew, we would inform the police for arrests.

The police, in fact, may have given the communists and others a convenient victim for their campaign against the government. The story is out today of the torture of a young waterworks engineer, Julio Arizaga, who was arrested several days ago. Today he went berserk in his cell at AVALANCHE headquarters and had to be taken to the military hospital. There he attacked his guard and managed to wound the guard with the guard's own weapon. He was subdued, however, and his conduct is being attributed to torture by the police. I'll check with Commissioner Otero on this because usually the police don't engage in torture of political prisoners.

Arizaga is a member of the pro-Chinese Movement of the Revolutionary Left (MIR) and former member of the PCU. He is also a former leader of the FEUU, but he has never been very active in union activity. In recent months Riefe has been guiding AVCAVE-1 as close to the MIR as possible while retaining good standing in the PCU. However, because the MIR favors rural action, including guerrillas, over trade-union organizing, AVCAVE-1 may be instructed to leave the PCU altogether and join the MIR. Meanwhile he is reporting good intelligence from former PCU colleagues like Arizaga who have joined the MIR, as well as information on the PCU.

Montevideo — 19 October 1965

Yesterday the NCG (Colorados abstaining) adopted an economic stabilization program that will enable the government to obtain an IMF stand-by credit which in turn will open the door to new private and official loans. Most observers agree that the state of siege was enacted not only to break the strikes but also to preclude violent opposition to these new economic measures that will be unpopular with the unions.

Latest problem: the Ministry of the Treasury has assigned one million pesos to the Ministry of the Interior for expenses relating to the stage of siege, but there's a severe shortage of banknotes. The British firm that prints Uruguayan money is holding up delivery because the Bank of the Republic can't pay for it—arrears amount to £100,000.

Montevideo — 22 October 1965

Commissioner Otero was vague about the torture of Julio Arizaga, the MIR activist and waterworks engineer, which was his way of confirming the story. On Monday Arizaga was taken before a judge for a hearing on the shooting of his guard, and his condition was so bad and the torture so evident that the judge ordered him to be freed. The police refused and he was returned to the military hospital where he is still incommunicado.

I asked Inspector Antonio Piriz about the case and he said Inspector Juan Jose Braga,‡ Sub-Director of Investigations, was the officer who ordered and supervised the torture. The purpose was to obtain information on the MIR and on the Tupamaros, whose identity and organizational structure are still unknown. He explained that the torture room is on the same corridor as the AVENGEFUL listening post in the isolated section above the offices of the Chief and the Deputy Chief of Police. I noticed the other rooms down the hall when I visited the LP, but I was told that those rooms are only used by Colonel Rodriguez and Colonel Martin during rest periods. Usually, according to Antonio, the subject of the interrogation is hooded and tied to a bed with the *piçana* (a hand-cranked electric generator) attached to his genitals. Since Tom Flores's‡ counter-terrorist operations with police ended, and General Aguerrondo‡ was replaced as Chief of Police, torture of political prisoners has been rare. However, the *picana* was still used on criminals (which is why thieves and robbers so often wound themselves before surrender—so that their first days under arrest will be in hospitals), and perhaps torture of Arizaga was an exception because of Braga's frustration over the inability to stop the Tupamaro bombings.

Montevideo — 28 October 1965

Until today the Blanco leadership was firm in resisting union demands on salary increases and sanctions, but the union leaders began cultivating support from Colorado legislators on the sanctions issue. Today the Blancos, fearing political gains by the Colorados, announced that only half the sanctions will be discounted from October salaries with the other half coming in November. They also let it be known that pay and benefits increases beyond 25 per cent may be possible but not until next June.

The security situation has eased so strikingly that it is difficult to imagine we're still in a state of siege. Practically all those arrested during the early days have been released, and the CNT even held a mass rally on the no-sanctions issue without interference from police. The only strike still in effect is the municipal workers' walk-out and today the Army began collecting garbage that's been piling up in the streets for the past week.

The only reason the state of siege hasn't been lifted is that Arizaga's condition is still too bad—if he were released the torture would be obvious. Blanco leaders are thus being forced to retain the state of siege in order to protect the Chief of Police, Ventura Rodriguez and the Minister of the Interior, Adolfo Tejera. The Arizaga case, in fact, is causing serious friction between the two, and the Colorados have seized it as a political issue. Tejera is conducting an in-house "investigation."

Through the Public Safety mission I've put in Commissioner Otero, Chief of Police Intelligence, for an International Police Academy course beginning in January in Washington. After about twelve weeks at the Academy, Otero will be given special training in intelligence operations by headquarters. I've asked that the Office of Training concentrate on physical surveillance and on penetration operations against communist parties—targeting, spotting, recruitments, agent-handling.

Maybe with enough training for officers like Otero the police will be able to recruit agents and pay for information instead of having to resort to torture.

God knows he needs this training. He's been bogged down in the Cukurs case since March (the kidnapping of an ex-Nazi that went awry) for the sake of publicity and a little travel. Cukurs was finally cremated and a few days ago Otero turned his ashes over to his son together with a dental bridge. The son and the Cukurs family dentist, however, told reporters that the dead man never wore a bridge so now Otero's looking for another body.

Montevideo — 4 November 1965

Today the state of siege was lifted—Arizaga's condition improved enough for him to be released. The Colorados continue to attack the government over torture but Tejera claims the Ministry is continuing the investigation. Nothing will come of it, of course, because the Chief of Police won't allow it. If pushed he can summon support from the Army command and the Blancos don't want to lose power to the military over a sordid case of torture. Neither do the Colorados so there's no danger to the torturers.

Throughout the state of siege the Blanco senators and deputies, by staying away from sessions called to consider the emergency decree, were able to prevent a quorum and a Colorado vote to lift the siege. On the negotiations, however, the Colorados are forcing the Blancos into a more compromising position. Yesterday the Colorado-dominated Senate passed an amnesty bill annulling all firings and sanctions against workers engaged in strikes. Similar action is expected in Deputies.

Montevideo — 10 November 1965

Negotiations have broken down, strikes are again under way and the state of siege may be reinstated. Although municipal workers throughout the country struck again, and the Montevideo transport system is striking for October salaries, the main attack now is back with the central administration unions. They rejected the proposed salary increases for next July and are striking for forty-eight hours today and tomorrow, seventy-two hours next week and an indefinite period the week after. Negotiations between the government and the unions of the autonomous agencies and decentralized services continue but without progress. The Chamber of Deputies passed the amnesty bill today, in spite of the strikes, and it now goes to the NCG, where anything less than a veto would indicate complete collapse of the dominant Blanco faction. The amnesty bill must have constitutional incongruities if strikes by government employees are illegal, but everything here seems so incongruous that an unconstitutional law would only be normal.

The Colorados are also taking up the Arizaga case in the Chamber of Deputies—certain of them want to make political gain by feigning shock and surprise—but a Deputies investigation stands no more chance of making headway in AVALANCHE than the Minister's investigation.

Montevideo — 16 November 1965

Otero and the police in general have pulled off another stunning bungle. Secretary of State Rusk is here on an official visit and this morning he laid a wreath at the monument to José Artigas, the father of Uruguayan independence, in Independence Plaza. For a week I've been insisting with Otero, who is in charge of security preparations, that all precautions be taken to avoid any incidents related to Rusk's visit. This morning Otero and about 300 other policemen were forming a cordon around the wreath-laying site when suddenly a young man slipped through the cordon and ran all the way up to Rusk, expelling an enormous wad of spittle in the Secretary's face. Otero was standing right next to Rusk in a stupor, but he recovered and with other police carried off the attacker while Rusk wiped his face dry and laid the wreath. Tonight Colonel Rodriguez‡ and other government officials formally called on the Embassy to apologize. The attacker, a member of the PCU youth organization, is in the hospital where he was taken after a police beating and is reported to be in a coma.

Montevideo — 19 November 1965

Several days ago an important student conference began here under sponsorship of the FEUU and the Prague-based International Union of Students. The conference is called the Seminar on Latin American Social and Economic Integration and has drawn about sixty student delegations from all over the hemisphere. Through AVBUZZ–1 we have put out adverse editorial comment in the Montevideo press, exposing the Seminar as organized, financed and directed by the Soviets through the IUS front and through PCU control of the FEUU. We also arranged for handbills on the same theme to be distributed, as well as a humorous facsimile of an Uruguayan 100-peso note labeled as the roubles with which the Soviets are financing the Seminar. We have also ordered from TSD copies of official letterhead stationery of the Seminar with the signature of the Seminar's Secretary for Foreign Affairs, Daniel Waksman, reproduced at various levels in order to coincide with whatever length of letter we decide to attribute to Waksman. If it comes soon we will have a black letter to add to the other propaganda against the Seminar. Waksman is a leader of the FEUU.

The breakthrough with the Bank of the Republic union failed and new strikes are spreading in protest against the NCG's veto of the amnesty bill. The central administration has been joined by government banks, the Clinics Hospital, primary and secondary schools, the University and the judicial system. Today and tomorrow the civil aviation workers are closing the airports. Other strikes to follow.

Only a week remains until the constitutional deadline

for increasing government employees' salaries because elections are scheduled for 27 November 1966. As no increases can be granted during the year before elections, the coming week is sure to be agitated.

Montevideo — 27 November 1965

The past week stands as another large question-mark for Uruguayan democracy. Beginning with the civil aviation strike on 19–20 November and ending with the passage by Congress of the bill for salary increases last night, not a day has passed without an important strike by government employees. Schools, banks, the University, the postal and telecommunications systems, printers, port workers, the central administration and others struck with increasing intensity until the entire country was paralyzed on 25 November by a CNT-organized general strike. The port of Montevideo was closed, the airports closed again, and no newspapers appeared on 25 or 26 November. Street marches and other demonstrations by thousands of workers were almost daily occurrences, usually ending at the Legislative Palace for speeches demanding benefits to offset inflation. Yesterday, the final day for salary increases for a year, the demonstrations culminated.

With the magic hour at midnight, the NCG convened at 7 p.m. while all the Blanco ministers were called to Government House and told to wait in an office adjacent to the NCG meeting-room. At 7:20 the seventy-two-page document consisting of 195 articles arrived at the NCG from the Chamber of Deputies. (The bill contains many provisions on government finances in addition to salary increases.) After a swift review it was approved. The Colorado Councillors were forced to vote for it without even having seen the text, and the Blanco ministers who also had not seen it (except the Treasury Minister) were also required to approve and sign it. At 8:55 the Minister of the Treasury arrived with the document back at the Chamber of Deputies where it was debated until finally approved at 11:34. Waiting just outside the Deputies' Chamber was the elderly President of the Senate who rushed the document over to the Senate, arriving at seventeen minutes before midnight. Although several Senators took the floor, there was no time even to read the document and at one minute to midnight the Senate voted approval.

The bill provides for significant salary increases for government employees, although not all that was demanded, together with new taxes on agricultural and livestock activities, wool exporters and the banking system. Even so the opposition has already denounced the bill as very inflationary. Today almost all the strikers have returned to work—the waterworks being the notable exception. Conflicts, however, haven't ended because the sanctions issue persists. Since the NCG veto of the amnesty bill, the Blanco legislators have prevented a quorum, and the Blanco NCG Counsellors are calling for new sanctions for the most recent strikes. Peace between the government and its workers is still remote.

Montevideo — 3 December 1965

For the Khalturin audio operation an apartment just above and to the side of the Salguero apartment was obtained for a listening post. My secretary was glad to move in for the time being, but the problem of an LP keeper hasn't been solved. According to the AVENGEFUL telephone tap on the Soviet Embassy Khalturin regularly spends Saturday afternoons at the apartment. His liaison with Borisova continues, but now his wife has arrived—although she is not happy and has hinted she may soon return to the Soviet Union.

Until a full-time LP keeper can be obtained this operation will be only marginal, although Conolly, the Soviet operations officer, goes to the LP on Saturdays and sometimes on Sundays to switch on the transmitters and, if Khalturin is there, to record what is said. Last Saturday I went with him after lunch. The transmitters for the switches are housed in grey Samsonite suitcases of the two-suit size. After opening them flat and setting up the antenna, taking care that it points in the direction of Khalturin's apartment, the operator pushes the transmitter button for five seconds. If the switch doesn't work the process is repeated until it does, though not too often because the transmitter can overheat. Included in the suitcase is a lead apron so that operators can avoid unwanted sterilization. Maybe Khalturin would like an apron, too, but Conolly didn't take my point. Another grey Samsonite suitcase contains the receiver-recorder and is similarly opened flat with special antenna raised. These technical operations are boring—no decent production from this one yet.

Montevideo — 6 December 1965

The Blancos on the NCG insist the sanctions remain and be increased with any new strike activity. Discounts from salary payments are to be made at the rate of four days per month until all sanctions are collected which in some cases now total eighteen days. Partial work stoppages have already started in the autonomous agencies and decentralized services and in the Ministry of the Treasury the union called for the Minister's resignation. The income tax collection office of the same Ministry paid him a similar compliment in declaring him *persona non grata*. The central administration employees joined the others in announcing new strikes and staged a march to the Ministry of the Treasury demanding a dialogue with the Minister on sanctions. Police broke up the march with considerable force.

The state of siege is going back into effect tomorrow. I've had calls both from Antonio Piriz and from Alejandro Otero advising that police tonight will start rounding up as many important labor leaders as possible. They are hoping that they will catch a number of important leaders by starting tonight instead of waiting until the NCG votes to reinstate the state of siege tomorrow.

According to the same police agents the Blanco leaders want to arrest the government union leaders before word gets around of the new stage of siege—

wishful thinking the way secrets are spread in this country. Nevertheless the Minister of the Treasury announced tonight that the latest plan by central administration employees for easing the sanctions had been rejected by the NCG—while he inferred that negotiations will continue tomorrow. Odds are good that the union leaders have already gone back into hiding.

Montevideo — 7 December 1965

As expected, practically all the government workers union leaders learned of the new state of siege and evaded police arrest. This morning, just as the street march by the central administration employees reached Independence Plaza in front of Government House, the Blanco NCG Councillors voted to reimpose the state of siege. Adolfo Tejera, Minister of the Interior, made the request on the grounds of preventing subversion of the national economy by organized labor. The decree was passed to the Legislature but again the Blancos are staying away from the meetings in order to prevent a quorum.

The police, especially Otero's department, looked pretty bad, although the demonstration outside the NCG offices this morning was broken up without violence. Only fifteen arrests have been made in spite of their early start, and already the PCU "self-defense" squads are back in action distributing propaganda and generally defying the state of siege. In order to help Otero and the police to save face, Horton agreed that I should pass to Otero the name and address of one of the leaders of the "self-defense" squads, Oscar Bonaudi, for preventive detention. As there are only three squads, AVCAVE–1 being on one and AVOIDANCE–9 being on another, the arrest of Bonaudi will cause a spy scare, and probably make the PCU decide to curb the squads' propaganda activities for a while. Riefe doesn't want Bonaudi arrested because he's afraid his agents will be jeopardized, but Horton wants to help the police, particularly Otero, to improve their image.

Montevideo — 10 December 1965

Big news! Alberto Heber, the Blanco NCG Councillor who will take over as NCG President in March, today proposed that Uruguay break diplomatic relations with the Soviet Union because of Soviet interference in Uruguayan labor troubles. We don't have direct access to Heber but can check with Colonel Rodriguez. I have no means of seeing the Soviet chauffeur until next week to discover their reaction, but Conolly is concentrating on the AVENGEFUL tapes. Headquarters is delighted and confirms that we should support the break in any way we can. Already Lee Smith,‡ the new covert-action operations officer, who recently replaced Alex Zeffer, is preparing a black letter linking the Soviet cultural attaché with leftist student activities. Lee is using the stationery with the letterhead of the Seminar on Latin American Social and Economic Integration that the TSD prepared for us last month.

My police are looking better than ever. Yesterday the newspaper printers' union had just voted *not* to strike when police broke into the union hall and arrested over 100 people. These were later released, however, but another vote was taken, this time the strike was on, and today and tomorrow Montevideo has no newspapers.

Montevideo — 11 December 1965

We have worked all day preparing a report for NCG Councillor Alberto Heber that will justify both a break in diplomatic relations with the Soviets and the outlawing of the PCU. We began the project last night when John Cassidy,‡ who replaced O'Grady as Deputy Chief of Station, got an urgent call from one of his contacts in the Uruguayan military intelligence service. They had been asked by Heber earlier yesterday for a report on the Soviets, but since they had nothing, they called on the station for assistance.

This morning all the station officers met to discuss

the problems of trying to write the Heber report. After we decided to write it on a crash basis, Conolly chose the names of four Russians to be in charge of their labor operations, and then went through his files to find concrete information to give weight to this fantasy report. Similarly Riefe selected certain key CNT and government union leaders as the Uruguayan counterparts of the Soviets, together with appropriate true background information that could be sprinkled into the report, such as trips by PCU leaders to Prague and Moscow in recent months. Cassidy, Conolly, Riefe and I then wrote the final version which Cassidy and I translated into Spanish. Tonight Cassidy took it out to AVBUZZ–1 for correction and improvement of the Spanish, and tomorrow he'll turn it over to the military intelligence service (cryptonym AVBALSA). For a one-day job the twenty-page report is not bad. Certainly it includes enough information that can be confirmed to make the entire report appear plausible.

We prepared this report with media operations in mind, apart from justifying the break with the Soviets and outlawing the PCU. Heber has already said publicly that he has strong evidence to support the break, though without the details which he hasn't yet got, but if the break is not made we can publish the report anyway and attribute it to Heber—he is unlikely to deny it. In that case it will cause a sensation and prepare the way for the later decisions we want, and also provide material for putting to the media by other stations, such as Buenos Aires and Rio de Janeiro. According to Heber, the Blanco NCG Councillors will meet tomorrow (Sunday) to decide on the break, and formal NCG action will follow on Monday or Tuesday. The Minister of Defense, meanwhile, has suggested outlawing the PCU and closing propaganda outlets such as *El Popular*.

The black letter connecting the Soviet cultural attaché with the Seminar on Social and Economic Integration will be put out in *El Plata*, the afternoon daily belonging to the Blanco faction led by the NCG President. The letter is a statement of appreciation for technical advice, and refers to instructions relating to the Seminar and brought by a colleague who recently returned to Montevideo. Thanks are also given for "other assistance." Although the letter is vague, Soviet financing and control of the Seminar is easily inferred. The forged signature is that of Daniel Waksman, the Seminar Secretary for Foreign Relations.

Tension on the labor front is higher than ever with mass arrests of workers (over 200 arrested at the Bank of the Republic and over 200 more at a tire company), and a call by the CNT for another general strike on 14 December. Lightning street demonstrations against the government continue and several residences of government leaders and political clubs of the traditional parties have been bombed. Our estimate is that if the new general strike is not called off, the Blancos will break relations with the Soviets, to be followed by strong measures against the PCU and leftist labor leaders.

Montevideo — 12 December 1965

This morning before Cassidy turned over the Heber report to military intelligence, Horton decided first to show it to Colonel Ventura Rodriguez, the Chief of Police, as the top military officer in public security. We took it over to Rodriguez's office, where we sat around the conference table with Rodriguez and Colonel Roberto Ramirez, Chief of the Guardia Metropolitana, who was listening to a soccer game on his little transistor radio.

As Rodriguez read the report, I began to hear a strange low sound which, as it gradually became louder, I recognized as the moan of a human voice. I thought it might be a street vendor trying to sell something, until Rodriguez told Ramirez to turn up the radio. The moaning grew in intensity, turning into screams, while several more times Rodriguez told Ramirez to turn up the soccer game. By then I knew we were listening to someone being tortured in the rooms next to the AVENGEFUL listening post above Rodriguez's office. Rodriguez at last finished reading the report, told us he thought it would be effective and Horton and I headed back for the Embassy.

On the way back Horton agreed that we had been listening to a torture session and I explained to him the location of the torture room with relation to the AVENGEFUL LP and Rodriguez's office. I wondered out loud if the victim could be Bonaudi, whose name I had given to Otero for preventive detention. Tomorrow I'll ask Otero, and if it was Bonaudi I'm not sure what I'll do. I don't know what to do about these police anyway—they're so crude and ineffectual. I ought to have known not to give any names to the police after the Arizaga case last month, without a full discussion, with the Chief if necessary, of what action the police would take.

Hearing that voice, whoever it was, made me feel terrified and helpless. All I wanted to do was to get away from the voice and away from the police headquarters. Why didn't Horton or I say anything to Rodriguez? We just sat there embarrassed and shocked. I'm going to be hearing that voice for a long time.

Back at the Embassy the Ambassador told Horton that the NCG President had just this morning asked him if he had any information that might be used to justify breaking relations with the Soviets. Horton showed him the Heber report and the Ambassador suggested he should give it to Washington Beltran, the NCG President. The Ambassador took the original out to Beltran's house while a copy went to the military intelligence service, with the warning that if it were passed to Heber he should be advised that Beltran already has a copy.

Giving the report to the Ambassador for Beltran has certain advantages but Heber may be reluctant to use it now. Too bad, because Heber is the councillor who convinced the others to reinstate the state of siege, the one who suggested the break, and will moreover be the NCG President in less than three months' time.

Montevideo — 13 December 1965

The impasse is broken and the break with the Soviets is off for the time being. Last night the government and bank unions reached agreement that the firings of previous months would be canceled and that sanctions against strikers will be spread out over many months as painlessly as possible. The agreement was followed last night by the release of all the bank workers who had been arrested late last week. Early this morning similar agreements were reached with central administration unions. Communist and other militant leaders of the CNT had no choice, as the government unions accepted these solutions, but to cancel the general strike scheduled for tomorrow.

With the general strike broken and agreements with unions being made, the government has dropped the threat of breaking relations with the Soviets. The report prepared for Heber will not be brought out by the government for the time being—we can do so later. The state of siege will continue until firm agreements with all the government unions are reached. The leftist daily *Epoca* is still closed for inflammatory propaganda, and almost 30 are still under arrest.

Somewhat anti-climactic but useful, our black-letter operation against the FEUU and the Soviet cultural attaché caused a sensation when it was published by *El Plata* this afternoon. Banner headlines announce "Documents for the Break with Russia" and similar treatment will be given in tomorrow morning's papers. Denials from Daniel Waksman, the FEUU leader to whom the letter is attributed, were immediate, but they will be given scant coverage except in the extreme-leftist press. AVBUZZ–1 has arranged for Alberto Roca, publisher of the station-financed student newspaper *Combate*, to take responsibility for the black letter in order to relieve *El Plata* of liability.

Through AVBUZZ–1 we'll place new propaganda, in the form of editorial comment, using the unions' "capitulation" to avoid the break with the Soviets as proof of Soviet influence over the unions (although in fact the government conceded quite a lot more than the unions).

Montevideo — 14 December 1965

More unexpected developments. Adolfo Tejera, the Minister of the Interior, tried to maneuver Colonel

Rodriguez, the Chief of Police, into a position where the Chief would be forced to resign. The ploy backfired, forcing the Minister to offer his resignation, as yet unaccepted, to the NCG. It's all so complicated and bizarre that not even after explanations by Otero and Piriz am I completely sure of what happened.

The episode began not long after midnight when Otero called to advise me that the Ministry of the Interior had just announced that certain union leaders were in the Soviet Embassy and that the Embassy was surrounded by police to prevent their escape. Otero said the report about union leaders having taken refuge in the Embassy is false, although police had indeed been ordered to surround the Embassy. We arranged to meet this morning for clarification.

This morning the sensational story of the union leaders' refuge in the Soviet Embassy is carried in the press. According to the Director-General of the Ministry of the Interior, who released the story to the press just before Otero's call last night, police had followed certain union leaders who are on their arrest list after a negotiating session between them and the Minister. The police reported that the union leaders had entered the Soviet Embassy which was then surrounded by police.

This morning Otero told me that police had not followed the union leaders after their meeting with the Minister, but that the Director-General of the Ministry had followed them. The Director-General lost them in the general vicinity of the Soviet Embassy and later, probably in consultation with the Minister, decided to order police to surround the Embassy and attribute the report of their being there to the police. The Director-General gave the order to the precinct involved rather than through the police headquarters, in order to have the Embassy surrounded before the story was checked. The purpose of the maneuver was to make the police look ridiculous, because Colonel Rodriguez has protested within his Blanco faction that the Minister has been negotiating directly with union leaders who are on the police arrest list.

Later today the police department issued a statement, authorized by Rodriguez, denying that the police gave any report to the Ministry of the Interior about persons seeking refuge in the Soviet Embassy, and also denying that police had followed union leaders after a meeting with the Minister. Also later today the police arrested one of the union leaders in question even though the Minister ordered that he be left alone, and only the intervention of two NCG Councillors obtained his release.

Otero told me the screams Horton and I heard were indeed Bonaudi's. Braga,‡ the Deputy Chief of Investigations, ordered the torture, which lasted for three days during which Bonaudi refused to answer any questions. Otero said Braga and others were surprised at Bonaudi's resistance. That's the last name I pass to the police as long as Braga remains.

Montevideo — 16 December 1965

The Blancos have accepted the resignations of both the Minister and the Chief of Police. The Ministry of the Interior now passes to the Blanco faction led by Alberto Heber, who is due to become NCG President in March. The new Minister is Nicolas Storace,‡ and the new Police Chief is Rogelio Ubach,‡ another Army colonel who is currently Uruguayan military attaché in Asuncion, Paraguay.

For some time yesterday it seemed as if the solidarity with Rodriguez expressed by senior military officers would result in only Tejera's dismissal, but first reports on Ubach from the Embassy military attaché office are favorable. Horton and I will call on him officially after he takes over, probably next week. Station files also reflect favorable information on Storace from a previous period as Minister of the Interior in the early 1960s. Next week we will also call on Storace, and in the meantime perhaps the police department will come out of the paralysis of the past three days and get on with enforcing the state of siege.

Besides Rodriguez, the rest of the military officers who form the police hierarchy have also resigned or will resign shortly—meaning we will have a new Chief of the Guardia Metropolitana as police supervisor for AVENGEFUL telephone tapping. There are no indications that problems will arise over continuing this operation.

We have had a short visit from the new Deputy Chief of WH Division, Jake Esterline.‡ He has replaced Ray Herbert who is retiring. He told me that I won't be able to return to Washington in three months as I had planned because my replacement will be delayed some six months. A disappointment as the situation at home is difficult, but I agreed to stay on as long as necessary.

Horton gave a buffet supper for Esterline and all the station personnel. During a heated conversation on why Holman was sent to a trouble-spot like Guatemala, Esterline admitted that he had tried to change Holman's assignment because news of Holman's incompetence in Montevideo had gradually gotten back to headquarters. However, Des FitzGerald who took over as DDP from Helms, was reluctant to change the assignment because agreement had already been obtained from the State Department. Esterline added, however, that he and the new Chief of WH Division, Bill Broe,‡ are making sure that Holman's criticism of station officers is offset by special memoranda for the personnel files.

I would have liked to talk to Esterline about matters of principle related to counter-insurgency—such as how we can justify our operations to support the police and beat down the PCU, FEUU and other leftists when this only serves to strengthen this miserable, corrupt and ineffectual Uruguayan government. If we in the CIA, and the other U.S. programs as well, seek to strengthen this and other similarly clique-serving governments only because they are anti-communists, then we're reduced to promoting one type of injustice in order to avoid another.

I didn't mention this to Jake for the same reason, I suppose, that none of us in the station discusses the problem really seriously, although cynicism and ridicule of the Blancos, Colorados, police, Army and others whom we support is stronger than ever in the station halls—ample proof that we all see the dilemma. But serious questioning of principles could imply ideological weakening and a whole train of problems with polygraphs, security clearance, career, personal security. For all of us the discussions remain at the level of irony.

Montevideo — 24 December 1965

Yesterday the state of siege was lifted by the NCG while the Bank of the Republic began delivering 500 million pesos to the various government offices for payment of Christmas bonuses. Today seven of the bankers imprisoned for the frauds discovered in April were released—not exactly harsh punishment considering all the savings lost.

Media promotion of the break with the Soviets continues through AVBUZZ–1 in the form of announcements by real and fictitious organizations backing the break. One typical announcement was made a few days ago by the National Feminist Movement for the Defense of Liberty‡ which tied the break in relations with "the great work of national recuperation."

The break is off for the foreseeable future, nevertheless, as Storace, the new Minister of the Interior, told Horton and me on our first visit. He is anxious to keep AVENGEFUL going and has so instructed the new Chief of Police. Storace is the government's chief negotiator with the unions. In order to keep up closely with the new Immigration Director, Luis Vargas Garmendia,‡ who is developing a new plan relating to communist diplomatic missions in Montevideo, Horton asked me to be in charge of working with Vargas whom we met at our second meeting with Storace.

Horton and I have also called on the new Chief of Police, Rogelio Ubach,‡ who presented us to Lieutenant-Colonel Amaury Prantl,‡ the new Chief of the Metropolitan Guard and supervisor of the AVENGEFUL listening post. Ubach wants to continue and expand the AID Public Safety program which is just now completing its first year. Emphasis is still on communications systems but special attention is now being given to the Metropolitan Guard, the anti-riot shock troops, for whom tear-gas, ammunition, helmets and gas-masks have been provided. In addition to training by Public Safety AID officers in Montevideo, ten police officers have been sent to the International Police Academy in Washington. Cost so far: about 300,000 dollars.

Another important weapons robbery occurred the other night—possibly the work of the Tupamaros. They got away with eighty-six revolvers, forty-seven shotguns, five rifles and ammunition, all taken from a Montevideo gun shop. Commissioner Otero leaves in three weeks for Washington. Headquarters decided to train him at the International Police Services School,‡ which is a headquarters training facility under commercial cover, instead of at the AID-administered International Police Academy. AID cover for the training, however, is retained.

Montevideo — 3 January 1966

Principal labor unrest since the general strike was broken last month has been in the Montevideo transport system. That dispute was solved but inflation is worse than ever which guarantees more labor trouble. According to government figures the cost of living went up 16.6 per cent in December alone, while inflation for all of 1965 was 85.5 per cent—twice the rate for 1964. The School of Economics of the University of the Republic, however, puts 1965 inflation at 99.6 per cent. No wonder the UPI put the Uruguayan social and economic crisis among the ten most important news stories of the year.

The main reason for the jump in inflation in November and December was the economic reforms adopted in October, particularly the freeing of the peso for imports which caused it to go from the old official rate of 24 up to about 60. These reforms were necessary for the Bank of the Republic to obtain refinancing, and cleared the way for the interim credit of 48 million dollars signed on 1 December. But more reforms will be needed for the IMF stamp of approval because another 50 million dollars' credit will be needed this year. Without IMF backing, credit can't be obtained except under shady or usurious conditions. Already the Minister of the Treasury has made another trip to Washington for meetings with the IMF. Trouble is that while the IMF-imposed reforms are supposed to stimulate exports, the immediate impact of stabilization falls on the lower middle class and the poor who can least cope.

For the Blancos this means trouble in this year's elections. Because of opposition by rural producers, mainly the sheep and wool ranchers, the new taxes created in November are inadequate to cover the salary and benefits increases for government employees. This means still more deficit and more inflation, and although rural producers were the most favored by the October measures, contraband exports to Brazil are expected to continue.

Salvation for the Blancos may be in constitutional reform, the movement for which continued to grow all last year. The Ruralistas are still leading the reform movement (today Juan Jose Gari‡ resigned as President of the State Mortgage Bank in protest over failure of his allied Blanco faction to declare for reform) but the movement is growing both in Blanco and Colorado circles. Chief among reforms would be the return to a one-man executive in order to facilitate decision-making. The ominous sign in the reform movement, however, is the predominance therein of rural producers. A Colorado newspaper in a recent editorial against return to the one-man presidency pointed out that practically all of the 200 families that own 75–80 per cent of Uruguay's rural lands are in favor of a one-man executive. It seems that if better decision-making is attained, land reform will only get further away. Happily for me, Horton agreed that I could drop the political-contact work altogether.

Stations all over the hemisphere are engaged in a propaganda campaign against the Tri-Continental Conference that opened yesterday in Havana. It's a meeting of over 500 delegates from seventy-seven countries —some delegates represent governments and some represent extreme-left political organizations. Themes of the Conference are not surprising: anti-imperialism; anti-colonialism; anti-neo-colonialism; solidarity with the struggles in Vietnam, Dominican Republic and Rhodesia; promotion of solidarity on the economic, social and cultural levels. It is a major event of the communist bloc and is supposed to last until 12 January.

For some months headquarters has been preparing the propaganda campaign and asked long ago for stations to try to place agents in the delegations. We had no agent in a position to go to the Conference, but AVBUZZ–1 is turning out plenty of material for the media. Our themes are two: exposure of the Conference as an instrument of Soviet subversion controlled by the KGB, and frank admission that the danger posed by the Conference calls for political, diplomatic and military counter-measures.

Since the purpose of the Conference is to create unity among the different dis-united revolutionary organizations, propaganda operations are also being directed at these organizations—mainly capitalizing on resistance to dominance by the Soviet line and Soviet-lining parties. The more we can promote independence and splits among revolutionary organizations the weaker they'll be, easier to penetrate, easier to defeat.

Luis Vargas,‡ the Director of Immigration, has agreed to review the case of the North Koreans who came temporarily and have been here for almost a year-and-a-half. For months we thought Tejera might take action, but nothing ever happened. Hopefully Vargas and Storace,‡ the Minister of the Interior, will now be willing to ask them to leave.

Montevideo — 7 January 1966

The Soviets at the Tri-Continental Conference have given our propaganda operations perfect ammunition in a speech yesterday by S. P. Rashidov, Chief of the Soviet delegation who is a member of the Presidium and Vice-Prime Minister. Rashidov affirmed the resolution of the Soviet Union to give maximum support in money, arms and munitions to insurrectional movements organized to promote social revolution. He said that right now the Soviets are backing liberation movements in

Guatemala, Peru, the Dominican Republic, Puerto Rico, Guyana and Venezuela.

The speech is carried by the wire services and headquarters wants prominent display in local newspapers. In countries maintaining diplomatic relations with the Soviet Union we are to make sure appropriate government officials get copies or résumés of the Rashidov speech, and editorial comment is to be produced calling for re-examination of relations with the Soviets in the light of the Rashidov admissions.

Khalturin's wife has decided to return to the Soviet Union because she can't stand the summer heat here. Although Dick Conolly,‡ the Soviet operations officer, has been able to monitor the audio installation in Khalturin's apartment only sporadically, he has come up with several meetings and occasional visits to the apartment by Nina Borisova. Because of transcribing difficulties the tapes are being pouched to headquarters and so far I've heard of no startling information. Khalturin, meanwhile, has begun to show interest in the wife of Carlos Salguero,‡ the owner of his apartment, and Conolly is working closely with them as access agents to Khalturin.

After thinking over how I might use my acquaintance with Borisov, the Soviet Consul and husband of Borisova, to exploit the triangle, I proposed to Conolly and Horton that I tell Borisov of his wife's infidelity more or less "as one man to another." The purpose would be to place Borisov in the difficult position of either not reporting something important that I tell him—dishonesty in reporting might be a first step to defection—or reporting that a CIA officer has told him that his wife is sleeping with his chief. Although sexual behavior is fairly relaxed among Soviets, the fact that the CIA is monitoring a liaison within the KGB office might make reporting difficult for Khalturin as well as Borisov. Possibly, if an honest report went to Moscow, either Borisov or Khalturin or both might be recalled with the attendant disruption and possible reluctance of either to return under a cloud. At Horton's instruction I made the proposal in writing to headquarters—both he and Conolly think it's a good idea.

Montevideo — 13 January 1966

Otero left today for training at the International Police Services School in Washington. Horton and I went to police headquarters to bid farewell and we took advantage of the meeting with Colonel Ubach,‡ the Chief of Police, to propose bringing down one of our officers to work full-time with police intelligence, using the AID Public Safety mission as cover. Ubach isn't terribly quick mentally, but he agreed, as he does to everything else we propose. Now we'll get approval from Storace, the Minister of the Interior, and advise headquarters to select someone. Once this matter is settled we'll begin working on the Minister, the Chief, and others in order to take the intelligence department out of the Investigations Division, preferably on an equal bureaucratic level as Investigations or at least with some autonomy. If approved we'll try to maneuver Inspector Piriz in as Intelligence Chief because he's much more experienced, mature and capable than Otero who suffers from impatience and is disliked by colleagues. Piriz, moreover, has already been on the payroll for some years and his loyalty and spirit of cooperation are excellent. While Otero is away I'll work closely with his deputy, Sub-Commissioner Pablo Fontana.‡

Montevideo — 20 January 1966

AVBUZZ–1 has been pounding away at the Tri-Continental Conference, which ended a few days ago, but he may have overplayed his hand a little. He arranged for a statement to be published in the name of an organization he calls the Plenary of Democratic Civic Organizations of Uruguay. The statement was perfect because it tied the Tri-Continental with the Congress of the People, the CNT and the waves of strikes during late last year. The problem was his vivid imagination in naming signatory organizations to demonstrate mass backing: the National Feminist Movement for the Defense of Liberty,‡ the Uruguayan Committee for Free Determination of Peoples,‡ the Sentinels of Liberty,‡ the Association of Friends of Venezuela,‡ the Uruguayan Committee for the Liberation of Cuba,‡ the Anti-Totalitarian Youth Movement,‡ the Labor Committee for Democratic Action,‡ the National Board for the Defense of Sovereignty and Continental Solidarity,‡ the Anti-Totalitarian Board of Solidarity with the People of Vietnam,‡ the Alliance for Anti-Totalitarian Education,‡ the Anti-Communist Liberation Movement,‡ the Free Africa Organization of Colored People,‡ the Student Movement for Democratic Action,‡ the Movement for Integral University Action.‡

Vargas, the Director of Immigration, is very excited about promoting action against communist bloc diplomatic and commercial missions in Montevideo. He showed me the Heber report of last month, without telling me how he got it—probably from Heber himself, and asked if I would use it and any other information we have in order to justify the expulsion of key Soviets instead of a break in diplomatic relations. He and Storace (and presumably Heber) now want us to prepare a report naming whichever Soviets we want as those responsible for meddling in Uruguayan labor and student organizations. At the appropriate moment the report will be used for declaring those Soviets *persona non grata*. Conolly, Riefe, Cassidy and I have already started on this new report. We will have to work fast to take advantage of the resentment caused by the Rashidov speech and the Tri-Continental and of Heber's clear intention to use expulsions and the threat of expulsions as a tool against the unions. Vargas is also going to begin action against the non-diplomatic personnel of communist missions, especially those who are here as officials of the commercial missions, which would include Soviets, Czechs, East Germans and the North Koreans. He's going to start with the North Koreans. He has discovered several ways in which he is going to prepare expulsions of Soviet bloc diplomatic and commercial officers. These expulsions will be mainly on technicalities he has found in the 1947 immigration law that forbids entry to persons who advocate the violent overthrow of the government, on irregularities in the issue of visas, and on interpretations of the status of Soviet bloc commercial officers. Little by little he hopes to cut down the official communist representation here by expelling the Koreans, East Germans and certain Czechs and Soviets—none of whom have diplomatic status—and by the *persona non grata* procedure where diplomatic officials are concerned.

I am encouraging Vargas to bring the approval authority for all visas to diplomats and others representing communist countries under his control. According to the current regulations he is supposed to have power of approval over all visas except diplomatic ones, but in recent years the Director of Immigration's office hasn't exercised this function. In order to obtain control of diplomatic visas, Vargas will prepare an instruction which Storace will get approved by the NCG. All this will take time but at least we're beginning to move. Our purpose is to get prior advice on visa requests and to give Vargas information about persons for whom the visas are requested. We will be able to delay the visas and to get visas refused where desirable—all of which will help to cut back the size of the communist missions, the numbers of intelligence officers in them, and the damage they can do.

In Havana yesterday it was announced that a new organization is being formed to coordinate revolutionary activities in Latin America. It will be a "solidarity" organization to channel assistance to liberation movements, and in the announcement Castro was quoted as praising the leadership of the revolutionary movement in Uruguay. Ambassador Hoyt asked us to prepare a report on these latest developments as well as on the Rashidov speech and other matters related to the Tri-Continental. He plans to give this material to the Foreign Minister because he says the NCG is going to take some kind of action.

Montevideo — 29 January 1966

Our use of the Rashidov speech and the Tri-Continental propaganda has produced a surprising show of strength by the Uruguayan government. Today the Foreign Minister called in Soviet Ambassador Kolosovsky and asked for an explanation of Soviet participation in the Conference, since Conference speeches and documents are flagrant violations of the principles of self-determination and non-intervention as expressed in the U.N. Charter. The Foreign Minister pointedly asked Kolosovsky if Rashidov, as Chief of the Soviet delegation, had been speaking on his own account or as a representative of the Soviet government. Kolosovsky answered that he will request clarification from Moscow. These exchanges have been reported in the media, especially Kolosovsky's failure to respond. Cables have gone to other WH stations for replay.

Other diplomatic moves include a statement by Venezuela that it will examine its diplomatic relations with countries represented at the Conference. In the OAS, Peru presented a resolution condemning the Conference, and ORIT headquarters in Mexico, together with member organizations in various countries, have sent telegrams to the OAS backing the Peruvian resolution. The U.S. representative in the OAS, speaking for the Peruvian resolution, said that the Alliance for Progress will make Latin America a lost cause for communism—he can't have spent much time in Latin America lately.

Manuel Pio Correa,‡ the Brazilian Ambassador sent by the military government to suppress exile plotting, returned permanently to Brazil last week. He has been rewarded for his work here by appointment as Secretary-General of the Brazilian Foreign Ministry—the number two post, equivalent to Under-Secretary. After he got back, a spokesman for the Brazilian Foreign Ministry commented that when Pio Correa made his final call at the Foreign Ministry here to bid farewell, he failed to deliver another protest note over the exiles.

Before leaving Montevideo Pio Correa told Horton that if things in Uruguay don't improve, sooner or later Brazil will intervene—perhaps not militarily but in whatever way is necessary to prevent its weak neighbor from falling victim to communist subversion. Well, at least we won't have to send troops as we did with the

Dominican Republic—the Brazilians will take care of those fifty-eight trained Uruguayan communists when the time comes.

Montevideo — 2 February 1966

Expulsion of the North Koreans was approved yesterday by Storace‡ and will be ordered by Vargas in a matter of hours. Vargas's investigation revealed that former Interior Minister Tejera had ordered them to detail their commercial activities in August last year, but the Koreans refused and Tejera asked in November for a report from the Bank of the Republic which was never made. Vargas's new query to the Bank of the Republic brought a reply that the North Koreans' only transaction since they arrived in 1964 was a small purchase of hides about a year ago. As their tourist visas expired long ago and they are making no commercial transactions, expulsion will provoke little opposition. What the North Koreans were doing all this time is a mystery; most likely intelligence support for the Soviets.

The Blanco NCG Councillors are keeping up the heat against the Soviets over the Tri-Continental and Rashidov's speech. In a well-publicized meeting yesterday they received from the Foreign Minister a group of documents on the Tri-Continental, including those we prepared for the Ambassador. A copy of Rashidov's speech was one of the documents and we are trying to get a recording of the speech to pass to the Foreign Minister through the Ambassador—hopefully the Miami station monitored the speech if it was broadcast. Although no decisions were reached, the meeting served to stimulate new speculation about a possible break in relations. This weekend the Argentine Foreign Minister will be in Punta del Este, and we are also creating press speculation that he and the Uruguayan Foreign Minister will be discussing the significance of Soviet diplomatic presence in the River Plate in the light of the Tri-Continental.

Today we helped to increase the tension even more by getting the military intelligence service to inspect a shipment of some thirty crates that recently arrived in the port from the Soviet Union. Through the AVENGEFUL telephone tap we learned about the crates and when the Army opened them today the Soviets protested loudly. They contained only tractors and parts but the incident contributed nicely to the current propaganda campaign.

Other propaganda on the Soviets and the Tri-Continental consists largely of press replay of significant articles published elsewhere—right now, in fact, stations all over the hemisphere are putting out a coordinated campaign to demonstrate that the channel for communist subversion begins in Moscow with the KGB and flows out through the Cubans and organizations like the Tri-Continental to the local organizations. Central to this campaign is a *Le Monde* article of 20 January on formation of the Latin American solidarity organization. Cleverer, perhaps, is the publication of a "secret" document through agents of the Caracas station in the Accion Democratica Party. The document, supposedly obtained at the Tri-Continental, purports to detail the formation of a Latin American solidarity organization and is being put out by various stations. Here we decided to use A. Fernandez Chavez,‡ one of our media agents and also the representative of ANSA, the Italian press service. In Fernandez's version the program of the solidarity organization is said to have been elaborated at a series of meetings in Montevideo, Rivera (on the Brazilian border) and Porto Alegre (capital of the Brazilian state bordering Uruguay). Officers of the Uruguayan–Soviet Cultural Institute were said to have participated.

Montevideo — 4 February 1966

The NCG President has raised suddenly the specter of a move against the Soviet mission again. Today he told newsmen at Government House that the Minister of the Interior, Storace, is preparing a new report on infiltration by communist diplomats in Uruguayan labor and student organizations. He also said that from what his own sources tell him, and from what Storace told him orally, there can be no doubt of illegal intervention by communist diplomats. He added that Storace's report will be presented to the NCG next week and will lead to an announcement of great moment.

The "Storace report" is the one we wrote for Storace and Vargas two weeks ago to justify the expulsion of eight Soviet and two Czech diplomats. This report is already in Storace's hands and if all goes well we should have some sensational expulsions next week. The Soviets were selected very carefully in order to produce the desired effects. Both Khalturin, the KGB chief, and Borisov, the Consul and a KGB officer, were left off the expulsion list, so that we can continue to monitor the liaison between Khalturin and Borisova. We included on the list, however, Khalturin's most effective and hard-working subordinates, including the cultural attaché whom we made trouble for in the spurious Waksman letter last year, so that Khalturin will have to take on an even greater work load. Reports from Salgueros‡ and from the AVBLIMP observation post reveal that Khalturin is working extremely long hours and appears to be under severe strain. By forcing still more work on him we might trigger some kind of breakdown. We also included the Embassy *zavhoz* (administrative officer) because his departure will cause irritating problems in the Soviet mission's housekeeping function. I added the two Czechs in order to demonstrate KGB use of satellite diplomats for their own operations and in order to get rid of the most active Czech intelligence officers.

Closely related to the new move against the Soviets was the decision by the NCG yesterday to instruct the Uruguayan mission at the OAS to support the Peruvian motion condemning the Tri-Continental and Soviet participation in it. The motion has passed the OAS and will be sent now to the U.N. Security Council.

The Soviets know what's coming, because AVAILABLE –1, my Soviet chauffeur, told me the whole mission is waiting under great tension to see how many and who are sent home.

Montevideo — 11 February 1966

The North Koreans are out but the Soviet expulsion is postponed. Vargas couldn't get the Koreans to go to his office to be advised, so he sent police to bring them in by force. The three officials and their families left today. Expulsion of the Soviets is postponed for the time being because Washington Beltran, the outgoing NCG President, wants Alberto Heber, who comes in as NCG President on 1 March, to make the expulsion. Storace's presentation of our report to the NCG is also postponed but Vargas assured me that action will be taken sooner or later. At the moment he is going to proceed with progressive harassment and expulsion—if politically acceptable—of the East German trade mission, the Czech commercial office and the Soviet commercial office. Because officials of these offices haven't got diplomatic status, Vargas can assert control without interference from the Foreign Ministry. He is also proceeding on the new decree granting the Ministry of the Interior and the Immigration Department equal voice with the Foreign Ministry for approval of all visas, diplomatic included, for communist country nationals.

Too bad about the expulsions because today Soviet Ambassador Kolosovsky replied to the Foreign Minister on the Rashidov speech. He said Rashidov was speaking at the Tri-Continental in the name of certain Soviet social organizations and not in the name of the Soviet government. Appropriate media coverage is following in order to ridicule Kolosovsky's answer and to applaud the North Korean expulsion.

Montevideo — 17 February 1966

Station labor operations continue to be centered on the Uruguayan Institute of Trade Union Education,‡ which is the Montevideo office of the AIFLD. Jack Goodwyn,‡ Director of the Institute, is working closely with Lee Smith,‡ the station covert-action officer, in order to develop a pool of anti-CNT labor leaders through the training programs of the Institute. The most effective program, of course, is the one in which trainees are paid a generous salary by the Institute for nine months after completion of the training course, during which time they work exclusively in union-organizing under Goodwyn's direction. It is this organizational work that is the real purpose of the AIFLD, so that eventually our trade unions can take national leadership away from the CNT. Goodwyn's job, in addition to the training program, is to watch carefully for prospective agents who can be recruited by Smith under arrangements that will protect Goodwyn.

The goals will take a long time to reach and progress often seems very slow. Nevertheless Goodwyn has already achieved several notable successes in the social projects field, which are showcase public-relations projects such as housing and consumer cooperatives. Using a four-million-dollar housing loan offer from the AFL–CIO, to be guaranteed by AID, Goodwyn has brought together a small number of unions to form the Labor Unity Committee for Housing. Some of these same unions have also formed what they call the Permanent Confederation, which is the embryo of a future national labor center that will affiliate with ORIT and the ICFTU.‡ Another housing project, also for about four million dollars, is being negotiated with the National Association of Public Functionaries—one of the two large unions of central administration employees. Goodwyn has also formed a consumer cooperative for sugar workers in Bella Union—the same region where the important revolutionary socialist leader, Raul Sendic, gets his support.

Station propaganda operations are now high-lighting the recent imprisonment by the Soviets of dissident writers Yuli Daniel and Andrei Sinyavsky as well as the Tri-Continental. Today the NCG discussed the Daniel and Sinyavsky cases and instructed the Foreign Minister to make a formal protest in UNESCO. NCG Councillors also harshly criticized Kolosovsky's reply that Rashidov was not speaking at the Tri-Continental for the Soviet government.

Montevideo — 25 February 1966

My little technical operation against the codes of the UAR Embassy is beginning to monopolize my time. For over a week two Division D technical officers, Donald Schroeder‡ and Alvin Benefield,‡ have been here planning the installation, and I've had to take them from shop to shop buying special glues, masking-tape and other hard-to-find items. Schroeder was here late last year for a short visit and at his request I sent the electric company inspector who is part of the AVENIN surveillance team into the Embassy for an inside casing. After his visit there was no doubt where the code-room is located—right over the office of Frank Stuart,‡ the Director of AID.

Some time ago Stuart received an instruction from AID headquarters in Washington to lend whatever cooperation is necessary to the station—although he doesn't seem to know exactly what is to happen. He's just nervous that some heavy instrument will come crashing down on his desk through the modern, hanging, acoustic-tile ceiling of the AID offices. I have arranged with him to get the keys to AID and for him to send away his watchman when we make the entry a few nights from now.

The installation will consist of two special contact microphones ("contact" meaning it is made to pick up direct vibrations instead of air vibrations, as in the case of a normal voice microphone) connected to small FM transmitters powered by batteries. Schroeder and Benefield will install the equipment right against the ceiling, as close as possible to the spot where the UAR code clerk has his desk. From my Embassy office which is across the street from the UAR Embassy and the AID offices, we will monitor the transmitter in order to record vibrations from the machine.

The UAR uses a portable Swiss-built encrypting machine which is like a combination typewriter and adding machine. Inside it has a number of discs that are specially set every two or three months. The code clerk, in order to encrypt a secret message, writes the message into the machine in clear text in five letter groups. Each time he completes five letters he pulls a crank which sets the inner discs whirling. When they stop the jumbled letters that appear represent the encrypted group. When the whole message is encoded the resulting five letter groups are sent via commercial telegraph facilities to Cairo.

The National Security Agency cannot break this code system mathematically but they can do so if sensitive recordings can be obtained of the vibrations of the encrypting machine when the discs clack to a stop. The recordings are processed through an oscilloscope and other machines which reveal the disc settings. Knowing the settings, NSA can put the encoded messages, which are intercepted through the commercial companies, into their own identical machines with identical settings, and the clear text message comes out. Although the Swiss manufacturer when selling the machine emphasizes the need to use it inside a sound-proof room on a table isolated by foam rubber, we hope this particular code clerk is careless. If we can discover the settings on this machine in Montevideo, NSA will be able to read the encrypted UAR messages on the entire circuit to which their Montevideo Embassy pertains. This circuit includes London and Moscow, which is why we have been pressured to get the operation going here. If successful, we will record vibrations from the machine every time the settings are changed in future. By reading these secret UAR messages, policymakers in Washington will be able to anticipate UAR diplomatic and military moves, and also to obtain an accurate reaction to U.S. initiatives.

In another day or two Schroeder and Benefield will have all their equipment ready. Our plan is to drive up Paraguay Street about 9 p.m. and enter normally through the front door of the AID offices, using Stuart's key. After checking security and closing blinds, I'll park the car just down Paraguay Street from AID for emergency getaway. While Schroeder and Benefield make the installation, I'll go up to my office in our Embassy and watch over the UAR Embassy and the AID office from my window. Horton also plans to be in the station when we make the installation. We'll have handie-talkies for communication between Schroeder and Benefield and Horton and me in the station. Very little risk in this one but plenty of advantage.

Montevideo — 1 March 1966

The technical installation under the UAR code-room took most of the night—Horton told Schroeder and Benefield that no matter what happens that equipment must not come loose and fall on to Stuart's desk. So they took their time and made it safe. Already we have recordings of the machine and after playing them through the oscilloscope of our communications room, Schroeder and Benefield are certain they will work. We pouched the tapes to headquarters for passage to NSA, who will advise on whether they can be used.

The sensitivity of the microphones is remarkable. Every time a toilet flushes, or the elevator goes up or down, even the structural creaks—every sound in this twelve-storey building is picked up.

Montevideo — 7 March 1966

Alberto Heber took over as President of the NCG and was greeted by the CNT with a call for another general strike for 16 March, in protest against continuing inflation and unemployment. The Montevideo transport strike is now three weeks old. Storace continues as chief government negotiator with the unions, and, with elections only nine months away, labor peace must be bought even at the price of still more concessions.

So today he settled the Montevideo transport strike. He also put to rest the sanctions issue. The unions of the autonomous agencies and decentralized services accepted his formula whereby all sanctions discounted for last year's strikes will be repaid to the workers and all other sanctions canceled.

The CNT then announced that the general strike called for 16 March is postponed until 31 March. Our

PCU penetration agents believe this was part of the bargain with Storace over sanctions and that the strike will probably not be held at all.

Montevideo — 12 March 1966

Luis Vargas, the Director of Immigration, has a new plan for reducing the numbers of commercial officers from the communist countries. These officers are more vulnerable than their colleagues with diplomatic status (although cover in the commercial departments is frequently used for intelligence officers) because Uruguayan law does not recognize "official" status for foreigners not having diplomatic passports. As almost all the Soviet, Czech and other communist trade officers carry service or special passports, which for them is between ordinary and diplomatic status, Vargas is going to apply the law which requires that foreigners who have completed the temporary residence period for purposes of commerce must solicit permanent residence in order to remain in Uruguay. As the request for permanent residence includes a statement of intention to become an Uruguayan citizen, Vargas is certain, as am I, that those officers affected will have to be transferred. By long delays of approval of visa requests for replacements, the numbers of officers in the commercial missions can be considerably reduced without outright expulsion. The first communist mission to feel this new procedure will be the East Germans whose four-man trade mission is functioning just like an embassy. Our Ambassador, in fact, is often embarrassed at diplomatic functions when the chief of the East German mission is present, and some time ago he asked us to see what could be done to get them thrown out.

Although I've also been trying to keep up pressure on Vargas and Storace for the expulsion operation against the Soviet officers, they have both said they want to hold this move in reserve to use when the unions start trouble again. Meanwhile, Vargas is proceeding with the special decree giving him and Storace approval power for all visas, including diplomatic, for nationals of the communist countries. The Foreign Ministry is opposed to giving the Interior Ministry a veto power on diplomatic visas, but Storace and Vargas, as men in Heber's confidence, are going to win.

Headquarters tell us that NSA is able to determine the code-machine settings with the tapes. We're going to leave the installation in place and when the settings are changed we will be advised and I will make some recordings in my office to be forwarded by pouch. At last I'll have these two Division D friends off my back. Benefield now goes to Africa for an operation against a newly-established Communist Chinese mission and Schroeder goes to Mexico City where he has been working for some time on an operation against the French code system.

Montevideo — 20 March 1966

Work with the police continues but with little real progress. Storace approved bringing down one of our officers under Public Safety cover and headquarters finally located an officer for the assignment: Bill Cantrell,‡ formerly with the Secret Service, then in the Far East Division after coming with the Agency. Unfortunately Cantrell will not arrive until September because he has to study Spanish, so I suppose I'll be working with police intelligence until I leave—with luck at the end of August.

Our efforts to convince Colonel Ubach to establish an intelligence division on a par with, or apart from, the ordinary Criminal Investigations Division haven't been successful. Horton, however, is determined to turn police intelligence into a British-style "special branch" like the one he dealt with in Hong Kong. I'm not sure whether he thinks this is needed because it will work better or because it's the British way—he seems even more anglophile than before: country walks, bird-watching, tennis, tea-time and quantities of well-worn tweeds that he wears in the hottest weather.

Establishing an autonomous "special branch" under

Inspector Piriz wouldn't be possible just now in any case because Piriz is still working on fraud cases and the other financial crimes that have continued since the first bank failures in April of last year. Heber on taking over as NCG President established a special Treasury Police under Storace with representation from the Bank of the Republic, the Ministry of the Treasury and the Montevideo Police Department. Piriz is the senior police officer in this new unit and it would be difficult to pry him away because his work on these cases has been excellent. As he is rather isolated from police headquarters his value as an intelligence source has come down, but I'm continuing his salary, in fact I've given him several raises to keep up with inflation, because of his long-range potential.

Frank Sherno, the regional technical officer stationed in Buenos Aires, sent us a portable Recordak document-copying machine which I hope to set up at the Montevideo airport as part of an improved travel-control operation. With this machine we can photograph all the passports from communist countries and that of anyone else on our watch list. Recently I've begun to work on this with Jaureguiza,‡ another Police Commissioner who is in charge of general travel control and the Montevideo non-domiciled population. Jaureguiza has agreed to obtain a convenient room at the Montevideo airport near the immigration counters to install the machine. When this is settled Sherno will come to set it up and train the operators. Hopefully we can get this done before Otero gets back from his training in Washington because he'll want to control it and his abrasive personality would hinder getting it started. By now he has finished the police training course at the International Police Services School and is undergoing special intelligence training by headquarters' OTR officers.

No wonder this passport photography has taken so long. Yesterday the Metropolitan Guard seized a large quantity of contraband at the airport and customs officers were revealed to be running a lucrative trade. Smuggling in fact is the reason why I've been delayed so often, because Piriz tells me the airport police are also in the business. Any tighter controls out there threaten their livelihood.

Montevideo — 30 March 1966

Headquarters thinks the operation against the UAR codes is so important that they asked that we buy or take a long lease on the apartment above the UAR Embassy. The reasoning is that in a couple of years we will be moving into the new Embassy now under construction on the Rambla and AID will also probably move at that time. As this operation could go on for many years, headquarters wants to be assured of access to the building and close proximity for a listening post. Bad news. Now I'll have to find someone to buy the apartment from the elderly couple living there, then someone to live in it as LP keeper. The apartment is enormous, as there is only one per floor in this building, so I'll need a family with some ostensible affluence.

Rio de Janeiro — 6 April 1966

Even from travel posters it's impossible to imagine the beauty of this city—mountains right in the middle of town, sparkling bays, wide, sandy beaches. The combination is simply spectacular.

All the case officers in charge of Cuban operations at the South American stations are here for a conference. The purpose is to stimulate new interest in recruiting agents who can go to Cuba to live, in recruitment operations against Cuban government officials who travel abroad, and in operations to penetrate Cuban intelligence activities in our countries of assignment. Tom Flores,‡ former Chief of Station in Montevideo, is now in charge of all Cuban affairs in headquarters and is running the conference—he held another one last week in Mexico City for Cuban operations officers in Central America, the Caribbean and Mexico.

In his introductory remarks, Flores lamented that the Agency still has practically no living agents reporting from within Cuba. Technical coverage from electronics and communications intercept ships like the *USS Oxford*, and from satellites and aerial reconnaissance, is good but not enough. Not surprisingly he carried on with the old theme of recruitment by secret writing through the mails. Then we had a full day on the structure and function of the Cuban intelligence service—more of the same information sent almost two years ago after the defection in Canada. Very boring.

Yesterday and today each of us has had a turn at describing our local operations against the Cubans—mine are still bogged down in following up the interminable leads on the counter-intelligence cases and in trying to get the government to take action against the Montevideo *Prensa Latina* office.

It was interesting, though, to hear of operations in Quito and Caracas. Fred Morehouse,‡ the former chief of the ZRBEACH communications monitoring team in Montevideo, was transferred to Caracas and there he managed to locate and identify two people who were operating clandestine radio communications circuits with Cuba. It wasn't said whether either of them was recruited, but in any case both circuits were neutralized.

Representing the Quito station is none other than old boss Warren Dean—the conference is for operations officers, but Dean wanted a few days' vacation in Rio. He explained that Rafael Echeverria went to Cuba after the military junta took over in 1963 and there he had an operation for a brain tumor. After recovery he was trained as a Cuban intelligence agent and he returned to Quito and was unmolested by the junta. Through Mario Cardenas, the Quito PCE penetration agent, Echeverria was discovered to have a secret-writing system for sending messages to Cuba and a radio signal plan for receiving them. The Office of Communications installed a transmitter in the radio Echeverria used to receive short-wave messages from Cuba, so that the station could record the messages in the apartment across the street where I had placed Luis Sandoval under commercial photography cover before Arosemena was overthrown. The station also copied Echeverria's cryptographic pads and thus was able to monitor his communications with the Cuban service in Havana. The Quito station's best new recruitment is Jorge Arellano Gallegos,‡ a PCE leader from years back on whom vulnerability data for recruitment has been collected for a long time.

We'll have another day or two here before the conference ends. Nobody is very excited except Cuban operations officers from headquarters such as Flores—the rest of us are increasingly absent at the beaches. When we finish I'll take a week off for fishing in the Caribbean with my father—then back to Montevideo to wait for my replacement. I am still uncertain about resigning when I return to Washington. I'll definitely separate from Janet but I'll have to find another job before resigning from the CIA.

Montevideo — 18 April 1966

The movement for constitutional reform has picked up surprising strength in recent months. The Ruralistas still are the most important group pushing for a strong, one-man executive but important Blancos and Colorados are joining the campaign. Some people, however, believe the problem of decision-making can be solved by retention of the collegiate executive but with all members from the same party. A one-man executive, many fear, would inevitably degenerate into some variety of dictatorship, as so much of Uruguayan and Latin American history suggests.

The PCU, through its political front, FIDEL, is conducting its own reform campaign—not for the one-man presidency because they know they'll be the first group suppressed when it degenerates. Their signature campaign is for a constitutional reform that would retain the weak executive, but provide for land reform and the nationalization of banking, foreign commerce, and the important industries still in private hands. They have no chance of winning, of course, but land reform is still the most important need in Uruguay. In the last census it was revealed that of the total rural population of 390,000 only about 3000—less than 1 per cent—

own some 70 per cent of the lands. If the rich ranchers pushing the Ruralista reform are successful, land reform will be as far away as ever under a one-man executive.

The Blancos' main problem is still inflation (13.6 per cent in January–March) and the ever-worsening economy. More IMF-dictated stabilization measures are coming up soon which will be unpopular and hurt the Blancos' electoral chances.

I have just finished one of the more disagreeable operations of my short career as a spy. Several months ago headquarters replied to one of my reports on the Yugoslav mission here—I had sent up to date information on all the mission personnel from the Foreign Ministry files—by proposing a recruitment. One of the attachés in the Yugoslav Embassy is an old personal acquaintance of DMHAMMER–1, a high-level defector of some years ago. The defector, now in his sixties, was the equivalent to the chief of administration in the Yugoslav Foreign Ministry and had provided excellent intelligence. In recent years he has been shuttled around the world making recruitment approaches to former colleagues—not all of them unsuccessful. Soon headquarters is going to retire him to pasture, but it was desired that he come to Montevideo for one last recruitment approach because the attaché is the code clerk.

Horton agreed and the headquarters' officer in charge came down to plan the approach with me. The AVENIN surveillance team established our target's daily routine, which involved a walk of several blocks from his apartment to the Embassy. He makes this walk in the morning, to home and back at lunchtime, and then again in the evening. The headquarters' officer brought the defector, a tall, handsome man with flowing white mane, over from Buenos Aires for the "chance" street encounter which would be on Boulevard España just a few blocks towards the beach from the Soviet Embassy.

As good fortune would have it, our target appeared right on time and the encounter, although lasting only about fifteen minutes, was very warm and animated. Our defector told the target that he was visiting Montevideo and Buenos Aires on a business trip from Paris where he now lives, and he invited the target to dinner the same day or the next. The attaché accepted the invitation for the following day, and we thought we might have a hit. We decided to use the same security precautions as on the first day, i.e. the headquarters officer and I on counter-surveillance in the street with Tito Musso,‡ the AVENIN team chief, near by in an escape vehicle.

The defector went to the elegant Aguila Restaurant the following night as agreed, but the attaché failed to appear. Although we suspected that the target had decided not to see our friend again—since the defector's unsuccessful recruitments are undoubtedly known to the Yugoslav service—we decided to arrange another street encounter just in case. This time the target simply told our defector that he understood and wanted nothing of the plan. He refused to speak more and continued on his way.

It was sad, almost pitiful, to see this very distinguished man lurking in the streets before pouncing on our target. The headquarters officer told me they have nothing more for him to do, and at his age he can scarcely learn another job, but they'll have to terminate his salary soon. He's now a U.S. citizen and will get some social security, but his last years are going to be difficult. No wonder most defectors either become alcoholics or suffer mental illness or both. Once they've been milked for all they're worth to us they're thrown away like old rags.

Montevideo — 25 April 1966

The Director of Immigration, Luis Vargas, has landed a blow on the East German commercial mission. He gave them the choice of requesting permanent residence or leaving with thirty days to decide. After a violent verbal encounter with the chief of the mission, Von Saher, he threw him out of his office and was about to start deportation proceedings when suddenly Von Saher and another officer of the mission, Spinder, returned to East

Germany. The other two East Germans, Kuhne and Vogler, have surprisingly requested permanent residence. They are still on their temporary permission, however, and as soon as that expires in a few months Vargas will deny the request for permanent residence.

One of my former agents has suddenly made much publicity in the newspapers. It's Anibal Mercader,‡ formerly AVBASK–1, who worked for us as a penetration agent of the Uruguayan Revolutionary Movement (MRO). Only a month or two after I arrived in Montevideo Mercader moved to Miami where he was employed in a bank. Now, two years later, he has disappeared with 240,000 dollars and is believed to be hiding in Buenos Aires with his wife, children and the money. This is a novel way to raise funds for the revolution, but maybe he was on the MRO's side all along. The FBI can figure this one out—we don't know him.

Montevideo — 12 May 1966

The PCU signature campaign on constitutional reform has been achieving considerable success—largely because the Party has drawn the CNT into the campaign. Through AVBUZZ–1, we have been trying to expose PCU use of organized labor for political ends. Yesterday his Plenary of Democratic Civic Organizations issued a "press statement" in which the leftist labor movement in Uruguay is denounced as an agent of international communism and the foreign conspiracy that has thrown itself into the political field in a confrontation, as equals, with the traditional democratic political parties over the constitutional reform issue. Because communists have been allowed to dominate the labor movement, the statement concludes, they have become a power among the powers of the state in a situation of "total subversion." I suppose AVBUZZ–1 knows his audience but sometimes he's embarrassing.

Commissioner Otero is back from the training course and is more enthusiastic than I've ever seen him. Reports from headquarters on his performance are very favorable. I was just able to get the airport photography operation started before he returned, but Otero is going to take care of the developing and printing work. As soon as possible Frank Sherno‡ will come back and will rearrange the police intelligence darkroom and order new equipment. I'm not sure how soon that will be because Sherno is spending almost all his time these days in Santiago, Chile where he and Larry Martin‡ are honeycombing a new building of the Soviet Mission with listening devices.

At the airport Sherno spent four days training the police officers who work with the immigration inspectors. Normally it takes a couple of hours to learn how to use this machine, but these men are special. I also arranged for a police courier to take the exposed film to Otero's office, and for the negatives and our prints to be sent over with the daily couriers from police headquarters. Such efficiency has its price, of course, and I've started monthly "expense" payments to the airport crew calculated on the numbers of passports and other travel documents photographed. It's as close to piecework incentive as I can get without calling it that, but without it the Recordak would just sit out there collecting dust. I also set up a travel watch list—simple at first to get them used to it—consisting of general categories of documents to photograph like the Soviets and satellites. Finally, I gave each of them a personal copy of the beardless Che Guevara photograph and asked that they imprint that face as deeply in their heads as possible. That won't be very deep, I'm afraid—these guys wouldn't recognize Che if he walked through with beard, beret, fatigues and automatic rifle.

The new police radio communications network is beginning to operate. Gradually the Public Safety mission technicians will expand it to the interior departments. The other day I got the frequencies from the Public Safety chief and we're getting our own receivers so that we can monitor the police frequencies.

Next week I'll give Otero a generous salary increase. While he was away I hooked Fontana,‡ his deputy, on the payroll but he doesn't want Otero to know—nor do I. From now on these people have got to concentrate on penetrating the Tupamaros, who seem to be the only organization following the "armed struggle" line right now. This would be like the Echeverria group in Quito, much more dangerous than the Soviet-line PCU, though nobody else in the station agrees with me on this. Otero, however, agrees to concentrate on the Tupamaros and somehow I've got to get him started on agent recruitments for intelligence so that the police won't have to resort to torture.

Montevideo — 19 May 1966

Headquarters turned down the suggestion that I speak to Borisov about the relationship between his wife and his chief. The affair goes on, however, and several times Horton has written nasty cables asking for reconsideration. The matter came to a head this week with the visit of the Chief of the Soviet Bloc Division, Dave Murphy,‡ and his deputy, Pete Bagley.‡ They're making the rounds of stations where there are Soviet missions. Between Conolly, the Soviet operations officer here, and Bagley the bad blood goes back many years and naturally there was a terrible scene of tempers. Although there were threats to get Conolly transferred back to headquarters, he's probably safe because Murphy and Bagley are already looking for a new Soviet operations officer for the Buenos Aires station. They were over there before coming here, and when they asked the Soviet operations officer to take them on a drive by the Soviet Embassy he couldn't find it. That was enough for his transfer.

Murphy wouldn't relent on the Borisov proposal. He's afraid Borisov would get violent and doesn't think a quick escape-route to avoid a fight is possible. I suppose he should know—he had beer thrown in his face a few years ago by a Soviet he was trying to recruit, and he still hasn't lived down the scandal.

Montevideo — 9 June 1966

Vargas has turned his attention to the Czech commercial mission and the Soviet *Tass* correspondent who is a KGB officer. When he called in the Czech commercial officers, the Consul, Franktisek Ludwig, came instead —insisting that the commercial officers belong to the Embassy mission and are subject to the Foreign Ministry rather than the Ministry of the Interior. Vargas would have none of it and told Ludwig that he would send the police for the commercial officers just as he had with the North Koreans if they refuse to appear. Ludwig protested, another violent argument followed, and afterwards Vargas began expulsion proceedings against Ludwig in the Foreign Ministry. Ludwig, however, returned quickly to Czechoslovakia before being ordered out. Perhaps he will return, perhaps not, but he was one of the two Czechs I put on the list for expulsion with the Soviets. I know him well from the diplomatic association. The commercial officers finally came to Vargas's office and requested permanent residence—to be denied by Vargas in due course.

Vargas insists that the Soviet diplomatic officers will be expelled as planned, but Heber wants to proceed slowly and save the Soviet expulsions for use against the unions. Meanwhile Vargas has required the *Tass* representative to seek permanent residence, but has allowed him a delay for decision.

We doubt if the *Tass* correspondent will seek permanent residence because he has been here for over five years and should be transferring home shortly. Even so, Vargas will deny the request if it is made.

Jack Goodwyn‡ has arranged for one of his AIFLD people to be named as the Uruguayan representative at the conference this month of the International Labor Organization in Geneva. The prestige appointment was made by the government, and Goodwyn's man is going as representative of the Uruguayan Labor Confederation‡ (CSU). The PCU and other leftists are squealing because the CSU is completely defunct and the CNT in any case represents 90–95 per cent of organized labor. The appointment is indicative of how the government increasingly sees the advantage of cooperation and even promotion of the AIFLD and related trade-union programs. Private industry is similarly well disposed.

In Washington the Agency has arranged with Joseph

Beirne,‡ President of the Communications Workers of America‡ (CWA), to have the CWA's training school at Front Royal, Virginia turned over to the AIFLD. This school has been used for years as the main center of the Post, Telegraph and Telephone Workers' International‡ (PTTI) for training labor leaders from other countries. Now the school will be the home for the AIFLD courses which until now have been held in Washington. Not a bad arrangement: seventy-six acres on the Shenandoah River where the isolation and control will allow for really close assessment of the students for future use in Agency labor operations. Also this year the AIFLD is starting a year-long university-level course in "labor economics" which will be given at Loyola University in New Orleans. AIFLD hasn't been exactly cheap: this year its cumulative cost will pass the 15 million dollar mark with almost 90 per cent paid by the U.S. government through AID and the rest from U.S. labor organizations and U.S. business. Since 1962 the annual AIFLD budget has grown from 640,000 dollars to almost 5 million dollars while the ORIT budget has remained at about 325,000 dollars per year. Millions more have been channeled through AIFLD in the form of loans for its housing programs and other social projects.

Montevideo — 24 June 1966

Vargas and Storace finally got the new procedure for issuing visas to nationals of communist countries approved by Heber and sent by the Foreign Ministry to all consular posts. The new procedure requires prior approval of all visas requested by citizens of communist countries. Approval procedure requires the Immigration Department and the Ministry of the Interior to check traces on the applicants with appropriate security offices —police and military intelligence—and none can be approved by the Foreign Ministry without prior approval in Immigration and Interior.

This is a very considerable victory because it opens the door to denials, delays and maneuvers that will harass and disrupt the Soviet and other communist missions here. In addition we will have plenty of time to get reports on visa applicants from headquarters and other stations, and we can influence decisions by preparing false reports. In order to protect himself Vargas asked me to channel our reports through military intelligence where he will initiate requests—he knows we are in regular contact with Colonel Zipitria.‡

Montevideo — 30 June 1966

I brought over Fred Houser‡ from the Buenos Aires station to serve as purchasing agent for the UAR code-room operation. As luck would have it the elderly couple had been thinking for some time of selling, and after a little negotiation we agreed on the equivalent of 35,000 dollars. The apartment is owned by a dummy corporation called Diner, S.A., and Houser simply purchased all the bearer shares of this company and the apartment was ours. I've got the shares locked up in my safe where they'll probably stay until the UAR gets another Embassy. Houser was perfect for the task because he has both U.S. and Argentine citizenship and easily passed as an Argentine in the purchasing operation. Now we are going to move in Derek Jones‡ and his family for cover. Jones is an old friend of Cassidy's‡ and has British as well as Uruguayan citizenship. As soon as they move in and our access is assured, Schroeder and Benefield will return to make a permanent installation of the microphone—possibly in the AID offices with a wire to the apartment but more probably directly from the apartment.

Montevideo — 3 July 1966

Yesterday the President of the Bank of the Republic and his re-financing team returned from the U.S. with a bundle of new sweets: postponement until December 1967 of payments totaling 47 million dollars that had been due to private New York banks before the end of this year; a new credit line of 22 million dollars from New York banks; a U.S. government stabilization loan of 7.5 million dollars; a 3-million-dollar loan for fertilizer from AID; a 1.5-million-dollar loan from the Inter-American Development Bank for economic development studies.

Thanks to the latest stabilization measures adopted, as a result of pressure from the IMF, in May, inflation in June was 14 per cent for a total cost-of-living increase during January–June of 36.3 per cent. As expected, the unions are making ever-more-ominous threats of new strikes while the Blancos are offering only the minimal increases provided for in the budget exercise of last year. Storace continues to be the government's chief negotiator but chances for averting another round of crippling strikes are very slight without substantial new benefits for the workers.

The PCU Congress is going to be held about the middle of next month and we have started a major propaganda campaign against it. The Party Congress, held only every few years, is the PCU's big event this year and they've invited a fraternal delegation from the Communist Party of the Soviet Union. Through Vargas I am trying to have the visas denied, but if this is impossible, as it now appears, we will hammer away at Soviet participation in the Congress as interference in Uruguayan politics.

Montevideo — 14 July 1966

Dominant factions of both the Colorados and the Blancos are now committed to a constitutional reform to return the country to the one-man presidency, although significant opposition continues in certain circles of both parties. Proponents of reform in the two parties are meeting regularly in order to agree on one constitutional reform project that will be approved in the Legislature and presented to the country by referendum. By agreeing on a joint reform pact the traditional parties will ensure that their version of reform will be the only one with a chance for adoption. Thus if voters reject the joint Colorado–Blanco project, which is unlikely, Uruguay will remain with the current collegiate system. The effect is to completely eliminate any possibility that the PCU reform project might be adopted, and the CNT has already denounced the Blanco–Colorado pact establishing a strong executive.

Meanwhile strikes are beginning again. The government employees' unions are asking for new benefits in the form of "loans"—in order to circumvent the constitutional prohibition of government salary increases before elections.

Montevideo — 27 July 1966

Storace was able to get a postponement of a government employees strike set for 21 July and of another strike in the Montevideo transport system that would have occurred today. Nevertheless municipal workers continue one-hour sitdowns per shift and tension is increasing over the "loans" and how the government can finance them.

In a secret meeting our proposals to deny visas to the Soviet faternal delegation to the PCU Congress next month were discussed by Storace and the Blanco NCG Councillors. It was decided, rightly I think, not to deny the visas but to use Soviet participation in the Congress as justification for action against the Soviet mission afterwards. Additionally, the government right now is studying a Soviet credit offer of 20 million dollars for purchase of Soviet machinery which can be repaid in non-traditional Uruguayan exports.

Don Schroeder and Al Benefield are back to improve the technical operation against the UAR code-room. By chance their trip has coincided with another change of the settings on the machine. From behind a screen they had built in our new apartment in the room above, and across a light well from the code-room, they were able to watch the code clerk making the new settings and to photograph him in the act. They don't even need the recordings now. The code clerk doesn't draw curtains or lower the blind. He couldn't make it much easier for us.

Montevideo — 10 August 1966

At last my replacement is here and I'll be able to leave by the end of the month. He is Juan Noriega,‡ a former Navy pilot, who recently finished his first tour at the Managua station where he was responsible for training the bodyguards for the President and the Somoza family.

Noriega got here just in time to see Uruguayan democracy hit another new low. All last week President Heber was out on his own protest strike—not against inflation but against his fellow Blanco NCG Councillors who were blocking certain of his military assignments. Several key assignments of strong military leaders by Heber, including the designation in June of General Aguerrondo‡ as Commander of the First Military Zone (Montevideo), had provoked rumors and speculation that Heber is planning a *coup* against his own government if the one-man executive is not adopted. We have no substantive reports to support this view, but Heber is definitely advancing strong, anti-communist officers into important positions. The NCG functioned without him until today, when he ended his strike and went on television to explain his actions.

Montevideo — 24 August 1966

I've turned over all my operations to Noriega and in a few days will be flying home. In two and a half years our station budget has gone up to almost a million and a half dollars while several new additions have been made to the station case officer complement. In a couple of weeks Bill Cantrell‡ arrives to work full-time with Otero's police intelligence department. Also due to arrive shortly is another non-official cover officer for operations against the PCU and related revolutionary organizations. This officer has been long-delayed in arriving—his cover was arranged by Holman with Alex Perry,‡ one of Holman's golfing companions, who is General Manager of the Uruguayan Portland Cement Co.,‡ a subsidiary of Lone Star Cement Corporation.‡ Approval from Lone Star headquarters was obtained last year also but many delays followed in finding the officer to fill the slot. Still another non-official cover officer is programed for Soviet operations.

What sharp contrast I feel on leaving compared to the excitement, optimism and confidence of that Sunday of arrival, watching the Pocitos crowd from O'Grady's apartment. While here, I've had another promotion and good fitness reports, but my sense of identification with the work and people of the CIA has certainly faded.

Holman's attitude and my deteriorating domestic situation have caused some hardening, perhaps even embitterment, but the more I see of this government the more urgent become the questions of whether and why we support such things.

Consider the new buses and trolleys for the Montevideo municipal transport system. When I went to the port to receive my car a few weeks after I arrived, I noticed a very large number of bright new blue and red vehicles parked ready to leave the port for service in the city's very crowded and over-taxed transport system. There were 124 of the buses and trolleys ordered in 1960 by Nardone, then NCG President, from Italy at a cost of several million dollars. They arrived at the end of 1963 but the Colorado-controlled municipal government was unable to pay the exorbitant unloading and customs costs levied by the Blanco-controlled port authority and customs administration. Because the Blancos resisted the political gain that would accrue to the Colorados when the buses and trolleys were put into service, even though they had been purchased by a Blanco administration, they sat in the port for seventeen months until the first group of four buses was released in May 1965. During that time they were sitting out of doors, deteriorating from the salt air and frequently stripped of parts and trimmings by vandals. Because of slow payment by the Blanco national government of the

Montevideo transport subsidy with which the customs and unloading charges would be paid, together with other red tape and slow paper-work, 104 of these units are still rusting in the port right now. Such subordination of the public interest to partisan political goals is not at all inconsistent with the rest of Colorado–Blanco governing in recent years. Uruguay, the model for enlightened democratic reforms, is the model of corruption and incapacity.

Part 4

Washington, D.C. — 15 September 1966

My assignment in headquarters is to the Mexico branch as officer in charge of support for operations against the Soviets in Mexico City. This first week, however, I'm making visits to arrange cover and other details. I'm keeping State Department cover, incidentally, and will ostensibly be assigned to the Research Assignments Office of the Bureau of Intelligence and Research. Central Cover Division still has that telephone system for cover calls and they gave me the usual two names that I'll use as my immediate superiors. The telephone number starts with DU–3, as all State Department numbers, but it rings in central cover in Langley.

I asked Jake Esterline,‡ the Deputy Division Chief, what the possibilities are that I'll be sent to Vietnam since all the divisions are being forced to meet a quota every three months for Vietnam officers. Jake said not to worry about it and he confirmed indirectly the general belief that most divisions are sending "expendables" to Vietnam. I wonder if I'd go if asked. With the special allowances most officers can save practically all their salary, and when the tour is up in eighteen months I'd have a little bundle to last until I find a new job. No, I've had all the counter-insurgency I want.

The Clandestine Services Career Panel also called me in for an interview. They told me I've been accepted in the Agency's new retirement program—meaning I can retire at age fifty with a handsome annuity. At thirty-one that seems like a long way off but it's nice to know you're in the most generous program. Yet not even this retirement program can keep me doing this same work for nineteen more years.

The officer I'm replacing on the Mexico branch is the same person who replaced me when I left Quito. He's being allowed to resign under a cloud because on the polygraph he wasn't able to resolve certain questions about finances in Quito. It's pretty sad because he's in his forties with a family to support and no job to enter. It makes me realize I'd better be careful about whom I discuss my doubts with—and I'd better get another job lined up before I start talking about anything.

Washington, D.C. — 4 October 1966

The headquarters organization of WH Division hasn't changed much from six years ago. In the executive offices, in addition to Bill Broe,‡ the Division Chief, and Jake Esterline, there are support officers for personnel, training, security and records. We have a Foreign Intelligence staff consisting of five officers, headed by Tom Polgar,‡ and a Covert-Action staff of four officers, headed by Jerry Droller, the famous "Mr. Bender" of the Bay of Pigs invasion. These staffs review projects and other documents from field stations that require division approval for funds and operational decisions. They also coordinate such matters with other headquarters offices outside WH Division.

The regional branches consist of the large Cuban branch with about thirty officers headed by Tom Flores, and smaller branches for Mexico, Central America, the Caribbean, the Bolivarian countries, Brazil, and the *cono sur* (Uruguay, Paraguay, Argentina and Chile). Altogether we have about 100 officers of the division at headquarters as opposed to a little over 200 officers at the stations. The division budget is about 37 million dollars for the financial year 1967—5.5 million dollars being spent in Mexico.

In the Mexico branch (WH/1) we are responsible for headquarters support to the vast and complicated operations of the Mexico City station. Our Chief, Walter J. Kaufman,‡ and our Deputy Chief, Joe Fisher,‡ head a team of about ten officers, each with responsibility for a different operational function at the station. Because of certain DDP office shifts in headquarters, our branch and the Cuban branch are temporarily being housed in the Ames building, one of several of the new high-rise office buildings in Rosslyn occupied by the Agency. Working just across the Potomac from Washington in many ways is more convenient than out in Langley, but the traffic coming and going is a disaster.

Joe Fisher gave me a briefing on the operations of the Mexico City station and I can understand why this station has the dubious reputation of too much bone and too little muscle. Operations are heavily weighted towards liaison (which rests on the unusually close relationship between Gustavo Diaz Ordaz,‡ the President of Mexico and Winston Scott,‡ the Chief of Station) and operational support (surveillance, observation posts, travel control, postal intercepts, telephone tapping). Badly lacking are good agent penetrations of the station's main targets: the Soviets, Cubans, local revolutionary organizations, and the Mexican government and political structure. The operations are dull because there are almost no political operations such as those we have in Ecuador and most Latin American countries. The reason is that the Mexican security services are so effective in stamping out the extreme left that we don't have to worry. If the government were less effective we would, of course, get going to promote repression.

My duties in support of the station Soviet/satellite section are to coordinate and process cases, which comes down to just keeping the paper moving. In some cases I have the action responsibility which I coordinate with the Soviet Bloc Division, and in others the SB Division has action responsibility and they coordinate with me. The operations leading into the target missions, but not dealing with an actual penetration or recruitment of target personnel, are generally my responsibility, whereas recruitments, provocations and more sensitive operations get SB Division action. In all cases we coordinate with each other. Telephone tapping, observation posts, surveillance teams, travel control, access agents and double-agent cases are my responsibility, but any operations to recruit or defect a Soviet would be handled by the Operations Branch, Western Hemisphere Office of Soviet Bloc Division (SB/O/WH). Satellite branches, e.g. SB/Poland, SB/Czechoslovakia, are the action or coordinating SB office for their particular countries. Happily for me, the SB Division people are responsible for compilation and updating of the SPR's (Soviet Personality Records) which is the very detailed analysis maintained on every Soviet of interest. Usually the information for the SPR is obtained over long periods of observation while the Soviet is assigned to a foreign mission. It includes his work habits, leisure activities, friends, personality, likes and dislikes, wife and family, health, vulnerabilities.

In the Mexico branch all the liaison and most of the support operations are under Charlotte Bustos‡ who has been in the branch for ten years and knows every detail of these complicated activities. Thus I only have to have a peripheral interest in these operations, even though they are targeted against the Soviets and satellites, because they are often used against many other targets. Nevertheless I look after the requirements related to the three observation posts overlooking the Soviet Embassy, together with the five or six houses we own on property next to it. There are also fifteen or twenty access agents, Mexicans and foreigners living in Mexico, who maintain personal relationships with the Soviets under one or another pretext, for whom I process operational approvals, name checks and other paper-work.

License-plate numbers of vehicles from the U.S., together with photographs of their occupants, are taken by the observation posts at the Soviet, satellite and Cuban embassies and forwarded to headquarters for additional investigation. The Office of Security obtains the names and other data from state office registration files and we forward to the FBI memoranda when the information involves U.S. citizens or foreigners resident in the U.S.

There are also a number of counter-intelligence cases involving U.S. citizens with known or suspected connections to Soviet or satellite intelligence operations in Mexico City. In some cases U.S. citizens were recruited while traveling in the Soviet Union and were given instructions for contact in Mexico City or some other city in Mexico. Usually in these cases the participants are considered to be under the control of the Soviets, or the satellite intelligence service as the case may be, as opposed to double-agent cases where control is supposed to be ours. One particularly complicated and lurid case came very close to home because it involved a sensitive experiment in cover.

About two years ago when Des FitzGerald was Chief of WH Division, he decided to make an experiment to see just how productive a group of CIA officers could be if they worked from a commercial cover office with very little direct contact with the CIA station under State cover in the Embassy. The experiment could have had a profound influence on the future of CIA use of State cover, which is the main type of cover used in countries where large U.S. military installations do not exist. Because the problem with non-official cover is that officers under official cover in embassies so often have to devote inordinate amounts of time to support of the non-official cover officers (security, communications, finance, reporting, name checks, etc.), non-official cover tends to be counter-productive. The experiment in Mexico City was to establish several officers under commercial cover with direct communication to headquarters and as little burden on the station as possible.

The LILINK‡ office—cryptograms for Mexico begin with LI—was set up for three operations officers under cover as import representatives. The Office of Communications designed a special cryptographic machine that looks like an ordinary teletype and that transmits and receives encoded messages via a line-of-sight infrared beam. The LILINK office is located in an office building that provides line-of-sight to a station office in the Embassy where similar transmitting and receiving gear is located. Secure communications exist without the need for personal meetings between the inside and outside officers. The LILINK office can also be hooked into the regular station communications system for direct communication with headquarters. Thus support duties for officers inside the Embassy have been reduced to the absolute minimum.

The experiment has been only partially successful. Our officers have had difficulties getting sufficient commercial representations to justify their cover, on the one hand, while station support for them has not been reduced as much as had been thought possible. The counter-intelligence case that I have inherited involved one of the officers of the LILINK office and led to the recent decision to close the office completely.

The officer in question has a serious drinking problem and was engaged in a liaison with a girl who was a clerk in the U.S. Embassy communications and records unit—not the station but the regular State Department unit. It was discovered that they had taken photographs and films of themselves and other couples in pornographic scenes, sometimes with the use of animals. One of the participants was a character of doubtful nationality who was connected with a combined Soviet–Polish espionage case in the U.S. several years ago but who had dropped out of sight.

When the photographs and films became known, along with the participation of the Soviet–Polish agent, headquarters decided to allow the officer to resign—a decision also taken by the State Department when advised of participation by their communications and records clerk. The other party—the ringer—again disappeared and the station has been vainly trying to locate him and the films. Neither our LILINK officer nor the girl were willing to discuss the matter prior to resignation and they have apparently floated off together to California. My job is now to coordinate the station investigation with the headquarters CI staff which handles the case with State Department security. No one has determined yet whether the Polish–Soviet agent recruited our officer or the girl—which is the main reason why LILINK is being closed. Already Arthur Ladenburg,‡ the junior officer under LILINK cover, has returned to headquarters.

In my dealings with the Counter-Intelligence staff on these sensitive cases I have discovered the solution to a seldom-discussed mystery in headquarters. During the weeks of study of the headquarters bureaucracy during formal training in 1959, there was never any mention of an Israeli branch or desk in the Near East Division. When someone once asked about this the instructor gave one of those evasive answers that suggests the question was indiscreet. Now I find that the Israeli branch is tucked away within the Counter-Intelligence staff so that its secrets are more secure from Israeli intelligence than they would be if the branch were in "open" view in the Near East Division. One of my CI staff contacts said that this is unfortunately necessary because of possible divided loyalties of Jewish employees of the Agency.

Washington, D.C. — 5 October 1966

At last I've found a small apartment and moved away from Janet. The strain of the moment of leaving the children was even worse than I'd expected—but I'll be going to see them regularly. With Janet I think I'm in for a long and bitter struggle. Leaving the children with her is going to take all the emotional control that I can muster—there simply is no way that I could obtain their custody in the face of tradition. Moreover, I don't want to create the kind of domestic fuss that will cause headquarters' security and cover people to worry. Better that I sacrifice some equity for the time being.

Washington, D.C. — 6 October 1966

This headquarters work is deadly—all I do is route paper for people to initial. But the truth is that it's not just boredom. Sooner or later things are bound to get worse. If I resign now I'll have to find a job in this wretched city, if only to be able to see my sons—and now Janet tells me she wants to wait a year or even longer for the divorce. What I would really like to do is go back to California to work, but then I would almost never see the children. If I don't resign I'll just stay bogged down in miserable work—and eventually I'll be assigned back to Latin America and be separated from the boys. Any way I look at it I get bad news.

But I'm going to resign from the CIA. I no longer believe in what the Agency does. I'm going to finish writing the résumé, advise Jake or Broe that I'm looking for another job, and then quit when something decent appears. I won't say exactly why I'm quitting, because if the truth were known my security clearance would be canceled and I would simply be released. I'll give "personal" reasons and relate them to my domestic situation. Otherwise I won't have an income while I look for another job.

The question is not whether, but when, to resign. I wonder what the reaction would be if I wrote out a resignation telling them what I really think. Something like this:

Dear Mr. Helms,‡

I respectfully submit my resignation from the Central Intelligence Agency for the following reasons:

I joined the Agency because I thought I would be protecting the security of my country by fighting against communism and Soviet expansion while at the same time helping other countries to preserve their freedom. Six years in Latin America have taught me that the injustices forced by small ruling minorities on the mass of the people cannot be eased sufficiently by reform movements such as the Alliance for Progress. The ruling class will never willingly give up its special privileges and comforts. This is class warfare and is the reason why communism appeals to the masses in the first place. We call this the "free world," but the only freedom under these circumstances is the rich people's freedom to exploit the poor.

Economic growth in Latin America might broaden the benefits in some countries but in most places the structural contradictions and population growth preclude meaningful increased income for most of the people. Worse still, the value of private investment and loans and everything else sent by the U.S. into Latin America is far exceeded year after year by what is taken out—profits, interest, royalties, loan repayments—all sent back to the U.S. The income left over in Latin America is sucked up by the ruling minority who are determined to live by our standards of wealth.

Agency operations cannot be separated from these conditions. Our training and support for police and military forces, particularly the intelligence services, combined with other U.S. support through military assistance missions and Public Safety programs, give the ruling minorities ever stronger tools to keep themselves in power and to retain their disproportionate share of the national income. Our operations to penetrate and suppress the extreme left also serve to strengthen the ruling minorities by eliminating the main danger to their power.

American business and government are bound up with the ruling minorities in Latin America—with the rural and industrial property holders. Our interests and their interests—stability, return on investment—are the same. Meanwhile the masses of the people keep on suffering because they lack even minimal educational facilities, health-care, housing, and diet. They could have these benefits if national income were not so unevenly distributed.

To me what is important is to see that what little there is to go around goes around fairly. A communist hospital can cure just like a capitalist hospital and if communism is the likely alternative to what I've seen in Latin America, then it's up to the Latin Americans to decide. Our only alternatives are to continue supporting injustice or to withdraw and let the cards fall by themselves.

And the Soviets? Does KGB terror come packaged of necessity with socialism and communism? Perhaps so, perhaps not, but for most of the people in Latin America the situation couldn't be much worse—they've got more pressing matters than the opportunity to read dissident writers. For them it's a question of day-by-day survival.

No, I can't answer the dilemma of Soviet expansion, their pledge to "bury" us, and socialism in Latin America. Uruguay, however, is proof enough that conventional reform does not work, and to me it is clear that the only real solutions are those advocated by the communists and others of the extreme left. The trouble is that they're on the Soviet side, or the Chinese side or the Cuban side—all our enemies.

I could go on with this letter but it's no use. The only real alternative to injustice in Latin America is socialism and no matter which shade of red a revolutionary wears, he's allied with forces that want to destroy the United States. What I have to do is to look out for myself first and put questions of principle to rest. I'll finish the résumé and find another job before saying what I really think.

Washington, D.C. — 7 October 1966

This morning at the Uruguay desk there was a celebration. The government at last expelled some Soviets—four left yesterday—and now the Montevideo press is speculating on whether the NCG will cancel a recent invitation to Gromyko to visit Uruguay. The expulsions are the result of Luis Vargas's‡ persistence—when I said farewell he told me that when the government unions started agitating again before the elections, the Soviets would suffer. (Before leaving Montevideo I wrote a memorandum recommending that Vargas be given a tourist trip to the U.S. as a reward if he finally got any thrown out, and it'll be small compensation since I never paid him a salary.)

The expulsion order was based on the same false report we prepared for Storace‡ last January, with minor updating, and it accuses the Soviets of meddling in Uruguayan labor, cultural and student affairs. Only four Soviets are being expelled right now because the cultural attaché and one other on the original list are on home leave in Moscow and their visa renewals can be stopped by Vargas. The other two not included in the expulsion are commercial officers and they will be expelled, according to Vargas, as soon as these four with diplomatic status leave.

The Montevideo station and others will be using the expulsions for a new media campaign against the Soviets. Our report for Storace ties the most recent wave of strikes to the PCU Congress in August and to the Soviet participation therein, together with the usual allegations of Soviet-directed subversion through the KGB, GRU and local communist parties. Proof of the authenticity of the subversion plan outlined in the report, according to Storace, are the eleven different strikes occurring in Uruguay at this moment. The Soviets were given forty-eight hours to leave Uruguay. Recently, too, the decree expelling the two remaining East Germans, Vogler and Kuhne, was approved. They were given thirty days to clear out. The gambit on Soviet expulsions may have worked against the unions last year but not this time. Strikes are spreading and the station reports street fighting between police and the strikers. Yesterday the Montevideo transport system, the banking system and many government offices were struck, while the CNT described Storace's report as an insult to the trade-union movement and pledged to continue the struggle against the government's economic policies—mainly the IMF-pressured reforms of the past year.

The pressure is showing again on President Heber. Last night in the NCG meeting he exchanged words with one of the Colorado Councillors who left the meeting but returned shortly to challenge Heber to a duel. The NCG meeting broke up as seconds were named, but later agreement was reached that the honor of neither man had been wounded. The seconds signed a document to that effect and the duel was canceled. What provoked the challenge was Heber's loss of temper when the Colorado Counselor reminded him that last year, two days before the first bank failed, Heber withdrew some 800,000 pesos from it.

Washington, D.C. — 15 October 1966

A curious cable from the Mexico City station started me thinking again. Kaufman gave me the action—it has the RYBAT indicator for special sensitivity—because it is a proposal for a CIA officer to be named as the U.S. Embassy Olympic attaché for the Games in 1968.

For some time the station has been reporting on the increasing number of coaches from communist countries contracted by the Mexican Olympic Committee to help prepare Mexican athletes for the Games. Six coaches from the U.S. were also contracted but they are outnumbered by the fourteen or fifteen communists—all of whom come from the Eastern European satellites. A little cold war is going on between several of the Americans and their communist colleagues, particularly in track and field, but the cold war chauvinism is really a degeneration of professional rivalry. The Embassy in Mexico City is involved because the USIS cultural section has given Specialist Grants to the Americans under the Educational Exchange Program. These grants supplement their salaries from the Mexican Olympic Committee and in several cases have been used as incentives to keep several coaches there who otherwise would have quit.

The station has also been reporting on the assignment of intelligence officers from the communist embassies to handle duties relating to preparations for the Olympics. These activities bring them into contact with a wide range of Mexican officialdom working on the Olympic Committee and the sports federations preparing the Mexican teams, and with an even larger number of people in the Olympic Games Organizing Committee preparing the Games themselves. The attraction to the communist intelligence services in using the Olympic Games as a vehicle for expanding operational potential among such a large group of government, business, professional and cultural leaders is obvious.

The cable from the Mexico City station describes a recent suggestion by the Ambassador, Fulton Freeman, that the CIA provide an officer to fulfil the duties as U.S. Embassy Olympic attaché. Such an assignment, the Ambassador reasons, would be logical since the CIA officer could keep an eye on the communist intelligence officers through the regular meetings of Olympic attachés—some of whom are private citizens resident in Mexico City while others are officers of diplomatic missions. The CIA officer would also be able to watch the communist Olympic attachés because his work with the Mexican Olympic Committee and the Organizing Committee would overlap with the communists. If the Agency is unable to provide an appropriate officer as Olympic attaché, the Ambassador will choose from among several possibilities he already has in mind, because increasing requests from the Mexicans to the Embassy on Olympic-related matters, together with the expected large influx of Americans for the Games, justifies an officer working full-time in the Olympics.

The Chief of Station, Win Scott,‡ comments in the cable that assigning an officer to this job would be advantageous to the station for a number of reasons. First, the station is handicapped because only three of its fifteen or twenty officers under Embassy cover are allowed to be placed on the diplomatic list. Such exclusion, a policy of successive Ambassadors, limits the mobility of station officers among the Diplomatic Corps, the governing (and only important) Mexican political party, the Foreign Ministry and other government offices, and professional organizations—all of which are important station targets for penetration and covert-action operations. An officer under Olympic cover would have ready access to these targets for spotting, assessment and recruitment of new agent assets in all these fields through his Olympic cover duties. Secondly, the officer would be close enough to monitor at least some of the communist Olympic attachés' more interesting developmental contacts as well as engaging them in direct personal relationships—right now practically no station officer has any direct personal relationship with communist counterparts. Thirdly, the station Olympics officer would be able to obtain information on the communist coaches training Mexican athletes, through the American coaches who already are beholden to the Embassy because of their Specialist Grants. The Chief of Station adds in the cable that the Olympic officer will have a separate office in the Embassy and will operate as an extension of the Ambassador's office—having of necessity a very discreet contact with the station.

I've ordered the files on past Olympics from Records Integration. It would be an exciting job.

Washington, D.C. — 25 October 1966

I've reviewed the files on operations connected with past Olympics—we've been in every Olympics since the

Soviets appeared in Helsinki in 1952. Melbourne, Rome, Tokyo—and now Mexico City. Provocations, defections, propaganda, recruitment of American athletes for Olympic Village operations, Winter Games and Summer Games—all the way with CIA.

I've written a memorandum to Bill Broe‡ and to Dave Murphy,‡ Chief of the Soviet Bloc Division, recommending approval of the Mexico City station's proposal. In my memorandum I said I might qualify to be the Ambassador's Olympic attaché as I have always been a great athlete—albeit in fantasy. I was only half serious and I thought they would laugh, but Murphy is interested. Broe was Chief of Station in Tokyo during the Olympics in 1964 and he's not too enthusiastic. But I sent another cable back to Mexico City telling them that the proposal is approved in principle and that headquarters will discuss with the State Department and look for a candidate. Kaufman says I've got better than a fifty-fifty chance of going. I think I'll postpone that resignation—maybe in the Olympics I could make a connection for a new job. Tonight I'll do some push-ups and maybe run around the block. They say Mexico City is a great place to live.

The other day a RYBAT cable arrived from Mexico City showing how the system works there. The Chief of Station advised that Luis Echeverria,‡ the Minister of Government (internal security), told him he has just been secretly selected as the next Mexican President. Echeverria is now the famous *tapado* (covered one) whom the top inner circle of the ruling party, the Revolutionary Institutional Party (PRI), select well in advance to be the next president. Although Echeverria said it in a somewhat indirect manner, the Chief of Station has no doubt that he was intentionally being let in on the secret—even though the elections won't be held until 1970.

The information in the cable is extremely sensitive, not so much because it's a secret but because presidential succession in Mexico is supposedly a decision made by a broad representation within the PRI. For years leaders of the PRI have been denying that presidential succession is determined secretly by the incumbent, ex-presidents, and a few other PRI leaders—they even have a nominating convention and all the appearances of mass participation. The Mexico branch Reports Officer sent a "blue stripe" report (very limited distribution) over to the White House and the State Department on Echeverria's good news.

Washington, D.C. — 1 December 1966

In last Sunday's elections in Uruguay the Blanco-Colorado constitutional-reform pact was adopted, and the Colorados won the presidency—it'll be General Gestido who resigned from the NCG last April to campaign for reform. The Colorados will also control the legislature so there will be no more excuses for lack of action. The PCU political front, FIDEL, made considerable gains. They won six seats in the legislature on 70,000 votes (5.7 per cent of the total) reflecting a gain from 41,000 votes (3.5 per cent) in 1962 and 27,000 votes (2.6 per cent) in 1958 when the Blancos took over. During these eight years the PCU has more than doubled its percentage of the vote and tripled its representation in the legislature.

Heber and Storace didn't fare very well. They were running together, Heber for President and Storace for Vice-President, and among Blanco lists they came in a distant third with only 83,000 of the over one million votes cast. Yesterday Heber decided to take a two-month vacation—his term as NCG President has only three months left—and Luis Vargas resigned as Director of Immigration.

It is unlikely that any additional action against the Soviets, East Germans or others will be taken, but the record for expulsions during the eleven months since we started working with Storace and Vargas is impressive: six Soviets, three North Koreans, two East Germans, and one Czech.

Washington, D.C. — 5 December 1966

My assignment to the Mexico City station under Olympic cover is still hopeful although there have been several delays caused by consultations between the station and the Ambassador and between headquarters and the department. Meanwhile I've embarked on a reading program that reveals Mexico to be just as interesting as Ecuador and Uruguay—perhaps more so because of the terrible failures of its violent movements for social justice.

As in Ecuador and other Latin American countries, Mexico had its "liberal revolution" during the nineteenth century, but here too it served mainly to curtail power of the Catholic Church. By the time the Revolution broke out in 1910, ending thirty-five years of dictatorship, over three-quarters of total investment in Mexico was in foreign hands, with U.S.-owned capital valued at close to one billion dollars. Not surprisingly, then, the two main forces in the 1910–20 Revolution were agrarian reform and economic nationalism, the latter of increasing importance after U.S. military occupation of Veracruz in support of the side seeking a return to pre-1910 conditions. However, struggles over the degree and immediacy of implementing the Revolution's goals produced a civil war that claimed over a million lives, perhaps two million, by the time it ended in the 1920s. Many of the Revolution's leaders were among its victims.

Most of the nationalist and agrarian ideals of the Mexican Revolution are embodied in the 1917 Constitution which is still in effect today. Specific implementation of the Constitution's principles, however, was left for later state and federal laws—what amounted to a gradualist approach that would allow for postponement and negotiations in the short run and major change in emphasis in the long run.

From the beginning of the Revolution, agrarian reform was considered as the basis for all other social and economic change, although there was plenty of disagreement over the degree and speed of land redistribution. The dominant theme was backward looking:

revindication for land deprivation of peasants caused by prior patterns of concentration. Possession of the land by peasants, it was thought, would increase production and above all would lead to dignity, the rural dignity that would serve as the foundation for the new sense of nationality, as the Revolution reversed the habit of exalting foreign things while denigrating things Mexican. Although private landholdings rose in number after redistribution began, the dominant institutional pattern for agrarian reform was the *ejido*: the communal lands owned by a village and divided among the peasants who could alienate their parcels only with great difficulty. The *ejido,* then, was in theory a return to the pre-Reforma tenure that was eliminated by the Constitution of 1857.

Agrarian reform proceeded slowly at first, restricted mainly to the "legitimizing" of land seizures made during the years of civil war. But in the late 1920s expropriations and redistribution accelerated, reaching a zenith during the presidency of Lázaro Cárdenas (1934–40) who distributed over forty million acres that affected more than two million people. Presidents who followed Cárdenas continued to redistribute land, although on a reduced level, while persistent mass rural poverty provoked criticism and allegations of failure in this most fundamental of the Revolution's programs.

In addition to being the high point for land redistribution, the Cárdenas régime is also considered to be the culmination of the Revolution's goal to recover industry and natural resources from foreign control. Nationalization of the American and British-owned petroleum industry in 1938 is the best-known of Cárdenas's applications of the 1917 Constitution's provisions for nationalist economic policies. World War II brought Mexico and the U.S. closer together again, and for many observers the original agrarian and nationalist drives ended during this period.

During the government of Miguel Alemán in 1946–52 foreign capital was invited back to Mexico and has been increasing steadily in spite of a "mexicanization" program requiring 51 per cent Mexican ownership of important firms. Alemán and the governments that followed channeled new investment into major mining and manufacturing industries as well as agriculture, irrigation, electric power and tourism. By 1965 foreign investment in Mexico had grown to 1.75 billion dollars, 80 per cent of which pertained to the hundreds of U.S. companies operating there. Also, since World War II, the Mexican government has constructed thousands of miles of roads, hundreds of new schools, and many social overhead projects such as potable water systems. By 1965 the coefficient of investment was up to 18.9 per cent following an average GDP growth rate during 1961–65 of 6.6 per cent, equivalent to 3 per cent *per capita.* Mexico's diversified exports (coffee, cotton, sugar, wheat, corn, fruits, sulphur, precious metals) rose in value an average of 8.5 per cent annually during the same period.

At first glance this would appear to be an optimistic situation with the land in the hands of the peasants and high agricultural and industrial growth rates. Surely the faster industry grows, the more resources will become available for investment in rural projects like irrigation and transportation, and in social overhead like education, housing and medical services. But a closer examination reveals the uneven nature of post-World War II developments in Mexico and lends credence to the view that the original goals of social justice and equitable distribution of income disappeared following the Cárdenas régime.

The central problem is similar to much of the rest of Latin American development: the emergence of a capital-intensive modern sector that provides employment for only a relatively small portion of the labor force—in the case of Mexico about 15 per cent. In spite of rapid expansion the modern sector seems unable to absorb a greater portion of the workers, leaving the vast majority bogged down in the primitive sector of unemployed and marginally employed, subsistence farming and menial services. Perhaps the best illustration of Mexico's uneven growth is found in the way its average *per capita* income of 475 dollars—slightly higher than the general Latin American average—is distributed. According to the Inter-American Development Bank the poorer half of Mexico's population receives only about 15 per cent of the total personal income—averaging about twelve dollars per person per month.

According to the United Nations Economic Commission for Latin America,[1] the 15 per cent of national income received by the lower-income 50 per cent of the population is less than is received by the same group in almost all the other countries of Latin America. In Mexico the poorest 20 per cent of the population receives only 3.6 per cent of total national income —lower than the comparable amount for El Salvador, Costa Rica and Colombia. The poorest 10 per cent of the Mexican population, who number some 4.2 million persons, receive an average income of only about five dollars per month. Moreover, both the shares of the poorest 20 per cent and the lower 50 per cent of the population have declined between 1950 and 1965—and the absolute value of the income of the poorest 20 per cent has also declined. Clearly the poor in Mexico have been getting poorer despite near-boom conditions in agriculture and industry.

What groups, then, has the Mexican government favored during the period since World War II? According to the same ECLA data, the high 5 per cent of the Mexican income scale receives almost 26 per cent of the national income—although the share of this group has fallen from about 33 per cent since 1950. The other 45 per cent of the top half of the population has increased its share and is now receiving about 55 per cent of the national income. In conclusion, ECLA reports that there is little indication of change in Mexican income distribution since 1950 except that the poor are somewhat worse off and the high 5 per cent has yielded some of its share while retaining over a quarter of the national income.

What to think about this disproportionate income distribution—an average *per capita* annual income of

---

1. *La Distribucion del Ingreso en America Latina,* Nacíones Unidas, New York, 1970, based on official Mexican statistics of the mid-1960s.

475 dollars yet with half the population receiving only about 150 dollars a year. Or put another way, the richest 20 per cent of the Mexican population receives about 55 per cent of national income whereas the poorest 20 per cent receives less than 4 per cent. Never mind material incentives and creation of internal markets—the Mexican Revolution, if it ever moved towards social justice, is clearly serving minority interests today.

Washington, D.C. — 10 December 1966

The more I learn of Mexico, the more the Mexican Revolution appears as empty rhetoric, or, at best, a badly deformed movement taken over by entrepreneurs and bureaucrats. For the decisions that have allowed such grossly out of proportion income distribution to develop have been brought about by the single political organization that evolved on the winning side during the Revolution and that became the umbrella for attracting the diverse sectors of Mexican society into the "revolutionary process." This party, now called the Revolutionary Institutional Party (PRI), has exercised a one-party dictatorship since the 1920s.

The PRI is a curious institution both because of its long monopoly of power and because of its heterogeneous composition. Theoretically it consists of three sectors, each embodied in a mass organization: the peasant sector in the National Campesino Confederation (CNC), the workers' sector in the Mexican Workers' Confederation (CTM) and the popular (middle class) sector in the National Confederation of Popular Organizations (CNOP). Each of the mass organizations has its own national, state and local bureaucratic structures that participate in the corresponding national, state and local PRI bureaucracy, lobbying for political decisions favorable to its interests. In reality, however, decisions of importance, including the naming of candidates for office, are usually made by the PRI headquarters in Mexico City, which is headed by a seven-man executive committee, often with participation by the Ministry of Government (internal security) or the Presidency. Lobbying by the mass organizations and the local PRI organizations assists in the decision-making process, but the direction of the process is clearly from the top down.

The PRI's effective use of its three mass organizations and its internal system of democratic centralism has enabled it to make good its claim to a monopoly on interpreting the goals and executing the programs of the Revolution. Advantages accruing from this success are political stability since the 1920s and the attractive climate for foreign investment since World War II. Efficiency has also been high inasmuch as the legislature and the judiciary are subordinate to the executive and under PRI control anyway. Suppression of the political opposition, especially communists and other Marxists, has been easy and effective whenever necessary.

Such political opposition that appears from time to time is still treated by the PRI in the traditional manner. First, an attempt is made to bring the opposition group into some form of inclusion or cooperation with the PRI itself. If this fails a close watch is maintained until the right moment arrives for repression. One recent example of the first method was the straying by former President Cárdenas in 1961 when he became a leader of the newly-formed and extreme-left National Liberation Movement (MLN). By 1964, after public attacks against him by PRI leaders, Cárdenas returned to the fold and supported the official PRI candidate for President—causing a serious split in the MLN. Another example was the Independent Campesino Confederation (CCI) set up in the early 1960s as a rival to the PRI's CNC. The CCI was led by Alfonso Garzon, a former CNC leader, and had a strong following with a radical agrarian program. A combination of government repression of the CCI and overtures to Garzon to return to the PRI succeeded in obtaining renewed support for the PRI by Garzon. Meanwhile Garzon caused a split in the CCI by trying to expel its communist leaders, who nevertheless continued active in the branch of the CCI they controlled.

Because the challenge to the PRI's leadership of the Revolution must obviously come from the left, both ideologically and in terms of specific social and economic programs, the PRI shows the least tolerance towards leftist groups that refuse to cooperate. Repression is regular and punishment is severe. A recent example is the jailing in 1964 of Ramón Danzos Palomino, leader of the pro-communist branch of the CCI, who campaigned for the presidency that year even though his communist-backed electoral organization was not allowed to be officially registered. His effectiveness in creating a following, however, led to the PRI decision to put him away for a while. Usually, the offense for undesirable opposition political activities is "social dissolution" of one kind or another.

The PRI, then, has its own version of democratic centralism and transmission belts through mass organizations. Political opposition that can be controlled or co-opted is tolerated, in fact encouraged, while adamant opposition is kept well in check through heavy-handed repression. Civil liberties are commensurate with toleration of dissent, variable from time to time, and public-information media are well trained in self-censorship. Prudence suggests working within the system in Mexico, and PRI slogans, not surprisingly, are coined on the themes of "social peace" and "national unity."

The seemingly simple questions cannot be avoided: if the PRI represents the campesinos, workers and popular classes as its mass organizations and propaganda would have them believe, how then has it allowed the business, industrial and professional leaders to corner such an inordinate share of the national income? Can it be that the PRI leaders themselves aspire to enter that top 5 per cent through their political activities? Or, perhaps more accurately, is not the PRI—and the revolutionary process earlier—simply the instrument of the industrial, professional and business communities and the servant of the top 5 per cent? Why, finally, are the supposed beneficiaries of the Mexican Revolution still the most deprived some fifty years after the fighting ended in victory?

Washington, D.C. — 15 December 1966

The Mexico and Cuba branches have returned to headquarters from the Ames building, which makes meetings with colleagues from the Soviet Bloc Division easier, but the daily routine involved in keeping paper moving is heavy and uninspiring. Reading the intelligence reports and the daily cable and dispatch correspondence between headquarters and the Mexico City station, and the operational files as well, reveals the same basic counter-insurgency approach as in Montevideo, Quito and other WH stations. We prop up the good guys, our friends, while we monitor carefully the bad guys, our enemies, and beat them down as often as possible.

In Mexico the government keeps our common enemy rather well controlled with our help—and what the government fails to do, the station can usually do by itself. The operational environment, then, is friendly even though the enemy is considerable in size, dangerous in intent and sensitive in its close proximity to the United States. The enemy in Mexico:

The Popular Socialist Party (PPS)

The largest of several extreme-left political groups is the PPS with an estimated membership of about 40,000. Founded in the late 1940s by Vicente Lombardo Toledano, who had reorganized Mexican labor into the Mexican Workers' Confederation (CTM) during the Cárdenas presidency, the PPS is the only communist party recognized by the Mexican government. During the transitional government following Cárdenas and preceding Alemán—the World War II years—Lombardo was eased aside as leader of the PRI labor sector, and during the years that followed he built the PPS into one of the largest Marxist parties in the Western Hemisphere. He was also the President of the Latin American Labor Confederation (CTAL), the regional affiliate of the Prague-based World Federation of Trade Unions (WFTU), until the CTAL was disbanded in 1964.

Although for CIA purposes the PPS is considered a

communist party, it is unorthodox because of its local character and autonomy, both features resulting from the forceful, caudillo-like personality of Lombardo. Nevertheless, it supports Soviet foreign policy and Marxist solutions to national problems while disdaining violent revolution for gradualist, peaceful tactics. It is strongly opposed to U.S. investment in Mexico and to the close ties between the Mexican and the U.S. governments.

The odd PPS autonomy in the international context is confused by its cooperative, though limited, support for the PRI at home. Thus the PPS is perhaps the best example of the PRI policy of allowing a controlled opposition to operate in order for dissidents to be attracted to the submissive opposition instead of to the uncompromising groups. Since the 1958 elections, for example, the PPS has publicly supported the PRI presidential candidates while running its own congressional candidates.

The PPS receives corresponding support from the PRI in several ways, apart from simply being allowed to operate. Mexican law requires 75,000 signatures for a political party to be registered officially for elections. Although the PPS membership is far below the required number, the PRI allows the fiction to exist that the PPS is entitled to registration. As a result, in the 1964 elections the PPS increased its representation in the Chamber of Deputies from one to ten, taking advantage of the new electoral law providing for special deputies' seats for minority parties. These ten seats of the PPS constitute 5 per cent of the Chamber's seats although the PPS polled less than 1 per cent of the votes. It is common belief, moreover, that the PPS receives a direct financial subsidy from the PRI although good intelligence on the subject is lacking.

The PPS has a youth wing, Juventud Popular, which has two to three thousand members and exerts some influence in the two main Mexican student organizations: The National Federation of Technical Students (FNET) and the University Student Federation (FEU). The PPS has supported the frequent student demonstrations this year although with care not to promote revolutionary violence.

The principal front work of the PPS is concentrated in the General Union of Workers and Peasants (UGOCM) formed by Jacinto Lopez, former leader of the CNC which is the PRI campesino front. The UGOCM has an estimated membership of 20,000, mostly campesinos, and is affiliated with the WFTU. With major strength in the state of Sonora, the UGOCM has sponsored land invasions by peasants but with little government repression—an indication of PRI tolerance and use of its controlled opposition. Lopez himself, although a defector from the PRI, was elected to the Chamber of Deputies in 1964 and is generally considered to be the PPS number two man. He too is a gradualist and clear beneficiary of working-within-the-system.

In spite of its tactical successes the PPS is considerably troubled by factionalism on the left. Recently a "leftist" PPS group led by Rafael Estrada Villa split from the PPS and took the name National Revolutionary Directorate (DNR). Estrada continues as a PPS Deputy although the DNR leans towards the more militant Chinese line.

The PPS, then, is the approved watering-hole on the left for those who find the PRI too moderate. Its voter attraction is slight, almost negligible, and in the PRI's eyes its function is tolerable as long as the PPS follows the rules. The PRI makes a few rewards available to keep the PPS leadership bought off—like the ten Deputies' seats—and the only danger is in the PPS's condition of unwilling gestator of dangerous factions such as the Estrada group.

The Communist Party of Mexico (PCM)

Although operating in Mexico since the 1920s, the PCM has never been able to attract a numerous membership—now estimated at about 5000, mostly from rural and urban lower middle and lower classes. The PCM also includes some professionals, intellectuals and cultural leaders, most notably the muralist David Alfaro Siqueiros, but for lack of members the PCM has never been able to register officially for elections.

The PCM closely follows the Soviet line with main emphasis on the legal struggle, leaving armed action for specific tactical purposes. Its domestic programs are founded on anti-U.S. nationalism while its foreign policy supports positions of the Soviet Union and defense of the Cuban revolution. Although party activities are seriously hampered by a lack of funds, the PCM manages to keep open a bookstore and to publish a weekly newspaper, *La Voz de Mexico*.

The party's youth wing, the Communist Youth of Mexico, has only about 500 members but exerts considerable influence in the important student organization, the National Center of Democratic Students (CNED), and in the colleges of law, political science and economics of the National University in Mexico City. Like the PPS, the PCM has supported the student protest demonstrations this year but is careful not to advocate violent revolutionary solutions publicly.

Until recently the PCM has been fairly successful in penetrating the petroleum workers', railway workers' and teachers' unions. However, PRI repression through the government of the PCM leaders of the petroleum and railway workers' strikes in 1958 has removed much of their influence from these two important unions. The party's influence in the National Union of Education Workers (SNET), an affiliate of the WFTU, remains.

In peasants' organizations the PCM has also been successful. In 1963 the party, together with the MLN and a peasant organization led by ex-PRI leader Alfonso Garzón, formed the Independent Campesino Confederation (CCI). When Garzón broke with the PCM later, the PCM leaders of the CCI under Ramón Danzos Palomino retained control of one CCI faction.

Also in 1963 the PCM, with the CCI and the faction of the MLN it controlled, formed the People's Electoral Front (FEP) in order to run candidates in the 1964 elections. The PRI, however, did not allow the FEP to register but Danzos obtained about 20,000 write-in votes in spite of the FEP ban. Not long after the elections, Danzos, who was uncompromising and hostile to the PRI, was arrested and he remains in jail today. Government repression of the PCM, the FEP and the PCM-controlled faction of the CCI continues, and the movement is kept well in hand. The repression itself, however, is indicative of PRI worry over PCM influence among the poverty-bound peasant masses.

The National Liberation Movement (MLN)

The MLN was formed at the Latin American Conference for National Sovereignty, Economic Emancipation and Peace held in Mexico City in 1961. Former President Lázaro Cárdenas, who headed the Conference, also became one of the leaders of the MLN. The idea behind the MLN was to form a political movement dedicated to extreme-left causes that would transcend the ideological differences then separating the established parties, like the PPS and the PCM, and independents.

Under Cárdenas the MLN had considerable initial success in uniting Marxists of many shades in its program of promoting Mexican nationalism, support for the Cuban revolution, denunciation of U.S. imperialism, freedom for political prisoners, redistribution of wealth, socialization of the land and similar causes. But in 1962 Vicente Lombardo Toledano, unable to control the MLN in his accustomed manner, withdrew the PPS from the MLN. Then in 1964 Cárdenas himself withered under PRI attacks and that year supported the PRI presidential candidate instead of Danzos Palomino who was running the "illegal" campaign of the People's Electoral Front with PCM and MLN support. Dissension over the FEP electoral campaign started a decline in the MLN although the Mexican delegation to the Tri-Continental Conference in Havana was headed by an MLN leader.

The semi-official journal of the MLN, *Politica*, continues to be published under the direction of Manuel Marcue Pardinas, formerly one of the intellectual leaders of the PPS. Partly because of Cárdenas's participation in the MLN, the PRI has not yet mounted really serious measures against it. Nevertheless, some MLN leaders come under regular fire from the PRI as a result of government repression against the PCM, FEP and CCI.

The Bolshevik Communist Party of Mexico (PCBM)

Some four splinter communist parties follow the Chinese line of which the PCBM is the most important. However, it is not thought to have more than a few hundred members.

The People's Revolutionary Movement (MRP)

Of three Trotskyist groups, the MRP is the most important although several of its leaders, including Victor Rico Galan, have been jailed this year for agitating in peasant communities. With Rico Galan out of action the MRP has started to decline.

The Soviet Mission

The Soviets have their largest mission in Latin America (not counting Cuba) in Mexico City with twenty-five diplomatic officials and about an equal number serving in administrative, trade, press and other non-diplomatic capacities. Of these approximately fifty officers, some thirty-five are known or suspected intelligence officers (about twenty-five KGB to ten GRU) which is a rather higher ratio of intelligence officers than the Latin American average for the Soviets. Both the KGB and the GRU missions are believed to have multiple-purpose programs, including penetration of the U.S. Embassy and the CIA station and intelligence collection on U.S. military installations in the south-west and western U.S. An unusual number of Soviet intelligence officers in Mexico City have served in the Soviet missions in Washington or New York prior to their Mexican assignments, and they are thought to be continuing to work against U.S. targets from their new vantage-points.

Additionally, the Soviet intelligence missions are also thought to be active in penetration operations against the PRI and the Mexican government through their "agents of influence" programs, in liaison and support for Mexican and Central American communist parties, propaganda, and the usual friendship and cultural societies.

The Czechoslovakian Mission

There are eight Czech diplomats and four or five others, of whom three are known and two are suspected intelligence officers. This intelligence mission is also thought to be targeted against the U.S. Embassy and against objectives in the U.S. proper. As elsewhere they are considered to be an auxiliary service of the Soviets, even though they engage in operations of their own peculiar interest such as the cultural exchange and friendship society programs.

The Polish Mission

The Poles have six diplomats and five non-diplomatic personnel. About half are known or suspected intelligence officers, and their functions are similar to the Soviet and Czech officers although they seem to be more active among Polish *émigrés* and other foreigners resident in Mexico City.

The Yugoslav Mission

There are also six Yugoslav diplomats and several additional officials. Three intelligence officers are in the mission and their operations, which are independent of the other communist intelligence services, are directed towards penetration of the local Yugoslav *émigré* community. U.S. targets are also on their list as are the Soviets, Poles and Czechs.

The Cuban Mission

The only Cuban diplomatic mission in Latin America is in Mexico City. They have thirteen diplomatic officials and an equal number of non-diplomatic personnel. Over half the officers in the mission are known or suspected intelligence officers. The main Cuban target is penetration of the Cuban exile communities in Mexico and Central America, but they also have operations in

Mexico City designed to penetrate the exile communities in the U.S., particularly Miami.

Other Cuban intelligence operations are for propaganda and support to the revolutionary organizations of their liking in Mexico and Central America. Traditionally, moreover, the Cuban mission in Mexico City supports the travel of revolutionaries from all over Latin America and the U.S. through the frequent Cubana Airlines flights between Mexico City and Havana.

The New China News Agency (NCNA)

The Chinese communists have had an NCNA office in Mexico City for several years. However, last month the three Chinese officials were expelled through station liaison operations on the grounds that they were engaged in political activities. The Chinese had, in fact, been using the NCNA office for propaganda and support to pro-Chinese revolutionary organizations in Mexico and Central America.

Central American Exiles

Mexico has traditionally been a haven for political exiles from Central American countries including communists and other extreme leftists. Several Central American parties, including the Guatemalans, maintain liaison sections in Mexico City in order to keep lines open to the Soviets, Cubans and others. They operate semi-clandestinely for the most part in order to avoid repression from the Mexican government.

Washington, D.C. — 20 December 1966

Because of the strategic importance of Mexico to the U.S., its size and proximity, and the abundance of enemy activities, the Mexico City station is the largest in the hemisphere. Altogether the station has some fifteen operations officers under State Department cover in the Embassy political section, plus about twelve more officers under assorted non-official covers outside the

Embassy. In addition, a sizeable support staff of communications officers, technical services, intelligence assistants, records clerks and secretaries bring the overall station personnel total to around fifty.

Liaison Operations

Dominating the station operational program is the LITEMPO‡ project which is administered by Winston Scott,‡ the Chief of Station in Mexico City since 1956, with the assistance of Annie Goodpasture,‡ a case officer who has also been at the station for some years. This project embraces a complicated series of operational support programs to the various Mexican civilian security forces for the purpose of intelligence exchange, joint operations and constant upgrading of Mexican internal intelligence collection and public security functions.

At the top of the LITEMPO operation is the Mexican President, Gustavo Diaz Ordaz,‡ who has worked extremely closely with the station since he became Minister of Government in the previous administration of Adolfo Lopez Mateos‡ (1958–64) with whom Scott had developed a very close working relationship. Scott has problems, however, with Luis Echeverria, the current Minister of Government, who is generally unenthusiastic and reluctant in the relationship with the station. Scott fears that Echeverria is following Diaz Ordaz's orders to maintain joint operations with the station only under protest and that the current happy situation may end when Echeverria becomes President in 1970.

Scott's chummy relationship with Diaz Ordaz none the less has its problems. In 1964 Fulton Freeman went to Mexico City as Ambassador to crown a Foreign Service career that had started in the same Embassy in the 1930s. He is expected to retire after the 1968 Olympic Games. At the time of his assignment to Mexico City Freeman's expectations of meaningful diplomatic relations with Diaz Ordaz collided with the President's preference for dealing with Scott, and Freeman was relegated to protocol contacts with the President while his diplomatic talents focused on the Foreign Minister. The problem of who would deal with the President was confused somewhat by the Ambassador's insistence, not long after arrival, on a detailed briefing about the station operational program, which Scott refused. Eventually both Scott and the Ambassador visited the White House, where President Johnson settled matters according to the wishes of the Agency and of his friend Diaz Ordaz. Scott continued, of course, to work with the President and the Ambassador never got the full briefing he had demanded. Since then the relations between Scott and the Ambassador have warmed, but the Ambassador forbids any station operations directed aginst the Mexican Foreign Ministry.

While Scott frequently meets the President and the Minister of Government, two non-official cover case officers handle the day-to-day contact with the chiefs of the security services subordinate to Echeverria. One of these officers is a former FBI agent who worked in the legal attaché's office in the Mexico City Embassy—the legal attaché is usually the FBI officer in an American embassy. The FBI officer had left the FBI to come with the station, but pains have been taken to conceal his CIA employment in order to avoid the bad blood that would result from the CIA's "stealing" of an FBI officer. The two non-official cover officers are the equivalent of an AID Public Safety mission but in Mexico this function is performed secretly by the station in deference to Mexican nationalist sensitivities—as is the case in Argentina. Through the LITEMPO project we are currently providing advice and equipment for a new secret communications network to function between Diaz Ordaz's office and principal cities in the rest of the country. Other joint operations with the Mexican security services include travel control, telephone tapping and repressive action.

The station also prepares a daily intelligence summary for Diaz Ordaz with a section on activities of Mexican revolutionary organizations and communist diplomatic missions and a section on international developments based on information from headquarters. Other reports, often relating to a single subject, are passed to Diaz Ordaz, Echeverria and top security officials. These reports, like the daily round-up, include information from station unilateral penetration agents with due camouflaging to protect the identity of the sources. The station is much better than are the Mexican services, and is thus of great assistance to the authorities in planning for raids, arrests and other repressive action.

Liaison between Scott and the Mexican military intelligence services consists mainly of exchange of information, in order to keep a foot in the door for future eventualities. The U.S. military attachés, moreover, are in constant contact with their Mexican military intelligence counterparts and their reports are received regularly by the station.

Stan Watson,‡ the Mexico City Deputy Chief of Station, has been meeting with a South Korean CIA officer who was recently sent under diplomatic cover to monitor North Korean soundings for establishment of missions in Mexico and Central America.

Communist Party Operations

The station CP section consists of two case officers, Wade Thomas‡ and Ben Ramirez,‡ both under Embassy cover, plus two case officers outside the station under non-official cover: Bob Driscoll,‡ a retired operations officer now working under contract, and Julian Zambianco who was transferred from Guayaquil to Mexico City about a year ago. These officers are in charge of agent and technical penetrations against the revolutionary organizations of importance. The quality of this intelligence is high, although not as high as it was before 1963. In late 1962 Carlos Manuel Pellecer,‡ the station's most important communist party penetration-agent, broke openly with communism by publishing a book. He was a leader of the Guatemalan Communist Party (PGT) and had been Minister of Labor in the Arbenz government during the 1950s. However, after the Agency-sponsored overthrow of the Arbenz government Pellecer made his way to Mexico City where for years he was the station's best source (cryptonym LINLUCK) on all the revolutionary organizations in Mexico, not just the Guatemalan exiles. His book, of course, was financed by the station and distributed by the Agency all over Latin America. Pellecer is still being used by the Mexico City station as a propaganda agent, as with other former penetration agents who formally break with communism without revealing their years of work as spies—Eudocio Ravines,‡ the well-known Peruvian defector from communism, is a parallel case. Another book by Pellecer, also financed by the station, has just appeared. This book is a continuation of CIA exploitation of the Marcos Rodriguez and Joaquin Ordoqui cases in Cuba, and is aimed at denigration of the Cuban revolution.

The station also collects information about communists from the U.S. living in Mexico. Many of them arrived during the McCarthy period and some have subsequently become Mexican citizens. Information about them is mainly of interest to the FBI, which calls them the American Communist Group in Mexico City (ACGMC). Information collected about them includes that obtained through the LIENVOY telephone-tapping operation described below.

The station also receives copies of reports from FBI penetration operations against Mexican revolutionary organizations. Mexico is the only country in Latin America, except Puerto Rico, where the FBI continued operations against the local left when the CIA took over in 1947. The FBI intelligence is of high quality.

Soviet/Satellite Operations

The largest section in the station is that covering Soviet/satellite operations. It has four case officers, three intelligence assistants and a secretary, all under Embassy cover, and four case officers under non-official cover. It is headed by Paul Dillon‡ and the other official cover case officers are Donald Vogel,‡ Cynthia Hausman‡ and Robert Steele.‡ A number of sensitive operations are underway.

The station has two observation posts in front of the

Soviet Embassy, which cover the entrances, plus a third observation post in the back of the Embassy to provide coverage of the gardens. The LICALLA observation post in the back is the closest of five houses bordering the Embassy property—all five are owned by the station. Several years ago films were made of Soviets conversing in the garden, but attempts by Russian lip-readers to discover their conversations were unsuccessful. From one of the front OP's, radio contact is maintained with the LIEMBRACE surveillance team for signaling when a particular Soviet surveillance target leaves the Embassy, his route and other data. Photos are regularly taken from all the OP's of Soviets and their families and all visitors to the Embassy. When visitors use vehicles, photographs are taken of their license plates for tracing. Occasionally the LICALLA OP is used for electronic monitoring, since it is close to the Embassy, but so far attempts to pick up radiations from Soviet cryptographic equipment have been unsuccessful.

In addition to the LIEMBRACE surveillance team, several other support operations include coverage of the Soviets. Through the LIENVOY operation, Soviet telephones are constantly monitored, and through the LIFIRE travel-control operation photographs of travel documents are obtained along with data on arrivals and departures. Monitoring of Mexican diplomatic communications reveals requests for Mexican visas by Soviet officials, including the diplomatic couriers. In addition, NSA is also monitoring several communications systems involving "burst" transmissions from the USSR to as yet unidentified agents believed to be in Mexico—possibly Soviet intelligence officers assigned abroad as "illegals," with false identity and non-official cover.

The station runs between fifteen and twenty access agents against the Soviets with varying degrees of effectiveness and reliability. Several of these agents are suspected of having been recruited by the Soviets for use as double agents against the station. Two of the most important of the current access-agents are Katherine Manjarrez,‡ Secretary of the Foreign Press

Association, and her husband—both of whom are targeted against the Soviet press attaché and the *Tass* correspondent. Others are LICOWL–1‡ and LIOVAL–1.‡

LICOWL–1 is the owner of a tiny grocery store situated in front of the Soviet Embassy where the Soviets buy odds and ends including their soft drinks—TSD is studying ways of bugging a wooden soft-drink case or the bottles themselves. More important, LICOWL–1 is involved at the moment in an operation against the Embassy *zavhoz* (administrative officer), who spends considerable time chatting with the agent. Because Silnikov, the *zavhoz*, has been on the prowl for a lover—or so he said to LICOWL–1—the station decided to recruit a young Mexican girl as bait. An appropriate girl was obtained through BESABER,‡ an agent who is normally targeted against Polish intelligence officers and who runs a ceramics business specializing in souvenirs. By loitering at LICOWL–1's store the girl attracted Silnikov's attention, and a hot necking session in a back room at the store led to several serious afternoon sessions at the girl's apartment nearby—obtained especially for this operation. Silnikov's virility is astonishing both the girl and the station, which is recording and photographing the sessions without the knowledge of the girl. Although promiscuity among Soviets is not abnormal, relationships with local girls are forbidden. Eventually it will be decided whether to try blackmail against Silnikov or to provoke disruption by sending tapes and photos to the Embassy if the blackmail is refused.

LIOVAL–1‡ is not as interesting a case but is more important. The agent is an American who teaches English in Mexico City and is an ardent fisherman. Through fishing he became acquainted with Pavel Yatskov, the Soviet Consul and a known senior KGB officer—possibly the Mexico City *rezident* (KGB chief). Yatskov and the agent spend one or two weekends per month off in the mountains fishing and have developed a very close friendship. When Yatskov is transferred back to Moscow—he has already been in Mexico for some years—we shall decide whether to try to defect him through LIOVAL–1. There is some talk of offering him $500,000 to defect. The Company is also willing to set him up with an elaborate cover as the owner of an income-producing fishing lodge in Canada. Recently Peter Deriabin,‡ the well-known KGB defector from the 1950s who is now a U.S. citizen and full-time CIA employee, went to Mexico City to study the voluminous reports on Yatskov written by LIOVAL–1. He concluded that there is a strong possibility that LIOVAL–1 has been recruited by Yatskov and is reporting on Paul Dillon, the station officer in charge of this case. Nevertheless, the operation continues while the counter-intelligence aspects are studied further.

The station double-agent cases against the Soviets, LICOZY–1,‡ LICOZY–3‡ and LICOZY–5,‡ are all being wound up for lack of productivity or problems of control. One of these agents, LICOZY–3, is an American living in Philadelphia who was recruited by the Soviets while a student in Mexico, but who reported the recruitment and worked for the Mexico City station. He worked for the FBI after returning to the U.S.—the Soviet case officer was a U.N. official at one time—but recently Soviet interest in him has fallen off and the FBI turned the case back over to the Agency for termination.

Against the Czechs and the Poles many of the same types of operation are targeted. Access agents, observation posts, telephone tapping, surveillance and travel control are continuous although with somewhat less intensity than against the Soviets. In the Yugoslav Embassy the code clerk has been recruited by the CIA as has one of the Embassy's secretaries.

Until the *New China News Agency* (NCNA) office was closed last month by the Mexican government, the Soviet/satellite section of the station was responsible for following the movements of the Chinese communists. Telephone intercepts through LIENVOY and occasional surveillance by the LIRICE team were directed against them, but the most important intelligence collected against them was from the bugging of their offices. The audio operation was supported by the Far East Division in headquarters, who sent an operations officer and transcribers to Mexico City. Now that the

NCNA offices are closed, the audio equipment will be removed and the station will continue to follow up the many leads coming from the bugging operation.

Cuban Operations

The Cuban operations section consists of two case officers, Francis Sherry‡ and Joe Piccolo,‡ and a secretary under Embassy cover and one case officer under non-official. An observation post for photographic coverage and radio contact with the LIEMBRACE surveillance team is functioning, as well as LIENVOY telephone monitoring and LIFIRE airport travel control. Through the LIFIRE team the station obtains regular clandestine access to the *Prensa Latina* pouch from Havana, and copies of correspondence between PL headquarters in Havana and its correspondents throughout the hemisphere are forwarded to the stations concerned.

Through the LITEMPO liaison operation the Mexican immigration service provides special coverage of all travelers to and from Havana on the frequent Cubana flights. Each traveler is photographed and his passport is stamped with arrival or departure cachets indicating Havana travel. The purpose is to frustrate the Cuban practice of issuing visas on separate slips of paper instead of in the passport so as to obscure travel. Prior to each Cubana departure the station is notified of all passengers so that name checks can be made. In the case of U.S. citizens, the Mexican service obliges by preventing departure when requested by the station.

The most important current operation targeted against the Cuban mission is an attempted audio penetration using the telephone system. Telephone company engineers working in the LIDENY tapping operation will eventually install new wall-boxes for the Embassy telephones in which sub-miniature transmitters with switches will have been cast by TSD. At the moment, however, the engineers are causing deliberate interference in Embassy telephones by technical means in the exchange. Each time the Embassy calls the telephone company to complain of interference on the lines, the engineers report back that everything in the exchange is in order. Eventually, as the interference continues, the engineers will check street connections and finally arrive to check the instruments in the Embassy. They will find the wall-boxes "defective" and will replace them with the bugged boxes cast by TSD. Right now, however, this operation (cryptonym: LISAMPAN) is still in the "interference-complaint-testing" stage.

Another important operation directed against the Cubans is a sophisticated provocation that won the CIA Intelligence Medal for Stan Archenhold,‡ the case officer who conceived it. The operation consisted of a series of letters sent to the Cuban intelligence service in their Mexico City Embassy from a person who purported to be a CIA officer trying to help them. The letters purport to implicate Joaquin Ordoqui, a respected, old-guard leader of the Cuban Communist Party and a high-ranking military leader, as a CIA agent. I haven't learned all the details of this operation, but my impression is that Ordoqui may have been an informant during the 1950s when exiled in Mexico, but that he refused to continue and was subsequently "burned" by the Agency to the Cubans. The letters continue to be sent to Cuban intelligence although Ordoqui was arrested in 1964, and the desired controversy and dissension in the Cuban revolutionary leadership followed.

As the cover of Sherry, the chief of the Cuban operations section, is in the Embassy consular section, he has been able to meet several of the Cuban consular officers directly. However, his main agent for direct assessment of the Cubans is Leander Vourvoulias,‡ Consul of Greece and President of the Consular Corps.

Support Operations

The support operations must also be detailed. The joint operation for telephone tapping, LIENVOY, is effected in cooperation with the Mexican authorities and has a capacity for about forty lines. The station provides the equipment, the technical assistance, couriers and transcribers, while the Mexicans make the connections in the exchanges and maintain the listening posts. In addition to monitoring the lines of the communist diplomatic missions and those of Mexican revolutionary groups, LIENVOY also covers special cases. For years the telephones of ex-President Cárdenas and his daughter have been tapped, and recently tapping has started on that of Luis Quintanilla, a Mexican intellectual who is planning a trip to Hanoi with the publisher of the *Miami News* and with a fellow of the Center for the Study of Democratic Institutions in Santa Barbara. Reports on plans for this trip are sent immediately to the White House.

The station also has its own unilateral telephone-tapping operation which is limited to special cases where the involvement of the Mexicans is thought to be undesirable. Connections for this operation are made outside the exchanges by telephone company engineers who work as station agents, as in the case of the bugging of the Cuban Embassy (LISAMPAN). However this is restricted as far as possible in order to avoid damaging relations with the Mexicans in the event of discovery.

Travel control, general investigations and occasional surveillance are the duties of a six-man team called LIFIRE. They obtain flight-travel lists from the airport, which are passed daily to the station and take photographs of passengers to and from communist countries and of their passports as they pass through immigration.

Another eight-man surveillance team, known as LIEMBRACE, has vehicles (including a Volkswagen photo-van) and radio-communications equipment and is mainly concerned with Soviet/satellite and Cuban targets. It is administered by Jim Anderson,‡ who also controls another eight-man team (LIRICE), similarly equipped, which deals with the Mexican revolutionaries and other miscellaneous targets.

Postal interception is mainly directed towards the mail from communist countries, but can occasionally be used to get correspondence from selected Mexican addresses.

As in every station, a variety of people assist in support tasks which they perform in the course of their ordinary jobs. For processing the immigration papers for station non-official cover personnel, for example, Judd Austin,‡ one of the U.S. lawyers in Goodrich, Dalton, Little and Riquelme (the principal law firm serving American subsidiaries) is used. The Executive Vice-President of the American Chamber of Commerce in Mexico City, Al Wichtrich,‡ channels political information to the station that he picks up in his normal work with American and Mexican businessmen. For technical support the station has an officer of TSD under Embassy cover with a workshop and qualifications in audio, flaps and seals, and photography.

Covert-Action Operations

The station covert-action operations section consists of Stanley Watson,‡ the Deputy Chief of Station, and two case officers under Embassy cover plus one case officer under non-official cover. Operations underway provide for placing propaganda in the major Mexico City dailies, several magazines and television. Student operations are centered mostly in the National University of Mexico (UNAM), while labor operations are concentrated on support for and guidance of the Mexico City headquarters of ORIT.‡ Station labor operations also include agents at the new ORIT school in Cuernavaca (built with CIA funds) for spotting and assessment of trainees for use in labor operations after they return to their country of origin. The Mexico programs of the American Institute for Free Labor Development‡ (AIFLD) are also under station direction.

Although the LITEMPO operation and others provide constant political intelligence on the Mexican situation, the station has one official cover case officer, Bob Feldman,‡ working full-time on LICOBRA, which is the operation for penetrating the PRI and the Mexican government. This officer works closely with the legitimate political section of the Embassy and is currently cultivating several PRI legislators for recruitment. Another LICOBRA target is an office in the Ministry of Government called the Department of Political and Social Investigations. This office, although part of a government ministry, is the main repository of the PRI for information on political officialdom (PRI and opposition) throughout the country. Still another LICOBRA target is the Foreign Ministry, where operations are now stalled because of the Ambassador's insistence that the station refrain from operations against this Ministry. It is in LICOBRA operations that the station and headquarters believe the Olympic attaché cover would be especially useful. By a determined effort at recruitment of unilateral penetrations of the PRI and the Mexican government, a better balance can be obtained between the excellent liaison operations and controlled agent sources. Rafael Fusoni,‡ an agent who has been in the LICOBRA program for some time, is already working as an agent in the Olympic Organizing Committee, as Assistant Director of Public Relations.

The Mexico City station, in spite of its wide-ranging operational activities and numerous personnel, is well known for its excellent administration. Two administrative officers and a secretary handle finances and property, but Win Scott, the Chief of Station, is exceptional in his attention to administrative details as well as to operations. Each officer in the station is required on leaving to advise the receptionist where he is going and when he will be back. Morning tardiness is not tolerated, cables and dispatches are answered promptly, and project renewals and operational progress reports are expected to be submitted on time. Considered altogether, the Mexico City station is a tight operation—it has to be with fifty employees and a budget of 5.5 million dollars.

The station also has a reports section that consists of one senior reports officer and an assistant. This office processes all information received by the station that can possibly be of interest to headquarters customers or other stations, writes the reports, and keeps appropriate files.

The records section is the largest and most efficient of any station in the hemisphere and is said to be Scott's pride. It contains detailed personality files on thousands of Mexicans and foreigners resident in Mexico, in addition to intelligence subject files, project files and extensive index files. The records section is administered by a qualified records officer with two full-time assistants and four working wives.

Such a large station obviously cannot get many more than half the employees integrated as State Department employees. Some of the secretaries and intelligence assistants who work in the station go to Mexico as tourists and are taken on the Embassy payroll as "local hire." Others work in the station without "normalization" as Embassy employees. Still others, who do not work in the Embassy, use cover as tourists, public relations representatives, businessmen, even retired people. Adequate cover is a continuing problem but solutions can usually be found. The nearness of Mexico to the U.S., the exceptional relations between the station and the Mexican government, and abundant U.S. tourism allow thin solutions that would be impossible in other countries.

Washington, D.C. — 15 January 1967

Still more delay on whether and when I'll go to Mexico City under Olympic cover. For the time being, unfortunately, attention in WH Division has turned to the Montevideo station where preparations have started for the conference of OAS Presidents to be held in Punta del Este in April, to which President Johnson will be going. In WH Division a special group has been formed to assign additional personnel to Montevideo, to set up a special base in Punta del Este, and to establish special liaison procedures with the Secret Service White House Detail. John Hanke,‡ the officer in charge of the headquarters task force, told me that the Montevideo station has asked that I go back to work with the police. Old bureaucrat Kaufman, however, doesn't want my desk empty any longer than necessary so he's going to delay my departure as long as he can. I'm not terribly cheered by the idea of working again with Otero and company but just getting back to Montevideo would be a joy compared with this headquarters work.

Before going I'll have to finish the paper-work on

two new officers going to Mexico City under non-official cover to work on Soviet operations. One is a contract agent who formerly trained infiltration–exfiltration teams for maritime operations against Cuba—he ran a special base on an island not far from Miami. The other is Jack Kindschi,‡ a staff officer who is being reassigned to Mexico City from the Stockholm station. Conveniently his cover as a public relations expert for the Robert Mullen Co.‡ will be the same in Mexico as in Sweden. While I'm away, my work will be handled by Bruce Berckmans,‡ a recent graduate of the Career Training Program, the new name given to the old JOT Program. Berckmans is an ex-Marine and will be going to Mexico City in a few months for communist party penetration-operations, which is his area of responsibility now in the branch. He'll have non-official cover as a marketing and agri-business consultant.

Montevideo — 1 March 1967

If Johnson gets assassinated it won't be for lack of protection. Our task force here has grown to about sixty people from headquarters and from other WH stations. Every nook and cranny in the station offices is filled with a desk or typing table. In Punta del Este we've set up a base in a house not far from where Johnson will stay which is almost next to the hotel where the conference sessions will be held.

The Secret Service advance party has set up an office in the station for quick passage of intelligence reports, which we are receiving from many other stations as well as from our own sources here. The object is to follow up all the leads on possible assassination attempts that turn up here or in other countries—all WH stations are reporting the travel of extreme-leftists or their sudden dropping out of sight. Two sections of the task force are doing most of the work in following up these leads and in other preparations with Uruguayan security people.

The station CP section under Bob Riefe is combing files on every important Uruguayan resident of far-left tendencies who might be involved in action against

Johnson or other presidents. Taking pains to avoid passing information that might jeopardize sources, reports for police intelligence are being prepared along with a master check-list for use at the control points separating the different security zones that increase in intensity from Montevideo to Punta del Este. The Liaison section, in which I am working, is in charge of writing these reports in Spanish and getting them over to Otero at police headquarters. Under normal circumstances we would not pass information from unilateral sources of high quality to the police, because there is high probability that the reports will seep out to the enemy through poor police security, but we're taking chances given the high stakes. Argentines, Paraguayans, Brazilians and others not resident in Uruguay but possible threats are included in this report procedure, and Otero's files are growing as never before. By the end of the month several hundred of these individual reports will have been passed along with many special leads from sources in Montevideo and other stations.

Montevideo — 2 April 1967

Each day, it seems, another wild story reaches the station on a terrorist plan to assault, bomb, poison or simply hex the conference. Checking these stories out has brought me into the homes of an array of weird people, sometimes with an over-eager Secret Service agent anxious to try thumbscrews to get the whole truth. One story, however, couldn't be taken lightly and for the past week I've been spending day and night trying to resolve it.

The original report came from BIDAFFY–1,‡ a penetration agent of the Buenos Aires station who is on the fringes of the terrorist group of John William Cooke. Cooke is a well-known extreme left-wing Peronist with close ties to Cuban intelligence. The report from BIDAFFY–1 alleged that Cooke and an unknown number of his followers are coming to Montevideo before the Conference in order to infiltrate the restricted Punta del

Este area for bomb attacks and such other terrorism as they can mount. The agent does not know the names of persons to accompany Cooke but the plan is first to operate from an apartment owned by Cooke in the Rambla Hotel, a twenty-storey decaying building on the beachfront in Pocitos.

Rather than pass this data to the police, which might jeopardize BIDAFFY–1, we decided to try to verify the report and call in the police after Cooke is here. Through the AVENIN surveillance team I obtained a hotel room on the same floor as Cooke's apartment and called over Frank Sherno, the regional technical support officer stationed in Buenos Aires. For two long nights Sherno tried unsuccessfully to open the lock to Cooke's apartment, using the battery-operated handgun vibrator with assorted picks. Then he made a key for the door—by the time it would work three more nights had passed. By this time our repeated trips between our room and the Cooke apartment had aroused the suspicions of the elevator operators, while the lobby employees were wondering out loud what three men were doing night after night in a room for two. My fear has been growing that the hotel manager might advise the police, which could reveal one or two of the AVENIN agents to Otero.

Last night, nevertheless, Sherno finally got Cooke's apartment open. On our first entry, after checking carefully for booby traps, we found a large wooden crate in the main room—just about the right length for rifles or other shoulder weapons. It was nailed shut and banded but the paneling was broken towards one of the corners and inside I could see books, magazines and other printed matter—possible filler or cover for more important objects underneath. I decided to leave the crate alone but we installed two battery-operated radio transmitters—one in the bedsprings and one above a curtain box. In our room we left receivers and recording equipment for the AVENIN agents who will alternate on monitoring duties.

This morning a cable arrived from Buenos Aires with another BIDAFFY–1 report: Cooke's daughter is coming today and will probably stay at the apartment—

possibly others of the group will follow shortly. I discussed the crate with the Secret Service chief who offered to lend us a portable X-ray machine that the Service uses on gifts given to President Johnson. Tonight the Secret Service agent who operates the machine will accompany me with the machine to our hotel room where we will stand by for a surreptitious entry. This afternoon Cooke's daughter did indeed arrive—with her lover. The AVENIN team will follow them when they leave the building and will advise us by radio when they begin to return. Meanwhile we will slip into the Cooke apartment and take X-ray pictures of the crate. I hope the elevator in the hotel will be able to lift this "portable" machine, never mind our wrestling it clandestinely down the hall. Anybody who interferes with us gets enough radiation to fry his bone marrow.

Montevideo — 4 April 1967

After a night and a morning of listening to regular concerts from the bedsprings, we finally heard Cooke's daughter and boyfriend leave the apartment. With great effort we got the X-ray machine into place, donned lead aprons and turned on the juice. With each picture—we had to take several because the crate was much larger than the X-ray negative—the lights dimmed and I thought we would blow the electrical system, but we were back in our room with the machine quite soon. The X-ray operator and I took the machine back to the station where he developed the film—fortunately nothing showed up except nails. This afternoon the couple returned to Buenos Aires without having made one remark about other people coming or even of the conference. They had a quiet little visit, our monitors learned a new trick or two, and in my report I'll recommend BIDAFFY-1 for a special bonus on account of his imaginative reporting.

Getting the reports and check lists to the police security force has been consuming more time during this final period. Now we have started to organize the procedures for Johnson's security on arrival at the

Montevideo aiport and for the helicopter flight to Punta del Este. John Horton,‡ the Chief of Station, will be at the aircraft parking site beside the terminal building with Secret Service agents while ten other CIA officers will be at strategic locations in the terminal building. Each of us will be responsible for watching certain windows and making certain that they are not opened. My post will be on the roof of the terminal building, just below the control tower. Each of us will have walkie-talkie communications with the rest of the airport team, and I will have a second, higher-powered walkie-talkie to report each detail to the station. Instantaneous reports will be sent by the station to Washington based on my indications of when Johnson's aircraft comes in sight, the moment of touch-down, parking, Johnson's descent and reception, his boarding of the helicopter, lift-off and disappearance. Other reports will follow from officers in cars on the highway to Punta del Este—Johnson's helicopters, in fact, will never be out of sight of CIA officers from before landing in Montevideo to the helicopter pad in Punta del Este, seventy miles away. Once Johnson is in Punta del Este, security will be less of a problem because of zonal restriction of movement in that area, the use of special badges and other precautions. As Johnson will be one of the last presidents to arrive, we will be able to practice on his colleagues during the two days before he gets here.

Montevideo — 14 April 1967

Both for Johnson's arrival three days ago and his departure today everything went perfectly. Back in the station during the party Horton handed me a cable from headquarters telling me that I should return immediately in order to prepare to go to Mexico City for the Olympic assignment. Tonight I'll try for a seat on one of the Air Force cargo planes flying back to Washington.

Results of the Conference? Well, they finally put to rest the original concerns of the Alliance for Progress for agrarian reform, income redistribution and social and economic integration. Just as well, I suppose, since none of the governments seem to have had a very serious concern for these matters anyway. Now the emphasis is on regional economic growth. Presumably economic growth alone will take care of the marginalized majority, and reform, in any case, will be easier to accept when there is more to spread around—meaning the privileged will be able to avoid significant cuts in consumption. Foreign aid will be channeled principally to education and agriculture which, in the absence of agrarian reform, means the development of high-productivity commercial farm operations. Those of the modern sectors should rejoice, for their increasing share of national income is sure to continue increasing. Forget the reforms—the pressure's off thanks to counter-insurgency.

Washington, D.C. — 30 April 1967

While I was in Montevideo several decisions on the Olympic cover job were made, both in the Agency and in the Department of State. Bill Broe, the WH Division Chief, had got lukewarm about sending me down because he had been Chief of Station in Tokyo during the 1964 Olympic Games and he believes the softening of political attitudes inherent in a cultural event like this will impede recruitments. Only if I stay on in the Mexico City station after the Games does Broe think I'll be able to justify the time spent between now and late next year on strictly Olympic cover matters. On the other hand Dave Murphy, Chief of the Soviet Bloc Division, believes that the bland political atmosphere will help me move in circles that might otherwise be closed to a U.S. government official. Besides, the Mexico City station has no contact operations under way between officers of the station and their Soviet counterparts. Since I am already known to the Soviets from Montevideo I'll be able to develop personal relationships with Soviet and satellite intelligence officers assigned to Olympic duties in their embassies. Murphy's opinion was shared by the Mexico City station which is anxious to use the Olympic job to develop agents for the LICOBRA targets: the PRI and the Mexican government.

The differences were resolved in my favor but then another problem arose. The Ambassador made it a condition of my assignment that I had never been exposed as a CIA officer to Latin American police officials. Kaufman, the Mexico Branch Chief, resolved this one by telling me to write a memorandum for Broe's signature assuring the State Department that I'm not known to any police. Kaufman reasoned that we could stretch the truth a little by claiming, if it's ever necessary, that any police officers who know me as a CIA officer are paid intelligence agents first and policemen second.

The most encouraging development is that the Ambassador has decided he wants two Olympic attachés—the other one will be Dave Carrasco, former basketball coach at the American University and now head of the Peace Corps sports program in Ecuador (who, of course, has no connection whatsoever with the Agency). Ostensibly I'll be his assistant, which will help me considerably because he has really legitimate sports credentials. Moreover he was born on the Mexican border, and has had friends for many years in Mexican sports circles. Next month Carrasco will come to Washington for discussions at the Department and with Kaufman and me. Barring other delays we should be opening the Embassy Olympic Games office in June.

Luis Vargas, my old Immigration Director in Montevideo, is here now on a trip with his wife financed by the station. It's the reward I recommended last year for his help in the expulsions and other action against the Soviets, East Germans, Czechs and North Koreans. As headquarters control officer for the visit I've taken them over to Senator Montoya's office for a chat, then out to Raymond Warren's‡ house for a cocktail party—he's Chief of the WH branch that includes Uruguay—then to the White House for a special tour conducted by Secret Service friends. In New York yesterday we watched the Loyalty Day Parade. Vargas was impressed at the magnitude of support demonstrated for the Vietnam War effort, as was I. If only these marchers knew the effects of counter-insurgency in Latin America.

Washington, D.C. — 5 June 1967

We have decided that Dave Carrasco should arrive in Mexico City a week or two before me, so while he arranges his personal affairs I have returned to paper shuffling at the Mexico branch. I have also just finished the Soviet Operations Course, a two-week full-time program ostensibly under the Office of Training but in fact controlled by the Soviet Bloc Division. I was to have taken the course last year but was able to plead personnel shortages at the Mexico branch. This time there was no begging off.

SB Division has been notably successful in peddling this course—they have, in fact, prevailed on the DDP to make the course compulsory for all Chiefs and Deputy Chiefs of Station being assigned to countries having Soviet missions, in addition to operations officers who will be engaging in Soviet operations. As I will probably be developing personal relationships with Soviet intelligence officers there was no way I could escape. However I was lucky because Jim Noland, my former Chief of Station in Quito, is back from an abbreviated tour in Santiago, Chile, and was also taking the course—prior to taking over the SB Division office that coordinates Soviet matters with the Western Hemisphere Division.

The Soviet Operations Course is the last word in the Agency on recruitment and defection of Soviets. It is based largely on the opinions and theories of Dave Murphy, SB Division Chief, which are highly controversial because of the dogmatic attitudes of Murphy and his subordinates, and the lack of demonstrated success. The majority of the officers taking the course were from area divisions other than SB, but most of us simply refrained from public dissent, knowing that SB would take note of dissidents and, given SB's weight within the DDP, such heresy would sooner or later reflect back on us.

Notably absent from the course are lectures and readings on Marx, Lenin and other communist theoreticians and leaders, although a thick paperback history of Russia was placed in our course kits for retention. What this course deals with are contemporary Soviet realities and how to use them to our advantage—how to get Soviets to commit treason by spying on their country.

But how to get to these Soviets, the most interesting of whom will be CPSU members? The most accessible and most vulnerable are those working in some capacity in the free world—more than 25,000 of them and still others who travel abroad on temporary assignments. Usually the accessible ones are on the staff of diplomatic, trade and technical assistance missions, including military personnel, but of special importance are Soviet scientists who attend conferences and congresses abroad. Of the Soviets stationed in a mission abroad for several years, the diplomats and intelligence officers are the most accessible and of these the most desirable recruitment, after the Ambassador, is a GRU officer—because of his military connections. Next in desirability would be a KGB officer because of his state security background.

The focus of the Soviet Operations Course, then, while taking into account the inestimable value of a recruitment of someone who is prepared to return to the Soviet Union, concentrates on the organization of Soviet communities in the non-communist countries and on the CIA operational programs to discover the vulnerable and disaffected. The theory is that the pressures built into the rigidly conformist routine for Soviets abroad, largely for internal security reasons, generates a natural disaffection by serving as a contrast with the relatively greater freedom of thought, movement and association that they usually see about them. Somewhere, the theory goes, there are Soviets who are already along the road to defection, and the CIA goal is to identify them and bring it about. The longer such a person can be persuaded to keep working (before "disappearing" and coming to the U.S.), best of all to return to the Soviet Union, the greater the possibilities for exploitation. But first to identify the candidates.

Most of the theory and doctrine for operations against Soviets has come from actual defectors as they have described their personal histories and the forces that brought them to defect. We studied, then, in considerable detail, the officially prescribed organization of both the professional and the leisure routines of the members of a Soviet mission. There usually is not much variation from one mission to another. First there is the overt diplomatic and administrative function of the mission, headed by the Ambassador, with sections dedicated to political, economic and cultural matters—normal in all respects. The administrative section under the *zavhoz* (chief) and his *komendants* (assistants) performs the housekeeping chores and attends to Embassy reception and other security functions. The commercial offices include representatives of Soviet enterprises peddling books, films, machinery and other goods, while arranging for imports of the host country's products.

More important is the other level of functions—the use of these overt positions as cover slots for KGB and GRU intelligence personnel. We reviewed the various techniques used to identify the *rezident* (intelligence chief) and his subordinates in each of the services. Of much interest also is the location of the restricted area where all classified documents are kept and where the cryptographic and radio communications activities take place. Identification of personnel in this section is obviously high priority. From the point of view of recruitment operations, however, prospects are limited because only designated persons in a Soviet mission are allowed to have personal relationships with foreigners, particularly non-communist foreigners, and each meeting with such people requires a full written report. Usually permission for such relationships is restricted to intelligence operations officers, diplomats and others such as the *zavhoz* who have legitimate need to deal with outsiders.

The restrictions on contact with the outside world by

most members of Soviet missions require rigid internal organization. The Komsomol, or communist youth organization, usually operates under "sports club" cover while the CPSU uses the cover of "trade union organization." The real trade-union organization is called the *mestkom*, or local committee, and the SK, or community security officer, is responsible for personnel security in each mission. Additionally, each mission has a club with a program of games, films, political studies and lectures, and social affairs—all centered around a designated clubroom. Participation in club activities is assigned and compulsory, and is designed to keep the group together and avoid wandering into temptations in the decadent bourgeois surroundings. Personal conflicts, gossiping, petty jealousies and backbiting are the usual product of such mental and emotional inbreeding as is, according to SB doctrine, the need to break out of it all.

Most CIA operations against the Soviet community abroad are designed to provide an orderly and complete body of working knowledge about the Soviet presence in the country of concern. Systematic organization is the theme, so that the extensive detail required can be effectively managed. Standard operations in the non-communist world are the kind we have in Mexico and Uruguay: travel control for arrivals and departures and for passport biographical data and photographs; observation posts for additional photographs, analysis of relationships within the community and support to surveillance teams; surveillance for discovery of overt and clandestine activities; telephone tapping for analysis of relationships and general information; audio penetrations for general information and secrets.

The better the access agent can cultivate a close personal relationship with the Soviet, the more the station can assess his vulnerability. Some of the best access agents are satellite officials serving in the same city as the target Soviet—often recruited to work against the Soviets for nationalistic motives. Still others are third-country diplomats, local politicians and government officials, and persons having the same hobby as a Soviet. Double agents, while primarily used to reveal Soviet intelligence requirements and *modus operandi*, and to occupy their time, also reveal the identities of intelligence officers and provide data on their professional competence and personality.

The access agent program is designed to provide disaffected Soviets with "channels for defection"—bridges to the other side—that they can build little by little while making up their minds. Access agents are people a Soviet can confide in, assuming the internal pressures create such a need. After a while, hours, months or even years, the access agents can initiate political discussions. The first rule of this game is never to denigrate Russia or things Russian. The key is to distinguish in the target's mind between Russia the homeland and Russia the subjected territory of the CPSU—to separate government from people and country. As most Soviet bureaucrats are thought to harbor some cynicism towards the CPSU bureaucracy, the good access agent can foment patriotic balances against the fostering of doubts towards the Party. One obvious and effective method is to combine praise for Russian cultural traditions with dismay over treatment of dissident writers and artists.

Covert-action operations against the Soviets are also varied: the Agency is deeply involved in the *samizdat* system of clandestine publishing in order to get dissident literature out of the Soviet Union for publication and to make books by banned writers available in the U.S.S.R. Major emphasis is also given to exposing Soviet subversive activities abroad and to circulating anti-Soviet propaganda to make them feel oppressed and disliked by the local community. Expulsions are constantly promoted in order to "prove" the Soviets are subversives.

The course also included a review of the procedures for keeping the Defector Committee of the U.S. mission in readiness, together with the rules for handling defectors: first efforts to get the Soviet to continue in his job as if nothing had happened, in order to make audio installations and rifle files; pre-planned safe places for keeping him hidden before departure for the U.S.; anticipation of violent reaction by the Soviet mission, with charges that the defector stole the cash-box; anticipation of procedures for letting the defector be interviewed by Soviet mission officials; initial debriefing requirements; military aircraft evacuation procedures.

Most of us took the course with some scepticism because SB lecturers refused to state the number of Soviets who have been snared through this vast effort. Surely there is some truth to the old saying that nobody recruits a Soviet—if they come over they recruit themselves, and this they can do without channels, bridges, OPS, surveillance teams, passport photography and insidious access agents.

And what happens when the dream agent comes along? Might not a Soviet so compromise their security that the CPSU would be obliged to take serious action? SB Division lecturers also avoided comment on how the recruitment of Colonel Oleg Penkovskiy‡ might have been related to the Cuban missile crisis. Here was a man embittered against the CPSU leadership who passed on information of great value about Soviet missiles: numbers, locations, accuracy, megatonnage, readiness factors. The Agency got valuable intelligence, Penkovskiy eventually got the firing squad—but did the Soviets send missiles to Cuba because they needed desperately to balance back from the damage caused by this intelligence breakthrough? Perhaps October 1962 was the price of that intelligence success.

If I were honest I would pull back from the Olympic cover assignment and ask for leave to find a new job. Working in the Olympics office with Carrasco, however, I'll be able to avoid close control by the station and concentrate on cover work. At the same time I'll also be watching for job opportunities after the Olympics—almost a year and a half from now and a lot can happen. And Mexico is just too attractive to refuse. I'll drive down during the first week of July.

Mexico City — 15 July 1967

This Olympics cover is extraordinary. Dave and I have been making the rounds together calling on the leaders of the different organizations involved in the Olympic preparations: the Organizing Committee, the Mexican

Olympic Committee and its vast new training center for Mexican athletes, the Mexican Sports Confederation and the individual sports federations. Each of these organizations seems to have some special needs that the U.S. Embassy Olympic Games office might help to fulfil. The Organizing Committee wants odds and ends related to putting on the sports events and major assistance in arranging for U.S. participation in the Olympic cultural program. The Mexican Olympic Committee, which is responsible for preparing the Mexican teams, needs help in getting several more coaches and additional State Department Specialist Grants for American coaches already here. After only five days on the job, access to an exceedingly large and varied range of people has suddenly opened up.

The officers in the station, from Win Scott down, are all excited about how my Olympic entrée can help them in their particular areas of responsibility. For his part, Scott told me first to concentrate on meeting as many people as possible and to establish my Olympic cover firmly. In the Soviet operations section, where I arranged for a desk and typewriter, the chief interest is on spotting and assessment of new access agents and on my establishing direct contact operations with the Soviet and satellite intelligence officers who are handling Olympic duties. The CP section wants me to spot possible recruitments for infiltration into revolutionary organizations, while the CA section wants assessment data on press officers of the Organizing Committee for use as media placement agents. The liaison section wants information on the Soviet and satellite Olympic attachés that can be passed to the Mexican services while the LICOBRA section wants me to spot possible agents for use in penetrating the PRI and the Mexican government. The Cuban operations section, probably the most destitute in agent material, wants personal data on the Cuban Olympic attaché, on leftists within the Olympic milieu who might eventually travel to Cuba, and on anyone at all who might be of interest to the Cubans. All these officers see my Olympic cover as promising for their operational goals.

No way to deny that this job could be valuable to

the station. General practice is to exchange calling cards with a new Olympic acquaintance, and so far a very high percentage of the people I've met have significant reports in station files. I've begun my own card file and am writing short memoranda on the people I meet. Perhaps if I keep producing memoranda to circulate among the different sections I can avoid making any recruitments for some considerable time—possibly right up to the Olympics. No problem getting discreetly up to the station from the Olympic office on the second floor, because the station's entrance is just to the side of the elevator in the back of the Embassy and not many people go up to the top floor.

New York — 13 December 1967

Events have taken several unexpected turns in recent months. Dave has assumed responsibility for Embassy support to the Olympic cultural program, which the Mexicans hope will add a dimension almost equal in importance to the sports program. The view in the Organizing Committee is that Mexico, in spite of sizable efforts under way in recent years to prepare teams, will be far down the list in national medal accumulation. Partly to overcome this deficit, and partly to excel in a different area, the Organizing Committee is putting on an impressive year-long Cultural Program of twenty events to correspond to the twenty sports events—although non-competitive. Officially the Organizing Committee has invited all the national Olympic committees to participate in the events in the Cultural Program, but many national committees, including the USOC, are not set up for such varied cultural activity. Response has therefore been slight, and the Organizing Committee has turned to the embassies in Mexico City to seek official support.

In our Embassy the cultural section has failed to become more than peripherally interested in the Cultural Program, so the Organizing Committee appointed a special representative to work with Dave and me on promoting wider participation by the U.S., especially the U.S. government, in the Cultural Program. I never thought I would be doing cultural attaché's work but Dave asked me to take responsibility for the Cultural Program, and since then I have been trying to generate interest in Washington and elsewhere for bringing participants to such events as a poets' encounter, theater and the performing arts, a folk arts festival, a stamp collectors' exhibit, a monumental sculpture program, a film festival, youth camp, atomic energy and space exploration exhibits, a children's painting festival, a popular arts and crafts exhibit, and other similar events.

I didn't like Dave asking me to work on the Cultural Program because it can easily take up all one's time, but after checking the names of Cultural Program officials in station files I immediately saw the advantage: the cultural section of the Organizing Committee is just loaded with people of established leftist credentials who would be very difficult for an American official to cultivate without suspicion. But in the Olympic atmosphere of peace and brotherhood, and given the Organizing Committee's dire need for U.S. government backing, I now have an open door to many more people of interest to different sections of the station. Moreover, by assuming these new, very time-consuming duties, I will have all the excuses needed for not making any recruitments. Up to now the station is very pleased, because I've also been regularly meeting Provorov and Belov, the Soviet Olympic officers (GRU and KGB, respectively) as well as the Czech, Pole and Yugoslav Olympic officers. My only problem is to keep away from DNNEBULA–1,‡ the Korean CIA officer who is also handling Olympic duties, and who corners me at every meeting. Generally, though, I'm only keeping up appearances with the station because I have no interest in developing operations.

The other unexpected development is a serious and deepening relationship with a woman I met on the Organizing Committee. I took a chance and told her I had worked for the CIA before, but in spite of her strong reaction she agreed to keep seeing me. She is one of the many leftists in the Cultural Program and she believes, with great bitterness, as do many other people, that the Agency was responsible for Che Guevara's execution.

Mexico City — 20 June 1968

One more CIA career comes to an end. It was a little earlier than I had expected, but Paul Dillon invited me for coffee the other day and told me Scott had asked him to make a proposal. He said that the station is very pleased with my work and that Scott would like me to transfer to the political section in the station after the Olympics, so that in the coming two or three years I will be able to make the recruitments and take part in other station operations for which I've been preparing since arrival last year. They especially want me to begin recruitments of some of the PRI bureaucrats I've met, such as Alejandro Ortega San Vicente, the Secretary-General of the Olympic Organizing Committee and former chief of the Ministry of Government's Department of Political and Social Investigations, which is really the PRI's information center on its own people. Scott said he will arrange for me to get another promotion and that the Ambassador has approved this plan.

I told Dillon that I appreciated the offer but that I planned to resign after the Olympics, to remarry, and remain in Mexico. He was startled, of course, because I hadn't mentioned this to anyone in the station yet. Later I spoke to Scott and wrote a memorandum for headquarters outlining my intentions. I was careful to cite my personal reasons as the only motive behind my decision, lest someone pounce on me as a security risk.

The sense of relief is very strong now that I have formally announced my intention to resign. Perhaps I should have done this on returning from Montevideo, because I have felt very strained beneath the surface since coming to Mexico—like being dishonest in a dishonest situation, except that the two negatives don't make a positive. The truth is that Bill Broe was right:

the Olympics aren't conducive to cold war politics. Working in the Cultural Program, moreover, has driven still another wedge between the rationale for counter-insurgency and the reality of its effects. It isn't just "them and us" but "all of us."

The cultural work has bridged many gaps; even though I've only been organizing rather than creating, the experience has been enough to ease the pains of increasing separation, of feeling a fraud, of isolation. Who knows if without it I could have given up all the security and comfort of continued CIA work. Headquarters and stations alike are peppered, as we all know, with officers who long ago ceased to believe in what they're doing—only to continue until retirement as cynical, bitter men anxious to avoid responsibilities and effort. I'll at least avoid joining them, no matter what happens.

Mexico City — 1 August 1968

This past week has seen a sudden flare-up of confrontation between students and university leaders and the government. It began with some confusion on 26 July when a street demonstration celebrating the anniversary of the Cuban Revolution clashed with a rival demonstration and then turned into a protest against the Mexican government. Two days later police entered buildings of the National University of Mexico (UNAM), and next day there was rioting in the streets by students and severe police repression. Three days ago another violent confrontation occurred in the streets and yesterday rioting spread to provincial university towns of Villahermosa and Jalapa. Today in Mexico City a peaceful protest march numbered at least 50,000 and was headed by the Rector of UNAM.

The original confused issues have broadened into more basic political demands, led on the student side by a national strike committee strongly influenced by former leaders of the National Liberation Movement (MLN) and the National Center of Democratic Students

(CNED)—both influenced in turn by the Communist Party of Mexico. Even so, the movement is a spontaneous popular demonstration against police violence with clear tendencies towards protest against the PRI's power monopoly and traditional service to the privileged. Demands formulated by the strike committee are impossible for the government to meet but are nevertheless popular: resignation of the police chiefs, disbanding of the riot police, repeal of the crime of "social dissolution" and compensation for the wounded and families of the dead—since 26 July, at least eight students have been killed, 400 injured and over 1000 arrested.

The government for its part has had to call in military forces several times when police have been unable to cope. Luis Echeverria is responsible as Minister of Government for re-establishing order but so far he has only made matters worse. He has publicly blamed the CNED and the PCM youth wing for the violence, which is only partly true—other demonstrators and the police too are to blame—while also claiming that five "riot coaches" from France, and other communist agitators, had plotted the insurrection from outside the country. No one believes such trash which makes the government look ridiculous and makes compromise more difficult. If Echeverria doesn't stop overreacting the situation will get even worse.

Last month I made a trip to Washington and New York for some final details on Cultural Program participation sponsored by the State Department. In Washington, not only would Janet not agree that I bring the boys here for the Olympics, she also made my seeing them very difficult. I decided to bring them anyway and had my lawyer telephone her to advise after we were on the flight. An uproar followed between headquarters and the State Department and between the Ambassador and Scott—all of whom have ordered me to send them back because Janet is threatening to expose me as a CIA officer. I have refused and told them to fire me if they want but that I believe I have a right to have my children in my home, whether in Mexico City or any other place. Besides, I'm sure the threat of exposure is only a bluff.

Mexico City — 1 September 1968

Throughout the greater part of August the government had taken a fairly gentle line about the massive demonstrations taking place. Then on 27 August a huge demonstration of some 200,000 marchers turned out to protest against the cost of the Olympics to Mexico which will be at least 175 million dollars. The turning-point in government policy came early the following morning when the considerable concentration of demonstrators that remained in the main downtown plaza was forcibly broken up. On the 29th another 3000 demonstrators turned up and were driven off. Today Diaz Ordaz, in his annual message to the country, pledged the use of the armed forces to ensure that the Games will be held. However he also promised to consider changing the penal code on "social dissolution." The strike committee has added to its demands the release of all political prisoners, and in this speech Diaz Ordaz took the trouble to claim that in Mexico there are no political prisoners—a claim so widely known to be false that it is ridiculous.

In the station the CP section is very busy getting information from agents on planning by the strike committee and on positions taken by the communists and other far-left groups. Highlights of this intelligence are being passed to Diaz Ordaz and Echeverria for use by the security forces. It's almost like being in Ecuador or Uruguay again—but I'm glad I'm not working on the government's side this time.

Mexico City — 19 September 1968

So far the only significant demonstration this month was a silent march of protest on the day that Diaz Ordaz opened the new Olympic sports installations. Protestors are increasingly saying that the police have burned the bodies of those students killed in repressive action and that the students' families have been frightened into silence. Student brigades have been going daily to factories, offices and homes to explain the student position and have been doing so with considerable effect. Last night, as a result of this activity, the government seized the National University in violation of the University's traditional autonomy. Echeverria justified this invasion by saying that the University has been used for political rather than for educational purposes.

Thousands of troops with tanks and armored cars were employed in the takeover of the University and although hundreds of people were arrested, the student strike leaders all escaped. The student brigades exposing government policies to serve minority interests have now made their headquarters in the Polytechnic Institute, where a battle is now going on between students and police.

Two of the big exhibits for the Olympic Cultural Program are being delayed because of the violence. At the National University we had a huge Jupiter Missile set up for the space exhibit, but it had to be taken down rather quickly before it got torn down by the demonstrators. The Organizing Committee is now looking for somewhere else to put it. Similarly the atomic energy exhibit at the Polytechnic has had to be put off while another site is found. The space exhibit was to be opened yesterday by Michael Collins, an Air Force astronaut, but I have had to cancel much of his program.

Mexico City — 25 September 1968

Each day since the UNAM was invaded has been filled with violence. Some ten to twenty more students have been killed and over 100 wounded in riots which have broken out in different parts of Mexico City but are now most frequent in the Plaza of the Three Cultures in the Tlatelolco section, where one of the main vocational schools of the Polytechnic Institute is located. Yesterday a pitched battle lasted about twelve hours as students defended the Polytechnic and the vocational school at the Plaza, but finally both were occupied by the Army and police. All street demonstrations are now being suppressed with much violence.

After a PRI campaign against him of several weeks, the Rector of UNAM resigned, but the professors association voted to resign with him if his resignation was accepted. Today the UNAM governing council refused the resignation and the Rector is expected to withdraw it. Increasingly the protest is turning towards the cost of the Olympic Games. Parents and teachers have joined the students, while vigilante groups controlled by the government have begun night raids on schools to intimidate the occupying students.

This afternoon I went up to the station offices to read the intelligence reports sent to headquarters over the past week. One report was on a meeting between Scott and President Diaz Ordaz in which Scott got the strong impression that the President is confused and disoriented, without a plan or decision on what to do next.

Mexico City — 3 October 1968

In one savage display of firepower at the Plaza of the Three Cultures, the government wiped out the protest movement and probably several hundred lives. The massacre yesterday afternoon came as a surprise, because for almost a week both the government and the strike committee had been backing off from confrontation and nearly everyone believed the crisis was passing. The Army had even evacuated the UNAM and the Rector withdrew his resignation.

Nevertheless, yesterday about 5 p.m. some 3000 people—students, teachers, parents and some workers and peasants—gathered at the Plaza of the Three Cultures for a march in protest against continued government occupation of the Polytechnic Institute and several of its vocational schools.

The first speaker at the rally, however, called off the march because of a concentration of about 1000 troops with armored vehicles and jeep-mounted machine-guns along the route. The rally continued peacefully but the military units surrounded the Plaza. Just after 6 p.m. the Army opened fire on the crowd and on the surrounding buildings believed to be sheltering sympathizers. Not until an hour later did the Army stop firing. Officially the toll is set at twenty-eight dead and 200 wounded, but several hundred were probably killed and many more wounded. Over 1500 were taken prisoner. Today mass confusion reigned as thousands of parents and relatives sought to find the bodies—already disappeared—of those unable to be located in hospitals or jails.

This morning the International Olympic Committee under Avery Brundage held a secret emergency meeting on whether to call off the Games. The IOC decision, according to a U.S. Olympic Committee member, was only one vote short of cancelation. Afterwards Brundage announced that the Games will proceed as scheduled and that local student problems have no connection with the Olympics.

Mexico City — 28 October 1968

Suddenly it's all over—capped by the gushing of color and sound from what must have been history's most spectacular display of fireworks. As of today we can all begin again to weigh whether this two-week circus was really worth all the bloodshed, and whether Mexico lost more prestige by killing protesters than it gained by putting on the Games.

My resignation will be effective early next year, although for practical purposes my service with the Agency is ending now. Perhaps I've been foolish dedicating all my time in recent months to the Olympics instead of finding a new job. But I have money saved that will allow time to find work although it won't be easy because combining two families and continuing to live like this will take a hefty income. My sons have asked to continue living here with me instead of returning to Washington, which didn't surprise me, so the legal measures I've taken will be useful. All the fuss by the Ambassador and Scott and headquarters was foolish because Janet's threat was only a bluff.

I try not to show it, but I feel unsure about finding satisfying work inside the same system I rejected long ago as a university student. The difficult admission is that I became the servant of the capitalism I rejected. I became one of its secret policemen. The CIA, after all, is nothing more than the secret police of American capitalism, plugging up leaks in the political dam night and day so that shareholders of U.S. companies operating in poor countries can continue enjoying the rip-off. The key to CIA success is the 2 or 3 per cent of the population in poor countries that get most of the cream —that in most places get even more now than in 1960, while the marginalized 50, 60 or 70 per cent are getting a lesser share.

There is a contradiction in what I'm doing but I don't have much choice given the plans we have and our need for income. One has to take the realistic view: in order to fulfil responsibilities you have to compromise with the system knowing full well that the system doesn't work for everybody. This means everybody has to get what he can within decency's limits—which can be stretched when needed to assure a little more security. What I have to do now is get mine, inside the system, and forget I ever worked for the CIA. No, there's no use trying to change the system. What happened at the Plaza of the Three Cultures is happening all over the world to people trying to change the system. Life is too short and has too many delights that might be missed. At thirty-three I've got half a lifetime to enjoy them.

Part 5

Mexico City — January 1970

I begin again after a year of great disappointment and sense of failure. My hopes for a new start and a future in Mexico were clouded with the failure of my marriage plans, and I am unsure of my direction. The reasons are a complex series of mistakes, perhaps even unrealistic hopes from the beginning, but with results too damaging to overcome. For now I continue to pick up the pieces and try to arrange them in a stable pattern.

I am also unsure of the work I chose although I had the good fortune of joining with a new company started by friends whom I met in the Olympics. From the point of view of finances I've had to retrench considerably, a distasteful process but one with definite blessings. The prospects in this new company, which processes and markets an entirely new product, are very encouraging and I've been given the opportunity to buy shares. My relationships with the owners and the general manager, who is my good friend, are excellent.

Working in commerce, however, is still as lacking in satisfaction as it was years ago, and I have decided to enter the National University of Mexico for an advanced degree. Perhaps I will return to the U.S. to seek a teaching career. Over the Christmas and New Year's break I also began working on an outline for a book on the CIA. This would have been impossible if my plans had succeeded, but the way is now clear and may well lead to my being forced to leave Mexico.

A book describing CIA operations might help to illustrate the principles of foreign policy that got us into Vietnam and may well get us into similar situations. Secret CIA operations constitute the usually unseen efforts to shore up unjust, unpopular, minority governments, always with the hope that overt military intervention (as in Vietnam and the Dominican Republic) will not be necessary. The more successful CIA operations are, the more remote overt intervention becomes—and the more remote become reforms. Latin America in the 1960s is all the proof one needs.

A book on the CIA could also illustrate how the interests of the privileged minorities in poor countries lead back to, and are identified with, the interests of the rich and powerful who control the U.S. Counter-insurgency doctrine tries to blur these international class lines by appeals to nationalism and patriotism and by falsely relating movements against the capitalist minorities to Soviet expansionism. But what counter-insurgency really comes down to is the protection of the capitalists back in America, their property and their privileges. U.S. national security, as preached by U.S. leaders, is the security of the capitalist class in the U.S., not the security of the rest of the people—certainly not the security of the poor except by way of reinforcing poverty. It is from the class interests in the U.S. that our counter-insurgency programs flow, together with that most fundamental of American foreign policy principles: that any government, no matter how bad, is better than a communist one—than a government of workers, peasants and ordinary people. Our government's support for corruption and injustice in Latin America flows directly from the determination of the rich and powerful in the U.S., the capitalists, to retain and expand these riches and power.

I must be careful to speak little of my ideas for the book. Jim Noland replaced Win Scott as Chief of Station here when Scott retired last September. Scott opened an office—in his old profession as an actuary. I imagine that he continues to work for the Agency though now on contract, because his knowledge and experience in Mexico, and his vast range of friends, are too valuable to lose. This is not the time for the Agency to learn of my intentions.

Mexico City — June 1970

Another failure which is difficult to understand. Last week I spoke to four editors in New York in the hope of getting a publishing contract and an advance to finish the book on the CIA. Unfortunately those editors mostly wanted a sensationalist exposé approach—divorced from the more difficult political and economic realities that give the operations meaning.

I'm not sure what to do now except begin again, reorganizing the material and trying to write more clearly. Perhaps I should try more modestly with a magazine or newspaper article on our operations to keep Allende out of the Chilean Presidency in 1964—he's running again right now and maybe exposure of the 1964 operations could help him. The trouble is that people may not believe me—in New York I felt the editors weren't really certain that I'm who I say I am.

The bad part of the New York trip is that I left copies of my material there, and despite assurances by the editors I'm afraid the Agency may learn of my plans for a book. One word by the station to the Mexican service and I get the one-way ride to Toluca—except it's a lonely way to go, disappearing down one of those canyons. In a few weeks the classes at the National University begin and I'll just have to hope no one finds out about me—neither the Agency nor the UNAM people. It's discouraging to be isolated like this but the renewed bombing in North Vietnam and the inability of the Nixon administration to admit defeat, coupled with the Cambodian invasion, have strengthened my determination to start again. The killings at Kent State and Jackson State show clearly enough that sooner or later our counter-insurgency methods would be applied at home.

Mexico City — January 1971

Recent months have brought important decisions and perhaps at last I am finding the proper course. Behind these decisions have been the continuation of the Vietnam war and the Vietnamization program. Now more than ever exposure of CIA methods could help American people understand how we got into Vietnam and how our other Vietnams are germinating wherever the CIA is at work.

I have resigned from my friends' company, and my sons are back in Washington—although I continue at the University. I sent the children for Christmas only but feared Janet would go back on her agreement that they return. When she did just that I relented without much choice—in any case they will have a better school and will learn English for a change. I, too, may leave Mexico if I can get financial support because my new plan for the book requires research materials unobtainable here.

I have decided now to name all the names and organizations connected with CIA operations and to reconstruct as accurately as possible the events in which I participated. No more hiding behind theory and hypothetical cases to protect the tools of CIA adventures. The problem now will be documentation. I have also decided to seek ways of getting useful information on the CIA to revolutionary organizations that could use it to defend themselves better.

The key to adopting increasingly radical views has been my fuller comprehension of the class divisions of capitalist society based on property or the lack of it. The divisions were always there, of course, for me to see, but until recently I simply failed to grasp their meaning and consequences: adversary relationships, exploitation, labor as a market-place commodity, etc. But by getting behind the liberal concept of society, that concept that attempts to paint out the irreconcilable class conflicts, I think I have grasped an understanding of why liberal reform programs in Latin America have failed. At the same time I have seen more clearly the identity of interests of the classes in Latin America (and other underdeveloped areas) with the corresponding classes in the U.S. (and other developed areas).

The result of this class conception, of seeing that class identity comes before nationality, leads to rejection of liberal reform as the continuous renovating process leading step by step to the better society. Reform may indeed represent improvement, but it is fundamentally a maneuver by the ruling class in capitalist society, the capitalists, to allow exploitation to continue, to give a little in order to avoid losing everything. The Alliance for Progress was just this kind of fraud—although it was heralded as a Marshall Plan for Latin America that would permit, indeed encourage, a Latin American New Deal to sweep through the region behind the leadership of liberals like Betancourt, Haya de la Torre, Kubichek and Muñoz Marin.

But the Alliance for Progress failed as a social reform program, and it failed also to stimulate sufficient *per capita* economic growth, partly because of high population growth and partly because of slow growth in the value of the region's exports. These two factors, combined with rising consumption by upper and middle classes, provided less for the investments on which growth must be founded.

Result? The division in Latin American society widened between the modern core, dependent largely on the external sector, and the marginalized majority. By 1969 over half the people in the labor market were unemployed or underemployed. Where progress occurred in education, health care and housing it accrued mostly to the core societies in cities. Flight to cities by rural unemployed continued with the cities unable to absorb them productively. The vicious circle of small internal markets and lack of internal growth momentum also continued.

Particularly in countries like Brazil, where economies have grown rapidly, wealth and income have tended to even greater concentration. Latest figures of the U.N. Economic Commission for Latin America (ECLA) show that the poorest 20 per cent of the Latin American population now receive only 3.1 per cent of total income and that the entire lower 50 per cent receives only 13.4 per cent of total income. The upper 5 per cent income bracket, on the other hand, receives 33.4 per cent of total income. The contrast between the high 5 per cent and the lower 50 per cent of the population according to ECLA rests on the dominance of the entrepreneurial class—the capitalists—in the upper 5 per cent whose extraordinary income results largely from distribution of profits which could be reinvested instead of being consumed. In Mexico, for example, 60 per cent of the income of the top 5 per cent is dividends, in El Salvador 80 per cent, in Argentina 85 per cent. Most important, income of the high 5 per cent is growing more rapidly than the middle- and lower-income levels—thus aggravating income imbalance still more. The assumption, therefore, that economic growth under the Alliance for Progress would result in higher standards of living for the poorer half of the population is now demonstrated to have been false.

Land-reform programs have also failed. During the 1960s virtually every country in Latin America began some program to reform restrictive, precarious and uneconomical tenure systems—long accepted as the most serious structural cause of imbalance in wealth and income. But with the exceptions of Cuba, Peru and Chile the impulse has been lost and little progress made where the bulk of the potential income-producing resources lies. Concentration continues: the upper 1.8 per cent of the rural income scale holds more than 50 per cent of the farmland while the small landholders who number 25 per cent of the farm population hold only 2.4 per cent of farmland.

During these past ten years, while Latin American countries failed to establish more equitable distribution of land, wealth and income, considerable success could be claimed in counter-insurgency—including propaganda to attract people away from the Cuban solution as well as repression. As part of the counter-insurgency campaign, the Alliance for Progress in the short run did indeed raise many hopes and capture many imaginations in favor of the peaceful reform solutions that would not fundamentally jeopardize the dominance of the ruling capitalist minorities and their system. Since the 1960s however, as the psychological appeal of peaceful reform diminished in the face of failure, compensatory measures have been increasingly needed: repression and special programs, as in the field of organized labor, to divide the victims and neutralize their leaders. These measures constitute the four most important counter-insurgency programs through which the U.S. government strengthens the ruling minorities in Latin America: CIA operations, military assistance and training missions, AID Public Safety programs to help police, and trade-union operations through ORIT,‡ the International Trade Secretariats‡ and the AIFLD‡—all largely controlled by the CIA. Taken together these are the crutches given by the capitalist rulers of the U.S. to their counterparts in Latin America in order to obtain reciprocal support against threats to American capitalism. Never mind all those marginals—what's good for capitalists in Latin America is good for capitalists in the U.S.A.

A liberal reform program like the Alliance for Progress is a safety-valve for capitalist injustice and exploitation—as the frontier served for release and escape from oppression in American cities during the last century. Such a program is only what the ruling-class will allow by way of redistribution during a time of danger to the system as a whole—something that runs against the current and the inherent drive to concentrate wealth and political power in ever fewer hands. Once the sense of urgency and danger fades, so also the pressure on the safety-valve declines and the natural forces for accumulation recuperate, soon wiping out the relative gains that the exploited obtained through reform. Reforms are temporary palliatives that can never eliminate the exploitative relationship on which capitalism is based.

Increasingly, as the oppressed in capitalist society comprehend the myth of liberal reform, their ruling minorities have no choice but to increase repression in order to avert socialist revolution. Eliminate CIA stations, U.S. military missions, AID Public Safety missions and the "free" trade-union programs and those minorities would disappear, faster perhaps, than they themselves would imagine.

My security situation is the same, although I am puzzled that the CIA does not seem to have discovered that I am writing, or if they know, why they haven't visited me. John Horton is now Chief of Station here, and others with whom I served at other stations have been assigned here although they have shown no interest in me. Through friends I have sent copies of my new outline to a publisher in Paris—perhaps at last I will get some encouragement.

Mexico City — March 1971

A quick trip to Montreal for conversations with a publisher's representative has given me new hope for both financial and research support. Although my outline and written material are acceptable, the problem remains where to find the information needed to reconstruct the events in which I participated in order to show precisely how the Agency operates. We discussed Paris or Brussels after agreeing that for security reasons anywhere in the U.S. would be unwise. We also discussed Cuba, where possibly the research materials could be found and even research assistance arranged.

I said I would be fearful of going to Cuba for several reasons: my past work against Cuba and communism, possible Soviet pressures, my reluctance to engage in sessions for counter-intelligence ploys, problems with the CIA afterwards. Mostly, I suppose, I am fearful that if the CIA learned that I had gone to Cuba they would begin a campaign to denigrate me as a traitor. As my hope is to return as quickly as possible to the U.S. after finishing, I would be increasing the odds for prosecution for publishing secrets if I had gone to Cuba.

There are some advantages, however, in going there. First, the security situation *vis à vis* CIA would be better and if the research materials are available I could work more calmly and faster. Moreover, in Havana I could arrange to get information on the CIA to interested Latin American revolutionary organizations through their representatives—efficiently and securely. Then, too, I would have the chance to see first hand what the Cuban Revolution has meant to the people and what their problems are. Such a trip is something I thought would be possible only after I finished.

After sleeping on the idea I agreed that I would go to Cuba if the trip can be arranged. Presumably the book will have to be politically acceptable to the Cubans and the research materials available. If I do not go to Cuba I will go to Paris to finish so my security situation will be improved in any case. At present I will say nothing, and hope that the CIA doesn't get wind of these plans.

Paris — August 1971

Great leaps of progress but so much work remains. In May I went to Havana to discuss the research materials needed, and they agreed to assist with what they have available—which appears to be a good deal. They also invited me to stay there to finish as much as possible, which I accepted. However, as I was committed to visit my sons in Washington, I returned to Paris for conversations with the publisher and then went to the U.S. for two weeks with the boys. I have returned to check availability of research materials here and will proceed shortly to Havana.

While in Cuba I traveled for several weeks around the island visiting a variety of development projects in agriculture, livestock, housing, health and education. The sense of pride and purpose evident in the Cubans is impressive. My worries about going to Cuba were unfounded and were more than replaced by fears of returning to the U.S. to see my sons. I shouldn't have returned, because I had gone to Cuba openly, but strangely I must have eluded the travel control—or the system failed to identify me in time. I wonder if my luck will make the Cubans suspicious.

Havana — October 1971

I begin to wonder whether writing this book was such a good idea. I have found considerable material to refresh my memory and to reconstruct events, and I have written a respectable number of pages. Trouble is that I'm running far afield into matters that are peripheral to my CIA work. At the same time the material here is more limited than I had thought, and I may have to risk returning to México and South America to continue the research. In any case I will return next month to Paris to continue there. My mood is gloomy as I feel disorganized and still quite far from having a presentable book. The events I want to describe get further into history each day—and each day the sense of urgency to finish quickly gets stronger.

Aside from specific information for reconstructing events, I have found here a number of excellent economic reports and essays on Latin American problems and their roots in U.S. exploitation of the region. One report by the Organization of American States describes clearly how the real beneficiary of the Alliance for Progress was the U.S. economy rather than the Latin American economies. This report[1] recognizes the failure to make substantial beginnings in land reform and income redistribution—similarly the failure of foreign aid and private investment to stimulate accelerated economic growth which the report projects as the key to integration of the masses.

The functioning of the external sectors of Latin American economies (excepting Venezuela as a special case) during these ten years demonstrates how these economies have supported the U.S. standard of living to the detriment of the Latin American people: Americans, in other words, can thank Latin American workers for having contributed to our ease and comfort. It is the external sector that counts because exports and foreign aid determine how much machinery and technology can be imported for economic growth, and during the past ten years the external sectors of Latin American economies failed to generate adequate growth.

---

1. *Analysis of the Economic and Social Evolution of Latin America Since the Beginnings of the Alliance for Progress*, Washington, 3 August, 1971.

From 1961 to 1970 Latin America paid out to other regions, mostly to the U.S., a little over 20 billion dollars, practically all in financial services (royalties, interest and repatriated profits to foreign capital). About 30 per cent of this potential deficit was offset by export surpluses, while the remaining 70 per cent was paid through new indebtedness, new private foreign investment and other capital movements. The new indebtedness, representing as it does new costs for financial services, raised still higher the proportion of export earnings required for repatriation of royalties, interest and profits to foreigners, mostly U.S., thus decreasing amounts available for investment.

During these ten years private foreign capital provided new investment of only 5.5 billion dollars while taking out 20 billion dollars. The lion's share went to U.S. investors whose investment, which averaged about 12 billion dollars in value, returned about 13 billion dollars to the U.S. Without the loans and grants from the U.S. under the Alliance for Progress, Latin America would have had to devote about 10 per cent more of its export earnings to the services account so that "fair return" on investment could be satisfied. Otherwise a moratorium or some other extreme measure would have been necessary—hardly conducive to new credit and investment.

The Alliance for Progress has been, in effect, a subsidy program for U.S. exporters and private investors—in many cases the same firms. For Latin America this has meant a deficit in the external sector of about 6 billion dollars that limited the importation of equipment and technology needed for faster economic growth—the deficit compensated by new indebtedness. For the United States this has meant a return to private investors of about five dollars for every dollar sent from the U.S. to Latin America during the period, plus a favorable trade balance, plus billions of dollars in loans that are earning interest and will some day be repaid. In other words Latin America through the Alliance for Progress has contributed to the economic development of the United States and has gone into debt to do it. No wonder we prop up these governments and put down the revolutionaries.

In contrast to the myth of the Alliance for Progress, which ensures that the gap between the U.S. and Latin American economies will grow, the interesting alternative does not assume that economic growth is the determinant for integration of the marginalized majority. Based on a distinction between *economic growth* and *social development*, the revolutionary solution begins with integration. The Cuban position paper for this year's sessions of ECLA, entitled *Latin America and the Second United Nations Decade for Development,* views social integration through structural changes in institutions—revolutionary change rather than reform—as the condition for development. Economic growth alone, with benefits concentrated in the modern core minority, cannot be considered as national development because the whole society doesn't participate. Institutional change, social integration and economic growth is the revolutionary order of priorities rather than economic growth, reform and eventual extension of benefits to the marginals—little by little so as not to affect the wealthy.

The institutional changes: first, the land tenure system must be altered to break the injustices and low productivity resulting from the latifundia–minifundia problem. Second, the foreign economic enterprises must be nationalized so that the product of labor is used for national development instead of being channeled to shareholders in a highly-developed, capital-exporting country. Third, the most important national economic activities must come under state control and be subjected to overall development planning with new criteria for marketing, expansion and general operations. Fourth, personal income must be redistributed in order to give purchasing power to the previously marginalized. Fifth, a real working union between government and people must be nurtured so that the sacrifices ahead can be endured and national unity strengthened.

During this early period of institutional change, attained with few exceptions, in the Cuban view, through armed struggle, the basic problems of priorities emerge: immediate development of social overhead projects in health and education *v.* expansion of consumption of the formerly marginalized *v.* investment in infrastructure. The redistribution of income, new costs of social projects, and increased internal consumption leave even less productive capacity for re-investment than before. High demand causes inflationary pressures and black markets, while rationing is necessary to assure equity in distribution.

The only source of relief to offset the investment deficit, according to the Cubans, is foreign aid. Aggravating the development problem is the exodus of managers and professionals who join the overthrown landed gentry and upper middle classes in seeking to avoid participation in national development by fleeing to "free" countries. Another drain on investment is the obvious need to maintain oversized military forces to defeat domestic and foreign counter-revolutionary forces.

The romantic stage of the revolution ends, then, as the realities of the long struggle for national development take root. Internally the revolution calls for ever-greater productivity, particularly in exports, so that dependence on external financing can be kept as low as possible. Nevertheless, years will pass before economic growth will reach the point of decreasing reliance on foreign aid. Sacrifice and greater effort are the order of the day, and neither can possibly result if the producers—the workers, peasants and others—fail to identify in the closest union with the revolutionary government. Mistakes will be made, as every Cuban is quick to admit, but there can be no doubt that national development here is well underway and accelerating.

In Cuba the people have education, health care and adequate diet, while long strides are being made in housing. When one considers that over half the population of Latin America, over 150 million people, are still deprived of participation in these minimal benefits of modern culture and technology, it becomes clear that the only country that has really attained the social goals of the Alliance for Progress is Cuba.

I still have no indication that the CIA knows I am

writing this book or that I have come to Cuba. During recent months I have tried to follow the growth of the Frente Amplio in Uruguay in preparation for the national elections next month. The situation is so ready for election operations by the Montevideo station that I have yielded to the compulsion to denounce this possibility. I wrote a letter to *Marcha* in Montevideo describing some of the standard covert-action operations and suggesting that the Agency may well be involved right now in operations against the Frente and in support of candidates of the traditional parties. If *Marcha* publishes even part of it, any doubts about my intentions on the part of the CIA must disappear.

Paris — January 1972

The letter to *Marcha* was a mistake. A couple of days after Christmas, while resting before dinner with my sons—they came for the vacation period—we had a knock at the door and who should appear but Keith Gardiner,‡ an old JOT and OCS colleague who spent some years in Brazil during the 1960s. I was unprepared for a visit from the CIA and I agreed, because my children live near him and play with his children, to accompany him to dinner. On leaving our hotel he disappeared for a few moments in order, he said, to release a colleague who was standing by in case I had received him in an unfriendly manner.

After dinner I agreed to speak privately to him. He surprised me with a machine copy of what *Marcha* had published of my letter, adding that Mr. Helms‡ wants to know just what I think I am doing. Not yet knowing that my letter to *Marcha* has been published, I decided to develop a bluff that might convince the Agency that there is nothing they can do to stop publication of the book. I told Keith that I have completed an over-sized draft that I am now editing down to appropriate size—the truth being that I have completed less than one-third of my research.

Gardiner admitted that the Paris station (Dave

Murphy, former Chief of the Soviet Bloc Division, is Chief of Station here now) located me through the French liaison service. Pointedly suggesting that I am being manipulated by the Soviets through my publisher, he said the Agency's chief concern is exactly what I have revealed in material already submitted or discussed—which I refused to talk about. I assured Keith, however, that I will be making no damaging revelations and will submit the final draft for approval before publication. On the *Marcha* letter he denied that the Montevideo station had engaged in any election operation, but he said the Bordaberry campaign (Bordaberry, a former Ruralista leader, won, running as a Colorado) received large infusions of Brazilian money —the role of the Brazilian military dictatorship as surrogate for U.S. imperialism in South America was also evident in the Bolivian rightist military *coup* a few months ago.

Gardiner told me that in September of this year he will enter the University of Wisconsin for a Master's Degree in Latin American studies—the first time a DDP operations officer has been sent for higher university study that either of us can remember. Then, again pointedly, he asked if I might reveal his name so as to expose him at the university. I assured him I wouldn't and suggested that while studying he keep in mind the possibility of joining the fight against the CIA and American imperialism. After all, why be a secret policeman for U.S. capitalists when the system itself is disappearing?

Not knowing to what ends the French service will go to please the Agency, I feared after meeting Keith that I might be deported under some pretext on a flight having New York as its first stop. So the next day I took the boys to Spain for the final week before their return to school. Now I continue here, and I must be careful to avoid provocation while finishing as fast as I can. I don't know if my bluff will work or whether the French service or the Agency will take action against me. I shouldn't have written the letter to *Marcha*.

Paris — August 1972

Events in the past three months have taken unfavorable turns, and I am fearful that the CIA is now closing in. My money has run out and I am living on small donations from friends, street surveillance has forced me to live in hiding, research still pending in Cuba was canceled, I still cannot find the information I need, and people who have befriended me and on whom I am depending show frequent signs of being infiltrators.

In May I went to Havana again for discussions on research left from last year, and on additional needs that have arisen since. For reasons I fail to understand there is a lack of confidence in my intentions about the book's political content. As a result, research I left pending with them last year has not been done—the same as cancelation if I have to do it myself. Very disappointing although understandable—the Cubans wouldn't want to be embarrassed by a politically unacceptable book, and political content is something that must come at the end, after the research is finished.

In June my publisher's advance ran out, and in order to get another advance I would have had to amend the contract to allow for publication first in France. It may be chauvinism, but as I am seriously criticizing American institutions, I'm determined to make every effort for publication there first, or at least simultaneously with publication elsewhere. I couldn't accept the amendment and I am depending on a few friends for sustenance.

A few days after returning from Cuba I suddenly began to recognize street surveillances in Paris, which I suspect may be the French service—possibly at CIA request. But being unsure of the sponsorship and purpose of the surveillance, I went to live secretly at the studio of a friend, Catherine, who agreed that I could stay there until the problem is resolved.

About the same time as the surveillance began I was befriended by several Americans, two of whom display excessive curiosity and other indications that suggest they may be CIA agents trying to get close to me for different purposes. One of these, a supposed freelance journalist named Sal Ferrera,‡ claims to write for College Press Service, Alternative Features Service and other "underground" organizations in the U.S. As a means to get some financial relief I agreed to an "interview" with Sal on my work in the CIA which he will try to sell. Meanwhile he gives me small loans and tries to find out where I am living.

With Sal I met Leslie Donegan‡ who claims to be a Venezuelan heiress, graduate of Boston University and currently studying at the University of Geneva. At Sal's suggestion I discussed the book and my financial situation with Leslie and allowed her to keep copies of the manuscript to read over a weekend. She agreed to finance me until I finish—right now I am rushing to prepare what I have written so far, for presentation to an American publisher who will be here in early October. Sal is also helping—he obtained a typewriter for me when I had to turn in my hired one for the deposit. Strangely, he refused to tell me where he got it—only that it's borrowed and that I may have to give it back quickly when the owner returns from London.

I shouldn't have allowed Leslie to read the manuscript, nor should I continue associating with either her or Sal. However, I need the "loans" they are giving me in order to survive until getting the contract with the American publisher in October. If indeed they are working for the CIA, relatively little harm is done because the cryptonyms and pseudonyms I have used will confuse, and I have assured them both that I do not intend to reveal true names—just as I did with Gardiner. I have also hidden away copies and preserved my notes so that the unfinished portions could be finished by someone else.

Leslie tried to persuade me to accompany her to Spain, but I begged off in order to work with Therese—another friend who is typing the manuscript for presentation to the American publisher, and who is being paid by Leslie. I certainly wouldn't go to Spain at Leslie's invitation. If she is working for the CIA they may have planned a dope plant with the cooperation of the Spanish service to get me put on ice for a few years. Under Spanish-style justice prisoners can probably be kept from writing books. If my suspicions about these two are ever confirmed, it will be ironic that the CIA, while trying to follow my writing and set a trap, actually financed me through the most difficult period.

Of all these recent problems the worst is that I haven't had the money for the boys to come for the summer. By Christmas, when they have their next vacation, a year will have passed without seeing them. Nevertheless, I'm sure that in October I'll get new financial support so that they can come in December. On no account can I return to the U.S. until I finish. After meeting with the publisher in October I'll go to London for final research at the British Museum newspaper library—they have all the newspapers from Quito, Montevideo and Mexico City for the periods when I was at those stations, and I will be able to reconstruct the most important operational episodes accurately.

These weeks are black. I am very unsure of what may happen.

Paris — 6 October 1972

How is it possible? I cannot believe that somewhere in the five or six hundred pages I've written, this editor couldn't see a book. Or if he could, perhaps he thinks I'm a bad risk. What he wants is drama, romance and glorification of what I did. When he left two days ago for Orly he barely showed any interest.

One can force a positive attitude at times, but to hit a new low after three years has its effects. Nevertheless I continue. Yesterday I began to record on tape the essential information that I can remember on what remains of the book in this version. These are descriptions of operations that I knew of or participated in and that will serve as illustrations. This is easily the most important part and will include eighty to ninety episodes that I will reconstruct from press reports in London, adding our role. By the end of next week the tapes will be finished, and I'll store copies in a safe place. The following week I'll go to Brussels for a short visit with my father who will be running through, and from there to London.

The CIA has been active in recent months trying to bring pressure. In September the General Counsel visited my father in Florida, and also Janet, to express Helms's concern over the book and my trips to Cuba. He also left copies of the recent court decision holding former CIA employees to the secrecy agreement and requiring submission of manuscripts for approval prior to publication. Sorry, but the national security for me lies in socialism, not in protection of CIA operations and agents.

Just after the General Counsel's visit to Janet I received a letter from my oldest son—almost eleven now—telling me of the visit:

> Hi,
>
> I wanted to tell you that a man from the government came to talk to mom about you, but she did not say anything except your address. What they told her is that they wanted to pay you money to stop and that they would offer another job (the job I'm not certain about).

I went to a telephone at the University of Paris where everyone calls overseas without paying—my son told me he had overheard the conversation while hiding after having been told to go away. The address doesn't matter because it's Sal's—he's been getting my mail since May so that I can keep Catherine's studio secret.

In order to keep money coming from Leslie and Sal during these final weeks I have kept up the fiction of following through with a team effort in London. They have both agreed to accompany me there—Sal will transcribe the tapes and Leslie will help with newspaper research at the British Museum. If I can get support in London I'll break with them completely but meanwhile I need their help. Today at a previously arranged meeting Leslie brought me a used typewriter that she bought only minutes before to replace the one Sal lent me last July. Apparently the owner of the borrowed typewriter called at Sal's and angrily demanded the immediate return of his machine. So I had to rush back to Catherine's studio for the borrowed typewriter which I returned right away to Sal. I don't need the one Leslie bought because I'm making the recordings, so I left it at Therese's apartment there in the Latin Quarter where Leslie gave it to me.

Little things about Sal and Leslie keep me suspicious. Often after pre-planned meetings with them I pick up surveillance and they continue to press me about where I'm living. I must hurry to finish the tapes— anyone would be able to use them to finish the research and the book. Things can only get better from now on.

Paris — 14 October 1972

Today my doubts about Sal and Leslie were resolved —in the case of Leslie, completely, and in the case of Sal, almost. It began two days ago over pizza when Leslie gave me money for the trip to Brussels and London. When she asked how I like the typewriter she bought me, I told her I haven't used it because of the recordings—adding that I left it at Therese's apartment. She seemed hurt that I had left it there, particularly as Therese never locks her apartment. Afterwards when Sal and I were alone, he said Leslie was very angry that I had left the typewriter with Therese, and, that if it disappears (Therese has already had several intrusions), Leslie will stop financing me.

Without reflecting properly I took the typewriter from Therese's apartment to Catherine's studio, although as usual I went through my counter-surveillance routine. I placed it under the table where I work and this afternoon after finishing the last tape I went out to buy a bottle of beer. When I returned I noticed a man and woman standing in front of Catherine's door, looking as if they had just knocked. As I approached the door, however, they backed away and began to embrace. I knocked and Catherine opened, laughing as she noticed the embrace in the dark hallway.

On glancing back at the couple with their full coats and large travel bags, I suddenly realized what was happening. After closing the door I took Catherine aside and whispered that the man and woman were probably monitors of a bugging operation to discover where I am living. She said she saw a hearing-aid in the ear of the man, which suggested that the irritating beeps causing interference on my radio over the past two days were the signal being monitored.

Catherine followed the couple down the steps to see where they went, and in their confusion they went all the way to the ground floor where the doorway is always locked with a key. This building, only a block from the Seine, has its regular entrance on the side away from the river and up the slope—corresponding to the third or fourth floor up from the ground floor where the monitors went. As they had no key they stood around for a moment, embraced again as Catherine passed, said nothing, and began to walk back up the stairs. Catherine, who had been watching them from the garbage-room, came back to the studio and told me that they seemed to have portable radios or cases beneath their coats.

Now it was clear. Since bringing the typewriter that Leslie bought for me to Catherine's studio, I have been hearing a beeping sound on my own portable FM radio. I paid little attention, however, because of the nearness to ORTF and the frequent other interference I get. I reached under the table, raised the typewriter case with the machine inside, and began to turn it. As I turned it the beeping sound on my radio got louder and softer in direct relation to the turning. Catherine carried it out of the building and the beeping completely disappeared. When she returned it began again. Later I tore open the lining of the inside roof of the case and found an elaborate installation of transistors, batteries, circuits, wiring and antennas—also a tiny microphone for picking up voices. The objects were all very small, mounted in spaces cut out of a piece of ¼-inch plywood cut exactly the size of the case and glued against the roof. Not only was the object designed to discover where I live through direction-finding, it appears also made for transmitting conversations.

I shall leave for Brussels in three days and Catherine will go to the country for a few days—there is certainly nothing they can do to her. Before leaving I shall stay in cheap hotels in Montmartre, changing each morning so that the police cannot find me through their registry slips. From London I will write to Sal and Leslie telling them that I prefer to work alone from now on—I can find some source of support for the two or three months until I finish. Leslie is a spy, and I will know for certain about Sal when I ask him where he got the first typewriter he lent me. Obviously that first machine was lent as a stand-in until the bugged typewriter was ready and they could effect a sudden switch. Leslie's feigned resentment when I left the typewriter at Therese's apartment was the ploy to get me to take the typewriter to where I live.

The damage may have been slight, but I've been foolish. From now on I take no chances.

London — 24 October 1972

Today, Tuesday, I arrived in London on the train from Paris. In order to avoid carrying the manuscript and other materials to Brussels—where the CIA might have tried to talk to me in my father's presence—I went back to Paris to get them and to proceed here. At the Gare du Nord this morning a friend was waiting to tell me that on Friday Therese was arrested and taken to an interrogation center at the Ministry of the Interior. For several hours she was questioned about me and the book—they know of my CIA background and said the U.S. government considers me an enemy of the state. They were most interested in discovering where I lived in Paris, but as Therese didn't know she couldn't tell them. Apparently she played dumb and was finally released. Tomorrow I will call to reassure her and to see if there are more details.

What is interesting about the arrest is that the French have continued to help the CIA—the surveillance and the crude opening of my correspondence sent c/o Sal were probably done by the French. However, by Friday—the day Therese was arrested—the CIA had known for a week where I was living. If the French service didn't know, it was only because the station hadn't told them—probably in order to avoid admitting that I caught the monitors and discovered the installation in the typewriter case. After having helped the Paris station, the French service might not like being kept on chasing around for my hideaway for days after it was known to the CIA.

Tonight by telephone Sal also told me of Therese's arrest, adding that Leslie "panicked" and went to Spain on Saturday. I feigned concern that she hadn't come here as planned, but Sal said he too was going to Spain —tomorrow if he can—in order to let things "cool off." I don't want them to know for sure that I am breaking with them, not yet anyway, so I protested to Sal that he must come here to help as planned. He insisted that he go to Spain in order to convince Leslie to come to London, and he will call by telephone later this week after seeing her.

The British service was well prepared for my arrival. My name was on the immigration check-list on the ship crossing the Channel, which caused me a long interview and then a longer wait. I can take no chances on jeopardizing my status here. Tomorrow I must begin looking for support, as I have money for only a few days.

London — 7 December 1972

Relief at last. After calling at the International Commission for Peace and Disarmament, a group that channels protest against U.S. crimes in Vietnam, I was sent to several other possible sources of support, finally to the editor who will help me finish. I now have a contract to publish here, with an advance sufficient to carry me through to the end as well as transcription service and other important support.

At the British Museum, moreover, I began reading the newspapers and discovered that here is the pot of gold I've been chasing for the past three years. In less than one week I discovered so many events in which we participated that I have decided to read all the newspapers, day by day, from the time I went to Ecuador until I returned to Washington from Uruguay. The Mexico City papers will also be valuable for selected events there. The editor accepts the added delay—this places completion from a few months to a year or more away—but it will be worth the effort. Sometimes I feel that I am reading the CIA files themselves, so much of what the Agency does is reflected in actual events. I may, in fact, be able to piece together a diary presentation to make the operations more readable.

I tried at first to live under an assumed name, more or less secretly as I had done in Paris. But each night as I left the Museum I was trailed by surveillance teams, and fatigue led me to give up the effort to conceal where I was living. My mail is again being opened, quite obviously, and meetings arranged by telephone have generated immediate surveillance once more. At times I wonder if the surveillance is mainly for harassment, as it is so clumsy and indiscreet, but if the British service does nothing more serious, I shall be able to finish in calm.

In telephone conversations with Sal and Leslie in Spain, she again tried to convince me to go there but she also refused to send me money. Sal eventually came to London to continue helping me—not knowing, perhaps, that I've solved the problem of support—but at our first meeting I refused his help unless he gave me certain information. Making it clear I thought Leslie was a spy, but without revealing how I found out, I asked Sal a series of questions on his university background and his connections with the underground press in the U.S. Eventually we came around to the first typewriter he lent me, and when he continued refusing to reveal who gave it to him (just as he had refused earlier in July) I told him we could go no further. I can only conclude that the CIA failed to establish a proper cover story for the first typewriter, since Sal could neither explain where it came from nor why he refused to explain. There is a remote possibility that Sal is the victim of an amazing chain of coincidences, but I can have nothing more to do with him.

In spite of the recent good news there is also a gloomy side. As soon as I had oral agreement on the new contract I telephoned the boys to tell them I have the money for them to come at Christmas. To my dismay Janet said she would not let them come, insisting that I go there to see them. She knows perfectly well that I cannot risk a trip to the U.S. until I have finished the book, so she must be cooperating with the CIA to ensure that in my desperation to see my sons I will risk a trip back now. It won't work.

London — October 1973

I hurry to finish, now more confident than ever that I really will see this project to the end. The *coup* in Chile, terrible as it is, has been like a spur for even faster work. Signs of preparations for the *coup* were clear all along. While economic assistance to Chile plummeted after Allende's election, military aid continued: in 1972 military aid to the Chilean generals and admirals was the highest to any country in Latin America; the growth of the CIA station since 1970 under the Chief of Station, Ray Warren;‡ the murder of General Schneider; the militancy of well-heeled "patriotic" organizations such as Patria y Libertad; the economic sabotage; the truckers' strike of 1972 with the famous "dollar-per-day" to keep the strikers from working; and the truckers' strike of this past June—both strikes probably were financed by the CIA, perhaps through the International Transport Workers' Federation‡ (ITF), perhaps through the AIFLD which had already trained some 9000 Chilean workers. Perhaps through Brazil. So many possible ways. Finally the Plan Z: so like our Flores document in Quito, our evidence against the Soviets in Montevideo, so typical of CIA black documents. Was it placed in the Minister's office by an agent in the Ministry? More likely the Chilean generals simply asked the station to write Plan Z, just as our Uruguayan liaison collaborators asked us to write the scenario for proof of Soviet intervention with trade unions in 1965 and 1966.

Brazilian participation in preparations for the *coup* and follow-up repression clearly demonstrates Brazil's subordinate but key role in the U.S. government's determination to retain capitalist hegemony in Latin America. Brazilian exiles arrested in Chile are recognizing their former torturers from Brazilian jails, as now they are again forced to submit to such horror. What we see in Chile today is still another flowering of Brazilian fascism.

Only a few more months and ten years will have passed since that 31 March when the cables arrived in the Montevideo station reporting Goulart's overthrow: Such joy and relief! Such a régime we created. Not just through the CIA organization and training of the military régime's intelligence services; not just through the military assistance programs—good for 165 million dollars in grants, credit sales and surplus equipment since 1964 plus special training in the U.S. for thousands; not just through the AID police-assistance program worth over 8 million dollars and training for more than 100,000 Brazilian policemen; not just the rest of the U.S. economic assistance program—worth over 300 million dollars in 1972 alone and over 4 billion dollars in the last twenty-five years. Not just the multi-lateral economic assistance programs where U.S. influence is strong—worth over 2.5 billion dollars since 1946 and over 700 million dollars in 1972. Most important, every one of the hundreds of millions of private U.S. dollars invested in Brazil is a dollar in support of fascism.

All this to support a régime in which the destitute, marginalized half of the population—some fifty million people—are getting still poorer while the small ruling élite and their military puppets get an ever larger share. All this to support a régime under which the income of the high 5 per cent of the income scale now gets almost 40 per cent of total income, while half the population has to struggle for survival on 15 per cent of total income. All this to create a façade of "economic miracle" where *per capita* income is still only about 450 dollars per year—still behind Nicaragua, Peru and nine other Latin American countries—and where even the U.N. Economic Commission for Latin America reports that the "economic miracle" has been of no benefit to the vast majority of the population. All this for a régime that has to clamor for export markets because creation of an internal market would imply reforms such as redistribution of income and a slackening of repression—possibly even a weakening of the dictatorship. All this to support a régime denounced the world over for the barbaric torture and inhuman treatment inflicted as a matter of routine on its thousands of political prisoners—including priests, nuns and many non-Marxists—many of whom fail to survive the brutality or are murdered outright. Repression in Brazil even includes cases of the torture of children, before their parents' eyes, in order to force the parents to give information. This is what the CIA, police assistance, military training and economic aid programs have brought to the Brazilian people. And the Brazilian régime is spreading it around: Bolivia in 1971, Uruguay in February of this year and now Chile.

Ecuador, too, has seen some remarkable events since I left. The reform program begun by the military junta in 1963 eventually led to the junta's own overthrow in 1966—the early relief of the ruling class because of the junta's repression of the left gave way to alarm over economic reforms and finally a combined opposition from left and right, similar to the forces that led to Velasco's overthrow in 1961. After a few months' provisional government, a Constituent Assembly convened to form a government and to write a new Constitution—Ecuador's seventeenth—which was promulgated in 1967. The 1968 election provided in the new Constitution developed into a new struggle between Camilo Ponce, on the right, and yes, Velasco, on the . . . well, wherever he happened to be. Velasco was elected President for the fifth time, but largely because he was supported by Carlos Julio Arosemena who had managed to recoup a considerable political following after his overthrow.

Velasco's fifth presidency began with the familiar spate of firings of government employees to make way for his own supporters, followed in 1970 by his closure of the Congress and assumption of dictatorial powers. Ecuador's seventeenth Constitution had a short life, although Velasco promised that elections would occur on schedule in 1972. Trouble was that Asaad Bucaram, the presidential candidate everyone knew would win, is too honest and too well known to favor the common people. (Carlos Arizaga Vega‡* was the leading Conservative Party candidate.) After Velasco failed to force Bucaram to stay in exile, or to prove through an elaborate campaign that Bucaram was not really born in Ecuador (both campaigns only strengthened Bucaram) all the traditional parties and economic élites —and eighty-year-old Velasco himself—combined to promote chaos and military intervention once again. In February 1972, a few months before the elections, the Ecuadorean military leaders took over and Velasco was overthrown for the fourth time in his five presidencies. During the years since I left there have been no meaningful reforms to ease the extreme injustices that prevailed when I first arrived in 1960.

Ecuador, however, after all these generations of political tragi-comedy and popular suffering has suddenly become the center of very great international attention. Petroleum! Ecuador this year became a major oil exporter, thanks to discoveries in the Amazonian jungles east of the Andes. Not that these discoveries were really so recent. It is now known that the oil was discovered by the cartel in explorations beginning in 1920, but was kept secret to avoid oversupply on the world market. By 1949 the petroleum companies had been so successful in keeping the fabulous reserves secret that Galo Plaza, then Ecuadorean President, diverted national attention from the eastern region by describing traditional hopes for oil or other resources

---

* The author has no knowledge that this person is in any way connected with the Agency at present.

in the oriente as one great myth. At the same time, under Plaza's leadership, Ecuador became the banana republic that it is—not surprising since Plaza had worked for United Fruit which, with Standard Fruit, became the dominant power for production and marketing of Ecuadorean bananas. Meanwhile the oil companies made millions by importing petroleum.

In March 1964, just after I left Ecuador, the military junta contracted for new exploration with the Texaco-Gulf consortium and subsequent contracts under other governments followed. But discoveries in the late 1960s could not be kept secret as in the past, and soon Ecuadorean reserves were being described as equal to or greater than those of Venezuela. By 1971 all the oriente region and all the coastal and offshore areas had been contracted for exploration and exploitation—in almost all cases with terms exceedingly prejudicial to Ecuador but with undoubted benefits to the government officials involved. All seven of the big companies got contracts, as did a number of smaller companies, and even Japanese concerns. By mid-1972 the pipeline from the oriente basin over the Andes and down to the Pacific port of Esmeraldas was completed, and oil started to flow—just a few months after the latest military takeover from Velasco. This year Ecuadorean income from oil exports is approaching the value of all the country's exports in 1972 when they were still dominated by bananas, coffee and cacao. Prospects for increased production and income (800,000 to 1,000,000 barrels daily) are almost beyond imagination.

First indications from the new military government created hope that a leftist nationalism of the Peruvian brand might channel benefits from petroleum exports to the masses of poor most in need of help. There was even talk of land reform and social justice and equal opportunity—familiar themes. Soon, however, a Brazilian-lining faction within the military leadership began to grow and struggles continue between these reactionary forces and the progressives who favor the Peruvian model. Nevertheless quite significant steps were taken to recover control of the petroleum industry and to reverse the shameful sell-outs made by the military junta in 1964 and by succeeding governments.

Several former government officials were even tried for their participation in the vast corruption connected with petroleum contracts between 1964 and 1972.

But so far the reactionary forces in the Ecuadorean government have been able to avoid agrarian reform, while military institutions take half of all the petroleum income—the other half being invested in electrification. Benefits from petroleum so far are best described by AID: "Initially, the beneficial effects of oil are being felt mainly in the more prosperous sectors of Ecuadorean society, while the poor half of the population remains virtually isolated from the economic mainstream. The rural and urban poor, with an average annual *per capita* income of less than eighty dollars, provide an inadequate market to stimulate the growth of the modern sector."

From a distance one can only imagine the struggle now under way between left and right within the context of Ecuadorean nationalism. Some of the forces involved, however, are evident. Brazilian support to reactionaries is part of larger efforts to get into active exploitation of Ecuador's petroleum—not surprising as Brazil must import 80 per cent of its oil. On the U.S. side, while military aid was suspended because of the tuna war, the Public Safety program goes on—worth about four million dollars in organization, training and equipment. The 1972 Public Safety project for Ecuador describes the program's purpose: "To assist the Government of Ecuador to develop and maintain an atmosphere conducive to increasing domestic and foreign investment, and the law and order necessary for a stable democratic society, by working through the National Police." The logic seems odd: the military government has declared its intention to remain in power indefinitely. The National Police enforces military rule. Therefore, strengthening the National Police will lead to a "stable, democratic society."

The CIA station also continues—now larger than ever with at least seven operations officers under Embassy cover in Quito (Paul Harwood‡ is now Chief of

Station) and four operations officers in the Guayaquil Consulate (Keith Schofield‡ is Chief of Base). By this year the AIFLD has trained almost 20,000 Ecuadorean workers while CEOSL‡ continues to make inroads against CTE dominance in the trade-union movement. In 1971 CEOSL and the International Federation of Petroleum and Chemical Workers‡ established the National Federation of Petroleum and Chemical Workers‡ with none other than Matias Ulloa Coppiano* as one of the main organizers. No question about the importance of Ecuador's petroleum workers now.

Perhaps in months to come the military government, using petroleum income, will commit itself to fairer distribution of income, and to programs that will benefit the mass of the population. The reforms—agrarian, economic and administrative—remain to be realized. Without doubt the chance that progressive forces will prevail underlies the policy of the Communist Party of Ecuador to support the current military government. Perhaps the government will fall under complete domination of its Brazilian-line faction. Perhaps it will continue without clear definition beyond continued favoring of the already wealthy class—allowing the petroleum bonanza to trigger extreme inflation and distorted economic development, as in Venezuela. But if it is to take a progressive path it will have to overcome not only the pro-Brazilians within its ranks, but also the U.S. government programs, not the least of which are put out by the CIA, including AIFLD, CEOSL and other reactionary organizations. In any case, events since I left demonstrate increasingly the triumph of those revolutionary ideas we fought so hard to destroy. Today Ecuador is immensely closer to the inevitable revolutionary structural changes than when I arrived.

Events in Uruguay since 1966 have been no less interesting than in Ecuador and considerably more revealing of the Brazilian military régime's readiness to fulfil the role of sub-imperialist power in South Amer-

* The author has no knowledge that this person is in any way connected with the Agency at present.

ica—remaining within and supporting continued U.S. hegemony.

In March 1967, Uruguay returned to the one-man executive as approved in the November 1966 elections. Nine months later, however, the moderate Colorado President died and was replaced by the rightist Vice-President, Jorge Pacheco Areco. Pacheco's four years in office were marked by continuing inflation, continuing financial and governmental corruption, no reforms, and failure to repress the Tupamaro movement in spite of widening use of torture, right-wing civilian terror organizations (of the type financed by the Montevideo station in the early 1960s), and police death-squads on the well known Brazilian model. The full flowering of the Tupamaro movement during the Pacheco presidency brought long periods of state of siege and suppression of constitutional liberties but with little success. Brazilian official policy of strengthening conservative influence in Uruguay—begun in 1964 by Manuel Pio Correa—resulted in the information during the Pacheco presidency of Brazilian-line factions, both in military institutions and in the traditional political parties.

In the November 1971 elections Pacheco was defeated in his attempt at re-election through constitutional amendment, but the winner was Juan Mana Bordaberry, Pacheco's next choice after himself. There was wide belief that the chief Blanco contender had actually won the close election, but through fraud the presidency was given to Bordaberry—an admitted advocate of "Brazilian-style solutions" and a prominent landowner. (In the early 1960s Bordaberry had been a leader of the Federal League for Ruralist Action dominated by Benito Nardone. He resigned his Senate seat in 1965 and in 1971 was running as a Colorado.)

Results of the 1971 elections indicate the remarkable growth of leftist sentiment in recent years. In 1958 the electoral front of the Communist Party of Uruguay received 2.6 per cent (27,000) of the total vote, in 1962 3.5 per cent (41,000), in 1966 5.7 per cent (70,000), and in 1971—strengthened with other groups in the

Frente Amplio—18.4 per cent (304,000). CIA estimates of PCU membership (published by the Department of State in *World Strength of Communist Organizations*) also grew correspondingly from 3000 in 1962 to 6000 in 1964 to 20,000 in 1969. With all this and the Tupamaros, too, something had to be done.

On taking office in March 1972 Bordaberry reportedly intensified the use of torture on Tupamaro prisoners which, in combination with errors by the Tupamaros themselves, led to severe setbacks for the movement. By September 1972 the Tupamaros were forced into a period of reorganization. Successes against the Tupamaros, however, created greater consciousness within the Uruguayan military of the injustices and corruption against which the Tupamaros had been fighting. Interrogations of Tupamaros led the military to uncover more stunning corruption than ever, and the trail began to lead back through the Pacheco régime to Pacheco himself and to Bordaberry who had been one of Pacheco's ministers. Investigations led to the arrest of some eighty business leaders in late 1972, and to an increasing tendency for military intervention in the civilian government.

In February 1973 the military finally took over but kept Bordaberry in office as chief executive, establishing a National Security Council as the mechanism for controlling the government.

The Uruguayan military justified their intervention as necessary for rooting out corruption and effecting agrarian, tax and credit reforms. Combating Marxism–Leninism was another justification offered by the military—which was itself divided among those under Brazilian influence, those favoring a leftist nationalism of the Peruvian variety, and those favoring closer relations with Argentina to preserve independence from Brazil. In June the Congress was closed and Brazilian-line military leaders were clearly in control.

With the ascendancy of Brazilian influence in Uruguay during the Pacheco and Bordaberry military governments, repression of the entire left has reached previously unimaginable proportions. Leftist parties have been proscribed, the National Workers' Convention outlawed, prisons overflow with political prisoners, freedom of the press has been eliminated, and left-wingers have been rooted out of the entire educational system. For having covered the Chilean *coup* three newspapers and one radio station were closed. The University of the Republic has been closed and the Rector and deans of all the faculties are facing military courts. Torture of political prisoners, already wide-spread under Pacheco, now seems to be equaling Brazilian proportions.

Meanwhile, since I left Uruguay in 1966, the economic crisis has deepened even more. *Per capita* economic growth during 1960–71 was zero. Inflation, according to the government's own figures, was 47 per cent in 1971, 96 per cent in 1972, and will reach 100 per cent this year—for 1962–72 inflation was near 6500 per cent. The peso, in the 70s when I left, is now down to 750 officially, and to over 900 on the black market. Purchasing power of the ordinary Uruguayan has declined 60–80 per cent in the past six years. Little wonder that latest polls indicate that 40 per cent of the population would emigrate if they could. In March this year it was revealed that Bordaberry had secretly sold 20 per cent of the country's gold reserves in order to pay foreign creditors, and he continues to pursue his admitted economic goal of integration with the Brazilian economy.

Assistance by the U.S. government to the Pacheco and the Bordaberry/military régime has of course not been lacking. Military aid to Uruguay during 1967–71 (grants, surplus equipment and credit sales) totalled 10.3 million dollars and for the financial year 1972 was just over 4 million dollars—equivalent to almost one and a half dollars for each Uruguayan. Training of the Uruguayan military also continues with a total of over 2000 trained since 1950. Economic assistance to Uruguay through AID and other official U.S. agencies rose from 6.5 million in 1971 to 10 million dollars last year. The Public Safety program also continues—worth 225,000 dollars last year with a cumulative total, since it was started by Ned Holman‡ in 1964, of 2.5 million dollars. About 120 Uruguayan policemen have been trained in the U.S., and over 700 in Uruguay, in riot control, communications and "investigative procedures."

CIA support? Montevideo station officers under Embassy cover grew from six to eight between 1966 and 1973, not to mention increases under non-official cover or within the AID Public Safety mission. Significantly, the Chief of Station since early this year, Gardner Hathaway, served in the Rio de Janeiro station during 1962–5 when the Goulart government was brought down and the military régime was cemented in power. Similarly, the Deputy Chief of Station, Fisher Ames,‡ served in the Dominican Republic during the repression following U.S. military invasion. Prominent among leaders of the Bordaberry/military government is Juan Jose Gari,‡* the old Ruralista political-action agent who is one of Bordaberry's chief advisors and, with Bordaberry, one of the leading opponents of the reforms mentioned but not yet started by military leaders. Important too is Mario Aguerrondo,‡* close liaison collaborator of the station when he was Montevideo Chief of Police in 1958–62. He's now a retired Army general and was a leader of the military *coup* in February.

Progress can also be noted in station labor operations. Since starting the AIFLD operation in Uruguay in 1963, over 7500 workers have been trained. This program enabled the station to form a new national trade-union confederation, finally replacing the old Uruguayan Labor Confederation (CSU) that was scrapped in 1967. The new organization, called the Uruguayan Confederation of Workers‡ (CUT), was formed in 1970 and is safely inside the fold of ORIT, ICFTU and the ITS. The pattern for formation of the CUT is almost a carbon copy of the formation of the CEOSL in Ecuador.

For the time being power lies with the Brazilian-line reactionary elements in the Uruguayan military. As in Ecuador the chance exists that those military officers who prefer a nationalist and progressive solution will

---

* The author has no knowledge that this person is in any way connected with the Agency at present.

eventually triumph, so that some of the reforms so drastically needed can be imposed. But as in Chile and in Brazil itself, this terrible repression only raises the people's consciousness of the injustices and can only speed the day for revolutionary structural transformation.

Events in Mexico have been less spectacular than in Ecuador and Uruguay—the one-party dictatorship of necessity lacks the violent lurches of political free-for-all and military *coup*—but no less indicative of rising revolutionary consciousness. While the country's remarkable *per capita* income growth (an average 3.2 per cent increase annually during 1960–71) reached just under 800 dollars last year, the benefits continue to be enjoyed by very few. The poorer half of the population gets only about 15 per cent of the total income and according to the Bank of Mexico half of the economically active population lack job security and earn under 80 dollars per month. A study by the National University revealed that of Mexico's twenty-four million people of working age, 9.6 million (40 per cent) are unemployed. As in the case of Brazil, Mexico's lack of an internal market because of income concentration in the privileged minority has forced the country to scramble for export markets in order to continue its economic growth and to meet payments on its enormous foreign debt contracted for development projects.

Surprise and alarm spread through Mexico's wealthy élite when Luis Echeverria* campaigned for the presidency in 1970 on a program for redistribution of income, so that workers and peasants would receive a fairer share. His intensive campaign throughout the country seemed designed for a candidate fighting an uphill battle against an overwhelming opposition—not altogether misleading since the opposition was the people's apathy rather than another candidate. His reformist policies were strongly opposed by Mexican business and industrial interests, and his new attempt to

---

* The author has no knowledge that this person is in any way connected with the Agency at present.

introduce democratic procedures within the PRI intensified divisions within the party. Although new statutes providing for greater internal democracy were adopted at the PRI convention in 1972, Echeverria has had scant success in trying to get a redistribution of income. Fears within the privileged minority that reforms might dangerously weaken the whole PRI power structure, together with resistance to the economic effect of redistribution, have effectively prevented significant reforms from starting.

Faced with the prospect of continuing injustice and failure of reform, Mexicans are increasingly turning to revolutionary action—and as revolutionary consciousness and action has grown, so too has the level of repression. The guerrilla movement in the Guerrero mountains continues to operate successfully against the discredited Mexican Army, in spite of the death of its principal leader, Genaro Rojas. Bank expropriations, executions, kidnappings and other direct action grow in intensity as urban guerrilla movements appear in the main Mexican cities.

The student movement, too, gains new strength in spite of regular right-wing violence. Just two months after I left Mexico another Tlatelolco-style massacre occurred when a peaceful student march of 8000 was attacked by some 500 plain-clothes para-police armed with machine-guns, pistols, chains, clubs and other weapons. The number killed was kept secret. Regular police forces were prevented from intervening even afterwards when the thugs invaded hospitals to prevent treatment to the injured students—roughing up doctors and breaking into operating rooms. Reaction to this carefully planned and officially sponsored attack caused the resignations of the Mexico City police chief and mayor, but Echeverria's promised investigation was predictably unsuccessful in finding those responsible.

One year later, in June 1972, dozens of students were injured when police attacked a demonstration commemorating companions killed at the Corpus Christi massacre. Since then repression of the student movement has been attempted alternately by the regular police forces and by the government-sponsored right-wing terror squads, with killings of students in August 1972 and February, May and August of this year. Two months ago the new right-wing rector of the National University in Mexico City called in the police to take over the campus, in order to enforce his program to "de-politicize" the University. Continuing student demands for justice have brought clashes in other university cities.

Meanwhile U.S. official support to the Mexican government and military continues. The CIA station in Mexico City remains the largest in Latin America. Strange that Jim Noland lasted only one year as Chief of Station and that John Horton lasted only two—replaced by Richard Sampson‡ (who in 1968 replaced Horton in Montevideo and who was transferred back to Washington not long after the Mitrione execution). Perhaps Echeverria has refused to have any contact with the station. ORIT‡ continues with its headquarters in Mexico City and with the Inter-American Labor College in Cuernavaca. Programs in Mexico of the AIFLD also continue, and one can assume the station's support to Mexican security services is as strong as ever.

The gap between rich and poor grows in developed countries as well as in poor countries and between the developed and underdeveloped countries. A considerable proportion of the developed world's prosperity rests on paying the lowest possible prices for the poor countries' primary products and on exporting high-cost capital and finished goods to those countries. Continuation of this kind of prosperity requires continuation of the relative gap between developed and underdeveloped countries—it means keeping poor people poor. Within the underdeveloped countries the distorted, irrational growth dependent on the demands and vagaries of foreign markets precludes national integration, with increasing marginalization of the masses. Even the increasing nationalism of countries like Peru, Venezuela and Mexico only yield ambiguous programs for liberating dependent economies while allowing privileged minorities to persist.

Increasingly, the impoverished masses are understanding that the prosperity of the developed countries and of the privileged minorities in their own countries is founded on their poverty. This understanding is bringing even greater determination to take revolutionary action and to renew the revolutionary movements where, as in Chile, reverses have occurred. Increasingly, the underprivileged and oppressed minorities in developed countries, particularly the U.S., perceive the identity of their own struggle with that of the marginalized masses in poor countries.

The U.S. government's defeat in Vietnam and in Cuba inspires exploited peoples everywhere to take action for their liberation. Not the CIA, police training, military assistance, "democratic" trade unions, not even outright military intervention can forever postpone the revolutionary structural changes that mean the end of capitalist imperialism and the building of a socialist society. Perhaps this is the reason why policymakers in the U.S. and their puppets in Latin America are unable to launch reform programs. They realize that reform might lead even faster to revolutionary awareness and action and their only alternative is escalating repression and increasing injustice. Their time, however, is running out.

London — January 1974

Six months to finish the research and six months to write this diary. If it is successful I shall be able to support other current and former CIA employees who want to describe their experiences and to open more windows on this activity. There must be many other CIA diaries to be written, and I pledge my support and experience to make them possible. Had I found the advice and support I needed at the beginning, I might have finished in two years rather than four, and many problems might have been avoided.

The CIA is still hoping to make me go back to the U.S. before publishing the diary, and I now find that my desperation to see the children was indeed what they thought might lure me back. Janet now admits that the Agency has been asking her for a long time not to send the children so that I would have to go there to see them. Although she refused to cooperate and sent them here last summer, she again refused to send them for the Christmas vacation while suggesting that I go there. Perhaps only when the children are no longer children will my seeing them become unraveled from the CIA.

For those who were unaware of the U.S. government's secret tools of foreign policy, perhaps this diary will help answer some of the questions on American domestic political motivations and practices that have arisen since the first Watergate arrests. In the CIA we justified our penetration, disruption and sabotage of the left in Latin America—around the world for that matter—because we felt morality changed on crossing national frontiers. Little would we have considered applying these methods inside our own country. Now, however, we see that the FBI was employing these methods against the left in the U.S. in a planned, coordinated program to disrupt, sabotage and repress the political organizations to the left of Democratic and Republican liberals. The murders at Kent and Jackson State, domestic activities of U.S. military intelligence, and now the President's own intelligence plan and "plumbers" unit—ample demonstration that CIA methods were really brought home. Prior restraints on using these methods against the "respectable" opposition were bound to crumble. In the early 1960s when the CIA moved to its new headquarters in Virginia, Watergate methods obtained final institutional status.

How fitting that over the rubble of the CIA's old temporary buildings back in Washington, the new building that rose was called "Watergate."

When the Watergate trials end and the whole episode begins to fade, there will be a movement for national renewal, for reform of electoral practices, and perhaps even for reform of the FBI and the CIA. But the return to our cozy self-righteous traditions should lure no one into believing that the problem has been removed. Reforms attack symptoms rather than the disease, and no other proof is needed than the Vietnam War and Watergate to demonstrate that the disease is our economic system and its motivational patterns.

Reforms of the FBI and the CIA, even removal of the President from office, cannot remove the problem. American capitalism, based as it is on exploitation of the poor, with its fundamental motivation in personal greed, simply cannot survive without force—without a secret police force. The argument is with capitalism and it is capitalism that must be opposed, with its CIA, FBI and other security agencies understood as logical, necessary manifestations of a ruling class's determination to retain power and privilege.

Now, more than ever, indifference to injustice at home and abroad is impossible. Now, more clearly than ever, the extremes of poverty and wealth demonstrate the irreconcilable class conflicts that only socialist revolution can resolve. Now, more than ever, each of us is forced to make a conscious choice whether to support the system of minority comfort and privilege with all its security apparatus and repression, or whether to struggle for real equality of opportunity and fair distribution of benefits for all of society, in the domestic as well as the international order. It's harder now not to realize that there are two sides, harder not to understand each, and harder not to recognize that like it or not we contribute day in and day out either to the one side or to the other.

London — May 1975

After a year of increasing doubt whether this diary would ever be published in the U.S. the way now looks clear. Had not Rep. Michael Harrington and Seymour Hersh and others made startling revelations in the year past, the political climate might not have permitted publication in the U.S. even now. Not that the CIA hasn't tried to delay and suppress this work: spurious leaks to discredit me, threats to enjoin publication, hints of expensive litigations. Yet in the end it is the CIA that gives way as its very institutional survival is brought into question. We already know enough of what the CIA does to resolve to oppose it. The CIA is one of the great forces promoting political repression in countries with minority regimes that serve a privileged and powerful elite. One way to neutralize the CIA's support to repression is to expose its officers so that their presence in foreign countries becomes untenable. Already significant revelations have begun and I will continue to assist those who are interested in identifying and exposing the CIA people in their countries.

Probably at no time since World War II have the American people had such an opportunity as now to examine how and why succeeding U.S. administrations have chosen, as in Vietnam, to back minority, oppressive and doomed regimes. The Congressional investigating committees can, if they want, illuminate a whole dark world of foreign Watergates covering the past thirty years, and these can be related to the dynamics within our society from which they emerged. The key question is to pass beyond the facts of CIA's operations to the reasons they were established—which inexorably will lead to economic questions: preservation of property relations and other institutions on which rest the interests of our own wealthy and privileged minority. This, not the CIA, is the critical issue.

Appendix 1

Alphabetical list of individuals who were employees, agents, liaison contacts or were otherwise used by or involved with the CIA or its operations; and of organizations financed, influenced or controlled by the CIA, as of the date or dates at which they are referred to in the main text, unless otherwise indicated. In some cases, the individuals referred to may have been "unwitting" of the CIA's sponsorship of their activities. The CIA's involvement with the organizations whose names follow was generally effected through key leaders of the organization or through other organizations controlled or influenced by the Agency. Thus only a very few members or leaders (sometimes none) of these organizations actually knew of their connection with the Agency. Moreover, many of the organizations listed were publicly revealed as having connections with the CIA and some have since severed relations with the Agency as a result. For example, the International Commission of Jurists (ICJ) has stated that, in 1967, on becoming aware of the ultimate source of some of its funding it took steps to insure that no further support from the Agency was accepted. Therefore the author wishes to underscore that none of the material in this Appendix and in the main text should be understood as referring to the present status of these individuals or organizations.

ACOSTA VELASCO, JORGE. Nephew of Ecuadorean President, Jose Maria Velasco. Minister of the Treasury and Minister of Government. Informant and political-action agent of the Quito station. *104, 122, 128–29, 134, 135, 167–68, 183, 198, 199–200, 201–4, 214–15*

AGENCIA ORBE LATINOAMERICANO. Feature news service serving most of Latin America. Financed and controlled by the CIA through the Santiago, Chile, station. *148, 235, 366*

AGRIBUSINESS DEVELOPMENT INC. (LAAD). Provided cover for CIA officer Bruce Berckmans, q.v. *552*

AGUERRONDO, MARIO. Uruguayan Army colonel and former Montevideo Chief of Police. Liaison contact. *390, 405, 456, 506, 610*

AIR AMERICA. CIA-owned airline for paramilitary operations, mainly in the Far East. *78*

ALARCON, ALBERTO. Guayaquil businessman and Liberal Party activist. Principal agent for CIA student operations in Ecuador. Cryptonym: ECLOSE. *125, 138, 171, 186, 207, 212, 247, 263, 303*

ALBORNOZ, ALFREDO. Ecuadorean Minister of Government (internal security). Liaison contact of the Quito station. *229, 231, 241–42*

ALLEN, JOHN. CIA operations officer at Camp Peary training base, formerly assigned in the Near East. *37*

ALLIANCE FOR ANTI-TOTALITARIAN EDUCATION. Propaganda mechanism of the Montevideo station. *479*

ALMEIDA, WILSON. Publisher and editor of *Voz Universitaria*, q.v., a university student newspaper. Propaganda agent for the Quito station. *122, 151, 302, 303*

ALONZO OLIVE, RAUL. Cuban engineer in sugar industry. Member of commerical delegation to Brazil and Uruguay. Recruited by the CIA in Montevideo before return to Cuba. *386*

AMADOR MARQUEZ, ENRIQUE. Labour and political-action agent of Guayaquil base. Minister of Economy. *124, 137, 214, 305*

AMERICAN FEDERATION OF STATE, COUNTY AND MUNICIPAL EMPLOYEES. The U.S. member of the Public Service International (PSI) q.v., which is the International Trade Secretariat for government employees. The CIA use of the PSI effected through the AFSCME. *69, 298, 416*

AMERICAN INSTITUTE FOR FREE LABOR DEVELOPMENT (AIFLD). CIA-controlled labour center financed through AID. Programs in adult education and social projects used as front for covering trade-union organizing activity, George Meany, q.v., President. *244–46, 252, 262, 305, 307, 311–12, 314, 321, 365, 376–77, 393, 485, 486, 501, 502, 549, 582, 610, 613*

immigration papers of non-official cover operation officers for Mexico City station. *549*

AVAILABLE–1. Chauffeur of the Commercial Department of the Soviet Embassy, Montevideo. Recruited by the Montevideo station. True name and cryptonym forgotten. *441, 484*

AVANDANA. Principal agent of the Montevideo station in postal intercept operation. True name forgotten. *349, 350, 367, 375, 376*

AVBANDY–1. An Uruguayan Army major who works for the Montevideo station as chief of the AVBANDY surveillance team assigned to Soviet-related targets. True name unknown. *356, 357, 361, 441*

AVBANDY–4. Member of the AVBANDY surveillance team in Montevideo and father of the team chief, also used in recruitment operations. True name forgotten. *441*

AVBLIMP–1 and 2. A husband/wife team who operate the observation post against the Soviet Embassy in Montevideo. True names unknown. *355–56, 484*

AVBLINKER–1 and 2. An American businessman and his wife in Montevideo who live in the station's observation post against the Cuban Embassy. True names and true cryptonym forgotten. *349*

AVBUSY–1. Letter carrier in Montevideo. CIA agent for letter intercept against Cuban intelligence agent. True name forgotten. *355, 412, 423, 424*

AVBUZZ–1. Principal Montevideo station agent for propaganda operations. True name forgotten. *364–65, 371–72, 382, 383, 389, 395, 397, 430, 436, 442, 443, 460, 469, 473, 476, 478, 498*

AVCASK–1. Montevideo station penetration agent against the Paraguayan leftist exile community. True name forgotten. *348–49, 367*

AVCASK–2. Penetration agent of the Montevideo station against the Paraguayan United Front for National Liberation (FULNA). True name forgotten. *349, 367*

AVCASK–3. Penetration agent of the Montevideo station against the Communist Party of Paraguay. True name forgotten. *349, 367*

AVCAVE–1. Penetration agent of the Montevideo station against the Communist Party of Uruguay. True name forgotten. *345, 347, 414, 415, 454, 455, 464*

AVDANDY–1. Montevideo station agent in the Uruguayan Foreign Ministry. True name and cryptonym forgotten. *357, 420*

AVENGEFUL–5. Transcriber of the AVENGEFUL telephone-tapping operation of the Montevideo station and sister of Mrs. Tomas Zafiriadis, q.v. Name forgotten. *392, 408, 413, 420, 422, 426, 444, 446, 456, 462, 465, 467, 468, 473*

AVENGEFUL–7. Wife of AVANDANA, q.v., and Montevideo station agent manning observation post against Cuban Embassy.

America (CWA) and Director of the American Institute for Free Labor Development. Important collaborator in CIA labor operations through the AIFLD and the Post, Telegraph and Telephone Workers International (PTTI), q.v. *245*

BENEFIELD, ALVIN. CIA technical officer specializing in operations against foreign diplomatic codes. *487, 488, 489, 505*

BERCKMANS, BRUCE. CIA operations officer in Mexico City under non-official cover. *552*

BERGER, MICHAEL. CIA operations officer in Montevideo. *347, 349, 367*

BESABER. Agent of the Mexico City station targeted against Polish intelligence officers under diplomatic cover. Owner of ceramics and tourist trinket business in Cuernavaca, Polish extraction. Name forgotten. *544*

BIDAFFY–1. Penetration agent of the Buenos Aires station against the revolutionary group of John William Cooke. True name and cryptonym forgotten. *553–54, 555*

BRAGA, JUAN JOSE. Deputy Chief of Investigations of the Montevideo Police Department. Close liaison collaborator of the Montevideo station. Torturer. *359, 456, 471*

BRAZILIAN INSTITUTE FOR DEMOCRATIC ACTION (IBAD). Anti-communist political-action organization of the Rio de Janeiro station. Used for financing and controlling politicians. *325*

BRESLIN, ED. U.S. Army major and intelligence adviser to the Ecuadorean Army. Close collaborator with the Quito station. *232, 234, 244*

BROE, WILLIAM V. Chief, Western Hemisphere Division. Former Chief of Station, Tokyo. *510, 516, 522, 557, 568–69*

BROWN, BILL. CIA staff operations officer, specialist in labor operations, assigned to the Panama station at Fort Amador, Canal Zone. *307*

BROWN, IRVING. European representative of the American Federation of Labor and principal CIA agent for control of the International Confederation of Free Trade Unions (ICFTU), q.v. *69*

BUCHELI, RAFAEL. Telephone company engineer in charge of the Quito exchanges. Quito station agent in charge of making telephone-tap connections. Cryptonym: ECWHEAT–1. *182, 183, 188, 240, 266, 302*

BURBANO DE LARA, MIGUEL (MIKE). Airport manager of Pan American-Grace Airways working for the Quito station as cutout to Luis Vargas, q.v. Cryptonym: ECACCENT. *110, 247–48, 283–84*

BURKE, JOHN. Quito station officer under AID Public Safety cover. *263, 264, 309, 310*

BURNS, PAUL. CIA operations officer in Montevideo. Specialist in CP penetration operations. *346, 350, 352, 354, 366, 380, 381, 391, 414*

BUSTOS, CHARLOTTE. CIA officer in charge of headquarters support to liaison and support operations in Mexico City. *512*

CABEZA DE VACA, MARIO. Quito milk producer working as Quito station agent. Cutout to Mario Cárdenas, q.v. Later used for funding and control of the Center for Economic and Social Reform Studies (CERES), q.v. *110, 247, 248*

CAMACHO, EDGAR. Stepson of Colonel Oswaldo Lugo of the Ecuadorean National Police. Quito station agent as cutout to Lugo. Later a transcriber for telephone-tapping operations. *211, 241, 267*

CAMARA SENA, -. Brazilian Army colonel sent to Brazilian Embassy in Montevideo as military attaché: liaison contact. *374, 387, 415, 419*

CANTRELL, WILLIAM. CIA operations officer in Montevideo under cover of the AID Public Safety Office. *491, 506*

CARDENAS, MARIO. Penetration agent of the Quito station against the Communist Party of Ecuador. Cryptonym: ECSIGIL–1. *110, 247, 272, 274, 283, 284, 290, 312, 494*

CARVAJAL, -. Uruguayan Army colonel and chief of military intelligence. Liaison contact. *358–59, 390*

CASSIDY, JOHN. Deputy Chief of Station, Montevideo. *465–67 479*

CASTRO, JUANA. Sister of Fidel Castro, used by CIA for propaganda. *396*

CATHOLIC LABOR CENTER (CEDOC). Labor organization in Ecuador supported by the Quito station. *See* JOSE BAQUERO DE LA CALLE, AURELIO DAVILA CAJAS and ISABEL ROBALINO BOLLO. *122, 236, 278, 305*

CATHOLIC UNIVERSITY YOUTH ORGANIZATION. Group used for propaganda through Aurelio Davila Cajas, q.v. *156, 163, 212–13*

CENTER FOR ECONOMIC AND SOCIAL REFORM STUDIES (CERES). Reformist businessman's organization financed and controlled by the Quito station. *247, 248*

CENTER OF STUDIES AND SOCIAL ACTION (CEAS). Reformist organization financed and controlled by the Bogotá station. *248*

CHIRIBOGA, OSWALDO. Velasquista political leader who recruited Atahualpa Basantes using "false flag" technique. Cryptonym: ECFONE. Later Ecuadorean Chargé d'Affaires in The Hague. *111, 141, 239*

CIVIL AIR TRANSPORT (CAT). CIA-controlled airline used for paramilitary operations, mainly in the Far East. *78*

CLERICI DE NARDONE, OLGA. Wife of Uruguayan President Benito Nardone. On death of Nardone continued as leader of the Federal League of Ruralist Action. Political contact of the Montevideo station. *366, 390*

Combate. Student publication of the Montevideo station financed and controlled through Alberto Roca, q.v. *405, 469*

tionary Left (MIR), recruited in Guayaquil as a penetration agent. Resettled by the CIA in Mexico. *270–71, 438, 452*

DULLES, ALLEN. CIA Director. *12, 21*

ECALIBY–1. Chauffeur of the Cuban Embassy in Quito. Quito station agent. True name and real cryptonym forgotten. *126*

ECBLISS–1. Manager of Braniff Airways in Guayaquil and support agent of the Guayaquil base. Name and true cryptonym forgotten. *315*

ECCLES, DR. Chief of the Junior Officer Training Program. *6, 8–9*

ECELDER. Secret printing operation for propaganda operations of the Quito station. *See* JORGE, PATRICIO, MARCELO, RODRIGO and RAMIRO RIVADENEIRA. True cryptonym forgotten.

ECHEVERRIA, LUIS. Mexican Minister of Government (internal security) and later President. Liaison contact of the Mexico City station. Cryptonym: LITEMPO–14. *522, 523, 539, 540, 570, 571, 611*

ECHINOCARUS–1. A penetration agent of the Guayaquil base against the Communist Party of Ecuador. True name unknown. *123*

ECJOB. Leader of a team of Quito station agents used for distribution of station-printed political handbills and for wall-painting. True name unknown. *119*

ECLAT. A retired Ecuadorean Army officer and leader of a surveillance and investigative team for the Guayaquil base. True name forgotten. *123*

ECOLIVE–1. A penetration agent of the Quito station against the Revolutionary Union of Ecuadorean Youth. Name forgotten. Planned to have been infiltrated into the Communist Party of Ecuador. *111*

ECOTTER–1 and ECOTTER–2. Travel-control agents of the Quito station. True names forgotten. *116*

ECSIGH–1. Mistress of Ricardo Vazquez Diaz, q.v., and chief stenographer of the Ecuadorean military junta. Recruited by the Quito station for political intelligence against the junta through Vazquez. True name and true cryptonym forgotten. *304*

ECSTACY–1 and ECSTACY–2. Agents of the Quito station who provided mail for monitoring. True names forgotten as well as original cryptonyms. *115–16, 144, 215*

ECUADOREAN ANTI-COMMUNIST ACTION. Name of fictitious organization used as ostensible sponsor of Quito station propaganda. *161*

ECUADOREAN ANTI-COMMUNIST FRONT. Name used as ostensible sponsor of Quito station propaganda. *154, 157, 161*

ECUADOREAN CONFEDERATION OF FREE TRADE UNION ORGANIZATIONS (CEOSL). National trade-union organization established and controlled by the Quito station. *213–14, 236, 237, 252, 258, 262, 278, 302, 304, 305, 306, 311, 314*

EDITORS PRESS SERVICE. CIA-controlled propaganda outlet based in New York. Material placed through CIA propaganda agents in Latin America. *389*

EGAS, JOSE MARIA. Leader of the Social Christian Movement. Quito station agent. *240, 257, 260*

ELSO, WILSON. Uruguayan Deputy. Leader of the Federal League for Ruralist Action. Under development by the Montevideo station for possible use as political-action agent. *390*

Ensayos. An intellectual journal financed and controlled by the Quito station through Carlos Vallejo Baez, q.v., and Juan Yepez del Pozo, Sr, q.v. *167*

ESTERLINE, JAKE. Deputy Chief of Western Hemisphere Division. *472, 509, 510*

ESTRADA ICAZA, EMILIO. General Manager of one of Ecuador's largest banks, collector of pre-Hispanic art. Guayaquil base political-action agent. *124, 212*

EUROPEAN ASSEMBLY OF CAPTIVE NATIONS. A CIA propaganda operation. *236*

FANNIN (or FANNON), LES. CIA polygraph operator. Caught in Singapore in 1960 by local police. Ransom attempted by the CIA but spurned by Singapore Prime Minister. *308*

FEDERATION OF FREE WORKERS OF GUAYAS (FETLIG). Provincial affiliate of the Ecuadorean Confederation of Free Trade Union Organizations (CEOSL), q.v., and controlled by the Quito station. *278*

FELDMAN, ROBERT. Mexico City station officer in charge of penetration operations against the Institutional Revolutionary Party (PRI) and the Mexican Foreign Ministry. *549*

FENETEL. The Ecuadorean national federation of communications workers affiliated with the PTTI and supported by the Quito station. *138, 252*

FERGUSON, JIM. Training officer in the CIA Junior Officer Training Program (JOTP, later called the Career Training Program). *6, 7–8, 9, 10, 16–21, 23, 93, 94*

FERNANDEZ CHAVEZ, A. Montevideo correspondent of *Agencia Orbe Latinoamericano*, q.v., and ANSA, the Italian wire service. Montevideo station propaganda agent. *365–66, 483*

FERNANDEZ, GONZALO. Retired Ecuadorean Air Force colonel, and former attaché in London. Quito station agent as cutout to CP penetration agent. *320*

FERRERA, SAL. Made efforts to divert author in Paris, believed by author to be at CIA's behest. *592, 594–600*

FIGUERES, JOSE. President of Costa Rica. Front man for CIA operations such as the American Institute for Free Labor Development, q.v., and the Institute of Political Education, q.v. *245*

FIRST NATIONAL CITY BANK. Used by the CIA for clandestine funding and for purchase of foreign currency. *326, 380, 391, 399*

José station. *See* SACHA VOLMAN; *see also* JOSE FIGUERES. *429*

INTER-AMERICAN FEDERATION OF WORKING NEWSPAPERMEN (IFWN). Journalists' trade union controlled by the CIA and financed through the American Newspaper Guild. *167*

INTER-AMERICAN LABOR COLLEGE. Training school of the Inter-American Regional Labor Organization (ORIT) in Cuernavaca, Mexico. Financed and controlled by the CIA. *237*

INTER-AMERICAN POLICE ACADEMY. Police training school at Fort Davis, C.Z. founded by the Panama station. Moved to Washington D.C. where renamed International Police Academy. Funded by AID but controlled by the CIA. *264, 309*

THE INTER-AMERICAN REGIONAL LABOR ORGANIZATION (ORIT). The regional organization of the ICFTU for the Western Hemisphere with headquarters in Mexico City. Founded by Serafino Romualdi, q.v., and a principal mechanism for CIA labor operations in Latin America. *69, 70, 125, 131, 237, 244–45, 307, 337, 365, 371, 376, 377, 393, 481, 486, 549, 582, 610, 613*

INTERNATIONAL CATHOLIC YOUTH FEDERATION. Youth organization of the Catholic Church used by the CIA for youth and student operations. *67*

INTERNATIONAL COMMISSION OF JURISTS (ICJ). An international association of lawyers in part indirectly financed by the CIA in the first decade of its existence, which the Agency hoped to use against the International Association of Democratic Lawyers. *73, 166, 239*

THE INTERNATIONAL CONFEDERATION OF FREE TRADE UNIONS (ICFTU). Labor center set up and controlled by the CIA to oppose the World Federation of Trade Unions (WFTU). Headquarters in Brussels. *68, 69, 131, 137, 237, 245, 337, 365, 376, 377, 393, 486, 610*

THE INTERNATIONAL FEDERATION OF CHRISTIAN TRADE UNIONS (IFCTU, later known as THE WORLD CONFEDERATION OF LABOR). The international Catholic trade-union organization used as a mechanism for CIA labor operations. *70*

THE INTERNATIONAL FEDERATION OF CLERICAL AND TECHNICAL EMPLOYEES (IFCTE). The ITS for white-collar workers used by the CIA for labor operations. *70*

INTERNATIONAL FEDERATION OF JOURNALISTS. CIA-influenced organization used for propaganda operations. Headquarters in Brussels. Established to combat the International Organization of Journalists. *72*

INTERNATIONAL FEDERATION OF PETROLEUM AND CHEMICAL WORKERS (IFPCW). The ITS for this industry set up originally by the CIA through the U.S. Oil Workers International Union. *70, 131*

INTERNATIONAL FEDERATION OF WOMEN LAWYERS. Organization used by the CIA for propaganda operations. *396*

INTERNATIONAL POLICE ACADEMY. CIA-controlled police training

LADD, RAYMOND. Quito station administrative officer also in charge of certain operations. *215, 241, 260, 262*

LADENBURG, ARTHUR. CIA operations officer in Mexico City under non-official cover. Later assigned to Santiago, Chile. *514*

LICALLA. One of three observation posts overlooking the Soviet Embassy in Mexico City. Names of agents forgotten. *543*

LICOBRA. Cryptonym for operations targeted by Mexico City station against the ruling Institutional Revolutionary Party (PRI) and the Mexican Foreign Ministry and Ministry of Government. *549–50, 558, 565*

LICOWL–1. Owner of small grocery store near Soviet Embassy, Mexico City. CIA agent. True name forgotten. *544*

LICOZY–1. Double-agent of Mexico City station against the KGB. True name forgotten. *545*

LICOZY–3. Double-agent of Mexico City station against the KGB. True name forgotten. *545*

LICOZY–5. Double-agent of the Mexico City station against the KGB. True name forgotten. *545*

LIDENY. Mexico City station unilateral telephone-tapping operation. True cryptonym and true names of agents unknown. *546*

LIEMBRACE. Mexico City station surveillance team. Names of team members unknown. *543, 546, 548*

LIENVOY. Joint telephone-tapping operation between Mexico City station and Mexican security service. Names of agents unknown. *542, 543, 545–48*

LIFIRE. Mexico City station travel control and general investigations team. True names unknown. *543, 546, 548*

LILINK. An operation in Mexico City to provide non-official cover for CIA officers with infra-red communications system to the CIA station in the Embassy. True name of cover business forgotten. *514*

LIOVAL–1. English teacher in Mexico City. U.S. citizen. CIA agent. True name forgotten. *544, 545*

LIRICE. Mexico City station surveillance team. True names of members unknown. *545, 548*

LISAMPAN. Mexico City station bugging operation against the Cuban Embassy. *547, 548*

LITEMPO. Cryptonym for all liaison operations with Mexican government. *539, 546, 549*

LONE STAR CEMENT CORPORATION. U.S. company whose Uruguayan subsidiary provided cover for CIA operations officer in Montevideo. *507*

LOPEZ MATEOS, ADOLFO. President of Mexico and close collaborator of the Mexico City station. Cryptonym: LIENVOY–2. *268, 539*

LOPEZ MICHELSON, ALFONSO. Leader of the Revolutionary Liberal Movement of Colombia which was supported by the

for Atahualpa Basantes. Cryptonym: ECCENTRIC. *111–12, 141, 147, 162, 308, 320*

PALADINO, MORRIS. Principal CIA agent for control of the Inter-American Regional Labor Organization (ORIT), q.v. ORIT Director of Education, Director of Organization, and Assistant Secretary-General. From July 1964 Deputy Executive Director of the American Institute for Free Labor Development (AIFLD), q.v. *237, 307*

PALMER, MORTON (PETE). Quito station operations officer. *309, 312, 313*

PAREDES, ROGER. Lieutenant-colonel in the Ecuadorean Army and Chief of the Ecuadorean Military Intelligence Service. *114–15, 117, 118, 150, 194, 231, 232, 240, 248*

PARKER, FRED. U.S. citizen resident in Quito. Furniture manufacturer. Quito station support agent. *275*

PAX ROMANA. International youth organization of the Catholic Church used by the CIA for student and youth operations. *67*

PELLECER, CARLOS MANUEL. CIA penetration agent of the Guatemalan Communist Party (PGT) and of the communist and related movements in Mexico City. Cryptonym: LINLUCK. *541–42*

PENKOVSKY, OLEG. Soviet Army colonel who spied for the CIA and British intelligence. *564*

PEREZ DROUET, RENATO. Quito travel agent and Secretary-General of the Ponce Administration. A leader of the Social Christian Movement. Quito station political-action agent. *120, 175, 220, 226, 236, 239, 242, 259*

PEREZ FREEMAN, EARLE. Chief of Cuban intelligence in Montevideo. Defected in Mexico City, then redefected. *327, 384–85, 388, 392–93, 398, 402, 409*

PERRY, ALEX (or ALEC). General Manager of Uruguayan Portland Cement Co. (subsidiary of Lone Star Cement Corporation) in Montevideo. Permitted CIA operations officer to be covered in his company. *507*

PHIPPS, RUSSELL. Montevideo station operations officer in charge of Soviet operations. *352, 396, 403, 417, 425, 441*

PICCOLO, JOSEPH. CIA officer in charge of operations against Cuba in Mexico City station. *546*

PILGRIM, VIRGINIA. Friend of author's family who recommended him for CIA employment. A CIA employee. *1, 5, 15–16*

PIO CORREA, MANUEL. Brazilian Ambassador to Mexico and to Uruguay, later Sub-Secretary of Foreign Affairs. CIA agent. *387, 402, 411, 415, 416, 418, 419, 422, 481, 607*

PIRIZ CASTAGNET, ANTONIO. Montevideo police inspector. Agent of the Montevideo station. Cryptonym: AVALANCHE–6. *367, 372, 383, 388, 392, 393, 401, 429, 453, 456, 463, 470, 478, 492–93*

PLENARY OF DEMOCRATIC CIVIC ORGANIZATIONS OF URUGUAY. Propaganda mechanism of the Montevideo station. *478, 498*

RODRIGUEZ, VENTURA. Uruguayan Army colonel and Chief of the Montevideo Police Department. Liaison contact of the Montevideo station. *359, 372, 383, 385, 386, 388, 390, 399, 400, 434, 451–52, 453, 456, 457, 460, 465, 468–71*

RODRIGUEZ, VLADIMIR LATTERA. First important defector from the Cuban intelligence service (DGI). Cryptonym: AMMUG–1. *412*

ROGGIERO, CARLOS. Retired Ecuadorean Army captain and leader of the Social Christian Movement. Quito station agent in charge of militant action squads. *240, 257*

ROMUALDI, SERAFINO. AFL representative for Latin America and principal CIA agent for labor operations in Latin America. *69, 131, 214, 245, 305, 376*

ROOSEN, GERMAN. Second Secretary, Uruguayan Embassy, Havana CIA agent targeted against the Cuban government. *329, 385, 386, 388, 392, 398, 402*

ROSETE, HADA. Leader of Cuban exile community in Montevideo and agent of the Montevideo station. *372, 377*

ROYAL BANK OF CANADA. Used by CIA as funding mechanism in Brazil. *326*

SALGADO, GUSTAVO. Ecuadorean journalist and principal Quito station propaganda agent. Regular columnist of *El Comercio* and provincial newspapers. True cryptonym forgotten, but ECURGE used for convenience. *119, 147–48, 154, 175, 180*

SALGUERO, CARLOS. Montevideo Station support agent. *446–47, 477, 484*

SAMPSON, RICHARD. CIA Chief of Station, Mexico City. *613*

SANDOVAL, LUIS. Lieutenant in the Ecuadorean National Police and chief technician of the police intelligence service. Quito station agent. *113, 169, 211, 213, 249, 275–76*

SANTANA, ROLANDO. Cuban diplomat in Montevideo. Defected to the CIA. *327, 372*

SAUDADE, GIL. Deputy Chief of Station in Quito. *146, 161–62, 166, 167, 174, 186, 187, 190–91, 198, 214, 218, 228, 235–36, 237, 242, 246, 247, 252, 258, 262, 278, 285, 292, 302, 304, 306, 308*

SCHOFIELD, KEITH. Chief of Base for CIA in Guayaquil. *606*

SCHROEDER, DONALD. CIA operations officer, specialist in operations against foreign diplomatic codes. *487–89, 491, 505*

SCOTT, WINSTON, Chief of Station, Mexico City. *268, 511, 521, 539–41, 550, 565, 568, 570, 573, 577*

SEEHAFER, RALPH. Chief of Base, Guayaquil. *269–70*

SENTINELS OF LIBERTY. Propaganda mechanism of the Montevideo station. *478–79*

SEVILLA, JUAN. Ecuadorean Minister of Labor, later Minister of the Treasury, later Ambassador to the German Federal Republic. Quito station agent for political action and propaganda. *242, 272, 281–83, 284, 285, 287–88, 290–92, 296, 310*

SHANNON, TED. Chief of Station, Panama, later involved in CIA police-training programs. *309*

SHAW, ROBERT. CIA operations officer. *327–28*

SHERNO, FRANK. CIA technical operations specialist, expert in audio (bugging) operations. Assigned to Buenos Aires station. *414, 415, 426, 447, 492, 499, 554*

SHERRY, FRANCIS. CIA officer in charge of operations against Cuba in Mexico City station. *546*

SIERO PEREZ, ISABEL. Cuban exile. Leader of the International Federation of Women Lawyers (IFWL). CIA propaganda agent. *396*

SIMMONS, CLARK. Deputy Chief of Station, Lima. *319*

SINCLAIR, WILLIAM. Inter-American Representative of the Public Service International (PSI), q.v. CIA agent for labor operations. *174*

SMITH, WILLIAM L. (LEE). CIA operations officer in Montevideo station. *485–86*

SNYDER, JOHN. Assistant Inter-American Representative of the Post, Telegraph and Telephone Workers International (PTTI), q.v. Agent of the Quito station in labor operations. *129, 137*

STEELE, ROBERT. CIA operations officer in the Soviet/satellite section in Mexico City station. *542*

STORACE, NICOLAS. Uruguayan Minister of the Interior and liaison contact of Montevideo station. *471, 476, 478, 485, 489–92, 502, 505, 518, 523*

STUART, FRANK. Director of AID in Montevideo. *487, 488*

STUDENT MOVEMENT FOR DEMOCRATIC ACTION. Propaganda mechanism of the Montevideo station. *479*

SVEGLE, BARBARA. Secretary-typist in the Quito station during the early 1960s. Served as courier to Aurelio Davila Cajas, q.v. *120*

TEJERA, ADOLFO. Uruguayan Minister of the Interior (internal security). Liaison contact of the Montevideo station. *386, 390, 399, 405, 406, 411, 415, 426, 428, 432, 433, 452, 454, 457, 458, 464, 469–70, 471, 476, 482*

TERRELL, EDWIN. Chief of the "Bolivarian" branch of Western Hemisphere Division. *98–99*

THOMAS, WADE. CIA operations officer, specialist in CP penetration operations. *541*

THORON, CHRISTOPHER. CIA operations officer assigned under State Department cover to the United Nations during 1960–65. Remained under State Department cover until 1969 when named President of American University in Cairo, which is possibly a CIA cover position. *99*

TORO, MEDARDO. Quito Station penetration agent of the Velasquista political movement. *257–58, 273, 291, 313, 314, 354*

TOROELLA, LUIS. Cuban arrested and executed for assassination attempt against Fidel Castro. Agent of the Miami Operations Base of the CIA and correspondent in secret writing with the Quito station. Cryptonym for convenience: AMBLOOD–1. *117, 165, 194*

TORRES, JUAN. Courier and assistant technician in the listening-

Appendix 2

*Alphabetical index of abbreviations. * indicates CIA use of organizations described in Appendix I.*

A and E	Assessment and Evaluation Staff of the Office of Training
ACOMC	American Communist Group in Mexico City
ADEP	Popular Democratic Action
AEC	Atomic Energy Commission
AF	Africa Division
AFL	American Federation of Labor
AID	Agency for International Development
*AIFLD	American Institute for Free Labor Development
ANCAP	National Administration of Petroleum, Alcohol and Cement
ANSA	Italian wire service
ARNE	Ecuadorean Nationalist Revolutionary Action
CA	Covert Action
CCI	Independent Campesino Confederation
*CEAS	Center of Studies and Social Action
*CEDOC	Catholic Labor Center
*CEOSL	Ecuadorean Confederation of Free Trade Union Organizations
*CERES	Center for Economic and Social Reform Studies
CFP	Concentration of Popular Forces
CI	Counter-Intelligence
CIA	Central Intelligence Agency
CI/ICD	Counter-Intelligence Staff, International Communism Division
CI/OA	Counter-Intelligence Staff, Operational Approval Branch
CIO	Congress of Industrial Organizations
CNC	National Campesino Confederation
CNED	National Center of Democratic Students
CNOP	National Confederation of Popular Organizations
CNT	National Workers Convention
*COG	Guayas Workers Confederation
COS	Chief of Station
*COSEC	Coordinating Secretariat of National Unions of Students
CPSU	Communist Party of the Soviet Union
CP	Communist Party

*CROCLE	Regional Confederation of Ecuadorean Coastal Trade Unions
CS	Clandestine Services (same as Deputy Directorate, Plans—DDP)
*CSU	Uruguayan Labor Confederation
CT	Career Training Program
CTAL	Latin American Labor Confederation
CTE	Ecuadorean Workers Confederation
*CTM	Mexican Workers Confederation
CTU	Uruguayan Workers Confederation
*CUT	Uruguayan Confederation of Workers
CWA	Communications Workers of America
DCI	Director of Central Intelligence
DCID	Director of Central Intelligence Directive
DDC	Deputy Directorate, Coordination
DDI	Deputy Directorate, Intelligence
DDP	Deputy Directorate, Plans (same as Clandestine Services—CS)
DDS	Deputy Directorate, Support
DDS & T	Deputy Directorate, Science and Technology
DOD	Domestic Operations Division
DRE	Revolutionary Student Directorate in Exile
ECLA	United Nations Economic Commission for Latin America
EE	Eastern Europe Division
FBI	Federal Bureau of Investigation
FBIS	Foreign Broadcast Information Service
FE	Far East Division
FENETEL	Ecuadorean Federation of Telecommunications Workers
FEP	People's Electoral Front
FETLIG	Federation of Free Workers of the Guayas Coast
FEU	University Student Federation
*FEUE	Ecuadorean Federation of University Students
FEUU	Federation of University Students of Uruguay
FI	Foreign Intelligence
FIDEL	Leftish Liberation Front
FIR	Field Information Report
FNET	National Federation of Technical Students
*FRD	Revolutionary Democratic Front
F and S	Flaps and Seals
FULNA	United Front for National Liberation
GRU	Chief Intelligence Directorate of the Soviet General Staff (Soviet Military intelligence organizations)
IAC	Intelligence Advisory Committee
IADL	International Association of Democratic Lawyers
*IBAD	Brazilian Institute for Democratic Action
ICA	International Cooperation Administration

	(predecessor of the Agency for International Development)
*ICFTU	International Confederation of Free Trade Unions
*ICJ	International Commission of Jurists
I & E	Intelligence and Liaison Department of the Montevideo Police
*IFCTU	International Federation of Christian Trade Unions
*IFJ	International Federation of Journalists
*IFPAAW	International Federation of Plantation, Agricultural and Allied Workers
*IFPCW	International Federation of Petroleum and Chemical Workers
*IFWN	Inter-American Federation of Working Newspapermen
IMF	International Monetary Fund
INR	Bureau of Intelligence and Research, Department of State
IO	International Organizations Division
IOJ	International Organization of Journalists
*ISC	International Student Conference
*ITF	International Transport Workers Federation
*ITS	International Trade Secretariats
IUS	International Union of Students
JCE	Communist Youth of Ecuador
JCS	Joint Chiefs of Staff
JOT	Junior Officer Trainee
KGB	Committee for State Security (Soviet intelligence and security service)
LP	Listening Post (for audio operations)
MAAG	Military Assistance Advisory Group
MIR	Movement of the Revolutionary Left
MLN	National Liberation Movement
MLR	Revolutionary Liberal Movement (of Colombia)
MRO	Uruguayan Revolutionary Movement
MRP	People's Revolutionary Movement
NCG	National Council of Government
NCNA	New China News Agency (*Hsinhua*)
NE	Near East Division
NIS	National Intelligence Survey
NPIC	National Photographic Interpretation Center
NSA	National Security Agency
*NSA	National Students Association (U.S.)
NSC	National Security Council
NSCID	National Security Council Intelligence Directive
NSD	National Security Directorate
OA	Operational Approval
OAS	Organization of American States
OBI	Office of Basic Intelligence
OC	Office of Communications (of the DDS)

OCB	Operations Coordination Board
OCI	Office of Current Intelligence
OCR	Office of Central Reference
OCS	Officer Candidate School
OF	Officer of Finance (of the DDS)
OL	Office of Logistics (of the DDS)
ONE	Office of National Estimates
OO	Office of Operations
OP	Office of Personnel (of the Deputy Directorate, Support)
OP	Observation post
ORIT	Inter-American Regional Labor Organization of the ICFTU
ORR	Office of Research and Reports
ORTF	French Radio and Television Service
OS	Office of Security (of the DDS)
OSI	Office of Scientific Intelligence
OSS	Office of Strategic Services
OTR	Office of Training (of the DDS)
OWVL	One way voice link (radio communications)
PCBM	Bolshevik Communist Party of Mexico
PCE	Communist Party of Ecuador
PCM	Communist Party of Mexico
PCP	Communist Party of Paraguay
PCU	Communist Party of Uruguay
*PLPR	Popular Revolutionary Liberal Party
POA	Provisional Operational Approval
POR	Revolutionary Workers Party
PP	Psychological and Paramilitary
PPS	Popular Socialist Party
PRI	Revolutionary Institutional Party
PRQ	Personal Record Questionnaire
PSE	Socialist Party of Ecuador
PSI	Public Service International
PSR	Revolutionary Socialist Party (of Ecuador)
PSU	Socialist Party of Uruguay
*PTTI	Post, Telegraph and Telephone Workers International
RF	Radio frequency
*RFE	Radio Free Europe
RID	Records Integration Division
RMD	Related Missions Directive
SAS	Scandinavian Airlines System
SATT	Strategic Analysis Targeting Team
SB	Soviet Bloc Division
SCWL	Subversive Control Watch List
SIME	Ecuadorean Military Intelligence Service
SK	Security Officer in a Soviet Community abroad
SNET	National Union of Education Workers

SPR	Soviet Personality Record
SR	Soviet Russia Division
SW	Secret writing
TASS	Soviet wire service
TSD	Technical Services Division
TUC	Trade Unions Council (Britain)
UAR	United Arab Republic (Egypt)
UGOCM	General Union of Workers and Peasants
UNAM	National Autonomous University of Mexico
UNESCO	United Nations Educational, Scientific and Cultural Organization
UPI	United Press International
URJE	Revolutionary Union of Ecuadorean Youth
USIA	United States Information Agency
USIS	United States Information Service (overseas offices of USIA)
USOC	United States Olympic Committee
USOM	United States Operations Mission (of ICA)
*WAY	World Assembly of Youth
WE	Western Europe Division
WFDY	World Federation of Democratic Youth
WFTU	World Federation of Trade Unions
WH	Western Hemisphere Division
WPC	World Peace Council

Appendix 3

Charts showing the bureaucratic structure of the CIA

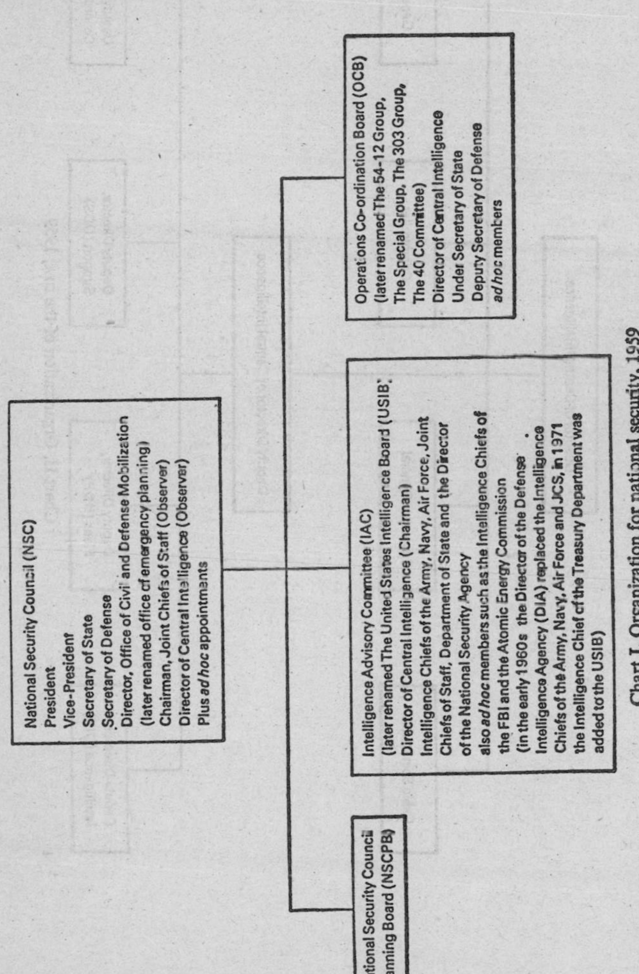

National Security Council (NSC)
President
Vice-President
Secretary of State
Secretary of Defense
Director, Office of Civil and Defense Mobilization
(later renamed office of emergency planning)
Chairman, Joint Chiefs of Staff (Observer)
Director of Central Intelligence (Observer)
Plus *ad hoc* appointments
National Security Council
Planning Board (NSCPB)
Intelligence Advisory Committee (IAC)
(later renamed The United States Intelligence Board (USIB)
Director of Central Intelligence (Chairman)
Intelligence Chiefs of the Army, Navy, Air Force, Joint
Chiefs of Staff, Department of State and the Director
of the National Security Agency
also *ad hoc* members such as the Intelligence Chiefs of
the FBI and the Atomic Energy Commission
(in the early 1960s the Director of the Defense
Intelligence Agency (DIA) replaced the Intelligence
Chiefs of the Army, Navy, Air Force and JCS, in 1971
the Intelligence Chief of the Treasury Department was
added to the USIB)
Operations Co-ordination Board (OCB)
(later renamed The 54-12 Group,
The Special Group, The 303 Group,
The 40 Committee)
Director of Central Intelligence
Under Secretary of State
Deputy Secretary of Defense
ad hoc members

Chart I. Organization for national security, 1959

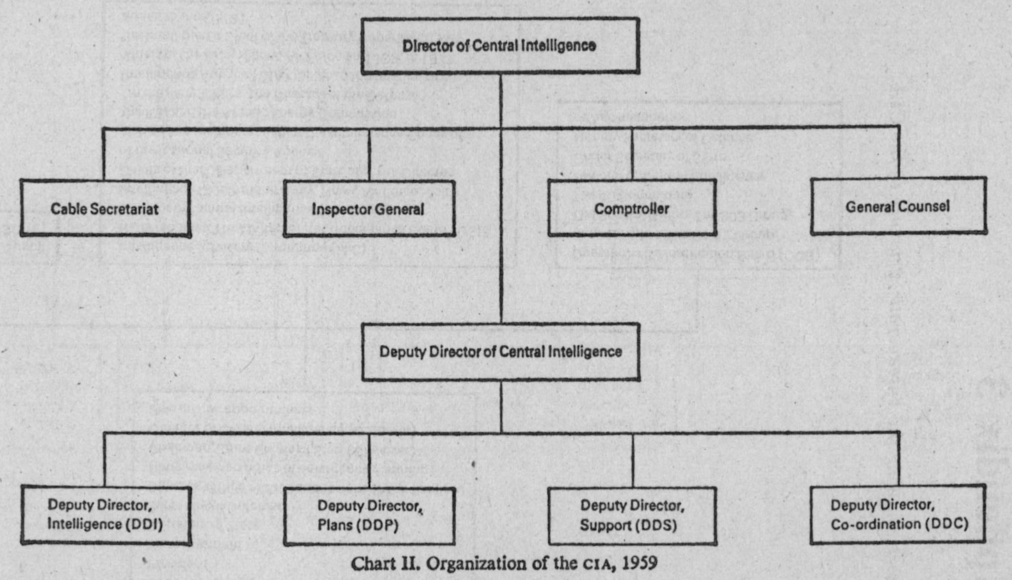

Chart II. Organization of the CIA, 1959

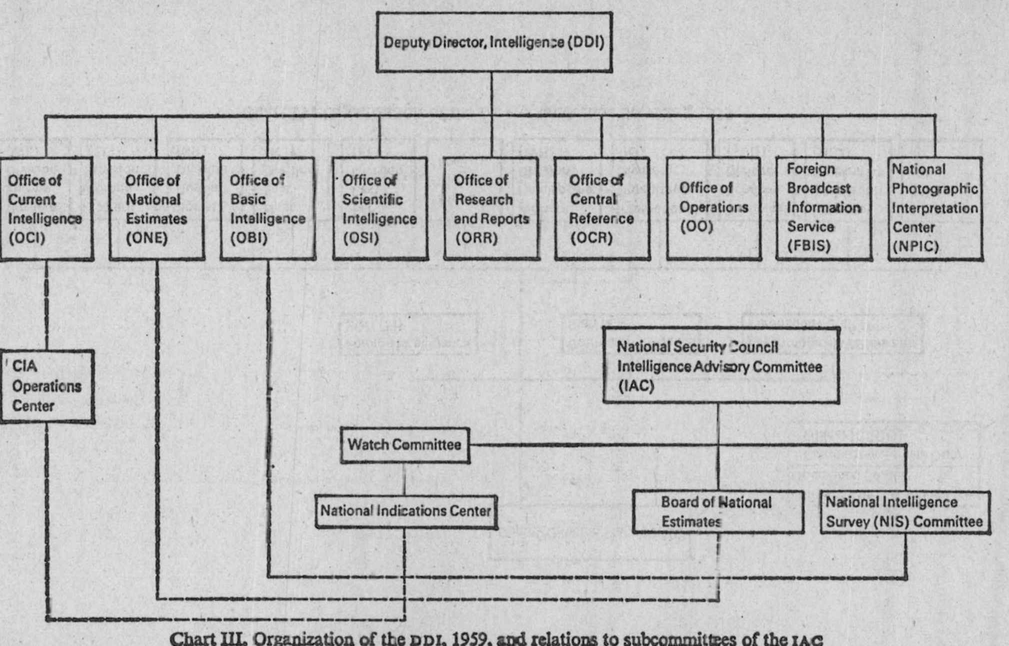

Chart III. Organization of the DDI, 1959, and relations to subcommittees of the IAC

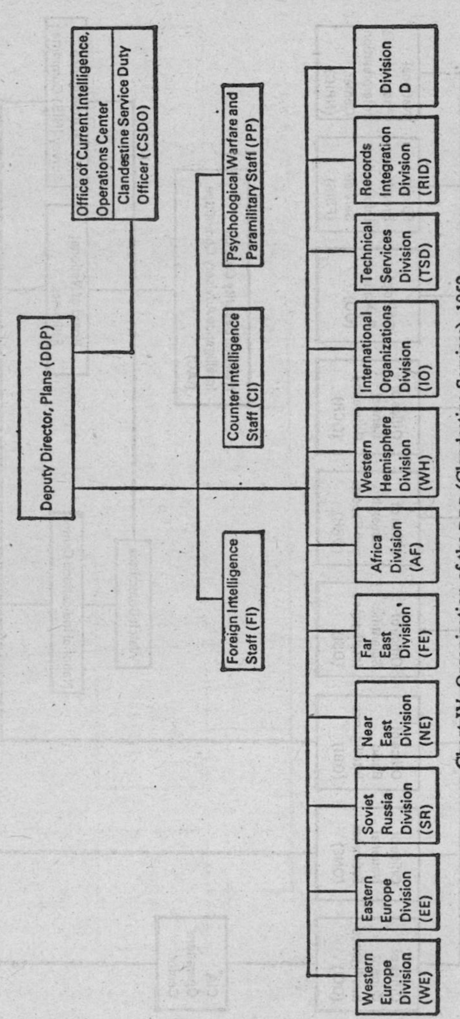

Chart IV. Organization of the DDP (Clandestine Services), 1959

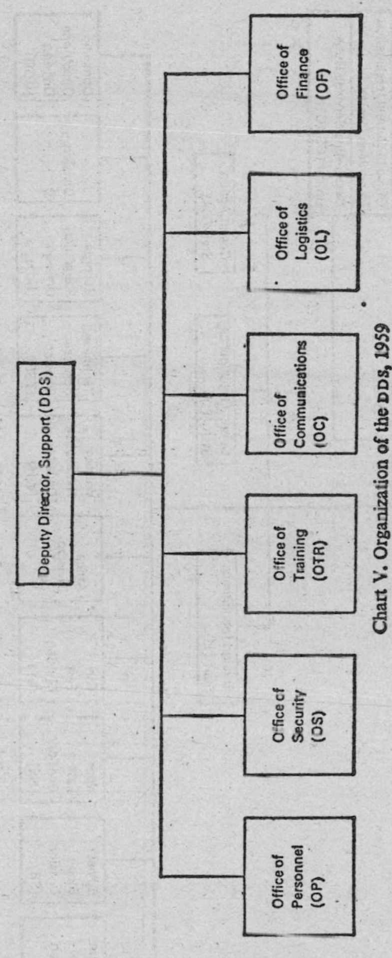

Chart V. Organization of the DDS, 1959

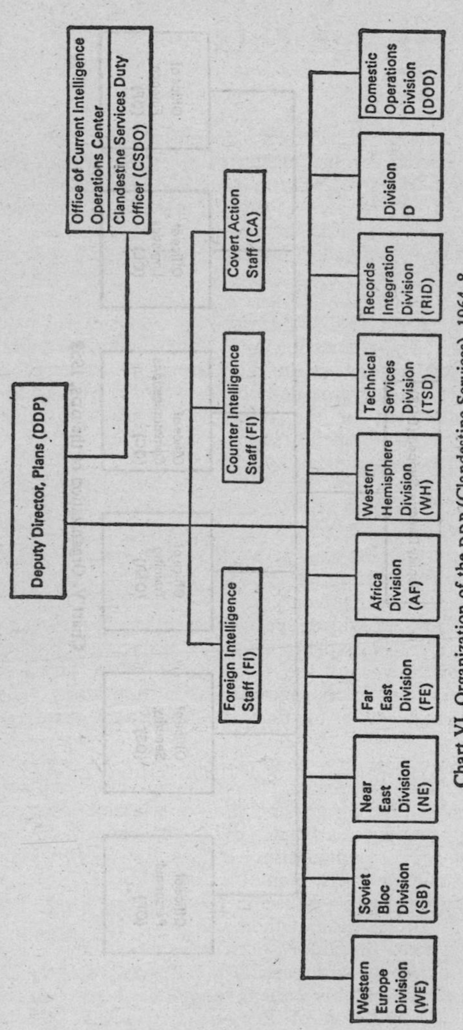

Chart VI. Organization of the DDP (Clandestine Services), 1964–8

Acknowledgments

Many people have helped in the search for the factual details needed to reconstruct the events in which CIA operations described herein occurred. Often they did not know the true purpose of the assistance they were providing. Others helped through moral encouragement and political orientation. I would now like to thank all those who helped and mention several in particular.

The libraries of the Universidad Nacional Autónoma de Mexico and the Colégio de Mexico, both in Mexico City, were valuable for early orientation and historical materials. During this period my professors in the Centro de Estudios Latinoamericanos of UNAM provided the inspiration needed to avoid early abandonment of the idea of writing this book. Encouragement and financial support from my father at this time was also very important.

Also during this early period, Francois Maspero helped me realize that I would have to leave Mexico to find adequate research materials. His advice was also of special value for the general focus and for the decision to concentrate on specific operations rather than types.

In Havana, the Biblioteca Nacional Jose Martí and the Casa de las Americas provided special assistance for research and helped find data available only from government documentation. Representatives of the Communist Party of Cuba also gave me important encouragement at a time when I doubted that I would be able to find the additional information I needed.

Several documentation centers in Paris gave me access to valuable research materials: the Bibliothèque Nationale, the Benjamin Franklin Library and the American Library, as well as the Institute d'Hautes Etudes de L'Amérique Latine and the Bibliothèque de Documentation Internationale Contemporarie of the Université de Paris, Nanterre.

In London the British Museum Newspaper Library provided invaluable documentation. Other material was obtained at the Hispanic and Luso Brazilian Council, Canning House.

Among the people who especially helped, I wish to mention Robin Blackburn and his colleagues at the *New Left Review*, London. Neil Middleton of Penguin Books gave the support and guidance needed for completion, and Laurence Bright, O.P., had the difficult task of reducing almost 500 diary entries totaling over 300,000 words to this edition—perhaps still too long but far superior to the early draft. John Gerassi and

Nicole Szulc obtained vital research materials in New York and Washington, D.C. Grateful thanks to *Playboy Magazine* for allowing the author to adapt certain portions of an interview for use in this edition. Finally, I wish to thank Catherine Beaumont who helped me through a very difficult period in Paris.

Without these people and institutions this diary would be far more incomplete than the present form and probably still unwritten.

ABOUT THE AUTHOR

PHILIP AGEE is a graduate of Notre Dame University and a twelve-year veteran CIA career officer with ten years as a covert operations officer in Ecuador, Uruguay, Mexico and Washington. He resigned from the CIA in 1969 and went abroad to write his account of the U.S. intelligence community. To circumvent prior censorship and possible U.S. government attempts to enjoin publication, *Inside the Company: CIA Diary* was first published in England, where it received widespread attention.